FUNDAMENTALS OF
INVESTMENT MANAGEMENT
AND STRATEGY

FUNDAMENTALS OF INVESTMENT MANAGEMENT AND STRATEGY

Geoffrey A. Hirt
Associate Professor of Finance
DePaul University

Stanley B. Block
Texas American Bank Chair of Finance
Texas Christian University

1983  Richard D. Irwin, Inc.
Homewood, Illinois 60430

ISBN 0-256-02623-8
Library of Congress Catalog Card No. 82–81641

Printed in the United States of America

2 3 4 5 6 7 8 9 0 K 0 9 8 7 6 5 4

PREFACE

In writing this book, we have attempted to develop a presentation that falls somewhere between the descriptive texts of the 1960s and the highly mathematical books designed primarily for graduate students. Thus, we hope to share financial theory with the students on a very readable basis.

While we accept many of the tenets and assumptions of an efficient market environment, we nevertheless carefully explain the importance of fundamental and technical analysis. Three chapters are devoted to the process of fundamental stock selection. Furthermore, we devote a chapter to special situations; we examine investment strategies for which the efficient market hypothesis may not be fully operative in that there may be superior returns even on a risk-adjusted basis.

As is true of most investment texts, the primary emphasis is on equity investments. The individual security as well as a potential portfolio of investments are considered. There is a strong emphasis on evaluating appropriate risk-return trade-offs and the implications of modern portfolio theory. The capital asset pricing model is introduced, explained, and critiqued.

Even though stocks are given the major attention throughout the text, a key strategy is to recognize all investment outlets as part of the feasible set. Some investments work best during inflation or other forms of economic upheaval, while others prosper in more stable times or even periods of disinflation. While we do not purport to be able to tell how to forecast the future with any high degree of certainty, the well-trained student should be aware of all options open for investment. For this reason, we take a hard look at the bond market and investment strategies that are appropriate for the type of volatile interest rates that we have had in the last decade.

We also examine such investment alternatives as real estate, commodities and financial futures, precious metals and gems, and collectibles (coins, stamps, art). We take a more systematic approach to these investments than most other texts by carefully evaluating risk-return trade-offs, trading costs, problems of illiquidity, and timing considerations. Whether the student chooses to engage in

v

these investments or not, he or she is almost certain to be approached with suggestions or proposals over a "lifetime of investments" and should be aware of the advantages and disadvantages of each.

We have also attempted to identify contemporary topics of particular importance and give them added attention. Chapter 13 on stock options is among the most up-to-date and comprehensive in any investment text on the market. There is strong coverage of the financial futures market in Chapter 17, with various hedge strategies suggested for portfolio managers and corporate financial officers. There is more than normal coverage of merger and acquisition investment strategy in Chapter 16, with attention devoted to premiums offered to target company stockholders, and the price movement impact of merger announcements or cancellations on the acquiring and acquired companies' stock values. Another contemporary issue of importance to the student is the 1981 Economic Recovery Tax Act. While parts of the act may yet be repealed, much of it will be with us in the future. We take a particularly hard look at its impact on estate taxes and estate planning.

The book is written primarily from the viewpoint of an individual investor or a financial advisor to an investor. For this reason, we stress the importance of setting investment objectives and also the various ways of participating in the market (cash versus margin accounts, long positions versus short positions, etc.). An entire chapter is devoted to important sources of investment information running the gamut from government documents to computer tapes.

All chapters conclude with a substantial body of questions or problems. The end-of-chapter material is carefully tailored to the text and can be a valuable asset to the instructor and students. A number of potential library projects are also suggested.

We wish to thank those who contributed directly to the preparation of the manuscript, particularly Roger Potter for his valuable help in the development of the material on estate planning and his supportive efforts in working with us on the questions and problems. For their valuable reviews and helpful comments, we are grateful to Keith E. Boles (University of Colorado, Colorado Springs), Jerry D. Boswell (College for Financial Planning), Ira Smolowitz (Siena College), Frank N. Tiernan (Drake University) and Paul Grier (SUNY-Binghampton).

We also wish to express our thanks to Dave Ritzwoller and Cheri Semans for their help in proofreading the manuscript and to Dean Ed Johnson and Dean Andrew Nappi for the administrative support provided by their institutions.

Finally, we are especially grateful to our families for their patience and tolerance throughout the endeavor.

Geoffrey A. Hirt
Stanley B. Block

CONTENTS

FUNDAMENTALS OF
INVESTMENT MANAGEMENT
AND STRATEGY

PART 1 INTRODUCTION TO INVESTMENTS

In Part 1 of the text, we establish the groundwork that is essential to the development of investment strategy and the management of financial resources.

The place to begin is with the setting of investment objectives. Not only is this the first step in any well-managed investment program, but it is often the most important ingredient. Among the factors the investor considers are willingness to take risks, desire for current income, need for liquidity, and tax considerations. In the first chapter, the reader is given an opportunity to catalog his or her own financial situation and relate this to investment alternatives. Career opportunities in the areas of investments and security analysis also are described in Chapter 1.

A discussion of security markets follows in Chapter 2. An important distinction is made between primary markets (for new issues) and secondary markets (for existing issues). We discuss the major organized exchanges, such as the New York Stock Exchange, the American Stock Exchange, and the Chicago Board Options Exchange, as well as the over-the-counter market. We also take a look at future developments in the securities industry relating to computerized security trading.

As part of the goal for establishing the groundwork for investment management in Part 1, sources of investment information are covered in Chapter 3. The reader is presented with an overview of aggregate economic data sources generated by the government and with industry/company data developed by investment advisory services, such as Value Line and Standard & Poor's. The uses of periodical indexes, journals, and data bases are also highlighted.

In Chapter 4, the actual steps necessary to participate in the market are considered with a description of the types of accounts that can be opened, the forms of orders that can be executed, and the commission costs involved. Tax considerations are also covered with an emphasis on the proper timing of investment decisions to minimize taxes. The issue of individually managed accounts versus mutual funds is the final item of consideration in Chapter 4.

The last topic for discussion in Part 1 is the development of investment strat-

egies for different economic environments. The relative performance of stocks, bonds, real estate, etc. are considered in times of high inflation, low inflation, boom, and recession. Long-term investment performance studies from the University of Chicago and elsewhere are reviewed.

1 The investment setting

In the last decade, we have seen an unusual series of economic events. Oil has gone from $2 to over $30 a barrel. Gold went from $35 an ounce to $875 and then fell by over 50 percent. Silver increased from $4 an ounce to over $50 an ounce and then declined by 80 percent. Interest rates have moved between 8 percent and 20+ percent, and inflation has been at double-digit levels only to moderate at later points in time. This is in sharp contrast to the stable economic environment of the 1950s and 1960s.

How does one develop an investment strategy in such an environment? Suggestions come to the investor from all directions. He or she is told how to benefit from the coming monetary disaster as well as how to grow rich in a new era of prosperity. The intent of this text is to help the investor sort out the various investments that are available and to develop analytical skills that suggest what alternates might be most appropriate for a given portfolio.

We shall define an investment as the commitment of current funds in anticipation of receiving a larger future flow of funds. The investor hopes to be compensated by forgoing immediate consumption, for inflation, and for taking a risk.

The process of investing may be both exciting and challenging. The first-time investor who pours over the financial statements of a firm and then makes a dollar commitment to purchase a few shares of stock often has a feeling of euphoria as he or she charges out in the morning to secure the daily newspaper and read the market quotes. Even the professional analyst may take pleasure in leaving his Wall Street office to evaluate an emerging high technology firm in Austin or Palo Alto. Likewise, the buyer of a rare painting or late 18th-century U.S. coin may find a sense of excitement in attempting to outsmart the market. Even the purchaser of a bond or money market instrument must do proper analysis to assure that anticipated objectives are being met.

However, the seasoned investor often learns that there are failures that go with successes. The professional money manager is under tremendous pressure to outperform the popular market averages, and failure to do so may mean loss

of a valuable account or perhaps a job. The individual investor may also feel a sense of frustration as he or she observes a "sure thing" go sour. The primary task is to establish your investment objectives so that both successes and temporary setbacks can be reasonably anticipated and accepted as part of the process.

FORMS OF INVESTMENT

In the text, we break down investment alternatives between financial and real assets. A financial asset represents a financial claim on an asset that is usually documented by some form of legal representation. An example would be a share of stock or a bond. A real asset represents an actual tangible asset that may be seen, felt, held, or collected. An example would be real estate or gold.

In Table 1–1, we list the various forms of financial and real assets.

Table 1–1

Overview of investment alternatives

A. Financial assets
   1. Equity claims—direct:
      Common stock.
      Warrants.
      Options.
   2. Equity claims—indirect:
      Investment company shares.
   3. Creditor claims:
      Savings accounts.
      Money market funds.
      Commercial paper.
      Treasury bills.
      Bonds (straight and convertible to common stock).
   4. Preferred stock (straight and convertible to common stock).
   5. Commodity futures.

B. Real assets
   1. Real estate—office buildings, apartments, shopping centers, personal residences.
   2. Precious metals—gold, silver.
   3. Precious gems—diamonds, rubies, sapphires.
   4. Collectibles:
      Art.
      Antiques.
      Stamps.
      Coins.
      Rare books.
   5. Other:
      Cattle.
      Oil.
      Common metals.

As indicated in part A of Table 1–1, financial assets may be broken down into five categories. *Direct equity claims* represent ownership interests and include common stock as well as other instruments that can be used to purchase common stock, such as warrants and options. Warrants and options allow the holder to buy a stipulated number of shares in the future at a given price. Warrants usually convert to one share and are long-term in nature, whereas options are generally based on 100 share units and are short-term in nature.

Indirect equity can be acquired through placing funds in investment companies (such as a mutual fund). The investment company pools the resources of many investors and reinvests them in common stock (or other investments). The individual enjoys the advantages of diversification and professional management (though not necessarily higher returns).

Financial assets may also take the form of *creditor claims* as represented by debt instruments offered by financial institutions, industrial corporations, or the government. The rate of return is often initially fixed, though the effective yield may vary with changing market conditions. Other forms of financial assets are *preferred stock,* which is a hybrid form of security combining some of the elements of equity ownership and creditor claims, and *commodity futures,* which represent a contract to buy or sell a commodity in the future at a given price. Commodities may include wheat, corn, copper, or even such financial instruments as Treasury bonds or foreign exchange.

As shown in part B of Table 1–1, there are also numerous categories of real assets. The most widely recognized investment in this category is *real estate,* either commercial property or one's own residence. For greater risk, *precious metals* or *precious gems* can be considered, and for those seeking psychic pleasure as well as monetary gain, *collectibles* are an investment outlet. Finally, the *other, all inclusive* category includes cattle, oil, and other items that stretch as far as the imagination will go.

Throughout the text, each form of financial and real asset is considered. What assets the investor ultimately selects will depend on his or her investment objectives as well as the economic outlook for the future. For example, if the investor believes that inflation will be relatively strong in the future, there may be a preference for real assets that have a replacement value reflecting increasing prices. In a more moderate inflationary environment, stocks and bonds may be preferred. In Chapters 5 and 6, we develop a further understanding of the relationship of economic circumstances to investment strategy.

THE SETTING OF INVESTMENT OBJECTIVES

The setting of investment objectives may be as important as the selection of the investment. In actuality, they tend to go together. A number of key areas should be considered.

Risk and safety of principal

The first factor that the investor must consider is the amount of risk that he or she is prepared to assume. In a relatively efficient and informed capital market environment, risk tends to be closely correlated with return. Most of the literature of finance would suggest that those who consistently demonstrate high returns of perhaps 20 percent or more are greater than normal risk takers. While there may be some clever investors who are able to prosper on their wits alone, most high returns may be perceived as compensation for risk.

And there is not only the risk of losing invested capital directly (a dry hole perhaps), but also the danger of a loss in purchasing power. A stock that is held for four years without a gain in value would represent a 36 percent loss in purchasing power with 8 percent inflation (compounded annually).

The investor who wishes to assume low risks will probably confine a large portion of his or her portfolio to short-term debt instruments in which the party responsible for payment is the government or a major bank or corporation. Some conservative investors may choose to invest in a money market fund, in which the funds of numerous investors are pooled together and reinvested in high-yielding, short-term instruments. More aggressive investors may look toward longer-term debt instruments and common stock. Real assets, such as gold, silver, or valued art, might also be included in an aggressive portfolio.

It is not only the inherent risk in an asset that must be considered, but also the extent to which that risk is being diversified away in a portfolio. Though an investment in gold might be considered risky, such might not be fully the case if it is combined into a portfolio of common stocks. Gold thrives on bad news, while common stocks generally do well in a positive economic development. An oil embargo or foreign war may drive down the value of stocks while gold is advancing, and vice versa.

The age and economic circumstances of an investor are important variables in determining an appropriate level of risk. Young, upwardly mobile people are generally in a better position to absorb risk than are elderly couples on a fixed income. Nevertheless, each of us, regardless of our plight in life, has different risk-taking desires. A surgeon earning $200,000 a year may be more averse to accepting a $2 per share loss on a stock than an aging taxicab driver.

One cruel lesson of the last decade is that those who thought they were buying conservative investments often found quite the opposite to be true. For example, an 8¾ percent U.S. government bond maturing in 1994 was trading at 72 percent of its stated value in mid-1981.

Current income versus capital appreciation

A second consideration in the setting of investment objectives is a decision on the desire for current income versus capital appreciation. Though this decision is closely tied to an evaluation of risk, it is a separate matter.

In purchasing stocks, the investor with a need for current income may opt for high-yielding, mature firms in such industries as public utilities, machine tools, or

apparel. Those searching for capital gains may look toward smaller, emerging firms in high technology, energy, or electronics. The latter firms may pay no cash dividend at all, but the investor hopes for an increase in value to provide the desired return.

Liquidity considerations

Liquidity is measured by the ability of the investor to convert an investment into cash within a relatively short period of time with a minimum capital loss on the transaction. Most financial assets provide a high degree of liquidity. Stocks and bonds can generally be sold within a matter of minutes at a price reasonably close to the last traded value. Such may not be the case for real estate. Almost everyone has seen a house or piece of commercial real estate sit on the market for weeks or months.

Liquidity can also be measured indirectly by the transaction costs or commissions involved in the transfer of ownership. Once again, financial assets generally trade on a relatively low commission basis (perhaps 1 or 2 percent), whereas many real assets have transaction costs that run from 5 percent to 25 percent or more.

In many cases, the lack of immediate liquidity can be justified if there are unusual opportunities for gain. An investment in real estate or precious gems may provide sufficient return to more than compensate for the added transaction costs. Of course, a bad investment will be all the more difficult to unload.

The investor must carefully assess his or her own situation to determine the need for liquidity. If you are investing funds to be used for the next house payment or the coming semester's tuition, then immediate liquidity will be essential, and financial assets will be preferred. If funds can be tied up for long periods of time, bargain-buying opportunities of an unusual nature can also be evaluated.

Short-term versus long-term orientation in measurement

In setting investment objectives, you must decide whether you will assume a short-term or long-term orientation in managing the funds and evaluating performance. You do not always have a choice. Those who manage funds for others may be put under tremendous pressure to show a given level of performance in the short run. The appliers of pressure may be a concerned relative or a large pension fund that has placed funds with a bank trust department. Even though you are convinced your latest stock purchase will double in the next three years, the fact that it is currently down by 15 percent may provide some discomfort to those around you.

Market strategies may also be short term or long term in scope. Those who attempt to engage in short-term market tactics are termed *traders.* They may buy a stock at 15 and hope to liquidate if it goes to 20. To help reach decisions, short-term traders often make use of technical analysis, which is based on evaluating market indicator series and charting. Those who take a longer-term per-

spective try to identify fundamentally sound companies for a buy-and-hold approach. A long-term investor does not necessarily anticipate being able to buy right at the bottom or sell at the exact peak.

Tax factors

Investors in high tax brackets will have different investment objectives than those in lower brackets or tax-exempt charities, foundations, or similar organizations. An investor in a high tax bracket may prefer municipal bonds (interest is not taxable), real estate (with its depreciation and interest write-off), or investments that provide tax credits or tax shelters, such as those in oil and gas or railroad cars.

In recent times, many investment advisors have cautioned investors not to be blinded by the beneficial tax aspects of an investment but to look at the economic factors as well.

Ease of management

A final item of consideration in setting up an investment program is ease of management. The investor must determine the amount of time and effort that can be devoted to an investment portfolio and act accordingly. In the stock market, this may determine whether you want to be a daily trader or to assume a longer-term perspective. In real estate, it may mean the difference between personally owning and managing a handful of rental houses or going in with 10 other investors to form a limited partnership in which a general partner takes full management responsibility and the limited partners merely put up the capital.

Of course, there is a minimum amount of time that must be committed to any investment program. Even when investment advisors or general partners are in charge, their activities must be monitored and evaluated.

PROFILE ANALYSIS

The editors of *Consumer Guide* have developed an interesting survey to see what types of investments are appropriate for investors based on their age and economic circumstances. The questionnaire is presented in Table 1–2. Try applying this survey to your own or your family's economic conditions. Of course, this survey represents only general guidelines.

NEW YORK STOCK EXCHANGE STUDY

The New York Stock Exchange has also done some interesting studies of investors in common stock. The information is presented in Table 1–3. Note that the number of individual shareowners dropped dramatically from 1970 to 1975. This was because of poor market conditions (the bear market of the mid-1970s)

| Table 1–2 | **Profile analysis: what should you invest in now?** |

Directions: Circle the answer that most nearly applies to you. Write that number in the space at right. Then add up the numbers and divide by 9 to get a median score.

AGE—My age is closest to:
(9) 30 (7) 40 (5) 50 (3) 60 (1) 70 _____

INCOME—My present annual income from all sources is nearest to (in thousands):
(2) 10 (4) 20 (5) 30 (6) 40 (8) 50 _____

ANNUAL EXPENSES—In relation to income, my annual expenses approximate:
(1) 100% (3) 90% (5) 80% (7) 70% (9) 50% _____

NUMBER OF DEPENDENTS—I presently have these dependents:
(9) 0 (8) 1 (6) 2–3 (4) 4–5 (1) 6 or more _____

ESTIMATED VALUE OF ASSETS—My house, insurance, savings, and investments total (in thousands):
(1) 50 (3) 100 (5) 250 (7) 350 (9) 500 or more _____

LIABILITIES—My bills, mortgages, installment payments, and debts in relation to assets approximate (in thousands):
(9) 30% (7) 50% (5) 75% (3) 90% (1) 100% _____

SAVINGS—I have cash on hand in savings or other liquid assets to equal this amount of expenses:
(1) 1 month (3) 2 months (5) 3 months (7) 4 months (9) 6+ months _____

LIFE INSURANCE—My life insurance coverage equals (in thousands):
(9) 250 (7) 150 (5) 100 (3) 50 (1) 25 or less _____

HEALTH INSURANCE—My health insurance coverage includes:
(9) Basic, major medical, catastrophic (5) Major medical plus basic (1) Basic _____

Add up your scores and divide by 9 to get the average. Then consider the investment strategies that follow.

The investment strategy rating numbers below correlate with the average score you got from the profile analysis. The investment strategy ratings indicate investment categories ranging from (1) ultraconservative to (9) highly speculative. By matching the profile score with the nearest investment strategy numbers, you get some feel for investments that may be appropriate for you. You would probably choose from two or three categories.

1. Insured savings accounts.
2. High-grade government securities.
3. High-quality corporate and municipal bonds, preferred stocks, investment trusts, and annuity income.
4. Lower-rated corporate and municipal bonds, preferred stocks, investment trusts, convertible bonds and preferred stocks, and variable insurance.
5. Higher-rated common stocks and investment trusts, and investment annuities.
6. Lower-rated common stocks and investment trusts.

Table 1–2 (concluded)   Investment strategy ratings

7. Speculative bonds, stocks, and investment trusts.
8. Gold and silver-related investments, and foreign investment trusts.
9. Rare and exotic investments: stamps, rare coins, art, antiques, gems and jewelry, rare books, autographs, prints, and lithographs.

SOURCE: The editors of *Consumer Guide,* with Peter A. Dickinson, *How to Make Money During Inflation Recession* (New York: Harper & Row, 1980).

and the increased enrollment of workers in pension and retirement plans, through which they had others managing their retirement funds. Stockholder participation did increase materially in the 1975–80 period due to somewhat improving market conditions and more generous tax legislation that lowered the capital gains tax rate on investments.

We also see in Table 1–3 that one out of every five adults owns common stock, that the median household income for common stockholders is $27,750, and that the median age of stockholders is 46 years (last line). This represents a sharp decline from 53 years in 1975. This reversal in age must be considered unusual in light of an ever increasing average age in the population. It is clear that more young people are coming into the market to replace older investors who have "lost the faith."

Also note the almost equal distribution between male and female stockhold-

Table 1–3   Highlights of eight NYSE shareholder surveys

	1952	1956	1959	1962	1965	1970	1975	1980
Number of individual shareowners (000s)	6,490	8,630	12,490	17,010	20,120	30,850	25,270	29,840
Number owning shares listed on NYSE (000s)	n.a.*	6,880	8,510	11,020	12,430	18,290	17,950	23,520
Adult shareowner incidence in population	1 in 16	1 in 12	1 in 8	1 in 6	1 in 6	1 in 4	1 in 6	1 in 5
Medium household income	$7,100	$6,200	$7,000	$8,600	$9,500	$13,500	$19,000	$27,750
Number of adult shareowners with household income:								
Under $10,000 (000s)	n.a.	n.a.	9,340	10,340	10,080	8,170	3,420	1,720
$10,000 and over (000s)	n.a.	n.a.	2,740	5,920	8,410	20,130	19,970	25,410
Number of adult female shareowners (000s)	3,140	4,260	6,350	8,290	9,430	14,290	11,750	13,530
Number of adult male shareowners (000s)	3,210	4,020	5,740	7,970	9,060	14,340	11,630	14,030
Median age	51	48	49	48	49	48	53	46

Note: Because of statistical adjustments not all subtotals add up to the totals for a given year.

*n.a. = Not available.

SOURCE: *New York Stock Exchange Fact Book* (New York: New York Stock Exchange, 1981).

ers—a clear indication that the stock market does not merely represent a man's world. More and more women are also going into investment advisory positions.

MEASURES OF RISK AND RETURN

The investor must compare the return potential from an investment to the risk that is involved. Return is usually measured as capital appreciation plus current income. In valuing common stock, a dividend valuation model is often used in which we show.

$$P_0 = \frac{D_1}{(1 + K_e)^1} + \frac{D_2}{(1 + K_e)^2} + \frac{D_3}{(1 + K_e)^3} + \ldots + \frac{D_\infty}{(1 + K_e)^\infty} \quad (1-1)$$

P_0 is the current price of the stock, D values represent subsequent dividend payments, and K_e is the expected rate of return or discount rate applied to future dividends. Under assumptions of a constant growth in dividends and a discount rate that exceeds that growth rate, K_e can be written to equal $\frac{D_1}{P_0} + g$. Thus, we speak of a total rate of return equaling the dividend yield (dividend payment divided by price), plus an anticipated growth rate *(g)* in stock value, earnings, and dividends. The growth in stock value is referred to as capital appreciation.

A stock that pays a $1 dividend and has a current price of $20 with an expected growth rate or capital appreciation of 4 percent is shown to provide a *total return* of 9 percent.

$$K_e = \frac{D_1}{P_0} + g = \frac{\$1}{\$20} + 4\% = 5\% + 4\% = 9\%$$

Figure 1–1   **Variability and return**

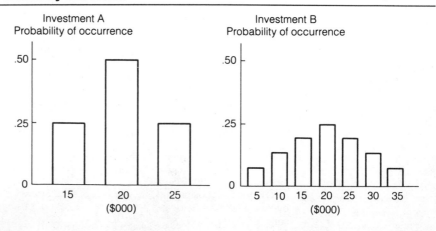

Risk measurement   Risk is generally defined as the degree of uncertainty about the outcome of a given event. The greater the variability of possible outcomes, the greater the risk. We introduce risk analysis by showing the two graphs in Figure 1–1.

While the two investments would appear to have the same expected value of $20,000, clearly investment B has the greater variability or dispersion around that expected value. Thus, we say it has the greater risk.

In the U.S. capital markets, returns on assets are assumed to be related to the risks that are involved. In Figure 1–2, we observe a theoretical risk-return relationship that is assumed to exist for various types of financial assets over the long term. Note the increasing return requirement associated with risk.

Major studies of rates of return in the financial markets tend to validate these patterns. As you will read in Chapter 5, Lorie and Fisher found that total returns on common stock averaged 9.1 percent from 1926 to 1976 and that long- and short-term debt provided considerably lower returns.[1]

Ibbotson and Sinquefield found a return of 8.5 percent on common stock between 1926 and 1974 with a similar drop-off in the return to debt instruments.[2] A graph of the results from the Ibbotson and Sinquefield study is presented in Figure 1–3. Of course, there are long-term studies, and large disparities can take place in the short run. For example, in many time periods during the 1970s, it was not unusual for short-term debt instruments to provide higher returns than common stock.

Systematic and   We have been discussing risks and returns for individual investments. Modern
unsystematic risk   capital market theory also requires that we consider the relationship between two or more investments to determine the combined risk level. Part of the risk of an individual investment may be diversified away. For this reason, not all risk associated with an investment may be thought to be compensated for by proportionally higher returns in the financial markets.

Financial theory can be used to break down risk which is systematic and non-systematic in nature. Systematic risk is the inherent risk in an investment and is related to movements in the market. Based on systematic risk, if the market goes up or down by 10 percent, our stock is assumed to go up or down by X percent. The joint movement between a security and the market in general is measured by the beta coefficient. Systematic risk is assumed to be compensated for by

---

[1]Lawrence Fisher and James H. Lorie, *A Half Century of Returns on Stocks and Bonds* (Chicago: University of Chicago Graduate School of Business, 1977). Also, James H. Lorie and Lawrence Fisher, "Rates of Return on Investment in Common Stock," *Journal of Business,* January 1964, pp. 1–17. Lawrence Fisher and James H. Lorie, "Rates of Return on Investment in Common Stock: The Year-by-Year Record 1926–1965," *Journal of Business,* July 1968, pp. 219–316.

[2]Roger G. Ibbotson and Rex A. Sinquefield, "Stocks, Bonds, Bills, and Inflation: Year-by-Year Historical Returns (1926–1974)," *Journal of Business,* University of Chicago January 1976, pp. 11–47.

Figure 1–2   **Risk and expected return for various security classes**

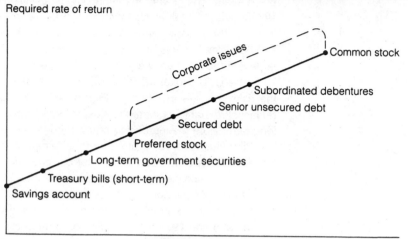

Figure 1–3   **Relative values of investments, 1926–1974**

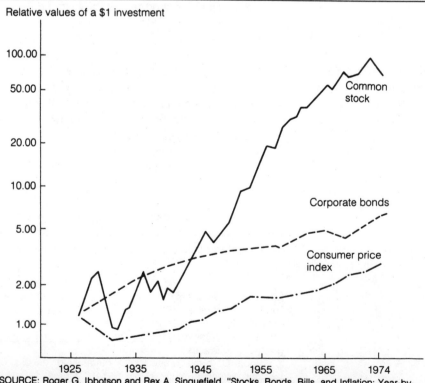

SOURCE: Roger G. Ibbotson and Rex A. Sinquefield, "Stocks, Bonds, Bills, and Inflation: Year-by-Year Historical Returns (1926–1974)," *Journal of Business* University of Chicago, January 1976, p. 36.

higher potential returns. That is, stocks that have high systematic risks or betas are assumed to provide higher returns to compensate for the additional risk. A second type of risk is unsystematic in nature. It is not related to general market movements but is random in nature and encompasses all the many nonmarket events that can influence a given company's stock (strikes, changes in raw material prices, lawsuits, etc.). Most of the unsystematic risk influencing a stock can be diversified away in an efficiently designed portfolio. For this reason, unsystematic risk is not assumed to receive additional compensation in the form of higher returns. These matters require further explanation and attention and are developed in subsequent parts of the text in which we also indicate some limitations to their utilization. We now briefly turn our attention to the accumulation of funds for investment in the financial markets.

FLOW OF FUNDS INTO THE FINANCIAL MARKETS

We basically have a three-sector economy; the participants are business, government, and households. Households tend to be net suppliers of funds, and business and government are net users. As households receive wages, dividends, and transfer payments from business and government, they generally save some portion of their income. These savings are funneled to financial intermediaries that in turn make investments in the financial markets as indicated in the top part of Figure 1–4. These financial intermediaries include banks, savings

Figure 1–4   **Flow of funds in the financial markets**

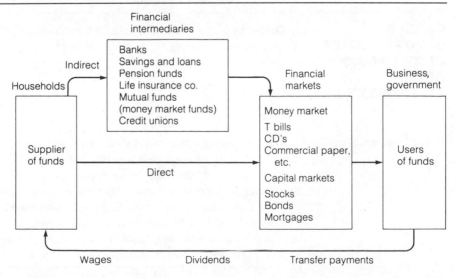

---

[3]Business also uses profits and the government uses taxation to increase their flows.

and loans, pension funds, insurance companies, mutual funds (including money market funds), credit unions, and other groups. Individuals may also invest directly in the financial markets and bypass the intermediaries. In either event, the funds are accumulated in the financial markets, then go to the net users of funds (business and government), and are once again recycled through the economy in the form of wages, dividends, and transfer payments.[3]

In recent times, there has been tremendous competition for funds among the financial intermediaries. The biggest battle is for fixed-income (interest-paying) dollars. The Monetary Deregulation Act mandated that all ceilings on interest rates (regulation Q) be lifted by 1986. (Traditionally there has been federally regulated interest rate ceilings on savings accounts and small certificates of deposit.) While banks and savings and loans have long battled for savings dollars, money market funds have added a new dimension to the picture. These funds take savings in initial amounts as small as $500, then pool them to buy high-yielding financial instruments that come in minimum amounts of $100,000 or more. The money market funds require no minimum holding period (such as on a certificate of deposit) and extend some check-writing privileges as well. Although money market funds are generally quite safe investments, they are not guaranteed by any federal regulatory agency. Some have argued that money market funds are allowed to compete directly with other financial intermediaries without the usual state or federal regulation or the necessity of setting up reserve requirements against their assets. Total assets of money market funds have grown from $3.7 billiion in 1977 to well in excess of $180 billion in mid-1982.

CAREER OPPORTUNITIES IN THE FIELD OF INVESTMENTS

Career opportunities in the field of investments include positions as a stockbroker, security analyst or portfolio manager, investment banker, or financial planner.

Stockbroker

A stockbroker generally works with the public in advising and executing orders for individual or institutional accounts. Although he or she may have a salary base to cushion against bad times, most of the compensation is in the form of commissions. Successful brokers do quite well financially.

Most brokerage houses look for people who have effective selling skills as well as an interest in finance. In hiring, some (though not all) brokerage houses require prior business experience and a mature appearance. A listing of the 30 largest brokerage houses is presented in Table 1–4. Further information on these firms (as well as others not included on the list) can be found in the *Securities Industry Yearbook* published by the Securities Industry Association, 20 Broad Street, New York, N.Y. 10005.

Table 1—4   Listing of 30 major brokerage houses

	1979		Offices		Employees	
	Capital	Rank	Number	Rank	Number	Rank
Merrill Lynch & Co., Inc.	$784,245,000	1	442	1	26,860	1
Shearson, Loeb Rhoades Inc.	246,254,559	2	266	2	8,595	4
Paine Webber Incorporated	245,200,000	3	229	6	8,982	3
The E. F. Hutton Group Inc.	237,954,000	4	249	4	8,582	5
Salomon Brothers	228,700,000	5	11	76	2,015	14
Dean Witter Reynolds Inc.	186,063,000	6	264	3	9,264	2
Goldman, Sachs & Co.	181,000,000	7	15	57	1,955	15
Bache Halsey Stuart Shields Incorporated	178,673,000	8	190	7	7,288	6
Stephens Inc.	145,097,750	9	1		134	
First Boston Inc.	127,213,217	10	14	61	1,332	19
Morgan Stanley & Co. Incorporated	107,542,000	11	7		1,661	18
The Drexel Burnham Lambert Group Inc.	104,362,000	12	38	23	3,059	9
Lehman Brothers Kuhn Loeb Incorporated	103,784,000	13	9		1,847	17
A. B. Becker Incorporated/Warburg Paribas Becker Incorporated	100,500,000	14	13	67	2,203	12
Kidder, Peabody & Co. Incorporated	92,389,138	15	59	12	3,150	8
Donaldson, Lufkin & Jenrette, Inc.	81,000,000	16	14	61	1,872	16
Bear, Stearns & Co.	73,675,000	17	11	76	2,156	13
Smith Barney, Harris Upham & Co. Incorporated	69,099,000	18	88	10	3,600	7
L. F. Rothschild, Unterberg, Towbin	66,285,000	19	9		1,239	21
Thomson, McKinnon Securities Inc.	61,589,000	20	113	9	2,815	10
A. G. Edwards & Sons, Inc.	54,038,000	21	161	8	2,355	11
Neuberger & Berman	47,261,538	22	1		293	68
Stern Brothers & Co.	45,623,000	23	4		64	
Brown Brothers Harriman & Co.	43,110,000	24	11	76	816	27
Oppenheimer & Co., Inc.	42,087,000	25	7		1,250	20
Aubrey G. Lanston & Co., Inc.	40,000,000	26	3		57	
John Nuveen & Co. Incorporated	38,750,732	27	12	70	317	62
Spear, Leeds & Kellogg	34,983,543	28	1		295	67
Dillon, Read & Co. Inc.	34,782,000	29	4		385	53
Alex. Brown & Sons	32,637,144	30	18	49	718	34

SOURCE: *Securities Industry Yearbook* (New York: Securities Industry Association, 1980), pp. 10–11.

More experienced brokers may specialize in institutional accounts, working with bank trust departments, mutual funds, and others. Though the percentage commission is much lower on these accounts, the volume is much greater.

Security analyst or portfolio manager

Security analysts study various industries and companies and provide research reports to their clientele. A security analyst might work for a brokerage house, a bank trust department, or any other type of institutional investor. Security analysts often specialize in certain industries, such as banking or the airlines.

They are expected to have an in-depth knowledge of overall financial analysis as well as the variables that influence their industry.

The role of the financial analyst has been upgraded over the years through the establishment of a certifying program in which one can become a Chartered Financial Analyst (CFA). To achieve this designation, there are minimum experience requirements and extensive testing over a three-year period. The exams are coordinated through the University of Virginia and given nationally to those who qualify. An example of the many areas covered by the exam is presented in Table 1–5.

Table 1–5   **The CFA candidate study program (Summary of the topic outline)**

Economics:
    Tools of analysis.
    Historical and structural perspective.
    Forecasting broad economic forces.
    Government economic policies and their implications.

Accounting:
    Principles and practices.
    Analysis of accounting statements.
    Judgment as to adequacy.
    Current problems.

Quantitative techniques:
    Compound growth and present value of stocks and bonds.
    Performance measurement.
    Hypothesis testing.
    Regression analysis.

Analysis of fixed income securities:
    Characteristics.
    Analysis of quality.
    Bond swaps and other techniques of management.
    Interest rate structure.

Analysis of equity securities:
    Industry appraisal.
    Company appraisal and evaluation.
    Ratio analysis.
    Management appraisal.
    Valuation techniques.

Portfolio management:
    Investor objectives and constraints.
    Institutions.
    Portfolio strategy.
    Modern portfolio theory.

Ethical standards and laws:
    Ethical standards.
    Treatment of ethical issues.
    Security laws and regulations.

SOURCE: W. Scott Bauman, "The CFA Candidate Program," *Financial Analysts Journal*, November–December 1974, p. 68.

While many security analysts are not CFAs, those that carry this designation tend to enjoy higher salary and prestige. It is interesting to note that those who are directly involved in the marketing of securities are not allowed to sit for the CFA exam. You must be an analyst or portfolio manager.[4]

The number of openings for security analysts has shrunk in recent times because of the tight research budgets of many brokerage houses. This came about in the mid-1970s when commission charges went from fixed to freely competitive and fewer dollars were allocated to research.

In spite of the tight situation, top analysts are still in demand. A magazine entitled the *Institutional Investor* actually picks an all-American team of security analysts, the best in energy, banking, and so on. As we will see later in the text, some academic researchers would question the legitimacy of such designations.

Portfolio managers have the responsibility for managing large pools of funds. They are generally employed by insurance companies, mutual funds, bank trust departments, pension funds, and other institutional investors. They often rely on the help of security analysts and brokers in designing their portfolios. They not only must decide which stocks to buy or sell, but also they must determine the risk level with the optimum trade-off between the common-stock and fixed-income components of a portfolio. Portfolio managers often rise through the ranks of stockbrokers and security analysts.

Investment banker

Investment bankers are primarily involved in the distribution of securities from the issuing corporation to the public. Investment bankers also advise corporate clients on their financial strategy and may help to arrange mergers and acquisitions.

The investment banker is one of the most prestigious participants in the securities industry. Although the hiring of investment bankers was once closely confined to Ivy League graduates with the right family ties, such is no longer the case. Nevertheless, an MBA and top credentials are usually the first prerequisites.

Financial planner

There is a new field of financial planning emerging to help solve the investment and tax problems of the individual investor. Financial planners may include specially trained representatives of the insurance industry, certified public accountants who have expertise in this area, and certified financial planners (the latter group is certified by the College for Financial Planning in Denver).

Those who achieve success in this area must be particularly adept at setting goals and objectives, analyzing diverse forms of investments, and assessing the tax consequences of investment decisions.

---

[4]Academic positions are also acceptable as a special category.

EMPHASIS IN THE TEXT

We recognize the existence of relatively efficient security markets in which assets may be thought to be properly valued at any point in time. However, we emphasize the techniques involved in fundamental analysis and, to some extent, technical analysis (to see if securities are, in fact, properly valued). We also point out areas where we feel the market may be less than completely efficient.

As a preview of the text, in Part 1 we examine the operations of the security markets, then consider sources of information on which to base investment decisions, as well as types and costs of transactions. We also look at investment strategy as it relates to the economic environment.

In Part 2 we actually go through the process of fundamental security analysis by examining the business cycle and its relationship to industry and company analysis. In analyzing the individual firm, we look at valuation considerations as well as financial statements. We then introduce technical analysis, which is based on the use of market indicators and charting. Finally, we go through a careful consideration of the efficient market hypothesis and its implications.

We then shift our attention from straight common stock issues to fixed-income securities (such as bonds) and leveraged securities (such as warrants and options) in Part 3. Many different investment and trading decisions are explained.

Portfolio management is considered in Part 4. We look at the literature on portfolio theory and its implications for those in charge of managing large pools of assets. A strong emphasis is placed on risk-return analysis (continuing our discussion from Chapter 1) and on the various techniques for measuring the performance of institutional portfolio managers.

We broaden our perspective of investment alternatives in Part 5. First of all, we look at special situations in the security markets, such as mergers and acquisitions, companies going public, or firms repurchasing their own shares. We then shift our attention to the commodities market with a look not only at traditional commodities, such as wheat or pork bellies, but also at financial futures, such as those related to bonds or foreign exchange. In this part of the text, we also take a hard look at real assets including real estate, precious metals, precious gems, and collectibles, and the advantages and disadvantages of each. In the concluding chapter of the text, we take a final overview of financial planning with an emphasis on retirement and estate planning.

IMPORTANT WORDS AND CONCEPTS

Investment	Systematic risk
Financial assets	Unsystematic risk
Real assets	Diversification
Direct and Indirect equity claims	Beta
Portfolio	Flow-of-funds analysis
Capital appreciation	Fundamental analysis
Liquidity	Technical analysis

Risk
Dividend valuation model

$$K_e = \frac{D_1}{P_0} + g$$

Variability

Security analyst
Portfolio manager
CFA
Investment banker

QUESTIONS AND PROBLEMS

1. How is an investment defined?

2. What are the differences between financial and real assets?

3. List some of the key areas relating to investment objectives.

4. Explain the concepts of direct equity and indirect equity.

5. How are equity and creditor claims different?

6. Do those wishing to assume low risks tend to invest long term or short term? Why?

7. How might investing in something generally considered to be risky actually decrease an investor's risk?

8. What are some types of appropriate investments for investors in high tax brackets who wish to diminish their tax obligation?

9. How is "liquidity" measured?

10. Explain why conservative investors who tend to buy short-term assets differ from short-term traders.

11. Why is there a minimum amount of time that must be committed to any investment program?

12. In a highly inflationary environment, would an investor tend to favor real or financial assets? Why?

13. If a stock pays a $2.50 dividend, has a price of $30 per share, and an expected growth rate of 5 percent per year, what will its total return be?

14. How is *risk* defined?

15. Over the long run, what have studies shown to be the relationship between risks and returns of financial assets?

16. Explain systematic and unsystematic risk.

17. Why is it thought that not all risk of an investment may be proportionately compensated for by higher returns?

18. What is meant by the three-sector nature of the economy in terms of the flow of funds?

19. What is a CFA?

20. What does a stock's beta indicate?

SELECTED REFERENCES

Bauman, W. Scott. "The CFA Candidate Program." *Financial Analysts Journal,* November–December 1974, pp. 68–70.

————. *Performance Objectives of Investors.* Occasional paper number 2. Charlottesville, Va.: Financial Analysts Research Foundation, 1975, pp. 29–50.

Blume, Marshall E., and Irwin Friend. "Risk, Investment Strategy and the Long-Run Rates of Return." *The Review of Economics and Statistics,* August 1974, pp. 259–69.

The editors of *Consumer Guide,* with Peter A. Dickinson. *How to Make Money during Inflation Recession.* New York: Harper & Row, 1980.

Eilbott, Peter. "Trends in the Value of Individual Stockholdings." *Journal of Business,* July 1974, pp. 339–48.

Fisher, Lawrence, and James H. Lorie. *A Half Century of Returns on Stocks and Bonds.* Chicago: The University of Chicago Graduate School of Business, 1977.

Ibbotson, Roger G., and Rex A. Sinquefield. "Stocks, Bonds, Bills, and Inflation: Year-by-Year Historical Returns (1926–1974)." *Journal of Business,* University of Chicago, January 1976, pp. 11–47.

Lease, Ronald C., Wilbur G. Lewellen, and Gary G. Schlarbaum. "The Individual Investor: Attributes and Attitudes." *Journal of Finance,* May 1974, pp. 413–33.

Lorie, James H., and Lawrence Fisher. "Rates of Return on Investment in Common Stock." *Journal of Business,* University of Chicago, January 1964, pp. 1–17.

————. "Rates of Return on Investment in Common Stock: The Year-by-Year Record 1926–1965." *Journal of Business,* July 1968, pp. 219–316.

New York Stock Exchange Fact Book. New York: New York Stock Exchange, 1981.

Pappas, James L., and George P. Huber. "Probabilistic Short-term Financial Planning." *Financial Management,* Autumn 1973, pp. 36–44.

Securities Industry Yearbook. New York: Securities Industry Association, 1980.

Treynor, Jack L. "Long Term Investing." *Financial Analysts Journal,* May–June 1976, pp. 56–59.

Weston, J. Fred. "Developments in Financial Theory." *Financial Management,* 10th anniversary issue, 1981, pp. 5–22.

2

Security markets— present and future

During the 1970s and early 1980's, many changes occurred in the security markets not only in the organization and competition between markets, but also in the increased array of securities from which to select. The market for stock options and financial futures are recent developments as is the increased popularity of mutual funds selling shares in portfolios of tax-free municipal bonds, short-term money market funds, and real estate investment trusts. Even the traditional markets for common stocks have changed with the advent of the composite tape linking several markets together, the elimination of fixed commissions, and the increased participation of financial institutions. Markets for corporate bonds, federal government securities, municipal bonds, and government-backed securities have all expanded as the use of debt has become more widespread. These events have all had an impact on the securities markets.

In this chapter, we examine how the market system operates, with an eye toward efficiency, liquidity, and allocation of capital. We then look at the role of the investment banker in the distribution of securities and the essential role of the secondary or resale market for stocks, bonds, and other securities. Finally, we examine some key protective legislation for the investor.

MARKET FUNCTIONS

Many times people will call their stockbroker and ask, How's the market? What they are referring to is usually the market for common stocks as measured by the Dow Jones Industrial Average, the New York Stock Exchange Index, or some other measure of common stock performance. The stock market is not the only market. There are markets for each different kind of investment that can be made.

A market is simply a way of exchanging assets, usually cash for something of value. It could be a used car, a government bond, gold, or diamonds. There doesn't have to be a central place where this transaction is consummated. As long as there can be communication between buyers and sellers, the exchange can occur. The offering party does not have to own what he sells. He can be an

agent acting for the owner in the transaction. For example, in the sale of real estate, the owner usually employs a real estate broker/agent who advertises and sells the property for a percentage commission. Not all markets have the same procedures, but certain trading characteristics are desirable for most markets.

Market efficiency and liquidity

In general, markets are efficient when prices respond quickly to new information, when each successive trade is made at a price close to the preceding price, and when the market can absorb large amounts of securities or assets without changing the price significantly. The more efficient the market, the faster prices react to new information, the closer in price is each successive trade, and the greater the amount of securities that can be sold without changing the price.

In order for markets to be efficient in this context, they must be liquid. Liquidity is a measure of the speed with which an asset can be converted into cash at its fair market value. Liquid markets exist when continuous trading occurs, and as the number of participants in the market becomes larger, price continuity increases along with liquidity. Transaction costs also affect liquidity. The lower the cost of buying and selling, the more likely it is that people will be able to enter the market.

Competition and allocation of capital

An investor must realize that all markets compete for funds; stocks against bonds, mutual funds against real estate, government securities against corporate securities, and so on. The competitive comparisons are almost endless. Because markets set prices on assets, investors are able to compare the prices against their perceived risk and expected return and thereby choose assets that enable them to achieve their desired risk-return trade-offs. If the markets are efficient, prices adjust rapidly to new information, and this adjustment changes the expected rate of return and allows the investor to alter his/her investment strategy. Without efficient and liquid markets, the investor would be unable to do this. This allocation of capital takes place on both secondary and primary markets.

Secondary markets

Secondary markets are markets for existing assets which are currently traded between investors. It is these markets that create the prices and allow for liquidity. If secondary markets did not exist, investors would have no place to sell their assets. Without liquidity, many people would not invest at all. Would you like to own $10,000 of Eastman Kodak common stock but be unable to convert it into cash if needed? If there were no secondary markets, investors would expect a higher return to compensate for the increased risk of illiquidity and the inability to adjust their portfolios to new information.

Primary markets

Primary markets are distinguished by the flow of funds between the market participants. Instead of trading between investors as in the secondary markets, participants in the primary market buy their assets directly from the source of the asset. A common example would be a new issue of corporate bonds sold by AT&T. You would buy the bonds through a brokerage firm acting as an agent for an investment banking firm or for AT&T. Your dollars would flow to AT&T rather than to another investor. The same would be true of buying a piece of art directly from the artist rather than from an art gallery. Primary markets allow corporations, government units, and others to raise needed funds for expansion of their capital base. Once the assets or securities are sold in the primary market, they begin trading in the secondary market. Price competition in the secondary markets between different risk-return classes enables the primary markets to price new issues at fair prices to reflect existing risk-return relationships. So far, our discussion of markets has been quite general but applicable to most free markets. In the following section, we will deal with the organization and structure of specific markets.

ORGANIZATION OF THE PRIMARY MARKETS—THE INVESTMENT BANKER

The most active participant in the primary market is the investment banker. Since corporations, states, and local governments do not sell new securities daily, monthly, or even annually, they rely on the expertise of the investment banker when selling securities.

Underwriting function

The investment banker acts as a middleman in the process of raising funds, and in most cases, he takes a risk by *underwriting* an issue of securities. Underwriting refers to the guarantee the investment banking firm gives the selling firm to purchase its securities at a fixed price, thereby eliminating the risk of not selling the whole issue of securities and having less cash than desired. The investment banker may also sell the issue on a "best efforts" basis where the issuing firm assumes the risk and simply takes back any securities not sold after a fixed period of time. However, this is not the usual practice.

The more risk the investment banker takes, the higher the selling fee to the corporation. Once the security is sold, the investment banker will usually make a market in the security, which means active buying and selling to insure a continuously liquid market and wider distribution.

Distribution

The distribution process is extremely important and one that an investment banker does not undertake by himself on large issues. More often, other invest-

ment banking firms will share the risk and the burden of distribution by forming a group called a syndicate. The larger the offering in dollar terms, the more participants there generally are in the syndicate. For example, the tombstone advertisement for Nevada Power Company's issue of common stock shows 34 participating investment bankers (Figure 2–1). The firms of Blyth Eastman Dillon & Co. (now Blyth Eastman Paine Webber), Merrill Lynch, and Dean Witter represent the managing underwriters, with the other 31 firms also participating in the syndicate. The firms at the top of the advertisement usually distribute the most shares, while the ones at the bottom, like Stix & Co. Inc., have the smallest amount. Each banker is responsible for the sale of an agreed-upon number of shares.

Nevada Power Company was already listed on the New York Stock Exchange and a market price was available, so the investment bankers did not have to make a market. Instead, the shares could be distributed directly from the investment banker to stock brokers and from them to the public. The advantage of having a large number of investment bankers is that more brokers are used and therefore more potential public buyers are available to improve the liquidity and geographic distribution of the issue. In the case of a new issue not previously trading in a public market like the New York Stock Exchange, the distribution process would include market makers (dealers) who would agree to buy and sell the securities over-the-counter. This would create a liquid market for the securities. The brokers would still enter into the process as they contacted their customers (J. Q. Public and Big Institutions) to see if they are interested in buying the new shares.

For most original, non-Treasury offers, the investment banker is extremely important as a link between the original issuer and the security markets. By taking much of the risk, the investment banker enables corporations and others to find needed capital and thus allows investors an opportunity to participate in the ownership of securities through purchase in the secondary markets.

Some initial offerings, such as Treasury bills or other federal government securities, do not use investment bankers. They rely on Federal Reserve banks to auction the securities to government securities dealers who make markets by buying and selling to large financial institutions. Individuals desiring to buy initial offerings from the Treasury can place orders directly with the nearest Federal Reserve branch bank.

ORGANIZATION OF THE SECONDARY MARKETS

Once the investment banker or the Federal Reserve (for U.S. government securities) has sold a new issue of securities, it begins trading in secondary markets that provide liquidity, efficiency, continuity, and competition. The *organized exchanges* fulfill this need in a central location where trading takes place between buyers and sellers. The *over-the-counter markets* also provide markets for exchange but not in a central location.

Figure 2–1   **Advertisement of distribution**

This announcement is not an offer to sell or a solicitation of an offer to buy any of these securities. The offering is made only by the Prospectus.

NEW ISSUE   August 22, 1979

750,000 SHARES

NEVADA POWER COMPANY

COMMON STOCK
(PAR VALUE $1 PER SHARE)

PRICE $26.625 PER SHARE

Copies of the Prospectus may be obtained in any State in which this announcement is circulated only from such of the underwriters as are qualified to act as dealers in securities in such State.

Blyth Eastman Dillon & Co.
Incorporated

Merrill Lynch White Weld Capital Markets Group.
Merrill Lynch, Pierce, Fenner & Smith Incorporated

Dean Witter Reynolds Inc.

Bache Halsey Stuart Shields   The First Boston Corporation   Bear, Stearns & Co.
Incorporated

Drexel Burnham Lambert   Goldman, Sachs & Co.   E. F. Hutton & Company Inc.
Incorporated

Kidder, Peabody & Co.   Lehman Brothers Kuhn Loeb   Loeb Rhoades, Hornblower & Co.
Incorporated   Incorporated

Paine, Webber, Jackson & Curtis   L. F. Rothschild, Unterberg, Towbin   Salomon Brothers
Incorporated

Shearson Hayden Stone Inc.   Smith Barney, Harris Upham & Co.   Warburg Paribas Becker
Incorporated   A. G. Becker

A. G. Edwards & Sons, Inc.   Robert W. Baird & Co.   William Blair & Company
Incorporated

Blunt Ellis & Loewi   Dain, Kalman & Quail   McDonald & Company   The Ohio Company
Incorporated   Incorporated

Piper, Jaffray & Hopwood   Prescott, Ball & Turben   D. A. Davidson & Co.
Incorporated   Incorporated

R. G. Dickinson & Co.   Howe, Barnes & Johnson, Inc.   The Milwaukee Company

Raffensperger, Hughes & Co., Inc.   Wm. C. Roney & Co.   Stix & Co. Inc.

This section updates significant occurrences in the securities markets during the 1970s and looks at the effects of the national market system in the 1980s. Since the secondary markets are often divided into the organized exchanges and the over-the-counter markets, each will be presented separately.

Organized exchanges

Organized exchanges are either national or regional, but both classifications are organized in a similar fashion. Exchanges have a central trading location where securities are bought and sold in an auction market by brokers acting as agents for the buyer and seller. Brokers are registered members of the exchanges, and their number is fixed by each exchange. The national exchanges are the New York Stock Exchange (NYSE) located at the corner of Broad and Wall Streets in New York City and the American Stock Exchange (AMEX) located at the corner of Hanover and Wall Streets, also in New York City. Both these exchanges are governed by a board of directors consisting of one-half exchange members and one-half public members.

The regional exchanges began their existence trading securities of local firms. As the firms grew, they became listed on the national exchanges, but they also continued to trade on the regionals. Many cities, such as Chicago, Cincinnati, Baltimore, Detroit, Boston, and others, have regional exchanges. Today most of the trading on these exchanges is done in nationally known companies. Trading in the same companies is common between the NYSE and such regionals as the Midwest Exchange in Chicago, the Pacific Coast Exchange in San Francisco and Los Angeles, and the smaller regionals. In fact, about 90 percent of the companies traded on the Midwest and Pacific Coast Exchanges are also listed on the NYSE. Using August 17, 1981, as a typical day, we see in Table 2–1 that 49,115,670 shares of firms listed on the New York Stock Exchange were traded. Since some of these shares are dually listed on other exchanges, not all volume was transacted in New York.

Consolidated tape

Although dual listing and trading has existed for some time, it was not until June 16, 1975, that a consolidated ticker tape was instituted. This allows brokers on the floor of one exchange to see prices of transactions on other exchanges in the dually listed stocks. Any time a transaction is made on a regional exchange or over-the-counter in a security listed on the NYSE, this transaction and any made on the floor of the NYSE are displayed on the composite tape. The composite price data keeps markets more efficient and prices more competitive between exchanges at all times. The middle part of Table 2–1 also shows the composite volume from January 1, 1981, to August 14, 1981, and the NYSE volume. Of the 8.592 billion shares traded on the composite tape, 7.484 billion shares, or 87.1 percent of the total volume, was accounted for by the NYSE.

The NYSE and AMEX are both national exchanges and for years did not allow dual listing of companies traded on their exchanges. As of August 1976, securi-

Table 2–1　　　　　　　**Data on trading volume**

Friday's Volume

49,115,670 Shares; 75,500 Warrants

TRADING BY MARKETS

	Shares	Warrants
New York Exchange	42,580,000	73,000
American Exchange	400	....
Midwest Exchange	2,256,800	....
Pacific Exchange	1,680,100	....
Nat'l Assoc. of Securities Dealers	1,043,470	2,500
Philadelphia Exchange	947,200	....
Boston Exchange	287,800	....
Cincinnati Exchange	228,900	....
Instinet System	91,000	....

NYSE – Composite

Volume since Jan. 1:	1981	1980	1979
Total shares	8,592,064,894	7,649,556,082	5,410,129,969
Total warrants	28,659,500	32,491,500	42,669,049

New York Stock Exchange

Volume since Jan. 1:	1981	1980	1979
Total shares	7,484,059,383	6,722,690,592	4,815,262,114
Total warrants	28,555,500	32,483,900	42,337,500

SOURCE: *The Wall Street Journal,* August 17, 1981.

ties were able to be dually listed between these exchanges. There doesn't seem to be any advantage to this since both are located in New York City, and traditionally, shares traded on one exchange are not traded on the other. As you can see from Table 2–1, there were only 400 shares of stock traded on the AMEX for firms also listed on the NYSE.

Listing requirements for firms

Securities can only be traded on an exchange if they have met the listing requirements of the exchange and have been approved by the board of governors. All exchanges have minimum requirements that must be met before trading can take place in a company's common stock. Since the NYSE is the biggest exchange and generates the most dollar volume in large, well-known companies, it is not surprising that its listing requirements are the most restrictive. According to the *NYSE Fact Book,* the requirements for a company to be listed for the first time are as follows:

1. The firm must have at least 2,000 stockholders owning 100 shares.
2. At least 1 million shares must be held by the public. Along with the first requirement, this insures a minimum level of liquidity and continuous trading.
3. Net tangible assets must be $16 million or more.
4. The firm must have $16 million in market value of publicly held stock.
5. The firm must have demonstrated earnings power under competitive conditions of $2.5 million before federal income taxes for the most recent year.
6. It also must have pretax income of at least $2 million for the previous two years.

The other exchanges have requirements covering the same areas, but the amounts are smaller.

Corporations desiring to be listed on exchanges have made the decision that public availability of the stock on an exchange will benefit their shareholders. The benefits will occur either by providing liquidity to owners or by allowing the company a more viable means for raising external capital for growth and expansion. The company must pay annual listing fees to the exchange and some fees based on the number of shares traded each year.

Membership for market participants

We've talked about listing requirements for corporations on the exchange; but what about the investment houses or traders that service the listed firms or trade for their own account on the exchanges? These privileges are reserved for a select number of people. The NYSE has 1,366 members, while the AMEX has only 650. These members can be divided into five distinct categories, each with a specific job to perform.

Commission brokers Commission brokers represent commission houses, such as Merrill Lynch or E. F. Hutton, that execute orders on the floor of the exchange for customers of that firm. Many of the larger retail brokerage houses have more than one commission broker on the floor of the exchange. If I call my account executive (stockbroker) and place an order to buy 100 shares of Minnesota Mining, he will teletype my order to the NYSE where it will be transmitted to one of the firm's commission brokers who will go to the appropriate trading post and execute the order.

Floor brokers You can imagine that a commission broker could get very busy running from post to post on a heavy volume day. In times like these, he will rely on some help from a floor broker, who is registered to trade on the exchange but is not an employee of a member firm. Instead, the floor broker owns his own seat and charges a small fee for his services (usually around $4 per 100 shares).

Registered traders Registered traders own their own seat and are not associated with a member firm (such as Merrill Lynch). They are registered to trade for their own accounts and, of course, do so with the objective of earning a profit. Because they are members, they don't have to pay commissions on these trades; but in so trading, they help to generate a continuous market and liquidity for the market in general. There is always the possibility that these traders could manipulate the market if they acted in mass, and for that reason, the exchanges have rules governing their behavior and limiting the number of registered traders at one specific trading post.

Odd-lot dealers Odd lots (less than 100 shares) are not traded on the main floor of the exchange, so if a customer wants to buy or sell 20 shares of AT&T,

the order will end up being processed by an odd-lot dealer. The dealer owns his own inventory of the particular security and buys and sells for his own account. If he accumulates 100 shares, he can sell them in the market, or if he needs 20 shares, he can buy 100 in the market and hold the other 80 shares in his inventory. A few very large brokerage firms, such as Merrill Lynch, have begun making their own odd-lot market in actively traded securities, and it is expected that this trend will become common practice at the other large commission houses. Odd-lot trading on other exchanges is usually handled by the specialist in the particular stock.

Specialists Specialists are a very important segment of the exchange and make up about one fourth of total membership. Each stock traded has a specialist assigned to it, and most specialists are responsible for more than one stock. The specialist has two basic duties with regard to the stocks he supervises. First, he must handle any special orders that commission brokers or floor brokers might give him. For example, a special order could limit the price someone is willing to pay for General Telephone stock at $28 per share for 100 chares. If the commission broker reaches the General Telephone trading post and GTE is selling at $31 per share, the broker will leave the order with the specialist to execute if and when the stock of GTE falls to $28 or less. The specialist puts these special limit orders in his "book" with the date and time entered so he can execute orders at the same price by the earliest time of receipt. A portion of the broker's commission is then paid to the specialist.

The second major function of specialists is to maintain continuous, liquid, and orderly markets in their assigned stocks. This is not a difficult function in the actively traded securities, such as General Motors, Du Pont, and American Telephone, but it becomes more difficult in those stocks where there are no large, active markets. For example, suppose you placed an order to buy 100 shares of Anacomp Inc. at the market price. If the commission broker reaches the Anacomp trading post and no seller is present, he can't wait for one to appear since he has other orders to execute. Fortunately, he can buy the shares from the specialist who acts as a dealer—in this case buying for and selling from his own inventory. To ensure his ability to maintain continuous markets, the exchange requires a specialist to have $500,000 or enough capital to own 5,000 shares of his assigned stock, whichever is greater. At times, specialists are placed under tremendous pressure to make a market for securities. A classic case occurred when President Eisenhower had a heart attack in the 1950s and specialists stabilized the market by absorbing wave after wave of "sell" orders.

OTHER ORGANIZED EXCHANGES

The American Stock Exchange trades in smaller companies than the NYSE and, except for a few dually listed companies on the NYSE, the stocks traded on the AMEX are completely different from those on any other exchange. Because

**The American
Stock Exchange**

the small companies on the AMEX do not meet the liquidity needs of large institutional investors, the AMEX has been primarily a market for individual investors. Nevertheless, the AMEX has seen strong growth in the late 1970s and early 1980s as many investors have sought out smaller firms.

In an attempt to differentiate itself from the NYSE, the AMEX traded warrants in companies for many years before the NYSE allowed them. Even now, the AMEX has warrants listed for stocks trading on the NYSE, while the NYSE has very few warrants listed at all. The AMEX also trades call options (as of 1982 the NYSE did not) in over 80 stocks with most of the underlying common stocks being listed on the NYSE. This market has been a stabilizing force for the AMEX. The AMEX (as well as the NYSE) has also recently entered into commodity futures trading through interest rate futures. Although the AMEX also trades about 200 corporate bonds, this is not the major market for corporate bonds.

**The Chicago Board
Options Exchange**

Trading in call options started on the Chicago Board Options Exchange (CBOE) in April of 1973 and proved very successful. The number of call options listed grew from 16 in 1973 to well over 200 in 1982. A call option gives the owner the right to buy 100 shares of the underlying common stock at a set price for a certain period of time. The establishment of the CBOE standardized call options into three-month, six-month, and nine-month expiration periods on a rotating monthly series. For example, one series is January, April, July, October. A second series is December, March, June, September, and the last series is November, February, May, August. When the CBOE began, only the first series was traded, but the growth in the market dictated the need for other dates. The CBOE and the AMEX currently have many options that are dually listed, and the competition between them is fierce. The two exchanges also have added put options (options to sell). A number of smaller regional exchanges also provide for option trading. More about these markets will be presented in Chapter 13.

Futures markets

The CBOE is a futures market for common stock but is usually referred to as the options market. Futures markets have traditionally been associated with commodities and more recently financial instruments. Purchasers of commodity futures own the right to buy a certain amount of the commodity at a set price for a specified period of time. When the time runs out (expires), the futures contract will be delivered unless sold before expiration. One major futures markets is the Chicago Board of Trade, which trades corn, oats, soybeans, wheat, silver, plywood, Ginnie Mae futures, and Treasury bond futures. There are also other important futures markets in Chicago, Kansas City, Minneapolis, New York, and other cities. These markets are very important as hedging markets and help set commodity prices. They are also known for their wide price swings and volatile speculative nature. We will spend more time discussing these markets in Chapter 17.

OVER-THE-COUNTER MARKETS

Unlike the organized exchanges, the over-the-counter markets (OTC) have no central location where securities are traded. Being traded over-the-counter implies that the trade takes place by telephone or electronic device and that dealers stand ready to buy or sell specific securities for their own accounts. These dealers will buy at a bid price and sell at an asked price that reflects the competitive market conditions. The National Association of Securities Dealers, a self-policing organization of dealers, requires at least two market makers (dealers) for each security, but often there are 5 or 10 or even 20 for government securities.

OTC markets exist for stocks, corporate bonds, mutual funds, federal government securities, state and local bonds, commercial paper, negotiable certificates of deposits, and various other securities. Altogether these securities make the OTC the largest of all markets in the United States in dollar terms.

In the OTC market, the difference between the bid and asked price is the spread; it represents the profit the dealer earns by making a market. For example, if ABC common stock is bid 10 and asked 10½, this quote simply means the dealer will buy at least 100 shares at $10 per share or will sell 100 shares at $10.50 per share. If his prices are too low, more buyers than sellers will appear, and he will run out of inventory unless he raises prices to attract more sellers and balance the supply and demand. If his price is at equilibrium, he will match an equal number of shares bought and sold, and for his market-making activities, he will earn 50 cents per share traded. Since this is his principal business, earnings on these transactions are taxed at ordinary income tax rates just like a wholesale distributor who buys nuts and bolts at cost and sells at retail, paying taxes on the profits.

Many of the 5,000+ common stocks actively traded over-the-counter repre-

Table 2–2

Over-the-Counter Markets

4:00 p.m. Eastern Standard Time Prices, Friday, August 14, 1981

Volume, All Issues, 29,447,200

SINCE JANUARY 1

	1981	1980	1979
Total sales	5,019,327,358	3,330,688,751	2,119,129,465

MARKET DIARY

	Fri	Thur	Wed	Tues	Mon
Issues traded	3,292	3,288	3,287	3,278	3,274
Advances	487	571	672	661	441
Declines	561	539	520	495	682
Unchanged	2,244	2,178	2,095	2,122	2,151
xNew highs	51	59	56	53	50
xNew lows	66	64	58	60	110

x-Based on 4 p.m. Eastern time bid quote.

ACTIVE STOCKS

	Volume	4:00 Bid	Chg.
Energy Reserves Grp	267,300	16¼	+ ⅛
Piezo Elec A	239,000	2⅝	....
Valex Petroleum	230,600	2¾	+3/16
Ferrofluidics Inc	213,300	1⅞	+ ¼
Applied Medical Dev	189,700	1 1/16	−1/16
Superior Care	187,900	3⅞	+11/16
Tyrex Oil	164,500	3 9/16	−1/16
Nicklos Oil Gas	156,900	32½	+ 2½
Tampax Inc	150,600	33	....
MCI Communications	149,900	23	+ ⅜

Issues selling for at least $1 a share.

SOURCE: Reprinted by permission of *The Wall Street Journal*, © Dow Jones & Company, Inc. (August 17, 1981). All rights reserved.

sent small companies and, in many cases, are closely held by insiders. There are actually several segments of the OTC stock market. There is a list of nationally traded companies like Tampax, Clevetrust, Econ Labs, etc., that have enough of a diversified shareholder base that they are considered national in scope. There are also small companies that only have local or regional interest. These may not appear in *The Wall Street Journal* but will be found on the financial pages of large city newspapers in Dallas, Cleveland, Chicago, Atlanta, Los Angeles, and other cities under the heading "Local Over-The-Counter Markets." OTC securities are also usually low priced as can be seen from the "Active Stocks" portion of Table 2–2, but the volume can be sizable.

Over-the-counter markets have always been very popular for bank stocks and insurance stocks. One reason is that these stocks do not generate enough trading volume or have enough stockholders to merit their listing on the organized exchanges. A second reason is that many are small and only have local interest.

Debt securities traded over-the-counter

Government securities of the U.S. Treasury provide the largest dollar volume of transactions on the OTC and account for billions of dollars in trades each week. These securities are traded by government securities dealers who are often associated with or a division of a large financial institution, such as a New York, Chicago, or West Coast money market bank or a large brokerage house like Merrill Lynch. These dealers make markets in government securities, such as Treasury bills, Treasury bonds, or federal agency securities like Federal National Mortgage Association issues.

Municipal bonds of state and local governments are traded by specialized municipal bond dealers who, in most cases, work for large commercial banks. Commercial paper, representing unsecured, short-term corporate debt, is traded directly by finance companies, but a large portion of commercial paper sold by industrial companies is handled by OTC dealers specializing in this market. Every security has its own set of dealers and its own distribution system. On markets where large dollar trades occur, the spread between bid and ask could be as little as 1/16 or 1/32 of $1 per $1,000 of securities.

NASDAQ

NASDAQ stands for the National Association of Securities Dealers Automated Quotations System. This system is linked together by a computer system and provides up-to-the-minute quotations on over 3,000 of the OTC stocks traded on the NASDAQ system. The National Association of Security Dealers requires firms trading on their automated quotation system to have at least 300 shareholders, 100,000 shares outstanding, $1 million in assets, and two registered market makers. NASDAQ only includes those firms of reasonable size and trading activity, while the OTC market includes many thousands more.

Before the new automated quotation system was installed in 1971, broker-dealers were required to telephone other competing dealers for quotations. This

was time-consuming and inefficient. If a large number of dealers made a market in a particular stock, it was almost impossible to trade actively and be sure you had the best price for your customer unless you called all the dealers. The NAS-DAQ eliminated this and now has available three different levels of quotations systems.

Level 1 is for users who are interested in receiving quotes for their customers but are not actively trading or acting as dealers. This level provides the median quote of all the market makers and therefore is a reasonable indicator of average prices, but not necessarily the best price available. To find the best price, you would need level 2.

Level 2 is primarily for broker-dealers who are active traders. Level 2 will provide a visual display of all the dealer bid-ask quotations and identify each dealer. Bid prices are listed in descending order, while ask prices are listed in ascending order. This makes it easy to find the best buy-or-sell price. The advantage of this system is that if a broker wants to place an order for a customer, he can immediately find the best price, call the dealer, and execute the transaction.

Level 3 is only for market makers. It provides all the same information as level 2 but enables the market maker to adjust his bid and ask price which instantaneously appears on other dealers' terminals. Changes in quotes can only be made for stock in which the dealer makes a market.

The third market

Prior to the mid-1970s, commissions on the NYSE were fixed. This meant that the same commission schedule applied to all transactions of a given size and one broker could not undercut the other on the New York Stock Exchange. Several OTC dealers, most notably Weeden & Co., decided to make a market in about 200 of the most actively traded NYSE issues and to do this at a much smaller cost than the NYSE commission structure would allow. This trading in NYSE-listed securities in over-the-counter markets became known as the third market. This market flourished until commission rates on NYSE-listed firms became fully competitive on May 1, 1975. The third market has since greatly diminished in importance. A similar rise and decline has taken place in the fourth market, in which institutions traded directly between themselves, bypassing the middleman broker.

THE TRANSFORMATION AND FUTURE OF THE CAPITAL MARKETS

Financial institutions, such as banks, pension funds, insurance companies, and investment companies (mutual funds), have always invested and traded in securities. However, the growth of these institutions and their participation in the capital markets has increased dramatically in recent years. Part of the increased share activity can be found in the accelerated growth of pension plans during this

period. Also, the rapid rise in stock prices during the post-World War II period attracted a lot of individual investors into mutual funds.

Table 2–3 on institutional activity shows a 289 percent increase between 1965 and 1980 in the size of the average number of shares per trade on the NYSE (224 to 872). This is one indication of the increasing role of financial institutions. An examination of the second column indicates an even more rapid increase in the number of block trades. A block trade is a single order of 10,000 shares or more. The average number increased from 9 per day in 1965 to 528 per day in 1980.

Perhaps a better indication of the increased dominance of market trading is the fact that block trades as a percentage of total NYSE volume increased from 3.1 percent in 1965 to 29.2 percent in 1980. During this time of increasing institutional activity, the small investor (100 to 200 shares) has seen his role decline. In 1965 individuals accounted for approximately 70 percent of the total NYSE volume, and by 1980, this had declined to 30 percent. This simply reinforces the idea of increased institutional presence.

In the early 1960s and before, the NYSE had been a market primarily for the individual investor. As this shift toward the institutions occurred, the market structure also changed. Because of fixed commissions on the NYSE, the third market and fourth market developed. The increased activity in these markets and federal legislation eventually forced the NYSE to eliminate its fixed commissions. When fixed commissions were replaced by negotiated rates, many smaller, research-oriented investment firms were unable to compete with the larger, retail brokerage houses. Before, they had received compensation in the form of give-ups for their research. The give-ups worked as follows. A research firm would provide institutions with specialized research, and when the firm made trades with large brokerage firms, the firm handling the transaction would give part of the commission to the research house. Negotiated commissions reduced commissions to

Table 2–3   **Institutional activity**

	Average number of shares per trade (NYSE)	Average number of block transactions per day (NYSE)	Block trades as a percent of reported NYSE volume
1965	224	9	3.1
1967	257	27	6.7
1969	356	61	14.1
1971	428	106	17.8
1973	449	116	17.8
1975	495	136	16.6
1977	641	215	22.4
1978	717	298	22.9
1980	872	528	29.2

SOURCE: *New York Stock Exchange Fact Book* (New York: New York Stock Exchange, 1981).

such an extent that trading houses no longer were able to give up enough to compensate the research house for its work. As a result, these smaller firms went out of business or merged with larger retail brokerage firms. A select few have been able to charge cash for their research and survive.

At the same time, many retail brokerage firms stopped providing free research to their individual customers. This forced the individual to either buy research or simply take their account executive's advice. This move to negotiated commissions also created the discount broker who will execute a trade for individuals at a discount from current rates of retail brokers. The market has not seen the end of the changes caused by the advent of negotiated rates. As more firms compete for business, the commissions on trades have gotten smaller, and several large brokerage firms have been forced to merge because they could not generate enough volume to cover their costs. In 1981, an additional trend has set in—other financial service firms have purchased brokerage houses in order to diversify their base. Examples include the purchase of Bache Halsey Stuart Shields by Prudential Insurance Company, Shearson, Loeb Rhoades by American Express, and Dean Witter Reynolds by Sears Roebuck & Co. These purchases are reflective of the tremendous competition among all forms of financial service firms (insurance companies, credit card firms, banks) to expand their base.

The national market system

A national market system was mandated by Congress In the Securities Amendments Act of 1975. This proposal was supported by the Securities Exchange Commission and by other key groups. While there has been some delay in the implementation of a national market system due to industry foot dragging and political changes in Washington, it is still a goal for the future. No one knows exactly what form this national market might take, but there are several things that will be required. Some are easily achieved, while others are not. The first is already in place, and that is the composite tape that reflects trades on all exchanges for listed NYSE companies. There will also have to be competition between specialists and market makers. This is already occurring between the regional exchanges and the NYSE in dually listed securities. The prices seem to be more stable and the spreads between the bid and ask prices are closer for securities with competing market makers. A third occurrence is that the NYSE will most likely have to abolish Rule 390, which prohibits members of the NYSE from trading off the board in NYSE-listed securities. This rule is currently undergoing change as Merrill Lynch and others challenge it.

Possibly the biggest dilemma in creating a national market system is fully developing a computerized system to execute limit orders. Currently, NYSE specialists execute most limit orders, which specify that a security must be bought or sold at a limited price or better. The national market system will need a computerized system to handle limit orders from all markets. Progress along these lines was being required by the SEC in mid-1982.

The national market system could take the form of NASDAQ where dealers

make markets and compete against one another. Most likely, the NYSE will not capitulate easily to an over-the-counter system of trading. The traditional auction markets have been able to absorb block trades without difficulty and serve the needs of institutional customers and individuals, and certainly the NYSE will not want to give up its dominant market position. One thing is sure; the markets of the future will rely on computers more than ever and be increasingly competitive and efficient.

REGULATION OF THE SECURITY MARKETS

Organized securities markets are regulated by the Securities and Exchange Commission (SEC) and by the self-regulation of the exchanges. The OTC market is controlled by the National Association of Securities Dealers. There are three major laws governing the sale and subsequent trading of securities. The Securities Act of 1933 pertains to new issues of securities, while the Securities Exchange Act of 1934 deals with trading in the security markets. The Securities Acts amendments of 1975 are the latest legislation, and their main emphasis is on a national securities market. The primary purpose of these laws was to protect unwary investors from fraud and manipulation and to make the markets more competitive and efficient by forcing corporations to make relevant investment information public.

Securities Act of 1933

The Securities Act of 1933 was enacted after congressional investigations of the abuses present in the securities markets during the 1929 crash and again in 1931. The act's primary purpose was to provide full disclosure of all pertinent investment information whenever a corporation sold a new issue of securities. For this reason, it is sometimes referred to as the "truth in securities" act. The Securities Act has several important features.

1. All offerings except government bonds and bank stocks that are to be sold in more than one state must be registered with the SEC.
2. The registration statement must be filed 20 days in advance of the date of sale and include detailed corporate information. If the SEC finds the information misleading, incomplete, or inaccurate, they will delay the offering until the registration statement is corrected. The SEC in no way certifies that the security is fairly priced but only that the information seems to be factual and accurate.
3. All new issues of securities must be accompanied by a *prospectus,* a detailed summary of the registration statement. Included in the prospectus is usually a list of directors and officers; their salaries, stock options, and shareholdings; financial reports certified by a CPA; a list of the underwriters; the purpose and use for the funds to be provided from the sale of securities; and any other reasonable information that investors may need to know before

they can wisely invest their money. A preliminary prospectus may be distributed to potential buyers before the offering date, but it will not contain the offering price or underwriting fees. It is called a "red herring" because stamped on the front in red letters are the words "Preliminary Prospectus."

4. For the first time, officers of the company and other experts preparing the prospectus or registration statement can be sued for penalties and recovery of realized losses if any information presented was fraudulent, factually wrong, or omitted.

Securities Exchange Act of 1934

This act created the Securities and Exchange Commission to enforce the securities laws. It was empowered to regulate the securities markets and those companies listed on the exchanges. Specifically the major points of the 1934 Act are as follows:

1. Guidelines for inside trading were established. Insiders must hold securities for at least six months before they can sell them. This is to prevent them from taking quick advantage of information which could result in a short-term profit. All short-term profits were payable to the corporation. Insiders were generally thought to be officers, directors, employees, or relatives. In the late 1960s, the SEC widened its interpretation to include anyone having information that was not public knowledge. This could include security analysts, loan officers, large institutional holders, and many others who had business dealings with the firm.

2. The Federal Reserve Board of Governors became responsible for setting margin requirements to determine how much credit you had available to buy securities.

3. Manipulation of securities by conspiracies between investors was prohibited.

4. The SEC was given control over the proxy procedures of corporations (a proxy is an absent stockholder vote).

5. In its regulation of companies traded on the markets, it required certain reports to be filed periodically. Corporations must file quarterly financial statements with the SEC, send annual reports to stockholders, and file 10-K Reports with the SEC annually. The 10-K Report has more financial data than the annual report and can be very useful to an investor or loan officer. Most companies will now send 10-K Reports to stockholders on request.

6. The act required all security exchanges to register with the SEC. In this capacity, they supervise and regulate many pertinent organizational aspects of exchanges, such as listing and trading mechanics.

The Securities Acts amendments of 1975

The major focus of the Securities Acts amendments of 1975 was to direct the SEC to supervise the development of a national securities market. No exact structure was put forth, but the law did assume that any national market would

make extensive use of computers and electronic communication devices. Additionally, the law prohibited fixed commissions on public transactions and also prohibited banks, insurance companies, and other financial institutions from buying stock exchange memberships to save commission costs for their own institutional transactions. This act is a worthwhile addition to the securities laws since it fosters greater competition and more efficient prices.

Other legislation

In addition to these three major pieces of legislation, a number of other acts deal directly with investor protection. For example, The Investment Advisor Act of 1940 is set up to protect the public from unethical investment advisors. Any advisor with over 15 public clients (excluding tax accountants and lawyers) must register with the SEC and file semiannual reports. The Investment Company Act of 1940 provides similar oversight for mutual funds and investment companies dealing with small investors. The act was amended in 1970 and currently gives the NASD authority to supervise and limit commissions and investment advisory fees on certain types of mutual funds.

A final piece of legislation dealing directly with investor protection is the Securities Investor Protection Act of 1970. The Security Investor Protection Corporation (SIPC) was established to oversee liquidation of brokerage firms and to insure investors' accounts to a maximum value of $50,000 in case of bankruptcy. It functions much the same as the Federal Deposit Insurance Corporation (for banks) and the Federal Savings and Loan Insurance Corporation. SIPC is an offshoot of the problems encountered on Wall Street during the period from 1967 to 1970. Share volume surged to then all-time highs, and many firms were unable to process orders fast enough. A back-office paper crunch caused Wall Street to shorten the hours the exchanges were formally open for new business but even this didn't help. Investors lost large sums, and for many months, they were unable to use or get possession of securities held in their names. Even though SIPC insures these accounts, it still does not cover market value losses suffered while waiting to get securities from a bankrupt brokerage firm.

On balance, all the legislation we have discussed has tended to increase the confidence of the investing public. In an industry where public trust is so critical, some form of supervision, whether public or private, is necessary and generally accepted.

SUMMARY

A smoothly functioning market is one that is efficient and provides liquidity to the investor. The success of a primary market, in which new issues are generally underwritten by investment bankers, is highly dependent upon the presence of an active resale (secondary) market.

Secondary markets may be established in the form of an organized exchange or as an over-the-counter market. The predominant organized market is the New

York Stock Exchange, but increasing attention is being directed to various other markets. The possibility of a true national market system looms as a consideration for the future, with the completed first step being the development of a consolidated tape among different markets. NASDAQ (National Association of Security Dealers Automated Quotations System) has done much to improve the communications network in the over-the-counter market and bring competition to the organized exchanges. Nevertheless, much remains to be done.

The dominant role of the institutional investor has had an enormous impact on the markets. The push by large investors for lower commission rates first created a third market, in which NYSE listed firms were traded over-the-counter by nonexchange members. This was ultimately followed by the elimination of the fixed commission system on the organized exchanges. Negotiated commissions have meant lower commissions for large institutional investors and thus less dollars to pay for organized research or to bankroll smaller brokerage firms. An enormous consolidation of market participants has taken place on Wall Street.

The term *market* seems to be broadening with different types of new investment outlets, as witnessed by the expansion of options and commodity trading mechanisms.

Finally, problems or imperfections in the marketplace during critical time periods have lead to a wide array of securities legislation. The legislation in the 1930s regulated the securities markets and created the SEC. Subsequent laws have dealt with restructuring the market and investor protection.

IMPORTANT WORDS AND CONCEPTS		
	Market	Odd-lot dealer
	Primary market	Specialists
	Secondary market	CBOE
	Third market	Options market
	Fourth market	NASDAQ
	Investment banking	SEC
	Underwriting	Securities Act of 1933
	Organized exchange	Prospectus
	OTC market	Red herring prospectus
	Commission broker	Securities Exchange Act of 1934
	Floor broker	Securities Exchange Act of 1975
	Registered trader	SIPC

QUESTIONS AND PROBLEMS

1. What is a *market*?
2. What is an efficient market?
3. What is the difference between primary and secondary markets?

4. What are the major functions of an investment banker?

5. How are organized exchanges and OTC markets related?

6. Briefly describe the participants on an exchange.

7. How does the American Stock Exchange differ from the New York Stock Exchange in terms of size of companies traded? Is the AMEX primarily a market for institutional investors or individuals?

8. What is meant by the dealer's spread in the OTC markets?

9. Explain how NASDAQ has replaced the telephone as a source of quotations for widely traded over-the-counter stocks.

10. What are the third and fourth markets? Why have they decreased in importance?

11. Define a block trade. What does the increase in block trades since 1965 tend to indicate about the nature of investors in the market?

12. What does the composite tape indicate?

13. What is likely to be the biggest dilemma in creating a national market system?

14. Indicate the primary purpose of the Securities Act of 1933. Why was it enacted? Under the act, does the SEC certify that a security is fairly priced?

15. Explain the purpose of the Security Investor Protection Corporation (SIPC).

SELECTED REFERENCES

Dann, Larry Y.; David Myers; and Robert J. Raab. "Trading Rules, Large Blocks, and the Speed of Price Adjustment." *Journal of Financial Economics,* January 1977, pp. 3–22.

Euback, Arthur E., Jr. "Risk/Return Contrast: NYSE, Amex, and OTC." *Journal of Portfolio Management,* Summer 1977, pp. 25–30.

Farrar, Donald E. "Toward a Central Market System: Wall Street's Slow Retreat into the Future." *Journal of Financial and Quantitative Analysis,* November 1974, pp. 815–27.

Feuerstein, Donald M. "Toward a National System of Securities Exchanges." *Financial Analysts Journal,* May–June 1972, pp. 28–34.

Freund, William C. "Issues Confronting the Stock Market in a Period of Rising Institutionalization." Supplement to *Journal of Financial and Quantitative Analysis,* March 1972, pp. 1687–90.

Friend, Irwin. "The Economic Consequences of the Stock Market." *American Economic Review,* May 1972, pp. 212–19.

Henning, C. N.; W. Pigott; and R. H. Scott. *Financial Markets and the Economy.* Englewood Cliffs, N.J.: Prentice-Hall, 1975.

Hershman, Arlene. "Here Comes the New Stock Market." *Dun's Review,* April 1978, pp. 65–70.

New York Stock Exchange Fact Book. New York: New York Stock Exchange, 1981.

Peake, Junius W. "The National Market System." *Financial Analysts Journal,* July–August 1978, pp. 25–33.

Securities and Exchange Commission. *The Future Structure of the Securities Market.* Statement. Washington, D.C.: Securities and Exchange Commission, February 2, 1972. Also, *White Paper on the Structure of a Central Market System,* March 30, 1973.

Stoll, Hans R. "The Pricing of Security Dealer Services: An Empirical Study of NASDAQ Stocks." *Journal of Finance,* September 1978, pp. 1153–72.

Tinic, S. M., and R. R. West. "Competition and the Pricing of Dealer Service in the OTC Market." *Journal of Financial and Quantitative Analysis,* June 1972, pp. 1707–28.

Van Horne, James C. The Function and Analysis of Capital Market Rates. Englewood Cliffs, N.J.: Prentice-Hall, 1970.

Welles, Chris. "The Showdown over Rule 390." *Institutional Investor,* December 1977, pp. 33–38.

3

Sources of investment information

We are continually exposed to much information in this world of expanding and rapid communications. As the scope of investments has grown to include more than stocks and bonds, investment information has expanded to cover assets, such as gold and silver, diamonds, original art, antiques, stamps and coins, real estate, farm land, oil and gas, tax shelters, commodities, mutual funds, and other specialized assets. The problem investors are faced with is not only which investments to choose from the many available, but also where to find relevant information on specific investments.

First of all, the investor needs a basic knowledge of the economic environment. After determining the economic climate, the investor will proceed to a more detailed analysis of industries and unique variables affecting a specific investment. It is often said that the sign of an educated person is whether he or she knows where to find information to make an intelligent decision. The rest of this chapter will attempt to provide a list and description of the basic information sources for some of the more common forms of investments as well as general economic sources. Appendix 3–A at the end of the chapter contains the addresses of many of the sources mentioned in this chapter.

AGGREGATE ECONOMIC DATA

Economic data are necessary for analyzing the past and predicting future trends of the economy. The economic environment that exists today and the one expected in the future will bear heavily on the types of investments selected when creating or managing an investment portfolio. Information on inflation, wages, disposable income, economic growth rates, interest rates, money supply, demographic trends and so on are important economic data that will influence investor decisions. This information is available in many publications from the government, commercial banks, and periodicals. What follows is a brief description of some of the major sources of economic data.

Federal Reserve Bulletin

The *Federal Reserve Bulletin* is published monthly by the Board of Governors of the Federal Reserve System, Washington D.C. It contains an abundance of monetary data, such as money supply figures, interest rates, bank reserves, and various statistics on commercial banks. Fiscal variables, such as U.S. budget receipts and outlays and federal debt figures are also found in the *Bulletin.* This publication also contains international data on exchange rates and U.S. dealings with foreigners and overseas banks.

Since a complete description of the *Federal Reserve Bulletin* is outside the scope of this chapter, a partial listing of the table of contents should suffice to provide a more complete idea of what information it contains. Each heading may be divided into more detailed sections that provide information for the previous month, the current year on a monthly basis, and several years of historical annual data.

Domestic Financial Statistics
Federal Reserve Banks
Monetary and Credit Aggregates
Commercial Banks
Financial Markets
Federal Finance
Securities Markets and Corporate Finance
Real Estate
Consumer Installment Credit
Domestic Non Financial Statistics
International Statistics
Securities Holdings and Transactions
Interest and Exchange Rates

The Federal Reserve Board also publishes a *Federal Reserve Quarterly Chart Book* and an annual *Historical Chart Book* depicting the data in the *Bulletin* in graphic form.

Federal Reserve Banks

There are 12 Federal Reserve Banks in the Federal Reserve System representing different geographical areas (districts) of the United States. Each bank publishes its own monthly letter or review which includes economic data about its region and sometimes commentary on national issues or monetary policy. The 12 banks by district are as follows: Boston (1), New York (2), Philadelphia (3), Cleveland (4), Richmond (5), Atlanta (6), Chicago (7), St. Louis (8), Minneapolis (9), Denver (10), Dallas (11), and San Francisco (12).

Federal Reserve Bank of St. Louis

One district bank, the Federal Reserve Bank of St. Louis, publishes some of the most comprehensive economic statistics on a weekly and monthly basis. *U.S. Financial Data* is published weekly and includes data on the monetary base,

bank reserves, money supply, a breakdown of time deposits and demand deposits, borrowing from the Federal Reserve Banks, and business loans from the large commercial banks. The publication also includes yields and interest rates on a weekly basis on selected short-term and long-term securities. An example of these published interest rates appears in Figures 3–1 and 3–2.

Figure 3—1

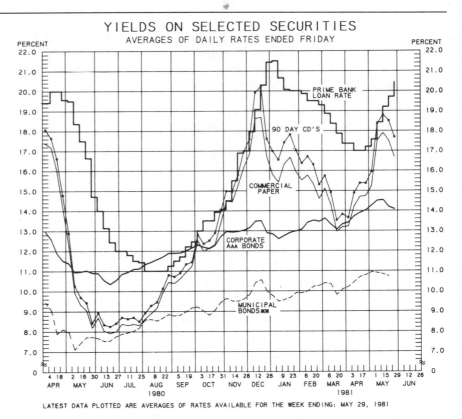

YIELDS ON SELECTED SECURITIES
AVERAGES OF DAILY RATES ENDED FRIDAY

LATEST DATA PLOTTED ARE AVERAGES OF RATES AVAILABLE FOR THE WEEK ENDING: MAY 29, 1981

1981	90 DAY CD'S	PRIME COMMERCIAL PAPER ✱✱✱	PRIME BANKERS' ACCEPTANCES	CORPORATE AAA BONDS	CORPORATE BAA BONDS	MUNICIPAL BONDS ✱✱
APR. 3	13.65	13.22	13.31	13.41	15.25	10.21
10	14.89	14.22	14.59	13.72	15.42	10.45
17	15.38	14.70	14.89	13.89	15.61	10.70
24	15.37	14.75	14.92	14.02	15.71	10.80
MAY 1	15.95	15.24	15.55	14.26	15.80	10.94
8	18.36	17.52	17.85	14.50	15.94	10.90
15	18.80	17.89	18.18	14.53	15.96	10.83
22	18.51	17.51	17.89	14.18	16.01	10.73
29 ✱	17.69	16.68	16.91	14.07	15.92	N.A.
JUNE 5						
12						
19						
26						

✱ AVERAGES OF RATES AVAILABLE.
✱✱ BOND BUYER'S AVERAGE INDEX OF 20 MUNICIPAL BONDS, THURSDAY DATA.
✱✱✱ DATA ARE 4-MONTH COMMERCIAL PAPER RATES.
N.A. - NOT AVAILABLE

PREPARED BY FEDERAL RESERVE BANK OF ST. LOUIS

Figure 3—2

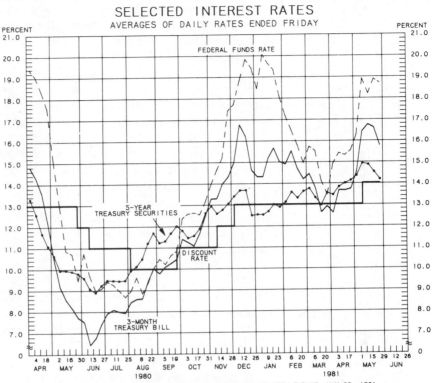

SELECTED INTEREST RATES
AVERAGES OF DAILY RATES ENDED FRIDAY

LATEST DATA PLOTTED ARE AVERAGES OF RATES AVAILABLE FOR THE WEEK ENDING: MAY 29, 1981

1981	FEDERAL FUNDS **	3-MONTH TREASURY BILL	6-MONTH TREASURY BILL ***	1-YEAR TREASURY BILL	5-YEAR TREASURY SECURITIES	LONG-TERM TREASURY SECURITIES
APR. 3	14.93	12.60	12.08	11.86	13.46	12.68
10	15.43	13.67	13.78	12.53	13.84	13.02
17	15.33	13.66	13.65	12.80	14.01	13.11
24	15.55	13.74	13.62	13.05	14.14	13.12
MAY 1	16.28	14.52	14.04	13.41	14.36	13.37
8	18.91	16.44	15.10	14.44	14.94	13.78
15	18.21	16.75	15.53	14.68	14.88	13.60
22	18.89	16.61	15.03	14.42	14.54	13.27
29 ✱	18.71	15.77	15.68	13.83	14.19	13.35
JUNE 5						
12						
19						
26						

✱ AVERAGES OF RATES AVAILABLE.
✱✱ SEVEN-DAY AVERAGES FOR WEEK ENDING WEDNESDAY TWO DAYS EARLIER THAN DATE SHOWN.
    CURRENT DATA APPEAR IN THE BOARD OF GOVERNORS' H.9 RELEASE.
✱✱✱ NEW ISSUE RATE
RATES ON LONG-TERM TREASURY SECURITIES ARE COMPUTED BY THE FEDERAL RESERVE BANK OF ST. LOUIS.
TREASURY BILL YIELDS ON DISCOUNT BASIS.

PREPARED BY FEDERAL RESERVE BANK OF ST. LOUIS

Monetary Trends is published monthly by the St. Louis Fed and includes charts and tables of monthly data. The information is similar to that found in *U.S. Financial Data* but covers a longer time period. The tables provide compound annual rates of change, while the graphs include the raw data with trend changes over time. Additional data are available on federal government debt and its composition by type of holder and on the receipts and expenditures of the government for both the National Income Account Budget and the High Employment Budget.

National Economic Trends is also published by the St. Louis Federal Reserve Bank and presents monthly economic data on employment, unemployment rates, consumer and producer prices, industrial production, personal income, retail sales, productivity, compensation and labor costs, gross national product, the implicit price deflator for the GNP, personal consumption expenditures, gross private domestic investment, government purchases of goods and services, disposable personal income, corporate profit after taxes, and inventories. This information is presented in graph form and in tables showing the compounded annual rate of change on a monthly basis. If raw data is needed, other economic publications are required.

Survey of Current Business

The *Survey of Current Business* is published monthly by the Bureau of Economic Analysis of the U.S. Department of Commerce. It contains monthly and quarterly raw data rather than compound annual growth rates as found in the St. Louis Federal Reserve's publications. The *Survey of Current Business* contains a monthly update and evaluation of the business situation analyzing such data as GNP, business inventories, personal consumption, fixed investment, exports, labor market statistics, financial data, and much more. For example, if personal consumption expenditures are broken down into subcategories, one would find expenditures on durable goods, such as motor vehicles and parts, and furniture and equipment; nondurables, such as food, energy, clothing, and shoes; and services.

The *Survey* can be extremely helpful for industry analysis as it breaks down data into basic industries. For example, data on inventory, new plant and equipment, production, and more could be found on such specific industries as coal, tobacco, chemicals, leather products, furniture, paper, and many others. Even within industries, such as lumber, production statistics can be found on hardwoods and softwoods right down to douglas fir trees, southern pine, and western pine. The Commerce Department publishes a weekly update to the *Survey* called *Weekly Business Statistics.* This publication updates the major series found in the *Survey of Current Business* and includes 27 weekly series and charts of selected series. To provide a more comprehensive view of what is available in the *Survey of Current Business* and *Weekly Business Statistics,* a list of the major series updates follows:

GNP	Housing Starts and Permits
National Income	Retail Trade

Personal Income
Industrial Production
Manufacturers Ship-
   ments, Inventories and
   Orders
Consumer Price Index
Producer Price Index
Construction Put in Place

Labor Force, Employment
   and Earnings
Banking
Consumer Installment Credit
Stock Prices
Value of Exports and Imports
Motor Vehicles

**Business
Conditions Digest**

Business Conditions Digest is published monthly by the Bureau of Economic Analysis of the U.S. Department of Commerce. The information provided is unique from the other publications previously discussed in that its primary emphasis is on cyclical indicators of economic activity. The National Bureau of Economic Research (NBER) analyzes and selects the time series data based on each series' ability to be identified as a leading, coincident, or lagging indicator over several decades of aggregate economic activity.

Over the years, the NBER has identified the approximate dates when aggregate economic activity reached its cyclical high or low point. Each time series is related to the business cycle. Leading indicators are those that move prior to the business cycle, coincident indicators move with the business cycle, and lagging indicators follow directional changes in the business cycle. Figure 3–3 represents the composite index of 12 leading, 4 coincident, and 6 lagging indicators that have consistently performed well relative to the general swings in the economy. The 22 indicators were selected out of several hundred found in the *Business Conditions Digest* and time-tested by the NBER. This publication can be very helpful in understanding past economic behavior and in forecasting future economic activity with a higher degree of success.

**Other sources of
economic data**

So far, we have presented the basic sources of economic data. Much other data is available or duplicated in other publications. What is available to each investor may vary from library to library, so here are some brief notes on other sources of data.

Many universities have bureaus of business research that provide statistical data on a statewide or regional basis. Major banks, such as Citicorp, Morgan Guaranty Trust, Harris Trust, and Bank of America, publish monthly or weekly letters or economic reviews including raw data and analysis. Several other government sources are available, such as *Economic Indicators* prepared by the Council of Economic Advisors and the *Annual Economic Report of the President.* Additionally, many periodicals, such as *Business Week, Fortune* and *Barrons,* contain raw data as well as economic commentary.

Figure 3—3

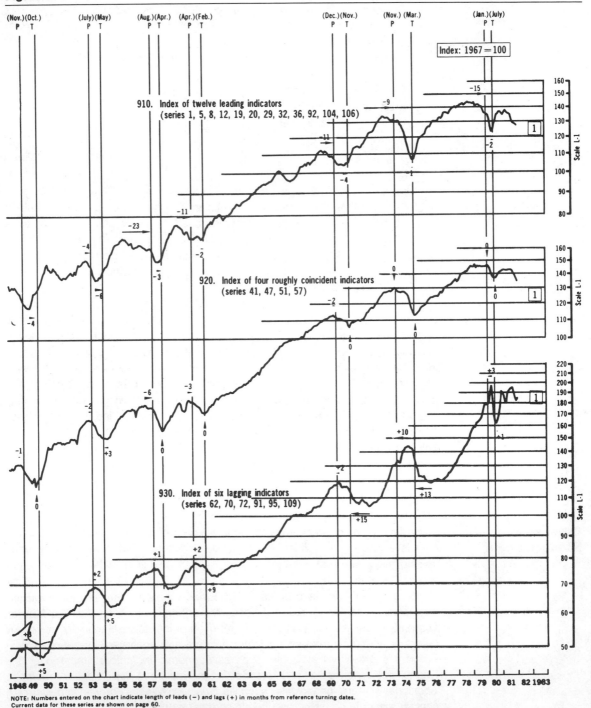

NOTE: Numbers entered on the chart indicate length of leads (−) and lags (+) in months from reference turning dates.
Current data for these series are shown on page 60.

SOURCE: *Business Conditions Digest* (U.S. Department of Commerce, Bureau of Economic Analysis, February, 1982).

INVESTMENT ADVISORY SERVICES

Investment information and advice is available from many sources, from large corporate financial services to individuals writing investment letters. A look through such financial magazines as *Barron's, Forbes,* and *Financial World* will turn up hundreds of investment services charging fees large and small for the information they sell. Most public libraries and universities subscribe to several of the major publications, such as Moody's, Standard & Poor's, or Value Line.

Moody's

Moody's is owned by Dun & Bradstreet and publishes several data bases for bonds and stocks. *Moody's Manuals* are widely used and present historical financial data on the companies listed as well as the officers and general corporate information. The *Manuals* are divided into several categories (Banks and Finance, Industrial, Municipals and Government, OTC Industrial, Public Utility, and Transportation). Each manual has a biweekly news supplement that updates quarterly earnings, dividend announcements, mergers, and other news of interest. *Moody's Manuals* are comprehensive, with each category including one or two volumes and over several thousand pages.

Moody's Bond Record contains data on corporates, convertibles, governments, municipals, and ratings on commercial paper and preferred stock. Corporate bond information includes the interest coupon, payment dates, call price, Moody's rating, and yield to maturity. The current price as well as the yearly and historical high-low price are presented. The total amount of the bond issue outstanding is given with a designation for a sinking fund and the original issue date. Data on convertible bonds also include the conversion price, conversion value, and conversion period. Information on industrial revenue and municipal bonds is usually limited to the Moody's rating. *Moody's Bond Record* also contains historical yield graphs for various types of bonds over at least 30 years. This is a monthly publication.

Moody's also publishes a weekly *Bond Survey* that reviews the week's activity in the bond market, rating changes, new issues, and bonds called for redemption. *Moody's Dividend Record* presents quarterly dividends and the date of declaration, date of record, date payable, and ex-dividend dates. This is an annual publication. *The Handbook of Common Stock* is an annual reference guide that summarizes a company's 10-year historical financial data along with a discussion of corporate background, recent developments, and prospects. Approximately 1,000 companies are listed in the *Handbook. Moody's Stock Survey* is a weekly publication that discusses the weekly investment climate and market performance. This publication also presents some selected stocks for purchase. Only a brief description has been given for each Moody's publication, but enough has been presented to know whether a particular one may be worth looking at further.

Standard & Poor's

A second major source of information is the Standard & Poor's Corporation, a subsidiary of McGraw-Hill. Standard & Poor's has very comprehensive coverage

of financial data. The following items will not all be discussed, but they provide a good look at what Standard & Poor's makes available to the investor.

Analysts Handbook
Bond Guide
Called Bond Record
Convertible Bond Reports
Corporation Records
Daily Stock Price Records
Dividend Record
Earnings Forecaster
Fixed Income Investor
Industry Survey
International Stock Reports
Investment Advisory Survey
Municipal Bond Selector

Opportunities in Convertible Bonds
The Outlook
Poor's Register of Corporations, Directors and Executives
Registered Bond Interest Record
The Review of Securities Regulation
Security Dealers Directory
Stock Guide
Stock Reports (A.S.E., N.Y.S.E., O-T-C and Regional Exchanges)
Stock Summary
Trade and Securities Statistics
Transportation Service
Trendline Charts

Standard & Poor's Corporate Records are similar to *Moody's Manuals* except they are organized alphabetically rather than by trade categories. The *Corporate Records* are published monthly, and the six volumes are updated by daily supplements. Information found in the volumes includes a historical company background, financial statements, news announcements, earnings updates, and other news of general interest. Companies found in the *Corporate Records* are listed, and their subsidiary companies are cross-listed.

Something that may be overlooked when examining the *Corporate Records* is the statistical section found in the T–Z volume. The statistical section includes a mutual fund summary, an address list of many no-load mutual funds, and foreign bond statistics. Special tables are contained in the T–Z volume listing new stock and bond offerings on a monthly basis. This volume also presents a classified index of industrial companies listed by Standard Industrial Classification code numbers (SIC). For example, if you want to find out about cereal breakfast food companies, you would first find the corresponding SIC number for cereal breakfast foods which is listed in alphabetical order. The number, 2043, then leads you to the cross-listing of companies in the *Standard & Poor's Corporate Records.* These are the companies one would find listed under *2043 Cereal Breakfast Foods:*

Carnation Co.
The Clorox Company
General Foods Corp.
General Mills, Inc.
Gerber Products Co.
Iroquois Brands, Ltd.
Kellog Company

Liggett Group Inc.
Nabisco, Inc.
Nestle S.A.
The Quaker Oats Co.
Ralston Purina Co.
George Weston Limited

All of these companies comprise an industry classification and may be found in the *Corporate Records.* This industry listing can certainly be helpful when trying to put together a list of companies for an industry analysis.

Several other Standard & Poor's publications are quite useful and present concise, thumbnail sketches of companies, common stock variables, and corporate bonds. Figure 3–4 depicts two pages from the *Stock Guide.* This is a monthly publication that enables investors to take a preliminary look at the common and preferred stock of several thousand companies and almost 200 mutual funds. The introduction to the *Stock Guide* presents recommendations of common stock for price appreciation and income and provides name changes, new exchange listings, common stock rating changes, and a graph of Standard & Poor's Stock Price Indexes.

The *Bond Guide* is of the same format as the *Stock Guide.* It is a monthly publication in booklet form that presents data on corporate and convertible bonds. Figure 3–5 shows one page on corporate bonds with a long list of American Telephone & Telegraph bonds. The Standard & Poor's rating is presented along with the bond form (either a coupon or registered bond), refunding dates, call prices, sinking fund, yields, prices, and other information. Figure 3–6 is one page on convertible bonds from the *Bond Guide.* Looking at the American Airlines convertible bond, one can find the coupon rate, interest dates, and maturity. Again, the Standard & Poor's rating is given along with the form of the bond. All the conversion data is presented with bond prices and common stock prices. Can you find how many shares of common stock an investor will receive for each $1,000 American Airlines convertible?[1]

One of the more popularly used Standard & Poor's publications is the *Corporate Reports.* These reports are often mailed out from brokerage houses to customers who want basic information on a company. In Figure 3–7, Texas Instruments provides a good example of what one would expect to find. This information can be compared to Figure 3–4, line 3, for Texas Instruments to see the difference in the depth of coverage between the *Corporate Reports* and the *Stock Guide.* The *Corporate Reports* are contained in three separate multiple-volume sets, the New York Stock Exchange Stocks, American Stock Exchange Stocks, and Over-the-Counter and Regional Stocks. Each company is updated quarterly with new earnings, dividends, and recent developments. About 1,020 NYSE stocks are selected and bound in an annual publication called the Standard & Poor's

---

[1] the answer is 40.

Figure 3—4   **Standard and Poor's Stock Guide**

216 Tex-T.I

STANDARD & POOR'S CORPORATION

I N D E X	Ticker Symbol	STOCKS NAME OF ISSUE (Call Price of Pfd. Stocks) Market	Com Rank & Pfd Rating	Par Val	Inst Hold Cos	Inst Hold Shs (000)	PRINCIPAL BUSINESS	1960-78 High	1960-78 Low	1979 High	1979 Low	1980 High	1980 Low	Nov. Sales in 100s	Nov. High	Nov. Low	Nov. Last	% Div Yield	P-E Ratio
1	TXG	Texas Gas Transmis ....NY,B,C,M,Ph,P	A	5	134	10135	Natural gas pipeline,barge	24⅛	9⅛	29	17¼	48	23¼	8106	48	34¼	37⅞	3.4	11
2	TXI	Texas Indus. ....NY,B,M	B+	1	21	611	Concrete & steel prod RE dev	20¾	1⅜	23¾	15⅝	38	18⅝	877	38	33¾	37¼	$2.1	12
3	TXN	Texas Instruments. ....NY,B,C,M,Ph,P	A	1	344	14871	Semiconductors:el'tronic eqp	138⅝	9¼	101	77	150¾	78¾	10572	150¾	126	149¼	1.3	16
4	TEI	Texas Int'l. ....NY,P,Ph,Tc	B	10¢	35	1595	Oil/gas:selling mfg div.	16¼	2⅜	20⅛	7	42⅛	12¼	12538	42⅛	36¾	42⅝		30
5	TXO	Texas Oil & Gas. ......NY,B,Ph	A	50¢	246	27570	Gas gathering:oil & gas	15	2⅜	29¼	14⅛	83⅜	26¾	16922	83⅜	64	79¾	0.5	27
6	TPL	Texas Pac Ld Tr Sub ....NY,B	B+	16²³¢	14	369	Holds surface rights:royalties	19	2½	31	15½	71	25	516	71	51	67¾	0.3	27
7	TXP Pr	Texas P&L$4.56Pfd(112) ......AS(²⁶)	AA	No	2	1	Elec sv:subsid of Texas Util	102	47	50¾	40⅝	45⅜	34⅜	10	39¼	34¾	36¾	12.4	
8	TXU	Texas Utilities. ......NY,B,C,M,Ph,P	A+	No	458	56711	Electric utility holding co.	36	15¼	20⅝	16⅝	19⅝	14⅜	23934	17⅞	16	16⅞	10.4	6
9	TG	Texasgulf Inc. ....NY,B,C,M,Ph,Mc,Tc	A+	No	142	6179	Metal producer: sulphur	55¾	3¼	36¼	18⅝	65	28	9299	65	54½	64¾	2.5	8
10	Pr	3.00 Cm Cv A Pfd(**43¼)vrtg ...NY,Mc		No	22	668	agri/ind'l chems: oil/gas	53⅝	33¾	57⅝	35	102	47	90	102	86	101B	3.0	
11	TXF	Texfi Indus ....NY,M	C	No	5	159	Fabrics for apparel indus	67¾	2⅛	11⅛	3¾	4⅛	2¾	2027	3¾	3¼	3¾		d
12	TXS	Texscan Corp ....AS	B—	No		103	CATV dstr eq/elect test eq.	9⅜	¾	5¼	1¾	23¾	4⅝	2579	23⅜	19½	21		25
13	TXTN	Textone, Inc. ....NY,B	B	20¢	141	10631	Wall paneling board: doors	19⅜	¾	1⅝	¾	3	1¾	1161	3	1¾	3B		
14	TXT	Textron, Inc. ....NY,B,C,M,Ph,P	A+	No			Consumer,metal,ind'l prod	57⅝	4¾	29¼	22¼	32¼	20¾	5722	32¼	26¼	31¾	5.7	8
15	WS	Wrrt Purch 1 com at $11¼) ...AS,M,P		25¢			aerospace (Bell Helicopter)	49¾	1⅜	18¾	12¼	20¾	10¾	51	20¾	16¾	20B		
16	Pr A	$2.08 cm Cv A Pfd (50)vrtg ....AS	A—	No	22	595	bearings,castings,zippers	68⅜	19	24¼	20¾	35	27¾	236	35	29¼	34¾	6.1	
17	Pr B	$1.40 cm Cv B Pfd (45)vrtg ....AS	BBB	No	7	122	investment company	50⅛	14	26¼	20¾	27¼	18½	27	37½	24¾	27¼	5.1	
18	TFI	TPI Co's ....AS	B	67¢			Building mtrs: food prod	30⅝	⅜	1⅝	¾	4½	1¾	378	3	2¾	2⅝		7
19	TMO	Thermo Electron ....NY,M	B+		35	831	Thermonic research: mfg	4	4¾	27¼	16⅜	39¼	20	2914	38½	30¾	33¾		18
20	THFR	Thetford Corp ....NY,M	C	25¢		214	Toilet sys:recreat veh,boat	29	1	9¾	4	6¾	2¾	565	4¾	3¾	4⅜B		d
21	THI	Thiokol Corp. ......NY,B,M,Ph,P	A	No	71	6244	Rocket mtrs/spec chemicals	26¾	3¾	24¼	14¼	26¾	22¾	3031	38¼	30¼	38¾	2.6	13
22	TDAT	Third Nat'l. ....NY,B,M,Ph,P	A	10		437	Multiple bank hldg:Tennessee	52¼	13¼	25¼	19¾	25¾	17¾	481	22	21½	21⅞B	5.5	4
23	TNB	Thomas & Betts ....NY,P,Ph	A	50¢	81	4067	Elec connectors, accessories	61⅝	3½	46¾	38⅝	55¾	35¾	1562	54	50¼	52¾	3.3	13
24	TII	Thomas Indus. ....NY,M	B+		20	1512	Lighting fix:decor hm:tools	22⅜	1¼	12¼	8⅝	16¼	7¾	1737	16¼	14¾	14¾	4.6	9
25	TNEL	Thomas Nelson. ....NY,M	B+			53	Book publ:prod'r,mktr-Bible	14¾	1¾	11¼	7¾	16¼	7¾	238	16¼	13¾	16⅝B	1.7	13
26	TMCI	Thompson Medical. ....N	NR	10¢	13	409	Appetite suppressants					8¾	10¾	1662	24	19¾	19¾B		8
27	THM.A	Thomson Newspaper A ....Tc,M	A+	No	56	2223	Large newspaper publisher	16⅝	1¾	17	13	26¾	13	1593	22¾	20¼	22¾B	3.6	12
28	THR	Thor Corp¹⁰ ....AS	C		2	38	Ice cream parlors:land:engr	11¾	1¾	1	1	2¾	1¾	947	3	3¾	2⅝B		
29	TMI	Thorofare Markets ....AS	B	20¢		10	Supermarkets mainly in Pa	26¾	2	5⅛	2¾	4¾	3¾	3	4¾	3¾	3⅞B	2.1	8
30	TRLS	Thousand Trails ....N	NR	No		10	Campground resorts, member			5¾	5¾	13¾	4¾	2871	12¾	10¾	12¾B		9
31	TDD	Three D Depts ....AS	C	25¢	4	5	Leas'd domestics,drapery dept	11¾	¾	4¾	¾	6¾	3	87	6¾	5½	5⅞	4.4	5
32	THRS	Threshold Technology ....AS	B	1¢		79	Automatic speech recog equip	14¾	3¾	10¾	6¾	14¾	4¾	2230	14½	11	14½B		d
33	TFT.A	Thriftimart Inc¹⁴ ....AS,P	A—		9	40	Food supermkts:Los Angeles	39¾	5¾	27¾	15¾	37¾	20	171	36¾	33¾	35	4.0	5
34	TFD	Thrifty Corp ....NY,B,P	B+	No	7	713	Drug & discount store chain	16¾	4	17¾	10¾	13¾	8¾	2249	13¾	11¾	11¾	6.4	7
35	TCX	Ti-Caro. ....NY,B,M	A—		142		Combed cotton yarns: threads	28¾	6¾	26	20¼	29¾	18¾	113	27¾	25¾	25¾B	8.5	4
36	TRTZ	Tidelands Rly Tr B SBI		No		10	Ministerial trust-oil & gas	32¾	12¾	42	26	45	33¾	301	45	43¾	45B	3.5	31
37	TDW	Tidewater Inc ....NY,B,M,P	A	50¢	86	6682	Supplies to offshore oil rigs	19¾	¾	23¾	13¾	54¾	19¾	6721	54¾	37	52½	1.4	20
38	TWI	Tidwell Indus ....NY,M	A—	10¢		648	Mobile & modular home mfr	33¾	¾	6¾	2¾	17¾	3¾	4246	17¾	6¾	16⅛		30
39	TIE	TIE/communications ....AS	NR	5¢	3	98	Key telephone systems			4¾	2¾	7¾	3¾	4246	17¾	14	14¾		32
40	TIERS	Tierco SBI ....NY,B,M,Ph,P	B+	1	3	81	Real estate investment trust	2¾	⅝	5¾	4¾	5¾	3¾	395	5¾	4¾	5⅛B		47
41	TGR	Tiger Int'l ....NY,B,M,Ph,P	B+	1	96	11562	Airfreight sv:leasing:insur	42	1¾	27¾	16¾	28¾	17¾	9259	24¾	21¼	23¾	3.5	9
42	TII	TII Indus¹⁶ ....N	B	50¢		2	Electronic devices,test lab	18	¾	3	3	20	4	1512	20	15¼	19¾B		21
43	TMB	Timberland Indus ....N	B	16¢		40	Door & cabinet mfr:hdware	18	⅞	8	2¾	8¾	4¾	648	8¾	6¾	4⅝B	4.7	28
44	TMDC	I.I.M.E. DC Inc. ....N	C	1		2	Transcontinental trucking	38	2¾	12¾	4¾	5¾	3	106	4	3¾	3⅞B		d

Uniform Footnote Explanations— See Page 1. Other: ¹Tc. ⁵¹△$1.75,'78. ⁵²⎿$0.02,'79. ⁵³Subsid Pfd in M5. ⁵⁴⎿$3.71,'79. ⁵⁵To 12-14-80, scale to $50 in '86. ⁵⁶⎿$2.40,'77. ⁵⁷⎿$0.40,'79.
⁵⁸△$0.27¼,'76. ⁵⁹Fiscal Dec.'76. ⁶⁰ASE trad'g halted Aug.27,'80. ⁶¹△$0.45,'80. ⁶²Defr.comp. ⁶³Fiscal July'76 & prior. ⁶⁴5% Ptc Cl A Stk. ⁶⁵⎿$1.81,⊛$6.16,'80. ⁶⁶△$1.67,'79. ⁶⁷⎿$0.29,'79.
⁶⁸△$2.35,'77. ⁶⁹△$0.65,'78. ⁷⁰Apply for ASE listing. ⁷¹⎿$0.05,'78. ⁷²⎿$0.06,'79.

SOURCE: *Standard & Poor's Stock Guide*, December 1980.

Figure 3—4 (concluded)

COMMON AND PREFERRED STOCKS

Tex—T.I 217

IDX	Cash Divs. Ea. Yr. Since	Latest Payment P Date	Latest Payment f $	Ex. Div.	So Far 1980	Total Ind. Rate	Paid 1979	Cash& Equiv.	Curr. Assets	Curr. Liabs.	Balance Sheet Date	Long Term Debt Mil-$	Shs 000 Pfd.	Shs 000 Com.	End	EARNINGS 1976	EARNINGS 1977	EARNINGS 1978	EARNINGS 1979	EARNINGS 1980	Last 12 Mos.	Period	INTERIM 1979	INTERIM 1980	IDX
1◆	1952	Q0.41	12-15-80 11-25	1.55	1.64	1.39	115.	494.	351.	8-1-80	377.	276	p20739	Dc	2.86	2.69	2.89	3.74	E4.30	4.32	12 Mo Sep	3.37	4.32	1
2◆	1962	Q0.20	11-28-80 10-31	s0.736	0.80	0.576	13.2	80.9	42.4	8-31-80	129.	19	6599	My	0.59	1.06	*2.13	4.31	6.04	5.70	12 Mo Aug	4.50	5.70	2
3◆	1962	Q0.50	10-27-80 9-30	2.00	2.00	2.00	135.	1323	1000	9-30-80	212.		23146	Dc	4.25	5.11	6.15	7.58	E9.10	8.93	9 Mo Sep	5.55	6.90	3
4		None Paid			Nil		11.8	90.1	80.2	6-30-80	91.2		9559	Dc	0.6	0.88△⁵¹d0.76⁵¹d0.54				1.41	9 Mo Sep	d0.61	□1.34	4
5◆	1965	Q0.09	10-31-80 10-9	0.29	0.36	0.186	30.0	285.	266.	8-31-80	464		47560	Au	1.02	1.40	1.61	2.04	2.96	2.96	9 Mo Sep			5
6◆	1956	A0.183	3-12-80 2-19	0.183	0.183	0.15	0.82	20.7	2.32	9-30-80			†4725	Dc	0.54	0.81	1.03	1.19		2.50	9 Mo Sep	0.66	1.97	6
7	1950	Q0.14	2-2-81 1-5	4.56	4.56	4.56	9.32	166.	226.	9-30-80	1016	†2874	34530	Dc	41.80	46.33	54.13	49.98			12 Mo Oct	2.48	3.04	7
8◆	1917	Q0.44	1-2-81 12-8	1.73	1.76	1.61	39.1	458.	428.	9-30-80	2699	⁵600	95261	Dc	2.29	2.40	2.54	2.45	E2.90	3.04	12 Mo Sep	3.14	△7.43	8
9	1921	Q0.44	12-15-80 11-17	1.50	1.60	1.20	53.4	501.	230.	9-30-80	346.	2603	p32894	Dc	1.98	1.21	1.33	*4.05	E△7.80	7.43				9
10	1977	Q0.75	12-15-80 11-17	3.00	3.00	3.00	15.7	1606	705.	10-4-80	311.	2603		Dc	20.28	15.43	16.70	45.62		4.30	9 Mo Sep	3.35	3.14	10
11		None Paid			Nil		0.97	44.6	18.1	8-1-80	56.4		3445	Oc	d1.63▲⁵⁸d1.63⁵⁸⁴3.79		0.97	d0.98		d6.95	9 Mo Jul	d0.19	▲46.16	11
12		None Since Public			Nil		0.23	9.97	7.13	7-31-80	p0.06	*1791	Ap	*0.03	*0.12	0.19	0.28	0.63	0.84	9 Mo Sep	0.13	0.34	12
13◆		5% Stk	4-25-73 3-28		Nil		0.48	5.89	3.26	6-30-80	1.94		918	Dc	0.64	0.34	0.35	d0.09		0.02	9 Mo Sep	d0.09	0.02	13
14◆	1942	Q0.45	1-1-81 12-9	1.80	1.80	1.75	15.7	1606	705.	10-4-80	311.	3486	33744	Dc	3.23	3.65	4.47	4.51	E4.15	4.30	9 Mo Sep	3.35	3.14	14
15		Terms&trad basis should be checked in detail Warrants expire May 1, 1984										68	Dc										15
16	1968	Q0.52	1-1-81 12-9	2.08	2.08	2.08	3.77	40.3	25.4	7-31-80	10.1	2530	1930	Ja	0.28	0.30	56.27 59.52		0.40	6 Mo Jul	0.17	0.09	16
17	1968	Q0.35	1-1-81 12-9	1.40	1.40	1.40	0.71	71.2	34.9	6-30-80	*46.3	956	4291	Je	0.28	0.66	55.37 118.4		1.89	3 Mo Sep	0.38	0.39	17
18		None Paid			Nil		1.87	16.3	9.90	6-30-80	7.49	3	1804	Sp	*0.89	1.08	1.09 1.60	*1.88	1.88	6 Mo Jul			18
19◆		None Paid			Nil													*d0.61	Pd0.56	0.56	3 Mo Sep			19
20◆		None Since Public			Nil																			20
21	1966	Q0.25	11-1-80 10-6	0.762	1.00	0.71¼	21.8	206.	.130	9-28-80	5.91		11419	Dc	59△1.49	1.87	*2.25	*3.47	3.00	3.00	9 Mo Sep	▲2.60	2.13	21
22	1929	Q0.30	1-2-81 12-5	1.15	1.20	1.00	21.9	119.	38.9	9-30-80	50.4		2386	Dc	△2.41	△2.78	□3.52	□4.82	5.42	5.42	12 Mo Sep	□4.44	□5.42	22
23	1934	Q0.43	1-2-81 12-5	1.67	1.72	1.47	6.97	83.6	21.5	9-30-80	29.2		7706	Dc	2.20	2.70	3.30	3.91	E4.20	4.21	9 Mo Sep	2.96	3.26	23
24◆	1955	Q0.16¾	1-1-81 12-8	0.547	0.66	0.461	n/a	23.9	8.26	9-30-80	22.7		5488	Dc	0.99	1.36	1.71	2.04	E1.60	1.99	9 Mo Sep	1.47	1.42	24
25◆	1975	Q0.07	11-10-80 10-21	0.238	0.28	0.208					10.3		1225	Mr	0.99	1.06	0.94	1.12		1.30	9 Mo Aug	0.55	0.73	25
26	1966	None Since Public			Nil		2.79	36.6	16.7	8-31-80	40.1	4000	Nv	**0.49	0.81	0.66	1.17		2.40	9 Mo Aug	0.83	2.06	26
27		g0.16	12-15-80 11-25	g0.61¾	0.64	g0.52¾	57.6	106.	43.1	12-31-79	1.77	216	†49236	Dc	0.81	0.95	1.13	1.31		1.46	9 Mo Sep	0.86	□1.01	27
28	1979	Q0.04	11-1-80 10-7	0.08	0.08	0.04	0.76	6.37	6.50	8-2-80	3.70	80	1990	Ja	d0.55	d1.00	d0.56	0.14		0.28	6 Mo Jul	d0.13	0.01	28
29◆		None Since Public			Nil		0.55	21.9	12.6	8-2-80	19.1	4	1245	Jl	▲*0.10	d0.11	d0.34	*0.61⁶¹*▲0.46	▲0.46		0.46				29
30◆		None Since Public			Nil		n/a	6.23	8.84				2538	Dc			d0.66	1.17		1.43	9 Mo Sep	1.14	1.40	30
31◆	1978	Q0.06	11-20-80 10-27	0.21	0.24	0.186	2.47	13.3	4.59	8-2-2-80	20.14	1516	Jl	*0.59	0.91	0.92	0.97	1.11	1.11	3 Mo Sep	d0.18	0.24	31
32		None Since Public			Nil		1.62	3.40	0.70	9-30-80	1.53	1969	Je	**d0.16	d0.42	d0.53	d0.36	d0.89	d0.89	24 Wk Sep	△3.04	△3.37	32
33◆	1977	Q0.35	12-1-80 11-3	1.40	1.40	1.05	7.59	38.2	24.2	9-14-80	10.7	*891	Mr	▲*2.49	△3.80	5.04	*6.29	6.62	6.62		d0.18	△3.37	33
34	1977	Q0.18	12-30-80 11-21	0.72	0.72	0.61½	3.07	186.	93.8	5-31-80	106.	9824	Au	0.80	0.88	1.09	*6.45	P1.50	5.75		3.04		34
35	1941	Q0.55	12-10-80 11-21	2.10	2.20	2.00	3.31	88.0	23.3	6-28-80	17.4	85	2713	Sp	4.30	4.90	6.06	5.34	P5.75	5.75				35
36	1977	Q0.31	10-14-80 9-24	1.58	1.58	1.85	0.54	0.80	0.49	9-30-80	1386	Mr	0.01	d1.33	1.57	1.84	1.43	9 Mo Sep	1.47	1.06	36
37◆	1962	Q0.18	10-10-80 9-24	0.66	0.72	0.583	22.9	74.8	74.8	6-30-80	*139	16193	Mr	1.78	*1.71	1.61	2.01	2.69	2.69	9 Mo Sep	0.72	1.40	37
38◆		Q0.068	9-29-73 9-10		Nil		1.25	15.8	15.8	9-30-80	5.42	1900	Dc	*0.06	*d0.38	d0.85	1.00	0.35	9 Mo Sep	1.10	0.45	38
39◆		None Paid			Nil		0.39	29.4	15.8	9-30-80	1.85	6849	Dc	0.05	*0.11	*0.22	⁶⁰0.33	0.46	9 Mo Sep	0.25	0.38	39
40		Q0.50	2-22-74 2-4		Nil		Equity per shr $9.73			6-30-80	10.5	2363	Dc	d0.72 ⁶¹d0.10		△*0.10⁶¹△d0.02		0.11	9 Mo Sep	△d0.18	d0.05	40
41	1973	Q0.20	1-15-80 10-20	0.80	0.80	0.75	70.9	399.	378.	p3-31-80	*1611	⁷%	16784	Dc	1.44	2.87	3.68	3.03	2.61	9 Mo Sep	2.03	1.61	41
42		None Since Public			Nil		0.52	8.60	2.62	9-26-80	3.62	968	Je	0.92	0.83	0.83	0.80	0.95	3 Mo Sep	0.26	*0.45	42
43◆	1977	Q0.05	12-22-80 11-24	0.20	0.20	0.17½	0.03	10.6	6.61	9-30-80	4.51	967	Dc	d0.06	0.70	□⁷¹1.36	0.76	0.15	9 Mo Sep	0.76	*0.45	43
44	1977	Q0.10	3-31-80 3-10	0.10	Nil	0.40	9.54	37.0	21.5	9-30-80	31.0	738	2612	Dc		0.74	1.21	J0.45		d0.09	9 Mo Sep	0.32	d0.22	44

◆ Stock Splits & Divs By Line Reference Index ¹²2-for-1,'79. ¹²2-for-1,'79. ²2-for-1,'78:Adj to 4%,'80. ⁹2-for-1,'79:10%,'79,'80. ¹¹3-for-1. ³3-for-1,'80. ¹²Adj for 3% & 10%,'79:6-for-5,'80. ¹³3-for-2,'79. ⁴²2-for-1,'80. ²²Adj for 4%,'76:10%,'77,'79,'80(ex)'79)Vote 10% stk,ex Dec 8. ⁶6-for-5,'76:3-for-2,'78:4-for-3,'79,5-for-4,'80. ²⁰10%,'80. ³⁶16-for-5,'77:10%,'79. ⁵⁹2-for-1,'76:3-for-2,'80. ⁴³10%,'80. ⁶⁰3-for-1 twice,'80. ⁷¹Adj for 5%,'78:6-for-5,'79.

Figure 3–5 Bond Guide—corporate bonds

16 Ame-Ang

STANDARD & POOR'S CORPORATION

Title-Industry Code & Co. Finances (In Italics) / Individual Issue Statistics: Exchange ↓	Ind / Interest Dates	Chgs. 1978 / S&P Quality Rating	Eligible ↓	Times Earn. 1979 / Bond Form	1980 Yr. End / Legality (Ct Ma NH NJ NY)	Cash &Eqv / Redemption Provisions: Refund Earliest/Other	Current Assets / Call Price For S.F.	Liabs	Date / Call Price Regular	L. Term Debt (Mil $) / Out-st'd'g (Mil $)	Debt % Prop / Underwriter Firm	Year	Interim Times Earn. Period / Price Range 1960-80 High	1960-80 Low	1980 / 1981 High	1981 / 1981 Low	1982 High	1982 Low	Mo. End Price Sale(s) or Bid	Curr Yield	Yield to Mat.
American Standard	*13g*	*4.52*		*5.00*	*5.80 Dc*	*35.3*	*938*	*523*	*9-81*	*271*	*50.8*		*9 Mo Sep*		*5.10*	*4.73*					
SF Deb 12⅜s 2010	fA	A+	X	R	- - √ - -	[1]106.06	[2]100		111.52	96.0	F2	'80	99¾	88	90	73¾	80	79½	79⅝	15.54	15.59
American Stores	*58*	*[3]4.98*		*2.27*	*2.14 Ja*	*37.9*	*711*	*569*	*10-81*	*390*	*60.9*		*9 Mo Oct*		*1.99*	*2.06*					
• SF Deb 9⅞s '90	fA	BBB+	X	R	- - - - -	....	100		102.775	14.5	L5	'70	114½	76	86⅛	83¾	85⅞	85¾	84	11.76	13.04
• SF Deb 9⅜s 2001	jJ	BBB+	X	R	- - - - -	[4]104.438	[5]100		106.656	50.0	G2	'76	110	65	68⅝	54¼	No Sale		63	14.88	15.41
• Notes 12s '90	Jd	BBB+	X	R	- - - - -	....	....		[6]100	75.0	L5	'80	101½	91	93	79⅞	80	80	∧80	15.00	16.50
American Sugar[7]	*27a*	*△3.98*		*△4.81*	*△12.83 Je*	*104*	*468*	*252*	*9-81*	*51.2*	*19.3*		*3 Mo Sep*		*9.76*	*29.44*					
• Sub SF Deb 5.30s '93	Ao2	BBB-	X	CR	- - - - -	....	100		102¾	20.2	Exch	'63	108	41¾	59	49⅝	51¼	49	s50¾	10.44	14.23
Amer Tel & Tel	*67a*	*3.01*		*2.89*	*2.66 Dc*	*N/A*	*10366*	*11391*	*11-81*	*47294*	*39.7*		*12 Mo Nov*		*2.63*	*2.59*					
• Deb 2¾s '82	Ao	AAA	X	CR	√√√√√	....	....		100	200	F2	'47	93	57	98	89¼	98½	97½	98¾	2.78	10.84
• Deb 3¼s '84	mS15	AAA	X	CR	√√√√√	....	....		100	250	H2	'54	88¼	56⅞	84½	74	80¼	78	s79½	4.09	12.69
• Deb 4⅜s '85	Ao	AAA	X	CR	√√√√√	....	....		100	250	M9	'57	103⅞	63½	82½	72⅛	79¾	76½	s78¼	5.59	12.98
• Deb 2⅝s '86	jJ	AAA	X	CR	√√√√√	....	....		100	125	H2	'46	77⅞	50	74	62¼	70⅞	67	s69	3.80	11.85
• Deb 2⅞s '87	Jd	AAA	X	CR	√√√√√	....	....		100.19	200	M9	'47	81	52	68½	59	65⅜	63	s64½	4.46	12.10
• Deb 3⅞s '90	jJ	AAA	X	CR	√√√√√	....	....		100.92	250	F2	'56	96	52¼	61⅝	50	56	53⅛	s55¼	7.01	12.68
Deb 4¾s '92	mN	AAA	X	CR	√√√√√	....	....		101.27	250	M9	'60	106	49¾	58¾	47⅜	54⅞	52¾	53⅝	8.86	12.81
Deb 4⅝s '94	Fa	AAA	X	CR	√√√√√	....	....		101.99	300	F2	'62	105¾	46¾	54	43⅞	50⅛	48½	49⅜	9.37	13.11
Deb 5⅝s '95	fA	AAA	X	R	√√√√√	....	....		102.20	250	M9	'66	104¾	51	57¾	47¼	53¼	51⅛	52	10.82	13.41
Deb 4⅜s '96	aO	AAA	X	CR	√√√√√	....	....		102.22	250	F2	'62	102⅜	41½	47¼	38⅛	43	41⅛	42	10.42	13.60
Deb 5½s '97	Jj	AAA	X	R	√√√√√	....	....		102.99	250	F2	'67	102⅞	48⅞	55	44⅝	50	48	48⅞	11.25	13.58
Deb 4¾s '98	Jd	AAA	X	CR	√√√√√	....	....		102.03	250	M9	'61	106¾	42½	47⅜	38½	42⅝	40⅞	41⅝	11.41	13.86
Deb 4⅜s '99	Mn	AAA	X	CR	√√√√√	....	....		102.41	250	M9	'63	100⅞	39¼	43⅜	35⅛	39	37¼	38⅛	11.48	13.93
Deb 6s 2000	fA	AAA	X	R	√√√√√	....	....		103.18	250	H2	'67	100¾	49⅞	53¾	44⅛	48½	46½	47⅜	12.66	14.04
• Deb 8¾s 2000	Mn15	AAA	X	R	√√√√√	....	....		104.90	[8]715	M9	'70	116⅜	67⅜	76	59⅝	64⅜	61½	s63	13.89	14.59
• Deb 7s 2001	Fa15	AAA	X	R	√√√√√	....	....		103½	500	B9	'71	104	55⅛	64⅞	48¾	54½	51⅝	s52⅜	13.37	14.36
Deb 5⅛s 2001	Ao	AAA	X	R	√√√√√	....	....		102.55	250	F2	'66	100⅞	43⅜	46¾	38⅛	41⅞	40⅛	40⅞	12.54	14.14
• Deb 7⅛s 2003	jD	AAA	X	R	√√√√√	....	....		104.49	350	M9	'72	98	55½	64¾	48¼	54⅜	51⅝	s53⅝	13.29	13.95
• Deb 8.80s 2005	Mn15	AAA	X	R	√√√√√	....	....		106.43	500	M9	'74	109¾	66½	75	58½	63⅛	61⅜	s63	13.97	14.31
• Debs 8⅝s 2007	Fa	AAA	X	R	√√√√√	....	....		106.39	300	S1	'75	109⅜	65⅛	74½	56¼	62¾	58½	s60½	14.26	14.54
• Notes 7¾s '82	Fa	AAA	X	R	√√√√√	....	....		100	300	S1	'75	106½	87	99.531	93¼	99.719	99.312	s99.719	7.77	Mat
• Notes 10⅜s '90	Jd	AAA	X	R	- - √√√	....	....		[9]101½	600	M9	'80	103⅛	81¾	91⅜	74	82¾	78	s80⅝	12.87	14.44
• Notes 13¼s '91	Ms15	AAA	X	R	- - √√√	....	....		[10]101½	600	S1	'81	....	....	100¾	86	94⅞	90½	s93½	14.17	14.55
[11]Amerifirst FedS&L(Miami)	*10b*	*1.13*		*1.09*	*1.04 Sp*					*371*											
Mtg-Back'A' 9¾s '87	jJ15	AAA	X	R	- - √ - -	....	....		[12]100	46.9	L7	'79	99¾	76¾	83½	71¾	79	78⅜	78⅜	12.44	15.81
Ames Dept.Stores	*58f*	*3.19*		*3.26*	*3.19 Ja*	*5.47*	*133*	*74.4*	*10-81*	*36.7*	*109*		*9 Mo Oct*		*2.64*	*3.04*					
• Sub SF Deb 10s '95	Jj15	NR		R	- - - - -	....	[13]100		100	2.54	Exch	'75	102½	70	75	60	65¾	65	65⅛	15.36	16.64
AMF Inc	*40*	*3.08*		*3.43*	*3.20 Dc*	*78.9*	*608*	*346*	*9-81*	*155*	*51.0*		*9 Mo Sep*		*2.95*	*3.59*					
• Notes 10s '85	Jd30	A-	X	R	- - √ - -	....	....		[14]100	60.0	L4	'75	108½	78	87⅞	79¼	86⅝	83¼	84¼	11.87	16.19
AMP Inc	*24b*	*11.57*		*13.12*	*10.22 Dc*	*140*	*646*	*248*	*9-81*	*55.4*	*15.5*										
• Notes 8⅝s '85	Ao	AA+	X	R	- - √√ -	....	....		[15]100	25.0	K2	'75	105	77	87¾	77	81⅝	81⅝	82⅝	10.44	15.82
Anaconda Co.	*44b*	*Now Atlantic Richfield,see*																			
SF Deb[16] 6⅝s '93	mN15	AA+	X	R	- √√√ -	....	100		102.144	122	F2	'68	99½	51	51	44	47	44½	44½	14.89	18.22
[17]Anadarko Production Co	*49*	*3.25*		*4.72*	*6.52 Dc*	*12.3*	*85.1*	*219*	*9-81*	*★265*	*15.3*		*9 Mo Sep*		*6.53*	*3.62*					
• SF Notes 14¾s '91	jD	A-	X	R	- - √ - -	....	[18]100		[19]100	100	M5	'81	....	....	100	97¼	96	93¾	93	15.86	16.19
Anchor Hocking	*16a*	*5.78*		*3.95*	*3.76 Dc*	*17.7*	*292*	*169*	*9-81*	*86.6*	*29.5*		*9 Mo Sep*		*3.29*	*2.96*					
(Glass)SFDeb 5⅛s '91	Ao15	AA	X	R	- - √√ -	....	*100		101.22	9.96	D4	'66	99¾	50	51	48	50	48	48	10.68	16.18
• SF Deb 8⅝s 2006	jJ	AA	X	R	- - √√ -	[4]104.73	[20]100		106.30	44.7	D4	'76	104¾	87	59	53⅞	No Sale		54¼	15.90	16.20
[21]Anglo Co., Inc	*49e*	*△2.78*		*△2.71*	*△2.41 Sp*	*8.91*	*123*	*93.6*	*9-81*	*97.7*	*50.8*										
◆Gtd Sub SF Deb 11⅞s '98	Jj15	B+	Y	R	- - - - -	[12]102.38	[22]100		108.31	17.5	D9	'78	104	80	80	73	No Sale		74½	15.94	16.39

Uniform Footnote Explanations—See Page 1. Other: [1]Fr 8-1-90. [2]Fr 8-1-91. [3]Yr Dec '78 & prior. [4]Fr 7-1-86. [5]Fr 7-1-82. [6]Fr 6-1-87. [7]Now Amstar Corp. [8]Call $785M 12-12-77 at 106.30. [9]Fr 6-1-85. [10]Fr 3-15-86. [11]Was First Fed'l S&L(Miami). [12]Fr 7-15-85. [13]Fr 1-15-86. [14]Fr 6-30-83. [15]Fr 4-1-82. [16]Gtd by Atlantic Richfield. [17]Subsid of Panhandle Eastern Corp. [18]Fr 12-1-89. [19]Fr 12-1-88. [20]Fr 7-1-87. [21]Subsid of Anglo Energy Ltd. [22]Fr 7-15-88.

Figure 3–6 Bond Guide—convertible bonds

II

STANDARD & POOR'S CORPORATION

CONVERTIBLE BONDS Issue, Rate, Interest Dates and Maturity	B F o o d m	S & P Quality Rating	Outstdg. Mil.-$	Conv. Ex- pires	Shares per $1,000 Bond	Price per Share	Div. Income per Bond	1982 RANGE Hi	Lo	Curr Bid Sale(s) Ask(A)	Curr. Return	Yield to Mat	Stock Value of Bond	Conv. Parity	STOCK DATA Curr. Price	P/E Ratio	Yr. End	1981	Last 12 Mos	1980 Dil-u'n
Acapulco Y LA Rest....13⅜s QJul 1996	R	NR	10.0	1996	108.70	9.20	....	88	85	86	15.7	16.0	40¾	7⅞	3¾	8 Dc	P0.47	P0.47	0.47	n/r
AccuRay Corp¹....5⅝s Jd 1991	C	CCC	13.2	1991	27.87	35.875	....	49	47	48	11.4	16.6	22⅜	17⅜	8⅛	10 Dc	0.68	0.84	90.84	n/r
Address Multi In 24¾s AnMy 1988	R	NR	11.0	1988	312.50	380.00	....	No Sale	32¾	28.4	5	26	●4	dⁱ Jl	*0.33	d21.9	d21.9	n/r
AEL Indus....6¾s iJ 1988	R	NR	1.05	1988	63.25	15.81	....	73	59	60	10.4	16.6	68	9½	10%	dⁱ Fb	Λ0.63	d21.9	d21.82	n/r
Aeroflex Labs....10s iD 1999	R	B	4.11	1999	110.25	9.07	....	No Sale	129%	7.72	7.06	129⅝	11¾	●11%	12 Je	0.51	0.95	121.01	n/r
Acronca....5¾s Ao 1982	R	NR	0.81	4-1-82	107.64	9.29	....	No Sale	93	6.18	19.1	32¼	8⅜	◆	25 Dc	Λ0.40	P0.12	n/r
⁴Alamand³ Corp⁶....6½s iD 1991	R	NR	8.77	1991	736.04	727.75	....	45	44¾	45	14.4	14.1	19%	12%	◆ 5%	7 Jl	d0.52	⁹0.74	⁹0.74	n/r
·Alexander's....5½s iJ 1996	R	B	18.0	1996	31.01	32.25	....	48½	48	48	8.84	25.6	26¾	11%	·8%	9 Dc	d0.23	dⁱ.10	⁹0.89	n/r
·All Amer Int....7⅞s Ao15 1983	R	NR	0.46	1983	74.07	13.50	....	82	82	82	8.84	25.6	74¾	11%	10	4 Dc	1.16	91.07	n/r
·Allegheny Beverage..6¾s iA 1988	R	B-	4.07	1988	123.46	8.10	49.38	98¾	93	95	6.58	7.22	95%	7%	·7%		1.41	91.76	1.28
·Allen Group....6s iJ 1987	R	NR	1.53	1987	54.20	18.45	54.20	86	84	84¾	7.11	9.78	83%	15%	·15%	8 Dc	2.03	E1.90	⁹2.04	1.89
·Allen Group....11½s iJ 1994	R	B+	3.75	1994	89.29	11.20	89.29	140	136	⁵136¾	8.46	7.09	137¾	15%	·15%	8 Dc	2.03	E1.90	⁹2.04	1.89
·Allied Stores....4½s mS15 1992	R	NR	2.35	1992	44.94	22.25	80.89	No Sale	118½	3.80	2.50	118%	26%	·26%	6 Ja	4.11	E1.90	⁹4.22	1.89
·Altec Corp....15s iD 1995	R	NR	2.71	1995	833.33	1.20	....	76	75	72	20.8	21.4	52%	%	·%	3 Sp	d0.11	P0.48	²d0.32	n/r
·Amerace Corp....5s mS 1992	R	BBB-	10.9	1992	27.03	37.00	35.68	67¾	67¾	67¾	7.43	10.1	49	24%	·18%	7 Dc	3.51	P2.77	2.77	2.84
·¹⁰Amer Airlines....5¾s mS 1998	R	NR	113	7-1-82	40.00	25.00	25.00	46	40	ˢ43	12.2	14.3	42%	10%	·10%	d Dc	d3.82	Pd3.82	⁹d0.58	6.47
·Amer Can Int¹⁸....4¾s Mn15 1988	R	NR	30.0	1988	17.09	58.50	49.56	No Sale	70¾	6.74	11.4	54¼	41¼	·31%	8 Dc	4.26	3.80	3.67	3.06
·Amer Century Tr⁹....7s Ao 1990	C	NR	2.40	1990	58.41	17.12	11.68	60¾	56⅝	57¾	12.1	6.1	48%	9%	·8%	17 Je	*1.87	*0.59	*0.48	n/r
·Amer Century Tr⁹....6¾s iJd15 1991	R	BB+	9.81	1991	41.91	23.86	8.38	55	55	55	12.2	16.2	35%	13%	·8%	17 Je	*1.87	*0.59	*0.48	n/r
·Amer City Bk....9¾s QJe30 1994	R	NR	5.00	1994	77.52	12.90	....	75	60	62	14.9	16.5	62	8	·18%	d Dc	Λ1.42		61.26	1.29
¹⁰Amer Gen'l....5⅛s mS 1987	R	NR	1.94	1987	51.70	181.70	39.78	61¾	61¾	⁸61¾	8.96	16.3	40%	50%	·32%	5 Dc	⁹6.56	P3.29	⁹6.65	6.47
·Amer Hoist & Der....4¾s iJd 1992	R	NR	0.68	1992	63.86	15.66	71.52	No Sale	78	4.61	4.38	54%	16%	·16%	5 Nv	3.41	P3.29	3.29	3.06
·Amer Hoist & Der....5⅛s iJd 1993	R	BB+	8.21	1993	50.25	19.90	11.68	87½	79¾	79½	6.95	8.39	81	15%	·16%	5 Nv	3.41	P3.29	3.29	3.06
·Amer Int'l Group....4s iJ 1997	R	AA-	28.7	1997	29.30	34.13	11.72	191¾	179¾	191%	2.09	16.9	191%	65%	·65%	2 Mr	4.71	5.83	9.60	4.57
·Amer Israeli Paper....11⅛s AnN15 1997	R		14.0	1997	58.58	17.07	5.27	72	70	⁸71¾	16.4		43%	12%	·7½					
·Amer Maize-Prod....11⅛s iA 2000	R	BB+	25.0	2000	255.61	218.18	28.61	84	82	82	14.3	14.5	57¾	14%	·10%	5 Dc	2.07	2.00	⁹2.00	1.96
·Amer Medical Int¹....8s iJd 2000	R	BBB	60.0	2000	52.99	18.87	27.55	126¾	119¾	117	6.84	6.41	129¾	22%	·24%	14 Au	1.23	1.60	11.74	1.56
·Amer Medical Int'l....9½s mN15 2001	R	BBB	125	2001	30.77	32.50	16.00	99¾	93	ˢ94	10.1	10.2	75¾	30%	·24%	14 Au	1.23	1.60	11.74	1.56
·Amer Medicorp¹³....9½s Ao 1989	R	NR	1.41	1989		Debs¹⁴	....	73	72	72	7.64	11.3	80%		·23.726	14 Au	1.02	1.55	11.73	1.56
·Amer Motor Inns....5½s Fa 1991	R	NR	3.58	1991	62.50	16.00	13.75	92	82	89¾	6.15	7.09	93	14%	·14%		1.31	1.73	101.84	1.66
·American Motors....5⅞s iD 1988	R	NR	21.0	1988	107.87	9.27	....	53½	49	ˢ52½	11.4	18.7	29%	4%	·2%	d Dc	d6.00	E2.00	⁹d2.22	n/r
¹⁵Amer Safety Eq....5⅞s iD 1983	R	NR	1.95	1983		Cv into $974.00	....	95	95	95	6.05	8.76	97%	38%	·37	d Dc	14.2	P4.68	13.0	n/r
·Amer Tobacco Int¹⁶..5¼s iA 1988	C	NR	3.35	1988	55.56	1718.00	194.46	No Sale	212¾	2.47	9.95	205¾	38%	·26%	6 Dc	◆6.50	P6.68	6.68	6.46
·Amfac....5s Ms 1989	R	BBB-	12.9	1989	28.00	35.714	40.32	75¾	73¾	75¾	6.64	9.68	75¾	26%	·26%	9 Dc	5.37	P2.84	2.84	5.05
·Amfac....5s Mn 1994	R	BBB-	33.3	1994	22.90	43.67	32.98	71	65¼	66¾	7.89	10.0	61%	29	·26%	9 Dc	5.37	P2.84	2.84	5.05
·Ampex¹⁸....5⅛s iA15 1994	R	BBB	54.0	1994	27.72	936.08	23.28	76¼	74	ˢ76¾	7.21	8.63	72¾	27%	·26%	9 Dc	Λ2.63	E2.90	⁹3.14	⁹0.83
·Anacomp, Inc....10s mN 1988	R	NR	0.88	1988	418.41	2.39	50.21	523	418¾	444¾	2.25	11.6	439%	10%	·10%	12 Je	0.74	0.88	⁹0.90	⁹0.83
·Anacomp, Inc....9⅜s mS 2000	R	B-	29.9	2000	67.57	14.80	8.11	94¾	84	84	11.3	15.9	71	12%	·10%	12 Je	0.74	0.88	⁹0.90	⁹0.83
·Anacomp, Inc....13⅜s iJl15 2002	R	B-	50.0	2002	57.14	17.50	6.86	87¾	85	87¾	15.8	15.9	60	15%	·9½	12 Fb	0.81	0.88	⁹0.90	⁹0.83
·Andersen Lab²⁰....6½s Ms 1988	R	NR	0.50	1988	95.24	10.50	....	102¾	98	98	6.25	6.52	90%	10%	·9½	10 Fb		10.96	10.96	n/r
·Anheuser-Busch....9s aO 2005	R	A	100	2005	27.82	35.94	35.61	123½	112	ˢ123¾	7.29	6.96	119¾	44%	·43	9 Dc	3.80	E4.65	⁹4.60	n/r
·Anthony Indus..11¼s ²¹Jd15 2000	R	B-	22.0	2000	250.33	19.87	22.15	66	63	ˢ66	17.0	17.5	33%	13%	·16%	9 Dc	1.14		9.84	2.08
·Apache Corp....6s iJl 1990	R	B+	4.06	1990	347.62	221.00	74.29	81	73	79¾	7.58	9.68	79¾	16%	·16%	6 Dc	2.13	E2.35	⁹2.24	2.08
·ARA Services....4⅞s iJd15 1996	R	A-	28.0	1996	9.87	101.35	19.74	48	45¾	45	10.2	13.3	25%	45%	·25%	6 Oc	5.33	▲4.00	4.00	n/r
·Arapaho Petrol....13s 24QMar31 1991	R	NR	1.12	1991	150.60	26.64	....	75	74¾	75	17.3	18.6	56%	3%	·3%	37 My	0.08	0.09	10.10	n/r

Uniform Footnote Explanations—See Page XVI. Other: ¹Was Ind'l Nucleonics. ²Cv into AM Int'l. ³Conv into AM Int'l. ⁴Was Beneficial Std Mfg. ⁵Cv into & data of Moraga Corp.
⁶Now Apex R.E.&T.sub of Apex Hldg. ⁷Cv into Moraga Corp.com. ⁸Offered outside U.S.;p&i in U.S.$. ⁹Was Amer Century Mfg inv. ¹⁰Was Lincoln Amer. ¹¹Cv into $3.25 Cv Jr pfd. ¹²Into Cl A.
¹³Now Humana Inc. ¹⁴Cv into $1119.48 prin amt 11.70% Deb98. ¹⁵Subsid & data of Marmon Group. ¹⁶Offered outside U.S.:Prin&Int pay in U.S.$. ¹⁷Cv into American Brands.
¹⁸Subsid & data of Signal Cos. ¹⁹Cv into Signal Cos. ²⁰Now Andersen Group. ²¹Due Jan 1. ²²Into Cl B. ²³Cv into & data of Continental Tel. ²⁴Due Oct 30. ²⁵To 10-29-83;then $7.64,etc.

Figure 3—7   **Standard & Poor's** *Corporate Reports*

Texas Instruments   2208

NYSE Symbol TXN   Options on CBOE

Price	Range	P-E Ratio	Dividend	Yield	S&P Ranking
Sep. 8'80 127³/₈	1980 130¹/₂–78⁵/₈	15	2.00	1.6%	A

Summary

Texas Instruments is the leading producer of semiconductor products, and has important representation in other segments of the electronics industry, in geophysical exploration, and in specialty metal products. Earnings improvement is expected for 1980, and further progress is possible for 1981. The impressive new products program enhances long-term prospects.

Current Outlook

Earnings for 1980 are estimated at about $8:80 a share, up from 1979's $7.58. Further moderate earnings progress is expected for 1981.

Dividends should continue at a minimum of $0.50 quarterly.

The growth of the semiconductor industry is expected to slow in the second half of 1980 and into the first half of 1981. Demand from the important military-aerospace and computer markets is expected to hold up. Integrated circuits should continue to show the fastest growth (although pricing should be more competitive), while further small gains are expected for discrete devices. In Digital Products, further progress is expected for minicomputers, but consumer products will be weak. Government electronics operations should show progress along with geophysical services, while metallurgical materials will be soft. Pretax margins are likely to show some further slippage in 1980 partly due to higher interest charges.

Net Sales (Million $)

Quarter:	1980	1979	1978	1977
Mar.	956	721	558	462
Jun.	1,007	784	615	493
Sep.		813	644	517
Dec.		906	733	575
		3,224	2,550	2,047

First half 1980 sales rose 30%, year to year. Pretax income was up 27%. After taxes at 44.0% in both periods, net income was also up 27%. Share earnings were $4.60, versus $3.63.

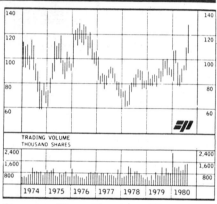

TRADING VOLUME
THOUSAND SHARES

| 1974 | 1975 | 1976 | 1977 | 1978 | 1979 | 1980 |

Common Share Earnings ($)

Quarter:	1980	1979	1978	1977
Mar.	2.20	1.68	1.35	1.20
Jun.	2.40	1.95	1.50	1.21
Sep.		1.92	1.56	1.29
Dec.		2.03	1.74	1.41
		7.58	6.15	5.11

Important Developments

Jul. '80—Capital spending of $570 million was planned for 1980. The backlog of orders at June 30, 1980 was $2.037 billion, versus $1.66 billion a year earlier, and up $44 million from March 31, 1980. Company funded research and development expenses in 1980 were expected to be $170 million, versus $134 million in 1979.

Next earnings report due in mid-October.

Per Share Data ($)

Yr. End Dec. 31	1979	1978	1977	1976	1975	1974	1973	1972	1971	1970
Book Value	41.75	37.12	32.64	28.89	25.53	23.67	20.61	16.67	14.87	13.74
Earnings	7.58	6.15	¹5.11	¹4.25	¹2.71	¹3.92	¹3.67	¹2.17	¹1.52	¹1.35
Dividends	2.00	1.76	1.41	1.08	1.00	1.00	0.72¹/₂	0.41¹/₂	0.40	0.30
Payout Ratio	26%	29%	28%	25%	37%	26%	20%	19%	26%	22%
Prices—High	101	92¹/₂	102¹/₄	129³/₄	119³/₈	115³/₄	138⁷/₈	95	64¹/₂	67¹/₄
Low	78	61³/₈	68⁵/₈	93¹/₈	61	58³/₄	74³/₈	58⁵/₈	39³/₄	30⁵/₈
P/E Ratio—	13–10	15–10	20–13	31–22	44–23	30–15	38–20	44–27	42–26	50–23

Data as orig. reptd. Adj. for stk. div(s). of 100% May 1973. 1. Ful. dil.: 6.12 in 1978, 5.10 in 1977, 4.23 in 1976, 2.70 in 1975, 3.91 in 1974, 3.64 in 1973, 2.16 in 1972, 1.52 in 1971, 1.35 in 1970.

SOURCE: *Standard & Poor's Corporate Reports*

Figure 3–7 (concluded)

2208

Texas Instruments Incorporated

Income Data (Million $)

Year Ended Dec. 31	Revs.	Oper. Inc.	% Oper. Inc. of Revs.	Cap. Exp.	Depr.	Int. Exp.	Net Bef. Taxes	Eff. Tax Rate	Net Inc.	% Net Inc. of Revs.
1979	3,224	507	15.7%	¹427	187	19.5	309	44.0%	173	5.4%
1978	2,550	385	15.1%	¹310	131	8.4	257	45.5%	140	5.5%
1977	2,046	319	15.6%	200	108	9.2	211	44.7%	117	5.7%
1976	1,659	250	15.1%	138	87	8.3	178	45.3%	97	5.9%
1975	1,368	207	15.1%	71	92	10.8	116	46.4%	62	4.5%
1974	1,572	257	16.3%	150	87	10.7	163	45.0%	90	5.7%
1973	1,287	205	15.9%	127	60	6.7	146	42.8%	83	6.5%
1972	944	131	13.9%	54	48	5.7	85	43.2%	48	5.1%
1971	764	110	14.4%	35	51	6.5	59	43.3%	34	4.4%
1970	828	109	13.2%	45	55	7.0	52	42.6%	30	3.6%

Balance Sheet Data (Million $)

Dec. 31	Cash	Current Assets	Current Liab.	Ratio	Total Assets	Ret. on Assets	Long Term Debt	Com-mon Equity	Total Cap.	% LT Debt of Cap.	Ret. on Equity
1979	117	1,083	882	1.2	1,908	10.1%	17.6	953	970	1.8%	19.2%
1978	115	915	637	1.4	1,518	10.1%	19.1	845	864	2.2%	17.7%
1977	257	815	467	1.7	1,255	9.8%	29.7	745	774	3.8%	16.6%
1976	294	783	418	1.9	1,128	9.4%	38.2	660	698	5.5%	15.7%
1975	267	663	302	2.2	941	6.5%	47.5	585	633	7.5%	11.0%
1974	155	656	342	1.9	965	10.0%	72.8	541	614	11.8%	17.7%
1973	179	590	283	2.1	828	11.3%	67.7	469	537	12.6%	19.6%
1972	196	470	188	2.5	634	7.9%	71.4	370	441	16.2%	13.7%
1971	186	415	153	2.7	580	6.1%	94.8	329	423	22.4%	10.7%
1970	124	350	139	2.5	531	5.6%	86.8	303	390	22.3%	10.2%

Data as orig. reptd. 1. Net of curr. yr. retirement and disposals.

Business Summary

Texas Instruments produces a variety of electrical and electronics products for industrial, consumer and government markets. Contributions by industry segment in 1979 were:

	Sales	Profits
Components	44%	55%
Digital Products	25%	14%
Government Electronics	17%	14%
Services	8%	9%
Metallurgical Materials	6%	8%

Operations outside the U.S. accounted for 38.6% of sales and 45.2% of operating profits.

Components include semiconductor integrated circuits (microprocessors, memories and digital and linear circuits), semiconductor discrete devices (transistors, diodes and optoelectronic products), assembled modules (microprocessor and memory printed circuit boards), magnetic bubble memory devices, and electrical and electronic control devices.

Digital products include minicomputers, electronic data terminals and peripherals, geophysical and scientific equipment, electronic calculators, home computers, time products, learning aids and other products.

Government Electronics products include radar, infrared surveillance systems and missile guidance and control systems.

Services mainly consist of the collection and electronic processing of seismic data in connection with petroleum exploration.

Metallurgical materials primarily involve clad metals which are used in variety of applications.

Employees: 85,779.

Dividend Data

Dividends have been paid since 1962.

Amt. of Divd. $	Date Decl.	Ex-divd. Date	Stock of Record	Payment Date
0.50	Sep. 28	Oct. 2	Oct. 9	Oct. 29'79
0.50	Dec. 21	Dec. 27	Jan. 3	Jan. 28'80
0.50	Mar. 14	Mar. 25	Mar. 31	Apr. 21'80
0.50	Jun. 27	Jul. 1	Jul. 8	Jul. 28'80

Next dividend meeting: late Sep. '80.

Capitalization

Long Term Debt: $217,092,000.

Common Stock: 22,947,373 shs. ($1 par).
Institutions hold about 64%.
Shareholders: 28,405.

Stock Market Encyclopedia, which contains end-of-the-year *Corporate Reports.* To develop an appreciation for the other Standard & Poor's services, try perusing this material at your library.

Value line

Value Line Investment Survey is a publication of Arnold Bernhard & Co. It is one of the most widely used investment services by individuals, stockbrokers, and small bank trust departments. The *Value Line Investment Survey* follows 1,700 companies, and each common stock is covered in a one-page summary (see the one for Texas Instruments in Figure 3–8). Value Line is noted for its comprehensive coverage, which can be seen by comparing Figure 3–8 to Figures 3–4 and 3–7. Raw financial data is available as well as trendline growth rates, price history patterns in graphic form, quarterly sales, earnings and dividends, and a breakdown of sales and profit margins by line of business. Value Line contains 13 sections divided into several industries each. The first few pages beginning an industry classification are devoted to an overview of the industry with the company summaries following. Each section is revised on a 13-week cycle.

Value Line has a unique evaluation system that is primarily dependent on historical relationships and regression analysis. From the valuation model, each company is rated 1 through 5 with 1 being the highest positive rating and 5 the lowest. Each company is rated on timeliness and safety. It should be noted that Value Line minimizes human judgment in making its evaluation, which is consistently mechanical from period to period.

The *Investment Survey* of Value Line also contains some information and advice on put and call options. This is updated weekly as are the stock rankings of the total sample. Data on options are presented in Figure 3–9. Value Line also publishes a separate *Convertible Bond Survey,* which analyzes and recommends action on convertibles based on the underlying common stock, interest rate movements, and related market behavior.

Other investment services

Dun & Bradstreet publishes *Key Business Ratios* in bound form. This publication contains 14 significant ratios on 800 different lines of business listed by SIC (standard industrial classification) code. Examples of ratios included are current assets to current debt, net profits on net sales, and total debt to tangible net worth. This publication has replaced the old Dun & Bradstreet 11-page pamphlet on key business ratios for 125 lines of business.

Dun's Marketing Services division of Dun & Bradstreet also publishes the *Million Dollar Directory* and *Billion Dollar Directory.* Companies are listed in alphabetical order, by geographical location by city and state, and by product classification. The data provide names, addresses and phone numbers, and sales for each company. This could be helpful in identifying companies in the same industry or in writing to request such information as annual reports or product lists.

Figure 3—8 The Value Line Investment Survey

TEXAS INSTR. NYSE-TXN

| RECENT PRICE | **83** | P/E RATIO **20.6** (Trailing: 18.4 / Median: 23.0) | EARN'S YLD **4.9%** | DIV'D YLD **2.4%** | 1071 |

Insider Decisions

	J A S O N D	J F M A M J	J A S
to Buy	1 2 4 2 1 1	1 1 0 2 2 1	0 0 4
to Sell	6 3 9 7 3 0	2 0 7 7 2 6	2 0 1

Institutional Decisions

	2Q'80	3Q'80	4Q'80	1Q'81	2Q'81
to Buy	82	94	73	106	77
to Sell	62	82	74	53	81
Hldg's(000)	13516	14738	14418	15090	14883

1984-86 PROJECTIONS

	Price	Gain	Ann'l Total Return
High	565	(+580%)	60%
Low	380	(+360%)	47%

Nov. 13, 1981 Value Line

TIMELINESS **4** Below Average (Relative Price Perform-ance Next 12 Mos.)
SAFETY **3** Average (Scale: 1 Highest to 5 Lowest)
BETA 1.15 (1.00 = Market)

BUSINESS: Texas Instruments is engaged in the development, manufacture, and sale of electronic equip., such as semiconductors, calculators, microprocessors, and small computers. Its equip. group fills military orders for missile guidance systems. International sales, about 35% of total. Has 44 plants in 18 countries. Employee costs, about 40% of sales; research and development, about 4.6%. Deprec. rate in 1980: 14.9%. Est'd plant age: 2.4 yrs. Has 89,875 empls., 26,427 shareowners. Insiders own 19% of outstanding stock. Pres.: J. Fred Bucy. Chrmn.: Mark Shepherd, Jr. Inc.: Del. Address: 13500 North Central Expressway (P.O. Box 5474), Dallas, Texas 75222.

Times are tough at TI. We think the semiconductor division is living hand-to-mouth these days. The European market is terrible. High interest rates and the specter of recession are keeping U.S. customers from building inventories. Orders aren't coming in as fast as chips are going out the door, so semiconductor revenues are falling. Price competition in some components hurts, too. These days, we suspect the semiconductor division is at best marginally profitable. **Computer products aren't faring much better.** Inflation is pushing up manufacturing costs. And TI is boosting spending on marketing and customer support. But the high cost of money and the weak economy have slowed bookings. So margins are getting squeezed. The pace of incoming business probably won't improve until mid-1982. In light of the dreary scenario for these two important divisions, this stock will probably trail the market averages.
Government electronics and geophysical services are holding up the bottom line. Increased defense spending, especially on electronic gear, is translating into higher sales and earnings for TI's government electronics division. The boom in oil and gas exploration

plus the soaring cost of drilling wells is spurring strong demand for seismic services. We expect these divisions will contribute over $3.00 of the company's 1981 share profits. **The 64K random access memory will mean big things to TI.** The company may capture the largest share among U.S. suppliers of this leading-edge memory chip. TI's product is smaller and faster than the competition's, and uses less power. The company has overcome some early manufacturing problems and is moving into high volume production. A lot of customers are currently designing the TI memory chip into their products, so **demand will probably surge in the first half of 1982.** If industry sales of 64Ks hit $1.5 billion by 1985 and TI can capture 10% of the market, this product would add plenty to profits by mid-decade. Appreciation potential to that time appears outstanding.
I.D.O./N.R.W.

CURRENT POSITION ($mill.)

	1979	1980	6/30/81
Cash Assets	116.6	139.8	58.3
Receivables	548.0	629.8	621.9
Inventory (FIFO)	340.3	442.7	409.1
Other	78.2	87.0	101.1
Current Assets	1083.1	1299.3	1190.4
Accts Payable	536.7	630.4	340.2
Debt Due	181.0	170.8	58.6
Other	164.7	170.2	457.0
Current Liab.	882.4	971.4	855.8

ANNUAL RATES of change (per sh)

	Past 10 Yrs	Past 5 Yrs	Est '78-'80 to '84-'86
Sales	15.0%	18.0%	15.5%
"Cash Flow"	16.0%	18.0%	15.0%
Earnings	19.0%	17.5%	14.0%
Dividends	17.0%	17.0%	12.0%
Book Value	12.5%	12.5%	14.5%

QUARTERLY SALES ($ mill.)

Calendar	Mar. 31	June 30	Sept. 30	Dec. 31	Full Year
1978	557.6	614.6	644.5	733.2	2549.9
1979	720.8	784.2	813.0	906.1	3224.1
1980	956.4	1007.2	1024.4	1086.7	4074.7
1981	1083.0	1055.6	1038.7	1042.7	4200
1982	1050	1090	1250	1300	4700

EARNINGS PER SHARE (A)

Calendar	Mar. 31	June 30	Sept. 30	Dec. 31	Full Year
1978	1.35	1.50	1.56	1.74	6.15
1979	1.68	1.95	1.92	2.03	7.58
1980	2.20	2.40	2.30	2.32	9.22
1981	1.47	.44	1.15	1.19	4.25
1982	1.25	1.35	1.90	2.50	7.00

QUARTERLY DIVIDENDS PAID (B)

Calendar	Mar. 31	June 30	Sept. 30	Dec. 31	Full Year
1977	.33	.33	.33	.33	1.32
1978	.42	.42	.42	.42	1.68
1979	.50	.50	.50	.50	2.00
1980	.50	.50	.50	.50	2.00
1981	.50	.50	.50	.50	

CAPITAL STRUCTURE as of 6/30/81
Total Debt $271.8 mill. Due in 5 Yrs $170.8 mill.
LT Debt $213.2 mill. LT Interest $26.0 mill.
(LT interest earned: 6.9x; total interest coverage: 4.3x) (15% of Cap'l)

Leases, Uncapitalized Annual rentals $24.5 mill.

Pension Liability None in '80 vs. None in '79

Pfd Stock None

Common Stock 23,530,905 shs. (85% of Cap'l)

(A) Based on avg. shares outstanding. Next egs. rep't due early Feb. Est'd constant-dollar egs./sh.: '80, $6.35. (B) Next div'd meet'g about Dec. 18. Goes ex div'd about Dec. 28. Approx. div'd payment dates: Jan. 24, Apr. 25, July 25, Oct. 25. (C) In millions, adjusted for stock splits and dividends. (D) Deprec. on accelerated basis.

Restated Sales (and Pretax Margins) by Business Line

	1978	1979	1980	1981
Elec Components	1094.0 (9.9%)	1422.4 (12.7%)	1774.1 (11.7%)	1650 (5%)
Digital Prods	674.0 (9.2%)	826.3 (3.9%)	982.8 (3.4%)	1050 (1.0%)
Government Elec	434.0 (10.1%)	532.8 (7.5%)	720.3 (9.1%)	830 (8.5%)
Metallurgical Mat	143.0 (11.9%)	193.8 (13.5%)	194.3 (10.8%)	200 (10.0%)
Services	204.9 (12.7%)	248.8 (12.0%)	403.3 (12.5%)	490 (12.0%)
Company	2549.8 (10.1%)	3224.1 (9.6%)	4074.7 (9.3%)	4200 (3.9%)

Company's Financial Strength A+
Stock's Price Stability 70
Price Growth Persistence 55
Earnings Predictability 70

SOURCE: *The Value Line Investment Survey*, November 14, 1980.

Figure 3—9

OPTIONS—RELEVANT INFORMATION FOR BUYERS AND WRITERS

The investor seeking to buy or write Call Options will find the tabulation below useful. Writers and buyers of Options should note that a Call's premium over its exercise value, *at a particular price for the common stock,* may tend to be greatest when the common stock is risky (Safety: 4 or 5; Stability: 5-25; Beta: well above 1.10); estimated Common Dividend Yield is relatively low; and Option has a long life (6 or 9 months). The premium may tend to be lowest when these conditions are reversed. . . . All other things being equal, an Option will rise or fall fastest (percentage-wise) and be riskiest when its price is low relative to the common stock price. . . . Buyers of 3- to 9-month Options regardless of the risk being assumed, may wish to concentrate in those Calls whose underlying com-

mon stocks are ranked 1 (Highest) or 2 (Above Average) for year-ahead relative market performance, ranked 1 (Highest) or 2 (Above Average) for 3- to 6-month technical market action and whose corresponding Industry Ranks for 12-month relative market performance are favorable (1-25). Options buyers should read the latest Value Line reports to improve their understanding of a company's near-term prospects; they should also be relatively confident that the Stock Market is poised to advance.

Investors who desire detailed evaluations of individual options are advised to consult the Option Evaluation Section in *Value Line Options & Convertibles.*

Ratings & Reports Page No.	Stock Name	Stock Ticker Symbol	Where Option Trades	Recent Stock Price	Stock Ranks Time- liness (3-6 mos)	Technical (3-6 mos)	Safety	Stock Stability Index	Stock Beta	Est'd Current P/E Ratio	Est'd Div'd Yield (next 12 mos)	Industry Group	Industry Rank
1752	AMF, Inc.	AMF	ASE (P)	27	3	2	3	60	1.10	9.7	5.0	Recreation	56
2092	ASA Ltd. (g)	ASA	ASE (P)	49	3	4	3	30	0.55	NMF	12.8	Investment Company	30
215	Abbott Labs.	ABT	PHL (P)	29	2	3	3	70	1.15	14.5	2.8	Health Care/Hosp. Supp.	32
1038	Advanced Micro Dev.	AMD	PAC (P)	19	4	4	4	10	1.75	54.3	NIL	Electronics	70
2068	Aetna Life & Casualty	AET	ASE (P)	45	2	2	3	75	1.15	7.3	5.4	Insurance (Diversified)	22
1892	Air Products & Chem.	APD	PHL (P)	38	2	3	3	70	1.00	8.7	2.6	Chemical/Diversified	80
1246	Allied Corp.	ALD	PHL (P)	47	2	3	3	65	1.20	4.6	5.3	Chemical (Basic)	44
1435	Allis-Chalmers	AH	PHL (P)	15	5	5	3	65	1.15	NMF	6.7	Agricultural Equip./Div.	91
1218	Aluminum Co. Of Amer.	AA	CBO (P)	23	3	4	3	75	1.10	6.1	8.0	Aluminum	87
625	Amax Inc.	AMX	ASE (P)	44	3	3	3	40	1.00	14.7	5.5	Lead. Zinc & Mining	88
1081	Amdahl Corp.	AMH	CBO (P)	31	3	3	4	5	1.60	21.8	1.5	Computer/Data Proc.	75
403	Amerada-Hess Corp.	AHC	PHL (P)	28	5	4	3	50	1.30	9.0	4.3	Petroleum (Integrated)	74
378	Amer. Broadc. Cos.	ABC	PAC (P)	35	2	2	3	65	1.05	6.3	4.6	Broadcasting	17
1893	Amer. Cyanamid	ACY	ASE (P)	27	3	3	3	50	1.05	7.2	6.5	Chemical/Diversified	80
180	Amer. Elec. Power	AEP	CBO	17	3	3	2	100	0.65	7.4	13.5	Electric Utility (East)	36
2071	Amer. Express	AXP	ASE,CBO (P)	48	3	2	3	70	1.10	8.2	4.4	Insurance (Diversified)	22
350	Amer. Home Products	AHP	ASE (P)	35	2	2	1	90	0.90	10.9	5.9	Drug (Proprietary)	7
216	Amer. Hospital Supply	AHS	CBO	37	3	3	2	80	1.00	10.2	3.1	Health Care/Hosp. Supp.	32
751	Amer. Tel. & Tel.	T	CBO (P)	60	3	1	1	100	0.65	6.7	9.5	Telecommunications	16
1040	AMP, Inc.	AMP	CBO	51	3	3	2	75	1.00	15.1	2.7	Electronics	70
1555	Anheuser-Busch	BUD	PHL (P)	43	1	1	3	70	0.90	9.0	3.0	Brewing	49
1830	Apache Corp.	APA	PHL (P)	21	3	3	3	20	1.35	15.6	1.4	Petroleum Producing	67
1458	Archer Daniels Midl'd	ADM	PHL (P)	18	2	4	3	40	1.15	6.9	0.8	Food Processing	42
1219	Asarco Inc.	AR	ASE (P)	28	4	4	3	20	1.35	19.7	5.0	Metals & Mining(General)	78
404	Ashland Oil	ASH	PHL (P)	30	4	4	3	55	1.00	10.0	8.0	Petroleum (Integrated)	74
405	Atlantic Richfield	ARC	CBO (P)	46	3	3	2	80	1.10	6.7	5.1	Petroleum (Integrated)	74
1083	Automatic Data Proc.	AUD	PHL (P)	29	2	2	2	70	1.00	17.5	1.6	Computer/Data Proc.	75
1380	Avco Corp	AV	PHL (P)	21	4	4	4	30	1.45	5.8	5.7	Multiform	54
1043	Avnet, Inc.	AVT	ASE (P)	49	4	3	3	50	1.45	11.4	2.1	Electronics	70
805	Avon Products	AVP	CBO (P)	32	4	3	1	90	0.90	8.2	9.8	Toiletries/Cosmetics	34
1849	Baker Int'l Corp.	BKO	PAC (P)	39	3	3	3	60	1.25	10.3	1.8	Oilfield Services	40
1772	Bally Mfg. Corp.	BLY	ASE,CBO (P)	30	1	2	4	10	1.30	9.7	0.5	Hotel/Gaming	35
2005	Bankamerica Corp	BAM	CBO	24	3	3	1	80	1.00	6.6	6.4	Bank	12
219	Bausch & Lomb	BOL	ASE (P)	48	4	4	3	40	1.05	10.8	3.6	Health Care/Hosp. Supp.	32
220	Baxter Travenol Labs.	BAX	CBO (P)	32	1	1	2	80	1.00	14.4	1.3	Health Care/Hosp. Supp.	32
1459	Beatrice Foods	BRY	ASE (P)	19	3	3	1	95	0.85	5.1	7.6	Food Processing	42
221	Becton Dickinson & Co	BDX	PHL (P)	46	3	3	2	85	0.80	11.6	2.4	Health Care/Hosp. Supp.	32
1422	Bethlehem Steel	BS	CBO (P)	21	3	4	3	50	1.25	4.1	7.6	Steel (Integrated)	51
1344	Black & Decker	BDK	CBO	14	4	4	3	65	1.15	12.0	5.7	Machine Tool	72
1604	Blue Bell, Inc.	BBL	PHL (P)	25	3	3	3	65	0.90	6.0	7.4	Apparel	13
554	Boeing	BA	CBO (P)	24	4	4	3	50	1.20	6.0	5.8	Aerospace/Diversified	76
928	Boise Cascade Corp	BCC	CBO	34	5	3	3	65	1.00	9.7	5.8	Paper & Forest Products	89
351	Bristol-Myers	BMY	CBO (P)	54	2	1	2	85	1.00	11.5	3.6	Drug (Proprietary)	7
361	Browning-Ferris Ind.	BFI	ASE (P)	32	2	2	3	40	1.30	11.8	3.0	Industrial Services	6
1754	Brunswick Corp.	BC	CBO (P)	20	2	3	3	50	1.10	6.6	4.5	Recreation	56
1361	Bucyrus-Erie	BY	ASE (P)	18	5	5	3	50	1.15	9.3	4.9	Machinery(Const.&Mining)	64
1238	Burlington Northern Inc.	BNI	CBO (P)	55	3	3	3	50	1.30	7.2	3.1	Railroad/Resources	63
1085	Burroughs Corp.	BGH	ASE,CBO (P)	31	4	5	3	75	1.00	7.8	8.4	Computer/Data Proc.	75
379	CBS Inc.	CBS	CBO	54	3	3	1	90	0.95	7.7	5.6	Broadcasting	17
309	CSX Corp.	CSX	PHL (P)	58	3	2	3	80	0.90	6.9	4.9	Railroad	11
1773	Caesars World	CAW	PHL (P)	8⅜	3	3	5	5	1.40	5.4	NIL	Hotel/Gaming	35
1362	Caterpillar Tractor	CAT	ASE (P)	54	2	4	1	90	1.00	7.2	5.0	Machinery(Const.&Mining)	64
555	Cessna Aircraft	CEA	CBO (P)	23	3	3	3	30	1.25	7.4	3.5	Aerospace/Diversified	76
929	Champion Int'l. Corp.	CHA	CBO (P)	20	4	4	3	65	1.10	9.2	7.5	Paper & Forest Products	89
409	Charter Co.	CHR	PHL (P)	9¾	4	4	5	5	1.35	54.4	10.2	Petroleum (Integrated)	74
2010	Chase Manhattan Corp.	CMB	ASE (P)	59	2	1	2	85	1.00	4.9	5.6	Bank	12
2012	Citicorp	FNC	CBO (P)	27	3	3	3	60	1.15	6.8	6.1	Bank	12
410	Cities Service	CS	PHL (P)	53	3	3	3	45	1.15	11.5	3.4	Petroleum (Integrated)	74
1387	City Investing Co.	CNV	PHL (P)	23	3	3	4	50	1.05	6.8	7.4	Multiform	54
411	Coastal Corp. (The)	CGP	ASE,CBO (P)	24	4	4	4	5	1.45	NMF	1.4	Petroleum (Integrated)	74
1548	Coca-Cola	KO	CBO (P)	36	▲2	2	1	90	0.90	9.4	6.8	Soft Drink	2
980	Colgate-Palmolive	CL	CBO (P)	16	3	3	2	85	0.90	7.3	7.5	Household Products	21
1308	Combustion Eng.	CSP	PAC (P)	36	3	4	3	60	1.15	8.1	4.9	Machinery	57
707	Commonwealth Edison	CWE	CBO (P)	22	2	2	1	100	0.65	6.6	12.7	Electric Util. (Central)	39
755	Communic. Satellite	CQ	PHL (P)	59	3	3	3	60	1.05	15.6	3.9	Telecommunications	16
1087	Computer Sciences	CSC	CBO (P)	13	5	4	4	15	1.30	9.3	NIL	Computer/Data Proc.	75
1088	Computervision Corp	CVN	PHL (P)	28	3	4	4	10	1.75	19.9	NIL	Computer/Data Proc.	75
188	Consol. Edison	ED	ASE (P)	33	1	1	1	100	0.65	5.1	9.8	Electric Utility (East)	36
756	Cont'l Telephone	CTC	ASE (P)	18	3	2	3	100	0.75	7.5	8.7	Telecommunications	16
1089	Control Data	CDA	CBO (P)	40	3	3	3	45	1.55	8.6	1.3	Computer/Data Proc.	75
1005	Corning Glass Works	GLW	CBO (P)	60	3	3	2	75	1.05	9.0	4.0	Electrical Equipment	55
1091	Data General Corp.	DGN	PAC (P)	53	3	3	3	40	1.20	12.4	NIL	Computer/Data Proc.	75
1092	Datapoint Corp.	DPT	CBO (P)	46	3		3	25	1.55	17.0	NIL	Computer/Data Proc.	75
1181	Dean Witter Reynolds	DWR	PHL (P)	50	—	2	3	25	1.55	12.3	2.0	Securities Brokerage	37
1436	Deere & Co.	DE	ASE (P)	36	3	4	2	85	0.90	7.2	5.6	Agricultural Equip./Div.	91
259	Delta Air Lines	DAL	CBO (P)	52	4	3	3	65	1.15	8.5	3.8	Air Transport	84
1248	Diamond Shamrock	DIA	CBO (P)	28	3	3	3	50	1.20	14.3	6.3	Chemical (Basic)	44
1095	Digital Equipment	DEC	ASE,CBO (P)	97	1	3	3	60	1.20	12.5	NIL	Computer/Data Proc.	75
1759	Disney (Walt) Prod.	DIS	ASE,CBO (P)	54	3	3	2	70	1.10	13.5	1.9	Recreation	56
1550	Dr Pepper	DOC	ASE (P)	13	2	2	3	60	1.05	8.7	6.3	Soft Drink	2
413	Dorchester Gas	DGS	PAC (P)	19	4	4	4	20	1.40	10.6	1.0	Petroleum (Integrated)	74
1249	Dow Chemical	DOW	CBO (P)	25	4	4	3	70	1.20	8.6	7.6	Chemical (Basic)	44
1853	Dresser Ind.	DI	PHL (P)	33	3	4	3	65	1.15	7.3	2.2	Oilfield Services	40
190	Duke Power	DUK	PHL (P)	22	3	1	1	95	0.65	6.7	10.0	Electric Utility (East)	36

ASE—American Stock Exchange   PAC—Pacific Stock Exchange   (P)—Put Options Also Traded
CBO—Chicago Board Options Exchange   PHL—Philadelphia Stock Exchange

SOURCE: Summary of Advices and Index, *The Value Line Investment Survey,* January 30, 1981.

Another publication is the *Dow Jones-Irwin Business Almanac.* Almost everyone has looked through an almanac at some time and probably remembers being overwhelmed by all the facts and figures. This almanac is no exception. For our specific purposes, there is a section on finance and accounting which covers key business ratios, financial statement ratios by industry, and corporate profits and margins. A section on the stock market covers 63 pages and includes market averages, mutual funds, dividends, common stock prices and yields, and much more. Information on commodities, banks, financial institutions, economic data, and a great deal more is contained in this 780-page business almanac.

Retail stockbrokers have long provided information to their clients. Of course, the more you can afford to pay and the bigger your account, the more research you may receive. Most large brokers, such as Merrill Lynch; Shearson/American Express; Bache, and E. F. Hutton, will provide investors information free and for a fee. You name what you want, and they have it—industry-company analysis, bond market analysis, futures and commodities, options advice, tax shelters in oil and gas and real estate and so on. The brokerage industry provides much more sophisticated coverage of investments outside of stocks and bonds than they have in the past. This is partly because investors themselves have become more sophisticated in response to inflation and partly because of the increasing numbers and complexity of alternative investments.

INDEXES, PERIODICALS, AND JOURNALS

Indexes

One way to find relevant articles in periodicals and journals is to use indexes. There are many that will lead an analyst to useful information. The *Business Periodicals Index* references subjects in approximately 170 periodicals in the fields of accounting, advertising, banking, communications, economics, finance, insurance, investments, labor management, marketing, taxation, and other specific topics. The *Funk and Scott Index of Corporations and Industries* indexes articles from over 750 publications in two volumes. Each article covered includes a brief description of the article's contents. The articles are taken from business, financial, and trade magazines, major newspapers, bank newsletters, and investment advisory services. One very popular index is *The Wall Street Journal Index,* which identifies the date, page, and column of articles appearing in *The Wall Street Journal.* The index is presented in two parts—corporate news and general news. Many libraries have several years of *The Wall Street Journal* on microfiche or microfilm. The *Disclosure Journal* presents data on companies filing Securities and Exchange Commission reports. It organizes the reports into subject headings, financial data, SIC, and company headings. These SEC reports are often found on microfiche. There are many other indexes, such as *Who's Who in Finance and Industry,* Dun & Bradstreet's *Reference Book of Corporate Management,* and Standard & Poor's *Register of Corporations, Directors and Executives.* These last three focus on people and can provide important qualitative information as to the capabilities of management.

Periodicals and newspapers

After using the *Business Periodical Index,* an investor will most likely be referred to several of the most popular business periodicals, such as *Fortune, Business Week, Forbes, Dun's Review, Financial World,* and others. *Fortune* is published biweekly and is known for its coverage of industry problems and specific company analysis. *Fortune* has several regular features that make interesting reading. One, called "Business Roundup," usually deals with a major business concern, such as the federal budget, inflation, productivity, etc. Another feature, "Personal Investing," is always a thought-provoking article presenting ideas and analysis for the average investor.

Forbes is also a biweekly publication featuring several company-management interviews. This management-oriented approach points out various management styles and provides a look into the qualitative factors of security analysis. There are several regular columnists who discuss investment topics from a diversified perspective. *Business Week* is somewhat more generally oriented than *Forbes.* It includes a weekly economic update on such economic variables as interest rates, electricity consumption, and market prices while also featuring articles on industries and companies. Many other periodicals, such as *Dun's Review, The Harvard Business Review,* and *Money Magazine,* are helpful to the financial manager or personal investor. Unfortunately, space limits describing too many.

Most major city newspapers (Chicago, Dallas, and Cleveland, to name a few) have good financial sections. The *New York Times* has an exceptional financial page. However, the most widely circulated financial daily is *The Wall Street Journal* published by Dow Jones. This is the paper that is read by millions of investors in order to keep up with the economy and business environment. Feature articles on labor, business, economics, personal investing, technology, and taxes appear weekly. Corporate announcements of all kinds are published. Figure 3–10, "Digest of Earnings Reports," is a daily feature that updates quarterly and annual earnings of firms.

New offerings of stocks and bonds are also advertised by investment bankers in the *Journal.* Prices of actively traded securities are presented by market. Common stock prices are organized by exchange and over-the-counter markets. Figure 3–11 is an example of common stock prices on the New York Stock Exchange. Along with the prices, notice that the most active securities for the day are listed in a table and that trading volume by market is also given.

Many other prices are printed in *The Wall Street Journal.* An investor will find prices of mutual funds, government Treasury bills, notes and bonds, put and call prices from the option exchanges, government agency securities, foreign exchange prices, and commodities future prices. Figure 3–12 is an example of the future prices from the *Journal.* The prices are listed by category and exchange. Because of the comprehensive price coverage on a daily basis and other features, it is hard to believe that an up-to-date intelligent investor would be able to function without *The Wall Street Journal.*

Barron's National Business and Financial Weekly is also published by Dow Jones every Monday. It contains regular features on dividends, put and call op-

Figure 3–10

Digest of Earnings Reports

ADVANCED SEMICONDUCTOR (O)
Year Dec 31: 1981   1980
Sales $37,600,000 $27,300,000
Net income .. 2,800,000   2,400,000
The above results have been computed at the guilder's current rate.

ALABAMA-TENN NAT GAS (O)
Year Dec 31: 1981 .   1980
Revenues $116,805,292 $91,907,047
Net income .. 5,786,491   5,265,689
Shr earns:
   Net income   5.36   4.88

ALTAMIL CORP. (A)
Quar Feb 28: 1982   1981
Sales $16,182,589 $19,013,968
Net loss a243,420   c94,487
Shr earns:
   Net loss c.06
   6 months:
Sales 35,333,322   37,732,624
Net income .. a2,102   543,480
Shr earns (primary):
   Net income 40
Shr earns (fully diluted):
   Net income 35
a-Includes pretax loss of $525,000 from expenses related to closing of three truck equipment facilities. b-Restated. c-Income.

AMERICAN BAKERIES CO. (N)
Year Dec 26: 1981   a1980
Sales $521,400,000 $492,506,000
Inco cnt op ... 2,232,000   1,983,000
Loss dis op ... 5,353,000   c26,000
Loss 3,121,000   c2,009,000
Extrd chg .. d2,491,000   ....
Acctg adj .. b2,078,000   ....
Net loss 7,690,000   c2,009,000
Shr earns:
   Inco cnt op ..   .85   .73
   Loss c.74
   Net loss c.74
   12 weeks:
Sales 121,677,000   113,429,000
Loss cnt op .. 362,000   c134,000
Loss dis op ... 661,000   c168,000
Loss 1,023,000   c302,000
Extrd chg .. d1,195,000   ....
Net loss 2,218,000   c302,000
Shr earns:
   Loss cnt op c.02
   Loss c.10
   Net loss c.10
a-Restated. b-Debit; cumulative effect on prior years of an accounting change. c-Income. d-Includes charges incurred in proxy fight.

AMERICAN PLAN CORP. (A)
Year Dec 31: 1981   1980
Income $1,016,556 $771,855
aExtrd cred .. 552,676   708,000
Net income .. 1,569,232   1,479,855
Shr earns (primary):
   Income 72   .67
   Net income   1.11   1.28
Shr earns (fully diluted):
   Income 59   .47
   Net income   .90   .87
a-Tax-loss carry-forward.

AMERICAN PACESETTER (Pa)
Year Dec 31: 1981   1980
Revenues $67,471,000 $80,752,000
Net income .. 3,416,000   5,828,000
Avg shares ... 2,396,000   2,818,000
... earns:

HI-SHEAR INDUSTRIES (N)
Quar Feb 28: 1982   1981
Revenues $21,811,000 $21,892,000
Net income .. a1,518,000   2,113,000
Avg shares .. 4,639,339   4,815,072
Shr earns:
   Net income   .33   .44
   9 months:
Revenues 78,394,000   68,140,800
Net income .. a6,983,000   7,301,000
Avg shares .. 4,757,920   4,571,206
Shr earns:
   Net income   1.47   1.60
a-Includes equity in net income of affiliate of $204,000 in the quarter and $1,099,000 in the nine months.

HICKORY FURNITURE CO. (O)
Year Dec 31: 1981   a1980
Sales $42,745,000 $40,369,000
Inco cnt op .. 2,964,000   2,446,000
Inco dis op .. 300,000   ....
Net income .. 3,264,000   2,446,000
Shr earns:
   Inco cnt op ..   2.67   2.17
   Net income   2.94   2.17
a-Restated to reflect change in fiscal year end to December 31 from July 31.

JACK WINTER INC. (N)
13 wk Feb 27: 1982   1981
Sales $7,459,000 $7,887,000
Net income .. 77,000   601,000
Shr earns:
   Net income   .02   .16

JENSEN INDUSTRIES (A)
Year Dec 31: 1981   1980
Sales ......,... $16,704,489 $12,169,019
Net income .. 1,072,474   117,145
Avg shares .. 1,161,473   1,523,171
Shr earns:
   Net income   .92   .08

KAUFMAN & BROAD INC. (N)
Quar Feb 28: 1982   a1981
Revenues $119,642,000 $98,028,000
Net loss 1,529,000   c1,241,000
Shr earns:
   Net loss c.09
a-Restated to reflect adoption of the new accounting change for foreign currency translation. c-Income.

LEGAL & GENERAL GROUP (F)
Year Dec 31: 1981   1980
Net income .. $52,400,000 $38,100,000
The above results have been computed at the pound's current rate.

LEUCADIA NATIONAL CORP. (N)
Year Dec 31: 1981   1980
Inco cnt op .. $5,056,000 $662,000
Loss dis op .. 1,700,000   c477,000
Income 3,356,000   1,139,000
Extrd cred .. a4,479,000   b753,000
Net income .. 7,835,000   1,892,000
Avg shares .. 3,099,000   3,209,000
...earns (co... ...equiv):

ORANGE-CO INC (N)
Quar Feb 28: 1982   1981
Revenues $30,268,000 $28,817,000
Inco cnt op .. 1,698,000   2,247,000
Loss dis op .. a3,740,000   ....
Net loss 2,042,000   c2,247,000
Avg shares .. 3,124,000   3,688,000
Shr earns:
   Inco cnt op   .53   .59
   Net loss c.59
   6 months:
Revenues 47,249,000   43,741,000
Inco cnt op .. 2,415,000   2,831,000
Loss dis op .. a3,740,000   ....
Net loss 1,325,000   c2,831,000
Avg shares .. 3,189,000   3,688,000
Shr earns:
   Inco cnt op   .72   .72
   Net loss c.72
a-Reflects write-off of investment in preferred stock of a former unit, Arthur Treacher's Fish & Chips Inc., including a reserve for losses on settlement of certain leases guaranteed by Orange-co. c-Income.

PATRICK PETROLEUM CO. (N)
8 mo Dec 31: 1981   1980
Revenues $89,743,164 $43,916,706
Net income .. 5,285,369   2,626,118
Avg shares ... 14,038,843   12,513,566
Shr earns (com & com equiv):
   Net income   .38   .21
The company has changed from an April 30 fiscal year to a calendar year.

PAY 'N PAK STORES INC. (O)
Year Feb 28: 1982   1981
Revenues $180,973,899 $151,765,190
Net income .. 7,198,966   6,448,801
Shr earns:
   Net income   1.63   1.46
   Quarter:
Revenues 38,436,401   32,759,212
Net income .. 1,773,713   1,666,663
Shr earns:
   Net income   .40   .38

PENNSYLVANIA ENGINEER (A)
Year Dec 31: 1981   1980
Sales $185,091,000 $216,076,000
Net income .. a7,348,000   5,402,000
Shr earns (primary):
   Net income   .50   .38
Shr earns (fully diluted):
   Net income   .39   .30
   Quarter:
Sales 58,660,000   57,300,000
Net income .. 1,026,000   796,000
Shr earns (primary):
   Net income   .07   .06
Shr earns (fully diluted):
   Net income   .06   .05
a-Includes net gain of $7,300,000 on sale of marketable securities.

PHOENIX RESOURCES CO. (O)
Year Dec 31: 1981   1980
Revenues $34,009,000 $28,961,000
Net income .. 2,142,000   5,229,000
Shr earns:
   Net income   .19   a.48
   Quarter:
Revenues 8,949,000   8,314,000
Net income .. 626,000   570,000
Shr earns:
   Net income   .05   a.05
a-Adjusted for a two-for-on... ...in July...

Figure 3–11 Common stock prices

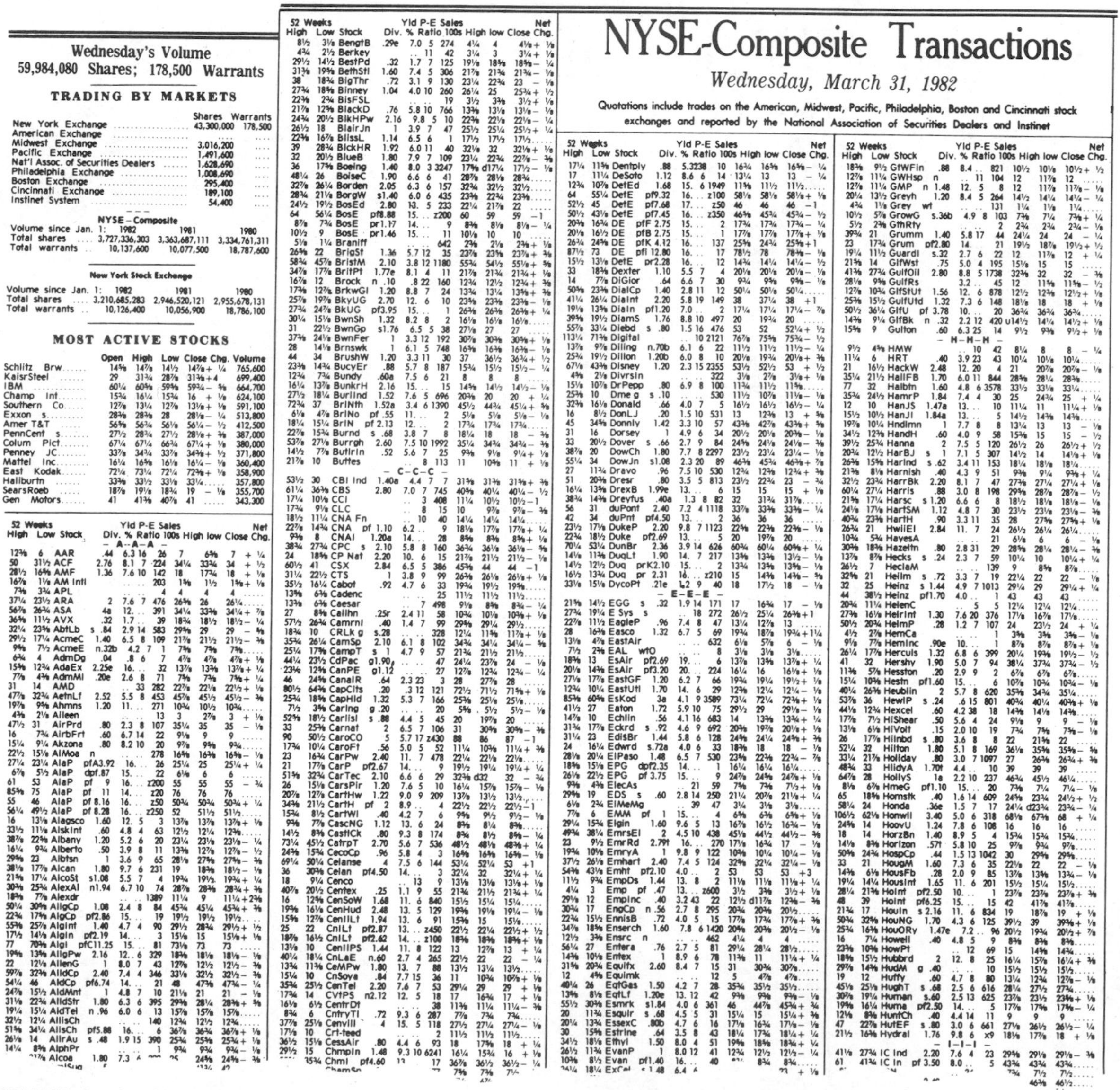

Wednesday's Volume
59,984,080 Shares; 178,500 Warrants

TRADING BY MARKETS

	Shares	Warrants
New York Exchange	43,300,000	178,500
American Exchange	....	....
Midwest Exchange	3,016,200	....
Pacific Exchange	1,491,600	....
Nat'l Assoc. of Securities Dealers	1,628,690	....
Philadelphia Exchange	1,008,690	....
Boston Exchange	295,400	....
Cincinnati Exchange	189,100	....
Instinet System	54,400	....

NYSE – Composite

Volume since Jan. 1:	1982	1981	1980
Total shares	3,727,336,303	3,363,687,111	3,334,761,311
Total warrants	10,137,600	10,077,500	18,787,600

New York Stock Exchange

Volume since Jan. 1:	1982	1981	1980
Total shares	3,210,685,283	2,946,520,121	2,955,678,131
Total warrants	10,126,400	10,056,900	18,786,100

MOST ACTIVE STOCKS

	Open	High	Low	Close	Chg.	Volume
Schlitz Brw	14⅝	14⅞	14½	14⅞	+ ¼	765,600
KaisrSteel	29	31¾	28⅞	31⅜	+4	699,400
IBM	60¼	60⅝	59⅝	59¾	− ⅝	664,700
Champ Int	15¾	16¼	15¾	16	+ ⅛	624,100
Southern Co	12⅞	13¼	12⅞	13⅛	+ ⅛	591,100
Exxon s	28⅜	28⅜	28	28⅛	− ¼	513,800
Amer T&T	56⅝	56¾	56⅛	56¼	− ½	412,500
PennCent s	27½	28¾	27½	28⅛	+ ⅜	387,000
Colum Pict	67¼	67¼	66¾	67¼	+ ⅛	380,000
Penney JC	33⅞	34¾	33⅞	34⅜	+ ½	371,800
Mattel Inc	16¼	16⅜	16⅛	16¼	− ⅛	360,400
East Kodak	72¼	73¼	72¼	72⅜	+ ⅛	358,900
Haliburtn	33⅜	33½	33⅛	33¼	.....	357,800
SearsRoeb	18⅞	19⅛	18¾	19	− ⅛	355,700
Gen Motors	41	41⅜	40⅞	41	.....	343,300

NYSE-Composite Transactions

Wednesday, March 31, 1982

Quotations include trades on the American, Midwest, Pacific, Philadelphia, Boston and Cincinnati stock exchanges and reported by the National Association of Securities Dealers and Instinet

tions, international stock markets, commodities, a review of the stock market, and many pages of prices and financial statistics. *Barron's* takes a weekly perspective and summarizes the previous week's market behavior. It also has regular analysis of several companies in its section called "Investment News and Views." The common stock section of *Barron's* not only provides weekly high-low-close

Figure 3–12

Futures Prices

Wednesday, March 31, 1982

Open Interest Reflects Previous Trading Day.

Left Column

	Open	High	Low	Settle	Change	Lifetime High	Low	Open Interest

—GRAINS AND OILSEEDS—

CORN (CBT)—5,000 bu.; cents per bu.

May	274	274¾	274	274¼	...	410¾	262¼	47,329
July	284¼	285	283½	284¼	+ ¼	399	267¾	40,274
Sept	288	289½	287½	288¾	+ ½	388½	268¾	7,561
Dec	293¼	295½	292¾	294½	+ ¾	345½	271	29,060
Mr83	307	309	306½	307¾	+ ½	320¾	293	6,254
May	315	317	315	316	+ ¾	317½	310	129

Est vol 18,451; vol Tue 32,662; open int 130,607, +1,262.

OATS (CBT)—5,000 bu.; cents per bu.

May	203	204¼	203	203¼	...	231½	177½	3,423
July	186½	188¼	186½	186¾	...	207	168½	3,203
Sept	179	180	178½	179	− ½	204¼	166	947
Dec	183½	184¼	182	182	− ½	199½	169	521
Mr83				187½	− ½	190	178	17

Est vol 933; vol Tue 1,516; open int 8,111, −19.

SOYBEANS (CBT)—5,000 bu.; cents per bu.

May	634	642	633	640	+ 6¾	922	605½	30,946
July	642	649½	641	647½	+ 5¾	866	615	28,861
Aug	646	652½	645	651½	+ 6¾	847	618½	3,354
Sept	647	654	646	652¾	+ 6¾	777	619	2,245
Nov	652	659	650	656¾	+ 6½	786	623½	16,142
Jn83	663	671½	663	669	+ 5½	783½	636	2,791
Mar	679	685½	679	684	+ 5½	744	649	382
May				696	+ 5½	746	670	31
July				704	+ 3½	700	700	5

Est vol 41,305; vol Tue 28,980; open int 84,757, −254.

SOYBEAN MEAL (CBT)—100 tons; $ per ton.

May	183.30	188.50	183.10	187.70	+ 4.30	260.50	178.40	18,022
July	185.60	190.00	185.50	189.50	+ 3.80	242.20	181.50	13,466
Aug	187.40	190.00	187.30	190.00	+ 2.50	244.00	183.00	2,292
Sept	188.50	191.50	188.30	191.50	+ 2.60	220.50	183.50	1,657
Oct	189.50	192.00	189.50	191.70	+ 1.70	226.00	184.00	2,737
Dec	192.00	195.00	191.50	194.70	+ 2.30	224.00	186.50	4,419
Jn83	196.00	197.90	193.50	197.00	+ 2.70	206.00	187.50	1,623
Mar	199.40	201.00	199.40	201.00	+ 2.80	201.00	191.50	39

Est vol 12,182; vol Tue 9,280; open int 44,255, +414.

SOYBEAN OIL (CBT)—60,000 lbs.; cents per lb.

May	18.85	18.95	18.75	18.88	+ .12	28.50	18.26	21,736
July	19.40	19.50	19.31	19.43	+ .10	29.50	18.67	15,223
Aug	19.57	19.73	19.57	19.70	+ .14	27.70	18.87	3,301
Sept	19.76	19.90	19.75	19.90	+ .17	25.38	19.05	2,263
Oct	19.98	20.10	19.98	20.10	+ .15	25.10	19.20	2,067
Dec	20.20	20.42	20.20	20.38	+ .16	25.30	19.45	3,708
Jn83	20.50	20.63	20.50	20.52	+ .07	23.00	19.70	1,191
Mar				20.80	− .03	22.90	20.00	217

Est vol 7,866; vol Tue 8,836; open int 49,706, −47.

WHEAT (CBT)—5,000 bu.; cents per bu.

May	368	371	367	370¼	+ 1¾	526	345	17,437
July	374	376¾	373½	376	+ 1¼	497½	352	20,357
Sept	386½	388¼	386	388¼	+ ¾	502	371½	5,859
Dec	405	406½	403¾	406½	+ 1¼	501	389	3,877
Mar83	418	420	417¼	419¾	+ 1¼	458	403½	1,579
May	424	426½	424	426½	+ 1	429½	419	41

Est vol 86,805; vol Tue 17,710; open int 49,150, +152.

WHEAT (KC)—5,000 bu.; cents per bu.

May	397	398	397	397¼	− ¼	495	388	8,843
July	394	394	392	393	− 2¼	496	382½	6,418
Sept	403	404	403	403½	− 3	502	393	465
Dec	418	418	418	418	− 1	495	407¾	412

Est vol 2,391; vol Tue 3,879; open int 16,138, −52.

WHEAT (MPLS)—5,000 bu.; cents per bu.

May	403½	403½	402	402¼	− 1½	485	388	2,642
July	403½	404	403	403¼	− ¼	457	389	1,356
Sept	407½	408¾	407½	408½	...	464	404	512
Dec	418½	419¾	418½	419¾	+ 1¼	441	414½	337
Mar83	427½	427½	427½	427½	...	427½	426	20

Est vol 840; vol Tue 1,142; open int 4,867, +29.

BARLEY (WPG)—20 metric tons; Cans per ton

Mar				123.30	+ 1.50	152.50	116.00	8
May	124.20	125.50	124.20	125.30	+ 1.30	144.20	118.00	2,622
July	125.80	125.80	125.80	125.80	+ 1.10	135.80	120.30	1,512
Oct	126.80	127.00	126.70	127.00	+ 1.00	135.80	121.50	2,612
Dec	126.80	127.00	126.80	127.00	+ 1.00	137.00	123.70	449

Est vol 270; vol Tue 670; open int 7,203, −11.

FLAXSEED (WPG)—20 metric tons; Cans per ton

May	339.00	343.90	339.00	343.70	+ 4.10	426.20	332.50	5,038
July	342.00	347.50	341.80	347.10	+ 3.30	426.00	339.00	2,091
Oct				350.00	+ 3.20	431.00	343.50	233
Dec				344.00	+ 1.00	402.50	339.50	316

Est vol 410; vol Tue 304; open int 7,678, −52.

RAPESEED (WPG)—20 metric tons; Cans per ton

June	324.00	327.00	324.00	327.00	+ 2.30	391.80	319.80	6,802
Sept	335.20	338.30	335.00	338.10	+ 2.70	367.00	328.50	2,762
Nov	332.00	334.90	332.00	334.90	+ 2.70	349.30	327.00	451

Est vol 1,600; vol Tue 1,373; open int 10,015, −18.

RYE (WPG)—20 metric tons; Can. $ per ton

May	160.50	161.20	160.10	160.30	− .20	232.50	158.50	1,942
July	162.50	163.00	162.40	162.50	+ .50	196.70	157.50	1,118
Oct	161.00	161.30	161.00	161.30	+ .80	180.00	155.50	89

Est vol 180; vol Tue 1,538; open int 3,149, −37.

—LIVESTOCK & MEAT—

CATTLE–FEEDER (CME)—44,000 lbs.; cents per lb.

Apr	66.75	67.00	66.45	66.95	− .15	70.80	54.30	2,437
May	66.45	66.70	66.10	66.67	− .17	72.00	54.20	4,768
Aug	65.20	65.20	64.50	64.92	− .42	70.00	55.52	1,507
Sept	64.05	64.20	64.05	64.20	− .30	69.00	55.60	339
Oct	63.75	63.85	63.50	63.70	− .35	64.00	55.70	361
Nov	64.25	64.35	64.40	64.30	− .15	64.65	57.25	91

Est vol 2,098; vol Tue 2,647; open int 9,511, +385.

CATTLE–LIVE (CME)—40,000 lbs.; cents per lb.

Apr	68.05	68.65	67.75	68.57	+ .32	72.40	53.50	15,663
June	66.50	66.50	65.85	66.42	− .25	72.30	54.75	24,027
Aug	63.25	63.50	62.95	63.32	− .32	66.85	54.30	13,540
Oct	62.00	62.10	61.60	61.92	− .22	65.90	53.70	57,555
Dec	62.40	62.55	62.05	62.35	− .25	64.65	54.90	2,234

Middle Column

	Open	High	Low	Settle	Change	Lifetime High	Low	Open Interest

—FOOD & FIBER—

COCOA (CSCE)—10 metric tons; $ per ton.

May	1,637	1,643	1,614	1,638	+ 5	2,394	1,606	6,282
July	1,684	1,685	1,655	1,678	+ 3	2,406	1,655	3,916
Sept	1,735	1,735	1,714	1,729	+ 4	2,436	1,710	2,167
Dec	1,785	1,792	1,779	1,792	+ 3	2,455	1,779	2,318
Mr83	1,850	1,850	1,841	1,854	+ 7	2,295	1,840	332

Est vol 1,734; vol Tue 2,637; open int 15,015, −15.

COFFEE (CSCE)—37,500 lbs.; cents per lb.

May	130.50	130.50	127.55	128.56	− 3.75	149.00	80.50	3,521
July	123.75	124.10	121.75	122.59	− 2.50	140.00	81.00	3,083
Sept	122.00	122.25	119.60	120.95	− 2.55	135.00	81.00	1,923
Dec	120.50	120.50	118.00	119.00	− 2.00	131.00	81.25	428
Mr83	118.00	118.25	116.00	117.38	− 1.12	130.00	113.50	114
May				114.76	− 1.74	115.80	115.80	1

Est vol 2,330; vol Tue 3,020; open int 9,070, −458.

COTTON (CTN)—50,000 lbs.; cents per lb.

May	65.80	66.10	65.61	65.92	+ .11	87.00	63.11	9,618
July	67.80	68.23	67.60	68.15	+ .31	86.10	64.60	9,509
Oct	70.50	70.73	70.40	70.60	+ .12	85.00	66.80	1,417
Dec	71.65	71.85	71.45	71.76	+ .16	86.85	67.71	8,836
Mr83	73.20	73.48	73.20	73.48	+ .20	75.70	69.12	534
May				74.53	+ .20	75.40	70.52	82
July	75.50	75.50	75.50	75.58	+ .20	76.25	74.50	13

Est vol 3,475; vol Tue 3,430; open int 30,009, −61.

ORANGE JUICE (CTN)—15,000 lbs.; cents per lb.

May	116.10	116.30	113.50	115.10	− 1.50	156.90	99.25	1,826
July	119.00	118.70	116.10	118.40	− 1.35	159.00	110.00	2,084
Sept	120.30	121.00	121.10	120.20	− 2.30	160.80	115.00	1,024
Nov	122.50	123.00	121.10	122.00	− 2.30	160.00	115.00	706
Jan83	124.50	125.00	123.30	124.00	− 2.30	162.50	118.00	476
Mar	126.00	126.00	125.75	125.75	− 2.30	163.75	122.00	310
May	126.90	126.90	126.90	127.50	− 2.30	163.75	122.00	123
July				129.25	− 2.30	142.20	139.00	5

Est vol 1,200; vol Tue 2,193; open int 6,616, −340.

POTATOES (NYM)—50,000 lbs.; cents per lb.

Apr	7.64	7.98	7.40	7.80	+ .16	12.44	7.40	618
May	7.85	7.90	7.80	7.81	...	8.00	7.50	227
Feb83				8.64	...	8.64	8.52	2
Mar	8.95	9.04	8.95	9.01	+ .06	9.04	8.50	57

Est vol 777; vol Tue 425; open int 904, −312.

SUGAR–WORLD (CSCE)—112,000 lbs.; cents per lb.

May	10.90	10.98	10.81	10.97	− .10	26.50	10.80	22,161
July	11.14	11.21	11.06	11.21	− .13	23.75	11.06	13,060
Sept	11.40	11.47	11.34	11.48	− .11	19.15	11.34	4,649
Oct	11.59	11.67	11.50	11.66	− .11	19.17	11.50	15,525
Jan83				11.88	− .11	14.00	12.55	3
Mar	12.47	12.50	12.38	12.49	− .17	15.15	12.48	6,418
May	12.65	12.65	12.65	12.71	− .16	14.90	12.47	793
July				12.80	− .20	13.41	12.80	40

Est vol 13,755; vol Tue 10,971; open int 62,649, +747.

—METALS AND PETROLEUM—

COPPER (CMX)—25,000 lbs.; cents per lb.

Apr	66.25	66.30	66.25	66.60	+ .15	73.10	66.45	33
May	67.10	67.80	66.85	67.55	+ .15	114.55	66.70	25,341
June				68.55	+ .15	...	...	0
July	69.05	69.70	68.80	69.50	+ .15	117.00	68.55	18,497
Sept	70.90	71.30	70.70	71.30	+ .15	106.00	70.30	4,800
Dec	73.45	74.10	73.20	73.85	+ .15	107.00	72.80	7,581
Jan83	74.50	74.50	74.50	74.70	+ .15	109.20	74.05	529
Mar	75.90	76.10	75.90	76.35	+ .15	107.00	75.25	1,840
May	77.60	77.60	77.50	78.00	+ .15	108.00	77.00	857
July				79.65	+ .15	103.00	78.45	377
Sept	80.90	80.90	80.75	81.30	+ .15	93.60	80.00	1,690
Dec	83.45	84.00	83.45	83.80	+ .15	93.00	82.25	591
Jan84	84.40	84.40	84.40	84.60	+ .15	89.15	83.65	106

Est vol 5,090; vol Tue 5,092; open int 62,242, +13.

GOLD (CMX)—100 troy oz.; $ per troy oz.

Apr	321.20	328.00	318.80	327.50	+ 8.00	898.00	312.50	10,658
May				330.70	+ 7.80	336.00	319.50	11
June	327.00	335.00	325.00	334.20	+ 7.70	925.00	319.00	43,412
Aug	334.00	340.00	333.50	341.90	+ 7.70	887.00	327.00	21,487
Oct	342.80	350.00	341.00	349.70	+ 7.70	842.00	333.00	18,018
Fb83	358.10	366.50	358.00	365.90	+ 7.70	660.00	347.50	17,741
Apr	366.50	366.50	366.50	374.10	+ 7.70	604.00	355.50	10,883
June	380.00	380.00	380.00	383.40	+ 7.70	596.00	365.00	2,251
Aug				392.40	+ 7.70	515.50	371.00	681
Oct				401.40	+ 7.70	500.00	388.00	565
Dec				410.40	+ 7.70	495.00	385.00	133

Est vol 55,000; vol Tue 53,538; open int 135,412, −6,574.

GOLD (IMM)—100 troy oz.; $ per troy oz.

June	327.50	335.50	325.80	334.40	+ 8.10	920.00	318.80	8,512
Sept	338.50	346.90	337.60	346.00	+ 8.20	948.00	329.50	2,686
Dec	350.00	359.00	350.00	359.70	+ 4.70	904.00	341.00	3,285
Mar83				370.10	+ 8.40	887.20	353.00	2,469
June				382.60	+ 8.50	674.50	365.50	1,092
Sept				395.40	...	20	388.00	...

Right Column

	Open	High	Low	Settle	Change	Lifetime High	Low	Open Interest

SILVER (CBT)—5,000 troy oz.; cents per troy oz.

Apr	702.0	719.0	700.0	719.0	+ 20.0	4562.0	690.0	272
May	729.0	729.0	728.0	728.0	+ 20.0	795.0	708.0	4
June	721.0	738.0	718.0	737.5	+ 20.5	4580.0	710.0	1,174
Aug	743.0	743.0	741.0	756.0	+ 21.0	4535.0	729.0	513
Oct				774.5	+ 21.5	3600.0	750.0	490
Dec	790.0	793.0	789.0	793.0	+ 22.0	3120.0	763.0	629
Fb83				811.5	+ 22.5	2728.0	790.0	804
Apr				830.0	+ 23.0	2666.0	807.0	1,202
June				848.5	+ 23.5	2307.0	815.0	698
Aug				867.0	+ 24.0	1874.0	845.0	248
Oct				885.5	+ 24.5	1743.0	861.0	167

Est vol 903; vol Tue 643; open int 6,201, −112.

SILVER (IMM)—1,000 troy oz.; cents per troy oz.

Apr	702.0	721.0	700.0	719.0	+ 20.0	1530.0	690.0	834
May	715.0	728.0	712.0	728.0	+ 20.0	808.0	700.0	46
June	721.0	739.0	718.0	737.5	+ 20.5	1565.0	709.0	5,512
Aug	738.0	759.0	735.0	756.0	+ 21.0	1470.0	726.0	818
Oct	762.0	778.0	762.0	774.5	+ 21.5	1420.0	740.0	188
Dec	778.0	793.0	775.0	793.0	+ 22.0	1530.5	761.0	1,068
Fb83				811.5	+ 22.5	1503.5	780.0	117
Apr	807.0	830.0	807.0	830.0	+ 23.0	1434.0	805.0	191
June				848.5	+ 23.5	1470.0	815.0	74
Aug				867.0	+ 24.0	1498.0	835.0	35
Oct	874.0	885.5	874.0	885.5	+ 24.5	1530.0	840.0	64

Est vol 2,784; vol Tue 2,238; open int 8,947, −502.

—WOOD—

LUMBER (CME)—130,000 bd. ft.; $ per 1,000 bd. ft.

May	142.80	143.00	141.60	142.40	− .40	220.30	137.50	2,995
July	152.50	152.80	151.50	152.40	− .40	224.50	147.60	1,895
Sept	160.00	160.00	159.20	159.60	− .20	229.50	155.30	865
Nov	160.50	160.70	159.80	160.50	− .30	224.50	157.10	662
Jn83	168.00	168.50	167.50	168.50	− .20	205.50	165.00	419
Mar	176.80	177.30	176.00	177.30	− .70	209.80	171.50	45
May	185.50	185.50	185.00	185.00	− 1.00	202.00	181.00	70
July	193.80	193.80	193.50	193.50	− 1.00	201.00	193.50	17

Est vol 1,063; vol Tue 1,579; open int 6,968, +94.

PLYWOOD (CBT)—76,032 sq. ft.; $ per 1000 sq. ft.

May	164.50	165.80	162.50	165.70	+ 1.20	241.00	162.50	2,195
July	169.50	170.80	167.80	170.70	+ 1.40	219.00	163.90	788
Sept	174.30	175.50	172.80	175.30	+ 1.30	224.50	172.80	457
Nov	179.00	179.70	176.50	179.50	+ 1.40	181.80	176.50	263
Jn83	181.50	183.00	180.00	183.00	+ 1.20	186.00	180.00	100
Mar	186.00	190.00	186.00	189.00	− 1.30	196.30	186.00	0

Est vol 645; vol Tue 551; open int 3,803, 96.

—FINANCIAL—

BRITISH POUND (IMM)—25,000 pounds; $ per pound

June	1.7890	1.7935	1.7875	1.7929	+.0035	1.9580	1.7835	20,327
Sept	1.7965	1.8020	1.7965	1.8000	+.0035	1.9580	1.7915	1,042
Dec	1.8065	1.8065	1.8030	1.8075	+.0030	1.9350	1.8000	103
Mr83				1.8140	+.0030	1.8050	1.8050	2

Est vol 3,788; vol Tue 4,311; open int 21,474, −482.

CANADIAN DOLLAR (IMM)—100,000 dlrs.; $ per Cans

June	.8118	.8136	.8102	.8135	+.0009	.8427	.7901	15,431
Sept	.8100	.8115	.8090	.8115	+.0006	.8380	.7890	658
Dec	.8070	.8080	.8070	.8090	+.0012	.8350	.8037	284
Mar83				.8060	+.0010	.8150	.8017	2

Est vol 3,557; vol Tue 5,071; open int 16,375, +34.

JAPANESE YEN (IMM)—12.5 million yen; $ per yen(.00)

June	.4099	.4117	.4095	.4106	−.0025	.4830	.4095	14,652
Sept	.4185	.4202	.4185	.4191	−.0028	.4775	.4185	467
Dec				.4270	−.0030	.4330	.4265	11

Est vol 5,646; vol Tue 6,364; open int 15,130, −240.

SWISS FRANC (IMM)—125,000 francs; $ per franc

June	.5270	.5295	.5263	.5283	+.0002	.5840	.4865	15,045
Sept	.5395	.5407	.5385	.5397	+.0002	.5845	.4975	455
Dec				.5497	...	.5920	.5470	29

Est vol 7,806; vol Tue 8,603; open int 15,529, −234.

W.GERMAN MARK (IMM)—125,000 marks; $ per mark

June	.4191	.4204	.4188	.4195	−.0004	.4720	.4135	13,467
Sept	.4253	.4263	.4253	.4255	−.0007	.4775	.4220	588
Dec				.4325	...	.4675	.4325	17

Est vol 4,542; vol Tue 4,616; open int 14,072, −17.

GNMA 8% (CBT)—$100,000 prncpl.; pts., 32nds of 100%

	Open	High	Low	Settle	Chg	Yield Settle	Chg	Interest
June	59-22	60-21	59-17	60-20	+ 25	15.476	−.210	17,484
Sept	59-10	60-11	59-07	60-11	+ 25	15.554	−.220	7,940
Dec	59-03	60-05	59-03	60-05	+ 25	15.606	−.221	8,161
Mr83	58-28	60-00	58-28	60-00	+ 25	15.650	−.222	6,359
June	59-04	59-28	59-04	59-28	+ 25	15.685	−.222	6,144
Sept	58-26	59-23	58-26	59-23	+ 25	15.712	−.223	4,399
Dec	58-26	59-23	58-26	59-23	+ 26	15.730	−.223	2,709
Mar84	58-24	59-21	59-00	59-21	+ 26	15.747	−.224	3,446
June	58-24	59-20	58-24	59-20	+ 26	15.756	−.224	1,491
Sept	58-23	59-19	58-23	59-19	+ 26	15.765	−.224	1,125
Dec	58-22	59-18	58-22	59-18	+ 25	15.774	−.224	731
Mar85	58-22	59-17	58-22	59-17	+ 25	15.783	−.224	75
June	58-20	59-16	58-20	59-16	+ 25	15.792	−.225	13

Est vol 7,000; vol Tue 7,147; open int 59,727, +855.

TREASURY BONDS (CBT)—$100,000; pts. 32nds of 100%

June	60-25	61-30	60-22	61-30	+ 31	13.567	−.214	64,630
Sept	61-04	62-09	61-00	62-08	+ 31	13.439	−.206	22,709
Dec	61-13	62-21	61-12	62-21	+ 28	13.419	−.196	16,072
Mar83	61-30	63-21	61-30	62-31	+ 28	13.346	−.187	15,433
June	62-10	63-10	62-10	63-10	+ 27	13.273	−.186	11,558
Sept	62-21	63-20	62-21	63-20	+ 27	13.208	−.184	16,203
Dec	63-09	63-29	63-08	63-29	+ 27	13.149	−.177	12,376
Mar84	63-14	64-13	63-13	64-05	+ 26	13.098	−.168	10,105
June	63-23	64-13	63-23	64-13	+ 26	13.047	−.161	5,452
Sept				64-20	+ 26	12.996	−.160	2,121
Dec	64-08	64-29	64-05	64-29	+ 25	12.945	−.159	1,057

Est vol 63,000; vol Tue 51,970; open int 177,716, −3,612.

TREASURY BILLS (IMM)—$1 mil.; pts. of 100%

| | | | | | | Discount | | Open |

prices and volume, but also informs investors as to the latest earnings per share and dividends declared as well as the dividend record and payable dates. This can be seen in Figure 3–13. Figure 3–14 presents *Barron's* tables of the weekly percentage leaders on the New York Stock Exchange, American Stock Exchange, and the over-the-counter market.

One unique feature of *Barron's* is the "Market Laboratory" covering the last three pages of each issue. Weekly data on major stock indexes are presented with the week's market statistics. Special weekly tables include: Economic and Financial Indicators, Pulse of Industry and Trade, and data on foreign markets as well as many other items. Figures 3–15 and 3–16 present a sample of a few tables from *Barron's* Market Laboratory. Careful reading of this publication will turn up useful data in a compact summary form not found in other publications.

Other major papers would be *The Wall Street Transcript* (weekly) and the *Commercial and Financial Chronicle* (weekly). *The Media General Financial Weekly* is an exceptional source of fundamental and technical indicators for the professional manager. Over 3,400 common stocks are divided into 60 industrial groups and analyzed based on relative strength (whether they are leading or lagging the market) trends, earnings, and other variables that may be useful to the analyst.

Journals

Most journals are academic and, because of this, are more theoretical than practical or trade oriented. However there are several that are industry oriented, such as the *Financial Analysts Journal* which is a publication of the Chartered Financial Analysts Federation, the professional organization giving the CFA designation. This journal has both academic and practitioner articles that deal mainly with analytical tools, new laws and regulations, and financial analysis. *The Journal of Portfolio Management* and the *Institutional Investor* are also well-read by the profession. The more scholarly, research-oriented academic journals would include the *Journal of Finance, Journal of Financial Economics, Financial Management,* and the *Journal of Financial and Quantitative Analysis.* These journals include information on the development and testing of theories, such as the random walk and efficient market hypothesis, capital asset pricing model, portfolio theories, and much empirical research on a variety of financial topics.

COMPUTER DATA BASES

More computer-accessible data bases are likely to become available during the 1980s as home computer usage soars and data-based storage management improves. Currently, there are several major sources of data that are available on magnetic tapes or that are accessible on an interactive, time-sharing basis.

Compustat is published by Investors Management Science Company, a subsidiary of Standard & Poor's Corporation. The Compustat tapes are very comprehensive, containing 20 years of annual financial data for over 3,000 companies.

Figure 3–13

NYSE—COMPOSITE TRANSACTIONS

Quotations include trades on the American, Midwest, Pacific, Philadelphia, Boston and Cincinnati stock exchanges and reported by the National Association of Securities Dealers and Instinet. Earnings as reported by company, omitting all non-recurring adjustments and potential dilution. Unless otherwise noted, rates of dividends in the following table are annual disbursements based on the last quarterly or semi-annual declaration. Where a stock dividend or split amounting to 25% or more has been paid the yearly high-low range is adjusted from the old stock; dividend begins with the date of split or stock dividend. Special or extra dividends or payments not designated as regular are identified as indicated below. **Note:** As a general rule, to be eligible to receive a newly declared cash dividend or stock dividend of less than 20% on a New York Stock Exchange-listed security (25% on the American Stock Exchange and over-the-counter), shareholders must have purchased their stock before the ex-dividend date, which is four trading days (exchanges and banks open) *prior to* the record date. For splits and stock dividends of 20% or more (on the Amex and OTC, it's 25%), the ex-dividend date is one business day *after* the payable date (when the new shares begin trading). Sales figures are unofficial. The 52 Weeks High and Low columns show the highest and the lowest price of the stock in consolidated trading during the preceding 52 weeks plus the current week.

a Also extra or extras
b Annual rate plus stock dividend
c Liquidating dividend
d New 52-week low
e Declared or paid in preceding 12 months
g Dividend or earnings in Canadian money. Stock trades in U.S. dollars. No yield or PE shown unless stated in U.S. money.
i Declared or paid after stock dividend or split up
j Paid this year, dividend omitted, deferred or no action taken at last dividend meeting
k Declared or paid this year, an accumulative issue with dividend in arrears
m Months for which share results are given
n New issue in the past 52 weeks. The high-low range begins with the start of trading in the new issue and does not cover the entire 52-week period.
q Quarterly
r Declared or paid in preceding 12 months plus stock dividend
rt Rights
s Stock split or stock dividend amounting to 25 per cent or more in the past 52 weeks. The high-low range is adjusted from the old stock. Dividend begins with the date of split or stock dividend.
sa Semi-annual
t Paid in stock in preceding 12 months, estimated cash value on ex-dividend or ex-distribution date
u New 52-week high
un Units
w Weeks for which share results are given
wd When distributed
wi When issued
wt Warrants
ww With warrants
x Ex-dividend or ex rights
x-dis Ex-distribution
xw Without warrants
y Ex-dividend and sales in full
z Sales in full
cld Called
vj In Bankruptcy or receivership or being reorganized under the Bankruptcy act, or securities assumed by such companies
D Deficit per share
Def Deficit
E Estimated
L Includes non-recurring loss
M Monthly
S Payments in stock
X Includes non-recurring profit
Y Latest dividend paid on date indicated
✚ Dividend declared
O Dividend omitted last week
➤ New earnings

52-Weeks High	Low	Stock (div.)	Sales 100s	Yield Pct.	P-E Ratio	Week's High	Low	Last	Net Chg.	EARNINGS Interim or Fiscal yr	Year ago	DIVIDENDS Latest dec	Stk of rec	Payment date
		—A—A—A—												
12¾	6	AAR .44	133	6.6	15	6¾	6¼	6⅝	−¼	✚ Feb9m.12	1.11	q.11	5-4	6-2
49½	31½	ACF 2,76	316	7.7	7	37¼	35¼	36	+¼	81DecX5.23	L5.02	q.69	3-5	3-15
28½	16⅝	AMF 1.36	3293	7.5	10	18½	17¼	18⅛	−⅜	81Dec2.95	2.39	q.34	2-24	3-10
16	1⅛	vjAMIn	3427			1½	1⅛	1⅛	−⅛	Jan6mD3.26		Y		10-10-80
7¼	3¾	APL	31			4⅛	4	4		Dec6mNil	Def	Y		4-1-80
37¼	23½	ARA 2	306	7.8	7	25⅞	24¾	25½	−⅛	Jan13w1.19	1.40	q.50	6-1	6-15
56½	26¾	ASA 4a	1744	11.5		35¾	33¾	34¾	+¼	Aug9m5.78	5.34	q1.00	2-18	2-26
36⅝	11½	AVX .32	563	1.6		20¼	18⅝	19¾	+¾	81DecD.62	1.56	q.08	4-23	5-7
32¼	23⅝	AbtLb s .84	x9051	2.8	14	29⅞	29	29¾	+½	➤Mar3m.52	.45	q.21	4-16	5-15
29½	17¼	AcmeC 1.40	286	6.4	7	22¼	21⅝	21⅞	−⅛	➤Mar6mX2.14	1.56	q.35	5-6	5-20
9⅝	7½	AcmeE n.32b	36	4.1	7	8¼	7⅝	7⅞	+⅛	Dec6m.53	.45	S5%	2-22	3-22
6¾	4	AdmDg .04	162	.8	6	5⅛	4⅞	5⅛	+⅛	81Dec.84	.77	q.01	3-15	3-31
15⅝	12¾	AdaEx 2.25e	154	16.5		13⅞	13⅜	13⅝	−⅛	81Dec1.03	.91	.12	3-22-82	4-19-82
8⅛	4⅜	AdmMl .20e	612	2.6	10	u 8⅛	7½	7⅝	−⅜	81Dec.64	.96	q.05	2-23	3-10
31	14	AMD	4655		44	24¾	23½	24⅜	+⅜	➤82Mar.55	1.55			
48¼	33½	AetnLf 2.52	16495	5.8	8	47¾	42½	43¾	−4	81Dec5.75	6.96	q.63	3-18	5-15
97	77	AetnL pf2										q.50	3-18	4-15
19½	9⅝	Ahmns 1.20	509	10.9		11⅛	10⅝	11	+¼	81DecDef	2.07	q.30	2-23	3-8
4¼	2⅛	Aileen	184			3	2⅝	2¾	−¼	Jan13wD.42	.05			
46⅞	31	AirPrd .80	1094	2.3	8	35¼	34⅜	35	−⅜	Dec3m1.21	1.13	q.20	4-2	5-3
16	7¾	AirbFrt .60	213	5.7	16	10⅞	10	10½	+⅝	81Dec.66	1.71	q.15	2-5	2-19
15¼	9¼	Akzona .80	286	8.3	21	10	9½	9⅝	−⅛	➤Mar3mD.22	.27	q.20	3-15	3-31
22½	15⅛	AlMoa n	2133			18½	17⅞	18¼	−¼	Sep3m.13				
27¼	23¼	AlaP pfA3.92	54	15.7		25¼	24¾	25				q.98	3-2	4-1
6⅞	5½	AlaP dpf .87	85	14.5		6⅛	5¾	6	+¼			q.218	3-2	4-1
61	53	AlaP pf 9	z650	15.7		57½	55½	57½	+1½	80Dec42.08	23.06	q2.25	3-2	4-1
85⅝	75	AlaP pf 11	z160	14.3		78	77	77	+⅜	80Dec42.08	23.06	q2.75	3-2	4-1
65½	55	AlaP pf 9.44	z280	15.7		61	59½	60	−1	80Dec42.08	23.06	q2.36	3-2	4-1
55	46	AlaP pf 8.16	z420	16.2		52½	50¼	50¼	−½	80Dec42.08	23.06	q2.04	3-2	4-1
56¼	49½	AlaP pf 8.28	z1400	15.8		52½	51¼	52½	+¾	80Dec42.08	23.06	q2.07	3-2	4-1
16	13⅛	Alagsco 1.60	50	11.4	5	14¼	13⅞	14	−⅛	✚➤Mar12m2.87	2.86	q.40	5-14	6-1
33½	11⅛	AlskInt .60	885	4.3	4	15	13¾	13⅞	−1	81Dec3.14	X6.37	q.15	3-9	3-22
37½	22⅝	Albany 1.20	940	4.8	6	25⅛	23⅞	25	+1⅜	81DecL4.15	3.87	q.30	3-11	4-1
16¼	9¾	Alberto .50	104	3.4	9	14¾	13½	14½	+¾	Dec3m.38	.29	q.12½	2-5	2-20
29⅝	23	Albtsn 1	1157	3.6	9	27⅞	26⅞	27¾	+¾	82Jan3.14	2.64	q.25	5-6	6-3
37¾	17⅞	Alcan 1.80	3527	10.0	6	18⅜	17⅞	18	−⅛	81Dec3.24	6.70	q.45	2-16	3-12
21⅝	17¼	AlcoStd 1.08	306	5.4	7	20⅛	19⅝	19⅞	−⅛	Dec3m.63	.61	q.27	2-22	3-10
30⅜	25¾	AlexAl n1.94	1061	6.7	10	29¾	28¾	29⅛	−½	81Dec2.98	2.98	q.48½	5-18	5-28
18⅜	7⅞	Alexdr	359			12	11¼	11⅝	−¼	Feb28w.72	.14	Y		9-9-80
50¼	31½	AllgCp 1.08	385	2.3	8	48¼	46	48	+2¼	81Dec6.07	4.79	q.27	2-23	3-3
22¾	17⅝	AlgCp pf2.86	97	14.9		19¾	19	19¼	+⅜			q.71½	2-26	3-8
54½	25⅞	AlgInt 1.40	600	4.6	4	31⅞	30½	30½	−¼	81Dec7.65	6.89	q.35	3-12	3-31
17	14⅛	AlgIn pf2.19	131	13.5		16½	15½	16¼	+⅞	80Dec12.22	7.92	q.54¾	3-12	4-1
77	70⅜	Algl pfC11.25	1247	15.1		74¾	74	74¾	+⅝			q2.81¼	3-12	4-1
19⅝	13⅝	AllgPw 2.16	4199	11.4	6	19⅛	18½	19	+⅜	81Dec3.03	2.59	q.54	3-15	3-31
22	12⅛	AllenG 1	181	6.9	8	14⅝	14	14½	+⅝	81Dec1.90	2.03	q.25	3-5	4-6
59⅞	32	AlldCp 2.40	1832	7.2	4	33⅞	33	33⅛	−¼	➤Mar3m1.38	2.33	q.60	2-10	3-10
54¼	46	AldCp pf6.74	286	14.3		47½	47	47¼	−⅛			q1.68½	4-15	5-14
96	83½	AldCp pf 12	19	13.7		87¾	87⅛	87½	+½			4.167	2-10	3-1
24⅞	15½	AldMnt 1	686	4.4	8	23	21⅞	22¾	+1⅛	Dec9m2.41	1.88	q.25	3-1	3-15
11	7	AlldPd .20	49	2.4	43	8¾	8¼	8½	+¼	81DecX.20	Def	q.05	4-23	5-14
31⅛	23¼	AlldStr 1.80	842	6.1	7	30½	29¼	29¾	−⅛	82Jan4.38	4.08	q.45	3-19	4-20
48⅞	15	AldTel n .96	148	6.3	6	15⅞	d15	15⅛	−¾	81Dec2.47	X2.21	q.24	3-15	3-31
32⅜	12¼	AllisCh	1241			15¼	12¾	15	+2½	81DecDef	3.56	Y		11-2-81
51⅝	34¼	AlisCh pf5.88	211	15.0		39½	37	39⅛	+1⅞			q1.46⅞	4-30	6-1
26⅛	14½	AllrAu s .48	510	2.0	14	25⅞	24¼	24⅜	−1⅜	Dec6mX1.10	X.61	q.12	3-31	4-15
14¼	8⅝	AlphPr	15			9⅞	9⅞	9⅞	−⅛	81DecDef	Def	Y		12-10-80
37½	21⅞	Alcoa 1.80	3804	7.2	6	25⅝	23¾	25⅛	−½	✚➤Mar3m.31	1.37	q.45	5-7	5-25
51⅞	29	AmlSug 5	x317	9.7	3	u51⅞	44¼	51½	+6½	➤Mar13w2.58	3.75	q1.25	4-16	5-1
67⅞	24½	Amax .60	2002	2.2	8	27⅝	26⅛	27⅜	+⅝	81DecX3.31	7.48	q.15	5-10	6-1
82½	35¼	Amax pf 3	175	7.7		39	38½	39	+½	80Dec68.31	43.62	q.75	8-10	9-1

52-Weeks High	Low	Stock (div.)	Sales 100s	Yield Pct.	P-E Ratio	Week's High	Low	Last	Net Chg.	EARNINGS Interim or Fiscal yr	Year ago	DIVIDENDS Latest dec	Stk of rec	Payment date
25	14¾	Amrce 1.32	22	8.4	6	16½	15½	15¾	−¾	81Dec3.51	3.57	q.33	3-15	4-15
40	25¾	Amrc pf2.60	5	9.6		27¼	26¾	27	−½	80Dec17.62	21.06	q.65	4-26	5-17
36⅛	15⅛	AmHes 1.10	6666	5.8	7	19¾	18½	18⅞	−⅞	81Dec2.53	X6.44	q.27½	3-19	3-31
156	66	AHes pf 3.50	x11	4.3		83½	79¾	81⅛	−2½	✚ 80Dec743.77	229.19	q.87½	4-19	4-30
8¾	2⅜	AmAgr s .10	1530	3.5	24	2⅞	2½	2⅞	+¼	Dec3mD.05	.09	q.02½	4-15	4-30
21⅝	9¼	AmAir	16514		88	15½	13¾	14⅛	−1¼	81DecX.16	Def	Y		2-15-80
9⅜	3¼	AAir wt	1161			5⅝	5	5⅛	−½					
14⅝	12⅜	AAir pf 2.18	148	16.6		13⅜	13	13⅛	−⅛	81Dec3.37	D30.33	q.546⅞	3-15	4-1
19¾	10¾	ABakr	227			13	12½	12⅝	+⅛	81Dec.85	.73	Y		12-31-81
46	34	ABrnd s3.50	1053	8.3	6	42⅜	41⅜	42	+⅛	81Dec6.68	6.50	q.87½	2-4	3-1
40¾	32⅝	ABrd pf1.70								81Dec48.61	43.04	q.42½	2-4	3-1
23⅛	18¼	ABrd pf 2.75	607	12.4		22½	22	22¼	+¼	81Dec48.61	43.04	q.68¾	2-4	3-10
45¾	34	ABrd pf 2.67	26	6.4		42	41¾	42	+¼	81Dec48.61	43.04	q.66¾	2-4	3-10
38¼	26¾	ABdcst 1.60	6482	4.4	7	36⅝	34¾	36½	+1⅜	✚ 81Dec5.13	5.18	q.40	5-21	6-15
22¼	15¾	ABldM 1	208	4.5	8	22	20⅝	22	+1¼	Jan3m.64	.60	q.25	4-15	4-30
16⅝	10½	ABusPd .56	53	4.7	6	12⅛	11⅞	12		81Dec1.87	2.15	q.14	3-1	3-15
43⅜	25¾	AmCan 2.90	x1455	10.8	7	28⅛	26⅝	26¾	−1	81DecL3.77	4.26	q.72½	4-16	5-25
22¾	19⅝	ACan pf 2.80	33	13.6		20⅞	19⅞	20⅝	+⅜	80Dec64.39		q.70	3-5	4-1
10½	6⅝	ACntry .20e	92	3.0	14	7	6⅝	6¾	−⅛	Dec6m.09	.20	.05	4-5-82	4-16-82
36½	24⅜	ACyan 1.75	4985	6.3	7	28¾	27⅜	27¾	−⅜	81Dec4.11	3.32	q.43¾	2-18	3-26
39⅞	26⅝	ADT 1.52	266	4.3	10	36¼	35½	35¾	−⅛	81Dec3.70	3.16	q.38	2-26	3-19
17⅞	15⅜	AEIPw 2.26	6973	12.6	8	u17⅞	17⅜	17⅞	+⅜	81Dec2.37	2.39	q.56½	2-10	3-10
54⅜	37½	AmExp 2.20	6446	4.4	9	50¼	48⅜	50	+¼	81Dec5.58	5.18	q.55	4-2	5-10
10	7	AFamil .60	1298	6.7	8	9¼	8	9	+¾	81Dec1.13	1.47	q.15	2-12	3-1
46½	37½	AGnCp 2.20	669	5.3	6	43½	41½	41½	−1⅞	81Dec6.42	9.06	q.55	2-17	3-1
37½	31⅝	AGn jpf 3.25	23	9.7		34½	33½	33½	−¾			q.81¼	2-17	3-1
17	14⅜	AGIBd 2.11e	337	13.0		16⅜	15¾	16¼	+¼	81Jun2.10	2.07	.17	4-8	4-30
29¾	23¼	AGnCv 1.80	193	6.2		29¼	27½	29⅛	+1⅝	✚ 81Dec2.42	1.74	.60+6.16	4-23	5-17
20	15	AHerit .72	145	3.7	10	u20	18½	19¼	+¾	81Dec2.02	2.22	M.06	4-12	4-23
23⅝	13½	AHoist 1.12	294	8.0	5	14⅜	13⅞	14	−⅛	Mar15w.21	.57	q.28	5-14	6-10
37¼	28¼	AHome 2	6155	5.4	12	36⅞	36	36⅞	+⅝	81Dec3.18	2.84	q.50	2-12	3-1
166½	133	AHme pf2								81Dec2824.61	2171.36	q.50	3-12	4-1
49⅞	31¼	AHosp 1.24	3120	2.7	15	45½	44⅝	45¼		81Dec3.08	2.72	q.31	5-28	6-21
32⅝	18¼	AMI s .52	3854	2.3	12	23⅝	21⅞	22¾	−⅝	Feb6m1.07	.78	q.13	4-12	5-5
4¾	2⅜	AmMot	2510			3¾	3⅝	3¾	+⅛	81DecD2.44	D6.10	Y		5-5-80
38½	31½	ANatR n 3	949	8.8	5	34½	33¾	34	−⅛	81Dec5.90	4.57	q.75	4-15	5-1
19¼	5½	ASLFla	278	10.9		6⅛	d 5½	5½	−¾	Dec3mD3.03	.81	Y		8-14-81
17	9⅝	AShp s .80a	279	6.8	6	12⅛	11¼	11¾		Dec3m.40	.60	q.20	2-11	2-25
43¾	24¼	AmStd 2.20	1294	8.2	7	28	26⅜	26⅞	−¾	81Dec4.07	5.00	q.55	3-18	4-5
14⅞	8¼	ASteril .38	1637	2.7	11	14½	13⅜	14⅛	−⅜	81Dec1.29	1.10	q.09½	2-26	3-15
37¾	21⅛	AmStr 1	183	2.7	7	u37¾	37	37¼	+¼	82Jan5.42	4.11	q.25	3-24	4-1
41	35¾	AStr pf 5.51	5	14.0		39½	39¼	39¼	−⅝	81Jan25.32	21.82	q1.37¾	5-24	6-10
61½	53⅝	ATT 5.40	21726	9.8	6	55⅝	54⅝	55⅜	+⅛	Feb12m8.70	8.10	q1.35	2-26	4-1
64¼	56⅛	ATT pf 4	91	6.9		58½	57⅜	58⅜	+⅜	81Dec258.09	219.00	q1.00	3-31	5-1
33½	27¼	ATT pf 3.64	98	12.4		29⅜	29⅛	29¼	+⅛	81Dec258.09	219.00	q.91	3-31	5-1
34½	27¾	ATT pf 3.74	74	12.4		30¼	29⅝	30¼	+½	81Dec258.09	219.00	q.93½	3-31	5-1
14¼	12	AWatr 1.20	20	8.7	4	14	13¾	13¾	−¼	✚ 81Dec3.13	3.09	q.30	4-30	5-14
17¾	15¼	AWat pf1.43	z270	8.1		17¾	17⅝	17⅝	+⅛	✚ 80Dec37.17	27.12	q.35⅞	5-14	6-1
9⅞	8¼	AWat pf1.25	z610	14.7		9⅛	8½	8½		✚ 80Dec61.32	48.15	q.31¼	5-14	6-1
10¼	8½	AWa 5pf1.25	z10	13.7		9⅛	9⅛	9⅛		✚ 80Dec49.85	37.15	q.31¼	5-14	6-1
34	21	Ameron 1.60	39	6.4	4	25⅛	24¼	25⅛	−⅛	Feb3m.85	.95	q.40	4-23	5-14
24¾	16⅛	AmesD s .40	561	1.7	8	24⅜	23½	24⅛	−⅛	82Jan2.84	2.32	q.10	5-21	6-25
35⅜	23	Ametk 1.20	719	4.3	11	28	25⅜	28	+1¼	81Dec2.44	2.02	q.30	3-17	3-31
30⅝	20⅛	Amfac 1.44	307	6.1	8	23¾	22	23⅝	+1⅜	81DecX2.88	X5.37	q.36	2-16	3-15
62½	43½	AMPIn 1.40	4744	2.3	16	59⅞	56¾	59⅝	+⅞	81Dec3.75	3.44	q.35	2-8	3-1
22	13	Ampco .60	6	4.4	4	13½	13¼	13½	+½	81DecX3.18	3.92	q.15	4-15	4-30
10¾	5⅝	Amrep	67		20	7⅞	7⅜	7⅜	−⅜	Jan9m.24	.50			
23½	18⅛	AmSth n1.60	103	8.4	5	19⅜	19	19⅛		✚➤Mar3m.96	1.07	q.40	6-11	7-1
29¾	18⅞	Amstar 1.90	579	8.2	3	24⅜	22¼	23⅛	−1½	➤Mar9m4.19	6.89	q.47½	3-11	4-2
5½	4¾	Amst pf .68	40	13.9		5⅛	4⅞	4⅞	−⅜	81Jun46.03	19.34	q.17	3-11	4-2
70½	62	Amst pf2.65								81Jun2822.29	928.02	q.66¼	3-11	4-2
47⅞	24⅜	Amsted 2.48	1141	10.0	7	26⅛	d24⅜	24⅞	−⅞	Dec3m.33	1.41	q.62	2-19	3-15
28	15½	Analog	28		42	23¼	22½	22½	−¾	Jan13w.21	.17			

Figure 3–14

Weekly Percentage Leaders Of NYSE-Listed Issues

The following list shows stocks that have gone up the most and down the most based on percent of change on the New York Stock Exchange regardless of volume.

Net and percentage changes are the difference between last week's closing price and this week's closing price.

UPS

Name	Sales(hds)	High	Low	Last	Chg.		Pct.
1 Geosource	8588	51⅛	31	50⅜	+18⅜	Up	57.4
2 GlfRes pfA	2	24	24	24	+ 8⅜	Up	53.6
3 NLT Corp	13127	29½	22¼	28⅞	+ 6¼	Up	27.6
4 Union Corp	1447	5¼	4⅛	5¼	+ 1⅛	Up	27.3
5 RB Ind	492	7⅜	6	7⅜	+ 1¼	Up	20.4
6 NoAmCoal	420	30½	25½	30½	+ 5⅛	Up	20.2
7 GearhInd	x7633	23⅛	18⅛	22⅜	+ 3¾	Up	20.1
8 Allis Chalm	1241	15¼	12¾	15	+ 2½	Up	20.0
9 GnDynam	x16548	29⅜	24⅞	29⅜	+ 4¾	Up	19.3
10 LevitzFrn	1431	25½	21	25	+ 4	Up	19.0
11 GlfRes pfB	12	22	18½	22	+ 3½	Up	18.9
12 Gulf Resrc	5970	17¾	14⅛	17½	+ 2¾	Up	18.6
13 WnAir Lin	2036	4⅜	3¾	4¼	+ ⅝	Up	17.2
14 AndrsnGrn n	237	13⅜	11⅜	13⅜	+ 1⅞	Up	16.3
15 Technicolor	4172	11¼	9¾	11¼	+ 1½	Up	15.4
16 OgdenCp pf	5	65½	61	65½	+ 8½	Up	14.9
17 PeaveyCo n	418	22¾	19¾	22⅝	+ 2⅞	Up	14.6
18 Amal Sug	x317	51⅞	44¼	51½	+ 6½	Up	14.4
19 ModMerch	749	9½	8⅜	9¼	+ 1⅛	Up	13.8
20 GNC s	248	10½	8¾	10⅝	+ 1¼	Up	13.7
21 CabotCp	667	23	19⅝	23	+ 2¾	Up	13.6
22 Benefl Cp	1621	18¼	15⅞	18	+ 2⅛	Up	13.4
23 MyersLE	220	8½	7⅜	8½	+ 1	Up	13.3
24 ToscoCp	3156	12⅜	10¾	11⅞	+ 1⅜	Up	13.1
25 LouLd Exp	10358	31½	27⅞	31½	+ 3½	Up	12.5
26 NtMedCare	1994	8¼	6¾	7⅞	+ ⅞	Up	12.5

DOWNS

Name	Sales(hds)	High	Low	Last	Chg		Pct.
1 IntlHarv 5.76pf	1062	11⅛	8⅜	9¼	− 2	Off	17.8
2 CharterCo wt	773	5⅛	4¼	4¼	− ⅞	Off	17.1
3 BiscayFSL	496	3⅜	2½	2⅝	− ½	Off	16.0
4 KDT Indust	1110	3⅜	2½	2⅝	− ½	Off	16.0
5 Hanna Mng	8636	36	31¾	32	− 4¾	Off	12.9
6 Intl Harv	3578	4⅞	4⅛	4¼	− ⅝	Off	12.8
7 Plan Resrch	5984	7¾	6¾	7	− 1	Off	12.5
8 Am SL Fla	278	6⅛	5½	5½	− ¾	Off	12.0
9 Webb DelE	761	8	7	7¼	− ⅞	Off	10.8
10 FlaEaCst s	223	16½	14½	14⅝	− 1¾	Off	10.7
11 Genesco Inc	883	4¾	4¼	4⅜	− ½	Off	10.3
12 GrtLakeInt	88	25⅞	22¾	23	− 2⅝	Off	10.2
13 Tidewatr	1239	27⅜	24⅜	24¾	− 2⅝	Off	9.6
14 ManorCare s	352	15½	14	14⅜	− 1½	Off	9.4
15 MarcadeGrp n	622	2¾	2½	2½	− ¼	Off	9.1
16 AmAirln wt	1161	5⅝	5	5⅛	− ½	Off	8.9
17 MoranEng	374	11½	10½	10½	− 1	Off	8.7
18 AetnaLfe	16495	47¾	42½	43¾	− 4	Off	8.4
19 Aileen Inc	184	3	2⅝	2¾	− ¼	Off	8.3
20 Avco 3.20pf	1550	35	31⅛	33¼	− 3	Off	8.3
21 DowChem	7772	24⅛	21⅞	22⅛	− 2	Off	8.3
22 FtBcpTex	2181	27¾	24⅛	24¾	− 2¼	Off	8.3
23 Sundstrand	4580	40¼	35	35¾	− 3¼	Off	8.3
24 EnterraCp	584	29	26½	26¾	− 2⅜	Off	8.2
25 FostrWhlr	2161	13⅝	12½	12⅝	− 1⅛	Off	8.2
26 Fruehf Corp	537	18½	16⅞	16⅞	− 1½	Off	8.2

Weekly Percentage Leaders Of AMEX-Listed Issues

The following list shows the American Stock Exchange stocks that have gone up the most and down the most based on percent of change regardless of volume.

No securities trading below $2 are included. Net and percentage change are the difference between the last week's closing price and this week's closing price.

UPS

Name	Sales(hds)	High	Low	Last	Chg.		Pct.
1 Std Metals	424	11½	6⅞	11⅛	+ 4⅛	Up	58.9
2 Spencer Cos	155	13	9⅜	13	+ 3⅛	Up	31.6
3 Acme Prec	142	2½	2⅛	2½	+ ½	Up	25.0
4 Topps Gum	466	6¼	4⅞	6¼	+ 1¼	Up	25.0
5 SMD Ind	290	2¾	1⅞	2⅝	+ ½	Up	23.5
6 OrroxCp	989	10	8	9¾	+ 1¾	Up	21.9
7 Alaska Airl	5404	6⅛	5	6	+ 1	Up	20.0
8 Lundy Elec	124	9⅛	7½	9	+ 1½	Up	20.0
9 PittWV Shrs	496	7½	6⅛	7½	+ 1¼	Up	20.0
10 Timeplex	589	11	8⅝	10½	+ 1¾	Up	20.0
11 Ultimate n	962	11⅝	9⅛	11¼	+ 1⅝	Up	16.9
12 Money Mgt	55	4¾	4¼	4¾	+ ⅝	Up	15.2
13 ElectrSnd	28	2⅞	2⅜	2⅞	+ ⅜	Up	15.0
14 MountMed n	464	12½	10¼	12	+ 1½	Up	14.3
15 Rex Noreco	46	3⅛	2¾	3	+ ⅜	Up	14.3
16 MeenanOil	224	7	5½	6⅛	+ ¾	Up	14.0
17 Verbatim s	1594	28⅜	24	27½	+ 3⅜	Up	14.0
18 Movielab	48	3⅛	2⅝	3⅛	+ ⅜	Up	13.6
19 Beehive n	408	7½	6¼	7⅜	+ ⅞	Up	13.5
20 GrantInd wt	304	2⅛	1⅝	2⅛	+ ¼	Up	13.3
21 KeyPharm s	4391	29½	26¼	29	+ 3⅜	Up	13.2
22 Digicon Inc	374	21⅞	19⅛	21⅞	+ 2½	Up	12.9
23 WorkWear	118	12	10½	12	+ 1⅜	Up	12.9
24 Genisco s	605	11¼	9¾	11¼	+ 1¼	Up	12.5
25 PostCorp	598	31½	26¼	29¼	+ 3¼	Up	12.5
26 Susquehan	46	2⅜	2	2¼	+ ¼	Up	12.5

DOWNS

Name	Sales(hds)	High	Low	Last	Chg		Pct.
1 Ampeco n	117	2⅝	2	2	− ⅝	Off	23.8
2 SFM Corp	57	7⅜	5⅞	6	− 1⅜	Off	18.6
3 Conroy Inc	195	10¼	8⅜	8⅝	− 1⅝	Off	15.9
4 DamsonO wt	84	2¼	1⅞	2	− ⅜	Off	15.8
5 ExplSurvy n	46	4⅛	3½	3½	− ⅝	Off	15.2
6 Parmnt Pkg	18	2¾	2½	2½	− ⅜	Off	13.0
7 BAT Indust	5	7⅜	6¾	6¾	− 1	Off	12.9
8 IntegrEntr	167	3⅞	3½	3½	− ½	Off	12.5
9 TexGnRs wt	185	3¼	2⅜	2⅝	− ⅜	Off	12.5
10 PeninResrcs	353	7⅜	6	6¼	− ⅞	Off	12.3
11 PremRsColo n	66	3⅛	2¾	2¾	− ⅜	Off	12.0
12 Univ Cigar	36	13⅛	11⅝	11¾	− 1½	Off	11.3
13 SageEnrgy	298	11	9⅝	9⅞	− 1¼	Off	11.2
14 BrigadierInd	49	3½	2⅞	3	− ⅜	Off	11.1
15 EngyMiner	402	4½	3¾	4	− ½	Off	11.1
16 Nelson LB	151	2¼	2	2	− ¼	Off	11.1
17 GatesLrjet s	325	16⅛	14	14⅛	− 1¾	Off	11.0
18 StatexPet n	55	11⅜	9⅞	10⅛	− 1¼	Off	11.0
19 TexGenRs	216	9⅝	8⅜	8⅜	− 1	Off	10.7
20 Thorof Mkt	62	3⅜	3⅛	3⅛	− ⅜	Off	10.7
21 Struth Well	1395	4¾	4	4¼	− ½	Off	10.5
22 SSP Ind	69	3½	3¼	3⅜	− ⅜	Off	10.0
23 Servo Corp	232	8⅝	7⅝	8	− ⅞	Off	9.9
24 StephnChm s	85	12⅞	11½	11⅝	− 1¼	Off	9.7
25 RatliffDril n	200	8	7	7⅛	− ¾	Off	9.5
26 UnitAsbestos	170	5¼	4¾	4¾	− ½	Off	9.5

Weekly Percentage Leaders Of Issues Traded O-T-C

The following list shows the Over-The-Counter stocks and warrants that have gone up the most and down the most based on percent of change regardless of volume.

No securities trading below $2 are included. Net and percentage change are the difference between the last week's closing price and this week's closing price.

UPS

Name	Last	Chg		Pct.
1 Isaly	2¾	+ 1¼	Up	83.3
2 VideoCp	9⅛	+ 3⅞	Up	73.8
3 Intfern	5¾	+ 2⅛	Up	58.6
4 PassptTr	2⅜	+ ⅞	Up	58.3
5 CamltInd	9¼	+ 3⅛	Up	51.0
6 DSI Cp	5⅝	+ 1⅞	Up	50.0
7 BioMd	2 3-16	+11-16	Up	45.8
8 Cognitrn	4⅜	+ 1⅜	Up	45.8
9 Dalco h	2⅞	+ ⅞	Up	43.8
10 ApldSolr	2½	+ ¾	Up	42.9
11 YorkRsh	2½	+ ¾	Up	42.9
12 Viragen	4⅝	+ 1⅜	Up	42.3
13 ApldSol un	3	+ ⅞	Up	41.2
14 TaylorDv	5	+ 1⅜	Up	37.9
15 Spex	7¾	+ 2	Up	34.8
16 MayfSup	4	+ 1	Up	33.3
17 Switcho	7	+ 1¾	Up	33.3
18 IntfcMec	8¾	+ 2⅛	Up	32.1
19 Codenol	8¼	+ 2	Up	32.0
20 GtrWash	2⅛	+ ½	Up	30.8
21 SunstFd	2⅛	+ ½	Up	30.8

DOWNS

Name	Last	Chg		Pct.
1 LevinCpt	2	− ⅞	Off	30.4
2 HiStoy un	2½	− 1	Off	28.6
3 NP Engy	2⅛	− ¾	Off	26.1
4 GulfNuc	6⅛	− 2	Off	24.6
5 Saxon s	5	− 1⅝	Off	24.5
6 Sykes s	14¾	− 4¼	Off	22.4
7 Patlx wt	3½	− 1	Off	22.2
8 Texon	6⅞	− 1⅞	Off	21.4
9 Patton	2⅜	− ⅝	Off	20.8
10 TransEx	4⅜	− 1⅛	Off	20.5
11 Biocl un	3	− ¾	Off	20.0
12 Minetnk	3¼	− ¾	Off	18.8
13 NestEn	2¾	− ⅝	Off	18.5
14 RepRscl	2¼	− ½	Off	18.2
15 StrutO	2¼	− ½	Off	18.2
16 US Antimy	3⅜	− ¾	Off	18.2
17 ClinicSci	4¾	− 1	Off	17.4
18 GilmSv	2⅜	− ½	Off	17.4
19 CompC s	12	− 2½	Off	17.2
20 BroadFn	2½	− ½	Off	16.7
21 Hadron	2½	− ½	Off	16.7

SOURCE: Reprinted by permission of *Barron's*, © Dow Jones & Company, Inc. (April 19, 1982).

Each year's data for the industrial companies includes over 120 balance sheet and income statement items and market data. Compustat has an industrial file that includes company data from the New York and American Stock Exchanges and the over-the-counter market. There is also a file on utilities and banks. Besides the annual file which is updated weekly, users can order tapes with quarterly data also updated weekly.

Figure 3–15

BARRON'S MARKET LABORATORY

Dow-Jones Hourly Averages

30 Industrials

	Apr. 12	13	14	15	16
Opening	842.56	839.71	839.80	837.61	839.42
11:00	840.37	840.37	836.19	836.47	840.75
12:00	840.18	841.04	836.76	836.57	841.23
1:00	842.18	841.89	836.76	836.95	841.04
2:00	841.99	845.13	837.71	836.57	843.04
3:00	841.32	843.51	836.57	837.71	844.94
Close	841.32	841.04	838.09	839.61	843.42
High (h)	847.32	847.89	844.46	842.85	848.36
Low (h)	836.38	836.19	831.91	832.38	836.85
Change	− 1.62	− 0.28	− 2.95	+ 1.52	+ 3.81

Wk's net change +0.48 (h) H 848.36 L 831.91

20 Transportation Cos.

Opening	348.77	348.09	347.60	345.47	345.20
11:00	348.77	348.16	345.26	343.96	345.33
12:00	347.54	348.29	345.68	344.30	344.99
1:00	347.54	349.26	345.68	345.06	345.26
2:00	347.95	350.70	347.26	345.06	345.13
3:00	347.05	350.01	345.61	344.99	346.57
Close	347.47	348.64	346.37	344.92	346.57
High (h)	351.12	352.90	350.43	347.60	348.50
Low (h)	345.06	345.33	342.92	342.17	342.65
Change	− 1.37	+ 1.17	− 2.27	− 1.45	+ 1.65

Wk's net change −2.27 (h) H 352.90 L 342.17

15 Utilities

Opening	110.52	111.26	111.66	112.03	111.78
11:00	110.56	111.42	111.91	111.74	111.87
12:00	110.65	111.38	111.70	111.95	112.03
1:00	110.69	111.46	111.70	111.70	111.99
2:00	110.81	111.58	111.91	111.99	112.23
3:00	110.77	111.62	111.99	111.87	112.23
Close	110.93	111.62	112.07	112.15	112.27
High (h)	111.54	112.35	112.48	112.52	112.84
Low (h)	110.20	110.52	111.17	111.30	111.42
Change	+ 0.41	+ 0.69	+ 0.45	+ 0.08	+ 0.12

Wk's net change +1.75 (h) H 112.84 L 110.20

65 Stocks

Opening	332.57	332.13	332.21	331.31	331.49
11:00	332.13	332.37	330.90	330.50	331.85
12:00	331.77	332.52	331.04	330.72	331.93
1:00	332.21	333.03	331.04	330.90	331.95
2:00	332.35	334.19	331.79	330.96	332.45
3:00	331.93	333.67	331.12	331.12	333.27
Close	332.13	332.75	331.69	331.63	332.97
High (h)	334.75	335.79	334.41	333.27	334.85
Low (h)	330.04	330.24	328.96	328.90	330.04
Change	− 0.54	+ 0.62	− 1.06	− 0.06	+ 1.34

Wk's net change +0.30 (h) H 335.79 L 328.90

(h)-Averages of the highs and lows reached at any time during the day by the individual stocks.

Shares Traded on N.Y. Exchange

	Thous. shares				
10-11	12,690	11,960	11,790	11,720	12,790
11-12	8,350	8,160	10,240	7,280	9,070
12- 1	7,240	6,730	5,920	6,960	8,570
1- 2	4,910	7,080	4,680	5,180	6,040
2- 3	5,940	7,360	4,950	6,180	9,440
3- 4	7,390	7,370	7,570	8,380	9,980
Total	46,520	48,680	45,150	45,700	55,890
	By Groups-Thous. shares				
30 Ind	4,158.1	3,877.8	4,545.4	4,037.4	5,367.8
20 Tran	1,615.9	1,862.8	1,280.9	980.5	1,538.5
15 Util	1,286.1	1,313.8	1,386.7	1,075.6	935.7
65 Stock	7,060.1	7,054.4	7,213.0	6,093.5	7,842.0

Ratio of 10 Most Active Stocks (Composite) to total trading, % of total:

9.56	9.94	13.40	12.02	11.39

Average closings (Composite) of 10 Most Active Stocks:

27.95	26.86	34.17	23.45	31.70

Weekly Trading by Markets in NYSE Listed Stocks

	Shares	Warrants
NYSE	241,929,480	502,100
Midwest	16,301,800	....
Pacific	10,530,200	....
NASDAQ	6,787,920	2,500
Phila.	4,658,800	....
Boston	1,680,000	....
Cincinnati	943,300	....
Instinet	764,100	....

NYSE Odd-Lot Trading

	Apr. 8	12	13	14	15
Purch th shs	115.2	137.1	123.4	120.7	111.2
Sales, th shs	294.8	365.6	316.7	307.1	277.3
Short sales, sh	925	1,050	442	791	660

Dow-Jones Weekly Averages

Stock Averages

	First	High	Low	Last	Chg.
Indus	841.32	843.42	838.09	843.42	+ 0.48
Trans	347.47	348.64	344.92	346.57	− 2.27
Utils	110.93	112.27	110.93	112.27	+ 1.75
Comp	332.13	332.97	331.63	332.97	+ 0.30

Bond Averages

20 Bonds	58.52	59.06	58.52	59.06	+ 0.67
10 Util	56.97	57.31	56.81	57.31	+ 0.58
10 Ind	60.07	60.81	60.07	60.81	+ 0.76

Dow-Jones Averages for 1982

Stock Averages

	First	High	Low	Last	Chg	%
Ind	882.52	882.52	795.47	843.42	−31.58	− 3.61
Trp	379.68	379.68	314.36	346.57	−33.73	− 8.87
Util	109.83	112.27	103.61	112.27	+ 3.25	+ 2.98
Cmp	349.60	349.60	311.19	332.97	−14.83	− 4.26

Stock averages are compiled daily by using the following divisors: Industrials, 1.314; Transports, 1.816; Utilities, 3.074; 65 Stks Comp., 6.255.

Bond Averages

20 Bds	56.93	59.06	55.67	59.06	+ 1.98	+ 3.47
10 Util	55.40	57.65	53.80	57.31	+ 1.45	+ 2.60
10 Ind	58.47	60.81	57.36	60.81	+ 2.50	+ 4.29

Dow-Jones Price-Earnings Ratio

	Apr. 16 1982	Mar. 16 1982	Apr. 16 1981	Apr. 16 1980
Industrials	7.4	7.0	8.3	6.2
Trnsprt Cos	7.5	7.0	10.4	5.7
Utilities	6.1	5.8	6.9	6.9

Per share earnings for 12 months ended Dec. 31.

NASDAQ OTC Indexes

Index	4/16/82	% Chg.
Industrial	208.40	+ 0.82
Composite	182.25	+ 0.61
Bank	138.20	....
Insurance	192.09	+ 0.04
Other Finance	168.62	− 0.01
Transportation	159.22	+ 2.43
Utilities	185.64	+ 3.52

(February 5, 1971, equals 100.00)

NYSE Most Active Stocks

Yearly High	Yearly Low		Sales	High	Low	Last	Chg.
17	9¾	Schlitz	4,575,300	16⅞	15¼	16⅞	+ 1
64⅞	48¾	IBM	3,837,300	64⅞	61¼	64½	+ 2¼
36	27¾	Exxon s	3,182,800	28⅝	28	28¼	− ¼
61½	53⅝	ATT	2,172,600	55⅝	54⅝	55⅜	+ ⅛
20¾	15⅝	Sears	1,960,400	19⅝	18¾	19¼	+ ¼
27½	16¼	RCA	1,942,900	23⅝	22	22⅞	+ ⅜
9⅝	4¼	Telex	1,825,600	9	7⅞	8⅞	+ ⅜
30⅞	21¾	Citicrp	1,654,900	27⅞	26⅞	27⅝	+ ⅛
35⅝	18¾	GnDyn	1,654,800	29⅝	24⅞	29⅝	+ 4¾
21⅝	9¼	AmAir	1,651,400	15½	13¾	14⅛	− 1⅛
48¼	33½	AetnLf	1,649,500	47¾	42½	43¾	− 4
26⅛	12	SonyCp	1,630,600	13¾	12¾	13¼	− ⅛
36½	17⅞	PogoPd	1,518,300	29½	26⅞	28	+ ¾
63¼	40½	WrnCm	1,503,200	57⅝	54	57½	+ 3
32	20¾	Mobil s	1,497,100	22⅛	21½	21⅞	+ ⅛
39⅛	26	Tandy s	1,423,700	33	31½	32⅞	+ ⅜
39½	29¼	Texaco	1,417,500	30⅛	29¾	30⅛	+ ¼
58	33⅞	GMot	1,325,100	42⅝	40⅛	41¼	− 1⅛
36⅜	20	NLT	1,312,700	29½	22¼	28⅞	+ 6¼
41¾	26⅜	Heublin	1,308,300	41¾	39	41¼	+ 1⅝

Week's Market Statistics

	Last week	Prev. week	Last year
Sales NYSE, th sh	241,929	203,436	207,233
Sales ASE, th sh	19,960	15,260	25,480
Sales OTC, th sh-a	134,791	104,556	142,559
Dow-Jones groups:			
30 Ind, th sh	21,986	19,585	18,197
20 Transp, th sh	7,279	6,619	10,768
15 Util, th sh	5,998	9,108	2,941
65 Stks, th sh	35,263	35,312	31,906
20 Most Active Stocks:			
Average price	31.27	29.89	38.69
% vol to total vol	13.77	16.00	15.08
20 Low Priced Stocks-v:			
Index	824.9	825.6	922.8
Volume, th sh	1,842.9	3,662.1	3,658.3
%vol to DJI vol	11.09	14.75	15.45
NYSE volume report, Apr. 2, 1982:			
Buy/sell, th sh-w	242,366	269,261	241,423
Total shorts, th sh	20,336.9	26,521.0	20,149.6
Public shorts, th sh	3,521.3	4,937.9	2,789.4
Member trading, Apr. 2, 1982:			
Member shrt, th sh-x	16,815.6	21,583.2	17,360.2
Speclst shrt, th sh	7,925.1	10,078.8	9,737.5
Purchases, th sh	62,944.3	66,326.9	60,013.5
Sales, th sh-z	68,352.8	80,567.0	66,682.3
Net buy/sell, th sh	− 5,408.5	− 14,240.1	− 6,668.8
% vol to NYSE-vol	27.09	27.28	26.24
Odd-lot trading, Apr. 2, 1982:			
Purchases, th sh	1,046	1,118	1,389
Purchases, th $	28,337	30,428	54,766
Sales, th sh-z	2,151	2,316	3,128
Sales, th $	65,108	69,339	116,057
Short sales, actual	4,396	6,007	7,822
Bond vol, NYSE, th$	116,758	89,058	76,925
Bond offerings, th$	1,588,965	753,785	2,110,800
Stock offerings th$	143,015	180,125	202,069
Barron's Best Gr bond yields-v	13.35	13.45	12.63
Barron's Intrm Gr bond yields-v	14.93	15.07	14.02
Barron's Confidence Index (Ratio Best Gr to Intrm Gr Bonds)	89.4	89.3	90.1
Spread between yields for Barron's Best Grade Bonds & Dow Jones Industrial Stock Avg.	− 6.74	− 6.84	− 7.12
Prices and Yields on Dow-Jones Averages:			
30 Ind	843.42	842.94	1005.58
30 Ind. %	6.61	6.61	5.51
20 Transp	346.57	348.84	447.38
20 Transp, %	4.49	4.46	2.95
15 Util	112.27	110.52	107.16
15 Util, %	10.66	10.81	9.80
20 Bonds, %-v	15.26	15.25	13.74
10 Util, %-v	13.90	14.08	14.53
10 Ind, %-v	14.58	14.67	12.95
Municipal Bond yield, %	13.25	13.66	11.69

a-NASDAQ. v-Week ended Thursday. w-Shares and warrants. x-Includes specialists short sales. z-Includes short sales.

Dow-Jones Bond Averages

	Apr. 12	13	14	15	16
20 Bonds	58.52	58.72	58.69	58.79	59.06
10 Util	56.97	57.03	56.81	56.90	57.31
10 Ind	60.07	60.41	60.57	60.60	60.81
U.S. Govts.	84.77	84.53	84.86	84.85	84.92

New York Exchange Bond Diary

Issues Traded	903	924	826	844	864
Advances	466	473	341	392	480
Declines	253	267	314	284	220
Unchanged	184	184	171	168	164
New Highs	19	23	16	21	14
New Lows	7	15	13	10	9
Sales, ths $	25,550	25,190	19,810	20,090	26,120

Weekly Composite Diary

	NYSE	AMEX	NASDAQ
	Week ended April 16, 1982		
Issues Traded	2,118	936	3,368
Advances	1,139	401	1,052
Declines	749	382	885
Unchanged	230	153	1,431
New Highs	112	31	....
New Lows	56	28	....

NYSE Common Stock Diary

	Apr. 12	13	14	15	16
Issues Traded	1,494	1,498	1,489	1,482	1,488
Advances	512	633	470	667	761
Declines	634	511	651	462	388
Unchanged	348	354	368	353	339

NYSE Composite Diary

Issues Traded	1,896	1,882	1,902	1,874	1,883
Advances	669	796	613	829	954
Declines	767	627	798	587	491
Unchanged	460	459	491	458	438
New Highs	47	40	30	28	55
New Lows	17	14	14	15	15
Sales, ths shs	53,733	57,557	53,488	53,528	65,280

Amex Composite Diary

Issues Traded	781	766	774	747	748
Advances	257	256	271	274	317
Declines	298	273	278	259	218
Unchanged	226	237	225	214	213
New Highs	11	11	8	11	15
New Lows	6	7	10	14	9
Sales th shs	4,555	5,041	4,069	3,835	4,168

NASDAQ OTC Market Diary

Issues Traded	3,370	3,369	3,370	3,369	3,368
Advances	465	554	474	575	644
Declines	531	467	540	390	364
Unchanged	2,374	2,348	2,356	2,404	2,360
New Highs	98	97	93	112	125
New Lows	36	41	63	48	53
Sales, ths shs	25,995	27,538	26,936	25,548	28,807

Other Market Indicators

NYSE Comp.	66.76	66.76	66.67	66.96	67.26
Ind.	75.35	75.31	75.16	75.58	75.97
Util.	38.94	39.05	39.15	39.18	39.27
Tran.	58.31	58.55	58.21	58.12	58.60
Fin.	71.60	71.54	71.37	71.43	71.63
Amex Index	272.88	274.94	274.41	273.48	274.15
OTC-a Comp.	180.89	180.76	180.41	181.12	182.25
Ind.	206.29	206.03	205.61	206.62	208.40
Insur.	191.12	191.49	191.42	191.50	192.09
Banks	138.11	138.28	137.77	137.86	138.20
S&P 500 Comp.	116.00	115.99	115.83	116.35	116.81
400 Ind.	128.79	128.73	128.56	129.24	129.77
Value Line	128.97	129.16	128.84	129.27	129.94

a-NASDAQ.

Amex Most Active Stocks

Yearly High	Yearly Low		Sales	High	Low	Last	Chg.
21¼	6½	DomeP s	2,246,800	9¼	8⅛	8¼	+ ¼
25⅝	8⅞	GlfCd g	620,700	12⅜	11⅛	11½	+ ⅜
8⅝	4⅝	AlskAir	540,400	6⅛	5	6	+ 1
301¾	24	Wang B	494,420	301¾	29¾	32	+ 1¼
29½	17⅛	KeyPh s	439,100	29½	26¼	29	+ 3⅜
13⅝	7⅞	OzarkA	373,800	12⅜	11⅝	11⅞	....
26⅜	12½	DorGas	360,400	18⅜	15⅞	18	+ ⅝
14¼	4⅛	RangrO	332,300	6¼	5½	5⅝	− ¼
35¾	10	HouOTr	318,300	13⅞	12⅞	13¼	....
17	8	HornHr	259,000	17	15⅝	16⅞	+ 1⅜

NASDAQ OTC Most Active Stocks

	Vol.	Last	Chg.
MCI Comm	11,900,200	36⅝	+ 3⅛
Intel Corp	4,640,000	32½	+ 2⅝
Apple Comp	3,755,400	16⅞	− ⅝
Tandem Comp	3,621,100	26¾	+ ½
Sykes Datatr	2,087,700	14¾	− 4¼
Tampax	1,714,400	37¾	+ 1¾
Pabst B	1,591,100	17⅝	+ 1¼
St Paul Cos	1,001,700	48⅝	− 1⅝
Amer Int'l Grp	906,200	68½	− ½
Tandon Corp	865,200	31	+ 2

STOCK EXCHANGE VOLUME TRENDS

	NYSE Up	NYSE Down	NYSE QCHA (%)	Amex Up	Amex Down	Amex QCHA (%)	NASDAQ Up	NASDAQ Down
April 12	17,602,900	20,986,300	-.12	2,073,400	1,412,300	+ .07	6,218,500	7,070,800
April 13	24,989,100	14,983,200	+ .21	2,976,900	984,300	+ .04	7,239,800	5,669,800
April 14	16,878,000	19,899,700	-.20	1,809,400	1,431,100	+ .14	7,151,900	6,287,600
April 15	26,310,400	10,937,000	+ .32	1,522,100	1,235,700	+ .17	8,929,700	3,769,300
April 16	32,524,200	15,308,200	+ .76	2,106,100	960,800	+ .58	11,655,300	5,330,600

Supplied by QUOTRON.

Figure 3–16 Barron's Market Laboratory—trade and foreign data

PULSE OF INDUSTRY AND TRADE

	Latest date	Latest period	Preceding period	Year ago
Production—What They Make:				
Auto output U.S.	Apr. 17	111,586	r88,225	119,551
Electric power prod, mil kw hrs	Apr. 10	42,072	41,234	40,461
Paper prod, th tons	Apr. 10	611	604	626
Paperboard prod, th tons	Apr. 10	568.5	604.6	632.3
Petroleum, dly ref. runs, th bbls	Apr. 9	11,390	11,272	12,072
Petroleum, refinery operations, %	Apr. 9	63.9	63.5	66.3
Steel production, th tons	Apr. 10	1,542	1,675	2,595
Steel capability utilization (AISI)	Apr. 10	52.1	56.6	86.7
GNP (adjusted annual rate)	4th qtr	– 4.5+	1.4+	3.8
Federal Res Bd index of prod a	Mar.	141.2	r142.3	152.1
Manufacturing prod	Mar.	139.7	r140.5	151.6
Durable	Mar.	128.6	r129.6	142.1
Non durable	Mar.	155.6	r156.4	165.3
Mining prod	Mar.	138.7	r142.3	143.2
Utilities	Mar.	168.7	r168.7	167.8
N'print output, U.S.&Can., th sh tons	Feb.	1,210	r1,165	1,165
Distribution—What They Sell:				
Carloadings, th cars	Apr. 10	354	386	379
Retail store sales bil $	Mar.	87.2	87.6	87.2
Mfg. sales, adj. bil $	Jan.	157.2	r161.1	161.2
Durable goods, bil $	Feb.	79.3	r77.9	82.2
Machine tool shipts, mil $	Feb.	359.5	383.6	422.2
Inventories—What's Left on Hand:				
Crude oil, th bbls	Apr. 9	378,381	380,522	394,323
Gasoline, th bbls	Apr. 9	247,651	249,086	278,891
Mfg Inventories, adj bil $	Feb.	276.4	r275.7	251.2
N'print stks, U.S.2Can., th sh tons	Feb.	1,543	r1,482	1,205
Orders Received:				
All manufacturing, adj bil $	Jan.	157.6	r159.5	162.1
Durable goods	Feb.	79.3	r78.1	82.2
Non-durable goods	Dec.	80.1	r80.0	79.3
Machine tools, mil $	Feb.	163.9	r205.2	280.1
Unfilled Orders:				
Durable goods	Feb.	309.8	309.9	382.0
Failures (D. & B.)				
Business failures, no.	Apr. 8	500	448	282
Business Incorporations (D. & B.)				
New Incorporations	Dec.	47,556	49,413	47,840
Purchasing Power:				
Whlesle Food Price Index (D&B) $	Apr. 13	17.46	17.55	17.37
Leading indicators a	Feb.	124.9	r125.3	135.2
Cons Price Index (USBLS) a	Feb.	283.4	282.5	263.2
Finished Goods Price Index a	Mar.	276.9	277.4	265.3
Employment:				
Civil labor force, th	Mar.	109,340	109,200	106,160
Employed, th	Mar.	99,490	99,600	98,400
Unemployed, th	Mar.	9,850	9,600	7,760
Constructiong				
Advance Planning (ENR), mil $	Apr. 15	2,730.3	2,645.8	3,497.8
Bldg contracts, (Dodge), mil $	Feb.	8,881	10,580	10,405
Lumber production, mil bd ft	Jan.	1,810	1,765	2,523
Lumber shipments, mil bd ft	Jan.	1,637	1,989	2,424
New housing starts, no ths	Mar.	947	953	1,289

a-1967 equals 100. e-Estimate. p-Preliminary. r-Revised.

FOREIGN

SOUTH AFRICAN ADR's

Closing prices of selected issues in U.S currency.

April 16, 1982

Name of Stock	Week's Close	Week's Change
Bracken	1.60	....
Deelkraal	2.60	+ .10
Doornfontein	12.50	– .25
Durban Deep	13.50	+ 1.50
East Rand Prop	7.625	– .375
Elandsrand	3.25	....
Elsburg	1.75	....
Ergo	5.125	+ .125
Gen Mining	14.50	+ .50
Grodtvlei	6.375	+ .125
Harmony	9.00	....
Hartebeestfontein	36.50	+ 2.50
Johannesb C	46.00	+ 1.00
Kinross	8.875	+ .50
Leslie	7.25	– .25
Libanon	12.50	– .25
Loraine	2.25	+ .10
Randfontein	43.00	+ 2.50
Sasol	2.35	+ .10
So. African Breweries	3.375	– .25
Southvaal	25.25	+ 1.00
Stilfontein	11.50	– .25
Unisel	8.00	....
Venterspost	6.125	+ .125
Western Areas	2.75	+ .10
Winkelhaak	20.25	– .75
Financial Rand	0.77375	+ .01875

x=Ex-Dividend.
Source: Cohn, Delaire & Kaufman, Inc.

STOCK INDEXES

	–1982– High	Low	Apr. 16 Close	Week's Change
Australia	595.50	455.60	477.30	+ 8.40
Austria	56.96	52.20	52.24	N.A.
Belgium	102.43	69.53	99.55	– 1.68
Canada	1,956.30	1,537.58	1,613.07	+ 7.06
France	113.18	97.88	109.32	+ 1.76
Italy	7,657.00	6,365.00	6,935.00	– 37.00
Japan	7,938.83	6,889.53	7,129.69	– 79.52
Netherl.	92.40	84.00	90.90	– 0.80
Switzerl.	237.20	217.20	232.30	– 1.80
U.K.	579.80	518.10	545.80	– 14.50
UK Kaf	302.00	209.20	265.50	+ 6.00
W.Grmny	729.80	666.70	716.40	– 8.30

N.A.-Not Available.

GOLD COINS

NAME OF COIN	Price	Premium Over the Value of the Gold Contained in Coin: In $ Per Coin	As a % of Gold Value
Krugerrand	371.00	11.25	3.13
Maple Leaf	370.50	10.75	2.99
Mexican 1 oz	370.50	10.75	2.99
Mexico Peso	444.00	10.25	2.36
Austria crown	350.00		
Sovereign	100.00	15.25	17.99

Wholesale dealer offering price on Friday.

Mocatta's spot Gold price: $359.75
Source: Mocatta Metals Corp.

GOLD AND SILVER PRICES

Handy & Harman's base for pricing gold content of shipments and for making refining settlements was $362.75 a troy ounce Friday. The company's silver price was $7.52 a troy ounce.

ECONOMIC AND FINANCIAL INDICATORS

	Latest period	Preceding period	Year ago
Federal Reserve Condition Report, Mil $, Mar. 31, 1982			
Loans and securities, total	611,707	603,883	566,607
U.S. Treasury securities, total	38,570	37,673	42,142
Other securities, total	79,346	79,620	79,143
Other loans, gross	472,258	467,404	426,278
Commercial & Industrial	202,624	200,036	173,195
Real estate	127,293	127,343	115,585
Financial institutions, total	41,803	41,072	38,276
Nonbank brokers & dealers	5,220	5,131	7,798
For purchasing & carrying sec	2,562	2,573	2,355
Total Assets	827,376	807,980	785,272
Demand deposits, total	172,731	157,859	207,545
Domestic commercial banks	19,684	17,218	38,488
Savings deposits, total	80,448	79,238	80,480
Time deposits, total	292,015	292,757	242,942
Total Liabilities	771,815	752,801	733,447
Federal Reserve Member Bank Changes, Mil $, Apr. 14, 1982:			
Gov't. securities bought outright	125,592	123,755	119,785
Federal agency issues bought outright	9,011	9,013	8,720
Borrowings from Fed	1,337	1,479	1,142
Seasonal Borrowings	154	166	149
Extended credit	234	279	
Float	3,480	3,027	3,510
Total reserve bank credit	148,641	147,465	143,305
Treasury gold stock-z	11,150	11,150	11,154
Currency in circulation	143,703	142,053	134,983
Treasury deposits with Fed banks	3,626	r3,314	3,033
Reserves with Fed banks	23,291	23,337	26,756
Total reserves including cash	38,655	38,495	40,128
Required reserves	38,389	38,169	39,727
Net borrowings from Fed	949	r1,034	993
Excess reserves	266	326	401
Free reserves	– 683	– 708	– 592
Money Supply (M1) bil $, Apr. 7, 1982:	453.6	r446.5	r432.2
Monetary Base, bil $, Apr. 14, 1982:	168.3	r169.1	161.8
Federal Reserve Interest Rates, % Apr. 14, 1982:			
Federal Funds	14.68	15.15	15.33
Treasury bill (90 day)	12.85	13.17	13.58
Commercial paper (dealer, 90 day)	14.21	14.18	14.66
Certfs of Deposit (resale, 90 day)	14.58	14.55	15.24
Eurodollar (90 days)	14.43	15.28	16.16
Money Market Funds, bil $, Apr. 14, 1982:			
Total Assets	192.3	193.3	117.3
Treasury Statement, bil $, Apr. 8, 1982:			
Gross Federal Debt	1,060.9	1,064.8	966.9
Statutory Debt Limit	1,079.8	1,079.8	985.0

p-Preliminary. r-Revised. sa-Seasonally adjusted. z-Actual.

MONEY RATES

April 16, 1982

Prime Rate	16½	16½	17-17½
Discount Rate	12	12	13
Fed Funds: High/Low	15¾-14½	14⅞-14¼	16-15¼
Fed Funds: Close/Offer	14¾-15	14½-14⅝	15-16
Call Money	16-17	14¾-16	16-16½
C.D.'s: One month	14.75	14.55	15.12
C.D.'s: One year	14.75	14.875	14.75
Accept: 30 days	14.50	14.50	15.10
Accept: 180 days	13.65	13.70	14.50
Short-term T-bills, Weekly Auction April 12, 1982:			
13 week bills	12.849	12.893	13.783
26 week bills	12.899	12.802	13.646
52 Week T-Bills, Latest Auction: April 15, 1982			
Average annual return	12.731	12.509	12.991
Average annual investment yield	14.81	14.519	
Savings Rates:			
Money market fund	13.49	12.70	13.85
6 month money market ctf.	13.154	13.170	13.896
30 month small-saver ctf.	14.10	14.05	12.0
1 year all-saver ctf.	10.37	10.16	
Savings passbook	5.5	5.5	5.5
US savings bonds	9.0	9.0	8.0

SOURCE: Reprinted by permission of *The Wall Street Journal*,

A second data base created by Compustat is called the Price-Dividend-Earnings tape (PDE) which contains monthly data on per-share performance. These tapes are leased to financial institutions for a fairly large sum or to nonprofit educational institutions for approximately $2,500 per year (a significant discount). The tapes may be paid for in cash or in soft dollars (commissions funneled through an S&P brokerage subsidiary).

These tapes are useful for the analysis of large numbers of companies in a short time period. Ratios can be created, analyzed, and compared. Trends and regression analysis can be performed. Searches can be implemented for specific kinds of companies. For example, one could read through the tapes and sort out companies meeting certain parameters, such as:

1. Dividend yield greater than 6 percent.
2. Earnings growth greater than 15 percent.
3. Price-earnings ratio less than the Standard & Poor's 500 Index.
4. Market price less than book value.

It should be noted that Interactive Data Corporation also provides the same information as the Compustat tapes on a time-sharing basis.

The *CRSP Tapes* are maintained by the University of Chicago in the Center for Research in Security Prices. The information provided is oriented to earnings, dividends, stock prices, and dates of mergers, stock splits, stock dividends, etc. The tapes are extremely useful (data begin in 1926) for historical research on stock performance. They are widely used in academia for research on the efficient market hypothesis, the capital asset pricing model, and other portfolio questions.

Value Line also has made computer tapes of its 1,700 companies available. Again these would have market price data as well as financial statement items. The Federal Trade Commission has industry trade topics available on aggregate industry data and the Federal Reserve Bank of St. Louis has been known to make tapes of monetary data available for academic researchers.

INFORMATION ON NONTRADITIONAL MARKETS

For the purposes of this section, we define nontraditional as being out of the realm of stocks, bonds, and government securities. A major area that has received increased attention during the 1970s has been commodities and financial futures. A major source of information on commodities is the *Commodity Yearbook*.

Commodity Yearbook

This is a yearly publication which can be supplemented by the *Commodity Yearbook Statistical Abstract* three times per year. The *Commodity Yearbook* runs several feature articles of educational interest covering commodities or situations that are currently in the forefront of commodity trading. For 1980, the

articles were "Understanding the London Metal Exchange," "Sugar and Its Shifting Role in the World Economy," "Spread Opportunities in Livestock Futures," and "The Role of Cycles in Commodity Price Forecasting."

In addition to the featured articles, the *Yearbook* covers each traded commodity from alcohol to zinc. For example, corn is covered in six pages. The first page is a description of the corn crop and relative occurrences for the 1979 year in review. The next five pages cover much data in tabular form for the last 13 years. The tables show world production of corn, acreage, and supply of corn in the United States, corn production estimates and disposition by value in the United States, corn supply and disappearance, distribution of corn in the United States, corn price support data, average price received by farmers for corn in the United States, and of course, weekly high-low-close of the nearest month's futures price. Each commodity has a similarly detailed evaluation and statistical summary.

Of course, there are other publications about commodities from main-line brokerage houses and specialty commodity brokers. In addition, the commodities exchanges publish educational booklets and newsletters. The International Monetary Market publishes the *I.M.M. Weekly Report,* which discusses the interest rate markets, foreign exchange markets, and gold. It also presents weekly prices for all interest rate futures, foreign exchange markets, gold, and selected cash market information, such as the federal funds rate and the prime rate. The Chicago Board of Trade also publishes the *Interest Rate Futures Newsletter.* As more investors become active in these markets, an investor (speculator) can be sure to find more available data.

Scott Publishing Company

The Scott Publishing Company has long been involved in the philatelic (stamp) market. They turn out annual catalogues with price data and pictures with descriptions. Recently, Scotts has added a *Stamp Market Update,* which is a quarterly report on current trends and prices. It features prices of major U.S. stamps and popular foreign stamps, information for specialized collectors, investment opportunities and strategies as stated by recognized experts, and special articles, statistical tables, and graphs.

SUMMARY

In summary, we can say that information is easy and yet difficult to find. The problem that beginners have is knowing where to look and what to look for, and this chapter has attempted to provide some guidance and sample data. The problem that advanced investors have is knowing what data is usable. This may also haunt beginners once they find the sources. To become proficient in finding data, spend a day in your library just looking through the volumes. This will increase your awareness of the types of information available. Then do some of

the exercises at the end of this chapter to see if you can find specific data. As for the problem of knowing what information is useful, the authors hope to shed some light on that as we proceed through the rest of the book.

<table>
<tr>
<td>

IMPORTANT WORDS AND CONCEPTS

</td>
<td>

Federal Reserve Bulletin
Survey of Current Business
Business Conditions Digest
Moody's Manuals
Standard & Poor's publications
Value Line Investment Survey
Business Periodicals Index

</td>
<td>

Funk and Scott Index of
  Corporations and Industries
The Wall Street Journal Index
Disclosure Journal
Compustat tapes
CRSP tapes

</td>
</tr>
</table>

QUESTIONS AND PROBLEMS

1. What type of information is part of aggregate economic data?

2. The Federal Reserve Bank of St. Louis has a number of comprehensive economic publications. What are they?

3. What is one of the major benefits provided by the *Survey of Current Business* in regard to industry data?

4. What makes *Business Conditions Disgest* unique among publications of economic data?

5. Of the major advisory services for investors, which ones would likely be found in most libraries?

6. What is special about the T–Z volume of Standard & Poor's *Corporate Records*?

7. What is the Standard & Poor's *Stock Guide*? What is included in the introduction.

8. Briefly describe the Value Line evaluation system.

9. Where can an investor look to quickly find information relating to reports filed with the SEC?

10. Under what category in *Barron's* would weekly data on stock market indexes and general market statistics be found?

11. What are the major computer data tapes available?

12. Choose a company and look it up in Moody's, Standard & Poor's, and Value Line to see the information provided and compare the data.

13. Select an industry and find the SIC code. Then look up all firms listed in this business. (Suggestion—the SIC code can be found in the T–Z volume

of Standard & Poor's *Corporate Records,* which will also provide the list of firms by the SIC number.)

14. Look up the implicit price deflator for GNP (one source is the St. Louis Federal Reserve Bank's *National Economic Trends*) and total corporate profits after taxes (same source). This data can be useful for current projects and will expose you to a good source for this type of information.

15. Select a company, go to *The Wall Street Journal Index* for the previous year, and identify the dates of all news stories about the company.

APPENDIX 3—A: NAMES AND ADDRESSES OF IMPORTANT DATA SOURCES

Federal Reserve Bank of:
   Atlanta, Ga. 30301
   Boston, Mass. 02106
   Chicago, Ill. 60690
   Cleveland, Ohio 44101
   Dallas, Tex. 75222
   Kansas City, Kans. 64198
   Minneapolis, Minn. 55480
   New York, N.Y. 10045
   Philadelphia, Pa. 19105
   Richmond, Va. 23219
   San Francisco, Calif. 94120
   St. Louis, Mo. 63166

Federal Reserve Bulletin
   Board of Governors of the
   Federal Reserve System
   Washington, D.C. 20551

Stock and commodity exchanges:
   American Stock Exchange
   86 Trinity Place
   New York, N.Y., 10006

   Chicago Board of Trade
   LaSalle at Jackson
   Chicago, Ill. 60604

   Chicago Mercantile Exchange
   444 West Jackson Blvd.
   Chicago, Ill. 60606

   New York Stock Exchange
   11 Wall Street
   New York, N.Y. 10005

U.S. government publications, such as:
   Survey of Current Business
   Weekly Business Statistics
   Business Conditions Digest
   Economic Indicators
   Economic Report of the President
   Statistical Abstract of the United States
   Statistical Bulletin

Can be requested from the:
   Superintendent of Documents
   U.S. Government Printing Office
   Washington, D.C. 20402

Periodicals:
   The Wall Street Journal and *Barron's*
   Dow Jones & Company
   Subscriptions Office
   200 Burnett Rd.
   Chicopee, Mass. 01021

   Changing Times
   The Kiplinger Magazine
   1729 H St., N.W.
   Washington D.C. 20006

   Disclosure Journal
   Disclosure Inc.
   1450 Broadway
   New York, N.Y. 10018

   Forbes
   60 5th Avenue
   New York, N.Y. 10011

Financial World
Macro Communications Inc.
150 East 58th Street
New York, N.Y. 10155

Business Week
1221 Avenue of the Americas
New York, N.Y. 10020

Money Magazine
Fortune
Time Inc.
3435 Wilshire Blvd.
Los Angeles, Calif. 90010

Media General Financial
    Services, Inc.
P.O. Box 26991
Richmond, Va. 23261

Financial Analysts Journal
1633 Broadway
New York, N.Y. 10019

Investment services:
  Moody's Investors Service
  99 Church Street
  New York, N.Y. 10007

  Standard & Poor's Corporation

345 Hudson Street
New York, N.Y. 10014

Value Line Services
Arnold Bernhard and Company
5 East 44th Street
New York, N.Y. 10017

Dun & Bradstreet
99 Church Street
New York, N.Y. 10007

Dun's Marketing Division
3 Century Drive
Parsippany, N.J. 07054

Computer data bases:
  Compustat
  P.O. Box 239
  Denver, Colo. 80201

  CRSP Tapes
  Center for Research in Security Prices
  University of Chicago
  Graduate School of Business
  Chicago, Ill. 60637

  Interactive Data Corporation
  122 East 42nd Street
  New York, N.Y. 10017

4

Participating in the market

There are many different kinds of investors participating in the market, from the individual to the professional, and each participant needs to know about the structure and mechanics of the market in which he or she might invest. In this chapter, we examine the use of indexes to gauge market performance, the rules and mechanics of opening and trading in an account, basic tax considerations for the investor, and the comparative features of investing individually or through mutual funds.

MEASURES OF PRICE PERFORMANCE— MARKET INDEX

We first look at tracking market performance for stocks and bonds. Each market has several market indexes published by Moody's, Standard & Poor's, Dow Jones, and other financial services. These indexes allow investors to measure their portfolio's performance against an index which approximates their portfolio composition; thus different investors prefer different indexes. While a professional pension fund manager might use the Standard & Poor's 500 Stock Index, a mutual fund specializing in small, over-the-counter stocks might prefer the NASDAQ (National Association of Securities Dealers Automated Quotations) index, and a small investor might use the Value Line average as the best approximation of his or her portfolio.

Stock market indexes and averages

Dow Jones Since there are many stock market indexes, we will cover the most widely used ones. Dow Jones, the publisher of *The Wall Street Journal and Barron's,* publishes several indexes of which the Dow Jones Industrial Average (DJIA) is one of the most popular. This average actually consists of 29 large industrial companies and American Telephone and Telegraph, a public utility, and is considered a "blue chip" index (stocks of very high

quality). Many people criticize the DJIA for being too selective and representing too few stocks. Nevertheless, the Dow Industrials do follow the general trend in the market, and these 30 common stocks comprise over 25 percent of the New York Stock Exchange value. Dow Jones also publishes an index of 20 transportation stocks, 15 utility stocks, and a 65-stock composite average. The companies that comprise these Dow Jones averages are shown in Table 4–1, while the listing of indexes that appear in *The Wall Street Journal* are shown in Table 4–2.

The Dow Jones Industrial Average used to be a simple average of 30 stocks, but when a company splits its stock price, the average had to be adjusted in some manner. For the Dow Jones Industrials, the divisor in the formula has been adjusted downward from the original 30 to slightly more than 1. Each time a company splits its shares of stock (or pays a stock dividend), the divisor is reduced to maintain the average at the same level prior to the stock split. If this were not done, the lower-priced stock after the split would lower the average, giving the appearance that investors are worse off. The method of adjusting the divisor, however, creates downward bias in the average over time and also gives higher-priced stocks more impact on the movement of the average. Figure 4–1 depicts the daily graph that appears in *The Wall Street Journal* covering the Dow Jones Averages.

Barron's, which is also a publication of Dow Jones, publishes *Barron's* 50 Stock Average and an index of low-priced securities which meets the needs of many small investors. *Barron's* also publishes a weekly average called *Barron's* Group Stock Averages covering 32 industry groups. These averages are especially useful to the analyst following the performance of a specific industry relative to the general market, and they are shown in Table 4–3.

Standard & Poor's Indexes

Standard & Poor's Corporation publishes several indexes, but two are most widely used—the S&P 400 Industrials and the S&P 500 Stock Index. These indexes are followed by professional investors and others as measures of broad stock market activity. The S&P 400 consists of 400 industrial common stocks of companies listed on the New York Stock Exchange and comprises over 50 percent of the market value of NYSE-listed companies. The S&P 500 Stock Index includes the 400 industrials plus utilities and transportation stocks.

These indexes are true indexes in that they are linked to some base value, in this case stock prices in the period from 1941 to 1943. The base period price in 1941 to 1943 was 10, so the S&P 500 Stock Index of 135.45 on April 21, 1981, indicates that the index has increased by 1,254.5 percent over this period. These indexes are weighted by the total market value of the companies in the index (value-weighted index), with large companies, such as IBM and AT&T, having a greater effect on the index than small companies. Nevertheless, these two indexes include many companies and provide a good measure of the direc-

Table 4—1   **Companies in the Dow Jones Averages**

Thirty stocks used in Dow Jones Industrial Average are:

Allied Chemical	General Foods	Owens-Illinois
Aluminum Co	General Motors	Procter & Gamb
Amer Brands	Goodyear	Sears Roebuck
Amer Can	Inco	Std Oil of Calif
Amer Tel & Tel	IBM	Texaco
Bethlehem Steel	Inter Harvester	Union Carbide
Du Pont	Inter Paper	United Technologies
Eastman Kodak	Johns-Manville	US Steel
Exxon	Merck	Westinghouse El
General Electric	Minnesota M&M	Woolworth

Twenty Transportation Stocks used are:

American Air	McLean Trucking	Santa Fe Indust
Burlington North	MoPac Corp	Southern Pacific
Canadian Pacific	Norfolk & West'n	Southern Railway
Consolid Freight	Northwest Air	Transway Int'l
CSX Corp.	Overnite Transp	Trans World
Delta Air Lines	Pan Am World Air	UAL Inc
Eastern Air Lines		Union Pac Corp

Fifteen Utility Stocks used are:

Am Elec Power	Consol Nat Gas	Panhandle EPL
Cleveland E Ill	Detroit Edison	Peoples Energy
Colum-Gas Sys	Houston Indust	Phila Elec
Comwlth Edison	Niag Mohawk P	Pub Serv E&G
Consol Edison	Pacific Gas & El	Sou Cal Edison

tion of the market for large New York Stock Exchange companies. Often the S&P 400 or S&P 500 is used as a proxy for market return when calculating the risk measure ("beta") of individual stocks and portfolios.

Value Line Average   The Value Line Average of 1,700 companies is a simple average of the price of 1,700 companies from the New York and American Stock Exchanges and the over-the-counter market. It is an unusual average in that it reflects three markets combined and is unweighted. Many individual investors use the Value Line Av-

Table 4—2   **Indexes and averages found in *The Wall Street Journal***

DOW JONES CLOSING AVERAGES

	– – – Thursday – – –			Yr. Ago	– –Since– –	
	1982	Change	%	1981	% Chg.	Dec. 31	%
Ind	828.96	+ 1.33	+0.16	933.36	−11.19	− 46.04	− 5.26
Trn	347.47	+ 0.62	+0.18	383.67	− 9.44	− 32.83	− 8.63
Utl	104.71	− 0.36	−0.34	107.49	− 2.59	− 4.31	− 3.95
Cmp	326.48	+ 0.28	+0.09	359.44	− 9.17	− 21.32	− 6.13

Ex-dividends of duPont Co. 60 cents lowered the industrial average by 0.48.

Ex-dividends of CSX Corp. 71 cents lowered the transportation average by 0.41.

The above ex-dividends lowered the composite average by 0.22.

OTHER MARKET INDICATORS

		1982	–Change–		1981
N.Y.S.E.	Composite	65.78	+ 0.07	+0.11%	72.53
	Industrial	74.45	+ 0.17	+0.23%	84.58
	Utility	37.84	− 0.24	−0.63%	37.28
	Transp.	58.66	+ 0.19	+0.33%	70.94
	Financial	70.04	+ 0 18	+0.26%	67.37
Am. Ex. Mkt Val Index		271.01	− 1 19	−0.44%	331.77
Nasdaq OTC Composite		181.38	+ 0.13	+0.07%	192.74
	Industrial	207.44	+ 0.23	+0.11%	241.84
	Insurance	188.62	+ 0.24	+0.13%	168.36
	Banks	140.13	− 0.26	−0.19%	123.23
Standard & Poor's 500		113.82	+ 0.13	+0.11%	126.61
	400 Industrial	126.86	+ 0.12	+0.09%	143.89
Wilshire 5000 Equity		1178.588	+ 1.144	+0.10%	1330.985

SOURCE: Reprinted by permission of *The Wall Street Journal,* © Dow Jones & Company, Inc. (February 19, 1982). All rights reserved.

Figure 4—1   **Dow Jones Averages**

The Dow Jones Averages

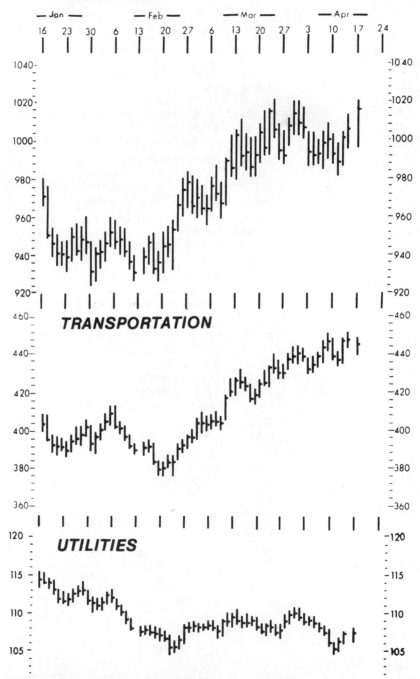

Table 4—3   **Barron's Group Stock Averages**

1980–1981 High*	Low*		February 12	February 5	Percent change
635.90	464.02	Aircraft manufacturing	524.59	567.59	−7.58
83.12	53.69	Air transport	82.25	83.34	−1.31
77.99	52.87	Automobiles	61.02	60.77	+0.41
197.60	142.38	Automobile equipment	183.87	183.74	+0.07
320.56	231.89	Banks	301.83	302.03	−0.07
271.56	199.82	Building material and equipment	252.70	255.44	−1.07
355.90	250.67	Chemicals	342.62	346.72	−1.18
50.28	30.96	Closed-End Invest	40.40	40.43	−0.07
1,520.94	932.59	Drugs	1,484.03	1,481.12	+0.20
613.73	373.59	Electrical equipment	570.09	570.09	. . .
705.44	451.01	Farm equipment	627.64	626.78	+0.14
332.46	231.67	Foods and beverages	315.19	319.39	−1.31
1,285.16	527.84	Gold mining	758.97	789.70	−3.89
302.69	233.84	Grocery chains	287.59	272.37	+5.59
202.95	148.54	Installment financing	178.40	180.94	−1.40
1,121.38	893.38	Insurance	1,005.42	1,030.66	−2.45
829.14	548.48	Liquor	732.70	737.34	−0.63
249.78	139.57	Machine tools	210.92	203.78	+3.50
304.27	138.87	Machinery (heavy)	215.36	223.39	−3.59
500.37	385.58	Motion pictures	499.88	500.37	−0.10
277.33	162.84	Nonferrous metals	211.13	222.00	−4.90
2,584.48	1,862.56	Office equipment	2,217.89	2,299.14	−3.53
837.30	515.50	Oil	668.26	696.49	−4.05
267.51	179.05	Packing	254.51	258.52	−1.55
292.50	212.07	Paper	288.22	288.83	−0.21
267.98	154.36	Railroad equipment	253.25	255.78	−0.99
390.56	315.06	Retail merchandise	364.91	362.89	+0.56
246.00	154.12	Rubber	238.87	243.47	−1.89
207.70	150.74	Steel and iron	192.73	195.89	−1.61
753.08	441.25	Television	710.37	679.75	+4.50
218.30	154.13	Textiles	208.78	208.39	+0.19
219.33	138.74	Tobacco	208.39	213.52	−2.40
1,004.69	759.13	Dow Jones Industrials	936.60	946.76	−1.07
425.68	233.69	Dow Jones Transportation	391.79	404.70	−3.19
117.81	96.04	Dow Jones Utilities	109.28	111.29	−1.81
388.87	271.73	Dow Jones Composite	363.37	370.25	−1.86

1980–81 high and lows through preceding week. In this table daily closings for trading week ended Friday used in the range for the Dow Jones Averages.

erage because it more closely corresponds to the variety of stocks the average investor may have in his or her portfolio.

Value Line weights each stock equally so that Genaral Motors has the same weight as a small company, such as Wendy's International. While changes in the Dow Jones averages and Standard & Poor's indexes reflect primarily the fluctuation in value of total shares outstanding, changes in the Value Line Average reflects more accurately the fluctuation of stock prices. Value Line may suit individual investor's needs, but professional managers have a tendency to weight their managed portfolio against the industry composition of the S&P 400 or 500 Index. Some managers have even gone so far as to construct portfolios where the industry weight equals the S&P index weight.

Other market indexes

Indexes are also computed and published by the New York Stock Exchange, American Stock Exchange, and the National Association of Security Dealers. Each index is intended to represent the performance of all the stocks traded in a particular exchange or market. As can be seen from the previously presented Table 4–2, the NYSE publishes a composite index as well as an industrial, utility, transportation, and financial index. Each index represents the stocks of a broad group or type of company. The NYSE Composite Index is market value weighted similar to the S&P 500 Stock Index and does not have to be adjusted for stock splits or stock dividends since these occurrences do not change total market value of the company. The American Stock Exchange also includes an index which is an unweighted index. The American Exchange Market Value Index simply adds or subtracts the daily net price change from the previous day's index. It is actually more like an average than an index since it does not have a base period.

The National Association of Securities Dealers, which is the self-governing body of the over-the-counter markets, also constructs several indexes to represent the companies in their market. They publish the NASDAQ OTC composite, industrial, insurance, and banking indexes which are also listed in Table 4–2.

The direction of the indexes are all closely related, but they do not necessarily move together all the time. If you are a pension fund manager trying to "outperform the market," then the choice of index may be crucial as to whether the fund manager maintains his or her accounts. The important thing for you as well as a professional when measuring success or failure of performance is to use an index that represents the risk characteristics of the portfolio being compared to the index. If you only want a general idea as to whether the market is going up or down over time, the choice of the average or index is not that critical since they all move fairly closely together.

Bond market averages   Performance in the bond market is not widely followed by way of an index or average but usually is gauged by interest rate movements. Since rising interest rates mean falling bond prices and falling rates signal rising prices, investors can usually judge the bond market performance by yield

curve changes or interest rate graphs. *Barron's* does publish an index of 20 bonds; 10 utility bonds, and 10 industrial bonds, but this is not widely used.

Mutual fund averages   Lipper Analytical Services publishes the Lipper Mutual Fund Investment Performance Averages shown in Table 4–4 taken from *Barron's.* Lipper publishes three basic fund indexes for growth funds, growth-with-income funds, and balanced funds. Additionally, the average performance on a year-to-date and weekly basis are included for 330 mutual funds covering several categories of investment objectives.

BUYING AND SELLING IN THE MARKET

Once you are generally familiar with the market and perhaps decide to invest directly in common stocks or other assets, you will need to set up an account with a retail brokerage house. Some of the largest and better-known retail brokers are Merrill Lynch; Shearson/American Express; Bache; and E. F. Hutton, but there are many other good houses both regional and national. When you set up your account, the account executive (often called stockbroker) will ask you to

Table 4–4   Lipper Mutual Fund Investment Performance Averages, Thursday November 19, 1981

	LIPPER FUND INDICES	Percentage Change			AVERAGE FUND PERFORMANCES	Percentage Change	
	Close	Year to date	Weekly	Number	Type of fund	Year to date	Weekly
Growth funds	147.73	− 9.63	−2.33	65	Capital appreciation	− 3.33	−2.46
				163	Growth	− 4.05	−2.03
Growth income	217.72	− 3.80	−1.44	81	Growth and income	− 1.21	−1.36
				24	Equity income	+ 8.25	−0.40
Balanced funds	182.49	− 2.78	−0.72	333	Average performance	−2.36	−1.84
OTHER MARKET INDICATORS				23	Balanced	+ 0.54	−0.48
Dow Jones Industrials	844.74	−12.37	−1.84	28	Income	+ 6.10	+0.84
				2	Insurance	+17.81	+0.14
S&P 500	120.71	−11.09	−2.01	8	Specialty	− 3.38	−0.82
				7	Gold	−26.20	−4.89
S&P 400	134.01	−13.23	−2.00	11	International	− 3.62	+0.65
				12	Option	+ 4.87	−0.78
N.Y.S.E. Composites	70.36	− 9.63	−1.86	93	Fixed income	+ 8.45	+1.45
				517	Average performance	+ 0.16	−0.98
AMEX Index	311.05	−10.87	−4.31	517	Median performance	+ 0.61	−1.09

Data supplied by Lipper Analytical Services. Year to date and weekly percentage changes on Thursday for mutual funds include reinvestment of income dividends and capital gains distributions, other market indicators do not. Only funds in existence for the entire period covered are included. Total number of funds, by objective, may include funds with net asset values unavailable at compilation time.

fill out a card listing your investment objectives, such as: conservative, preservation of capital, income oriented, growth plus income, or growth. The account executive will also ask for your social security number for tax reporting, the level of your income, net worth, employer, and other basic information. Basically he or she needs to know the client's desire and ability to take risk in order to give good advice and proper management of the investor's assets.

Cash or margin account

The account executive will need to know if you want a cash account or margin account. Either account allows you five business days to pay for any purchase. A cash account requires full payment, while a margin account allows the investor to borrow a percentage of the purchase price from the brokerage firm. The percentage of the total cost the investor must pay is called the margin and is set by the Federal Reserve Board. During the great crash in the 1920s, margin was only 10 percent, but it was as high as 80 percent in 1968. It has been at 50 percent since January 1974. The margin percentage is used to control speculation. When the Board of Governors of the Federal Reserve System thinks that the markets are being pushed too high by speculative fervor, they raise the margin requirement, which means that more cash must be put up. The Board of Trade did this to the silver and gold markets in 1980 to quell the rapid rise in silver prices from $9 to $50 per ounce. The Hunt brothers of Texas felt the pinch when their margined silver contracts fell from $50 to $20 an ounce over several months, and they incurred substantial losses on borrowed money (the price of silver actually fell below $8 an ounce in 1982).

Margin accounts are used mostly by traders and speculators or by investors who think their long-run return will be greater than the cost of borrowing. Most brokerage houses require a $2,000 minimum in an account before loaning out money, although many brokerage houses have higher limits. Here is how a margin account works. Assume you purchased 100 shares of IBM at $60 per share on margin and that margin is 50 percent.

Purchase: 100 shares of IBM at $60 per share	$6,000
Borrow: Cost (1 − margin percentage)	−3,000
Equity contributed, cash or securities	$3,000

You can borrow $3,000 or (1 − margin percentage) times the total cost. The cost of borrowing is generally 1 to 2 percent above the prime rate depending upon the size of the account. Rather than putting up $3,000 in cash, a customer could put $3,000 of marginable stock into his account to satisfy the margin. Not all stocks may be used for margin purchases. The Securities and Exchange Commission publishes a list of approved securities which may be borrowed against.

One of the reasons people buy on margin is to leverage their returns. Assume that IBM rises to $80 per share. The account would now have $8,000 in stock

and an increase in equity of $2,000, or a 67 percent increase over the original cash invested.

100 shares of IBM at $80	$8,000
Loan	−3,000
Equity	$5,000

Leverage creates a 67 percent gain on a 33 percent increase in the stock price. The customer now can purchase $2,000 more in securities since the equity of $5,000 will support $10,000 of securities (equity divided by margin = initial market value of securities).

Margin is a two-edged sword however, and what works out to your advantage in up markets, works to your disadvantage in down markets. If IBM had gone to $40, your equity would decrease.

100 shares of IBM at $40	$4,000
Borrowed	−3,000
Equity	$1,000

Your equity would now be at minimum maintenance standards where the equity of $1,000 equals 25 percent of the market value. A fall below $1,000 would bring a margin call for more cash or equity. Many brokerage firms have maintenance requirements above 25 percent, and when margin calls are made, the equity often needs to be increased to 35 percent or more of the portfolio value. In this particular example, we assume you must maintain a $2,000 minimum in your account, so you would have been called for more equity when the stock was at $50 even though the minimum maintenance requirement had not yet been reached.

An important feature of a margin account is that securities may not be delivered to the customer. In this case, the IBM would be kept registered in the street name of your retail brokerage house (e.g., Shearson, Loeb Rhoades), and your account would show your claim on 100 shares which are held as collateral for the loan. It is much like an automobile loan; you don't hold title to the car until you have made the last payment. In the use of margin, however, there is no due date on the loan. The use of margin increases risk and is not recommended for anyone who cannot afford large losses or who has no substantial experience in the market.

Long or short?— that is the question

Once you have opened the account of your choice, you are ready to buy or sell. When investors establish a position in a security, they are said to be "long" if they purchase the security for their account. It is assumed that the reason they purchased the security was to profit on an increase in price over time and/or to

receive dividend income. An investor who is long may take delivery of the securities (keep them in physical possession) if he or she has a cash account. An investor with a cash account may also choose to keep them on deposit in his/her brokerage account to facilitate bookkeeping, dividends, safekeeping, and ease of sale. A margin account user has no choice but to keep them with the broker in "street name."

Sometimes investors anticipate that the price of a security may drop in value. If they are long in the stock, some may sell out their position. Those who have no position at all may wish to take a "short" position in order to profit from the expected decline. When you short a security, you are borrowing the security from your broker and selling it with the obligation to replace the security at a future time. How you can sell something you don't own is an obvious question. Remember the margin account and the fact that securities must be kept by the broker. Your broker will simply loan you the security from the brokerage house inventory. If your brokerage house doesn't have an inventory of the particular stock you want to short, the firm will borrow the stock from another broker.

A short sale may only be made if you have a short sale margin account, and you must put up the value of the security the same way as if it were a purchase except that the accounting is different. An investor would need to have a margin account (type 2) and a short sale margin account (type 5) in order to sell short. Let us look at a short sale of 100 shares of Litton at $70 per share. The sale would net $7,000 in cash which would show up as a credit in your type 5 account, and at the same time, you would incur a $7,000 debit by being short 100 shares at $70 per share. Additionally, this transaction has to be margined, and your margin account (type 2) would have to have $3,500 of equity available. Essentially, the brokerage firm has a total of $10,500 available to cover the repurchase of the stock which eventually has to be replaced. The type 5 account (short sale margin account) is always balanced where the debit equals the credit. Any increase in equity is transferred to the type 2 margin account, and any decrease in equity is borrowed from the type 2 margin account. Let us follow an example over several time periods. In time period 1, the investor establishes a short position.

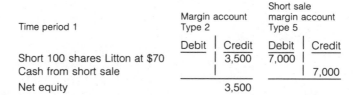

Time period 1	Margin account Type 2		Short sale margin account Type 5	
	Debit	Credit	Debit	Credit
Short 100 shares Litton at $70		3,500	7,000	
Cash from short sale				7,000
Net equity		3,500		

In the second time period, Litton rises to $90 and the short position remains open, but $2,000 has to be borrowed from the margin account to balance the type 5 account.

Time period 2	Type 2		Type 5	
	Debit	Credit	Debit	Credit
Short 100 shares Litton at $90		3,500	9,000	
Cash from short sale				7,000
Borrowed on margin	2,000	__ transferred __		2,000
Net Equity		1,500		

The net equity position declines to $1,500 because of the $2,000 loss of equity as Litton rose $20 per share. Notice the type 5 account stays balanced. Finally, Litton falls to $50 per share in the third time period providing a net credit in the type 5 account of $4,000. This is transferred into the type 2 account to pay off the $2,000 loan and increase the equity.

Time period 3	Type 2		Type 5	
	Debit	Credit	Debit	Credit
Short 100 shares Litton at $50		3,500	5,000	
Cash from short sale				7,000
Borrowed	2,000			2,000
Increased equity		4,000 transferred 4,000		
Net equity		5,500		

If the investor closes his position at the end of time period 3, the type 5 account would cancel out as the $5,000 available cash is used to repurchase $5,000 of Litton stock. The investor would be left with an increased equity of $2,000 up to $5,500.

Time period 3 ending balance	Type 2		Type 5	
	Debit	Credit	Debit	Credit
Short 100 shares Litton		3,500	5,000	
Cash from short sale to repurchase				5,000
Increased equity		2,000		
Net equity		5,500		

Investors sometimes sell short to establish beneficial tax positions. For example, if you had bought Digital Equipment at $60 and seven months later it was $100, you would have a $40 per share short-term profit on paper. If you want to preserve the profit but wait until next year to pay the tax, you can "sell short against the box." This means you can short shares against those you already hold. Since you own the stock and also have a short position, you can neither gain nor lose by price movements in the stock. In the following tax year, you can

deliver the shares you hold to cover your short position. At that point, you will incur the tax obligations associated with the transactions. The total net profit will still be $40.

TYPES OF ORDERS

When an investor places an order to establish a position, he or she has many different kinds of orders from which to choose. When the order is placed with the account executive on a NYSE-listed stock, it is teletyped to the exchange where it is executed by the company's floor broker in an auction market. Each stock is traded at a specific trading post on the floor of the exchange, so the floor broker knows exactly where to go to find other brokers buying and selling the same company's shares.

Most orders placed will be straightforward market orders to buy or sell. The market order will be carried by the floor broker to the correct trading post and will usually trade close to the last price or within ¼ of a point. For example, if you wanted to sell 100 shares of AT&T at market, you would probably have no trouble finding a ready buyer since AT&T may be trading 300,000 to 500,000 shares per day. On the other hand, if you wanted to sell 100 shares of Bemis, there might be as little as only 1,000 shares traded in a day, and no other broker would be waiting at the Bemis post to make a transaction with the floor broker. If the broker finds no one else wishing to buy the shares he is selling, he will transact the sale with the specialist who is always at the post ready to buy and sell 100-share "round lots." If the broker wants to sell, the specialist will either buy the shares for his own account at ⅛ to ¼ less than the last trade or will buy out of his book in which special orders are kept.

There are two basic special orders, the "limit order" and the "stop order." A limit order limits the price at which you are willing to buy or sell and assures you that you will pay no more than the limit price on a buy or receive no less than the limit price on a sell. Assume you are trying to buy a thinly traded stock that fluctuates in value and you are afraid that with a market order you might risk paying more than you want. So, you would place a limit order to buy 100 shares of Bell Industries at 16½ or a better price. The order will go to the floor broker who goes to the post to check the price. The broker finds Bell Industries trading at its high for the day of 16⅞, and so he leaves the limit order with the specialist who records it in his book. The entry will record the price, date, time, and brokerage firm. There may be other orders in front of yours at 16½, but once these are cleared and assuming the stock stays in this range, your order will be executed at 16½ or less. Limit orders are used by investors to buy or sell thinly traded stocks or to buy securities at prices thought to be at the low end of a price range and to sell securities at the high end of the price range. Investors who calculate fundamental values have a basic idea of what they think a stock is worth and will often set a limit to take advantage of what they view to be discrepancies in values.

Many traders are certain that they want their order to be executed if a certain price is reached. A limit order does not guarantee execution if orders are ahead of you on the specialist's book. In cases where you want a guaranteed "fill" of the order, a stop order is placed. A stop order is a two-part mechanism. It is placed at a specific price like a limit order, but when the price is reached, the stop turns into a market order which will be executed at close to the stop price but not necessarily at the exact price specified. Often there will be a common price that many short-term traders will view with optimism for a certain trading strategy. When the stock hits the price, it may pop up on an abundance of buy orders or decline sharply on a large volume of sell orders, and your "fill" could be several dollars away from the stop price. Assume that AXE Corporation stock has been trading between $25 and $40 per share over the last six months reaching both these prices three times. A trader may follow several strategies. One strategy would be to buy at $25 and sell at $40 using a stop buy and a stop sell order. There may be some traders putting in a stop buy at $41 thinking that if the stock breaks through its peak trading range it will go on to new highs, and finally some may put in a stop sell at $23 to either eliminate a long position or establish a short position with the assumption that the stock has broken its support and will trend lower. When used to eliminate a long position, a stop order is often called a stop-loss order.

Limit orders and stop orders can be "day orders" that expire at the end of the day if not executed, or they can be GTC (good til cancelled) orders. GTC orders will remain on the specialist's books until taken off by the brokerage house or executed. If the order remains unfilled for several months, most brokerage houses will send reminders that the order is still pending so that the client does not get caught buying stock for which he is unable to pay. Orders have been known to stay on the specialist's books for years.

If a customer really wants to create a position at a limit price with certainty of it being executed upon hitting the price, he or she may place a limit order for an odd lot. An odd lot is an order for less than the 100-share round lot. Odd-lot orders are executed off the exchange by an odd-lot dealer, or in the case of Merrill Lynch, odd lots are executed by the brokerage firm itself without the customary $\frac{1}{8}$ to $\frac{1}{4}$ extra cost. The important point for this example is that odd-lot prices are related to round-lot prices on the floor of the exchange, and an order to sell 99 shares at 50 will be executed off the floor at 50 whenever the price on the floor hits 50. This does not facilitate larger block trades by institutional investors but does help individuals trade without stop orders if necessary.

COST OF TRADING

Since May 1, 1975, commissions have been negotiated between the broker and customer with larger orders getting smaller percentage charges. Before "May Day" commissions were fixed, and all brokers charged the same fee out of a published table. Now there are individual variations, so check with several bro-

kers. If commissions are of concern, you may want to do business with a "discount" broker who charges a discount of up to 70 percent from the old fixed-commission schedule.

Discount brokers have sprung up as bare-bones operators providing only transactions but no research. They have found a niche with those investors who make up their own minds and do not need advice or personal service. Discount brokers do not have many regional offices located around the country (but may be represented in some of the largest cities like New York, Chicago, and Los Angeles). Instead, they rely on toll-free, long distance "WATS" lines for their customers.

Regular brokerage houses still offer more personal service and more variety of services and are often part of a financial corporation involved in underwriting and investment banking, managing mutual funds, pension funds, economic advising, government bond dealings, and more. Unfortunately, you pay extra when dealing with a full-service broker. Table 4–5 sets forth the fees for one national brokerage house.

Most full-service brokers still use a formula for computing commissions, but they also negotiate rates on large, block transactions of from $300,000 to $500,000 and are willing to give actively trading customers discounts from the formula if their business over the year makes them a large trader in volume.

The fees in Table 4–5 are not necessarily an industry standard, and you may find variations of these fees from broker to broker. However, most firms will have a similar structure charging a commission based on the dollar value of the transactions and the number of shares purchased. Don't be embarrassed to ask your broker what the commission will be before you make any trades.

TAXES

In the previous sections, we discussed trading strategies and different types of orders that can be used to transact purchases and sales. In the brief example about selling short against the box, it was indicated that for tax reasons an investor would choose to defer taxes. As we go through this section, the basics of taxation on investment income will be considered.

Short-term versus long-term gains and losses

There are different effective tax rates on short-term and long-term holdings. The Internal Revenue Service defines long-term as being over one year for stocks, bonds, and other physical assets, such as a house, antiques, stamps, coins, etc. On commodity futures contracts, the break between long-term and short-term is six months.

Short-term gains are taxed as ordinary income, which is at the effective marginal tax rate of the investor. Short-term losses may be used to offset short- or long-term gains. Any net loss that is short-term may be deducted from ordinary income—up to $3,000 per year. For example, if an investor incurred a $10,000

Table 4—5   **Example of round-lot commissions**

Trades	Commissions
Under → $800	2.500% + $11
801–2,500	1.875 + 16
2,500–5,000	1.395 + 28
5,000–20,000	1.255 + 35
20,000–30,000	0.910 + 104
Over 30,000	0.560 + 209

short-term loss in 1982, he could deduct $3,000 in 1982 and carry forward the $7,000 difference into 1983, which could again be used to offset gains. Net short-term losses can be carried forward indefinitely until used up.

Long-term gains receive preferential tax treatment. The IRS allows 60 percent of long-term gains to be excluded from taxation so that the maximum tax an investor will pay is his or her marginal tax rate times $(1 - .6)$. If you are in the 40 percent marginal bracket, your maximum tax would be $40\% \times (1 - .6)$, or 16 percent. This reduced rate makes long-term gains very advantageous and is one good reason to prefer long-term gains to short-term gains. Table 4—6 sets forth the tax liability of different gains demonstrating the advantages of long-term gains.

Timing of gains and losses

Because of the tax laws, the best kind of gain is long-term which minimizes the tax and the best kind of loss is short-term because it maximizes your deductions. The worst tax combination would be to take long-term gains and short-term losses in the same year because they are netted out before the long-term gains receive any exclusion. Examples of these points are presented in Table 4—7.

By separating the gain and loss in different years (alternative 1), the total tax savings is $1,200 minus $480, or $720 in reduced taxes. When the short-term loss is combined with the long-term gain in the same year (alternative 2), the tax savings evaporates as they are netted off against one another. This demonstrates the advantages of timing the gains and losses. There are many other combinations that could be covered. If you want to match up short-term gains and long-term losses or any other combinations and compute the tax savings or liabilities, we leave that up to you.

Table 4—6   **Short-term versus long-term gains**

Short-term gain	$10,000	Long-term gain	$10,000
No exclusion	–0–	60% excluded	6,000
Taxable gain	$10,000	Taxable gain	$ 4,000
Marginal tax rate	40%	Marginal tax rate	40%
Tax	$ 4,000	Tax	$ 1,600
Effective tax rate	40%	Effective tax rate	16%

Table 4—7   **Short-term loss and long-term gain**

Alternative 1

Short-term loss, year 1	($3,000)
Marginal tax rate 40%	
Tax savings on ordinary income	1,200
Long-term gain, year 2	3,000
Exclusion 60%	1,800
Taxable income	1,200
Marginal tax rate 40%	(480) Tax

Alternative 2

Short-term loss, same year	($3,000)
Long-term gain, same year	3,000
Net taxable gain or loss	0 No tax

There are many other tax consequences an individual should be aware of, such as tax shelters, estate planning, and gift taxes. These will be covered more completely in the final chapter on estate planning.

INDIVIDUAL INVESTMENTS OR MUTUAL FUNDS

The investor must also determine whether he or she will participate in the market individually or through a mutual fund. We will explore the implications of investments through mutual funds.

A mutual fund or investment company professionally manages an investor's money in a portfolio consisting of many securities, sometimes numbering in the hundreds. The investor owns a share of the portfolio assets equal to his number of shares in the fund. There are several advantages to this approach. An investor with a small amount of money (under $10,000) can achieve diversification through the large number of securities in the portfolio. This diversification eliminates the risk of being concentrated in two or three securities. Other people may have larger sums of money to invest but not have the time or skill to manage it as well as a professional.

The performance of equity mutual funds follows the stock market in general, and since the 1974 market drop, mutual funds have not been very popular vehicles for investment as more investors in funds redeemed their old shares than bought new ones. Figure 4–2 shows the relationship between 1975 and 1980 of redemptions versus sales.

In Chapter 15, we will go through a thorough review of the performance of mutual funds in comparison to popular market indicators. For now, we would say that the long-term performance has not been particularly impressive, although some mutual funds have turned in good performances in the last few years, specifically the aggressive, growth-oriented funds.

Figure 4—2   **Mutual fund sales and redemptions**

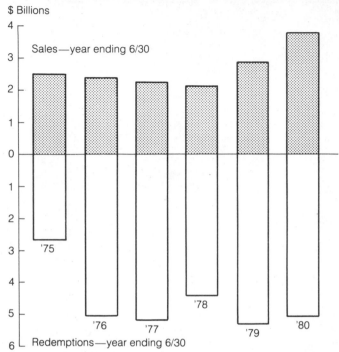

Note: Figures are for equity funds only.

SOURCE: *Investment Company Institute,* presented in *Forbes,* September 1, 1980, p. 69.

Closed versus open-end funds

A closed-end mutual fund is similar to the common stock of corporations. The supply is fixed, and the only way an investor can purchase the fund shares is from another investor. Some closed-end funds trade on the New York Stock Exchange and others over-the-counter. Many are bond funds. Closed-end funds usually sell at a discount from the market value of assets held (net asset value) because they are not as liquid as open-end funds. Of the 22 closed-end funds in *Forbes'* 1980 annual mutual fund survey, each one sold at a discount from net asset value. Occasionally, a closed-end fund may sell at a premium over net asset value because one or more stocks in the portfolio is not publicly traded and is carried on an artificially low-cost basis. It is felt by the market that the true value of the shares is much greater than cost, so a premium in the portfolio occurs.

Open-end funds comprise the majority of investment funds and allow investors to buy and sell shares at the net asset value (NAV) plus a possible commission for the trade. There is no limitation on the number of shares. The open-end mutual fund stands ready to redeem shares or sell new shares at the net asset value per share. This NAV per share is equal to the market value of the portfolio minus

liabilities divided by the total shares outstanding in the mutual fund. If a mutual fund owner wants to sell his or her shares, the money is paid out, and the shares are retired. This does not cause any change in net asset value per share or penalize other investors in the fund. *The Wall Street Journal* lists the daily prices of open-end funds. An example appears in Figure 4–3.

Load versus no-load funds

Load and no-load funds both do the same thing in terms of managing an investor's money, but the load fund charges a commission (called a load) of between 7.25 and 8.5 percent on stock funds but occasionally as little as 2.5 percent on bond funds. According to *Forbes'* 1980 Annual Mutual Fund Survey, Affiliated Fund was the largest stock fund with $1.570 billion in assets and a load of 7.25 percent. It was followed by The Dreyfus Fund at $1.512 billion with a maximum load of 8.5 percent. Load funds are the predominant type of stock fund based on asset size and numbers of investment companies. There is a good

Figure 4–3

Mutual Funds

Tuesday, April 28, 1981

Price ranges for investment companies, as quoted by the National Association of Securities Dealers. NAV stands for net asset value per share; the offering includes net asset value plus maximum sales charge, if any.

	Offer NAV	
	NAV	Price Chg.
Able Assoc	23.85	N.L.– .36
Acorn Fnd	28.14	N.L.– .36
ADV Fund	15.41	N.L.– .14
Afuture Fd	15.48	N.L.– .23
AIM Funds:		
Conv Yld	15.42	16.49– .16
Edsn Gld	13.97	14.94– .23
HiYld Sc	9.10	9.73– .06
Alpha Fnd	17.82	N.L.– .24
Am Birthrt	12.27	13.41– .09
American Funds Group:		
Am Bal	9.00	9.84– .06
Amcap F	12.47	13.63– .09
Am Mutl	12.66	13.84– .11
An Gwth	10.24	11.19– .09
Bnd FdA	11.22	12.26– .01
Fund Inv	9.01	9.85– .11
Gth FdA	13.13	14.35– .13
Inc FdA	8.29	9.06– .04
I C A	9.38	10.25– .11
Nw Prsp	8.31	9.08– .05
Wash Mt	7.77	8.49– .08
American General Group:		
A GnCBd	6.10	6.67– .03
AG Entp	15.05	16.45– .19
Gn Exch	40.63	N.L.– .47
Growth	27.66	N.L.– .57
High Yld	9.11	9.77– .03
G Mun	15.60	16.38 ...
...	22.41	24.49– ...

	Offer NAV	
	NAV	Price Chg.
Direct Cap	2.36	N.L. ...
DodgC Bal	24.12	N.L.– .14
DodgC Stk	21.45	N.L.– .23
Drx Burnh	15.48	N.L.– .14
Dreyfus Group:		
A Bonds	12.27	N.L.– .01
Dreyf Fd	15.57	17.02– .15
Dreyf Lv	22.52	24.61– .13
Numbr 9	12.43	N.L.– .07
Spl Incm	7.55	N.L.– .03
Tax ExB	10.15	N.L. ...
Third Cn	8.81	N.L.– .06
Eagle Gth	9.77	10.68– .15
Eaton & Howard:		
Balncd F	8.26	8.91– .03
Foursq	10.36	N.L.– .09
Growth	21.30	22.96– .24
Income	4.13	4.45 ...
Spec Fnd	14.28	15.40– .15
Stock Fd	11.56	12.46– .08
Eberstadt Group:		
Chem Fd	10.44	11.41– .09
Enrgy R	14.61	15.97– .05
Surveyr	17.34	18.95– .15
Elfun TIF	(z)	(z) ...
Elfun Trst	(z)	(z) ...
Evrgrn Fd	35.88	N.L.– .41
Fairfld		11.16– .12
F		.11

	Offer NAV	
	NAV	Price Chg.
Inv Indicat	1.59	(z) – .05
Inv Qualty	8.75	9.16 ...
Inv Tr Bos	13.05	14.07– .16
Investors Group Funds:		
IDS Bnd	4.10	4.24+ .01
IDS Gth	15.17	16.49– .27
IDS HYd	3.61	3.76 ...
IDS nwD	10.25	11.14– .11
IDS Prog	5.18	5.63– .09
IDS Tax	3.12	3.25 ...
Mutual	9.47	10.30– .05
Stock Fd	21.32	23.18– .18
Selectv	6.58	7.07 ...
Var Pay	10.28	11.17– .11
Inv Resrch	5.79	6.33– .11
I S I Group:		
Growth	6.11	6.68– .06
Income	3.43	3.75– .02
TrPa Shr	(z)	(z) ...
Trust shr	9.79	10.70– .04
Istel Fund	32.54	N.L.– .38
Ivy Fund	10.41	N.L.– .05
JP Growth	12.92	14.04– .08
JP Income	7.03	7.64– .01
Janus Fnd	10.38	N.L.– .15
John Hancock Funds:		
Balanc	8.37	9.10– .06
Bond Fd	12.48	13.57– .06
Growth	11.57	12.58– .19
Tax Ex	8.83	9.60– .02
Kauf Fund	2.34	N.L.– .03
Kemper Funds:		
Income	7.32	7.79– .03
Growth	11.98	13.09 ...
High Yld	8.51	...
Mun		...

	Offer NAV	
	NAV	Price Chg.
Price Rowe:		
Growth	14.49	N.L.– .18
Income	7.95	N.L. ...
New Era	21.57	N.L.– .06
Nw Horz	18.33	N.L.– .23
Tax Free	7.84	N.L.– .01
Pro Services Funds:		
Med Tec	17.46	N.L.– .22
Pro Fnd	9.16	N.L.– .13
Pro Inco	7.39	N.L.– .01
Prud SIP	13.48	14.73– .11
Putnam Funds:		
Convert	13.92	15.21– .04
George	13.04	14.25– .11
Growth	12.08	13.20– .07
High Yld	14.55	15.60– .07
Income	5.55	5.95– .02
Intl Equi	17.69	19.33– .07
Investr	10.14	11.08– .16
Option	14.12	15.43– .11
Tax Ex	17.59	18.47– .01
Vista Fd	17.35	18.96– .24
Voyage	16.64	18.19– .36
Rainbw Fd	3.79	N.L.– .01
Revere Fd	8.48	N.L.– .08
Safeco Group:		
Equity	12.40	N.L.– .09
Growth	17.51	N.L.– .13
Income	11.70	N.L. ...
St Paul Funds:		
Captl Fd	15.01	15.97– .15
Growth	15.09	16.05– .34
Cd	24.89	N.L.– .50
		N.L.– .14
		– .70

Note: N.L. = No-load (no commissions).

reason for this since load funds are sold by salesmen who collect a portion of the commission. Many load funds have declining sales charges as larger amounts of money are invested.

No-load funds do not charge commissions and are sold directly by the investment company through advertisements, prospectus, and (800) WATS-line telephone orders. As of June 30, 1980, no-load funds comprised about 25 percent of all stock fund assets, and during the third quarter of 1980, they accounted for 43 percent of all new stock fund sales. The controversy for years has always been which type of fund performs better. Many feel that load funds, because of their larger size, have better management, while others feel that small funds have better potential to outperform the market. Actually, some of the no-load funds are not that small; T. Rowe Price Growth Stock Fund had $919.4 million in assets as of June 30, 1980. This popular no-load fund also has a fairly low annual expense per $100 of assets. In fact, notwithstanding size differences, both types of funds perform about the same—there is no significant statistical difference between them. Given that performance is approximately equal, most astute investors will shop around for a no-load fund to fit their needs rather than pay a commission.

Choosing a fund to meet your objectives

For years, equity funds and bond funds have been the stable old favorites of mutual fund portfolios, but in recent years, an emphasis on tax-free income funds and money market mutual funds have given new impetus to investment companies. Let's look at a number of different types of funds, moving from the stock funds to the less traditional areas. The reader may also wish to consult the Wiesenberger Financial Services *Investment Companies* guide for additional information on individual mutual funds (published annually by Warren, Gorham & Lamont, Boston).

Stock funds Investors can find any kind of stock fund to meet their needs for growth, income, high risk, high technology, natural resources, or other very specific investment strategies. For example, funds investing in international securities like the Templeton Growth Fund may provide an investor additional diversification as well as professional management in securities an investor is unable to get research on or unable to keep up with because of the time and expense involved in following international securities. Often mutual fund names indicate the emphasis or objectives of the fund. The following list of mutual funds will give you an idea of the variety.

American Insurance and Industrial Fund	L
Franklin Custodian Funds Utilities Series	L
ISI Income Fund	L
Over-The-Counter Securities Fund	L
Technology Fund	L
United Science & Energy Fund	L
Energy Fund	N.L.

Financial Industrial Income Fund	N.L.
Johnston Capital Appreciation Fund	N.L.
Rowe Price New Horizon Fund	N.L.
Steadman Oceanographic Technology & Growth Fund	N.L.

Note: L = Load fund; N.L. = No-load fund

Index funds Many research studies have examined the ability of mutual fund managers to outperform the broad market as measured by the S&P 500. The findings indicate that some funds do outperform the market and some do not, but there is no statistical significance to prove that professional managers can do better than the market year after year.

In response to these realities, some mutual funds have been started where the portfolio is weighted by company to be exactly equal to the S&P 500 Stock Index weights or any other index used for a market measure. This has stirred much controversy because it is a tacit admission that you can't outperform the market. The question is, should the manager of this kind of fund be paid when in fact there is no analysis or decision making necessary? Management fees should be at a minimum. If you believe that common stocks are good long-term investments but that you can't outperform the market on a consistent basis, maybe you could be comfortable with an index fund.

Balanced funds These funds combine investments in common stock and bonds and often preferred stock, and try to provide income plus some capital gains. But on the whole, they have not performed as well as the S&P 500 Stock Index. Forbes Balanced Fund average total return between 1968 and 1980 was 4.1 percent versus 4.5 percent for the S&P 500. Funds that invest in convertible securities are also considered to be balanced since the convertible security is a combination fixed-income security with the chance for appreciation if the underlying common stock rises.

Bond and preferred stock funds These funds invest in both bonds and preferred stock with the emphasis on income rather than growth. In the period of the late 1970s with interest rates reaching 20 percent on short-term securities and 14 to 15 percent on long-term bonds, many new mutual funds of this type were started. Between June 1979 and June 1980, these funds on average earned high interest but also lost between 4 and 13 percent on declining portfolio values.

Money market funds These funds have been the phenomenon of the late 1970s and early 1980s. *Forbes'* Mutual Fund Survey lists 81 money market mutual funds with the largest by far being Merrill Lynch Ready Asset Trust at over $11 billion and three others at over $3 billion. Money market mutual funds invest in short-term government securities, commercial paper, and repurchase agreements and have been very popular during periods of high short-term interest rates. Since most funds offer check-writing privileges in minimums of $500, many

people have taken their funds out of banks and savings and loans to take advantage of rates never before available to small investors.

The benefits of a money market fund are the high return that is related to interest rates and also the rate of inflation. Money market funds are no-load, and most require a minimum deposit of $1,000 (many require $5,000). This is to discourage those who would use these funds as a bank account. Length of time to maturity on money market portfolios averages between 20 and 50 days. When rates are expected to come down, the maturity lengthens, and vice versa. These funds have definitely provided the small investor an opportunity to invest in securities that were out of reach before money market funds (T bills have a minimum investment of $10,000). Over three fourths of mutual fund assets are now invested in money market funds.

Municipal bond funds These provide the investor tax-free income, liquidity, and a diversified portfolio of municipal securities that are somewhat illiquid when held in small amounts by individuals. *Forbes* lists 40 such tax-free bond funds. The average load runs about 4 percent, but 15 are no-load funds.

Many of the municipal bond funds are specializing in short-term municipals, which eliminate the wild fluctuations in long-term bond prices. These funds are of greatest use to investors in high marginal tax brackets since the aftertax income on a tax-free portfolio may be better than the aftertax return on a taxable bond portfolio. For example, if an investor is in the 50 percent marginal tax bracket, he or she would be indifferent between an 8 percent tax-free yield and a 16 percent taxable yield.

Final comment on funds

An investment in mutual funds offers the investor the advantages of diversification and professional management, though mutual funds are unlikely to provide returns that are superior to the popular market averages over a long period of time. The individual must assess his or her own desires to determine if this is the optimum vehicle for market participation. Some individuals thrive on the idea of placing their own orders, charting their own performance, and generally determinating their own fate. For them, a mutual fund deprives them of these opportunities. However, there are others who wish to delegate the difficulties and time-consuming activities of money management to others, and mutual funds serve as an excellent outlet.

SUMMARY

The investor should have a basic understanding of measures of market performance, the rules and mechanics of opening and trading in an account, basic tax considerations, and the comparative advantages of investing individually through mutual funds.

In gauging the movements in in the market, the investor may view the Dow Jones Industrial Average, the Standard & Poor's 400 Industrials, the Standard & Poor's 500 Stock Index, the Value Line Average of 1,700 companies, or the NASDAQ averages (to name but a few). To evaluate various industry securities, the investor may turn to *Barron's* Group Stock Averages and for mutual funds to the Lipper Mutual Fund Investment Performance Averages. The investor will try to evaluate his or her performance in light of an index that closely parallels the makeup of his or her portfolio.

With some understanding of the various markets and the related means of measurements for those markets (such as the DJIA), the potential investor is now in a position to consider opening up an account. The investor may establish either a cash or margin account and use the account to buy securities or to sell short (in which case a margin account is necessary). The investor can also execute a number of different types of orders, such as a market order, a limit order, and a stop order. The latter two specify prices where the investor wishes to initiate transactions.

The investor must also consider the tax consequences of his or her actions. Important distinctions must be made between short-term and long-term capital gains and losses, with the latter representing a holding period in excess of one year. The IRS allows 60 percent of long-term capital gains to be excluded from taxation, so that the maximum the investor will have to pay on such a transaction is his or her marginal tax rate times 40 percent. Generally, it is best to establish long-term capital gains where possible and take losses short-term. If there are only short-term losses, $3,000 may be written off annually against ordinary income, with the balance carried forward.

While some investors prefer to directly manage their own financial resources, others look to the mutual fund industry for help. The fund may be either a closed-end investment company or an open-end mutual fund (with unlimited shares available). Mutual funds may be either loads (requiring commissions) or no-loads, and there is no discernable difference in performance between the two. Because of this, the investor is advised to consider going the no-load route and avoiding the commission. There are all types of funds available including those that specialize in common stocks, corporate bonds, preferred stock, and municipal bonds (and combinations thereof). Money market funds, which are no-load mutual funds specializing in short-term, high-yielding securities, have become particularly popular in the last few years.

IMPORTANT WORDS AND CONCEPTS	Dow Jones Industrial Average	Sell short against the box
	Barron's Group Stock Averages	Limit order
	Standard & Poor's 400 Industrials	Stop order
	Standard & Poor's 500 Stock Index	Long-term gains and losses

True Index
Value Line Average
NYSE Index
American Stock Exchange Index
Weighted Index
NASDAQ OTC Indexes
Lipper Mutual Fund Investment
  Performance Averages
Margin account
"Long" position
"Short" position

Short-term gains and losses
Investment company
Mutual fund
No-load fund
Open-end fund
Closed-end fund
Net asset value
Index fund
Balanced fund
Money market fund

QUESTIONS AND PROBLEMS

1. What four stock indexes comprise the Dow Jones Averages?

2. How is the Dow Jones Industrial Average adjusted for stock splits?

3. What are the criticisms and defenses of the DJIA?

4. Suggest an index that would be appropriate for measuring industry performance.

5. What types of stocks are included in the S&P 500 Stock Index that are not part of the S&P 400 Industrials?

6. If the S&P 500 Stock Index is 140, what percent is this above the base period value for the 1941–43 period?

7. What is a value-weighted index? Are the Standard & Poor's Indexes value weighted? Is the Value Line Average value weighted?

8. Explain the difference between a cash and a margin account.

9. Assume you buy 100 shares of stock at $50 per share on margin (50 percent). If the price rises to $60 per share, what is your percentage gain in equity? Disregard interest costs.

10. In the problem above, what would the percentage loss be if the price had decreased to $35?

11. Explain how a short sale works.

12. Assume a short sale of 100 shares of stock at $50 per share. There is a margin requirement of 50 percent.
    a. How much net equity must you initially show in the type 2 margin account?
    b. If the price of the stock goes to $60, what will your net equity position be?

13. Explain what is meant by a limit order.

14. What is difference between day orders and GTC orders?

15. If your marginal tax rate is 43 percent, what is the maximum tax you would pay on a long-term capital gain?

16. Assume an investor in a 45 percent tax bracket has a $4,000 short-term gain and a $5,000 long-term gain. How much total tax will be paid?

17. An investor has a $12,000 short-term loss in 1983. What is the maximum deduction he can take against ordinary income? How much will be carried forward into future years?

18. Assume the same investor in problem 17 had short-term gains of $15,000 in 1984. If he is in a 40 percent marginal tax bracket, how much total tax will he pay?

19. Another investor has short-term losses of $3,000 in 1983. She is trying to decide whether to take a $5,000 long-term capital gain in the same year or wait until January of the following year to take the gain. She is in a 45 percent tax bracket. If she takes the gain and loss in the same year, how much tax will she pay?

20. Assume the same investor in problem 19 waits until 1984 to take the gain. Compare the tax savings in 1983 on the $3,000 write-off to the taxes paid in 1984 on the long-term capital gain. What is the net value? Comparing the answers in questions 19 and 20, should the investor wait until January of 1984 to take her gain?

21. Assume the same circumstances in problem 20, except that the investor is in a 50 percent tax bracket in 1984. Should she still wait until 1984 to take her long-term capital gains or take them in 1983?

22. Contrast closed- and open-end mutual funds.

23. Why might someone want to invest in a mutual fund? Does statistical evidence indicate that mutual funds outperform the general market?

24. Contrast load and no-load funds. Does one tend to show superior performance over the other?

25. What are some of the different types of mutual funds?

26. Why have money market funds been popular with small investors?

SELECTED REFERENCES

Branch, Ben, and Walter Freed. "Bid-Asked Spreads on the AMEX and the Big Board." *Journal of Finance,* March 1977, pp. 159–63.

Butler, Hartman L., Jr., and J. Devon Allen. "The Dow Jones Industrial Average Reexamined." *Financial Analysts Journal,* November–December 1979, pp. 23–30.

Groth, John C.; Wilbur G. Lewellen; Gary G. Schlarbaum; and Ronald C. Lease. "An Analysis of Brokerage House Securities Recommendations." *Financial Analysts Journal,* January–February 1979, pp. 32–40.

Grube, R. Corwin; O. Maurice Joy; and Don B. Panton. "Market Response to Federal Reserve Changes in the Intitial Margin Requirement. *Journal of Finance,* June 1979, pp. 659–74.

Hopewell, Michael H., and Arthur L. Schwartz, Jr. "Temporary Trading Suspensions in Individual NYSE Securities." *Journal of Finance,* December 178, pp. 1355–73.

Latane, Henry A.; D. L. Tuttle; and W. E. Young. "Market Indices." *Financial Analysts Journal,* September–October 1971, pp. 75–85.

Lewellen, Wilber G.; Ronald C. Lease; and Gary G. Schlarbaum. "The Personal Investments of Professional Managers." *Financial Management,* Winter 1979, pp. 28–36.

Lorie, James H., and Mary T. Hamilton. "Stock Market Indexes." In *Modern Developments in Investment Management,* ed. James H. Lorie and Richard Brealey. New York: Praeger Publishers, 1972.

Mahon, Gigi. "Sunny Side of the Street: Discount Brokers Increase Share of Trade." *Barron's,* June 11, 1979, p. 11.

Molodovsky, Nicholas. "Building a Stock Market Measure." *Financial Analysts Journal,* May–June 1967, pp. 43–48.

Reilly, Frank K. "Stock Price Changes by Market Segment." *Financial Analysts Journal,* March–April 1971, pp. 54–59.

Regan, Patrick J. "The 1976 BEA Pension Fund Survey." *Financial Management,* Spring 1977, pp. 48–65.

Rudd, Andrew. "The Revised Dow Jones Industrial Average: New Wine in Old Bottles?" *Financial Analysts Journal,* November–December 1979, pp. 57–63.

Schultz, John W. "Misleading Averages." *Barron's,* July 7, 1977, p. 5.

Shepard, Lawrence. "How Good is Investment Advice for Individuals?" *Journal of Portfolio Management,* Winter 1977, pp. 32–36.

West, Richard R., and Seha M. Tinic. "Institutionalization: Its Impact on the Provision of Marketability Services and the Individual Investor." *Journal of Contemporary Business,* Winter 1974, pp. 25–48.

5

Investment strategy in differing economic environments

The frequent stories in the newspaper about the impact of inflation on our lifestyles has, at times, dulled our sensitivity. One might say, so what if the cost of housing went up by 10 percent last year or the price of gasoline is over $1 a gallon? However, there is a very real problem, and it rests on the long-term, all-pervasive effect that inflation has on our ability to purchase needed goods and services and make rational decisions. In Table 5–1, we see the impact of an 8 percent rate of inflation on the cost or valuation of certain key economic variables over a 20-year period.

Though arguments can be made that the 8 percent rate should be lower or higher, the results are worthy of observation. For example, we note that the average, run-of-the-mill, three-bedroom, two-bath house would cost over $300,000 at the end of 20 years. In the San Francisco Bay Area, the figure would be closer to half a million dollars. While not everyone will opt to own his or her own home and alternate lifestyles may become necessary, the fact remains that those who do wish to acquire ownership of a $300,000 house will face a down payment of perhaps $60,000 and annual mortgage payments of $20,000 to $25,000 per year.

Table 5–1   **Potential impact of inflation**

	1981	2001
Existing three-bedroom home	$68,200.00	$317,880.00
Automobile	7,000.00	32,627.00
Gallon of gasoline	1.25	5.83
Dinner for two at a nice restaurant	25.00	116.52
Movie for a family of four	14.00	65.24
Visit to the doctor	18.00	84.00
Average private school tuition	3,750.00	17,475.00
Textbooks for the semester	125.00	582.63
Starting salary—bachelor's degree in business	17,000.00	79,237.00
Midlevel executive salary	35,000.00	163,135.00
Poverty level (family of four)	8,414.00	39,218.00

Other items in Table 5–1 follow a similar pattern—a routine trip to the doctor will cost $84, and the anticipated poverty level income for a family of four will be $39,218. We wish to point out to students that these numbers do not relate to some futuristic concept that would apply to their great-grandchildren, but could relate to the time period in which they will make many of their major purchases. In order to acquire some historical perspective, rates of inflation over a 35-year time period are presented in Figure 5–1.

INVESTMENT STRATEGIES

The student should realize that there are investment strategies for every circumstance. A 1980 study by Salomon Brothers, a prestigious bond underwriting house, indicates the results shown in Table 5–2 for different types of investments over a 10-year time period.

First of all, note that these returns were earned in an inflationary period in which overall consumer price increases averaged 6 to 8 percent annually. Strategies that worked well during the late 1960s and 70s may not be the solutions for the 80s and 90s if inflation diminishes. In a later section of this chapter, we will take a hard look at investment strategies that are appropriate for an economy in which inflation is abating.

STOCKS AND INFLATION

Because a primary investment outlet discussed in the text is common stocks, we deem it particularly important that students understand how stocks perform in an inflationary environment. As indicated in Table 5–2, equities were the third lowest performers in the 10-year inflationary period (though they did quite well in 1980). First of all, we examine why this is the case and also some of the accounting and valuation problems related to the corporation in an inflationary environment. We then examine how stocks have performed over a half century in which there was inflation, deflation, and stable prices, and we see that their comparative performance was good. Finally, we look at some of the causes and cures for inflation so that the student can draw his or her own conclusions about the likelihood for the persistence of inflation in the future.

THE DIVIDEND VALUATION MODEL AND INFLATION

As discussed in Chapter 1, under the dividend valuation model, the price of a share of stock is equal to:

$$P_0 = \frac{D_1}{(1 + K_e)^1} + \frac{D_2}{(1 + K_e)^2} + \frac{D_3}{(1 + K_e)^3} + \ldots + \frac{D_\infty}{(1 + K_e)^\infty} \quad (5-1)$$

D (dividends) are assumed to be growing at the rate of g each year, and if g is

Figure 5—1   **Rates of inflation in the U.S. economy, 1946—1981**

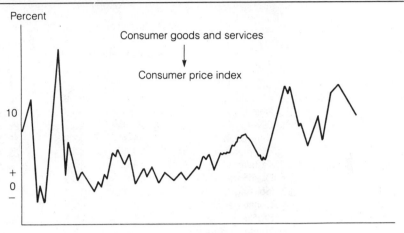

SOURCE: *Federal Reserve Historical Chart Book* (Washington, D.C. Federal Reserve Board of Governors), 1981.

reasonably constant and $K_e > g$ (the discount rate exceeds the growth rate), the equation may be rewritten as:

$$P_0 = \frac{D_1}{K_e - g} \qquad (5-2)$$

Shifting terms, we then show:

$$K_e = \frac{D_1}{P_0} + g \qquad (5-3)$$

K_e refers to the required return (or discount rate) on an investment in common

Table 5–2   **Annualized returns on alternate investments, 1971–1980**

	10 years (1971–80)	5 years (1976–80)	1 year (1980)
Oil	30.8%	20.9%	14.3%
Gold	28.0	30.9	−13.9
Oriental carpets	27.3	20.9	−0.2
U.S. coins	27.1	29.7	−8.0
U.S. stamps	23.5	32.9	18.0
China, ceramics	22.9	30.7	36.5
Silver	21.5	20.1	−26.6
Rare books	16.8	13.8	18.0
Old masters	15.4	16.8	22.9
Farmland	14.6	14.8	9.7
Diamonds	14.5	16.9	0.0
Housing	10.3	11.6	8.1
Consumer price index	8.3	9.7	10.0
Stocks	5.8	9.8	25.3
Foreign exchange	5.3	3.1	−17.3
Bonds	3.8	1.1	−9.6

SOURCE: Robert S. Salomon, Jr., Salomon Brothers.

stocks. It represents the anticipated yield in cash dividends (D_1/P_0) plus a growth *(g)* or increase in earnings, dividends, and associated valuation.

In order to assess the ability of stocks to serve as a hedge against inflation, we must study the impact of inflation on required return (K_e). Let us assume that with no inflation, K_e is equal to 4 percent.[1] But with 6 percent inflation, the investor requires a 10 percent return to compensate for inflation and still provide a 4 percent real return.

How can this increased return to 10 percent be best achieved? Examining the definition of K_e, we see that either the current dividend yield must be increased or the growth rate must be accelerated.

$$\overset{\text{Dividend yield}}{} \quad \overset{\text{Growth rate}}{}$$

$$K_e = \frac{D_1}{P_0} + g$$

In terms of numbers, assume:

$$K_e = \frac{\$2}{\$100} + 2\% = 4\% \text{ (0 inflation)}$$

But now K_e must increase to 10 percent to compensate for inflation. Assuming the current expected dividend (D_1) to be essentially a constant, this can only be achieved in the equation by lowering P_0 or by increasing g, the growth rate of future earnings or dividends.

---

[1]This is an assumed value. We could begin our analysis by using other values, such as 6 percent or 8 percent, and the conclusions would still be basically the same.

If the former is necessary, that is, P_0 must be lowered to compensate for inflation, then clearly stocks are a poor hedge against inflation. In this case, the price of a share of stock would have to go from $100 to $25.

$$\frac{\$2}{\$25} + 2\% = 10\%$$

$$8\% + 2\% = 10\%$$

The question then becomes, do corporations enjoy sufficient growth in an inflationary environment so as to increase g to the point where K_e is adjusted upward without affecting P_0? That is, can we reasonably expect:

$$\frac{\$2}{\$100} + 8\% = 10\%$$

No downward change in price · · · · · because of accelerating growth

Inflation and the growth rate

As the U.S. economy moved into the time period of the late 1960s, there was a shift from very moderate inflation of about 2 percent to an annualized rate of 7 percent as indicated in Table 5–3. This would indicate the growth rate *(g)* would have to increase by 5 percent to compensate for 5 percent greater inflationary expectations and the associated required return expectations.

What has been the pattern of increase in corporate profits and dividends during the time periods under study? We see in Table 5–4 that the *increased* rate

Table 5–3 **GNP price deflator 1958–1980**

	Annualized increase 2 percent		Annualized increase 7 percent
		1968	4.5%
		1969	5.0
1958	2.2%	1970	5.4
1959	2.2	1971	5.1
1960	1.7	1972	4.1
1961	.8	1973	5.8
1962	1.8	1974	9.7
1963	1.4	1975	9.6
1964	1.6	1976	5.3
1965	2.2	1977	5.5
1966	3.3	1978	7.5
1967	2.9	1979	8.5
		1980	9.0

SOURCE: U.S. Department of Commerce.

Table 5–4   **Change in corporate profits, 1958–1980**

Rate of growth in reported corporate profits (1968–1980)	Rate of growth in reported corporate profits (1958–1967)	Increased rate of growth	Increased inflationary expectations	Difference
9.3%	8.2%	1.1%	5%	−3.9%

SOURCE: U.S. Department of Commerce.

of growth in corporate profits (1.1 percent) has not kept pace with increased inflationary expectations (5.0 percent), in fact it has fallen behind by 3.9%.

A similar pattern prevails for corporate dividends as indicated in Table 5–5 with a shortfall of 3.5 percent between the increase in dividend payments and the increase in inflation.

Returning to the earlier equation $(K_e = \frac{D_1}{P_0} + g)$, it would appear that de-

mands for a higher K_e have not been met by g alone. Inflation has increased by 5 percent while g has only increased at a rate of about 1.5 percent (1.1 percent for earnings, 1.5 percent for dividends). Thus, the higher returns demanded by stockholders have also been partially achieved by lowering the price of the stock and increasing the current divided yield.

The irony is that old stockholders who need a higher return to compensate for inflation are actually burdened with a decrease in value of their holdings so that the current return offered to prospective investors is in line with returns in the marketplace.

**REPORTED
VERSUS
ADJUSTED
EARNINGS
IN AN
INFLATIONARY
ENVIRONMENT**

Even the earnings patterns depicted in Table 5–4 do not portray the full effect of inflation. The values are assumed to be based on historical cost accounting methods. While historical cost accounting was not a major problem between 1958 and 1967, it was in the 1968–80 era. In the latter time period, there were substantial phantom profits that were the results of FIFO (first-in, first-out) inventory accounting and the underdepreciation of plant and equipment.

Inventory that was purchased a year ago at $1 and sells today at $1.25 may appear to bring 25 cents in profit, but perhaps 15 cents of the gain is simply the result of inflation. The problem is increased by the fact that in 1980, two thirds of all U.S. companies used FIFO accounting (representing one half of total inventories). While LIFO (last-in, first-out) accounting would more closely match current costs to current prices, many companies fear the initial shock effect on reported performance to shareholders.

Corporations have less choice in the matter of depreciation. Assets are gen-

Table 5—5   **Change in corporate dividends, 1958—1980**

Rate of growth in corporate dividends (1968–1980)	Rate of growth in corporate dividends (1958–1967)	Increased rate of growth	Increased inflationary expectations	Difference
8.0%	6.5%	1.5%	5%	−3.5%

Payout rates (1958)	Payout rates (1968)	Payout rates (1980)		
51.1%	41.6%	34.3%		

SOURCE: U.S. Department of Commerce.

erally depreciated on a historical cost basis, which may provide an asset value below that required to replace plant and equipment in the future. A $1 million, 10-year asset that is depreciated at the rate of $100,000 per year may not reflect the true cost of, perhaps, $2.5 million dollars to replace the asset after its anticipated life.

The Bureau of Economic Analysis of the U.S. Department of Commerce collects data on corporate profits based on reported earnings and adjustments for inflation (related to inventory gains and underdepreciation). Values for 1958 through 1980 are reported in Table 5–6.

Of particular interest is the year 1974. In 1974, profits before taxes were $126.9 billion, but over a third of this amount was inflation-induced with an inventory valuation adjustment figure of $40.4 billion and underdepreciation of $2.9 billion.

Although the Securities and Exchange Commission and the Financial Accounting Standards Board have endorsed supplemental reporting requirements that use measures besides historical cost, the reported bottom-line figure in the annual report is essentially based on historical cost data. Hopefully, much more progress and acceptance will take place along the lines of additional reporting.

The corporation further suffers in that taxes are paid on the inflated rather than the adjusted values in Table 5–6. The 1980 corporate tax bill was $20 billion greater based on earnings related to historical costs (column 1) than it would have been on earnings adjusted for inflation (column 4). While the effective tax rate was a mere 34% of reported profits based on historical costs in 1980, the effective tax rate actually represented 43% of income after inflation adjustments as indicated in Figure 5–2.[2] The same basic points can be made for the individual who enjoys illusory gains during inflation.[3]

On an adjusted basis, corporate dividends also consume a much larger per-

---

[2] The effective rate is the average rate paid by all corporations and is not the same as the maximum corporate tax rate.

[3] The individual suffers even more in that inflation continually takes him into higher marginal tax brackets as his income increases during inflation. The 1981 tax legislation will alleviate part of this problem.

Table 5—6   **Reported and adjusted corporate profits (billions of dollars)**

Year of reporting	(1) Profit before taxes	(2) Inventory valuation adjustment	(3) Underdepreciation (capital consumption allowance)	(4) Profit before taxes—adjusted for inflation
1958	41.1	−0.3	−3.4	37.4
1959	51.6	−0.5	−2.9	48.2
1960	48.5	0.3	−2.3	47.8
1961	48.6	0.1	−1.8	47.8
1962	53.6	0.1	1.2	55.8
1963	57.7	−0.2	2.1	59.6
1964	64.7	−0.5	2.8	67.0
1965	75.2	−1.9	2.8	76.1
1966	80.7	−2.1	3.9	82.5
1967	77.3	−1.7	3.7	79.3
1968	85.6	−3.4	3.7	85.9
1969	83.4	−5.5	3.5	81.4
1970	71.5	−5.1	1.5	77.9
1971	82.0	−5.0	0.3	77.3
1972	96.2	−6.6	2.5	92.1
1973	115.8	−18.6	1.9	99.1
1974	126.9	−40.4	−2.9	89.4
1975	123.5	−12.0	−12.2	99.3
1976	155.9	−14.5	−14.4	127.0
1977	173.8	−14.8	−14.9	144.1
1978	223.3	−24.3	−13.5	185.5
1979	255.4	−42.6	−15.9	196.9
1980	245.9	−45.7	−17.2	183.0

SOURCE: U.S. Department of Commerce.

centage of income as indicated in Figure 5–3. A dramatic example is 1974 when dividends represented 40 percent of reported earnings but almost 100 percent of inflation-adjusted aftertax income.

Net debtor—creditor hypothesis

To ensure that we are not overly negative in looking at the effects of inflation, there is a potentially positive benefit that should be examined. A firm is said to be in a net debtor position when monetary liabilities exceed monetary assets. By this, we mean accounts payable, bank loans, and long-term debt exceed receivables or other forms of credit extension. To the extent a firm is in a net debtor position, it can benefit from inflation. Why? Because loans on the books are being repaid with cheaper dollars. If inflation has increased by 100 percent since a loan was negotiated 10 years ago and the dollar thus shrinks to 50 percent of its former value, the debtor can repay each dollar of the loan with current dollars that are the equivalent of 50-cent pieces at the time the loan was negotiated. Equipment that had a real value of $1 million when purchased in 1970 may be paid off in the equivalent of $500,000 of real purchasing power.

Of course, the lender will attempt to protect against this form of benefit to the

Figure 5—2 **Corporate taxes as a percentage of reported and inflation-adjusted profits**

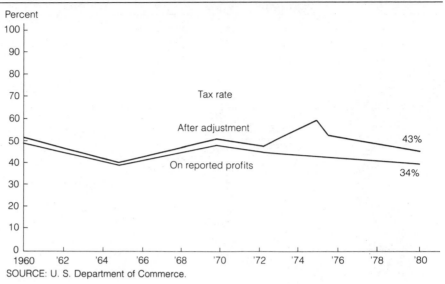

SOURCE: U. S. Department of Commerce.

debtor by charging a sufficiently high interest rate to provide not only for a real return, but also for some measure of compensation for inflationary expectations. Thus, the lender may have a desired real rate of return of 3 percent[4] and also require an additional 5 percent as an inflation premium to compensate for the loss of purchasing power in an inflationary environment. If the rate of inflation meets the lender's expectations of 5 percent, the net debtor position loses its advantage. The lender has been compensated for his inflationary expectations. What has happened, however, is that the lender has consistently guessed too low on inflation and allowed the debtor to benefit. Perhaps only 8 percent was charged when it should have been 12 percent.

Real return	3%	Real return	3%
Inflation expectation	5	Actual inflation	9
Rate changed	8%	Correct rate	12%

Thus, the borrower continues to pay off the loan on a less than fully compensated basis to the lender. Some researchers have suggested that the benefits to net debtor corporations have been substantial and tend to mitigate many of the drawbacks of inflation.[5] This would tend to be true for large industrial corpora-

---

[4]A lender generally has a lower real return requirement than a stockholder.

[5]Franco Modigliani and Richard A. Cohn, "Inflation, Rational Valuation and the Market," *Financial Analysts Journal*, March–April 1979, pp. 24–42.

Figure 5—3

Dividends as a percentage of reported and inflation-adjusted aftertax profits

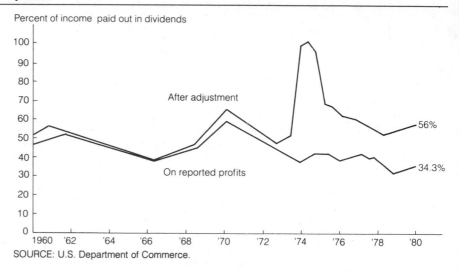

Percent of income paid out in dividends

SOURCE: U.S. Department of Commerce.

tions who are heavy borrowers. Even when creditors are wise enough (which they seldom are) to charge an interest rate that fully compensates for inflation, net debtors still benefit from the fact that interest payments are fully tax deductible as a current business expense even though part of the compensation really represents a repayment of "real principal" to the lender. A $100,000 loan that carries a 12 percent interest rate allows the borrower a $12,000 tax deduction when, in fact, he is paying $3,000 in real interest and $9,000 toward the erosion

Table 5—7

Stock prices and the rate of inflation

	Average annual percent increase in prices*	Average annual percent change in Dow Jones Industrial Average
1952–55	1.4%	16.1%
1956–57	3.8	(5.3)
1958–65	1.6	10.5
1966–70	4.3	(3.5)
1971–72	2.9	12.3
1973–74	8.9	(10.3)
1975–76	6.2	15.1
1977–80	8.2	3.0

Note: The dates do not coincide with exact calender periods but represent approximations of the beginning and ending of inflationary patterns.
*Measured by government's implicit price deflator for GNP.

of the lender's real capital (hardly a business expense!). One might pity the lender who is paying taxes on the full $12,000 as if it were profit.

Though the net debtor-creditor hypothesis may serve as a partially mitigating factor to the ravages of inflation, there are winners as well as losers. If borrowers benefit, then surely lenders must sacrifice. What is gained by an airline is lost by a bank or manufacturer carrying heavy receivables. Both Kessel[6] and DeAlessi[7] found almost an even split between the number of net debtors and net creditors among U.S. corporations over a long period of time. Perhaps, the increased corporate borrowing of the 1970s, funded in part by private lenders, has created more net debtors for now, but the basic pattern remains intact.

A long-term view of the stock market and inflation

A number of arguments have been made to the effect that the stock market is not a good inflation hedge. Let us take a harder look at the evidence. In Table 5–7, we see the relationship between rates of inflation and stock prices between 1952 and 1980. In every time period chronicled, as the rate of inflation increased from its prior level, stock prices did not do as well. As the inflation rate abated from its prior level, the market rallied.

A similar pattern can be viewed in Table 5–8, in which we examine stock prices during five key inflationary periods between 1941 and 1973. In column 1, we see the nominal total returns on stocks as measured by five different indicators. The term *nominal* refers to actual reported dollars unadjusted for inflation. In column 2, we have total real returns which are equal to total nominal returns (column 1) minus the rate of inflation during the period of time under study. On the bottom sector of the table, the weighted average return for all five of these time periods is presented.

We see the weighted average for the Dow Jones (DJ) Industrial Average was 5.1 percent on a nominal basis, but adjusting for inflation, it was a negative 1.6 percent. A similar pattern prevails for most of the other indexes, with the Standard & Poor's Utilities Index showing the weakest nominal and real returns. Public utilities suffer the most since they must continually go before regulatory commissions to achieve price increases in an inflationary environment. Although they tend to benefit from being in a net debtor position on older, outstanding debt they also face the prospect of higher costs on new financing.

EXPANDING THE PERSPECTIVE

Most of our inflation and market analysis has covered the post-World War II time period with particular emphasis on the era beginning in the mid-to-late 1960s.

[6]Reuben A. Kessel, "Inflation Caused Wealth Redistribution: A Test of Hypothesis," *American Economic Review,* March 1956, pp. 128–41.

[7]Louis DeAlessi, "Do Business Firms Gain from Inflation?" *Journal of Business,* April 1964, pp. 162–66.

Table 5—8   **Indicators of market performance during periods of inflation**

Market indicators	(1) Nominal return	(2) Real return
3/31/41 to 6/30/43:		
DJ Industrials	12.8%	2.7%
S&P 425 Industrials	17.6	7.1
S&P Utilities	6.5	−3.1
S&P Rails	21.3	10.5
S&P 500 Stocks	16.6	6.2
3/31/46 to 9/30/48:		
DJ Industrials	0.2	−11.0
S&P 425 Industrials	−0.7	−11.7
S&P Utilities	−5.8	−16.3
S&P Rails	−6.0	−16.4
S&P 500 Stocks	−1.5	−12.5
3/31/50 to 12/31/51:		
DJ Industrials	24.9	16.9
S&P 425 Industrials	31.5	23.1
S&P Utilities	8.5	1.5
S&P Rails	30.1	21.8
S&P 500 Stocks	28.4	20.2
3/31/56 to 3/31/58:		
DJ Industrials	−2.1	−5.6
S&P 425 Industrials	−6.2	−9.5
S&P Utilities	7.2	3.4
S&P Rails	−16.0	−19.0
S&P 500 Stocks	−3.1	−6.5
12/31/65 to 12/31/73:		
DJ Industrials	1.9	−2.8
S&P 425 Industrials	4.4	−0.4
S&P Utilities	−0.8	−5.3
S&P Rails	2.9	−1.8
S&P 500 Stocks	4.0	−0.8
Weighted average:*		
DJ Industrials	5.1	−1.6
S&P 425 Industrials	7.0	0.3
S&P Utilities	1.4	−4.9
S&P Rails	4.7	−1.9
S&P 500 Stocks	6.6	−1

*Weights are equal to number of months in each
inflationary period.
SOURCE: Updated results of Frank K. Reilly, Glenn L.
Johnson, and Ralph E. Smith, "Inflation, Inflation Hedges
and Common Stock," *Financial Analysts Journal.*
January—February 1970, pp. 107.

A number of studies go all the way back to the 1920s and provide a half century of perspective. As one expands the time horizon for viewing data, common stocks become a much more attractive investment vehicle. Studies by Lorie and Fisher at the University of Chicago indicate that between 1926 and 1976, stocks have provided a 9.1 percent return on investment on a nominal basis and a 6.6 percent real return after a 2.5 percent inflation adjustment.[8] Of the 9.1 percent nominal return, 4.6 percent was in the form of price appreciation and 4.5 percent in the form of dividends.

During the time span of the Lorie and Fisher study, stocks outperformed debt instruments as indicated below.

	Stocks	Long-term debt	Intermediate-term debt	Short-term debt
Nominal return	9.1%	3.4%	3.6%	3.0%
Real return	6.6	1.1	1.2	0.7

The long-term return on stocks is even more attractive when one considers that the capital gains component of the total return is taxed at a substantially lower tax rate than the interest on debt instruments.

Another study by Ibbotson and Sinquefield at the University of Chicago indicated similar results. Their study covered the 1926–74 time period, with nominal returns on common stocks averaging 8.5 percent as indicated in the first column of Table 5–9. The returns on debt instruments are also shown to be lower.[9]

INVESTMENT RETURNS AND ABATING INFLATION

Long-term observers of the market maintain that the investor should not be overly influenced by the last decade of high inflation and relatively weak equity values. The stock market made a strong comeback after the post-World War II inflationary period as the Dow Jones Industrial Average went from 300 to 900 from the mid-1950s to the mid-1960s.

---

[8]Lawrence Fisher and James H. Lorie, *A Half Century of Returns on Stocks and Bonds,* (Chicago: University of Chicago Graduate School of Business, 1977). Also, James H. Lorie and Lawrence Fisher, "Rates of Return on Investment in Common Stock," *Journal of Business,* January 1964, pp. 1–17; Lawrence Fisher and James H. Lorie, "Rates of Return on Investment in Common Stock: The Year-by-Year Record 1926–1965," *Journal of Business,* University of Chicago, July, 1968, pp. 219–316.

[9]Most market studies relating to common stock primarily focus on stocks that trade on the New York Stock Exchange. In recent times, stocks that trade on the American Stock Exchange or over-the-counter have turned in a much better performance. Of course, they represent a small percentage of total trading volume.

Table 5–9   Rates of return (1926–1974)—Ibbotson–Sinquefield study

Series	Annual rate of return	Number of years returns are positive	Number of years returns are negative	Highest annual return (and year)	Lowest annual return (and year)
Common stocks	8.5%	32	17	54.0% (1933)	−43.3 (1931)
Long-term government bonds	3.2	37	12	16.8 (1932)	− 9.2 (1967)
Long-term corporate bonds	3.6	39	10	18.4 (1970)	− 8.1 (1969)
U.S. Treasury bills	2.2	48	1	8.0 (1974)	− 0.0 (1940)
Consumer Price Index	2.2	39	10	18.2 (1946)	−10.3 (1932)
Common stocks—inflation adjusted	6.1	31	18	53.3 (1954)	−37.4 (1931)
Long-term government bonds— inflation adjusted	1.0	29	20	30.2 (1932)	−15.5 (1946)
Long-term corporate bonds— inflation adjusted	1.4	31	18	23.5 (1932)	−13.9 (1946)
U.S. Treasury bills—inflation adjusted	0.1	29	20	12.6 (1932)	−15.2 (1946)

SOURCE: Roger G. Ibbotson and Rex A. Sinquefield, "Stocks, Bonds, Bills, and Inflation: Year-by-Year Historical Returns (1926–1974)," *Journal of Business*, University of Chicago, January, 1976.

Even moderate abatement from inflation can trigger off substantial rallies. If investors anticipate a 10 percent rate of inflation and it is only 8 percent, this will lower their total required return by 2 percent. With an assumed 4 percent required real return, this means K_e, or the total required return on common stock, would go from 14 percent to 12 percent. Using the formula

$$K_e$$
(Total required return) = real return + return to compensate for inflation

then at 10 percent inflation

$$4\% + 10\% = 14\%$$

and at 8 percent inflation

$$4\% + 8\% = 12\%$$

Though it would appear that K_e still remains high with 8 percent inflation, the really significant fact is that it is coming down from 14 percent to 12 percent.[10] Since stocks were previously valued using a 14 percent discount rate and are now valued using a 12 percent discount rate, they should go up in price.

---

[10]No explicit risk premiums are considered here.

Using a previously developed formula (Equation 5–3), we see that with D (dividends) and growth (g) assumed to be constant, in order for the K_e (required return) to decrease, P_0 (price) must increase.

$$K_e = \frac{D_1}{P_0} + g$$

Constant

Constant

Decline

Must increase for K_e to decline

Thus it is not the absolute level of inflation that is critical, but rather the adjustment from prior levels and expectations. Eight percent inflation following 10 percent inflationary expectations may be a more positive market influence than 4 percent inflation following 2 percent inflationary expectations. In the latter case, overall stock prices might be higher, but they would probably be moving in a downward direction. Perhaps the Dow Jones Industrial Average would be going from 1,100 to 1,000.

Bond prices

Bond prices should also benefit from abating inflation. The required return on a debt instrument also includes a real rate of return plus compensation for inflation. With lesser inflationary expectations, the required return will diminish, and this means that future interest payments and the maturity value of a bond will be discounted at a lower rate providing a higher present value or price. Longer-term debt instruments are particularly sensitive to inflationary influences on the required rate of return.

Once again, we would emphasize that it is the change in inflationary expectations that is most important rather than absolute levels. A 2 percent drop in inflationary expectations may raise a bond price from 800 to 900. Although it is still trading below par value, a 100-point gain has taken place.

Bond traders tend to be somewhat cynical about changes in inflationary expectations. Because of their sophisticated training and many scars from past false movements in the financial markets, they desire concrete evidence of fundamental changes in the inflationary environment before taking action. Both bond and stock traders tend to be particularly concerned about large federal budget deficits and their long-term effect on inflationary expectations.

Real assets

Real assets tend to be victims of abating inflation. Since gold, silver, and various forms of collectibles are hedges against inflation, their values may decline with perceptions ot lessening inflation. This was certainly the case with the price of gold and silver in the early 1980s. After increasing from $35 an ounce to

$875 an ounce in the 1970s, gold prices declined by 60 percent. Silver made a similar ascent from $4 to over $50 an ounce, only to retreat by 80 percent due to economic circumstances.

Not all real assets are quite so volatile, and some collectibles may hold their value reasonably well in abating inflation if they are of high quality. Actually, real estate may benefit from a slight reduction in inflation because the associated lower interest rates may mean greater ease in financing property. However, a major decline in inflation would hurt real estate values as well.

INFLATIONARY CONSIDERA-TIONS FOR THE PRESENT

Perhaps the most distressing feature in the inflationary environment of the 1970s was the inability of the 1973–75 recession to break the inflationary spiral. Data for real gross national product and rate of inflation are presented in Table 5–10 for the 1957–80 period.

In the mid-1970s, in spite of the worst economic retraction since the Depression, prices continued upward during the recession, and the rate of increase only slowed down moderately thereafter. From 1978 to 1980, prices were once again increasing rapidly. In 1981 and 1982, some relief from inflation was once again in sight. Part of this was attributed to a recessionary environment and part to a consistent, tight money policy on the part of the Federal Reserve system.

The means of controlling current attitudes and policies toward inflation go beyond the scope of this book and are more appropriately covered in a course on economics. Nevertheless, we do wish to point out that more strategies are being proposed and adopted to increase our *supply* capability in the United States. High energy and food prices, combined with shortages of key industrial materials, have had more to do with the double-digit inflation and recessions of the 1970s

Table 5–10   Economic growth and inflation, 1957–1980

	Year	Real GNP	GNP price deflator (percent)		Year	Real GNP	GNP price deflator (percent)
Recession → (	1957	680.9	3.4%		1968	1,051.8	4.5%
	1958	679.5	2.2	Recession → (	1969	1,078.8	5.0
	1959	720.4	2.2		1970	1,075.3	5.4
Recession → (	1960	736.8	1.7		1971	1,107.5	5.1
	1961	755.3	.8		1972	1,171.1	4.1
	1962	799.9	1.8		1973	1,235.0	5.8
	1963	830.7	1.4		1974	1,217.8	9.7
	1964	874.4	1.6	Recession → (	1975	1,202.1	9.6
	1965	925.9	2.2		1976	1,271.0	5.3
	1966	981.0	3.3		1977	1,332.7	5.5
	1967	1,007.7	2.9		1978	1,385.7	7.5
					1979	1,483.0	8.5
				Recession → (	1980	1,480.7	9.0

Figure 5—4   **Personal savings as a percentage of disposable income, (five-year average, 1973—1977)**

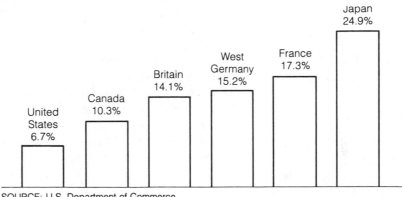

SOURCE: U.S. Department of Commerce.

than the inadequate *demand* problems of the 1930s and 1950s for which many of our current economic policies were developed.

If we can create goods and services at a more efficient and productive level, perhaps some long-term abatement of inflation is possible. Modernization of plant and equipment will require greater savings and capital formation in the United States. Personal savings as a percentage of personal disposable income has continually declined in the United States and is lower than that in most industrialized nations as indicated in Figure 5—4.

The 6.7 percent value for the United States is influenced by earlier years of relatively higher savings; in the 1981—82 period it was at a 4 to 5 percent level, making the situation even worse. There must be some reversal of this pattern if badly needed capital is to be invested and inflation brought under control.

Solutions to the savings problem include lowering taxes on earned income to increase disposable income available for savings and the reduction of taxes on earned interest to encourage savings. Increased corporate investment can also be encouraged through more rapid depreciation of plant and equipment and additional tax credits for new purchases. Some tax legislation toward this end has already been passed, but it's ultimate effectiveness remains to be seen.

Other solutions to inflationary problems include the development of a more competitive marketplace through appropriate antitrust enforcement and the decontrol of various protected industries. These, of course, are very difficult decisions and are dependent on the political philosophy of the electorate. Everyone's viewpoint must be carefully considered.

The economic outlook for the 1980s is very much dependent on our success in producing goods and services more efficiently. The question becomes, can we find ways to produce housing, energy, automobiles, industrial materials, and other goods and services in such a way that the inflation psychology will be moderated

or eliminated? It is up to the investor to make his or her decision on the probable outcome and to choose the best investment strategy based on that decision.

SUMMARY

In this chapter, we observed investments that do well in an inflationary environment and others that do not. Stocks have been a relatively poor performer in recent inflationary times because of the increasing required return (K_e) on equities dictated by a higher expected rate of inflation. This return has not been supplied by a sufficiently increased rate of growth (g) in earnings and dividends, and therefore current price (P_0) has declined or remained constant.

When one looks at earnings adjusted for FIFO inventory gains and inadequate depreciation based on historical cost accounting, the evaluation of reported earnings is downgraded. A partially balancing factor may be the net debtor position in which many corporations find themselves. To the extent that old debt obligations are currently being paid off with cheaper dollars in an inflationary environment, the corporation may benefit. Though lenders try to protect themselves by charging a sufficiently high interest rate to cover the erosion in purchasing power, their inflationary expectations have historically been set at too low a level to provide full compensation.

Even though stocks have not served as good inflation hedges in the last decade, studies by Fisher and Lorie and Ibbotson and Sinquefield indicate stocks have provided returns above the rate of inflation and above that of other liquid investments over the last 50 years. The data were compiled over a time period in which there was inflation, deflation, and price stability.

Furthermore, an abatement of inflation from high levels of expectation generally produces capital appreciation potential for equities. The investor's required rate of return should be lowered in recognition of less inflationary expectations, and this in turn produces higher stock prices. The same basic proposition applies to the bond market, though sophisticated investors may remain cynical about the economic outlook. Real assets, which thrive in an inflationary environment, will show some decline in value as inflation abates.

IMPORTANT WORDS AND CONCEPTS

Inflation
GNP implicit price deflator
Consumer price index
Dividend valuation model
Annualized rate
FIFO
LIFO
Nominal return
Real return

Lorie and Fisher study
Ibbotson and Sinquefield study
Personal savings/personal
 disposable income
Reported earnings versus
 adjusted earnings
Inflationary expectations
Net debtor—creditor
 hypothesis

QUESTIONS AND PROBLEMS

1. What key factors cause a difference between reported and adjusted earnings in an inflationary environment (that is, phantom profits)?

2. What might be the implications for tax and dividend purposes of a large difference between reported and adjusted income?

3. What is the difference between a nominal return and a real return?

4. Using the concept of the dividend valuation model, explain why stock prices tend to decrease as the rate of inflation increases.

5. If long-term inflationary expectations were to decline from 10 percent to 8 percent, what would be the probable outlook for the stock market?

6. What do the Lorie and Fisher and Ibbotson and Sinquefield studies indicate about comparative returns between common stocks, long-term debt, and short-term debt over the long term?

7. What are some possible ways to encourage savings and corporate capital investment in the United States?

8. What is the net debtor-creditor hypothesis?

9. Assessing the evidence, are common stocks a good investment as a hedge against inflation?

10. "The absolute level of inflation is not the critical factor for stock market increases." Explain.

11. How do bonds react to lessening rates of inflation?

12. How do real asset prices react to lessening rates of inflation?

13. Considering the present economic and financial environment, outline an investment strategy related to inflationary expectations.

14. Assume $K_e = \$5/\$100 + 3\%$. Growth is stable. If K_e is to go to 10 percent due to inflationary expectations, what would the price of a share of stock fall to if dividends do not increase?

15. "Even if lenders charge high rates of interest, they may not be fully compensated for the impact of inflation because of taxing considerations." Explain the meaning behind this statement.

SELECTED REFERENCES

DeAlessi, Louis. "Do Business Firms Gain from Inflation?" *Journal of Business,* April 1964, pp. 162–66.

Fisher, Lawrence, and James H. Lorie. *A Half Century of Returns on Stocks and Bonds.* Chicago: University of Chicago Graduate School of Business, 1977.

Freund, William C. "The Historical Role of the Individual Investor in the Corporate Equity Market." *Journal of Contemporary Business,* Winter 1974, pp. 1–12.

Gray, William S. III. "Developing a Long-Term Outlook for the U.S. Economy and Stock Market." *Financial Analysts Journal,* July–August 1979, pp. 29–39.

Ibbotson, Roger G., and Rex A. Sinquefield. "Stocks, Bonds, Bills, and Inflation: Year-by-Year Historical Returns (1926–1974)." *Journal of Business,* University of Chicago, January 1976, pp. 11–47.

Kessel, Reuben A. "Inflation Caused Wealth Redistribution: A Test of Hypothesis." *American Economic Review,* March 1956, pp. 128–141.

Lorie, James H., and Lawrence Fisher. "Rates of Return on Investment in Common Stock." *Journal of Business,* University of Chicago, January 1964, pp. 1–17.

————Rates of Return on Investment in Common Stock: The Year-by-Year Record 1926–1965." *Journal of Business,* July 1968, pp. 219–316.

Modigliani, Franco, and Richard A. Cohn. "Inflation, Rational Valuation and the Market." *Financial Analysts Journal,* March–April 1979, pp. 24–42.

Reilly, Frank K.; Glenn L. Johnson; and Ralph E. Smith. "Inflation, Inflation Hedges and Common Stock." *Financial Analysts Journal,* January–February 1970, pp. 104–110.

Soldofsky, Robert M., and Dale F. Max. "Securities as a Hedge against Inflation: 1910–1969." *Journal of Business Research,* April 1975, pp. 165–172.

Umstead, David A. "Forecasting Stock Market Prices." *Journal of Finance,* May 1977, pp. 427–41.

PART 2

ANALYSIS AND VALUATION OF EQUITY SECURITIES

While we often praise the investor who is fortunate enough to receive a hot tip and capitalize on it, in the real world, events do not normally follow this course. In the second section of the text, we examine the in-depth analytical process that the typical security analyst must pursue.

Initially, we look at key variables influencing the economy. The security analyst must consider the role of fiscal and monetary policy and their impact on economic conditions in the near term and over a long period of time. The security analyst also must examine business cycles, their length, and causation. An understanding of leading indicators and their ability to provide warnings about peaks and troughs in the economy is also important. We take a look at many of these items, although clearly we are drawing from a vast body of knowledge (exact and inexact) from which we can only consider the most relevant material.

As part of the consideration of economic movements, we also evaluate industry patterns. What industries peak with the economy, which go against the grain? Not only are industries influenced by the business cycle, but also by their own life cycle which is related to the ability to adjust to technological change.

The evaluation of the individual firm is the next logical step in the valuation process. We first examine valuation procedures based on the future dividends and earnings of the firm. The widely used concept of the price-earnings ratio (earnings multiplier) is also a major item for consideration.

In assessing value, the security analyst also devotes much time and attention to the examination of the financial statements of the firm. Key ratios must be computed and additional analysis done. Very little on the financial statements is accepted at face value.

Finally, a key question for any security analyst is whether the security markets are assumed to be "efficient." In an efficient market environment, securities are assumed to be correctly priced at any point in time. All relevant information is thus presumed to be impounded into the value of the security at a given point in time. At the end of this section, we will consider the pros and cons of the arguments related to this efficient market hypothesis. We also present a discus-

sion of technical analysis (the use of charting and key indicator series to predict stock prices) and its role in investment analysis.

6

Economic and industry analysis

To determine the value of the firm, the process of fundamental analysis relies on long-run forecasts of the economy, the industry, and the company's financial prospects. Short-run changes in business conditions are also important in that they influence investor's required rates of return and expectations of corporate earnings and dividends. This chapter presents the basic information for analysis of the economy and industry, while the next chapter focuses specifically on the valuation of the individual firm. In Chapter 8, we extend our discussion to include financial statement and ratio analysis for the firm.

Figure 6–1 presents an overview of the valuation process as an inverted triangle. The process starts with a macro analysis of the economy and then moves into industry variables. Next, common stocks are individually screened out according to expected risk-return characteristics, and finally the surviving stocks are combined into portfolios of assets (portfolio management is discussed in Part 4). This figure is not inclusive of all variables considered by an analyst but is intended to indicate representative areas applicable to most industries and companies.

ECONOMIC ACTIVITY AND THE BUSINESS CYCLE

An investor begins the valuation process with an economic analysis. The hope is that an accurate forecast and examination of economic activity will provide the basis for accurate stock market predictions and indicate which industries may prosper. The analyst needs information on present and expected interest rates, monetary and fiscal policy, government and consumer spending patterns, and other economic data. To be successful, investors must understand business cycles and be able to forecast accurately. Unfortunately, these are not easy tasks, but the rewards can be significant if the timing is right.

Whether or not an analyst uses statistical methods, such as regression analysis and probability theory, or simply seat-of-the-pants judgment, he or she is still

Figure 6—1　　　　　　　　**Overview of the valuation process**

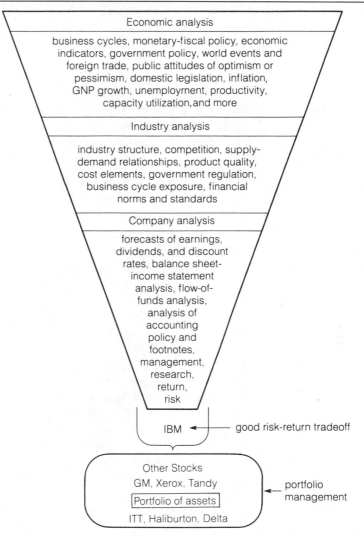

basing the forecast on expectations related to past data and experiences. Past information usually is not extrapolated into the future without being adjusted to conform with the subjective beliefs of the decision maker. Even when highly sophisticated statistical methods are used, subjectivity enters into the decision in some fashion.

Most likely, past knowledge will be helpful, but modifications for the present effects of worldwide inflation and oil cartels, which were not so important previously, need to be included in any forecast now. Since most companies are influ-

enced to some degree by the general level of economic activity, a forecast will usually start with an analysis of the government's economic program.

FEDERAL GOVERNMENT ECONOMIC POLICY

Government economic policy is guided by the Employment Act of 1946 and subsequent position statements by the Federal Reserve Board, the President's Council of Economic Advisors, and other acts of Congress. The goals established by the Employment Act still hold and cover four broad areas. These goals are the focus of monetary and fiscal policy, and they are as follows:

1. Stable prices.
2. Business stability at high levels of production and employment.
3. Sustained economic growth.
4. A balance in international payments.

These goals are often conflicting in that they do not all respond favorably to the same economic stimulus. Therefore, goal priorities and economic policies change to reflect current economic conditions. In the 1950s and early 1960s, the United States did not have an international trade problem or spiraling inflation, so the focus of economic policy was on employment and economic growth. The economy grew rapidly between 1961 and 1969, and because of the Vietnam War, unemployment reached very low levels. The demand for goods and competition for funds was very high during the war, and eventually war expenditures, large budget deficits, full employment, and large increases in the money supply caused many problems. Inflation accelerated to high levels, interest rates reached record heights, and an imbalance of international payments finally resulted in two devaluations of the U.S. dollar in the early 1970s.

By the time Jimmy Carter took office in January 1977, it was recognized that the primary goals were once again to reduce unemployment, control inflation, and create a moderate level of economic growth that could be sustained without causing more inflation (a very difficult task indeed!). The achievement of these goals was thrown into the hands of the Federal Reserve Board. The Fed's tight money policy caused a rapid increase in interest rates in order to control inflation. These high rates depressed common stock prices as the required rate of return by investors reached record levels. Ronald Reagan inherited most of the same problems as Carter but tried new ways of reaching the goals. As the early 1980s began, Reagan would rely more on fiscal policy than previous administrations in his desires to increase economic growth and control inflation. An aggressive use of both *fiscal* and *monetary* policy by the Reagan administration has been the object of both praise and criticism.

Fiscal policy

Fiscal policy can be described as the government's taxing and spending policies. These policies can have a great impact on economic activity. One must

realize at the outset that fiscal policy is cumbersome. It has a long implementation lag and is often motivated by political rather than economic considerations since Congress must approve budgets and develop tax laws. Figure 6–2 presents a historical picture of government income and expenditures. When the government spends more than it receives, it runs a deficit which must be financed through the Treasury. Deficits may be a sign that the government desires to stimulate the growth of the economy.

A forecaster must pay attention to the size of the deficit and how it is financed in order to measure its expected impact on the economy. If the deficit is financed by the Treasury selling securities to the Federal Reserve, it is very expansive. The money supply will increase without having any significant short-run effects on interest rates. If the deficit is financed by selling securities to individuals, there is not the same expansion in the money supply, and short-term interest rates will rise unless the Federal Reserve intervenes with open-market trading.

A look at Figure 6–2 shows that surpluses have occurred very infrequently from 1950 to 1980. Surpluses have a tendency to reduce economic growth as

Figure 6–2 Federal budget seasonally adjusted annual rates (quarterly)

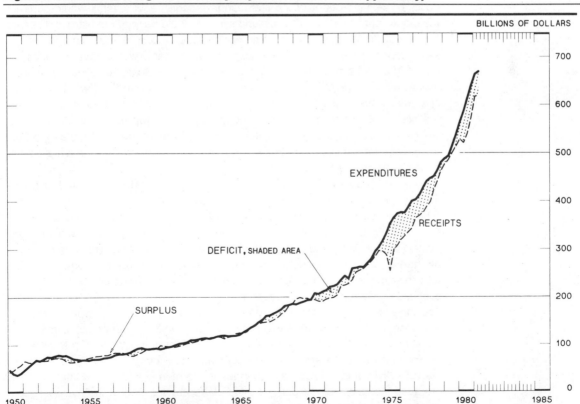

SOURCE: *Federal Reserve Quarterly Chart Book* (Washington D.C.: Federal Reserve Board of Governors, 1981).

the government slows its demand for goods and services relative to its income. In an analysis of fiscal policy, the important consideration for the investor is the determination of the flow of funds. In a deficit economy, the government usually stimulates GNP by spending on socially productive programs or by increasing spending on defense, education, highways, or other government programs. The Reagan administration instituted budget cuts in education, revenue sharing, and a rash of social programs at the same time that it reduced tax revenues through tax cuts. This strategy was one that attempted to shift GNP growth from the government sector into the private sector.

Monetary policy

Monetary policy is conducted by the Federal Reserve Board of Governors through several methods of controlling the money supply and interest rates. There are lags in the effectiveness of monetary policy, but it can be implemented very quickly to reinforce fiscal policy or, when necessary, to offset the effects of fiscal policy.

The Federal Reserve has several ways to influence economic activity. First of all, it can raise or lower the reserve requirements on commercial bank time deposits or demand deposits. An increase in reserve requirements would contract the money supply. Why? The banking system would have to hold larger reserves for each dollar deposited and would not be able to loan as much money on the same deposit base. A reduction in reserve requirements would have the opposite effect. The Fed also changes the discount rate periodically to reflect its attitude toward the economy. This discount rate is the interest rate the Federal Reserve charges commercial banks on very short-term loans. The Fed does not make a practice of loaning funds to a single commercial bank for more than two or three weeks, and so this charge can influence an individual bank's willingness to borrow money for expansionary loans to industry. The Fed can also influence bank behavior by issuing policy statements or jawboning.

Beyond these monetary manipulations, the tool most widely used is open-market operations in which the Fed buys and sells securities for its own portfolio. When the Fed sells securities in the open market, purchasers write checks to pay for their securities, and demand deposits fall causing a contraction in the money supply. At the same time, the increase in the supply of Treasury bills sold by the Fed will force prices down and interest rates up to entice buyers to part with their money. The Fed usually accomplishes its adjustments by selling securities to commercial banks, government securities dealers, or individuals. If the Fed buys securities, exactly the opposite occurs; the money supply increases, and interest rates go down. As you will see in the next chapter on stock valuation, the interest rate is extremely important in determining the required rate of return or discount rate for a stock. Many economists feel that Federal Reserve open-market activity and the resultant changes in the money supply and interest rates are good indicators of the policy position taken by the Fed. If the money supply increases and interest rates fall, the general consensus is that the Fed is encouraging economic expansion. As the money supply decreases or increases

slowly and interest rates rise, the expectation is that the Fed is "tightening up" monetary policy to restrict economic growth and inflation. It should be pointed out that the Federal Reserve can not totally control the money supply. Money market funds, the resultant monetary expansion created by banks lending money, and changing spending patterns by the population all contribute to the difficulty in controlling the money supply.

In the early 1980s, the Federal Reserve began to direct substantially more attention to controlling steady growth in the money supply rather than attempting to control interest rates. Historically, the policy had been the opposite. Thus the Fed, in recent times, has attempted to control the growth rate in the monetary aggregates of M1 (currency in circulation plus private checking deposits, including those in interest-bearing NOW accounts) and M2 (M1 plus savings accounts and money market mutual funds).

The desired growth rates for the monetary aggregates might be 3 to 5 percent for M1 and 8 to 10 percent for M2, and in the process of attempting to achieve these growth rates, interest rates might be allowed to fluctuate widely. This new era of highly volatile interest rates calls for particular adeptness by the investor.

Government policy, real growth, and inflation

There is always the danger that fiscal or monetary policy can be too stimulative. This can cause rapid economic growth, demand for goods greater than supply, rising inflation, and eventually an economy that ends up in a recession. Figure 6–3 depicts almost 30 years of gross national product (GNP) in current dollars and in inflation-adjusted 1972 dollars. In the bottom portion of the figure, we see changes in the annual growth rate for real GNP.

Figure 6–4 shows the annual percentage change in the consumer price index.

In comparing the bottom half of Figure 6–3 to Figure 6–4, notice that there is a close relationship between real GNP and inflation. The change in real GNP is inversely related to the rate of inflation. As inflation rises, real GNP falls (as indicated in 1973–75 and 1980). Since real GNP is the measure of economic output in real physical terms, it does not do any good to stimulate the economy only to have all the gains eroded by inflation. These graphs demonstrate the conflict between the goals of economic growth and stable prices. You cannot grow *too* fast without paying a price.

BUSINESS CYCLES AND CYCLICAL INDICATORS

So far we have discussed the government's impact on the economy. Fiscal policy and monetary policy both provide important clues to the direction and magnitude of economic expansions and contractions. There are other measures used to evaluate the direction of the business cycle. These measures are called economic indicators, and they are divided into leading, lagging, and coincident indicators. The National Bureau of Economic Research (NBER) classifies indicators

Figure 6—3   Gross national product seasonally adjusted annual rates (quarterly)

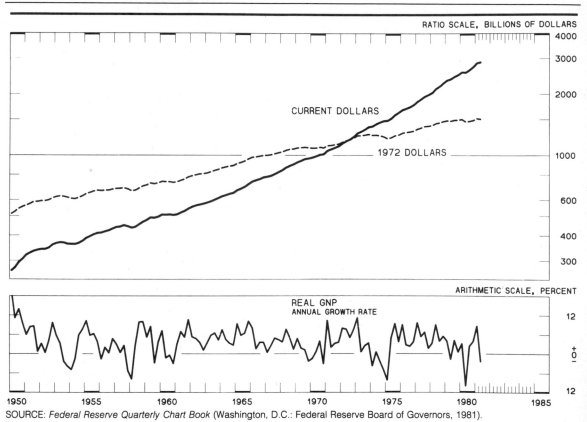

SOURCE: *Federal Reserve Quarterly Chart Book* (Washington, D.C.: Federal Reserve Board of Governors, 1981).

relative to their performance at economic peaks (end of economic expansion and beginning of recession) and troughs (end of recession and beginning of expansion).

Leading indicators change direction in advance of general business conditions and are of prime importance to the investor who wants to anticipate rising corporate profits and possible price increases in the stock market. Coincident indicators move roughly with the general economy, and lagging indicators usually change directions after business conditions have turned around.

The NBER publishes it's indicators in the monthly publication, *Business Conditions Digest* (BCD). This publication includes moving averages, turning dates for recessions and expansions, cyclical indicators, composite indexes and their components, diffusion indexes,[1] and information on rates of change. Many of the

[1]A diffusion index shows the pervasiveness of a given movement in a series. If 100 units are reported in a series, the diffusion index will indicate what percentage followed a given pattern.

Figure 6–4   **Consumer price index change in annual rates, seasonally adjusted (quarterly)**

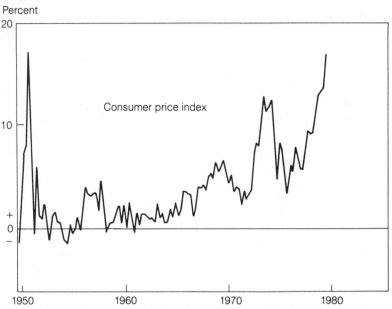

SOURCE: *Federal Reserve Quarterly Chart Book* (Washington, D.C.: Federal Reserve Board of Governors, 1981).

series are seasonally adjusted and are maintained on a monthly or quarterly basis.

Figure 6–5 presents a summary of cyclical indicators by economic process and cyclical timing with the first half (part A) of the figure presenting timing at business cycle peaks and the second half (part B) showing timing at business cycle troughs. Thus, in the upper half, we see the leading, coincident, and lagging indicators for business cycle peaks and, in the lower half, similar indicators for the bottoming out of business cycles (troughs). While we would not expect you to study or learn all the leading or lagging indicators for a cyclical peak or trough, it is important that you know that they are heavily relied upon by economists and financial analysts. Let's look more specifically at how they are used.

Leading indicators   Of the 109 leading indicators shown in the Figure 6–5, 62 lead at peaks and 47 lead at troughs. Of these, 12 basic indicators have been reasonably consistent in their relationship to the business cycle. These 12 leading indicators have been standardized and used to compute a composite index that is widely followed. It is a much smoother curve than each individual component since erratic changes in one indicator are offset by movements in other indicators. The same

Figure 6–5 Cross-classification of cyclical indicators by economic process and cyclical timing

A. Timing at business cycle peaks

Economic process ╲ Cyclical timing	(1) Employment and unemployment (18 series)	(2) Production and income (10 series)	(3) Consumption, trade, orders, and deliveries (13 series)	(4) Fixed capital investment (18 series)	(5) Inventories and inventory investment (9 series)	(6) Prices, costs, and profits (17 series)	(7) Money and credit (26 series)
Leading (L) indicators (62 series)	Marginal employment adjustments (6 series) Job vacancies (2 series) Comprehensive employment (1 series) Comprehensive unemployment (3 series)	Capacity utilization (2 series)	New and unfilled orders and deliveries (6 series) Consumption (2 series)	Formation of business enterprises (2 series) Business investment commitments (5 series) Residential construction (3 series)	Inventory investment (4 series) Inventories on hand and on order (1 series)	Stock prices (1 series) Commodity prices (1 series) Profits and profit margins (7 series) Cash flows (2 series)	Money flows (3 series) Real money supply (2 series) Credit flows (4 series) Credit difficulties (2 series) Bank reserves (2 series) Interest rates (1 series)
Roughly coincident (C) indicators (23 series)	Comprehensive employment (1 series)	Comprehensive output and real income (4 series) Industrial production (4 series)	Consumption and trade (4 series)	Backlog of investment commitments (1 series) Business investment expenditures (5 series)			Velocity of money (2 series) Interest rates (2 series)
Lagging (Lg) indicators (18 series)	Duration of unemployment (2 series)			Business investment expenditures (1 series)	Inventories on hand and on order (4 series)	Unit labor costs and labor share (4 series)	Interest rates (4 series) Outstanding debt (3 series)
Timing unclassified (U) (8 series)	Comprehensive employment (3 series)		Trade (1 series)	Business investment commitments (1 series)		Commodity prices (1 series) Profit share (1 series)	Interest rates (1 series)

B. Timing at business cycle troughs

Economic process / Cyclical timing	(1) Employment and unemployment (18 series)	(2) Production and income (10 series)	(3) Consumption, trade, orders, and deliveries (13 series)	(4) Fixed capital investment (18 series)	(5) Inventories and inventory investment (9 series)	(6) Prices, costs, and profits (17 series)	(7) Money and credit (26 series)
Leading (L) indicators (47 series)	Marginal employment adjustments (3 series)	Industrial production (1 series)	New and unfilled orders and deliveries (5 series) Consumption and trade (4 series)	Formation of business enterprises (2 series) Business investment commitments (4 series) Residential construction (3 series)	Inventory investment (4 series)	Stock prices (1 series) Commodity prices (2 series) Profits and profit margins (6 series) Cash flows (2 series)	Money flows (2 series) Real money supply (2 series) Credit flows (4 series) Credit difficulties (2 series)
Roughly coincident (C) indicators (23 series)	Marginal employment adjustments (2 series) Comprehensive employment (4 series)	Comprehensive output and real income (4 series) Industrial production (3 series) Capacity utilization (2 series)	Consumption and trade (3 series)	Business investment commitments (1 series)		Profits (2 series)	Money flow (1 series) Velocity of money (1 series)
Lagging (Lg) indicators (40 series)	Marginal employment adjustments (1 series) Job vacancies (2 series) Comprehensive employment (1 series) Comprehensive and duration of unemployment (5 series)		Unfilled orders (1 series)	Business investment commitments (2 series) Business investment expenditures (6 series)	Inventories on hand and on order (5 series)	Unit labor costs and labor share (4 series)	Velocity of money (1 series) Bank reserves (1 series) Interest rates (8 series) Outstanding debt (3 series)
Timing unclassified (U) (1 series)							Bank reserves (1 series)

SOURCE: *Business Conditions Digest* (U.S. Department of Commerce Bureau of Economic Analysis), 1981.

can be said for a similar index of four coincident indicators and six lagging indicators.

Figure 6–6 shows the performance of the composite index of leading, lagging, and coincident indicators over several past business cycles. The bracketed areas are recessions as defined by the NBER. The minus figures indicate how many months the index preceded the economy. (For lagging indicators there are plus signs.)

While the composite index of leading indicators has been a better predictor than any *single* indicator, it has varied widely at peaks, with the longest lead time being 23 months before the peak in 1957 and the shortest being 4 months in 1953. At troughs, the longest lead has been six months before the bottom in 1954 and the shortest, one month in 1974–75. Table 6–1 presents the components of the 12 leading indicators.

It can be seen by examining Table 6–1 that the 12 leading indicators do not exhibit the same notice at peaks as they do at troughs. In general, the notice prior to peaks is quite long, but the warning prior to troughs is very short, which means that it is very easy to miss a turnaround to the upside, but on the downside, you can be more patient waiting for confirmation from other indicators. It should also be noted that the indicators occasionally give false signals. Sometimes the indicators give no clear signal at all, and with the large variability of leads and lags versus the average lead time, an investor is lucky to get close to

**Table 6–1   Performance record of twelve leading indicators
1945–1971**

Series name	Mean lead time,* peaks (months)	Mean lead time,* troughs (months)	False signals (number)	Failure to signal (number)	Average score† (percent)
Average workweek, production workers, manufacturing	11	2	3	0	66%
Average weekly initial claims, state unemployment insurance	15	1	2	0	73
New building permits, private housing units	16	7	2	0	67
Net business formation	15‡	2	2	0	68
New orders, durable goods industries	7	3	2	0	78
Contracts and orders, plant and equipment	6	2	2	1	64
Change in book value, manufacturing, and trade inventories	6	1	4	0	65
Industrial materials prices	12	4	2	0	67
Stock prices, 500 common stocks	9	5	2	0	81
Corporate profits after taxes	9	2	2	0	68
Ratio, price to unit labor cost, manufacturing	14	0	1	0	69
Change in consumer installment debt	13	3	3	0	63
Composite index, reverse trend adjusted	5	4	2	0	

*The 1948–49, 1953–54, 1957–58, 1960–61, 1969–70 recessions were used to determine lead times.

†Based on a range of 0 to 100 percent. See Geoffrey H. Moore and Julius Shiskin, *Indicators of Business Expansions and Contractions* (New York: National Bureau of Economic Research, 1967.)

‡Index of net business formations was not available in determining lead time prior to the 1948 peak.

SOURCE: Clyde Farnsworth, *Monthly Review*, Federal Reserve Bank of Richmond, August 1971.

Figure 6—6 Composite indexes (leading, lagging, and coincident indexes)

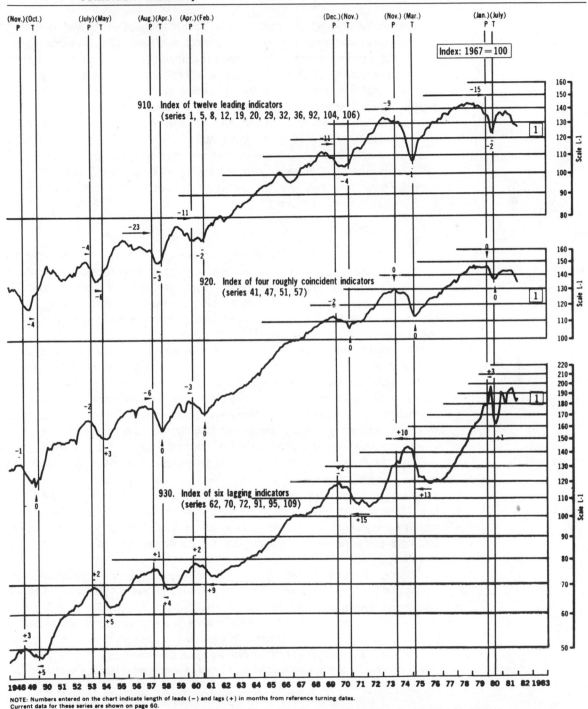

NOTE: Numbers entered on the chart indicate length of leads (−) and lags (+) in months from reference turning dates. Current data for these series are shown on page 60.

SOURCE: *Business Conditions Digest* (U.S. Department of Commerce Bureau of Economic Analysis, February, 1982).

predicting economic activity within three or four months of peaks and troughs. It becomes clear that despite economic indicators and forecasting methods, investors cannot escape uncertainty in an attempt to manage their portfolios of assets.

One very important fact that you may have noticed is that the stock market is the most reliable and accurate of the 12 leading indicators (Table 6–1). This, of course, presents a very real problem for us because our initial objective is to forecast (as well as we are able) changes in common stock prices. In order to do this, we are constrained by the fact that the stock market is anticipatory and has worked on a lead time of nine months at peaks and five months at troughs. Clearly, we need to find some variables that give longer leads than the stock market. From Table 6–1, we can see that there are several indicators that do this, but they are not always reliable.

MONEY SUPPLY AND STOCK PRICES

One variable that has been historically popular as an indicator of the stock market is the money supply. The money supply is supposed to influence stock prices in several ways. Studies of economic growth and the money supply from 1867 to 1960 by Milton Friedman and Anna Schwartz found a long-term relationship between these two variables.[2]

Why does money matter? If you are a monetarist, money explains much of economic behavior. The quantity theory of money holds that as the supply of money increases relative to the demand for money, people will make adjustments in their portfolios of assets. If they have too much money, they will first buy bonds (a modification of the theory would now include Treasury bills or other short-term monetary assets), stocks, and finally real assets. This is the direct effect of money on stock prices sometime referred to as the liquidity effect.

The indirect effect of money on stock prices would flow through the GNP's impact on corporate profits. As money influences economic activity, it will eventually influence corporate earnings and dividends and thus returns to the investors. Many studies have found that a significant relationship exists between the money supply variable and stock prices, but unfortunately, money supply growth and stock prices have turning points that are too similar to be really helpful to the investor.

Observe Figure 6–7 which includes the money supply, stock prices, and corporate profits on the same graph. It can be noted that in the 1969–70 and 1974–75 periods, the drop in the money supply did not lead the decline in stock prices enough to be helpful. In fact, during 1978 when the money supply began declining, stock prices continued to rise. This pattern of contrary movements is one that was of great interest to economists and financial analysts.

We question whether investors should react to short-term changes in the money

---

[2]Milton J. Friedman and Anna J. Schwartz, "Money and Business Cycles," *Review of Economics and Statistics,* Supplement, February 1963.

**Figure 6—7 Money supply, stock prices, and corporate
profits cyclical indicators**

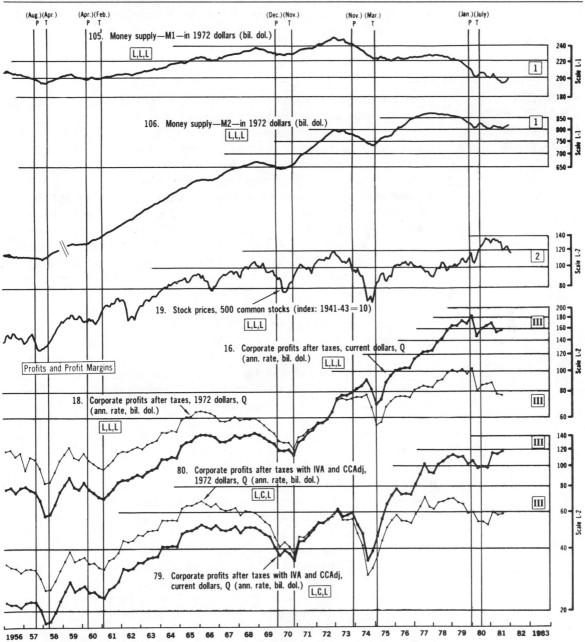

¹This is a weighted 4-term moving average (with weights 1,2,2,1) placed on the terminal month of the span.
²Beginning with data for June 1981, this is a copyrighted series used by permission; it may not be reproduced without written permission from Commodity Research Bureau, Inc.
Current data for these series are shown on page 69.

SOURCE: *Business Conditions Digest* (U.S. Department of Commerce Bureau of Economic Analysis, February, 1982).

supply. Present wisdom would suggest that the most positive long-term sign may simply be a *slow,* steady, predictable growth in the money supply—which will tend to moderate inflationary influence through restricted growth in the available dollars to purchase a limited supply of goods.

BUSINESS CYCLES AND INDUSTRY ANALYSIS

Each industry may be affected by the business cycle differently. Industries where the underlying demand for the product is consumer oriented will quite likely be sensitive to short-term swings in the business cycle. These industries would include durable goods, such as washers and dryers, refrigerators, electric and gas ranges, and automobiles. Changes in the automobile industry will also be felt in the tire and rubber industry as well as auto glass and other automobile suppliers. Figure 6–8 shows the automobile industry's sales from 1973 to mid-1981 relative to the real GNP's growth rate. Notice the similarity of the pattern. From the beginning of 1973 to the beginning of 1975, both GNP and automobile sales show steep declines. A recovery begins in 1975 and peaks in 1978 before declining again. This same type of pattern also continues into the 1980's. This close relationship is why it is often said that the United States lives in an automobile economy.

Not all industries are so closely related to the business cycle. Necessity-oriented industries, such as food and pharmaceuticals, are consistent performers since people do have to eat and illness is not dependent upon the economy. Industries that have products with low price elasticities[3] that are habitual in nature, such as cigarettes and alcohol, do not seem to be much affected by business cycles either. In fact, there are some industries that do better during a recession. The movie industry prospers during a recession as more people substitute low-cost entertainment for more expensive forms. This is one pattern that may not remain the same, however. As cable television and pay TV come into their own with satellite hook-ups, people may find it even more convenient to stay at home than go to the movies when money is tight. This is one thing that makes investments exciting—the ever changing environment.

Housing is another example of an industry that historically has done well in recessionary environments. As the economy comes to a standstill, interest rates tend to come down, and prospective home purchasers are once again able to afford mortgage rates on a home. In the period of extremely high mortgage rates in the early 1980s, it was felt that a precipitous drop in mortgage rates would be necessary to once again stimulate the growth in the housing market.

The Federal Reserve tracks data on various types of consumer expenditures. In Figure 6–9, we see the pattern for personal consumption expenditures on durable goods, nondurables, and services. Durable goods have fared relatively poorly during the period of the 1970s and been the most susceptible to down-

---

[3]Price elasticity represents the sensitivity of quantity purchased to price.

Figure 6—8   **New auto sales and real GNP, 1973–1981**

Annual rates, millions of units

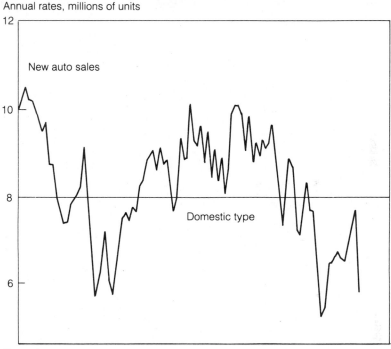

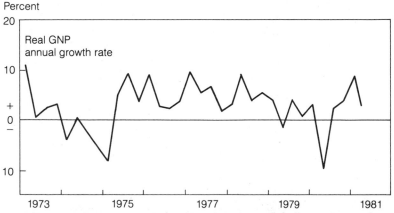

SOURCE: *Federal Reserve Quarterly Chart Book* (Washington, D.C.: Federal Reserve Board of Governors, July 1981).

turns, while nondurables have done quite well, with services leading the growth for personal expenditures.

Sensitivity to the business cycle may also be evident in industries which produce *capital* goods for other business firms (rather than consumer goods). Examples would be manufacturers of business plant and equipment, machine tools,

Figure 6—9   **Personal consumption expenditures (services, nondurable goods, and durable goods)**

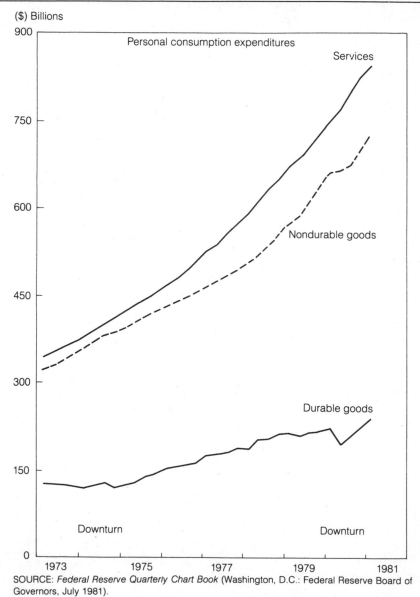

($) Billions

Personal consumption expenditures

SOURCE: *Federal Reserve Quarterly Chart Book* (Washington, D.C.: Federal Reserve Board of Governors, July 1981).

or pollution control equipment. There often is a lag effect between the recovery from a recession and the increased purchase of capital goods, so that recoveries within these industries may be delayed. Computers and other high-technology industries tend to be less cyclical in nature and not as sensitive to the ups and down of the economy.

We do not mean to imply that cyclical industries are bad investments or that they should be avoided. We merely point out the cyclical influence of the economy. Often cyclical industries are excellent buys in the stock market because the market does not look far enough ahead to see a recovery and its very leveraged impact on cyclical profits.

INDUSTRY LIFE CYCLES

Life cycles are created because of economic growth, competition, availability of resources, and the resultant market saturation of the particular goods and services offered. Life-cycle growth influences many variables considered in the valuation process. The particular phase of the life cycle that an industry or company is in determines the growth of earnings, dividends, capital expenditures, and market demand for products.

Figure 6–10 shows an industry life cycle (although it could very well be a company life cycle) and the corresponding dividend policy that is most likely to be found at each stage. A small firm in the initial stages of development (Stage I) pays no dividends because it needs all of its profits (if there are any) for reinvestment in new productive assets. If the firm is successful in the market place, the demand for its products will create growth in sales, earnings, and assets, and the industry will move into stage II. At this stage, sales and returns on assets will be growing at an increasing rate, and earnings will still be reinvested. In the early part of Stage II, stock dividends (distributions of additional shares) may be instituted, and in the latter part of Stage II, *low* cash dividends may be started to inform investors that the firm is profitable.

Obviously, industries in Stage I or early Stage II are very risky, and the investor does not really know if growth objectives will be met or dividends will ever be paid. But if you want to have a chance to make an investment (after careful research) in a high-growth industry with large potential returns, then Stage I or II industries will provide you with opportunities for gains or losses. Since actual dividends are irrelevant in these stages, an investor will be purchasing shares for capital gains based on expected growth rather than current income. As the industry enters Stage III, the growth rate is still positive, but the rate of change starts declining. This is often the point where investors do not recognize that the growth rate has begun to decline, and they still pay large premiums over the regular market for stocks in these industries. However, when the market does realize that the growth rate in fact is diminishing, stock prices can take a sizable tumble.

In Stage III, the expansion of sales continues but at a decreasing rate, and

Figure 6—10   **Industry life cycle**

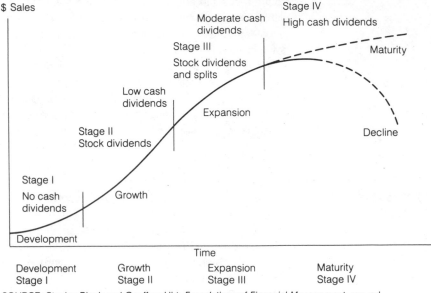

SOURCE: Stanley Block and Geoffrey Hirt, *Foundations of Financial Management,* rev. ed. (Homewood, Ill.: Richard D. Irwin, 1981).

returns on investment may decline as more competition enters the market and attempts to take away market share from existing firms. The industry has expanded to the point where asset expansion slows in line with production needs, and the firms in the industry are more capable of paying cash dividends. Stock dividends and stock splits are still common in Stage III, and the dividend payout ratio usually increases from a low level of 5 to 15 percent of earnings to a moderate level of 25 to 40 percent of earnings. Finally, at Stage IV, maturity, the firm maintains a stable growth rate in sales similar to that of the economy as a whole, and when risk premiums are considered, its returns on assets level out to those of the economy. Automobiles might be a good example of a mature industry.

In unfortunate cases, industries suffer declines in sales (passenger railroads) if product innovation has not increased the product base over the years. In Stage IV, assuming maturity rather than decline, dividends might range from 40 to 60 percent of earnings. Of course, these percentages will be different from industry to industry depending on individual characteristics.

It is also important to realize that growth companies can exist in a mature industry and that not all companies within an industry experience the same growth path in sales, earnings, and dividends. Some companies are simply better managed, have better people, more efficient assets, and have put more money into productive research and development that has created new products or improved products.

For example, electric utilities are generally considered mature, but some utilities exist in states like Florida, Texas, and California that have undergone rapid population explosions over the last decade. These utilities would still have higher growth rates than the industry in general. Computer companies, such as IBM, were fast approaching maturity until technical innovations created new markets. Now personal computers and word processors have not only added vitality to older markets, but also created new industries of their own. You can trace the histories of many industries to see that this pattern repeats itself over and over.

The warning to the investor is not to become too enamored with a company just because it is in a "growth industry." It's time of glory may have passed. Other investors improperly ignore companies that are in the process of revitalization because they no longer carry the growth-stock tag. More will be said about growth stocks in the next chapter.

Other industry factors to consider

There are other significant factors that a financial analyst may wish to evaluate for a given industry. For example, is the industry structure monopolistic like a regulated utility, oligopolistic like the automobile or steel industry, partially competitive like the drug industry, or very competitive like the market for farm commodities? Questions of industry structure are very important in analyzing pricing structures and price elasticities that exist because of competition or lack of it.

Questions of supply and demand relationships are very important as they affect the price structure of the industry and its ability to produce quality products at a reasonable cost. The cost variable can be affected by many factors. For example, high relative hourly wages in basic industries, such as steel, autos, rubber, and others, are somewhat responsible for the inability of the United States to compete in world markets for these products. Availability of raw material is also an important cost factor. Industries like aluminum and glass have an abundance of low-cost bauxite and silicon to produce their products. Unfortunately, the aluminum industry uses very large amounts of electricity in the production process, and so the low cost of bauxite is offset by the high cost of energy. Energy costs are of concern to all industries, but the availability of reasonably priced energy sources is particularly important to the airline and trucking industries. The list could go on and on, but as an analyst becomes familiar with a specific industry, he or she learns the crucial variables.

Government regulation is another area where most industries are affected. This applies to the automobile industry where safety and exhaust emmissions are regulated and to all industries where air, water, and noise pollution are of concern. Many industries engaged in interstate commerce are strongly regulated by the government, such as utilities, railroads, and telephone companies. Many industries, such as airlines, trucking, and natural gas production companies, are being deregulated, and these industries will be facing a new climate where the old game plan may no longer prove successful. Pharmaceutical firms and food companies are regulated through the Food and Drug Administration. Most indus-

tries are affected by government expenditures, but this is especially true for industries involved in defense, education, and transportation.

These are but a few examples to alert you to the importance of having a thorough understanding of your industry. This is why in many large investment firms, trust departments, and insurance companies, analysts are assigned to only one industry or to several related industries so that they may concentrate their attention on a given set of significant factors.

SUMMARY
The primary purpose of this chapter is to provide you with a process of valuation and an appreciation of some of the variables that should be considered. The valuation process is based upon fundamental analysis of the economy, industry, and company. This method assumes decisions are made based on economic concepts of value over the long-term trend of the stock market. The purpose of the process is to eliminate losers from consideration in your portfolio and to thereby provide you with a good opportunity to build a sound portfolio.

The first step in the valuation process is an analysis of the economy and long-term economic trends. The difficulties of attaining government policy goals are discussed as a trade-off between conflicting objectives (high growth versus low inflation). Fiscal and monetary policy are discussed as the primary tools used to stimulate economic activity. Interest rates are influenced by inflation, with the end result being a higher required rate of return for the investor.

Business cycles are short-term swings in economic activity; they have impacts on stock prices because they change investor expectations of risk and return. In order to forecast economic activity, cyclical indicators are presented as leading, lagging, and coincident indexes. The one index potentially most valuable to an investor is the composite index of 12 leading indicators. Unfortunately, stock prices are one of the most accurate leading indicators, and we must find another indicator that leads stock prices. The most popular and economically rational leading indicator is the money supply. The money supply influences economic activity by increasing or decreasing interest rates and corporate profits, which in turn eventually affect corporate dividends. Money also has a direct effect on stock prices by changing liquidity. An investor cannot escape risk, however, and the money supply is no sure way to forecast stock prices. The leads are too similar, and many factors have clouded the effect of changes in the money supply on the economy and stock prices.

The sensitivity of various types of industries to the business cycle is also examined. Firms in consumer durable goods as well as those in heavy capital goods manufacturing (plant and equipment) are perhaps most vulnerable to the business cycle. Industries are also examined from the standpoint of their life-cycle growth path. This growth path affects earnings, dividends, and market valuation and provides a perspective on the valuation process which will be continued in the next chapter.

IMPORTANT WORDS AND CONCEPTS	Fundamental analysis	Open-market operations
	Valuation	Cyclical Indicators
	Monetary policy	Peaks and troughs
	Fiscal policy	Monetarist
	Federal deficit and surplus	Money supply
	Business cycles	Industry factors
	Fed	Cyclical industries
	Reserve requirements	Industry life cycle
	Discount rate	

QUESTIONS AND PROBLEMS

1. As depicted in Figure 6–1, what are the three elements in the valuation process?

2. What are the four goals under the Employment Act of 1946?

3. What is fiscal policy? Did Reagan or Carter place more emphasis on fiscal policy?

4. What is monetary policy?

5. How specifically can the Fed influence economic activity?

6. In regard to Federal Reserve open-market activity, if the Fed buys securities, what is the likely impact on the money supply? Is this likely to encourage expansion or contraction of economic activity?

7. In the early 1980s, how did the Federal Reserve redirect policy in regard to the money supply and interest rates?

8. What is the historical relationship between real GNP and inflation? What lesson might be learned from observing this relationship?

9. What is the advantage of using a composite of indicators (such as the 12 leading indicators) over simply using an individual indicator?

10. Do leading indicators tend to give longer warning before peaks or before troughs? What is the implication for the investor?

11. Give some examples of how different types of industries would relate to the business cycle.

12. Why do industry life cycles exist? How does the dividend policy generally relate to the life cycle of the firm or industry?

13. How has the computer industry avoided moving into Stage IV of maturity?

14. Develop a list of industries in each phase of the life cycle, and look up their dividend record to see if they correspond to the general view of the chapter.

15. Observe the performance of the 12 leading indicators for the next month. Compare this to changes in stock prices and interest rates.

SELECTED REFERENCES

Cairncross, Alec. "Economic Forecasting." *Economic Journal,* December 1969, pp. 797–812.

Elliott, J. W. "A Direct Comparison of Short-Run GNP Forecasting Models." *Journal of Business,* January 1973, pp. 33–60.

Federal Reserve Historical Chart Book and *Federal Reserve Quarterly Chart Book.* Washington, D.C.: Federal Reserve Board of Governors, selected issues.

Friedman, Milton J., and Anna J. Schwartz. "Money and Business Cycles." *Review of Economics and Statistics,* supplement, February 1963.

Heathcotte, Bryan, and Vincent P. Apilado. "The Predictive Content of Some Leading Economic Indicators for Future Stock Prices." *Journal of Financial and Quantitative Analysis,* March 1974, pp. 247–58.

Hickman, B. G., ed. *Econometric Models of Economic Behavior.* New York: National Bureau of Economic Research, 1971.

Kenan, Michael W. "Expectations, Money, and the Stock Market." *Federal Reserve Bank of St. Louis Review,* January 1971, pp. 16–31.

Latane, Henry A., and Donald L. Tuttle. "Profitability in Industry Analysis." *Financial Analysts Journal,* July–August 1968, pp. 51–61.

Livingston, Miles. "Industry Movements of Common Stocks." *Journal of Finance,* June 1977, pp. 861–874.

Mennis, Edmund A. "The Practical Use of Economic Analysis in Investment Management." *The Economic Framework for Investors.* Charlottesville, Va.: The Financial Analysts Research Foundation, 1975.

Moor, Roy E. "The Use of Economics in Investment Analysis." *Financial Analysts Journal,* November–December 1971, pp. 63–69.

Nelson, Charles R. "Rational Expectations and the Predictive Efficiency of Economic Models." *Journal of Business,* July 1975, pp. 331–43.

Reilly, Frank K., and Eugene Drzycimski. "Alternative Industry Performance and Risk." *Journal of Financial and Quantitative Analysis,* June 1974, pp. 423–46.

Rozeff, Michael S. "Money and Stock Prices: Market Efficiency and the Lag in Effect on Monetary Policy." *Journal of Financial Economics,* September 1974, pp. 245–302.

Rogalski, Richard J., and Joseph D. Vinso. "Stock Returns, Money Supply and the Direction of Causality." *Journal of Finance,* September 1977, pp. 1017–30.

Spiro, Harvey M. "The Use of Economics in Portfolio Decisions." *Journal of Portfolio Management,* Spring 1976, pp. 34–38.

Sprinkel, Beryl W. *Money and Markets: A Monetarist View*. Homewood, Ill.: Richard D. Irwin, 1971.

Tysseland, Milford S. "Further Tests of the Validity of the Industry Approach to Investment Analysis." *Journal of Financial and Quantitative Analysis,* March 1971, pp. 835–47.

Wenglowski, Gary M. "Industry Profit Analysis—A Progress Report and Some Predictions." *The Economic Framework for Investors*. Charlottesville, Va.: The Financial Analysts Research Foundation, 1975.

7

Valuation of the individual firm

The analysis in Chapter 6 centered on economic activity and the resultant swings in the business cycle which affected industries and corporate profitability and influenced the purchase of common stocks. The valuation of the individual firm was depicted as the last major step of the valuation process (Figure 6–1).

Valuation is based upon economic factors, industry variables, and an analysis of the financial statements and the outlook for the individual firm. The purpose of valuation is to determine the long-run fundamental economic value of a specific company's common stock. This process tries to determine whether a common stock is undervalued, overvalued, or fairly valued relative to its market price. As will be indicated in Chapter 9, there is a continuing controversy in academic circles over the ability of security markets to correctly price securities. This has lead to debate over the efficient market hypothesis, which states that all securities are correctly priced at any point in time (there is no secret information to be uncovered by the enterprising analyst). For purposes of this chapter, we shall not be fully bound by the limiting assumptions of the efficient market hypothesis—though they are carefully considered in Chapter 9. Furthermore, most of the orientation in this chapter is to long-run concepts of valuation rather than to the determination of short-term market pricing factors.

REVIEW OF BASIC VALUATION CONCEPTS

There are several ways to approach the valuation of common stock. Some models rely solely on dividends expected to be received during the future, and these are usually referred to as dividend valuation models. A variation on the dividend model is the earnings model, which substitutes earnings as the main income stream for valuation. Other methods may include the market value of assets, such as cash and liquid assets, replacement value of plant and equipment, and other hidden assets, such as timber. For the first part of our discussion, we develop the dividend valuation model and earnings models.

Dividend valuation models

The value of a share of stock may be interpreted by the shareholder as the present value of an expected stream of future dividends. Although in the short run, stockholders may be influenced by a change in earnings or other variables, the ultimate value of any holding rests with the distribution of earnings in the form of dividend payments. Though the stockholder may benefit from the retention and reinvestment of earnings by the corporation, at some point the earnings must generally be translated into cash flow for the stockholder.[1]

General dividend model

A generalized stock valuation model based on future expected dividends can be stated as follows:

$$P_0 = \frac{D_1}{(1 + K_e)^1} + \frac{D_2}{(1 + K_e)^2} + \frac{D_3}{(1 + K_e)^3} + \cdots + \frac{D_\infty}{(1 + K_e)^\infty} \quad (7-1)$$

where:

P_0 = Present value of the stock price.

D_i = Dividend for each year.

K_e = Required rate of return (discount rate).

This model was first presented in Chapter 1 and again in Chapter 5 under our discussion of the dividend valuation model and inflation. This model is a very general model and assumes that the investor can in fact determine the right dividend for each and every year as well as the annualized rate of return that an investor requires.

Constant growth model

Rather than predict the actual dividend each year, a more widely used model includes an estimate of the growth rate in dividends. This model assumes a constant growth rate in dividends to infinity.

If a constant growth rate in dividends is assumed, Formula 7–1 can be expressed as:

$$P_0 = \frac{D_0(1 + g)^1}{(1 + K_e)^1} + \frac{D_0(1 + g)^2}{(1 + K_e)^2} + \frac{D_0(1 + g)^3}{(1 + K_e)^3} + \cdots + \frac{D_0(1 + g)^\infty}{(1 + K_e)^\infty} \quad (7-2)$$

where:

$D_0(1 + g)^1$ = Dividends in the initial year.

$D_0(1 + g)^2$ = Dividends in year 2, and so on.

g = Constant growth rate in the dividend.

The current price of the stock should equal the present value of the expected

---

[1] Some exceptions to this principle are noted later in the chapter.

stream of dividends. If we can correctly predict the growth of future dividends and determine the discount rate, we can attempt to ascertain the value of the stock.

For example, assume that we wanted to determine the present value of ABC Corporation common stock based on this model. We shall assume that ABC anticipates an 8 percent growth rate in dividends per share, and we use a 12 percent discount rate as the required rate of return. We can put our projections into tabular form and come up with the following present value analysis (see Table 7–1).

The present value of the expected dividends for the next 20 years is $43.60. This does not include the additional $40.90 coming in from year 21 to infinity. This additional $40.90 is arrived at by subtracting dividends in the first 20 years from the total value of dividends equaling $84.50, as indicated in Formula 7–3. Formula 7–3 includes all dividends to infinity assuming constant dividend growth and is a reduction of Equation 7–2.

Table 7–1   **Present value analysis of ABC Corporation**

Year	Expected dividends $g = 8\%$	Present value factor $K_e = 12\%$*	Present value of dividends
1982	$ 3.38	.893%	$ 3.02
1983	3.65	.797	2.90
1984	3.94	.712	2.81
1985	4.25	.636	2.70
1986	4.59	.567	2.60
1987	4.96	.507	2.51
1988	5.36	.452	2.42
1989	5.79	.404	2.34
1990	6.25	.361	2.26
1991	6.75	.322	2.17
1992	7.29	.287	2.09
1993	7.87	.257	2.02
1994	8.50	.229	1.95
1995	9.18	.205	1.88
1996	9.91	.183	1.81
1997	10.70	.163	1.74
1998	11.56	.146	1.69
1999	12.48	.130	1.62
2000	13.48	.116	1.56
2001	14.56	.104	1.51
Present value of dividends for years 1982–2001			43.60
Present value of dividends for years 2002 to infinity			40.90
Total present value of ABC common stock			$84.50

*Figures are taken from Appendix B at the end of the book.

$$P_0 = D_1/(K_e - g) \qquad\qquad (7\text{--}3)$$
$$= \$3.38/(.12 - .08)$$
$$= \$3.38/.04$$
$$P_0 = \$84.50$$

D_1 represents the initial dividend. One limiting factor of Formula 7–3 is that the required rate of return, K_e, must always be larger than the growth rate, g.

We must also be aware that there are several things that could be wrong with our analysis. First, our expectations of dividend growth may be too high for an infinite period of time. Perhaps 6 percent is a more realistic estimate of expected dividend growth. If we substitute our new estimate into Formula 7–3, we can measure the price effect as dividend growth changes from an 8 percent rate to a 6 percent rate.

$$P_0 = \$3.38/(.12 - .06)$$
$$= \$3.38/.06$$
$$= \$56.33$$

A 6 percent growth rate cuts the present value down substantially from the prior value of $84.50.

We could also misjudge our required rate of return, K_e, which could be higher or lower. A lower K_e would increase the present value of ABC Corporation, while a higher K_e would reduce its value. We have made these points to show how sensitive stock prices are to the basic assumptions of the model. Even though you may go through the calculations, the final value is only as accurate as your inputs. This is where a security analyst's judgment and expertise are important— in justifying the growth rate and required rate of return.

A nonconstant growth model

Most analysts do not accept the premise of a constant growth rate in dividends or earnings. As we examined in Chapter 6, industries go through a life cycle in which growth is nonlinear. Growth is usually highest in the infancy and growth phases of the life cycle, and as expansion is reached, the growth rate slows until the industry reaches maturity. At maturity, a constant, long-run growth rate that approximates the long-run growth of the macro economy may be appropriate for a particular industry.

It should be remembered that some companies in an industry may not behave like the industry in general. Companies constantly try to avoid maturity or decline, and so they strive to develop new products and markets to maintain growth.

In situations where the analyst wants to value a company without the constant growth assumption, a variation on the constant growth model is possible. Growth is simply divided into several periods with each period having a present value. The present value of each period is summed to attain the total value of the firm's share price. An example of a two-period model may illustrate the concept. As-

sume that JAYCAR Corp. is expected to have the following growth pattern in Figure 7–1.

Assume that JAYCAR will have a dividend growth rate of 20 percent for the next 10 years of its life and an 8 percent perpetual growth rate after that. JAYCAR's dividend is expected to be $1 next year, and the appropriate required rate of return (discount rate) is 12 percent. Using the constant growth model for years 1 through 10 and years 11 through infinity, we would end up with a present value of $57.18, which can be substantiated as follows:

Present value of the first ten years of dividends

Year	Dividends (20 percent growth)	PV factor (12 percent)*	Present value of dividends
1	$1.00	.893%	$ .89
2	1.20	.797	.96
3	1.44	.712	1.03
4	1.73	.636	1.10
5	2.07	.567	1.17
6	2.48	.507	1.26
7	2.98	.452	1.35
8	3.58	.404	1.45
9	4.29	.361	1.55
10	5.15	.322	1.66
			$12.42

*Figures are taken from Appendix B.

The dividend in year 11 is expected to be $5.56 or $5.15 (for year 10) compounded at the new, lower 8 percent growth rate ($5.15 × 1.08). Since the rest of the dividend stream will be infinite, Formula 7–3 can provide the value of

Figure 7–1   **JAYCAR growth pattern**

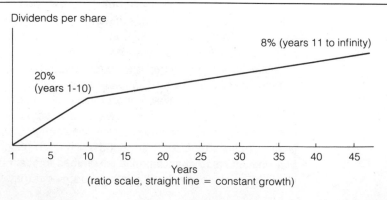

Dividends per share

8% (years 11 to infinity)

20% (years 1-10)

1   5   10   15   20   25   30   35   40   45

Years
(ratio scale, straight line = constant growth)

JAYCAR at the end of year 10 based on a discount rate of 12 percent and an expected growth rate of 8%.

$$P_{10} = D_{11}/(K_e - g)$$
$$P_{10} = \$5.56/(.12 - .08)$$
$$= \$5.56/.04$$
$$= \$139$$

An investor would pay $139 at the end of the 10th year for the future stream of dividends from year 11 to infinity. In other words, this price can be viewed as a function of expected dividends. To get the present value of the 10th-year price, the $139 must be discounted back to the present by the 10-year PV factor for 12 percent from Appendix B (.322). This part of the answer is $139.00 × .322 or $57.18. The two parts of this analysis can be combined to get the current valuation per share.

Present value of the dividends from years 1 to 10	$12.42
Present value of 10th year price ($139.00 × .322)	44.76
Total present value of JAYCAR common stock	$57.18

Do dividends really matter?

Dividend valuation models estimate the present value from an expected future stream of dividends. If the predictions are correct, the valuation will probably be reasonably accurate, but if the forecast is off its target, such would not be the case.

If a firm fails to pay dividends, then dividend valuation makes little sense. If a firm were never to pay a dividend, would the company cease to have value? Probably not! As long as the expectation existed (born out by reality) that retained earnings were being reinvested to increase the asset base of the company, the firm would have some value.

Dividends are currently taxed at 2½ times the rate for long-term capital gains. In this environment, many investors prefer to have capital gains from appreciating stock prices rather than dividends. There has always been the "bird-in-the-hand theory" that dividends are worth more than earnings because, once paid to the stockholder, the company cannot take them away. While it is true that dividends do have information content and thus influence expectations, rising dividends are no guarantee that the common stock will also rise in the short run.

Fortune magazine compiled a list of companies with no dividends and with rising dividends for the period from 1970 to 1980. The results are not necessarily what one might expect. Table 7–2 shows 12 companies that paid no dividends over the entire 10-year period. The median annual return for these companies was 18.7 percent versus 9.4 percent for the Fortune 500 as a whole.

Table 7–2   **A dozen that paid no dividends**

Company	Total return to investors, 1970–80	
	Annual average, compounded (percent)	Rank in Fortune 500
NVF	41.7%	2
National Semiconductor*	33.3	7
Teledyne*	32.2	9
Tosco*	28.9	17
Data General*	25.3	34
Penn Central	19.9	78
Digital Equipment*	17.4	96
Lockheed	13.9	143
Median for 500	9.4	
LTV	6.9	284
Crown Cork & Seal	4.6	342
DPF*	(5.7)	451
Memorex*	(13.9)	463

*Company has never paid a cash dividend.

SOURCE: "Fresh Evidence that Dividends Don't Matter," *Fortune,* May 4, 1981, p. 351. *Fortune* Magazine Art Department. © 1981 Time Inc. All rights reserved.

Table 7–3 presents 19 companies with rising dividends over this decade. The 19 companies with rising dividends performed rather poorly on the basis of total return because of declining stock prices.

While increased dividends generally increase common stock value, we see that this is not always the case. If a company's overall performance is questionable, then raising dividends may not encourage investors. Although the examples in Table 7–3 represent exceptions to the rule, they occur frequently enough to encourage investor caution.

EARNINGS VALUATION MODELS

Dividend valuation models are best suited for those companies that are in the expansion or maturity phase of their life cycle. Dividends of these companies are more predictable and usually comprise a larger percentage of the total return than capital gains. Earnings per share models are also used for valuation. For example, the investor may take the present value of all future earnings to determine a value.

The combined earnings and dividend model

Another, more comprehensive valuation model relies on earnings per share and a price-earnings ratio (earnings multiplier) combined with a finite dividend model. The value of a common stock can be viewed as a dividend stream plus a market price at the end of the dividend stream. Using Procter & Gamble as an example, we develop a present value for the stock at the beginning of 1982 (actual numbers are shown in Table 7–4).

Table 7–3   **Growing dividends didn't save these stocks**

Company	Growth in cash dividends, Average annual rate, compounded 1971–80 (percent)	Decline in stock price 1970–80 (percent)	Total return to investors, 1970–80 Annual average return, compounded (percent)	Rank
Burroughs	26.6%	(1.4%)	1.2%	398
Brunswick	24.7	(17.3)	1.3	396
Economics Laboratory	16.7	(13.2)	.8	404
Jim Walter	16.3	(16.4)	1.9	386
Georgia-Pacific	14.0	(4.1)	2.4	381
Nashua	13.5	(16.8)	1.5	392
Coca-Cola	11.8	(21.2)	1.0	402
Brockway Glass	10.4	(36.4)	.7	411
Avon Products	10.0	(61.4)	(5.2)	449
Colgate-Palmolive	9.9	(8.1)	3.0	375
Quaker Oats	9.0	(6.4)	2.9	376
Warner-Lambert	8.7	(41.2)	(1.8)	432
ITT	8.5	(40.7)	.5	413
Owens-Illinois	8.4	(10.5)	3.3	370
Champion Spark Plug	8.0	(11.5)	4.2	350
Heublein	7.7	(38.3)	(1.3)	428
National Service Industries	7.3	(9.3)	5.0	324
Sybron	6.8	(45.4)	(1.7)	431
Squibb	4.9	(17.9)	.8	405

SOURCE: "Fresh Evidence that Dividends Don't Matter" *Fortune,* May 4, 1981, p. 354. *Fortune* Magazine Art Department. © 1981 Time Inc. All rights reserved.

Procter & Gamble has an expected growth rate in earnings per share of 10.5 percent and has historically had a dividend payout ratio (dividends per share/ earnings per share) of approximately 45 percent. Its normal price-earnings ratio (P/E) is estimated to be 12, which is used as the earnings multiplier. Although we use a required rate of return for this company of 13 percent, it might be pointed out that required rates of return may differ from investor to investor as they evaluate their risk-return trade-offs differently. The present value of the stock will be equal to the present value of the dividend stream for five years in this case plus the present value of the stock price at the end of the five-year period. The analysis is presented in Table 7–4. Note that the present value of the dividend stream is $17.74, and the present value of the future price is $90.38 for a total current value of $108.12.

The pure, short-term earnings model

Often, investors/speculators take a very short-run view of the market and simply ignore using present value analysis with its associated long-term forecasts of dividends and earnings per share (EPS). Instead they only use next year's earnings per share and apply an appropriate multiplier to compute the estimated value.

Table 7—4   **Procter & Gamble present value analysis**

A. Present value of dividends for five years

Year	Estimated earnings per share (10.5% growth)	Estimated payout × ratio	Estimated dividend = per share	PV factor × (13%)*	Present = value
					$ 3.71
1982	$ 9.30	.45%	$4.19	.885%	3.63
1983	10.28	.45	4.63	.783	3.54
1984	11.36	.45	5.11	.693	3.47
1985	12.55	.45	5.67	.613	3.39
1986	13.87	.45	6.24	.543	$17.74

B. Present value of common stock price

Year	EPS	× P/E	= Price	× PV factor (13%)	
1986	$13.87	12	$166.44	.543%	= 90.38

A + B = Total present value of Procter and
Gamble common stock at the beginning of
1982 $108.12

*Figures are taken from Appendix B at the end of the book.

Using this method for Procter & Gamble would provide a 1982 valuation of $111.60 per share if we use expected 1982 earnings of $9.30 and a normalized P/E of 12×.

$$P_0 = EPS \times P/E$$
$$= \$9.30 \times 12$$
$$P_{1982} = \$111.60$$

Of course, every method of valuation has its limitations. Although this method is simplified by ignoring dividends and present value calculations, earnings need to be correctly estimated, and the appropriate price-earnings ratio must be applied. Unfortunately, just as in the dividend models, even if the estimated EPS is correct, there is no assurance that the market will agree with your P/E ratio.

THE PRICE-EARNINGS RATIO

The price-earnings ratio is simply the price per share divided by the earnings per share. Predicting the appropriate price-earnings ratio is not easy because in a sense you are trying to pick an earnings multiple that is based on long-run value and trends. The P/E is a function of two fluctuating variables—price and earnings—so it often has wide fluctuations during the year.

The bottom of Figure 7–2 shows the high and low price-earnings ratios for the Standard & Poor's 500 Stock Index for the years 1964 through 1981 (based on the right-hand scale). From 1964 through 1972, the high P/E was close to 20 times earnings, while the low P/E was close to 12 in 1970. It seems as though

Figure 7–2   **Standard & Poor's 500 Stock Index and price-earnings ratios**

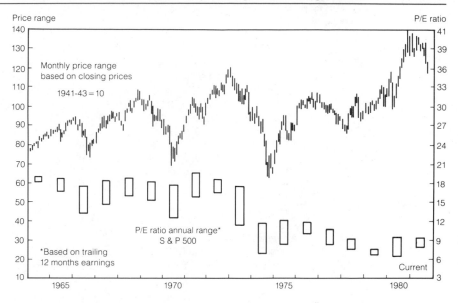

1973 was a transition year with the P/E falling dramatically. During the next eight years, it barely hit 12× and usually stayed between 7× and 9×. This, of course, is an average figure; many firms trade at higher or lower values.

It is interesting to note, however, that the market was rising between 1974 and 1981 while price-earnings ratios have been falling (compare the top and bottom part of Figure 7–2). The year 1973 was the start of particularly high inflation, which has continued into 1981, with economic policy trying to reduce its impact. With high rates of inflation and resultant high interest rates, price-earnings ratios have declined. The market has viewed common stock as risky creating risk-adjusted expected rates of returns that are commensurate with returns in the bond and money markets.

On a historical basis, the stock market is undervalued in terms of P/E ratios, but in the early 1960s when price-earnings ratios were higher, the United States was not faced with high inflation or high interest rates. If inflation permanently subsides and interest rates fall, it may very well be that the market will return to its former P/E levels.

If it is usually true that "a bad market also spoils good stocks," then individual firms' price-earnings ratios will be affected by the market. How do we judge whether an individual company's P/E is too high or low or what is the normal P/E? One way is to examine the historical level of a firm's P/E ratio and to also compare each company's historical price-earnings ratios to the market. General Signal, a diversified capital goods company, is used as an example. Table 7–5 provides a summary of earnings per share, high-low price, high-low P/E ratio, and the high-

Table 7–5 **General Signal—EPS, price, P/E and P/E relative**

Year	EPS	Price		P/E		P/E relative to S&P's 500	
		High	Low	High	Low	High	Low
1971	1.01	19.10	13.80	18.9	13.6	1.11	.80
1972	1.20	29.60	17.00	24.7	14.2	1.44	.82
1973	1.26	28.60	18.20	22.8	14.5	1.75	1.11
1974	1.35	26.50	8.60	19.6	6.4	2.14	.70
1975	1.59	21.20	11.90	13.3	7.5	1.28	.72
1976	2.00	28.40	17.10	14.2	8.6	1.42	.85
1977	2.43	29.50	22.70	12.1	9.4	1.34	1.03
1978	2.93	33.70	23.50	11.5	8.0	1.47	1.02
1979	3.52	39.10	25.0	11.1	7.1	1.60	1.02
1980	4.01	54.20	28.20	13.5	7.0	1.48	.77

Average high P/E for last five years	12.5
Average low P/E for last five years	8.0
Average P/E for last five years	10.25
Average P/E relative to S&P's 500 for last five years	1.20

low P/E relative to the Standard & Poor's 500 Index P/E. The second part of the table provides average values for the last five years.

Based on an analysis of the high and low P/E ratios for the last five years shown in the second part of Table 7–5 and a present and future analysis of earnings, we derive the following:

Year	Estimated EPS	P/E		Anticipated stock price	
		High	Low	High	Low
1981	$4.34	12.5	8.0	$54.25	$34.72
1982	5.21	12.5	8.0	65.12	41.68
1983	6.34	12.5	8.0	79.25	50.72
1984	7.30	12.5	8.0	91.25	58.40
1985	7.98	12.5	8.0	99.75	63.84

The earnings forecast are based on an analysis of growth prospects. Since the stock was trading in the mid-30s at the time this analysis was made in late 1981, it would appear the stock is trading at the lower end of its normal trading range based on historical P/E ratios. Furthermore, if future earnings projections come through, higher stock value may be expected in the future.

What about a comparison of General Signal's P/E ratio to the Standard & Poor's 500? As indicated in the second part of Table 7–5, General Signal carries a premium multiple of 1.20 times the average S&P 500. With the Standard & Poor's selling at 7.5 times earnings per share in late 1981, General Signal would

normally have a P/E of 9. This would imply a 1981 stock price of $39.06 (9 × $4.34). Whether this is reasonable or not would require much further analysis. As discussed in Chapter 9, advocates of the efficient market hypothesis would argue that the only meaningful price is the one that exists in the marketplace.

Anytime historical data is to be used for decision making, the question is always the same. How many years of historical data is relevant? That depends on the expectations of the future. We used the last five-year average because we wanted to be conservative in our estimate of the economy and inflation over the next several years. If you thought the economy was returning to the days of low inflation, earlier data might have been used. There are other questions that need to be asked when determining the P/E ratio and estimating EPS.

1. Is it still the same company as it was 5 or 10 years ago?
2. Are the products, markets, and potential the same, better, or worse?
3. How does the expected growth rate in earnings, sales, and dividends compare to historical rates?
4. What is the competition doing?

There are many more questions that could be added to the list, but these should stimulate your imagination.

Generally, all else being equal, firms with higher growth rates in earnings per share have higher price-earnings ratios than slow-growth firms. It makes sense to pay more for a company that is growing faster than another. Unfortunately, it is not usual to find comparable companies on the basis of all else being equal. Companies have different capital structures, products, markets, variations in earnings growth, and different accounting practices, and this often makes comparisons difficult. It also makes P/E estimation very tricky and not without complications.

Since growth is one of the more important influences on the P/E, Table 7–6 relates historical growth, expected growth, and price-earnings ratios.

Several points can be made concerning Table 7–6. Companies with the same

Table 7–6 P/E and growth in EPS

Industry	Company	Five-year EPS growth (percent)	1976–80 P/E	Expected five-year growth in EPS (percent)	Current P/E	Expected normal P/E
Trucking	Roadway	14.5%	12.9×	16.0%	11.5×	16.0×
Airlines	Delta	12.0	7.8×	15.0	8.6×	9.0×
Railroads	Southern RR	14.5	7.0×	11.5	7.1×	5.5×
Fast foods	McDonald's	22.5	13.1×	17.0	10.1×	17.0×
Tobacco	Reynolds	9.5	6.8×	12.5	6.3×	6.0×
Drugs	Bristol Myers	13.5	11.6×	12.0	10.9×	10.5×
Brokerage	Merrill Lynch	17.5	8.5×	15.0	6.5×	8.3×
Radio-TV	CBS	13.5	7.9×	13.0	7.8×	8.0

SOURCE: *Value Line Investment Survey* (Arnold Bernard & Co., selected issues).

historical growth rates in EPS, like Bristol Myers and CBS, do not have the same historical price-earnings ratio or the same current P/E. More than growth creates differences in price-earnings ratios. In the case of CBS, the growth rate in the future is expected to remain about the same as in the past, and there is very little difference in the three price-earnings ratios shown in Table 7–6. Some companies (such as Roadway, with an increase in expected growth versus growth during the past five years) have a higher expected normal P/E (which is what we would expect), and others, like McDonald's, have slower growth but a higher expected P/E (which is certainly not what we would anticipate). Only after careful analysis of all the factors can you make an appropriate judgment concerning a firm's P/E, ratio.

FORECASTING EARNINGS PER SHARE

The other side of choosing an appropriate P/E is forecasting the earnings per share of a company with the proper growth rate. There are several ways investors can get earnings forecasts. They can rely on professional brokerage house research, investment advisory firms like Value Line, financial magazines like *Forbes* or *Business Week,* or they can do it themselves.

Investment advisory services

Standard & Poor's Earnings Forecaster is a service that provides estimated earnings per share data from several different sources. Table 7–7 shows a few forecasts from this S&P publication for GEO International and Georgia Pacific. The company providing the forecast is listed as well as the date the forecast was made (i.e., Advest, Sept. 15 for GEO International). There can be a wide difference of opinion with some companies, such as Georgia Pacific in the lumber-housing industry. The estimates for 1982 vary from $2.25 per share to $3.75 per share. Obviously, Bache Halsey Stuart Shields has a different concept of interest rates and the housing industry than Shearson, Loeb Rhoades.

Least squares trendline

One of the most common ways of forecasting earnings per share is to use regression or least squares growth analysis. This involves a statistical method whereby a trendline is fitted to a time series of historical earnings. This trendline, by definition, is a straight line which minimizes the distance of the individual observations from the line. Figure 7–3 depicts a scattergram for the earnings per share of General Signal previously discussed. The earnings of this company have been fairly consistent, and so we get a very good trendline with a minimum of variation. The compounded growth rate for the whole 10-year period was 16.5 percent, with 9.8 percent for the first 5 years and 20.4 percent for the last 5 years. This shows up in Figure 7–3 as two distinct five-year trendlines. Most universities have statistical programs that run regression analysis, and even hand-held calculators have the ability to compute a growth rate from raw data.

Table 7–7   Standard & Poor's earnings forecaster

Company and fiscal year ending date	Stock price	Estimated date	P/E ratio	Earnings per share 1980*	1981	1982
GEO International (September)	34		8 ×	2.31		
Advest		September 15			4.00–4.25	—
Bacon, Whipple		September 16			4.20	—
A. G. Edwards		October 7			4.10	5.70
Howard, Weil, Labouisse, Freidrichs		October 14			4.00	5.75
Georgia Pacific (December)	20		9 ×	2.34		
Bache Halsey Stuart		September 3			1.65†	2.25
E. F. Hutton & Co.		September 20			1.60†	2.50
Shearson, Loeb Rhoades		August 1			2.75†	3.75
United Business Service		October 5			2.10†	—

*Actual.

†Fully diluted.

SOURCE: Standard & Poor's Earnings Forecaster, October 23, 1981.

Whenever a mechanical forecast is made, subjectivity still enters the decision in choosing the data which will be considered in the regression plot. Always be careful not to extrapolate a trend from a peak to a trough or a trough to a peak. This can be extremely misleading for a cyclical industry. Be sure to use enough data points to get a good line, and in cyclical industries, plot out your line for several business cycles to get a long-run average.

Using Georgia Pacific, a cyclical, interest-sensitive stock, and American Home

Figure 7–3   Least squares trendline for EPS of General Signal

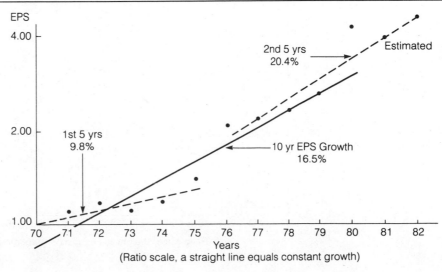

(Ratio scale, a straight line equals constant growth)

Products, a consistently performing proprietary drug company, we compare earning trends.

Year	Earnings per share Georgia Pacific (past 10-year EPS)	Earnings per share American Home Products (past 10-year EPS)
1972	$1.38	$1.08
1973	1.82	1.25
1974	1.76	1.42
1975	1.56	1.58
1976	2.12	1.75
1977	2.54	1.94
1978	2.93	2.21
1979	3.12	2.51
1980	2.34	2.84
1981*	2.00*	3.15*

*Estimated.

From Figure 7–4, it is clear that American Home Products would provide the most reliable forecast based on past data. In order to forecast Georgia Pacific, you would not start in 1975 and end in 1981 (trough to trough). You would also

Figure 7–4   **Georgia Pacific and American Home Products EPS trendlines**

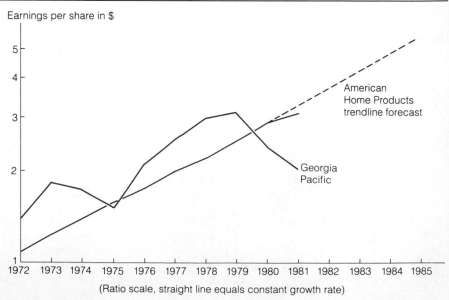

Earnings per share in $

American Home Products trendline forecast

Georgia Pacific

(Ratio scale, straight line equals constant growth rate)

not start in 1978, 1979 or 1980 because they would each create a downward-sloping trendline with negative growth. Clearly, a 10-year forecast with Georgia Pacific is more reliable than a 5-year forecast.

The income statement method

A more process-oriented method of forecasting earnings per share is to start with a sales forecast and create a standardized set of financial statements based on historical relationships. Of course, the sales forecast must be accurate if the earnings estimates are to have any significance. This method can be very involved and provides a student with a very integrated understanding of the relationships that go into the creation of earnings. For a firm like American Home Products, there would not be much gained from an income statement forecast, but for Georgia Pacific, the cyclical nature of profitability would be brought out.

Several important factors are included in this method of forecasting. The analyst is forced to examine profitability and the resultant fluctuations in profit margins before and after taxes. The impact of short-term interest expense and any new bond financing can be factored into the analysis as well as any increase in shares of common stock from new equity financing.

Most analysts use an abbreviated method of forecasting earnings per share. They use a sales forecast combined with aftertax profit margins. For example, let us assume that the Hutchins Corporation has a sales and profit margin history as set forth in Table 7–8. The sales have been growing at a perfect 10 percent growth rate, and so the forecast is a simple extrapolation. However, the profit margin has fluctuated between 6.5 percent and 9.1 percent, with 8.2 percent being the average. Common stock outstanding has also grown consistently by an average of 1.4 million shares per year. Given the cyclical nature of the profit margin, 8.2 percent was used for 1982, which is expected to be an average year. Nine percent was used for 1983, a year expected to be economically more robust. Multiplying the profit margin times the estimated sales produced an esti-

Table 7–8   **Abbreviated income statement method—Hutchins Corporation**

Year	Sales ($000s)	Aftertax profit margin	Earnings ($000s)	Shares (000s)	Earnings per share
1976	$1,250,000	7.9%	$ 98,750	30,000	$3.29
1977	1,375,000	9.1	125,125	31,500	3.97
1978	1,512,500	8.5	128,562	33,200	3.87
1979	1,663,750	6.5	108,143	35,000	3.08
1980	1,830,125	8.3	151,900	35,200	4.31
1981	2,013,137	8.7	175,142	37,000	4.73
1982*	2,214,452	8.2	173,958	38,400	4.53
1983*	2,435,896	9.0	219,230	39,800	5.50

*Estimated.

mate of earnings which was divided by the number of shares outstanding to find the earnings per share. Once the EPS is found, it still must be plugged into a valuation model to determine a normal value.

GROWTH STOCKS AND GROWTH COMPANIES

A "growth stock" may be defined as the common stock of a company generally growing faster than the economy or market norm. These companies are usually predictable in their earnings growth. Many of the more popular growth stocks, such as 3M, Eastman Kodak, and McDonald's, are really in the middle to late stages of the expansion phase. They tend to be fully valued and recognized in the marketplace.

"Growth companies," on the other hand, are those companies that exhibit rising returns on assets each year and sales that are growing at an increasing rate (growth phase of the life-cycle curve). Growth companies may not be as well known or recognized as growth stocks. Companies that may be considered to be growth companies might be in such industries as cable television, word processors, personal computers, medical electronics, and so on. These companies are growing very rapidly, and extrapolations of growth trends can be very dangerous if you guess incorrectly. There are many things that growth companies have in common. Usually, they have developed a proprietary product that is patented and protected from competition like the Xerox process (now other companies can use the dry process). This market protection allows a high rate of return and generates cash for new-product development.

One of the things that growth stocks and growth companies have in common is good research and development (R&D). Each company tries to prolong the growth and expansion phase of its life cycle as long as possible with new products or improved products. Value Line's November 13, 1981, issue of *Selection and Opinion* featured an article entitled "R&D: Key to Growth." Value Line took 409 companies over the 1978–80 period and measured research and development expenditures as a percentage of sales. They then ranked these 409 companies from the highest to lowest (R&D/sales) ratio. The top 10 R&D companies' average spending was 11 percent of sales dollars on research and development, which generated an earnings per share growth of 33.7 percent over the last 10-year period. The bottom 10 companies spent less than .12 percent on average, and EPS grew at only 8.3 percent. A further test with the top 100 companies showed R&D/sales averaged 5.6 percent with a resultant 15.2 percent growth in EPS, while the bottom 100 companies' R&D/sales averaged .44 percent and increased earnings 11.3 percent.

Besides research and development, there are other indicators of growth potential. Companies should have sales growth greater than the economy by a reasonable margin. Increasing sales should be translated into similar earnings

growth, which means consistently stable and high profit margins. Additionally, the earnings growth should show up in earnings per share growth (no dilution of earnings through unproductive stock offers). The firm should have a low labor cost as a percentage of total cost, since wages are prone to be inflexible on the downside but difficult to control on the upside.

The biggest error made in searching for growth-oriented companies is that the price may already be too high. By the time you identify the company, so has everyone else, and the price is probably inflated. If the company has one quarter where earnings do not keep up with expectations, the stock price could tumble. The trick, of course, is to find growth companies before they are generally recognized in the market, and this requires taking more risk in small companies trading over-the-counter.

ASSETS AS A SOURCE OF STOCK VALUE

Corporate assets take many forms—cash and marketable securities, buildings, land, timber, old movies, oil, and other natural resources. Sometimes these assets, rather than earnings, dominate a firm's stock price. Also companies with heavy cash positions are attractive merger and acquisition candidates because there is a possibility that a firm with highly liquid assets could be taken over and its own cash used to pay back debt incurred in the takeover.

Natural resources

Natural resources, such as timber, copper, gold, and oil, often give a company value even if the assets are not producing an income stream. This is because of the present value of the future income stream that is expected as these resources are used up. Companies like International Paper, Weyerhaeuser, and other forest-product companies have timberlands with market values far in excess of their book values and, in some cases, in excess of their common stock prices.

Oil companies with large supplies of oil under the ground may have to wait 20 years before some of it is pumped, but there may be substantial value there. In the case of natural-gas pipeline companies, increasing reserves have changed the way these companies are viewed by the market. They used to be considered similar to utilities because of their natural gas transmission system, but now they are also being valued based on their hidden assets (called energy reserves). Table 7–9 gives a list of pipeline companies and the present value of their proven reserves compared to the common stock price (in the third and fourth column).

Investors should not overlook hidden assets because of naive extrapolation of past data or failure to understand an industry or company. Furthermore, assets do not always show up on the books of a company. They may be fully depreciated, like the movies *Sound of Music, Jaws,* or *Star Wars,* but still have plenty of value in the television market.

Table 7–9 Value from energy reserves

Company (1980 revenues in $ millions)	(1) Operating income percent — Pipelines	(2) Operating income percent — Oil and gas production	(3) Present value of proven reserves on 12/31/80 (per share)	(4) Stock price (early March)	(5) Price as multiple of estimated 1981 earnings*	(6) Yield (percent)
Interstate transmission:						
Texas Eastern ($4,272)	35%	54%	$178.17	$57.00	6.1	5.6
United Energy Resources ($4,135)	91	9	14.49	42.75	6.3	3.6
Transco Companies ($2,628)	85	15	43.19	47.00	9.4	3.1
Panhandle Eastern Pipe Line ($2,472)	56	44	25.17	42.00	6.7	4.1
Southern Natural Resources ($1,798)	58†	8†	16.21	67.25	8.9	2.8
Intrastate transmission:						
ENSERCH ($2,695)	41	35	27.06‡	50.25	10.1	3.4
Houston Natural Gas ($2,358)	54	18	12.49§	49.50	8.5	2.6
Texas Oil & Gas ($1,191)	40‡	55‡	15.02‖	37.25	19.4	.5

*Source for earnings: Institutional Brokers Estimate System.

†Percent of net income.

‡Estimate.

§On July 31, 1980.

‖On August 31, 1980.

SOURCE: "There is Still a Glow in Gas Pipelines," *Fortune,* April 6, 1981, p. 96. *Fortune* Magazine Art Department. © 1981 Time Inc. All rights reserved.

SUMMARY

This chapter presents several common stock valuation models that rely on dividends and earnings per share. The point is made in all of them that, in order for the valuation to be accurate, the forecast of earnings and dividends needs to be correct.

Firms can be valued in many ways, and an analyst may choose to use several methods to substantiate his or her estimates. Valuation models based primarily on dividends look at future projections of dividends and the associated present values of the dividends. Assumptions must be made as to whether the dividend growth pattern is constant, accelerating, or decreasing.

Valuation using the earnings method requires that a price-earnings ratio be used as a multiplier of EPS. Price-earnings ratios are influenced by many variables, such as growth in earnings per share, capital structure, level of the market in general, industry factors, profitability, and more. A careful study of each situa-

tion must be concluded before choosing the appropriate P/E. The price-earnings ratio is a function of two fluctuating variables—earnings and price. The two variables combine together to form a ratio that is primarily future oriented. High price-earnings ratios usually indicate positive expectations of the future, while low price-earnings ratios connote negative expectations.

In order to choose a P/E that is reasonable, the analyst must have some idea about the expected growth rate in earnings per share. Investors may find earnings estimates in investment advisory services, statistical forecasts by brokerage houses through their own time series statistical regression analysis, or by using the income statement method. Growth stocks were discussed more with the view of alerting the student what to look for when trying to identify a growth stock or company than with the concept of valuation. The previously developed methods of valuation can be used on growth stocks as long as care is taken to evaluate the duration and level of growth.

We also presented some basic ideas about the value of companies based not on their earnings or dividend stream but on their assets, such as cash or natural resources. Throughout the chapter, it was pointed out that every industry and company is unique. Management, products, organization structure, accounting systems, and philosophy are different for each. The role of an analyst is to understand the intricacies of several related industries and companies so as to enlighten the investing public.

IMPORTANT WORDS AND CONCEPTS	Valuation	Growth company
	Fundamental analysis	Hidden asset values
	Valuation models	Constant growth model
	Dividend valuation models	Nonconstant growth model
	Earnings valuation models	Combined earnings and dividend
	P/E ratio	model
	Income statement method	Least squares trendline
	Growth stock	

QUESTIONS AND PROBLEMS

1. How is value interpreted under the dividend valuation model?

2. Assume $D_1 = \$1.60$, $K_e = 10\%$, and $g = 6\%$. Using Formula 7–3 for the constant growth dividend valuation model, compute P_0.

3. If a higher growth rate than 6 percent can be assumed in problem 2, will the value of the stock go up, down, or remain unchanged?

4. The Walton Corporation anticipates a nonconstant growth pattern for dividends. Dividends at the end of year 1 are $2 per share and are expected to grow by 16 percent per year until the end of year 5 (that's four years of

growth). After year 5, dividends are expected to grow at 5 percent as far as the company can see into the future. All dividends are to be discounted back to the present at a 10 percent rate ($k_e = 10\%$).

a. Project dividends for years 1 through 5 (the first year is already given). Round all values that you compute to two places to the right of the decimal point.

b. Find the present value of the dividends in part a.

c. Project the dividend for the sixth year (D_6).

d. Use Formula 7–3 to find the present value of all future dividends beginning with the sixth years' dividend. The present value you find will be at the end of the fifth year.

Use Formula 7–3 as follows: $P_5 = D_6/(K_e - g)$.

e. Discount back the value found in question d for five years at 10 percent.

f. Observe that in part b you determined the present value of dividends for the first five years and, in part e, the present value of an infinite stream after the first five years. Now add these together to get the total present value of the stock.

5. Rework problem 4, following the same steps, with a new assumption that dividends after the first year are $1.20 and that they will grow at 20 percent per year until the end of the fifth year, at which point they will grow at 6 percent per year for the foreseeable future. Use a discount rate of 12 percent throughout your analysis. Round all values that you compute to two places to the right of the decimal point.

6. What does the price-earnings (P/E) ratio indicate? Why have P/E ratios tended to be lower in the 1970s and early 1980s than in prior time periods?

7. How does a firm's growth rate influence its P/E ratio?

8. What is the characteristic(s) of a least squares trendline?

9. Security analysts following the Mitchell Corporation use a simplified income statement method of forecasting. Assume that current sales (1982) are $15 million and are expected to grow by 12 percent in 1983 and 1984. The aftertax profit margin is projected at 6.1 percent in 1983 and 5.9 percent in 1984. The number of shares outstanding is anticipated to be 500,000 for 1983 and 510,000 for 1984. Project earnings per share for 1983 and 1984.

10. The average price-earnings ratio for the industry that the Mitchell Corporation is in is $8\times$. If the company has a P/E ratio 20 percent higher than the industry in 1983 and 25 percent higher than the industry ratio of 8 in 1984, (a) indicate the appropriate P/Es for the firm in 1983 and 1984; (b) combine this with the earnings per share data in question 9 to determine the anticipated stock price for 1983 and 1984.

11. As relates to questions 9 and 10, assume that you wish to determine the

probable price range in 1984 if the P/E ratio is between 9.5 and 11. What is this price range?

12. What is the difference between a growth company and a growth stock? What are some industries that growth companies are in?

13. Why might a firm with highly liquid assets be an attractive merger or acquisition candidate?

14. How should a firm with natural resources be valued?

15. What is an example of a valuable asset that might not show any "value" on a balance sheet?

SELECTED REFERENCES

Basu, S. "Investment Performance of Common Stocks in Relation to Their Price-Earnings Ratios: A Test of the Efficient Market Hypothesis." *Journal of Finance,* June 1977, pp. 663–82.

Beaver, William, and Dale Morse. "What Determines Price-Earnings Ratios?" *Financial Analysts Journal,* July–August 1978, pp. 65–76.

Benishay, Haskell. "Market Preferences for Characteristics of Common Stocks." *Economic Journal,* March 1973, pp. 173–191.

Black, Fischer. "The Dividend Puzzle." *Journal of Portfolio Management,* Winter 1976, pp. 5–8.

Chung, Peter S. "An Investigation of the Firms Effect Influence in the Analysis of Earnings to Price Ratios of Industrial Common Stocks." *Journal of Financial and Quantitative Analysis,* December 1974, pp. 1009–29.

Friend, Irwin, and Marshall Puckett. "Dividends and Stock Prices." *American Economic Review,* September 1964, pp. 656–82.

Graham, Benjamin. "The Future of Common Stocks." *Financial Analysts Journal,* September–October 1974, pp. 20–30.

Latane, Henry A.; O. Maurice Joy; and Charles P. Jones. "Quarterly Data, Sort-Rank Routines, and Security Evaluation." *Journal of Business,* October 1970, pp. 427–38.

Litzenberger, Robert H., and O. Maurice Joy. "Further Evidence on the Persistence of Corporate Profitability Rates." *Western Economic Journal,* June 1970, pp. 209–12.

Mao, James C. T. "The Valuation of Growth Stocks: The Investment Opportunities Approach." *Journal of Finance,* March 1966, pp. 95–102.

Miller, Merton, and Franco Modigliani. "Dividend Policy, Growth, and the Valuation of Shares." *Journal of Business,* October 1961, pp. 411–33.

Reilly, Frank. "The Misdirected Emphasis on Security Evaluation," *Financial Analysts Journal,* January–February 1973, pp. 54–60.

Robichek, Alexander A., and Marcus C. Bogue. "A Note on the Behavior of

Expected Price/Earnings Ratios Over Time." *Journal of Finance,* June 1971, pp. 731–35.

Walter, James E. "Dividend Policy: Its Influence on the Value of the Enterprise." *Journal of Finance,* May 1963, pp. 280–91.

Wendt, Paul F. "Current Growth Stock Valuation Models." *Financial Analysts Journal,* March–April 1965, pp. 91–103.

Wippern, Ronald F. "Financial Structure and the Value of the Firm." *Journal of Finance,* December 1966, pp. 615–33.

8

Financial statement analysis

Financial statements present a numerical picture of a company's financial and operating health. Since each company is different, an analyst needs to examine the financial statements for industry characteristics as well as for differences in accounting methods. The major financial statements are the balance sheet, income statement, and the sources and uses of funds statements. A very helpful, long-term overview is usually provided by a 5 or 10-year summary statement found in the corporate annual report. One must remember that the footnotes to these statements are an integral part of the statements and provide a wealth of in-depth explanatory information. More depth can often be found in additional reports, such as the 10-K filed with the Securities and Exchange Commission and obtainable on request (free of charge) from most companies.

Fundamental analysis depends on variables internal to the company, and the corporate financial statements are one way of measuring fundamental value and risk. Financial statement analysis must be combined with economic and industry analysis before a final judgment is made to purchase or sell a specific security. Chapter 7 presented methods of valuation that used forecasts of dividends and earnings per share. Earnings per share combined with an estimated price-earnings ratio were also used to get a current and future price. Careful study of financial statements provides the analyst with much of the necessary information to forecast earnings and dividends, to judge the quality of earnings, and to determine financial and operating risk.

THE MAJOR FINANCIAL STATEMENTS

In the first part of this chapter, we examine the three basic types of financial statements—the income statement, the balance sheet, and the sources and uses of funds statement—with particular attention paid to the interrelationships among these three measurement devices. In the remainder of the chapter, ratio analysis is presented in detail, and deficiencies of financial statements are discussed along with inflation and the role of the security analyst in interpreting financial statements.

Income statement   The income statement is the major device for measuring the profitability of a firm over a period of time. An example of the income statement is presented in Table 8–1 for Heublein, Inc. First of all, note that the income statement is for a defined period of time, whether it be one month, three months, or a year. The statement is presented in a stair-step or progressive fashion so that we may examine the profit or loss after each type of expense item is deducted.

For 1981, Heublein, Inc., had net sales of $1,984,396,000 with an additional $65,725,000 in franchise and license fees. The firm's operating income was $224,300,000, and net income after taxes was $88,379,000. Primary earnings per share were $4.09, and fully diluted earnings per share were $3.93. Are these good income figures or bad? As we shall later see, the analyst's interpretation of the numbers will depend on historical figures, industry data, and on the relationship of income to balance sheet items, such as assets and net worth.

Table 8–1

HEUBLEIN, INC.
Income Statement
For the Years Ended June 30, 1981, 1980, and 1979
($000s except per share data)

	Year ended June 30		
	1981	1980	1979
Revenues:			
Net sales	$1,984,396	$1,865,474	$1,719,222
Franchise and license fees	65,725	56,405	49,852
Total revenues	2,050,121	1,921,879	1,769,074
Costs and expenses:			
Cost of sales	1,381,606	1,325,293	1,222,693
Selling, advertising, administrative, and general expenses	444,215	401,384	376,405
Total costs and expenses	1,825,821	1,726,677	1,599,098
Operating profit	224,300	195,202	169,976
Other deductions:			
Interest expense:			
Long-term debt	12,636	14,315	13,077
Other	15,945	11,046	10,029
Corporate and miscellaneous—net	27,378	23,783	15,851
Total deductions	55,959	49,144	38,957
Income before income taxes	168,341	146,058	131,019
Income taxes	79,962	68,647	62,889
Net income	$ 88,379	$ 77,411	$ 68,130
Earnings per share:			
Primary	$4.09	$3.62	$3.19
Fully diluted	$3.93	$3.48	$3.09

SOURCE: Heublein Annual Report, 1981.

Balance sheet

The balance sheet indicates what the firm owns and how these assets are financed in the form of liabilities or ownership interest. While the income statement purports to show the profitability of the firm, the balance sheet delineates the firm's holdings and obligations. Together these statements are intended to answer two questions: How much did the firm make or lose, and what is a measure of its worth? A balance sheet for Heublein Inc., is presented in Table 8–2.

Note that the balance sheet is given at one point in time, in this case the most recent is June 30, 1981. It does not represent the result of transactions for a specific month, quarter, or year but rather is a cumulative chronicle of all transactions that have affected the corporation since its inception. This is in contrast to the income statement, which measures results only over a short, quantifiable period of time. Generally, balance sheet items are stated on an original-cost basis rather than at market value.

As mentioned earlier, every company is different. Heublein was chosen because its annual report demonstrates a few industry differences that might not show up in an automobile firm, for example. Heublein's balance sheet differentiates inventories much more than most companies. Because the process of making distilled spirits is quite long and takes many years, inventories are divided into separate categories, such as finished products, products in process, bulk whiskey and wine, and raw materials. For an industry such as this, it may not be surprising that total inventories are almost as large as property, plant, and equipment.

Another variable that is unique to the industry shows up under taxes in the current liabilities section. Because alcohol is taxed at many levels, Heublein's excise taxes are greater than its income taxes, a very unusual situation and one that could be misleading if the analyst were not aware of industry factors.

Sources and uses of funds statements

The third major financial statement is the sources and uses of funds statement. This statement supplements the income statement and balance sheet. As indicated in Figure 8–1, the sources and uses of funds statement allows us to measure how changes in the balance sheet were financed over a period of time. While the balance sheet is nothing more than a snapshot of the firm at a point in time, if we put together two such snapshots, we can ascertain significant changes.

Sources of funds   In constructing a sources and uses of funds statement, an increase in stockholders' equity is considered a source of financing. This may include additional profit, new preferred or common stock, and other types of capital infusion into the firm. In the case of Heublein in Table 8–3, profit accounted for $88 million in sources for 1981, and sale of common stock amounted to $5 million in the same year. Another source of financing, albeit indirect, is a reduction in assets (book value of assets sold), which accounted for $8 million for Heublein. To the extent that a company reduces its financial commitments to receivables, inventory, or plant and equipment, it frees up funds for use else-

Table 8—2

HEUBLEIN, INC.
Consolidated Balance Sheet
June 30, 1981, and 1980
($000)

	June 30	
	1981	1980
Assets		
Current assets:		
Cash and temporary investments	$ 74,761	$ 37,884
Accounts and notes receivable	199,497	195,780
Inventories:		
Finished products	97,646	101,158
Products in process	7,157	8,237
Bulk whiskey and wine	165,433	156,964
Raw materials	34,133	34,312
Total inventories	304,369	300,671
Deferred income tax benefits	19,015	20,834
Prepaid expenses	11,947	9,378
Total current assets	609,589	564,547
Investments in and advances to affiliated companies	20,978	19,826
Property, plant, and equipment—net	388,594	372,043
Other assets:		
Cost in excess of net assets of purchased businesses	53,070	53,833
Trademarks, contracts, and franchises	13,645	2,675
Other	35,063	34,095
Total other assets	101,778	90,603
Total assets	$1,120,939	$1,047,019
Liabilities and Shareholders' Equity		
Current liabilities:		
Notes payable	$ 34,204	$ 28,177
Current portion of long-term debt	4,305	5,572
Current obligations under capital leases	2,616	2,900
Accounts payable	77,491	80,061
Accrued expenses	90,181	81,898
Taxes:		
Federal, state, and foreign income taxes	44,942	28,189
Excise taxes	50,877	54,846
Other taxes	8,628	9,019
Total taxes	104,447	92,054
Dividends payable	9,794	8,886
Total current liabilities	323,038	299,548
Long-term debt due after one year	199,649	201,306
Capital lease obligations	24,262	24,132
Other long-term liabilities	15,536	20,328
Minority interest in foreign subsidiaries	6,723	5,347
Shareholders' equity:		
Preferred stock:		
Series A	866	927
Series B	220	244
Common stock	10,760	10,673
Additional paid-in capital	152,606	147,578
Retained earnings	387,279	336,936
Total shareholders' equity	551,731	496,358
Total liabilities and shareholders' equity	$1,120,939	$1,047,019

SOURCE: Heublein Annual Report, 1981.

Table 8—3

HEUBLEIN, INC.
Sources and Uses of Funds
For the Years Ended June 30, 1981, 1980, and 1979
($000)

	Year ended June 30		
	1981	1980	1979
Sources of working capital:			
Operations:			
Net income	$ 88,379	$ 77,411	$ 68,130
Charges (credits) not requiring funds:			
Depreciation and amortization	42,722	39,806	33,837
Deferred income taxes	2,857	1,608	(1,186)
Equity in unremitted earnings of unconsolidated affiliates			
Minority interest in earnings of foreign	(4,428)	(3,559)	(4,033)
subsidiaries	1,376	228	821
Total funds from operations	130,906	115,494	97,569
Book value of assets sold	8,036	10,402	11,164
Increase in long-term debt	5,791	5,426	13,032
Increase in investments in and advances to affiliated companies	3,013	3,751	2,250
Increase in common stock and additional paid-in capital resulting from exercise of stock options and issuance of restricted stock	5,112	2,889	541
Other—net	104	154	1,027
Total sources of working capital	152,962	138,116	125,583
Uses of working capital:			
Additions to property, plant, and equipment	63,984	73,854	72,896
Dividends declared	38,036	34,566	31,631
Additions to cost in excess of net assets of purchased businesses, trademarks, contracts, and franchises	12,889	357	7,674
Reduction of long-term debt	7,448	12,496	3,353
Increase in other assets	1,534	8,384	538
Decrease (increase) in other long-term liabilities	7,519	520	(2,812)
Total uses of working capital	131,410	130,177	113,280
Increase in working capital	$ 21,552	$ 7,939	$ 12,303
Changes in working capital:			
Cash and temporary investments	$ 36,877	$(14,958)	$(12,653)
Accounts and notes receivable	3,717	15,387	9,475
Inventories	3,698	25,819	57,155
Deferred income tax benefits	(1,819)	10,390	4,050
Prepaid expenses	2,569	2,580	(2,468)
Notes payable, current portion of long-term debt and current obligations under capital leases	(4,476)	(12,553)	5,390
Accounts payable, accrued expenses, and taxes	(18,106)	(17,970)	(47,989)
Dividends payable	(908)	(756)	(657)
Increase in working capital	$ 21,552	$ 7,939	$ 12,303

SOURCE: Heublein Annual Report, 1981.

Figure 8—1   **Relationship of funds statement to balance sheet**

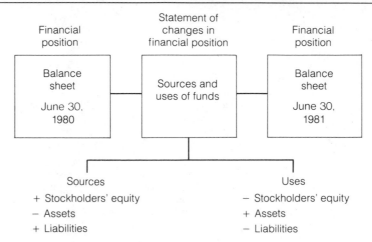

where—perhaps in new product development or in other asset accounts. Finally, an increase in liabilities represents a flow of new funds into the business. Heublein had only a $5.8 million increase in long-term debt in 1981, which is a rather small amount of the total sources of funds.

Uses of funds   Now look at the opposite side of the coin. A use of funds could come about from a reduction in stockholders' equity from losses to the firm, a reduction of outstanding shares, or the payment of dividends. An increase in the cash account as well as an increase in any asset account, such as inventory or plant and equipment, is also a use of funds. Another use of funds is a reduction in liability accounts (In 1981, Heublein retired $7.4 million of long-term debt, or $1.6 million more than it borrowed).

Analysis of funds statements   In analyzing a sources and uses of funds statement, the analyst examines how the buildup (or reduction) in assets was accomplished. For example, are increases in long-term assets being supported by profits and long-term borrowing, or are they being financed by the more dangerous route of short-term borrowings? In the case of Heublein for 1981, the major uses of funds were to add $64 million in plant and equipment and pay dividends of $38 million. These payments were more than adequately covered by net income and depreciation, leaving a $21 million increase in working capital, a healthy financial picture.

Heublein also provided an analysis of how the increase in working capital was being deployed labeled "changes in working capital" at the bottom of table 8–3. For the time being, the firm was content to increase cash and temporary investments until the funds were needed in other areas.

KEY FINANCIAL RATIOS FOR THE SECURITY ANALYST

We have just summarized the three major financial statements that will be the basis of your analysis in this section emphasizing financial ratios. Ratio analysis brings together balance sheet and income statement data to create a better understanding of the firm's past and current health, and this will aid you in forecasting the future outlook.

Ratio analysis

Ratios are used in much of our daily life. We buy cars based on miles per gallon; we evaluate baseball players by earned run averages and batting averages and basketball players by field-goal and foul-shooting percentages; and so on. These are all ratios constructed to judge comparative performance. Financial ratios serve a similar purpose, but you must know what is being measured in order to construct a ratio and to understand the significance of the resultant number.

Financial ratios are used to weigh and evaluate the operating performance and capital structure of the firm. While an absolute value, such as earnings of $50,000 or accounts receivable of $100,000, may appear satisfactory, its acceptability can only be measured in relation to other values.

For example, are earnings of $50,000 actually good? If a company earned $50,000 on $500,000 of sales (10 percent "profit margin" ratio), that might be quite satisfactory. But earnings of $50,000 on $5 million could be disappointing (a meager 1 percent return). After we have computed the appropriate ratio, we must compare the firm's results to those achieved by similar firms in our industry as well as our own firm's past record of performance. Even then, this "number crunching" process is not always adequate since we are forced to supplement our financial findings with an evaluation of company management, physical facilities, and numerous other factors.

Ratio analysis will not discover "gold mines" for the analyst. It is more like a physical exam at the doctor's office. You hope you are all right, but if not, you are content to know what is wrong and what to do about it. Just like with medical illness, some diseases are easier to cure than others, and the same is true of financial illness. The analyst is the doctor. He or she determines the illness and keeps track of management to see if they can administer the cure. Sometimes ailing companies can be very good values. Penn Central went into bankruptcy, and its common stock could have been purchased at $2 per share for several years. In 1981, 10 years later, Penn Central stock traded in the $40–$50 range. It was one sick company that got cured, and any investor willing to take a risk would have profited nicely.

Bankruptcy studies

In a sense, ratio analysis protects an investor from picking losers more so than it guarantees picking winners. Several studies have used ratios as predictors of financial failure. The most notable studies are by William Beaver and

Edward Altman. Beaver found that ratios of failing firms signal failure as much as five years ahead of bankruptcy, and as bankruptcy approaches, the ratios deteriorate more rapidly with the greatest deterioration in the last year.[1] The Beaver studies also found that: (1) "Investors recognize and adjust to the new solvency positions of failing firms. (2) The price changes of the common stocks act as if investors rely upon ratios as a basis for their assessments, and impound the ratio information in the market prices."

The Altman research indicated that ratios were 95 percent accurate in predicting failure one year ahead of bankruptcy and 72 percent accurate two years head of failure, with the average lead time for the ratio signal being 20 months.[2] Altman developed a Z score, which was an index developed through multiple discriminate analysis that predicted failure. The Z score relied on the following ratios:

1. Net working capital/total assets (liquidity).
2. Retained earnings/total assets (cumulative profitability).
3. Earnings before interest and taxes (EBIT)/total assets (productivity of assets).
4. Market value of equity/book value of debt (debt utilization).
5. Sales/total assets (competitive position).

The greater the firm's bankruptcy potential, the lower its Z score. The ratios were not equally significant, but together they separated the companies into a correct bankruptcy group and nonbankruptcy group 95 percent of the time. One interesting result that demonstrates relationships is that a negative relationship existed between items 3 and 5. As profits declined (3), sales/total assets (5) rose. The explanation? Failing firms do not replace their assets, and so assets either decline faster than sales or sales stay level on a smaller asset base. Normally, rising asset turnover would indicate a positive picture, but when combined with other ratios, the picture changes. In the next section, we present six classifications of ratios that ought to be helpful to the analyst. Many more could be used, but we leave you to your own inventions if you need to create a measurement device that is not satisfied by the following list.

Classification system

We divide 20 significant ratios into six primary groupings.

A. Profitability ratios:
    1. Operating margin.
    2. Aftertax profit margin.
    3. Return on assets.
    4. Return on equity.

---

[1]William H. Beaver, "Market Prices, Financial Ratios, and the Prediction of Failure," *Journal of Accounting Research,* Autumn 1968, pp. 179–92.

[2]Edward I. Altman, "Financial Ratios, Discriminant Analysis and the Prediction of Corporate Bankruptcy," *Journal of Finance,* September 1968, pp. 589–609.

B. Asset utilization ratios:
  5. Receivable turnover.
  6. Inventory turnover.
  7. Fixed asset turnover.
  8. Total asset turnover.
C. Liquidity ratios:
  9. Current ratio.
  10. Quick ratio.
  11. Net working capital to total assets.
D. Debt utilization ratios:
  12. Long-term debt to equity.
  13. Total debt to total assets.
  14. Times interest earned.
  15. Fixed charge coverage.
E. Price ratios:
  16. Price to earnings.
  17. Price to book value.
  18. Dividends to price (dividend yield).
F. Other ratios:
  19. Average tax rate.
  20. Dividend payout.

The interpretation of ratios is as much a science as an art, and one can compare ratio analysis to putting together a puzzle. It takes all the pieces of a puzzle to make a complete picture, and so it is with ratios—only with ratios, whether the picture is in focus depends on the interpretative skill of the analyst.

The users of financial statements will attach different degrees of importance to the six categories of ratios. To the potential investor, the critical consideration is profitability and debt utilization. For the banker or trade creditor, the emphasis shifts to the firm's current ability to meet debt obligations in terms of liquidity ratios. The bondholder, in turn, may be primarily influenced by debt to total assets—while also eyeing the profitability of the firm in terms of its ability to cover interest payments in the short term and principal payments in the long term. Of course, the shrewd analyst looks at all the ratios with different degrees of attention.

A. Profitability ratios The profitability ratios allow the analyst to measure the ability of the firm to earn an adequate return on sales, total assets, and invested capital. The profit margin ratios (1, 2) relate to income statement items, while the two return ratios (3, 4) relate the income statement (numerator) to the balance sheet (denominator). Many of the problems related to profitability can be explained, in whole or in part, by the firm's ability to effectively employ its resources. We shall apply these ratios to Heublein's income statement and balance

sheet previously presented in Tables 8–1 and 8–2 for 1981. The values are further rounded for ease of computation ($'s in millions).

Heublein ratios.

A. Profitability ratios (1981)

1. Operating margin $= \dfrac{\text{Operating income}}{\text{Sales (revenue)}} = \dfrac{\$\ 224}{\$2050} = 10.92\%$

2. Aftertax profit margin $= \dfrac{\text{Net income}}{\text{Sales (revenue)}} = \dfrac{\$\ 88}{\$2050} = 4.29\%$

3. Return on assets

    (a) $\dfrac{\text{Net income}}{\text{Total assets}} \qquad\qquad = \dfrac{\$\ 88}{\$1121} = 7.85\%$

    (b) $\dfrac{\text{Net income}}{\text{Sales}} \times \dfrac{\text{Sales}}{\text{Total assets}}$

         $4.29\% \times 1.83 \qquad\qquad = 7.85\%$

4. Return on equity

    (a) $\dfrac{\text{Net income}}{\text{Stockholders' equity}} = \dfrac{\$\ 88}{\$\ 552} = 15.95\%$

    (b) $\dfrac{\text{Return on assets}}{(1 - \text{Total debt/Total assets})} = \dfrac{7.85\%}{1 - .508} = 15.95\%$

The profitability ratios indicate some slippage of income between operating margin and aftertax profit margin that is more than one would expect with a 46 percent tax rate. This leads us to suspect that interest expense, excise taxes, lease expense, or other charges significantly reduced aftertax income.

Du Pont analysis. Notice that the return on assets and return on equity have a part *(a)* and *(b)*, or two ways to determine the ratio. The method employed in part *(b)*, which originated in the Du Pont Company's financial system, helps the analyst see the relationship between the income statement and the balance sheet. For example, the return on assets is generated by multiplying the aftertax profit margin (income statement) by the asset turnover ratio (combination income statement-balance sheet ratio).

The Du Pont Company was a forerunner in stressing that satisfactory return on assets may be achieved through high profit margins, or rapid turnover of assets, or a combination of both. The Du Pont system causes the analyst to examine the sources of a company's profitability. Since the profit margin is an income statement ratio, a high profit margin indicates good cost control, whereas a high asset turnover ratio demonstrates efficient use of the assets on the balance sheet. Different industries have different operating and financial structures. For example, in the heavy capital goods industry, the emphasis is on a high profit

margin with a low asset turnover—while in food processing, the profit margin is low, and the key to satisfactory returns on total assets is a rapid turnover of assets.

Du Pont analysis further stresses that the return on equity stems from the return on assets adjusted for the amount of financial leverage by using the total debt-to-asset ratio. Over one half of Heublein's assets are financed by debt (50.8 percent), and the return on equity reflects this method of financing by being more than twice as large as the return on assets (15.95 percent versus 7.85 percent). As a detective, the financial analyst can judge how much debt a company employs by comparing these two measures of return. Of course, you will want to check this clue with the debt utilization ratios. The total relationship between return on assets and return on equity under the Du Pont system is depicted in Figure 8–2.

In computing return on assets and equity, the analyst must be sensitive to the age of the assets. Plant and equipment purchased 15 years ago may be carried on the books far below its replacement value in an inflationary economy. A 20 percent return on assets purchased in the late 1950s or early 60s may be inferior to a 15 percent return on newly purchased assets.

B. Asset utilization ratios Under this heading, we measure the speed at which the firm is turning over accounts receivable, inventory, and longer-term assets. In other words, asset utilization ratios measure how many times per year a company sells its inventory or collects its entire accounts receivable. For long-term assets, the utilization ratio tells us how productive the fixed assets are in terms of sales generation.

Figure 8–2   **Du Pont analysis**

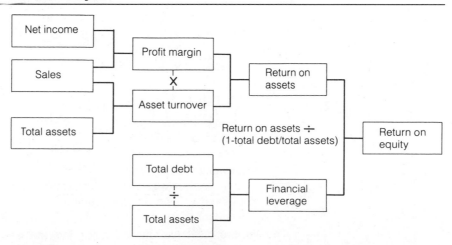

B. Asset utilization ratios (Heublein, 1981)

5. Receivables turnover $= \dfrac{\text{Sales}}{\text{Receivables}} = \dfrac{\$2050}{\$\ 199} = 10.30\times$

6. Inventory turnover $\ \ = \dfrac{\text{Sales}}{\text{Inventory}} = \dfrac{\$2050}{\$\ 304} = \ 6.74\times$

7. Fixed asset turnover $= \dfrac{\text{Sales}}{\text{Fixed assets}} = \dfrac{\$2050}{\$\ 389} = \ 5.27\times$

8. Total asset turnover $\ \ = \dfrac{\text{Sales}}{\text{Total assets}} = \dfrac{\$2050}{\$1121} = \ 1.83\times$

The asset utilization ratios further relate the income statement (numerator) to the various assets on the balance sheet. Heublein seems to be utilizing its assets fairly well.

We have not yet discussed Heublein's markets, but at this point, it seems appropriate to point out that Heublein sells such products as wines, Smirnoff vodka, grocery items, and Kentucky Fried Chicken. Now what does this add to your knowledge and interpretation of the above ratios? These ratios are a combination of two industries—the distilling industry, which has large investments in receivables and inventory, and the fast-food industry, which has very little receivables and large investments in fixed assets. The receivable turnover would be much higher than other distillers because of the Kentucky Fried Chicken business, and therefore, industry comparison would not be helpful in this case.

C. Liquidity ratios The primary emphasis of the liquidity ratios is a determination of the firm's ability to pay off short-term obligations as they come due. These ratios can be related to receivables and inventory turnover in that a faster turnover creates a more rapid movement of cash through the company and improves liquidity. Again, remember that each industry will be different. A jewelry store chain will have much different ratios than a grocery store chain.

C. Liquidity ratios (Heublein, 1981)

9. Current ratio $= \dfrac{\text{Current assets}}{\text{Current liabilities}} \qquad = \dfrac{\$610}{\$323} \qquad = 1.89$

10. Quick ratio $= \dfrac{\text{Current assets} - \text{Inventories}}{\text{Current liabilities}} = \dfrac{\$305}{\$323} \qquad = \ .94$

11. Net working capital to total assets $=$
$\dfrac{\text{Current assets} - \text{Current liabilities}}{\text{Total assets}} = \dfrac{\$610 - 323}{\$1121} = \ .26$

The first two ratios (current and quick) indicate whether the firm can pay off its short-term debt in an emergency by liquidating its current assets. The quick

ratio looks only at the most liquid assets, which include cash, marketable securities, and receivables. Cash and securities are already liquid, but receivables usually will be turned into cash during the collection period. If there is concern about the firm's liquidity, the analyst will want to cross-check the liquidity ratios with receivable turnover and inventory turnover to determine how fast the current assets are turned into cash during an ordinary cycle.

The last liquidity ratio is a measure of the percentage of current assets (after short-term debt has been paid) to total assets. This indicates the liquidity of the assets of the firm. The higher the ratio, the greater the short-term assets relative to fixed assets and the safer the position of the company. This ratio was used by Altman in his bankruptcy studies and was quite significant.

Heublein seems to be in reasonable shape. Alcohol is not a perishable good and could be sold to other distilling companies if necessary. This makes the current ratio quite safe, and when combined with a quick ratio of almost 1, the firm would not cause its creditors any concern.

D. Debt utilization ratios The debt utilization ratios provide an indication of the way the firm is financed between debt (lenders) and equity (owners) and therefore helps the analyst determine the amount of financial risk present in the firm. Too much debt can not only impair liquidity with heavy interest payments, but can also damage profitability and the health of the firm during an economic recession or industry slowdown.

D. Debt utilization ratios (Heublein, 1981)

12. Long-term debt to equity

$$\frac{\text{Long-term liabilities}}{\text{Stockholders' equity}} = \frac{\$200}{\$552} = .36$$

13. Total debt to total assets

$$\frac{\text{Total debt}}{\text{Total assets}} = \frac{\$569}{\$1121} = .508$$

14. Times interest earned

$$\frac{\text{Income before interest and taxes}}{\text{Interest}} = \frac{\$224}{\$28} = 8.0 \times$$

15. Fixed charge coverage[3]

$$\frac{\text{Income before fixed charges and taxes}}{\text{Fixed charges}} = \frac{\$224}{\$28 + 19} = 4.7 \times$$

We have already discussed the impact of financial leverage on the return on equity, and the first two ratios in this category indicate to the analyst how much

---

[3]Fixed charges in 1981 were $19 million in lease expenses. There were no sinking fund payments.

financial leverage is being used by the firm. The more debt, the greater the interest payments and the greater the impact on the firm's earnings. Companies with stable sales and earnings, such as utilities, can afford to employ more leverage than those in cyclical industries, such as automobiles or airlines. Ratio 12, long-term debt to equity, provides information concerning the long-term capital structure of the firm. In the case of Heublein, long-term liabilities represent 36 percent of the stockholders' equity base provided by the owners of the firm. Ratio 13, total debt to total assets, looks at the total assets and the use of borrowed capital. Each firm must consider its optimum capital structure, and the analyst should be aware of industry fluctuations in assessing the firm's proper use of leverage. Heublein seems quite safe given that its business is not subject to large swings in sales.

The last two debt utilization ratios indicate the firm's ability to meet its cash payments due on fixed obligations, such as interest, lease payments, licensing fees, or sinking fund charges. The higher these ratios, the more protected the creditor's position. Use of the fixed charge coverage is more conservative than interest earned since it includes all fixed charges. Now that leases are capitalized and show up on the balance sheet, it is easier to understand that lease payments are similar in importance to interest expense. Charges after taxes, such as sinking fund payments, must be adjusted to before-tax income. For example, if a firm is in the 40 percent tax bracket and must make a $60,000 sinking fund payment, the firm would have had to generate $100,000 in before-tax income to meet that obligation. The adjustment would be as follows:

$$\text{Before-tax income required} = \frac{\text{After tax payment}}{(1 - \text{tax rate})}$$
$$= \frac{\$60,000}{(1 - .40)}$$
$$= \$100,000$$

Heublein's fixed charge coverage is quite a bit less than its interest earned ratio, but it still provides reasonable protection for its leaseholders and creditors. In this case, the company had no sinking fund charges.

E. Price ratios   Price ratios relate the internal performance of the firm to external judgment of the marketplace in terms of value. What is the firm's end result in market value? The price ratios indicate the expectations of the market relative to other companies. For example, a firm with a high price-to-earnings ratio has a higher market price relative to $1 of earnings than a company with a lower ratio.

E.   Price ratios (Heublein, June 30, 1981)

$$16. \quad \text{Price to earnings} = \frac{\text{Common stock price}}{\text{Earnings per share}} = \frac{\$30.95}{\$\ 3.93} = 7.9\times$$
$$\text{(fully diluted)}$$

17. Price to book value $= \dfrac{\text{Common stock price}}{\text{Book value per share}} = \dfrac{\$30.95}{\$24.50} = 1.26 \times$

18. Dividends to price (dividend yield)

$= \dfrac{\text{Dividends per share}}{\text{Commons stock price}} = \dfrac{\$1.78}{\$30.95} = 5.8\%$

Heublein's price-earnings ratio indicates that the firm's stock value is $7.90 for every $1 of earnings. This number can be compared to other companies in the distilling industry and/or fast-food industry. As indicated in Chapter 7, the price-earnings ratio (or P/E ratio, as it is commonly called) is influenced by the earnings and the sales growth of the firm, the risk (or volatility in performance), the dividend payment policy, the quality of management, and a number of other factors. The P/E ratio indicates expectations about the future of a company. Those firms which are expected to provide returns greater than those for the market in general with equal or less risk often have P/E ratios higher than the market P/E ratio.

Expectations of returns and P/E ratios do change over time as Table 8–4 illustrates. A selected list of price-earnings ratios for U.S. firms at the end of 1975 and 1981 shows that during this six-year period, price-earnings ratios generally fell. A change in investor philosophy may have substantially lowered the P/E ratio of many of the traditional growth stocks, such as IBM, McDonald's, and Texas Instruments. On the other hand, the rising price of oil helped the oil-service industry, and this may be why Haliburton's P/E held constant in an environment of generally lower P/E ratios.

The price-to-book-value ratio relates the market value of the company to the historical accounting value of the firm. In a company that has old assets, this ratio may be quite high, but one with new, undepreciated, fixed assets might

Table 8–4   **Price-earnings ratios for selected U.S. corporations**

		P/E ratio	
Corporation	Industry	December 31, 1975	December 10, 1981
Exxon	International oil	8	5
Texas Utilities	Public utility	9	6
Union Carbide	Chemical	9	5
Bank America	Banking	10	7
CBS	Broadcasting	11	7
Haliburton	Oil service	12	12
Winn-Dixie	Retail	14	8
IBM	Computers	17	9
Upjohn	Ethical drugs	18	10
McDonald's	Restaurant franchises	26	10
Texas Instruments	Semiconductors	34	15

have a lower ratio. This ratio needs to be combined with your knowledge of the company's assets and industry norms.

The dividend yield is part of the total return that an investor receives along with capital gains or losses.

F. Other ratios The other ratios presented in category F are to help the analyst spot special tax situations that affect the profitability of an industry or company, and to determine what percentage of earnings are being paid to the stockholder and what is being reinvested for internal growth.

F. Other ratios

$$19. \quad \text{Tax rates} = \frac{\text{Income tax}}{\text{Taxable income}} = \frac{\$\ 79.9}{\$168.3} = 47.5\%$$

$$20. \quad \text{Payout ratio} = \frac{\text{Dividends per share}}{\text{Earnings per share}} = \frac{\$1.78}{\$3.93} = 45.3\%$$

These ratios are calculated to provide the analyst with information that may indicate unusual tax treatment or reinvestment policies. For example, the tax ratio for forest products companies will be low because of the capital gains treatment given to timber cuttings. A company's tax rate may decline in one year due to heavy capital expenditures and the resultant investment tax credits. Earnings per share may rise, but we need to know if it is from operations or favorable tax treatment. If it is from operations, we will be more sure of next year's forecast, but if it is from tax benefits, we cannot count on them to be continual except for an industry like forest products.

The dividend payout ratio provides data concerning the firm's reinvestment strategies. A high payout ratio tells the analyst that the stockholder is receiving a large part of the earnings and that the company is not retaining much income for new plant and equipment or product development. High payouts are usually found in industries that do not have great growth potential, while low payout ratios are associated with firms in growth industries.

USES OF RATIOS

The previous section presented 20 ratios that may be helpful to the analyst in evaluating a firm. In a healthy firm, ratios may not tell us much except that the firm is not in trouble, and that can be good news. How do we use the data we have gathered to check the health of companies we are interested in analyzing?

One way is to compare the company to the industry. This is becoming more difficult as companies diversify into several industries. Twenty years ago, firms competed in one industry, and ratio comparisons were more reliable. Now companies have a wide range of products and markets. Heublein is a case in point. Table 8–5 presents the business segments that Heublein operates.

Table 8–5

HEUBLEIN, INC.
Business Segments
For the Years Ended June 30, 1981, 1980, and 1979
($000)

The Company operates worldwide principally in four business segments: production and marketing of distilled spirits and prepared cocktails (spirits), production and/or marketing of wines and brandies (wines), production and sale of specialty food products (grocery) and operating and franchising principally Kentucky Fried Chicken restaurants (restaurants). The business segment information for each of the three years ended June 30 is presented below:

	1981	1980	1979
Revenues:			
Spirits	$ 876,546	$ 883,419	$ 819,563
Wines	378,497	386,938	368,972
Grocery	153,552	131,511	114,193
Restaurants	641,526	520,011	466,346
Consolidated	$2,050,121	$1,921,879	$1,769,074
Operating profit:			
Spirits	$ 107,078	$ 93,341	$ 85,570
Wines	26,551	32,655	31,451
Grocery	21,545	17,904	17,989
Restaurants	69,126	51,302	34,966
Consolidated	224,300	195,202	169,976
Interest expense	28,581	25,361	23,106
Corporate and miscellaneous—net	27,378	23,783	15,851
Income before income taxes	$ 168,341	$ 146,058	$ 131,019
Identifiable assets:			
Spirits	$ 318,695	$ 320,379	$ 300,703
Wines	318,137	308,445	282,559
Grocery	61,601	63,219	66,696
Restaurants	316,519	276,682	244,330
Corporate	105,987	78,294	82,545
Consolidated	$1,120,939	$1,047,019	$ 976,833
Capital expenditures:			
Spirits	$ 4,386	$ 5,825	$ 6,980
Wines	7,148	14,885	20,414
Grocery	3,514	3,087	5,456
Restaurants	48,686	49,721	38,987
Corporate	250	336	1,059
Consolidated	$ 63,984	$ 73,854	$ 72,896
Depreciation and amortization:			
Spirits	$ 6,422	$ 6,393	$ 5,648
Wines	8,429	8,910	6,784
Grocery	3,143	3,644	3,243
Restaurants	23,546	19,616	16,766
Corporate	1,182	1,243	1,396
Consolidated	$ 42,722	$ 39,806	$ 33,837

SOURCE: Heublein Annual Report, 1981.

Heublein has four principal business segments consisting of spirits, wine, grocery, and restaurants. This additional data adds a new dimension to our analysis. Although spirits is the largest segment in terms of revenues and profits, it is third in capital expenditures. This implies that Heublein is changing the makeup of the firm's assets. Over the last several years, it has been upgrading its Kentucky Fried Chicken restaurants to recapture market share lost to McDonald's and other fast-food chains. It has been successful in doing so as indicated by the improvement in the profitability of the restaurant segment from 1979 through 1981.

If we look further, we can tell that it takes less investment to generate one dollar of sales in spirits than in restaurants. The assets employed in spirits, wines, and restaurants are almost exactly the same, and yet the revenues are significantly different. The most productive assets in terms of sales generation are in the grocery segment. After examining Table 8–5, an analyst realizes that Heublein's ratios reflect a composite of several industries. Familiarity with all four segments makes the analyst more capable of interpreting the significance of these ratios. It may be that the analyst will compare the ratios with two or more industries rather than one. Table 8–6 compares selected Heublein ratios with the spirits and fast-food industries.

Heublein's profit margins are not as high as either the fast-food or spirits industry, and some improvement in pricing or cost control could benefit bottom-line profits. However, return on equity is between the two industries, and Heublein's use of long-term debt is more conservative.

COMPARING TRENDS

Over the course of the business cycle, sales and profitability may expand and contract, and ratio analysis for any one year may not present an accurate picture of the firm. Therefore, we look at trend analysis of performance over a number of years.

Table 8–6   **Selected ratio comparisons for Heublein, 1981**

	Heublein	Spirits industry	Fast-food industry
Operating margin	10.92%	12.50%	17.50%
Aftertax profit margin	4.29%	8.10%	6.00%
Return on equity	15.95%	12.50%	18.00%
Long-term debt to equity	36.00%	42.10%	84.25%
Price to earnings	7.90×	10.70×	8.50×
Price to book value	1.26×	1.33×	1.53×
Dividend yield	5.80%	3.30%	2.10%
Tax rate	47.50%	47.00%	45.00%
Payout ratio	45.30%	22.00%	18.00%

SOURCE (for industry data): *Value Line Investment Survey* (Arnold Bernard & Co., October 9, 1981).

First examine the 10-year summary of selected financial data for Heublein in Table 8–7. One can see an overall growth in sales with a small decline in sales in 1977. Also note in the middle of the table that the company reached fully diluted earnings per share of $3.27 in 1976 and did not surpass that until four years later in 1980. A more complete understanding of Heublein would indicate market troubles with the Kentucky Fried Chicken operations beginning in 1977 and the cure taking several years. After three years of upgrading the fried chicken units, their profitability had improved greatly by 1981.

While the trends provide even more information concerning Heublein's cyclical nature, trend comparisons with other companies in the industry or other industries would also be helpful.

A GENERAL STUDY OF INDUSTRY TRENDS

In this section we shift our attention slightly to four very different industries and look at their comparative trends over time based on the ratios of return on equity and long-term debt to equity. The specially picked industries are airlines, brewing, chemicals, and drugs. By studying these important industries, the analyst develops a feel for comparative performative in our economy.

The return on equity for the four separate industries shown in Table 8–8 exhibits some wide differences in profitability. Table 8–8 is graphed in Figure 8–3, and the trends are more visible. It is clear that the drug industry has the highest and most consistent returns on equity with very little variation due to industry or economic effects. The chemical industry has the next highest returns but a little more volatility than drugs. Brewing is next followed by airlines, which show a cyclical character and very low returns.

Although it may be easy to generalize about industries and their relationship to economic cycles, individual companies within each industry seem to stand out. The benefit of looking at the industry together is that the best and worst become apparent to the trained analyst. The best and most consistent airline is Delta while American, Eastern and others have had profit squeezes (not included in this analysis is Braniff which went bankrupt in 1982).

In the brewing industry, Heileman stands head and shoulders over the others in terms of return on equity even though it uses very little long-term debt, while Schlitz and Pabst have both deteriorated. Dow has the highest returns in the chemical industry, which on the whole seems not to have any real losers even though Allied had one bad year in 1979. Again, the drug industry has no consistent loser, but Merck seems to be the highest and most consistent of the best.

In Table 8–9 and Figure 8–4, the same four industries' long-term debt-to-equity ratios are given which might explain the impact of financial leverage on the return on equity and possibly explain why some companies and industries are more volatile than others. In general, the airline industry has the

Table 8–7 Consolidated selected financial data ($000 except per share data)

	1981	1980*	1979	1978	1977	1976	1975	1974	1973	1972
Revenues	$2,050,121	$1,921,879	$1,769,074	$1,620,112	$1,550,902	$1,583,133	$1,414,415	$1,240,142	$966,139	$814,000
Costs and expenses:										
Cost of sales	1,381,606	1,325,293	1,222,693	1,139,387	1,094,151	1,100,170	998,872	854,504	661,806	547,065
Selling, advertising, administrative, and general expenses	444,215	401,384	376,405	334,065	318,098	323,151	277,943	255,998	201,776	172,124
Total costs and expenses	1,825,821	1,726,677	1,599,098	1,473,452	1,412,249	1,423,321	1,266,815	1,110,502	863,582	719,189
Operating profit	224,300	195,202	169,976	146,660	138,653	159,812	147,600	129,640	102,557	94,811
Income before income taxes	168,341	146,058	131,019	109,300	95,998	130,286	121,477	111,024	89,544	79,773
Income from continuing operations	88,379	77,411	68,130	56,290	48,617	65,881	59,907	52,341	42,667	38,299
Net income	$ 88,379	$ 77,411	$ 68,130	$ 56,290	$ 41,417	$ 73,065	$ 61,405	$ 54,410	$ 30,411	$ 22,442
Earnings per common and common equivalent share:										
Continuing operations	$4.09	$3.62	$3.19	$2.65	$2.27	$3.06	$2.82	$2.47	$2.04	$1.94
Net earnings	$4.09	$3.62	$3.19	$2.65	$1.93	$3.39	$2.89	$2.57	$1.45	$1.13
Earnings per common share assuming full dilution:										
Continuing operations	$3.93	$3.48	$3.09	$2.58	$2.22	$2.96	$2.71	$2.40	$1.99	$1.87
Net earnings (fully diluted)	$3.93	$3.48	$3.09	$2.58	$1.91	$3.27	$2.78	$2.49	$1.45	$1.11

Statistics:

Dividends declared	$ 38,036	$ 34,566	$ 31,631	$ 29,269	$ 27,333	$ 24,838	$ 22,711	$ 20,497	$ 18,095	$ 15,921
Dividends declared per common share	1.78	1.625	1.49	1.38	1.29	1.175	1.075	.98	.91	.87
Earnings retained in the business†	50,343	42,845	36,499	27,021	21,284	41,043	37,196	31,844	24,572	22,085
Taxes of all kinds†	563,835	588,007	554,484	506,726	469,903	486,338	452,885	421,249	341,247	292,349
Capital expenditures	63,984	73,854	72,896	68,931	56,858	54,215	59,164	59,259	38,954	30,325
Depreciation and amortization†	42,722	39,806	33,837	30,413	27,211	25,052	24,131	14,919	10,750	10,267
Net property, plant, and equipment	388,594	372,043	345,109	313,665	288,062	279,327	252,932	189,880	148,858	149,052
Total assets	1,120,939	1,047,019	976,833	883,246	842,193	848,871	769,985	677,564	532,382	471,428
Long-term obligations and redeemable preferred stock	224,997	226,609	236,172	225,566	226,890	231,888	237,453	202,268	120,646	128,055
Working capital	286,551	264,999	257,060	236,418	232,405	228,948	217,297	212,800	124,800	147,530
Common and common equivalent shares (thousands)	21,626	21,404	21,363	21,251	21,435	21,537	21,217	21,166	20,932	19,608
Common shareholders	22,485	24,328	26,620	28,247	29,071	24,769	27,174	27,493	28,537	30,044
Worldwide employment	28,540	27,062	24,922	22,817	22,789	24,871	25,912	24,711	18,300	17,452

Ratios:

Current ratio	1.9 to 1	1.9 to 1	2.0 to 1	2.0 to 1	2.1 to 1	2.0 to 1	2.1 to 1	2.2 to 1	1.8 to 1	2.4 to 1
Return on shareholders' equity†	16.9%	16.3%	15.8%	14.1%	12.8%	19.0%	19.6%	19.3%	17.8%	18.8%
Income as a percent of revenues†	4.31%	4.03%	3.85%	3.47%	3.13%	4.16%	4.24%	4.22%	4.42%	4.71%

*After giving effect to a change to the LIFO method of valuing certain inventories.

†Based on continuing operations.

SOURCE: Heublein Annual Report, 1981.

Table 8—8   Return on equity (percent)

Industry	1973	1974	1975	1976	1977	1978	1979	1980
Airline	4.3%	6.6%	NMF	7.3%	11.9%	16.6%	6.8%	NMF
American	NMF	3.6	NMF	9.2	10.2	16.2	9.8	NMF
Delta	18.1	20.4	10.2	13.0	14.9	17.8	16.0	10.1%
Eastern	NMF	2.3	NMF	10.4	9.1	15.3	11.8	NMF
Pan American	NMF	NMF	NMF	NMF	2.5	18.3	10.5	10.0
Brewing	11.5	10.0	8.8	11.7	11.1	10.3	10.1	12.5
Anheuser-Busch	13.1	11.9	14.3	9.0	13.5	14.7	15.8	16.6
Coors	14.6	11.3	14.1	15.4	12.2	9.2	10.4	9.1
G. Heileman	16.4	12.3	13.3	21.7	22.8	23.2	27.4	27.3
Pabst	10.5	8.2	8.8	12.6	8.1	4.1	3.5	4.5
Schlitz	19.3	15.5	9.5	14.0	5.5	3.4	NMF	8.3
Chemical	14.5	16.9	13.2	14.1	12.9	13.6	15.0	13.0
Allied	10.6	14.9	11.1	11.3	11.6	9.5	.8	15.0
Dow	17.7	29.8	25.1	21.4	17.8	16.9	20.1	18.1
Du Pont	16.3	10.8	7.1	11.4	12.8	16.5	17.7	12.6
Monsanto	16.1	18.4	15.5	16.3	11.5	11.7	11.9	5.3
Union Carbide	13.8	21.2	13.9	14.4	11.3	10.8	13.8	14.1
Drug	19.6	19.4	18.5	18.1	16.6	19.2	20.0	19.4
Lilly	21.3	21.1	18.9	18.6	18.1	20.1	21.0	19.7
Merck	25.7	25.6	24.1	23.2	22.8	21.1	22.9	22.3
Pfizer	15.9	15.9	15.9	15.7	25.6	16.5	16.8	16.2
Searle (G. D.)	22.2	21.3	20.2	14.1	NMF	16.9	18.0	17.9
Upjohn	19.0	17.1	15.1	15.8	16.7	20.2	20.1	19.7

Note: NMF = No profit.

SOURCE: *Value Line Investment Survey* (Arnold Bernard & Co., selected issues).

most debt by a large margin, followed by the chemical, brewing, and drug industries.

The basic business of airlines requires a large capital commitment in terms of airplanes, and therefore, a large amount of debt is needed to finance them since profitability is not sufficient to provide enough internal funds. Delta is the exception, and because of the low level of debt (its been declining), its returns are more stable.

All the other industries are in safe territory. Coors has no debt, while Anheuser-Busch has a rising ratio due to its rapid expansion during the last half of the 1970s. Dow leads the chemicals with the highest debt-to-equity ratio, and Du Pont is the lowest. The drug industry in general has low levels of debt mostly because their consistently high returns allow internal generation of funds and little reliance on the debt markets.

These tables and figures only cover two ratios, but they should get across the point that industry comparisons allow you to pick the quality companies and find the potential losers. These two ratios can be extremely important when making risk-return choices between common stocks.

Figure 8—3   Return on equity

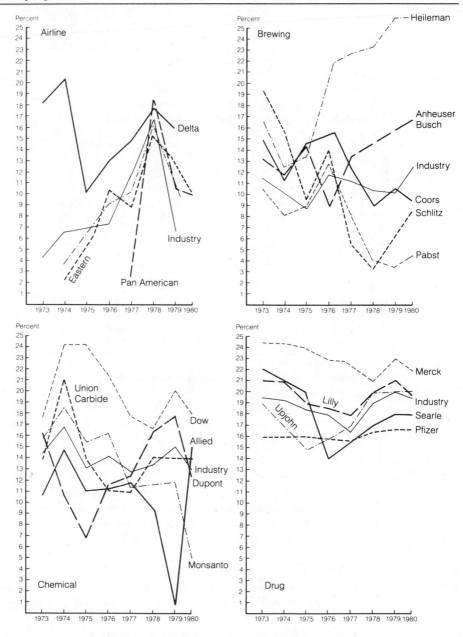

Table 8–9 Long-term debt to equity (percent)

Industry	1973	1974	1975	1976	1977	1978	1979	1980
Airline	143.0%	130.3%	136.0%	111.0%	91.4%	106.0%	118.6%	140.0%
American	108.5	84.3	83.4	68.2	59.7	119.3	131.0	158.2
Delta	46.0	77.7	82.2	64.7	38.3	22.7	14.7	16.0
Eastern	235.0	204.0	214.5	167.0	116.0	213.0	256.6	250.9
Pan American	224.6	277.8	314.8	206.5	303.6	132.3	138.4	175.8
Brewing	20.9	29.5	39.0	35.5	31.7	32.0	32.7	39.4
Anheuser-Busch	18.6	35.9	57.6	53.7	48.6	55.7	55.2	71.0
Coors	—	—	—	—	—	—	—	—
G. Heileman	48.2	38.2	40.2	29.0	22.2	21.2	31.5	35.8
Pabst	—	—	—	—	7.3	9.5	7.5	5.2
Schlitz	12.7	45.6	65.0	61.8	54.2	38.0	43.8	36.8
Chemical	36.9	38.3	43.2	44.7	51.2	50.0	46.6	45.3
Allied	47.7	43.3	59.0	57.3	69.4	74.6	66.7	46.0
Dow	80.2	66.2	63.8	65.6	76.1	86.5	78.6	77.7
Du Pont	6.6	21.1	23.2	31.7	30.0	23.1	20.8	19.4
Monsanto	39.0	33.4	42.8	40.6	42.9	47.4	43.2	48.8
Union Carbide	44.6	35.7	46.5	51.5	47.0	40.7	43.9	38.9
Drugs	12.5	16.6	24.9	25.8	23.8	22.5	20.2	18.9
Lilly	.8	.6	1.2	1.8	—	.3	.2	1.9
Merck	4.0	5.2	23.0	19.7	16.7	14.5	12.8	11.3
Pfizer	18.4	29.9	50.7	45.7	41.2	42.8	40.0	37.1
Searle (G. D.)	73.9	60.5	87.0	78.8	90.2	80.2	50.3	16.5
Upjohn	17.0	14.3	41.0	46.0	41.2	33.6	29.8	35.3

Note: — = No long-term debt.

SOURCE: *Value Line Investment Survey* (Arnold Bernard & Co., selected issues).

DEFICIENCIES OF FINANCIAL STATEMENTS

Several differences occur between companies and industries, and inflation has additionally clouded the meaning of accounting statements. Some of the more important difficulties occur in the area of inflation-adjusted accounting statements, inventory valuation, extraordinary gains and losses, pension fund liabilities, research and development, deferred taxes, and foreign exchange accounting. We do not have space to cover all of them, but we will touch on the most important ones.

Inflation effects

As previously indicated in Chapter 5, inflation causes phantom sources of profit that may mislead even the most alert analyst. The major problem is that revenue is almost always stated in current dollars, whereas plant and equipment or inventory may have been purchased at lower price levels. Thus, profit may be more a function of increasing prices than of satisfactory performance.

Much of the distortion of inflation shows up on the balance sheet since most of the values on the balance sheet are stated on a historical- or original-cost

Figure 8—4 Long-term debt to equity

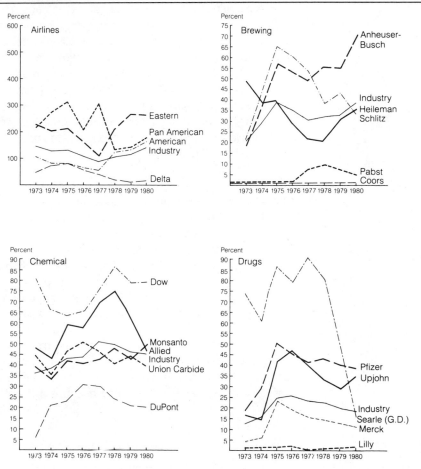

basis. This may be particularly troublesome in the case of plant and equipment and inventory, which may now be worth two or three times the original cost or—from a negative viewpoint—may require many times the original cost for replacement.

The accounting profession has been groping with this problem for decades, and the discussion becomes particularly intense each time inflation rears its ugly head. In October 1979, the Financial Accounting Standards Board (FASB) issued a ruling *(Statement No. 33)* that required about 1,300 large companies to disclose inflation-adjusted accounting data in their annual reports. This information is disclosed in addition to the traditlonal historical cost data, and it could show up in obscure footnotes or in a separate full-fledged financial section with detailed explanations.

Inflation-adjusted accounting is a relatively new concept in accounting prac-

tice, and most likely, it will undergo many modifications over time. To begin, the FASB is requiring the use of two separate methods. The first, called the constant-dollar method, adjusts statements by using the consumer price index. The second, called the current-cost method (sometimes referred to as replacement cost), requires assets to be revalued at their current cost. This will affect inventory and plant and equipment the most, thus affecting overall balance sheet accounts and the total asset value of the firm. The revaluation will also affect inflation-adjusted profits through adjustments to depreciation expense and cost of goods sold, and profits will be smaller than they would be on a historical-cost basis. Appendix A presents Heublein, Inc., 1981 inflation-adjusted data provided to the stockholders in the company's annual report.

Many financial executives think that the new data will simply confuse most investors, but others see benefits. The most important benefit will be the ability to determine if a company is generating enough cash flow from internal operations to replace worn-out equipment and maintain existing levels of production. Another benefit to investors will come from being able to measure dividends, income, and stock prices in dollars adjusted for inflation.

From a study of 10 chemical firms and eight drug companies using current-cost (replacement-cost) data found in the financial 10-K Statements that these companies filed with the Securities and Exchange Commission, it was found that the changes shown in Table 8–10 occurred in their assets, income, and selected ratios.

The comparison of replacement-cost and historical-cost accounting methods shows that replacement cost reduces income but at the same time increases assets. This increase in assets lowers the debt-to-assets ratio since debt is a monetary asset that is not revalued because it is paid back in nominal dollars.

Table 8–10 **Comparison of replacement cost accounting versus historical cost accounting**

	Ten chemical companies		Eight drug companies	
	Replacement cost	Historical cost	Replacement cost	Historical cost
Increase in assets	28.4%	—	15.4%	—
Decrease in net income before taxes	(45.8%)	—	(19.3%)	—
Return on assets	2.8%	6.2%	8.3%	11.4%
Return on equity	4.9%	13.5%	12.8%	19.6%
Debt to assets ratio	34.3%	43.8%	30.3%	35.2%
Interest coverage ratio (times interest earned)	7.1×	8.4×	15.4×	16.7×

Note: Replacement cost is but one form of current cost. Nevertheless, it is widely used as a measure of current cost.

SOURCE: Jeff Garnett and Geoffrey A. Hirt, "Replacement Cost Data: A Study of the Chemical and Drug Industry for Years 1976 through 1978" (Working paper).

The decreased debt-to-assets ratio would indicate that the financial leverage of the firm is decreased, but a look at the interest coverage ratio tells a different story. Because the interest coverage ratio measures the operating income available to cover interest expense, the declining income penalizes the ratio, and the firm shows a decreased ability to cover its interest cost.

As long as prices continue to rise in an inflationary environment, profits appear to feed on themselves. The main objection is that when prices do level off, there is a rude awakening for management and unsuspecting stockholders as expensive inventory is charged against softening retail prices. A 15 to 20 percent growth rate in earnings may be little more than an "inflationary illusion." Industries most sensitive to inflation-induced profits are those with cyclical products, such as lumber, copper, rubber, and food products, as well as those in which inventory is a significant percentage of sales and profits. Reported profits for the lumber industry have been influenced as much as 50 percent by inventory pricing, and a number of other industries' profits have been influenced by 15 to 20 percent.[4]

Inventory valuation

The income statement can show considerable differences in earnings depending upon the method of inventory valuation. The two basic methods are FIFO (first-in, first-out) and LIFO (last-in, first-out). In an inflationary economy, a firm could be reporting increased profits even though no actual increase in physical output took place. The example of the Rhoades Company will illustrate this point. We first observe their income statement for 1981 in Table 8–11. They sold 1,000 units for $20,000 and show earnings after taxes of $4,200 and an operating margin and aftertax margin of 35 percent and 21 percent, respectively.

Assume that in 1982 the number of units sold remains constant at 1,000 units. However, inflation causes a 10 percent increase in price, from $20 to $22 per unit. Total sales will go up to $22,000, but with no actual increase in physical

Table 8–11

RHOADES CORPORATION
First-Year Income Statement
Net income for 1981

Sales	$20,000 (1,000 units at $20)
Cost of goods sold	10,000 (1,000 units at $10)
Gross profit	10,000
Selling and administrative expense	2,000
Depreciation	1,000
Operating profit	7,000
Taxes (40 percent)	2,800
Earnings after taxes	$ 4,200

Operating margin $7,000/20,000 = 35%
Aftertax margin $4,200/20,000 = 21%

[4]Ronald M. Copeland, Joseph F. Wojdak, and John K. Shank, "The Use of Lifo to Offset Inflation," *Harvard Business Review,* May–June 1971, pp. 91–100.

volume. Further assume the firm uses FIFO inventory pricing, so that inventory first purchased will be written off against current sales. We will assume that 1,000 units of 1981 inventory at a cost of $10 per unit are written off against 1982 sales revenue. If Rhoades used LIFO inventory, and Cost of Goods Sold went up 10 percent also, to $11 per unit, income will be less than under FIFO. Table 8–12 shows the 1982 income statement of Rhoades under both inventory methods.

Table 8–12 demonstrates the differences between FIFO and LIFO inventory methods. Under FIFO, Rhoades Corporation shows higher profit margins and more income even though no physical increase in sales occurs. This is because FIFO costing lags behind current prices, and the company generates "phantom profits" due to capital gains on inventory. Unfortunately, this inventory will need to be replaced next period at higher costs. When and if prices turn lower in a recessionary environment, FIFO will have the opposite effect and show a more negative performance. LIFO inventory costing, on the other hand, relates current costs to current prices, and although profits rise in dollar terms, the margins stay basically the same. The only problem with LIFO inventory accounting is that low-cost layers of inventory build up on the balance sheet of the company and understate inventory. This will cause inventory turnover to appear higher than under FIFO.

Extraordinary gains and losses

Nonrecurring gains or losses may occur from the sale of corporate fixed assets, lawsuits, or similar events that would not be expected to occur often, if ever again. Some analysts argue that such extraordinary events should be included in computing the current income of the firm, while others would leave them off in assessing operating performance. The choice can have a big impact on ratios that rely on earnings or earnings per share. Extraordinary gains can inflate returns, reduce price-earnings ratios, and lower payout ratios if they are included in earnings. The analyst concerned about forecasting should only include those

Table 8–12

RHOADES CORPORATION
Second-Year Income Statement Using FIFO and LIFO
Net Income for 1982

	FIFO	LIFO
Sales	$22,000 (1,000 at $22)	$22,000 (1,000 at $22)
Cost of goods sold	10,000 (1,000 at $10)	11,000 (1,000 at $11)
Gross profit	12,000	11,000
Selling and administrative expense	2,200 (10% of sales)	2,200 (10% of sales)
Depreciation	1,000	1,000
Operating profit	8,800	7,800
Taxes (40 percent)	3,520	3,120
Earnings after taxes	$ 5,280	4,680
Operation margin	$8,800/22,000 = 40%	$7,800/22,000 = 35.4%
Aftertax margin	$5,280/22,000 = 24%	$4,680/22,000 = 21.2%

earnings from continuing operations; otherwise, the forecast will be seriously off its mark. Unfortunately, there is some inconsistency in the manner in which nonrecurring losses are treated in spite of determined attempts by the accounting profession to ensure uniformity of action.

Pension fund liabilities

One area of increasing concern among financial analysts is the unfunded liabilities of corporate pension funds. These funds eventually will have to pay workers their retirement income from the pension fund earnings and assets. Currently, most funds operate in a surplus position as more contributions are received than benefit payments made. Eventually, they will have to pay the piper, and if the money is not available from the pension fund, the company is liable to make the payments. These unfunded pensions may have to come out of earnings in future years, which would penalize shareholders and limit the corporation's ability to reinvest in new assets. The September 14, 1981, issue of *Business Week* pointed out some of the controversy surrounding the FASB's new disclosure requirements. The new accounting rule does not base pension benefits on worker's future earnings, and so the rule understates pension liabilities.[5] However, the FASB did increase the amount of information that corporations must report.[6]

Other distortions

There are always problems in accounting statements and methods of reporting earnings. Space does not permit us to cover each and every area of potential earnings distortion, but a mention of some of them might provide you with areas that require further investigation. As the tax laws change from year to year, so do the possibilities of changes in accounting methods. Some other areas for detective work could be in accounting methods for the following: investment tax credit, research and development expenditures, deferred taxes, foreign exchange currency translations, merger accounting, intangible drilling and development costs, and percentage depletion allowances. As you can see, there are many issues that cause analysts to dig further and to be cautious about accepting bottom-line earnings per share.

SUMMARY

Chapter 8 presents the basics of accounting statements and ratio analysis. After going through an income statement, balance sheet, and the sources and uses of funds statements, ratios are presented that help tie together these statements.

Ratio analysis is used to evaluate the operating performance and capital

---

[5]"Pension Liabilities: Improvement is Illusory," *Business Week,* September 14, 1981, pp. 114–18.

[6]Additional changes by the FASB in the pension fund area can be expected in future.

structure of a firm. Ratios will not help you find a gold mine, but they can help you avoid the trap of buying sick companies. Using ratio analysis, a brief description of two bankruptcy studies was given which emphasized the ability of ratios to spot troubled firms with a potential for failure.

Twenty ratios were classified into six categories which measured profitability, asset utilization, liquidity, debt utilization, relative prices, and taxes and dividend policy. Heublein, Inc., was used as an example as we went through the computation of each ratio. The Du Pont method was presented to demonstrate the relationship between assets, sales, income, and debt for creating returns on assets and equity.

Ratios are best used when compared to industry norms, company trends, and economic and industry cycles. It is becoming more difficult to use ratio analysis on an industry basis as firms become more integrated and diversified into several industries. Four industries were used—airlines, brewing, chemicals, and drugs—to examine industry trends and differences. Each company was compared to industry norms, and the difference between companies and industries was easily seen.

Finally, the deficiencies of financial statements were discussed with major emphasis on inflation. Accounting statements adjusted for inflation appear in Appendix 8–A. The effect on ratios was examined for replacement-cost versus historical-cost data. Inflation also affects inventory valuation, and an example of income and profit margins was created for FIFO and LIFO inventory methods. Other distortions were discussed, such as extraordinary gains and losses and pension fund liabilities.

Financial analysis is a science as well as an art, and experience certainly sharpens the skills. It would be unrealistic for someone to pick up all the complex relationships involved in ratio analysis immediately. This is why analysts are assigned industries which they learn inside and out. After much practice, the detective work is easier, and the true picture of financial performance becomes focused.

IMPORTANT WORDS AND CONCEPTS		
	Income statement	Dividend yield
	Balance sheet	Payout ratio
	Sources and uses of funds statement	Trend analysis
	Net working capital	Inflation-adjusted accounting
	Profitability ratios	Constant-dollar method
	Du Pont analysis	Current-cost method
	Asset utilization ratios	Extraordinary gains and losses
	Liquidity ratios	Operating margin
	Debt utilization ratios	Return on equity
	Price ratios	Current ratio
		Quick ratio

QUESTIONS AND PROBLEMS

1. Why is a reduction in assets considered a source of funds?

2. Is ratio analysis likely to be more valuable in picking winners or avoiding likely losers?

3. According to the Altman study, how accurate are ratios in predicting bank-ruptcy?

4. What ratios are likely to be of greatest interest to the banker or trade creditor? To the bondholder?

5. If a firm's operating margin and aftertax margin are almost the same (an unusual case), what can we say about the firm?

6. If a firm has a high return on assets and a low net income to sales margin, what can the analyst infer about the firm?

7. Contrast the capital goods industry and the food processing industry using ratio 3 *(b)*. (You need only provide comments—no numbers are expected.)

8. In computing return on assets and return on equity, how does the age of the assets influence the interpretation of the values?

9. Given the following financial data: net income/sales = 5%; sales/total assets = 2.5; debt/total assets = 60%; compute:
   a. Return on assets.
   b. Return on equity.

10. Explain in problem 9 why return on equity was so much higher than return on assets.

11. A firm has a return on assets of 12 percent and a return on equity of 18 percent. What is the debt-to-total-assets ratio?

12. How do the asset utilization ratios relate to the liquidity ratios?

13. Can public utility firms better justify the use of high debt than firms in the automobile or airline industry? Comment.

14. Given the following financial data:

Assets:		Liabilities and stockholders' equity:	
Cash	$ 1,000	Short-term debt	$ 2,000
Accounts receivable	3,500	Long-term debt	1,000
Inventory	1,500	Stockholders' equity	7,000
Fixed assets	4,000	Total liabilities and	
Total assets	$10,000	stockholders' equity	$10,000

Income before fixed charges and taxes	$4,000
Interest payments	500
Lease payment	700
Taxes (45% tax rate)	1,260
Net income (after taxes)	$1,540

Compute:
a. Quick ratio.

     b. Return on equity.

     c. Fixed charge coverage.

15. Assume in part *c* of problem 14 that the firm had a sinking fund payment obligation of $200. How much before-tax income is required to cover the sinking fund obligation? Would higher tax rates increase or decrease the before-tax income required to cover the sinking fund?

16. What might a high dividend payout ratio suggest to an analyst about a company's growth prospects?

17. In what way does the general trend to corporate diversification over the last 20 years make ratio comparison more difficult?

18. In Table 8–8, the chemical industry shows a higher return on equity than the brewing industry for 1980 (13 percent versus 12.5 percent). Can we necessarily say that the chemical industry also has a higher return on assets for 1980? Use information in Table 8–9 to help clarify or support your answer.

19. Why is the airline industry so much more subject to the effects of a recession than the drug industry?

20. Explain the probable impact of replacement-cost accounting on the ratios of return on assets, debt to total assets, and times interest earned for a firm that has substantial, old, fixed assets.

21. Can you think of some industries where replacement-cost accounting would have a large impact on the financial statements?

22. In examining Table 8–11 and the first column of Table 8–12, explain why earnings after taxes and the ratios have improved in spite of a constant unit sales volume.

23. In the first column of Table 8–12, if the sales price had gone to $23.50 per unit, what would the aftertax margin be?

24. What is the drawback or danger of having unfunded pension fund liabilities?

SELECTED REFERENCES

Backer, Morton, and Martin L. Gosman. "The Use of Financial Ratios in Credit Downgrade Decisions." *Financial Management,* Spring 1980, pp. 53–56.

Barefield, Russell M., and Eugene E. Comiskey. "The Smoothing Hypothesis: An Alternative Test." *Accounting Review,* April 1972, pp. 291–98.

Bernstein, Leopold A., and Joel G. Siegel. "The Concept of Earnings Quality." *Financial Analysts Journal,* July–August 1979, pp. 72–75.

Chen, Kung H., and Thomas A. Shimerda. "An Empirical Analysis of Useful Financial Ratios." *Financial Management,* Spring 1981, pp. 51–60.

Copeland, Ronald M.; Joseph F. Wojdak; and John K. Shank. "The Use of Lifo to Offset Inflation." *Harvard Business Review,* May–June 1971, pp. 91–100.

Edwards, James Don, and John B. Barrack. "Last-In, First-Out Inventory Valuation As a Way to Control Illusory Profits." *MSU Business Topics,* Winter 1975, pp. 19–27.

Horngren, Charles T. "Accounting Principles: Private or Public Sector?" *Journal of Accountancy,* May 1972, pp. 37–41.

Joy, O. Maurice; Robert H. Litzenberger; and Richard W. McEnally. "The Adjustment of Stock Prices to Announcements of Unanticipated Changes in Quarterly Earnings." *Journal of Accounting Research,* Autumn 1977, pp. 207–25.

Modak, N. D. "Corporate Planning and the Securities Analyst." *Financial Analysts Journal,* September–October 1974, pp. 51–54.

"Pension Liabilities: Improvement is Illusory." *Business Week,* September 14, 1981, pp. 114–18.

Stauffer, Thomas R. "The Measurement of Corporate Rate of Return: A Generalized Formulation." *Bell Journal of Economics and Management Science,* Autumn 1971, pp. 434–69.

Terborgh, George. "Inflation and Profits." *Financial Analysts Journal,* May–June 1974, pp. 19–23.

Walker, Ernest W., and J. William Petty II. "Financial Differences Between Large and Small Firms." *Financial Management,* Winter 1978, pp. 61–68.

APPENDIX 8–A: HEUBLEIN INFLATION-ADJUSTED FINANCIAL DATA

Supplementary information on the effects of changing prices (unaudited)

As required by *Financial Accounting Standard No. 33,* "Financial Reporting and Changing Prices," the company is presenting supplementary information designed to represent the effect of inflation on its operations.

Certain amounts appearing in the primary financial statements (inventories, property, plant, and equipment, cost of sales, and depreciation and amortization expenses) have been restated to two bases: "historical cost/constant dollars" and "current costs". The constant dollars restatement, through the use of the consumer price index for all urban consumers, adjusts transactions recorded in actual dollars at different times to dollars having the same general purchasing power. The restatement to current costs is intended to reflect changes in specific prices. The use of various indices measuring price changes for specific types of assets was the principal technique used in estimating current costs. These costs are meant to indicate the amount needed to replace existing inventories and production facilities at current prices.

Depreciation and amortization expenses are adjusted under both bases by restating the historical cost of property, plant, and equipment to constant dollars and current costs for 1981. These restated costs become the base from which depreciation and amortization are calculated utilizing the same methods and asset lives used in historical-cost statements. Cost of sales is adjusted under both

---

SOURCE: Heublein Annual Report, 1981.

methods by restating the historical cost of inventories at the beginning and end of the year. No adjustment has been made for that portion of the company's inventories valued by the LIFO method, since these amounts already approximate average fiscal 1981 dollars.

In accordance with *Standard No. 33,* no adjustments to income tax expense reported in the primary financial statements have been made in determining net income in the restated income statements. This provision is consistent with present tax laws which do not allow deductions for inflation-adjusted costs. As a result, the consolidated effective income tax rate rises from 47.5 percent on the historical cost basis to 61.9 percent on the constant-dollars basis and to 64.2 percent on the current-costs basis.

Net monetary liabilities were held during a period in which the purchasing power of the dollar declined. As a result, the company experienced a gain, since those monetary liabilities will be paid with dollars having decreased purchasing power. It should be noted that this purchasing power gain on net monetary liabil-

HUEBLEIN, INC.
Consolidated Statement of Income
Adjusted for General Inflation and Specific Prices
Years ended June 30, 1981, and 1980
($000 except per share data)

	1981			1980*
	As reported in financial statements	Adjusted for general inflation (constant dollars)	Adjusted for specific prices (current costs)	Adjusted for specific prices (current costs)
Revenues	$2,050,121	$2,050,121	$2,050,121	$2,144,817
Cost of sales	1,381,606	1,411,337	1,418,348	1,514,299
Selling, advertising, administrative, and general expenses	444,215	453,745		456,757
Other deductions	55,959	55,959	55,959	54,845
Income before income taxes	168,341	129,080	124,510	118,916
Income taxes	79,962	79,962	79,962	76,611
Net income	$ 88,379	49,118	44,548	42,305
Gain on net monetary items		21,632	21,632	34,634
Net income plus gain on net monetary items		70,750	66,180	76,939
Increase in specific prices†			83,943	114,271
Less: Effect of increase in general price level			81,326	119,734
Amount of increase in specific prices over (under) increase in the general price level			2,617	(5,463)
Net change in shareholders' equity from above	$ 88,379	$ 70,750	$ 68,797	$ 71,476
Per common share:				
Net income	$4.09	$2.27	$2.06	$1.98
Net income plus gain on net monetary items		$3.27	$3.06	$3.59
Net assets at year-end	$ 551,731	$ 772,682	$ 781,509	$ 771,087

*Amounts shown are stated in average fiscal 1981 dollars.

†At June 30, 1981, and 1980 the current costs of inventory were $361,938,000 and $377,720,000 and the current costs of property, plant, and equipment, net of accumulated depreciation, were $550,569,000 and $581,269,000, respectively.

ities does not represent receipt of cash and should not be considered as providing funds for subsequent reinvestment in the company.

Both general and specific inflation adjustments involve estimates, assumptions, and subjective judgments which should be viewed only as an attempt to approximate the effects of inflation. Clearly, these amounts are experimental in nature and may not represent the actual impact of inflation on the company.

The adjustment to depreciation and amortization in 1981 increased cost of sales by $5,176,000 and $3,862,000 for constant dollars and current costs, respectively. Selling, advertising, administrative, and general expenses were increased by $9,530,000 for constant dollars and by $7,089,000 for current costs, for a total depreciation and amortization effect of $14,706,000 and $10,951,000 under each basis. In 1980, the adjustment to current costs depreciation and amortization increased cost of sales by $4,793,000 and selling, advertising, administrative, and general expenses by $8,900,000, for a total depreciation and amortization effect of $13,693,000.

Five-year comparison of selected financial data adjusted for effects of changing prices* ($000 except per share data)

	Year ended June 30				
	1981	1980	1979	1978	1977
Revenues	$2,050,121	$2,144,817	$2,236,110	$2,240,615	$2,289,131
Historical cost information adjusted for general inflation (constant dollars):					
Net income	49,118	51,958			
Net income per common share	$2.27	$2.43			
Net assets at year-end	772,682	753,841			
Historical cost information adjusted for specific prices (current costs):					
Net income	44,548	42,305			
Net income per common share	$2.06	$1.98			
Amount of increase in specific prices over (under) increase in the general price level	2,617	(5,463)			
Net assets at year-end	781,509	771,087			
Other information:					
Gain from decline in purchasing power of net amounts owed	21,632	34,634			
Dividends declared per common share	$1.78	$1.81	$1.88	$1.91	$1.90
Marked price per common share at year-end	$30.95	$33.83	$33.02	$37.34	$36.53
Average consumer price index	259.4	232.5	205.2	187.6	175.8

*Amounts shown are stated in average fiscal 1981 dollars.

**Report of certified
public accountants**

ARTHUR YOUNG & COMPANY

277 PARK AVENUE

NEW YORK, NEW YORK 10172

The Board of Directors and Shareholders
Heublein, Inc.

We have examined the accompanying consolidated balance sheet of Heublein, Inc., at June 30, 1981 and 1980, and the related consolidated statements of income, additional paid-in capital, retained earnings, and changes in financial position for each of the three years in the period ended June 30, 1981. Our examinations were made in accordance with generally accepted auditing standards and, accordingly, included such tests of the accounting records and such other auditing procedures as we considered necessary in the circumstances.

In our opinion, the statements mentioned above present fairly the consolidated financial position of Hueblein, Inc., at June 30, 1981 and 1980, and the consolidated results of operations and changes in financial position for each of the three years in the period ended June 30, 1981, in conformity with generally accepted accounting principles applied on a consistent basis during the period except for the change, with which we concur, to the LIFO method of accounting for certain inventories in the year ended June 30, 1980, as described in the Inventories note to the consolidated financial statements.

Arthur Young & Company

July 20, 1981

9

A basic view of technical analysis and market efficiency

In the preceding three chapters, we have followed a fundamental approach to security analysis. That is, we have examined the fundamental factors that influence the business cycle, the performance of various industries, and the operations of individual firms. We have further examined the financial statements and tools of measurement that are available to the security analyst. In following a fundamental approach, one attempts to evaluate the appropriate worth of a security and perhaps ascertain whether it is under- or overpriced.

In this chapter, we shall examine a technical approach to investment timing. In this approach, analysts and market technicians examine prior price and volume data, as well as other market-related indicators, to determine past trends in the belief that they will help forecast future ones. Technical analysts place much more emphasis on charts and graphs of *internal market data* than on such fundamental factors as earnings reports, management capabilities, or new product development. They believe that even when important fundamental information is uncovered, it may not lead to profitable trading because of timing considerations and market imperfections.

We shall also devote much time and attention in this chapter to the concept of market efficiency; that is, the ability of the market to adjust very rapidly to the supply of new information in valuing a security. This area of study has led to the efficient market hypothesis, which states that all securities are correctly priced at any point in time.

At the outset, be aware that there are many disagreements and contradictions in the various areas that we will examine. As previously implied, advocates of technical analysis do not place much emphasis on fundamental analysis, and vice versa. Even more significant, proponents of the efficient market hypothesis would suggest that neither technical nor fundamental analysis Is of any great value in producing superior returns.

In light of the various disagreements that exist, we feel it is important that the student be exposed to many schools of thought. For example, we devote the first part of the chapter to technical analysis and then later offer research findings that

relate to the value of the technical approach as well as the fundamental approach. Our philosophy throughout the chapter is to recognize that there is a gap between practices utilized by brokerage houses (and on Wall Street) and beliefs held in the academic community, yet the student should be exposed to both.

TECHNICAL ANALYSIS

Technical analysis is based on a number of basic assumptions:

1. Market value is determined solely by the interaction of demand and supply.
2. Demand and supply are governed by both rational and irrational factors.
3. It is assumed that though there are minor fluctuations in the market, stock prices tend to move in trends that persist for long periods of time.
4. Reversals of trends are caused by shifts in demand and supply.
5. Shifts in demand and supply can be detected sooner or later in charts.
6. Many chart patterns tend to repeat themselves.[1]

For our purposes, the most significant items to note are the assumptions that stock prices tend to move in trends that persist for long periods and that these trends can be detected in charts. The basic premise is that past trends in market movements can be used to forecast or understand the future. The market technician generally assumes that there is a lag between the time he perceives a change in the value of a security and when the investing public ultimately assesses this change.

In developing the tools of technical analysis, we shall divide our discussion between the *(a) use of charting,* and *(b) key indicator series* to project future market movements.

THE USE OF CHARTING

Charting is often linked to the development of the Dow theory in the late 1890s by Charles Dow.[2] Mr. Dow was the founder of the Dow Jones Company and editor of *The Wall Street Journal.* Many of his early precepts were further refined by other market technicians, and it is generally believed that the Dow theory was successful in signaling the market crash of 1929.

Essential elements of the Dow theory

The Dow theory maintains that there are three major movements in the market: daily fluctuations, secondary movements, and primary trends. According to the theory, daily fluctuations and secondary movements (covering two weeks to a month) are only important to the extent that they reflect on the long-term pri-

---

[1]R. D. Edwards and John Magee, Jr., *Technical Analysis of Stock Trends* (Springfield, Mass: John Magee, 1958).
[2]*The Wall Street Journal,* December 19, 1900.

mary trend in the market. Primary trends may be characterized as either bullish or bearish in nature.

In Figure 9–1, we look at the use of the Dow theory to analyze a market trend. Note that the primary movement in the market is positive in spite of two secondary movements that are downward. The important facet of the secondary movements is that each low is higher than the previous low and each high is higher than the previous high. This tends to confirm the primary trend, which is bullish.

Under the Dow theory, it is assumed that this pattern will continue for a long period, and the analyst should not be confused by secondary movements. However, the upward pattern must ultimately come to an end. This is indicated by a new pattern in which a recovery fails to exceed the previous high (abortive recovery) and a new low penetrates a previous low as indicated in the top part of Figure 9–2. For a true turn in the market to take place, the new pattern of movement in the Dow Jones Industrial Average must also be confirmed by a subsequent movement in the Dow Jones Transportation Average as indicated on the bottom part of Figure 9–2.

A subsequent change from a bear to a bull market would require similar patterns of confirmation. While the Dow theory has proved helpful to market technicians, there is always the problems of false signals. For example, not every abortive recovery is certain to signal the end of a bull market. Furthermore, the investor may have to wait a long time to get full confirmation of a change in a primary trend. By the time the Transportation Average confirms the pattern in the Industrial Average, important market movements may have already taken place.

Support and resistance levels

Chartists attempt to define trading levels for individual securities (or the market) where there is a likelihood that price movements will be challenged. Thus,

Figure 9–1   **Presentation of the Dow theory**

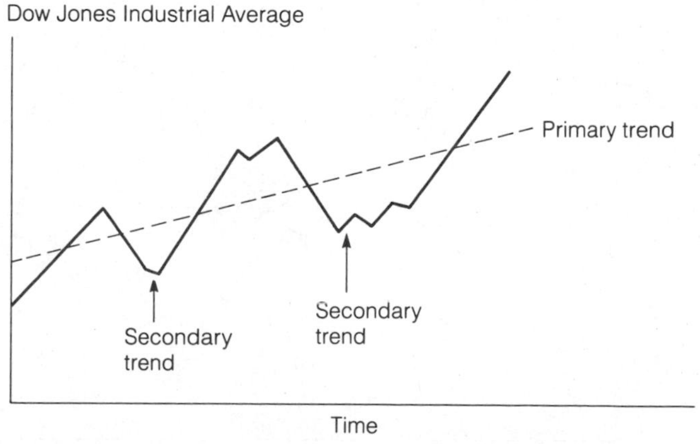

Dow Jones Industrial Average

Primary trend

Secondary trend

Secondary trend

Time

Figure 9—2   **Market reversal and confirmation**

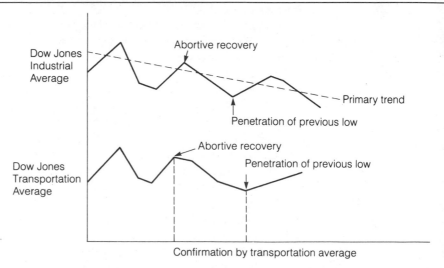

Confirmation by transportation average

in the daily financial press or on television, the statement is often made that the next barrier to the current market move is at 960 (or some other level). This assumes the existence of support and resistance levels. As indicated in Figure 9—3, a support level is associated with the lower end of a trading range and a resistance level with the upper end.

Support may develop each time a stock goes down to a lower level of trading because investors who previously passed up a purchase opportunity may now choose to act. It is a signal that new demand is coming into the market. When a stock reaches the high side of the normal trading range, resistance may develop

Figure 9—3   **Support and resistance**

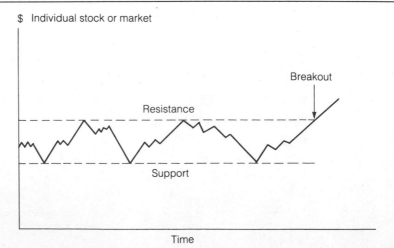

because some investors who bought in on a previous wave of enthusiasm (on an earlier high) may now view this as a chance to get even. Others may simply see this as an opportunity to take a profit.

A breakout above a resistance point (as indicated in Figure 9–3) or below a support level is considered significant. The stock is assumed to be trading in a new range, and higher (lower) trading values may now be expected.

Volume

The amount of volume supporting a given market movement is also considered significant. For example, if a stock (or the market in general) makes a new high on heavy trading volume, this is considered to be bullish. Conversely, a new high on light volume may indicate a temporary move that is likely to be reversed.

A new low on light volume is considered somewhat positive because of the lack of investor participation. On the other hand, when a new low is established on the basis of heavy trading volume, this is considered to be quite bearish.

In the early 1980s, the New York Stock Exchange has been averaging a volume of 40 to 45 million shares daily. When the volume jumps to 70 or 80 million shares, analysts take a very strong interest in the trading pattern of the market.

Types of charts

Up until now, we have been using typical line charts to indicate market patterns. Technicians also use bar charts and point and figure charts. We shall examine each.

Bar chart A bar chart shows the high and low price for a stock with a dash along the line to indicate the closing price. An example is shown in Figure 9–4.

Figure 9—4   **Bar chart**

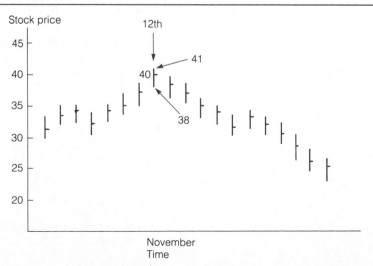

We see on November 12, the stock traded between a high of 41 and a low of 38 and closed at 40. Daily information on the Dow Jones Averages are usually presented in the form of a bar chart, with daily volume shown at the bottom as indicated in Figure 9–5.

Trendline, published through a division of Standard & Poor's, provides excellent charting information on a wide variety of securities traded on the major exchanges and is available at many libraries and brokerage houses. Market technicians carefully evaluate the charts looking for what they perceive to be significant patterns of movement. For example, the pattern in Figure 9–4 might be interpreted as a head and shoulder pattern (note the head in the middle) with a lower penetration of the neckline to the right indicating a sell signal. In Figure 9–6, we show a series of price movement patterns presumably indicating market bottoms and tops.

Though it is beyond the scope of this book to go into interpretation of chart formations in great detail, special books on the subject are suggested at the end of our discussion of charting.

Point and figure chart

A point and figure chart (PFC) emphasizes significant price changes and the reversal of significant price changes. Unlike a line or bar chart, there is no time dimension. An example of a point and figure chart is presented in Figure 9–7. The assumption is that the stock starts out at 30. Only moves of two points or greater are plotted on the graph (some may prefer to use one point). Advances are indicated by X's and declines are shown by O's. A reversal from an advance to a decline or vice versa calls for a shift in columns. Thus, the stock initially goes from 30 to 42 and then shifts columns in its subsequent decline to 36 before moving up again in column 3. A similar pattern persists throughout the chart.

Chartists carefully read point and figure charts to observe market patterns (where there is support, resistance, breakouts, congestion, etc.). Students with a strong interest in charting may consult such books as Edwards and Magee, *Technical Analysis of Stock Trends*[3] and Zweig, *Understanding Technical Forecasting.*[4] The problem in reading charts has always been to analyze patterns in such a fashion that they truly predict stock market movements before they unfold. In order to justify the effort, one must assume that there are discernable trends over the long term.

KEY INDICATOR SERIES

In the television series, "Wall Street Week," host Louis Rukeyser has a number of technical indicators that he watches on a weekly basis. He refers to them

[3]R. D. Edwards and John Magee, Jr., *Technical Analysis of Stock Trends,* 5th ed. (Springfield, Mass: Stock Trends Service, 1966).

[4]Martin E. Zweig, *Understanding Technical Forecasting* (Princeton, N.J.: Dow Jones, 1978).

Figure 9—5   **Bar chart of market averages**

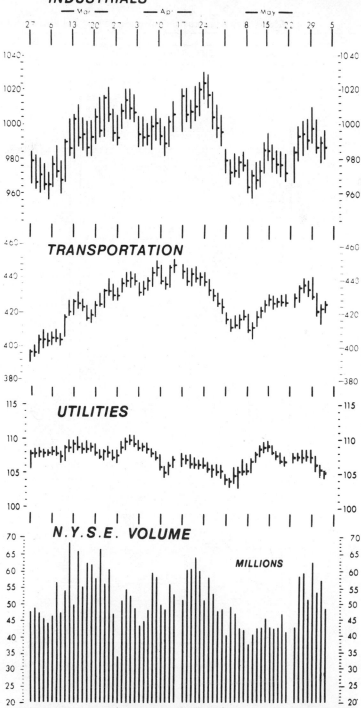

The Dow Jones Averages

HIGH →
CLOSE →
LOW →

INDUSTRIALS
TRANSPORTATION
UTILITIES
N.Y.S.E. VOLUME

MILLIONS

Following are the Dow Jones averages of industrial, transportation and utility stocks with the total sales of each group for the period indicated.

Figure 9—6   **Chart representation of market bottoms and tops**

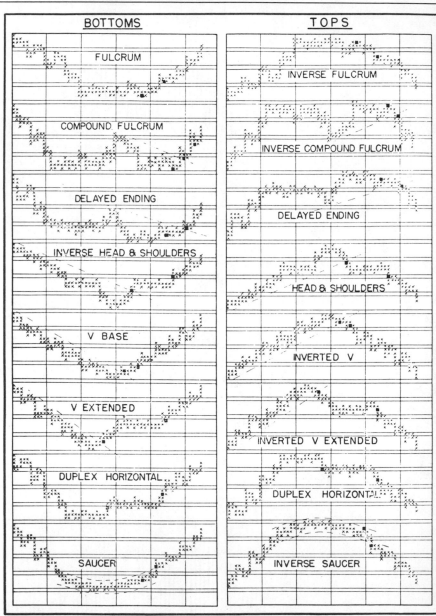

SOURCE: Irwin Shishko, "Techniques of Forecasting Commodity Prices," *Commodity Yearbook* (New York: Commodity Research Bureau, 1965), p. 4.

Figure 9–7   **Point and figure chart**

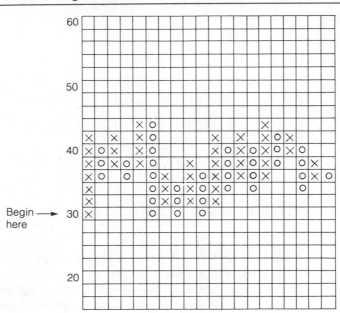

Begin here → 30

as his elves and compares the bullish and bearish indicators to determine what the next direction of the market might be.

In this section, we will examine similar bullish and bearish technical indicator series. We will first look at contrary opinion rules, then smart money rules, and finally overall market indicators.

Contrary opinion rules

The essence of a contrary opinion rule is that it is easier to figure out who is wrong than who is right. If you know your neighbor has a terrible sense of direction and you spot him taking a left at the intersection, you automatically take a right. In the stock market, there are similar guidelines.

Odd-lot theory   An odd-lot trade is one of less than 100 shares, and only small investors tend to engage in odd-lot transactions. The odd-lot theory suggests that you watch very closely what the small investor is doing and then do the opposite. *The Wall Street Journal* reports odd-lot trading on a daily basis, and *Barron's* reports similar information on a weekly basis. It is a simple matter to construct a ratio of odd-lot purchases to odd-lot sales. For example, on June 3, 1981, 186,526 odd-lot shares were purchased, and 382,020 shares were sold, indicating a ratio of .488. The ratio generally fluctuates between .40 and 1.60.

The odd-lot theory actually suggests that the small trader does all right most of the time but badly misses on key market turns. As indicated in Figure 9–8, the

Figure 9—8   **Comparing Standard & Poor's 500 Index and the Odd-lot Index**

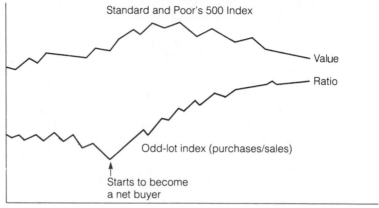

odd-lot trader is on the correct path as the market is going up; that is, selling off part of the portfolio in an up market (the name of the game is to buy low and sell high). This net selling posture is reflected by a declining odd-lot index (purchase/ sales ratio). However, as the market continues upward, the odd-lot trader suddenly thinks he or she sees an opportunity for a killing in the market and becomes a very strong net buyer. This precedes a fall in the market.

The odd-lot trader is also assumed to be a strong seller right before the bottom of a bear market. Presumably, when the small trader finally gets grandfather's 50 shares of AT&T out of the lockbox and sells them in disgust, it is time for the market to turn upward.

As if to add injury to insult, there is a corollary to the odd-lot theory that says one should be particularly sensitive to what odd-lot traders do on Monday because off-lotters tend to visit with each other over the weekend, confirm each others opinions or exchange hot tips, and then call their brokers on Monday morning. The assumption is that their chatter over the barbeque pit or in the bowling alley is even more suspect than their own individual opinions.

While the odd-lot theory appeared to have some validity in the 1950s and 1960s, it has not been a particularly valuable tool in the 1970s and early 1980s. For one thing, the odd-lotters outguessed many of the professional money managers in selling off before the stock market debacle of the mid-1970s, and they began buying in advance of a recovery. Another problem is that odd-lotters have been fairly consistent net sellers since the late 1960s, so there is not a balanced movement in the index.

Short sales position   A second contrary opinion rule is based on the volume of short sales in the market. As you will recall from Chapter 4, a short sale represents the selling of a security you do not own with the anticipation of purchas-

ing the security in the future to cover your short position. An investor would only engage in a short sale transaction if he believed the security would, in fact, be going down in price in the near future so that he could buy back the security at a lower price to cover his short sale. When the aggregate number of short sellers is large (that is they are bearish), this is thought to be a bullish signal.

The contrary opinion stems from two sources: first, that short sellers are sometimes emotional and may overreact to the market; second and more important, that there now is a built-in demand for stocks that have been sold short by investors who will have to repurchase the shares to cover their short positions.

Daily short sale totals for the New York Stock Exchange are recorded in *The Wall Street Journal.* Also once a month (around the 20th), *The Wall Street Journal* provides a report on total short sale figures for the two major exchanges as well as securities traded on those exchanges (based on mid-month data). This feature usually contains comments about current trends in the market.

Technical analysts compute a ratio of the total short sales positions on an exchange to average daily exchange volume for the month. The normal ratio is between 1.00 and 1.75. A ratio of 1.00 would indicate that the current short sales position is equal to one day's average trading volume.

As the short sales ratio (frequently called the short interest ratio) approaches the higher end of the normal trading range, this would be considered bullish (remember this is a contrary opinion trading rule). As is true with many other technical trading rules, its use in predicting future performance has produced mixed results.[5]

Investment advisory recommendations A further contrary opinion rule states that you should watch the predictions of the investment advisory services and do the opposite. This has been formalized by Investors Intelligence (an investment advisory service itself) into the Index of Bearish Sentiment. Abraham W. Cohen, president of Investors Intelligence, suggests that when 42 percent or more of the advisory services are bearish, you should expect a market upturn. Conversely, when only 17 percent or fewer are bearish, you should expect a decline.[6]

Lest one take investment advisory services too lightly, however, observe the market impact of a recommendation by Joseph Granville, publisher of the *Granville Market Letter.* On Tuesday, January 6, 1981, Mr. Granville issued a late evening warning to his subscribers to "sell everything." He helped cause a next-day decline in the Dow Jones Industrial Average of 23.80 points on a new record volume of 92,890,000 shares on the New York Stock Exchange. Forty billion ($40,000,000,000) in market value was chopped off the total value of stocks traded on U.S. security exchanges and the over-the-counter market.

---

[5]Randall Smith, "Short Interest and Stock Market Prices," *Financial Analysts Journal,* November–December, 1968, pp. 151–54. Barton M. Briggs, "The Short Interest—A False Proverb," *Financial Analysts Journal,* July–August, 1966, pp. 111–16.

[6]"How to Read Stock Market Indicators," *Business Week,* December 8, 1980, p. 14.

Although market events did not immediately confirm Mr. Granville's pessimism (and brought much criticism), the fact that one man could trigger such a reaction is an indication of the number of people that are influenced by the suggestion of an advisory service.

Smart money rules

Market technicians have long attempted to track the pattern of sophisticated traders in the hope that they might provide unusual insight into the future. We shall briefly observe theories related to bond market traders and stock exchange specialists.

Barron's Confidence Index   The *Barron's* Confidence Index is used to observe the trading pattern of investors in the bond market. The theory is based on the premise that bond traders are more sophisticated than stock traders and will pick up trends more quickly. The theory would suggest that if one can figure out what bond traders are doing today, he may be able to determine what stock market investors will be doing in the near future.

Barron's Confidence Index is actually computed by taking the yield on *Barron's* 10 top-grade corporate bonds and dividing by the yield on the Dow Jones broadly based 40 bond average and multiplying by 100.

$$\begin{matrix} Barron's \\ \text{Confidence} \\ \text{Index} \end{matrix} = \frac{\text{Yield on } Barron's \text{ 10 top grade corporate bonds}}{\text{Yield on Dow Jones 40 bond average}} (100) \quad (9-1)$$

The index is published weekly in the "Market Laboratory" section of *Barron's* magazine. What does it actually tell us? First of all, we can observe that the top-grade bonds in the numerator will always have a smaller yield than that of the more broadly based Dow Jones 40 bond average in the denominator. The reason is that the higher-quality issues can satisfy investors with smaller returns. The bond market is very representative of a risk-return trade-off environment in which less risk requires less return and higher risk necessitates a higher return.

With top-grade bonds providing smaller yields than lower-grade bonds, the Confidence Index will always be less than 100 (percent). The normal trading range is between 80 and 95, and it is within this range that technicians look for signals on the economy. If bond investors are bullish about future economic prosperity, they will be rather indifferent between holding top-grade bonds and average-grade bonds, and the yield differences between these two categories will be relatively small. This would indicate that the Confidence Index may be close to 95. An example is presented below in which top-grade bonds are providing 11.4 percent and average-grade bonds are yielding 12 percent.

$$\begin{matrix} Barron's \\ \text{Confidence} \\ \text{Index} \end{matrix} = \frac{\text{Yield on } Barron's \text{ 10 top-grade corporate bonds}}{\text{Yield on Dow Jones 40 bond average}} (100)$$

$$= \frac{11.4\%}{12\%} (100) = 95 \ (\%)$$

Now let us assume that investors become quite concerned about the outlook for the future health of the economy. If events go poorly, some weaker corporations may not be able to make their interest payments, and thus, bond market investors will have a strong preference for top-quality issues. Some investors will continue to invest in average or lower-quality issues but only at a sufficiently high yield differential to justify the risk. We might assume that the *Barron's* Confidence Index will drop to 84 because of the increasing spread between the two yields in the formula.

$$\begin{array}{c}Barron's \\ \text{Confidence} \\ \text{Index}\end{array} = \frac{\text{Yield on } Barron's \text{ 10 top grade corporate bonds}}{\text{Yield on Dow Jones 40 bond average}} (100)$$

$$= \frac{11.6\%}{13.8\%} (100) = 84 \, (\%)$$

The average yield on the Dow Jones 40 bond average is now 2.2 percent higher than that on *Barron's* 10 top-grade bonds, and this is reflected in the lower Confidence Index reading. Of course, as confidence in the economy is once again regained, the yield spread differential will narrow, and the Confidence Index will go up.

Market technicians assume that there is a few months of lead time between what happens to the Confidence Index and what happens to the economy and stock market. As is true with other such indicators, it has a mixed record of predicting future events. One problem is that the Confidence Index is only assumed to consider the impact of investors' attitudes on yields (their demand pattern). We have seen in the late 1970s and early 1980s that the supply of new bond issues can also influence yields. Thus, a very large bond issue by AT&T or General Motors may drive up high-grade bond yields even though investor attitudes indicate they should be going down.

Short sales by specialists Another smart money index is based on the short sales positions of specialists. Recall from Chapter 2 that one of the roles that specialists perform is to make markets in various securities listed on the organized exchanges. Because of the uniquely close position of specialists to the action on Wall Street, market technicians ascribe unusual importance to their decisions. One measure of their activity that is frequently monitored is the ratio of specialists' short sales to the total amount of short sales on an exchange.

When we previously mentioned short sales in this chapter, we suggested that a high incidence of short selling might be considered bullish because short sellers often overreact to the market and provide future demand potential to cover their short position. In the case of market specialists, this is not necessarily true. These sophisticated traders keep a book of limit orders on their securities so that they have a close feel for market activity at any given point in time, and their decisions are considered important.

The normal ratio of specialist short sales to short sales on an exchange is

about 55 percent. When the ratio goes up to 65 percent or more, market technicians interpret this as a bearish signal. A ratio under 40 percent is considered bullish.

Overall market rules

Our discussion of key indicator series has centered on both contrary opinion rules and smart money rules. We now briefly examine two overall market indicators; the breadth of the market indicator series and the cash position of mutual funds.

Breadth of the market   A breadth of the market indicator attempts to measure what a broad range of securities are doing as opposed to merely examining a market average. The theory is that market averages, such as the Dow Jones Industrial Average of 30 stocks or the Standard & Poor's 500 Stock Average, are weighted toward large firms and may not be representative of the entire market. In order to get a broader perspective of the market, an analyst may examine all stocks on an exchange. In Figure 9–9, we see an example of daily advances and declines for all stocks on the New York Stock Exchange.

The technician often compares the advance-declines with the movement of a popular market average to determine if there is a divergence between the two. Advances and declines usually move in concert with the popular market averages but may move in the opposite direction at a market peak or bottom. One of the possible signals for the end of a bull market is when the Dow Jones Industrial Average is moving up but the number of daily declines consistently exceeds the number of daily advances. This indicates that conservative investors are investing in blue chip stocks but that there is a lack of broad-based confidence in the market. In Table 9–1, we look at an example of divergence between the advance-decline indicators and the Dow Jones Industrial Average (DJIA).

In column 4, we see the daily differences in advances and declines. In column 5, we look at the cumulative pattern by adding or subtracting each new day's value from the previous total. We then compare the information in column 4 and column 5 to the Dow Jones Industrial Average (DJIA) in column 6. Clearly, the strength in the Dow Jones Industrial Average is not reflected in the advance-decline data, and this may be interpreted as signaling future weakness in the market.

Figure 9–9   **Advance—decline data on the New York Stock Exchange**

MARKET DIARY

	Thu.	Wed.	Tue.	Mon.	Fri.	Thu.
Issues traded	1,922	1,897	1,943	1,948	1,943	1,928
Advances	785	653	478	927	772	900
Declines	751	845	1,134	689	802	657
Unchanged	386	399	331	332	369	371
New highs	66	41	69	173	126	149
New lows	22	69	56	37	29	21

SOURCE: Reprinted by permission of *The Wall Street Journal*, Dow Jones & Company, Inc. (June 5, 1981). All rights reserved.

Table 9—1 **Comparing advance—decline data and the Dow Jones Industrial Average**

Day	(1) Advances	(2) Declines	(3) Unchanged	(4) Net advances or declines	(5) Cumulative advances or declines	(6) DJIA
1	850	750	350	+100	+100	+7.09
2	800	810	340	− 10	+ 90	+4.52
3	792	821	337	− 29	+ 61	+3.08
4	780	828	342	− 48	+ 13	+5.21
5	719	890	341	−171	−158	−2.02
6	802	812	336	− 10	−168	+5.43
7	783	824	343	− 41	−209	+3.01
8	692	912	340	−226	−435	+ .52

Breadth of the market data can also be used to analyze upturns in the market. When the Dow Jones Industrial Average is going down but advances consistently lead declines, the market may be positioned for a recovery. Some market technicians develop sophisticated weighted averages of the daily advance-declines to go along with the data in Table 9–1.

While a comparison of advance-decline data to market averages can provide important insights, there is also the danger of false signals. Not every divergence between the two signals a turn in the market, so the analyst must be careful in his or her interpretation. The technical analyst generally looks at a wide range of variables.

Mutual fund cash position Another overall market indicator is the cash position of mutual funds. This measure indicates the buying potential of mutual funds and is generally representative of the purchasing potential of other large institutional investors. The cash position of mutual funds, as a percentage of their total assets, generally varies between 5 percent and 20 to 25 percent.[7]

At the lower end of the boundary, it would appear that mutual funds are fully invested and can provide little in the way of additional purchasing power. As their cash position goes to 15 percent or higher, market technicians assess this as representing significant purchasing power that may help to trigger a market upturn. While the overall premise is valid, there are problems in identifying just what is a significant cash position for mutual funds in a given market cycle. It may change in extreme market environments.

EFFICIENT MARKET HYPOTHESIS We shift our attention from technical analysis to that of examining market efficiency. As indicated at the beginning of the chapter, we shall now view many contradictions between the assumptions of fundamental or technical analysis and findings of the efficient market hypothesis.

---

[7]The cash dollars are usually placed in short-term credit instruments, as opposed to stocks and bonds.

We previously said that an efficient market is one in which new information is very rapidly processed so that securities are properly priced at any given point in time. An important premise of an efficient market is that there are a large number of profit-maximizing participants concerned with the analysis and valuation of securities. This would seem to describe the security market environment in the United States. Any news on IBM, AT&T, an oil embargo, or tax legislation is likely to be absorbed and acted upon very rapidly by profit-maximizing individuals. For this reason, the efficient market hypothesis (EMH) assumes that no stock price can be in disequilibrium or improperly priced for very long. There is almost instantaneous adjustment to new information. The efficient market hypothesis applies most directly to large firms trading on the major security exchanges.

The efficient market hypothesis further assumes that information travels in a random, independent fashion and that prices are an unbiased reflection of all currently available information.

More generally, the efficient market hypothesis is stated and tested in three different forms: the weak form, the semi-strong form, and the strong form. We shall examine each of these and the related implications for technical and fundamental analysis.

WEAK FORM OF THE EFFICIENT MARKET HYPOTHESIS

The weak form of the efficient market hypothesis suggests that there is no relationship between past and future prices of securities. They are presumed to be independent over time. Because the efficient market hypothesis maintains that current prices reflect all available information and information travels in a random fashion, it is assumed that there is little or nothing to be gained from studying past stock prices.

The weak form of the efficient market hypothesis has been tested in two different ways. First, researchers have attempted to determine the actual independence of price changes over time.

Tests of independence

Tests of independence have examined the degree of correlation between stock prices over time and have found the correlation to be consistently small (between $+.10$ and $-.10$) and not statistically significant. This would indicate stock price changes are independent.[8] A further test is based on the frequency and extent of runs in stock price data. A run occurs when there is no difference in direction between two or more price changes. An example of a series of data and some runs is presented below.

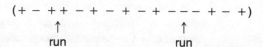

$$(+ - + + - + - + - + - - - + - +)$$

run   run

---

[8]Sidney S. Alexander, "Price Movements in Speculative Markets: Trends or Random Walks," *Industrial Management Review*, May 1961, pp. 7–26. Eugene F. Fama, "The Behavior of Stock Market Prices," *Journal of Business*, January 1965, pp. 34–105.

Some amount of runs can be expected in any series of data through chance factors, but an independent data series should not produce an unusual amount of runs. Statistical tests have indicated that security prices generally do not produce any more runs than that which would be expected through the process of random number generation.[9] This would also tend to indicate that stock price movements are independent over time.

Trading rule tests

A second method of testing the weak form of the efficient market hypothesis (that past trends in stock prices are not helpful in predicting the future) is through trading rule tests. Because practicing market technicians maintain that tests of independence (correlation studies and runs) are too rigid to test the assumptions of the weak form of the efficient market hypothesis, additional tests by academic researchers have been developed. These are known as trading rule or filter tests. The purpose of these tests is to determine whether a given trading rule based on past price data, volume figures, etc. can be used to beat a naive buy-and-hold approach. The intent is to simulate the conditions under which a given trading rule is used and then determine if superior returns were produced after consideration of transaction costs and the risks involved.

As an example of a trading rule, if a stock moves up 5 percent or more, the rule might be to purchase it. The assumption is that this represents a breakout and should be considered bullish. Similarly, a 5 percent downward movement would be considered bearish and call for a sell strategy (rather than a buy-low/sell-high strategy, this is a follow-the-market-trend strategy). Other trading rule tests might be based on advance-decline patterns, short sales figures, and similar technical patterns. Research results have indicated that in a limited number of cases, trading rules may produce slightly positive returns, but after commission costs are considered, the results are neutral and sometimes negative in comparison to a naive buy-and-hold approach.[10]

Implications for technical analysis

The results of the *tests of independence* and *trading rules* would seem to uphold the weak form of the efficient market hypothesis. Security prices do appear to be independent over time or, more specifically, move in the pattern of a random walk.

Some challenge the research on the basis that academic research in this area does not capture the personal judgment that an experienced technician brings forward in reading his charts. There is also the fact that there are an infinite

---

[9]Sidney S. Alexander, "Price Movements in Speculative Markets: Trends or Random Walks," *Industrial Management Review,* May 1961, pp. 7–26. Eugene F. Fama, "The Behavior of Stock Market Prices," *Journal of Business,* January 1965, pp. 34–105.

[10]Eugene F. Fama and Marshall Blume, "Filter Rules and Stock Market Trading Profits," *Journal of Business,* supplement, January 1966, pp. 226–41. George Pinches, "The Random Walk Hypothesis and Technical Analysis," *Financial Analysts Journal,* March–April 1970, pp. 104–10.

number of trading rules, and not all of them can or have been tested. Nevertheless, research on the weak form of the efficient market hypothesis would seem to suggest that prices move independently over time, that past trends cannot be used to predict the future, and that charting and technical analysis may have limited value.

SEMI-STRONG FORM OF THE EFFICIENT MARKET HYPOTHESIS

The semi-strong form of the efficient market hypothesis maintains that all public information is already impounded into the value of a security, and therefore, one cannot use fundamental analysis to determine whether a stock is under- or overvalued.

Basically, the semi-strong form of the efficient market hypothesis would support the notion that there is no learning lag in the distribution of public information. When a company makes an announcement, investors across the country assess the information with equal speed. Also, a major firm listed on the New York Stock Exchange could hardly hope to utilize some questionable accounting practice that deceptively leads to higher reported profits and not expect sophisticated analysts to pick it up. (This may not be equally true for an obscure firm that trades over-the-counter and enjoys little investor attention.)

Researchers have tested the semi-strong form of the efficient market hypothesis by determining whether investors who have acted on the basis of newly released public information have been able to enjoy superior returns. If the market is efficient in a semi-strong sense, this information is almost immediately impounded in the value of the security, and there would be little or no trading profits available. The implications would be that one could not garner superior returns by trading on public information about stock splits, earnings reports, or other similar items.

Tests on the semi-strong form of the efficient market hypothesis have generally been on the basis of market and risk-adjusted returns. Thus, the return from a given investment strategy must be compared to the performance of popular market indicators with appropriate risk adjustments. As will be described in Chapter 14, the risk measurement variable is usually the beta. After such adjustments are made, the question becomes, Are there abnormal returns that go beyond explanations associated with risk? If the answer is yes and can be shown to be statistically significant, then the investment strategy may be thought to refute the semi-strong form of the efficient market hypothesis. The investor must also cover transaction costs in determining that a given strategy is superior.

The risk adjustment measure may be viewed as:

$$K_i = a_i + b_i k_M + e_i$$

| Actual return | Inter-cept | Risk vari-able | Market return | Abnormal return |

Each of these items will receive further attention in Chapter 14. For now, our concern is whether our investment strategy can produce consistently superior, abnormal returns *(e$_i$)*.

Tests examining the impact of such events as stock splits and stock dividends, earnings announcements, and changes in accounting policy have generally indicated that the market is efficient in a semi-strong sense. For example, a study by Fama, Fisher, Jensen, and Roll indicated that almost all of the market impact of a stock split takes place before public announcement.[11] There is little to be gained from acting on the announcement.

Other studies have indicated that favorable or unfavorable earnings reports have generally been considered prior to public announcement, and there is little or no price change after announcement (unless there is a very large deviation from expected results).[12]

According to the semi-strong form of the efficient market hypothesis, investors not only digest information very quickly, but they are able to see through more changes in accounting information that do not have economic consequences. For example, the switching from accelerated depreciation to straight-line depreciation for financial reporting purposes (but not tax purposes) would tend to make earnings per share look higher but would provide no economic benefit for the firm. Research studies indicate this would have no positive impact on valuation.[13]

Similarly, investors are not deceived by mere accounting changes related to inventory policy, reserve accounts, exchange translations, or other items that appear to have no economic benefits. The corporate treasurer who switches from LIFO to FIFO accounting to make earnings look better in an inflationary economy will probably not see his or her firm's stock price rise as investors look at the economic consequences of higher taxes associated with the action and disregard the mere financial accounting consequences of higher reported profits.[14] Under this circumstance, the effect on stock price may be neutral or negative.

Implications for fundamental analysis

If stock values are already based on the analysis of all available public information, it may be assumed that there is little to be gained from additional fundamental analysis. Under the semi-strong form of the efficient market hypothesis, if General Motors is trading at $50, the assumption is that every shred of public

---

[11]Eugene F. Fama, Lawrence Fisher, Michael G. Jensen, and Richard Roll, "The Adjustment of Stock Prices to New Information," *International Economic Review,* February 1969, pp. 2–21.

[12]Ray Ball and Phillip Brown, "An Empirical Evaluation of Accounting Income Numbers," *Journal of Accounting Research,* Autumn 1968, pp. 159–78.

[13]T. Ross Archibald, "Stock Market Reaction to Depreciation Switch-Back," *Accounting Review,* January 1972, pp. 22–30. Robert S. Kaplan and Richard Roll, Investor Evaluation of Accounting Information: Some Empirical Evidence," *Journal of Business,* April 1972, pp. 225–57.

[14]Shyam Sunder, "Stock Price and Risk Related to Accounting Changes in Inventory Valuation," *Accounting Review,* April 1975, pp. 305–15.

information about GM has been collected and evaluated by thousands of investors, and they have determined an equilibrium price of $50. The assumption is that anything you read in *The Wall Street Journal* or *Standard & Poor's* publications has already been considered many times over by others and is currently impounded in the value of the stock. If you were to say that you think GM is really worth $52 because of some great new product, proponents of the semi-strong form of the efficient market hypothesis would suggest that your judgment cannot be better than the collective wisdom of the marketplace in which everyone is trying desperately to come out ahead.

Ironically, although many would suggest that fundamental analysis may not lead to superior profits in an efficient market environment, it is fundamental analysis itself which makes the market so efficient. Because everyone is doing fundamental analysis, there is little in the way of unabsorbed or undigested information. Therefore, one extra person doing fundamental analysis is unlikely to achieve superior insight.

Although the semi-strong form of the efficient market hypothesis has strong research support and would generally be considered valid, there are exceptions. For example, Basu has found that stocks with low P/E ratios consistently provide better returns than stocks with high P/E ratios on both a nonrisk-adjusted and risk-adjusted basis.[15] Since a P/E ratio is publicly available information that may be used to generate superior returns, this flies in the face of the more common conclusions on the semi-strong form of the efficient market hypothesis. Oppenheimer and Schlarbaum have also shown that investors can generate superior risk-adjusted returns by following widely disseminated rules by Graham and Dodd on such factors as dividends, capitalization, firm size and P/E ratios, and by using only public information.[16] Additional evidence of this nature continues to accumulate, and in Chapter 16, under the discussion of special situations, we present other possible contradictions to the majority viewpoint of the semi-strong version of the efficient market hypothesis.

Even if the semi-strong form of the efficient market hypothesis is generally valid, other types of exceptions can be noted. These exceptions extend to the type of securities being evaluated. While one would generally expect closely watched firms on the New York Stock Exchange to exhibit a high degree of pricing efficiency, smaller firms, perhaps trading over-the-counter, have less institutional following and are less likely to be correctly evaluated and priced at a given point in time. Firms with hidden assets in the ground may also be difficult to evaluate.

---

[15]S. Basu, "Investment Performance of Common Stocks in Relation to Their Price-Earnings Ratios: A Test of the Efficient Market Hypothesis," *Journal of Finance,* June 1977, pp. 663–82. Also, S. Basu, "The Information Content of Price-Earnings Ratios," *Financial Management,* Summer 1975, pp. 53–64.

[16]Henry R. Oppenheimer and Gary G. Schlarbaum, "Investing with Ben Graham: An Ex Ante Test of the Efficient Market Hypothesis," Forthcoming issue of the *Journal of Financial and Quantitative Analysis.*

Similarly, while many analysts may not be able to add additional insight through fundamental analysis, there are exceptions to every rule. It can be assumed that some analysts have such *extraordinary* insight and capability in analyzing publicly available information that they can perceive what others cannot. Also, if you take a very long-term perspective, the fact that a stock's value is in short-term equilibrium may not discourage you from taking a long-term position or attempting to find long-term value.

STRONG FORM OF THE EFFICIENT MARKET HYPOTHESIS

The strong form of the efficient market hypothesis goes beyond the semi-strong form to state that stock prices reflect not only all public information, but *all* information. Thus, it is hypothesized that insider information is also immediately impounded into the value of a security. In a sense, we go beyond the concept of a market that is highly efficient to one that is perfect.

The assumption is that no group of market participants or investors has monopolistic access to information. If this is the case, then no group of investors can be expected to show superior risk-adjusted returns under any circumstances.

Unlike the weak and semi-strong form of the efficient market hypothesis, major test results are not generally supportive of the strong form of the hypothesis. For example, specialists on security exchanges have been able to earn superior rates of return on invested capital.[17] The book they keep on unfilled limit orders would appear to provide monopolistic access to information. An SEC study actually found that specialists typically sell above their latest purchase 83 percent of the time and buy below their latest sell 81 percent of the time.[18] This implies wisdom that greatly exceeds that which would be available in a perfect capital market environment. Likewise, an institutional investor study, also sponsored by the SEC, indicated that specialists average return on capital was over 100 percent.[19]

Another group that appears to use nonpublic information to garner superior returns is corporate insiders. An insider is considered to be a corporate officer, member of the board of directors, or substantial stockholder. The SEC requires that insiders report their transactions to that regulatory body. A few weeks after reporting to the SEC, the information becomes public. Researchers can then go back and determine whether investment decisions made by investors appeared, on balance, to be wise. Did heavy purchases by insiders precede strong upward price movements, and did sell-offs precede poor market performance? The an-

---

[17]Victor Niederhoffer and M. F. M. Osborne, "Market-Making and Reversal on the Stock Exchange," *Journal of the American Statistical Association,* December 1966, pp. 897–916.

[18]Securities and Exchange Commission, *Report of the Special Study of the Security Markets,* part 2 (Washington, D.C.: U.S. Government Printing Office, 1965).

[19]Securities and Exchange Commission, *Institutional Investor Study Report* (Washington D.C.: U.S. Government Printing Office, 1971).

swer appears to be yes. Research studies indicate insiders consistently achieve higher returns than would be expected in a perfect capital market.[20] Although inside traders are not allowed to engage in short-terms transactions (of six months or less) to generate trading profits, they are allowed to take longer-term positions, which may well prove to be profitable. It has even been demonstrated that investors who follow the direction of inside traders after information on their activity becomes public may enjoy superior returns.[21] (This, of course, represents contrary evidence to the semi-strong form of the efficient market hypothesis as well.)

Even though there is evidence on the activity of specialists and insiders that would cause one to reject the strong form of the efficient market hypothesis (or at least not to accept it), the range of participants with access to superior information is not large. For example, tests on the performance of mutual fund managers have consistently indicated that they are not able to beat the market averages over the long term.[22] Although mutual fund managers may get the first call when news is breaking, that is not fast enough to generate superior returns.

While the strong form of the efficient market hypothesis suggests more opportunity for superior returns than the weak or semi-strong form, the premium is related to monopolistic access to information rather than other factors.

SUMMARY

Following the discussion of fundamental analysis in Chapters 6 through 8, we examine technical analysis in this chapter and, more significantly, the impact of the efficient market hypothesis on both fundamental and technical analysis.

While fundamental analysis deals with financial analysis and determinants of valuation, technical analysis is based on the study of past price and volume data as well as associated market trends to predict future price movements. Technical analysis relies heavily on charting and the use of key market indicators to make forecasts.

Charting came into prominence with the development of the Dow theory in the late 1800s by Charles Dow. The theory stresses the importance of primary trends that may be temporarily obscured by daily and secondary movements. In order for a long-term, bullish trend to be reversed, there must be an abortive recovery followed by penetrations of previous lows, and patterns in the Dow Jones Indus-

[20]James H. Lorie and Victor Niederhoffer, "Predictive Statistical Properties of Insider Trading," *Journal of Law and Economics,* April 1966, pp. 35–53. Joseph E. Finnerty, "Insiders and Market Efficiency," *Journal of Finance,* September 1976, pp. 1141–48. Jeffrey Jaffe, "Special Information and Insider Trading," *Journal of Business,* July 1974, pp. 410–428. Shannon P. Pratt and Charles W. DeVere, "Relationship Between Insider Trading and Rates of Return for NYSE Common Stocks, 1960–1966," in *Modern Developments in Investment Management,* ed. James H. Lorie and Richard Beasley (New York: Praeger Publishers, 1972), pp. 268–79.

[21]Pratt and DeVere, "Relationship," pp. 268–79.

[22]Michael Jensen, "The Performance of Mutual Funds in the Period 1945–1964," *Journal of Finance,* May 1968, pp. 389–416.

trial Average must be ultimately confirmed by the Dow Jones Transportation Average. Similar patterns of movement in the opposite direction would signal the end of a bear market.

Technical analysts also observe support and resistance levels in the market as well as data on volume. Line, bar, and point and figure charts are used to determine turns in the market.

Market technicians also follow a number of key indicator series to predict the market. There are contrary opinion indicators, smart money indicators, and general market indicators.

Although there have been traditional arguments about whether fundamental or technical analysis is more important, a great deal of current attention is directed to the efficient market hypothesis and its implications for all types of analysis.

The efficient market hypothesis (EMH) maintains that the market adjusts very rapidly to the supply of new information, and because of this, securities tend to be correctly priced at any given time (or very rapidly approaching this equilibrium value). The EMH further assumes that information travels in a random, independent fashion and that prices are an unbiased reflection of all currently available information. Furthermore, past trends in prices mean little or nothing.

The efficient market hypothesis has been stated and tested in three different forms.

a. The weak form states that there is no relationship between past and future prices (they are independent over time).
b. The semi-strong form suggests that all public information is currently impounded in the price of a stock and there is no concept of under- or over-valuation based on publicly available information.
c. The strong form suggests that *all* information, public or otherwise, is included in the value of a security. The implication of the strong form is that security prices are not only highly efficient, they are perfect.

Substantial research tends to support the weak form of the efficient market hypothesis, which causes many researchers to seriously question the overall value of technical analysis. However, many on Wall Street would vigorously debate this position. The semi-strong form of the efficient market hypothesis is also well supported by research, and this fact would tend to question the value of fundamental analysis by the individual investor. (It is, however, the collective wisdom of all fundamental analysis that leads to the efficient market hypothesis in the first place.) There are a few contradictions to the semi-strong form of the efficient market hypothesis, and much research is aimed at supplying additional contradictory data. The semi-strong form probably does not apply with equal emphasis to smaller firms that are not in the institutional investor's limelight.

The strong form of the efficient market hypothesis is not generally accepted. Thus, the market does not perfectly adjust to all information (insider as well as public). Evidence suggests that stock exchange specialists and corporate insid-

ers may be able to achieve superior returns based on the monopolistic use of nonpublic data. However, there are very few groups who demonstrate successful access or use of nonpublic information.

<table>
<tr>
<td>**IMPORTANT WORDS AND CONCEPTS**</td>
<td>

Technical analysis
Charting
Key indicators
Dow theory
Support and resistance levels
Contrary opinion rules
Odd-lot theory
Short sales position
Smart money rules
</td>
<td>

Barron's Confidence Index
Overall market rules
Breadth of market
Advances and declines
Efficient market hypothesis
Mutual fund cash position
Weak form of EMH
Semi-strong form of EMH
Strong form of EMH
</td>
</tr>
</table>

QUESTIONS AND PROBLEMS

1. What is technical analysis?

2. What are the views of technical analysts toward fundamental analysis?

3. Outline the basic assumptions of technical analysis.

4. Under the Dow theory, if a recovery fails to exceed the previous high and a new low penetrates a previous low, what does this tell us about the market?

5. Also under the Dow theory, what other average is used to confirm movements in the Dow Jones Industrial Average?

6. What is meant by a support level for a stock or a market average? When might a support level exist?

7. In examining Figure 9–7, if the next price movement is to 34, will a shift to a new column be indicated? (Assume the current price is 36.)

8. What is the logic behind the odd-lot theory? If the odd-lot index starts to move higher in an up market, what does the odd-lot theory indicate the next movement in the market will be?

9. How reliable has the odd-lot theory been in recent times?

10. What is the logic behind *Barron's* Confidence Index?

11. If the advance-decline movement in the market is weak (more declines than advances) while the DJIA is going up, what might this indicate to a technician about the market?

12. Categorize the following as either contrary opinion or smart money indicators (as viewed by technicians).
    a. Short sales by specialists.
    b. Odd-lot positions.

c. Short sales positions.

d. *Barron's* Confidence Index.

e. Investment advisory recommendations.

13. Under the efficient market hypothesis, what is the assumption about the processing of new information, and what effect does this have on security pricing?

14. What does the weak form of the efficient market hypothesis suggest? What are the two major ways in which it has been tested?

15. Would low correlation coefficients over time between stock prices tend to prove or disprove the weak form of the efficient market hypothesis?

16. What is the essence of the semi-strong form of the efficient market hypothesis? Does this necessarily apply with equal force to a small company trading in the over-the-counter market?

17. Under the semi-strong form of the efficient market hypothesis, is there anything to be gained from a corporate treasurer changing accounting methods to increase earnings per share when there is no associated true economic benefit or gain?

18. Why does fundamental analysis tend to make the market so efficient?

19. Suggest some studies that would indicate that the market is not completely efficient in the semi-strong form.

20. What does the strong form of the efficient market hypothesis suggest? Are major test results generally supportive of the strong form?

21. How do specialists, insiders, and mutual fund managers fare in terms of having access to superior information to generate large returns? (Comment separately.)

22. Project: Follow a number of technical indicators over the next few weeks, and compare actual market performance to suggested market performance (by the indicators).

SELECTED REFERENCES

Alexander, Sidney S. "Price Movements in Speculative Markets: Trends or Random Walks." *Industrial Management Review,* May 1961, pp. 7–26.

Archibald, Ross T. "Stock Market Reaction to Depreciation Switch-Back." *Accounting Review,* January 1972, pp. 22–30.

Ball, Roy, and Phillip Brown. "An Empirical Evaluation of Accounting Income Numbers." *Journal of Accounting Research,* Autumn 1968, pp. 159–78.

Basu, S. "Investment Performance of Common Stocks in Relation to Their Price-Earnings Ratios: A Test of the Efficient Market Hypothesis." *Journal of Finance,* June 1977, pp. 663–82.

————. "The Information Content of Price-Earnings Ratios." *Financial Management,* Summer 1975, pp. 53–64.

Briggs, Barton M. "The Short Interest—A False Proverb." *Financial Analysts Journal,* July–August 1966, pp. 111–16.

Edwards, R. D., and John Magee, Jr. *Technical Analysis of Stock Trends,* 5th ed. Springfield, Mass: Stock Trends Service, 1966.

Fama, Eugene F. "The Behavior of Stock Market Prices." *Journal of Business,* January 1965, pp. 34–105.

Fama, Eugene F., and Marshall Blume. "Filter Rules and Stock Market Trading Profits." *Journal of Business,* supplement, January 1966, pp. 226–41.

Fama, Eugene F.; Lawrence Fisher; Michael G. Jensen; and Richard Roll. "The Adjustment of Stock Prices to New Information." *International Economic Review,* February 1969, pp. 1–21.

Finnerty, Joseph E. "Insiders and Market Efficiency." *Journal of Finance,* September 1976, pp. 1141–48.

Jaffe, Jeffrey. "Special Information and Insider Trading." *Journal of Business,* July 1974, pp. 410–28.

Jensen, Michael. "The Performance of Mutual Funds in the Period 1945–1964." *Journal of Finance,* May 1968, pp. 389–416.

Kaplan, Robert S., and Richard Roll. "Investor Evaluation of Accounting Information: Some Empirical Evidence." *Journal of Business,* April 1972, pp. 225–57.

Lorie, James H., and Victor Niederhoffer. "Predictive Statistical Properties of Insider Trading." *Journal of Law and Economics,* April 1966, pp. 35–53.

Niederhoffer, Victor, and M. F. M. Osborne. "Market-Making and Reversal on the Stock Exchange." *Journal of the American Statistical Association,* December 1966, pp. 897–916.

Oppenheimer, Henry R., and Gary G. Schlarbaum. "Investing with Ben Graham: An Ex Ante Test of the Efficient Market Hypothesis." Forthcoming issue of the *Journal of Financial and Quantitative Analysis.*

Pinches, George. "The Random Walk Hypothesis and Technical Analysis." *Financial Analysts Journal,* March–April 1970, pp. 104–10.

Pratt, Shannon P., and Charles H. DeVere. "Relationship between Insider Trading and Rate of Return for NYSE Common Stocks, 1960–1966." In *Modern Developments in Investment Management,* ed. James H. Lorie and Richard Beasley. New York: Praeger Publishers, 1972, pp. 268–79.

Shishko, Irwin. "Techniques of Forecasting Commedity Prices." *Commodity Yearbook.* New York: Commodity Research Bureau, Inc., 1965, pp. 30–41.

Smith, Randall. "Short Interest and Stock Market Prices." *Financial Analysts Journal,* November–December 1968, pp. 151–54.

Sunder, Shyam. "Stock Price and the Risk Related to Accounting Changes in Inventory Valuation. *Accounting Review,* April 1975, pp. 305–15.

Securities and Exchange Commission. *Institutional Investor Report.* Washington D.C.: U.S. Government Printing Office, 1971.

Zweig, Martin E. *Understanding Technical Forecasting.* Princeton, N.J.: Dow Jones & Company, Inc., 1978.

PART 3 FIXED INCOME AND LEVERAGED SECURITIES

We now shift our attention from stocks to fixed-income and leveraged securities. Fixed-income securities include bonds, preferred stock, certificates of deposit, and even money market funds. In the high interest rate environment of the last decade, many investors have increased their emphasis on fixed-return investments. However, we shall see that fixed-income securities are not without risk or uncertainty as to outcome.

In Chapter 10, we look at the organization of the debt markets and the elements that define the basic debt instrument. The functions of the bond rating agencies are also explored along with the perceived efficiency of the bond market. In Chapter 11, we assume the role of the bond investor and examine a number of strategy considerations for optimizing return on investment.

The second half of this section covers leveraged securities, that is, securities in which there is a magnified return or loss potential for a given level of investment ("maximum bang for the buck"). The discussion begins with convertibles and warrants in Chapter 12. We examine the valuation of these securities and the existence of speculative premiums (the difference between market value and intrinsic value). We also look at the advantages and disadvantages of convertibles and warrants to the investor as well as to the corporation. A recurring question is, are we dealing with fool's gold? While the answer is no, it is a qualified no that can only be fully understood after you have examined the in and outs of investing in these securities.

The stock option became highly popular with the founding of the Chicago Board Options Exchange in 1973. Options allow the investor to buy and sell stock at a specified future price, and they may be used as a form of speculation or as a defensive tool. In Chapter 13, we examine the basic types of options (puts and calls), the operations of the options market, how option prices are established, and the use of leverage in the option contract. We also examine how "option plays" can be tailored to the overall objectives of the portfolio. We conclude with a discussion of some of the more sophisticated option strategies in which there is multiple trading of options on a given stock at one time.

10 Bond and fixed-income fundamentals

As the reader will observe in various sections of this chapter, bonds actually represent a more substantial portion of new offerings in the capital markets than common stock. Some of the most financially rewarding positions on Wall Street go to sophisticated analysts and dealers in the bond market. Though high interest rates periodically choke off the market and bring predictions of doom for "bond instruments in the future," such is not likely to be the case. Rather, the trend is more likely to focus on a wiser and more adaptive use of the debt instrument.

In this chapter, we will examine the fundamentals of the bond instrument for both corporate and government issuers, with an emphasis on the debt contract and security provisions. We will also look at the overall structure of the bond market and the ways in which bonds are rated. The question of bond market efficiency is also considered. While most of the chapter deals with corporate and government bonds (and various government debt issues), other forms of fixed-income securities also receive attention. Thus, there is a brief discussion of short-term, fixed-income investments (such as certificates of deposit and commercial paper) as well as preferred stock.

In Chapter 11, we will shift the emphasis to actually evaluating fixed-income investments and devising strategies that attempt to capture profitable opportunities in the market. We begin our present discussion by considering the key elements that go into a bond contract.

THE BOND CONTRACT

The major provisions in a bond agreement are spelled out in the *bond indenture,* a complicated legal document often over 100 pages in length, administered by an independent trustee. We shall examine some important terms and concepts associated with a bond issue.

Par value—the face value of a bond. Most corporate bonds are traded in $1,000 units, while many federal, state, and local issues trade in units of $5,000 or $10,000.

Coupon rate—the actual interest rate on the bond usually payable in semiannual installments. To the extent that interest rates in the market go above or below the coupon rate after the bond is issued, the market price of the bond will change from the par value. A bond initially issued at a rate of 8 percent will not fare well in a market where 14 percent is the currently demanded rate of return. We will eventually examine how the investor makes and loses substantial amounts of money in the bond market with the swings in interest rates. A few existing corporate bonds are termed *variable rate notes,* meaning that the coupon rate is only fixed for a short period of time and then varies with a stipulated short-term rate, such as the rate on U.S. government Treasury bills. In this instance, the interest payment varies up and down rather than the price of the bond, and most of the bonds can be redeemed at par early in the life of the issue at the option of the holder. This type of issue is likely to become increasingly popular in the future. In recent times, zero coupon rates have also been issued at values substantially below maturity value. The investor generally receives his or her return in the form of capital appreciation over the life of the bond.

Maturity date—the date on which final payment is due at the stipulated par value.

Methods of repayment—repayment of the bond can take place under many different arrangements. Some bonds are never paid off, such as selected *perpetual* bonds issued by the Canadian and British governments in which there are no maturity dates. A more normal procedure would simply call for a single-sum lump payment at the end of the obligation. Thus, the issuer may make 40 semiannual interest payments over the next 20 years plus one lump-sum payment of the par value of the bond at maturity. There are three other significant means of repayment.

The first is the *serial* payment, in which bonds are paid off in installments over the life of the issue. Each serial bond has its own predetermined date of maturity and receives interest only to that point. Although the total bond issue may span over 20 years, 15 to 20 maturity dates are assigned. Municipal bonds are often issued on this basis. Second, there may be a *sinking fund* provision in which semiannual or annual contributions are made by a corporation into a fund administered by a trustee for purposes of debt retirement. The trustee takes the proceeds and goes into the market to purchase bonds from willing sellers. If no sellers are available, a lottery system may be used among outstanding bondholders.

Finally, debt may be retired under a *call provision.* A call provision allows the corporation to call or force in all of the debt issue prior to maturity. The corporation usually pays a 5 percent to 10 percent premium over par value as part of the call provision arrangement. The ability to call is often *deferred* for the first five years of an issue (it can only take place after this time period).

SECURED AND UNSECURED BONDS

We have discussed some of the important features related to interest payments and retirement of outstanding issues. At least of equal importance is the nature of the security provision for the issue. Bond market participants have a long-standing practice of describing certain issues by the nature of asset claims in liquidation. In actuality, only infrequently are pledged assets sold off and the proceeds distributed to bondholders. Typically, the defaulting corporation is reorganized, and existing claims are partially satisfied by issuing new securities to the participating parties. Of course, the stronger and *better secured* the initial claim, the higher the quality of the security to be received in a reorganization.

There are a number of terms used to denote collateralized or secured debt. Under a *mortgage* agreement, real property (plant and equipment) is pledged as security for a loan. A mortgage may be *senior* or *junior* in nature, with the former requiring satisfaction of claims before payment is given to the latter. Bondholders may also attach an *after-acquired property clause* requiring that any new property be placed under the original mortgage.

A very special form of a mortgage or collateralized debt instrument is the *equipment trust certificate.* It is used by firms in the transportation industry (railroads, airlines, etc.). Proceeds from the sale of the certificate are used to purchase new equipment, and this new equipment in turn serves as collateral for the trust certificate.

Not all bond issues are secured or collateralized by assets. Certainly, most federal, state, and local government issues are unsecured. A wide range of corporate issues also are unsecured. There is also a set of terminology referring to these unsecured issues. A corporate debt issue that is unsecured is referred to as a *debenture.* Even though the debenture is not secured by a specific pledge of assets, there may be priorities of claims among debenture holders. Thus, there are senior debentures and junior or subordinated debentures.

If liquidation becomes necessary because all other avenues for survival have failed, secured creditors are paid off first out of the disposition of the secured assets. The proceeds from the sale of the balance of the assets are then distributed among unsecured creditors, with those holding a senior ranking being satisfied before those holding a subordinate position (subordinated debenture holders).[1]

Unsecured corporate debt may provide slightly higher yields because of the greater suggested risk. However, this is partially offset by the fact that many debenture issuers have such strong financial statements that security pledges may not be necessary.

Companies with less favorable prospects may issue *income bonds.* These bonds specify that interest is to be paid only to the extent that it is earned in current income. There is no legally binding requirement to pay interest on a regular basis, and failure to make interest payments cannot trigger bankruptcy proceedings. These issues appear to offer the corporation the unusual advantage of

---

[1]Those secured creditors that are not fully satisfied by the disposition of assets may also participate with the unsecured creditors in the remaining assets.

paying interest as a tax-deductible expense (as opposed to dividends) combined with freedom from the binding contractual obligation of most debt issues. But any initial enthusiasm for these issues is quickly reduced by recognition of the fact that they have very limited appeal to investors. The issuance of income bonds is usually restricted to circumstances where new corporate debt is issued to old bondholders or preferred stockholders to avoid bankruptcy or where a troubled corporation is being reorganized.

THE COMPOSITION OF THE BOND MARKET

Having established some of the basic terminology relating to the bond instrument, we now are in a position to take a more comprehensive look at the bond market.

While there may be a tendency to think of corporate issues as making up a large percentage of the bond market, this is simply not the case. Corporate issues must vie with offerings from the U.S. Treasury, federally sponsored credit agencies, and state and local governments (municipal offerings). The total dollar amount of *new* security issues from these four sources (with a maturity of at least one year) rose from $40 billion in 1966 to $204 billion in 1980. The relative importance of the four types of issues is indicated in Figure 10–1. Over the 14-year period, new issues of corporate securities averaged only 33 percent of the total, while government securities (federal, state, and local) made up the other 67 percent. It is interesting to note the dramatic recent rise in long-term U.S. government securities (top portion of Figure 10–1). Large deficits, beginning in the mid-1970s, have steadily increased the U.S. government's portion of new financing.

In the following section, we will briefly discuss the various forms of debt instruments available to the investor.

U. S. government securities

U.S. government securities take the form of Treasury bills, Treasury notes, and Treasury bonds (only the latter two are considered in Figure 10–1). The distinction between the three categories relates to the life of the obligation.

Treasury bills are short-term in nature with a maximum maturity of one year and common maturities of 91 and 182 days. Treasury bills (T bills) are unique in that they trade on a discount basis—meaning that the yield the investor receives takes place as a result of the difference between the price paid and the maturity value (and no actual interest is paid). Thus, a $10,000 Treasury bill quoted to pay 10 percent annualized interest over a six-month period will initially sell for $9,500. The investor receives $500 on the $10,000 face amount, or 5 percent for six months, which is translated into a 10 percent annualized rate. Actually, the true rate is slightly higher than the 10 percent quoted rate. The investor is receiving $500 interest on the $9,500 discounted price ($500/$9,500) or 5.26 percent, which translates into 10.52 percent.

Treasury bills trade in minimum units of $10,000, and there is an extremely

Figure 10-1 Long-term funds raised by business and the government

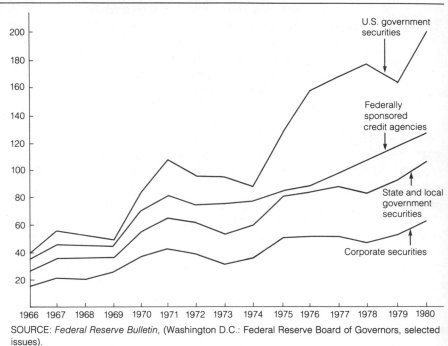

SOURCE: *Federal Reserve Bulletin,* (Washington D.C.: Federal Reserve Board of Governors, selected issues).

active secondary or resale market for these securities. Thus, an investor buying a Treasury bill from the government with an initial life of approximately six months would have no difficulty in selling it to another investor after two or three weeks. Since the T bill now has a shorter time to run, its market value would be a bit closer to par.

A second type of U.S. government security is the *Treasury note,* which is considered to be of intermediate term and generally has a maturity of one to seven years. Finally, *Treasury bonds* are long-term in nature and span from 7 to 25 years or longer. Unlike Treasury bills, Treasury notes and bonds provide direct interest and trade in units of $1,000 and higher. Because there is no risk of default (unless the government stops printing money or the ultimate bomb explodes), U.S. government securities provide lower returns than other forms of credit obligations. Interest on U.S. government issues is fully taxable for IRS purposes but is exempt from state and local taxes.

Federally sponsored credit agency issues

Referring back to Figure 10-1, observe the rapid growth in securities issued by federal agencies. New issues have been running at the rate of approximately $20 billion per year. These issues represent obligations of various agencies of the government, such as the Federal Home Loan Bank, the Federal National

Mortgage Association (FNMA), and the Federal Housing Administration (FHA). Although these issues are authorized by an act of Congress and used to finance federal projects, they are not direct obligations of the Treasury but rather of the agency itself.

Though the issues are essentially free of risk (there is always the implicit standby power of the government behind the issues), they carry a slightly higher yield than U.S. government securities simply because they are not directly issued by the Treasury. Agency issues have been particularly active as a support mechanism for the housing industry. The issues generally trade in denominations of $5,000 and up and have varying maturities of from 1 to 40 years with an average life of approximately 15 years. Examples of some agency issues are presented below.

	Minimum denomination	Life at issue
Federal Home Loan Bank	$10,000	12–25 years
Federal Intermediate Credit Banks	5,000	Up to 4 years
Federal Housing Administration	50,000	1–40 years
Export-Import Bank	5,000	Up to 7 years
U.S. Postal Service	10,000	25 years

Interest on agency issues is fully taxable for IRS purposes and is generally taxable for state and local purposes although there are exceptions. (For example, interest on obligations issued by the Federal Housing Administration are subject to state and local taxes, but those of the Federal Home Loan Bank are not.)

One agency issue that is of particular interest to the investor because of its unique features is the GNMA ("Ginnie Mae") pass-through certificate. These certificates represent an undivided interest in a pool of federally insured mortgages. Actually, GNMA, the Government National Mortgage Association, buys a pool of mortgages from various lenders at a discount and then issues securities to the public against these mortgages. Security holders in GNMA certificates receive monthly payments that essentially represent a pass through of interest and principal payments on the mortgages. These securities come in minimum denominations of $25,000, are long-term in nature, and are fully taxable for federal, state, and local income tax purposes. A major consideration in this investment is that the investor has fully consumed his or her capital at the end of the investment. (Not only has interest been received monthly, but all capital has been returned over the life of the certificate.)

State and local government securities

Debt securities issued by state and local governments are referred to as municipal bonds. Examples of issuing agencies include states, cities, school districts, toll roads, or any other type of political subdivision. The most important

feature of a municipal bond is the tax-exempt nature of the interest payment. Dating back to the United States Supreme Court opinion of 1819 in *McCullough* v. *Maryland,* it was ruled that the federal government and state and local governments do not possess the power to tax each other. An eventual byproduct of the judicial ruling was that income from municipal bonds cannot be taxed by the IRS. Furthermore, income from municipal bonds is also exempt from state and local taxes if bought within the locality in which one resides. Thus, a Californian buying municipal bonds in that state would pay no state income tax on the issue. However, the same Californian would have to pay state or local incomes taxes if the originating agency were in Texas or New York.

We cannot overemphasize the importance of the federal tax exemption that municipal bonds enjoy. The consequences are twofold. First of all, individuals in high tax brackets may find highly attractive investment opportunities in municipal bonds.[2] Some have referred to municipal bond investments as "welfare for the rich." The formula used to equate interest on municipal bonds to other investments is:

$$y = \frac{i}{(1 - t)} \qquad (10-1)$$

where:

y = Equivalent before-tax yield on a taxable investment.
i = Yield on the municipal obligation.
t = Marginal tax rate of the investor.

If an investor has a marginal tax rate of 45 percent and is evaluating a municipal bond paying 10 percent interest, the equivalent before-tax yield on a taxable investment would be:

$$\frac{10\%}{(1 - .45)} = \frac{10\%}{.55} = 18.18\%$$

Thus, the investor could choose between a *non*-tax-exempt investment paying 18.18 percent and a tax-exempt municipal bond paying 10 percent and be indifferent between the two. Table 10–1 presents examples of trade-offs between tax-exempts and non-tax-exempt (taxable) investments at various interest rates and marginal tax rates. Clearly, the higher the marginal tax rate, the greater the advantage of tax-exempt municipal bonds.

A second significant feature of municipal bonds is that the yield that the issuing agency pays on municipal bonds is lower than that on taxable instruments. A municipal bond paying 10 percent may be quite competitive with taxable instruments paying considerably more. Average differentials are presented in Table 10–2.

---

[2]It should be noted, however, that any capital gain on a municipal bond is taxable as would be the case with any investment.

Table 10—1   **Marginal tax rates and return equivalents**

Yield on municipal (percent)	Comparable yield on taxable investment (in percent for each marginal tax bracket)			
	35 percent bracket	40 percent bracket	45 percent bracket	50 percent bracket
8.0%	12.3%	13.3%	14.5%	16.0%
9.0	13.8	15.0	16.4	18.0
10.0	15.4	16.6	18.2	20.0
11.0	16.9	18.3	20.0	22.0
12.0	18.5	20.0	21.8	24.0
13.0	20.0	21.7	23.6	26.0
14.0	21.5	23.3	25.5	28.0

The difference is of a 2.5 to 5 percent magnitude, and this is extremely important to issuing agencies. The ability of a city, state, or political subdivision to save 2.5 to 5 percent from normal bond market yields is critically important to municipal issuers. During those time periods when an overly aggressive Congress has attempted to propose legislation that might overturn the tax-exempt features of municipals, the cries of anger from mayors and governors is loud and clear. A major distinction that is also important to the bond issuer and investor is whether the bond is of a general obligation or revenue nature.

General obligation versus revenue bonds   A general obligation issue is backed by the full faith, credit, and "taxing power" of the governmental unit. For a revenue bond, on the other hand, the repayment of the issue is fully dependent on the revenue-generating capability of a specific project or venture, such as a toll road, bridge, or municipal colosseum.

Because of the taxing power behind most general obligation (GO) issues, they tend to be of extremely high quality. Approximately three fourths of all municipal bond issues are of the general obligation variety, and very few failures have

Table 10—2   **Comparable yields on municipals and taxable corporates**

January	Municipals Aa	Corporates Aa	Difference
1974	5.13	8.00	2.87
1975	6.57	9.13	2.56
1976	6.60	9.13	2.53
1977	5.41	8.16	2.75
1978	5.40	8.59	3.19
1979	6.01	9.48	3.47
1980	6.72	11.56	4.84
1981	10.12	13.52	3.40

SOURCE: *Moody's Bond Record* published by Moody's Investor's Service, Inc., New York, New York (selected issues).

taken place in the post-World War II era. Revenue bonds tend to be of more uneven quality, and the economic soundness of the underlying revenue-generating project must be examined (though most projects are quite worthwhile).

One special form of revenue bond that has gained popularity in the late 1970s and 80s is the pollution and environmental control revenue bond. A political subdivision offers the issue with the backing of a long-term pledge or guarantee from an industrial firm who will use the proceeds. Essentially, the political subdivision serves as a funneling device for the corporate entity and, through this approach, allows for the utilization of tax-exempt funds by the corporation. Well over 1,000 such issues are currently in existence (see examples presented in Table 10–3).

Congress has been highly supportive of this activity as a means of providing less expensive financing for low dollar return projects that provide benefits to society. In an earlier era, industrial revenue bonds, tax-exempt issues used to attract industry into a given area through low-cost financing, enjoyed a similar popularity. However, since the net benefit to society of one city stealing another city's factory and payroll is nil, severe restrictions were put on industrial revenue bonds in 1968, and the maximum size issue allowed now is only $5 million dollars.

Municipal bond guarantee A growing factor in the municipal bond market is the third-party guarantee. Whether dealing with a general obligation or revenue bond, a fee may be paid by the originating governmental body to a third party insurer to guarantee that all interest and principal payments will be made. A number of states, including California and Michigan, now have provisions to guarantee payments on selected issues. There are also two large private insurers. The first is a consortium of four insurance companies that market their product under the name of the Municipal Bond Insurance Association (MBIA). The second is the American Municipal Bond Assurance Corporation (AMBAC). Both will insure general obligation or revenue bonds.

A bond that carries a guarantee will have a slightly lower yield and a better secondary or resale market. This may be important because municipal bonds, in

Table 10–3 Examples of industrial revenue bonds

Amount	State/municipality	Lessee/guarantor
$ 35,000,000	Escambia County, Fla.	St. Regis Paper Co.
60,000,000	Gary, Ind.	Standard Oil of Indiana
110,000,000	East Baton Rouge, La.	Exxon Corp.
40,000,000	Ohio Air Quality Authority	Republic Steel Corp.
60,000,000	Gulf Coast Waste Disposal	Shell Oil Co.
75,000,000	Allegeheny County—Pennsylvania	U.S. Steel Corp.

SOURCE: *Moody's Bond Record*, published by Moody's Investors Service, Inc., New York, New York (selected issues).

general, do not provide as strong a secondary market as U.S. government issues. The market for a given municipal issue is often small and fragmented, and there are high indirect costs associated with reselling the issue.

Corporate securities

While corporate bonds represent only 33 percent of the total bond market (which also includes U.S. government securities, federally sponsored credit agencies, and municipal bonds), they are still the dominant source of new financing for the U.S. corporation. That is, corporate bonds have been the most significant form of new financing for U.S. corporations as indicated in Figure 10–2.

Between 1964 and 1981, corporate bonds represented 77 percent of the total volume of long-term corporate securities sold. In tight money periods, such as 1974–75, the ratio approached 87 percent. Whether this overall pattern will continue into the future is an open question, depending on the status of the bond and equity markets in competing for funds.

The corporate market may be broken down into a number of subunits including *industrials, public utilities, rails* and *transportation,* and *financial issues* (banks, finance companies, etc.). The industrials are a catchall category that includes everything from high technology companies to discount chain stores. Public utilities represent the largest segment of the market and have issues that run up to

Figure 10–2   **Long-term corporate financing, 1964–1981**

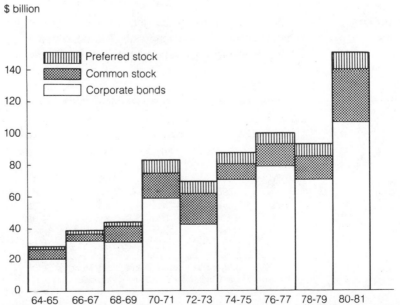

SOURCE: *Federal Reserve Bulletin* (Washington, D.C.: Federal Reserve Board of Governors, selected issues).

40 years in maturity. Because public utilities are in constant need of funds to meet ever expanding requirements for power generation, telephone services, and other essentials, they are always in the bond market to raise new funds. The needs associated with rails and transportation as well as financial issues tend to be less than those associated with public utilities or industrials. In Table 10–4, we see the comparative yields from three of the categories and for all corporations.[3]

The higher yields on public utility issues represent a supply-demand phenomenon more than anything else. A constant stream of new issues to the market can only be absorbed by a higher yield pattern. In other cases, the higher required return also may be associated with quality deterioration as measured by profitability and interest coverage.

Corporate bonds of all types generally trade in units of $1,000, and this is a particularly attractive feature to the smaller investor who does not wish to purchase in units of $5,000 to $10,000 (which is necessary for many Treasury, federally sponsored credit agency issues, and municipals). Because of higher risk relative to government issues, the investor will generally receive higher yields on corporates as well. All income from corporates is taxable for federal, state, and local purposes. Finally, corporate issues have the disadvantage of being subject to calls. When buying a bond during a period of high interest rates, the call provision must be considered a negative feature because the high-yielding bonds may be called in as interest rates go down.

Bond market investors

Having considered the issuer or supply side of the market, we now comment on the investor or demand side. The bond market is dominated by large institutional investors (insurance companies, banks, pension funds, mutual funds) even

Table 10–4   **Comparative yields on Aa bonds among corporate issuers (percent)**

January	Industrial	Public utility	Rails and transportation	Average corporations
1974	7.85%	8.15%	7.92%	8.00%
1975	8.81	9.45	8.70	9.13
1976	8.87	9.39	8.45	9.13
1977	7.90	8.41	7.52	8.16
1978	8.42	8.76	7.93	8.59
1979	9.24	9.70	8.33	9.48
1980	11.16	11.95	10.90	11.56
1981	13.01	14.03	12.69	13.52

SOURCE: *Moody's Bond Record* published by Moody's Investors Service, Inc., New York, New York (selected issues).

---

[3]Financial issues are generally not broken out of the published data.

more than the stock market. Institutional investors account for 90 to 95 percent of the trading in key segments of the bond market.[4] However, the presence of the individual investor is partially felt in the corporate and municipal bond market where the incentives of low denomination ($1,000) corporate bonds or tax-free municipal bonds have some attraction.

Institutional investors' preferences for various sectors of the bond market are influenced by their tax status as well as the nature of their obligations or liabilities to depositors, investors, or clients. For example, banks traditionally have been strong participants in the municipal bond market because of their substantial tax obligations. Their investments tend to be in short- to intermediate-term obligations because of the short-term nature of their deposit obligations (the funds supplied to the banks). One problem that banks find in their bond portfolios is that such investments are often preferred over loans to customers when the economy is weak and loan demand is sluggish. Not so coincidentally, this happens to be the time period when interest rates are low. When the economy improves, interest rates go up, and so does loan demand. In order to meet the loan demand of valued customers, banks liquidate portions of their bond portfolio. The problem with this recurring process is that banks are buying bonds when interest rates are *low* and selling them when interest rates are *high*. This can cause losses in the value of the portfolio. This concept is more fully developed in Chapter 11, "Principles of Bond Valuation and Investment."

The bond market investor must be prepared to deal in a relatively strong primary market (new issues market) and a relatively weak secondary market (resale market). While the secondary market is active for many types of Treasury and agency issues, such is not the case for corporate and municipal issues. Thus, the investor must look well beyond the yield, maturity, and rating to determine if a purchase is acceptable. The question that must be considered is: How close to the going price can I dispose of the issue should that be necessary? If a 5 or 10 percent discount is involved, that might be unacceptable. Unlike the stock market, the secondary market in bonds tends to be dominated by over-the-counter transactions (although there are listed bonds traded as well).

Finally, a number of bond offerings are sold to investors as a private placement. That is, they are sold privately to investors rather than through the public markets. Historically, private placements have equaled 30 to 35 percent of new debt issues. Private placements are most popular with such investors as insurance companies and pension funds. They are primarily offered in the corporate sector by industrial firms rather than public utilities. The lender can generally expect to receive a slightly higher yield than on public issues to compensate for the extremely limited or nonexistent secondary market and the generally smaller size of the borrowing firm in a private placement.

---

[4]Sidney Homer, "Historical Evolution of Today's Bond Market," *Journal of Portfolio Management,* Spring 1975, pp. 6–11.

BOND RATINGS

Bond investors tend to place much more emphasis on independent analysis of quality than do common stock investors. For this reason, both corporate financial management and institutional portfolio managers keep a very close eye on bond rating procedures. The difference between an AA and an A rating may mean the corporation will have to pay ¼ percent more interest on the bond issue (perhaps 13½ percent rather than 13¼ percent). On a $100 million, 20-year issue, this represents $250,000 per year (before tax), or a total of $5 million over the life of the bond.

The two major bond rating agencies are Moody's Investors Service (a subsidiary of Dun & Bradstreet, Inc.) and Standard & Poor's (a subsidiary of McGraw-Hill, Inc.). They rank thousands of corporate and municipal issues as well as a limited number of private placements, commercial paper, and preferred stock issues and offerings of foreign companies and governments. U.S. government issues tend to be free of risk and therefore are given very little attention by the bond rating agencies. Moody's, founded in 1909, is the oldest of the two bond rating agencies and covers twice as many securities as Standard & Poor's (particularly in the municipal bond area). A third agency, Fitch Investors Service, Inc., is an old-line rating agency that, except in bank securities, currently has a small position in the market.

The bond ratings, generally ranging from an AAA to a D category, are decided on a committee basis at both Moody's and Standard & Poor's. Many corporate treasurers and bond investors are shocked to find out that both firms employ under 100 analysts (and that their average age is in the late 20s) to make monumental decisions that can have a profound effect on a corporation or municipality approaching the financial markets.[5]

There are no fast and firm quantitative measures that specify the rating that a new issue will receive. Nevertheless, measures pertaining to cash flow and earnings generation in relationship to debt obligations are given strong consideration. Of particular interest are coverage ratios that show the number of times that interest payments, as well as all annual contractual obligations, are covered by earnings plus depreciation. A coverage of two or three may contribute to a low rating, while a ratio of 5 to 10 may indicate the possibility of a strong rating. Operating margins, return on invested capital, and returns on total assets are also evaluated along with debt-to-equity ratios.[6] Financial ratio analysis makes up perhaps 50 percent of the evaluation. Other factors of importance are the nature of the industry in which the firm operates, the relative position of the firm within the industry, the pricing clout that the firm has, and the quality of management.

Decisions are not made in a sterile, isolated environment. Thus, it is not unusual for corporate management or the mayor to make an actual presentation to

---

[5]Irwin Ross, "Higher Stakes in the Bond Rating Game," *Fortune,* April 1976, pp. 133–42.

[6]Similar appropriate measures can be applied to municipal bonds, such as debt per capita or income per capita within a governmental jurisdiction.

the rating agency, and on-sight visitations to plants or cities may take place. Corporations or municipalities have been known to change their operating or financial policies in order to satisfy people at the rating agencies. Perhaps the size of the issue will be pared down to provide for better interest coverage, or an increase in cash dividends will be delayed to strengthen the internal financing position of the firm.

The overall quality of the work done by the bond rating agencies may be judged by the agencies' acceptance in the business and academic community. In truth, their work is very well received. Although Paine, Webber, Kuhn, Loeb & Co. and some other investment houses have established their own analysts to shadow the activities of the bond rating agencies and look for imprecisions in their classifications (and thus potential profits), the opportunities are not great. Academic researchers have generally found that accounting and financial data were well considered in the bond ratings and that rational evaluation appeared to exist.[7]

One item lending credibility to the bond rating process is the frequency with which the two major rating agencies arrive at exactly the same grade for a given issue (and this occurs well over 50 percent of the time). When "split ratings" do occur (different ratings by different agencies), they are invariably of a small magnitude. A typical case might be AAA versus AA rather than AAA versus BBB. While one can question whether one agency is looking over the other's shoulder or "copying its homework," this is probably not the case in this skilled industry.

Nevertheless, there is room for criticism. While initial evaluations are quite thorough and rational, the subsequent monitoring process may not be wholly satisfactory. Subsequent changes in corporate or municipal government events may not trigger a rating change quickly enough in all cases. One sure way that a corporation or municipal government will get a reevaluation is for them to come out with a new issue. This tends to generate a review of all existing issues.

Actual rating system   In Table 10–5, we see an actual listing of the designations used by Moody's and Standard & Poor's. Note that Moody's combines capital letters and small *a*'s, and Standard & Poor's uses all capital letters.

The first four categories are assumed to represent investment-grade quality (high or medium grades). Large institutional investors (insurance companies, banks, pension funds) generally confine their activities to these four categories. The next two B grades are considered speculative in nature, while C and D rated issues are generally in default and may trade flat (without interest). More involved rating systems utilizing pluses, minuses, or other symbols are sometimes used for finer

[7]James O. Horrigan, "The Determination of Long Term Credit Standing with Financial Ratios," *Empirical Research in Accounting: Selected Studies,* supplement to *Journal of Accounting Research,* 4 (1966), pp. 44–62. Thomas F. Pogue and Robert M. Soldofsky, "What's in a Bond Rating?" *Journal of Financial and Quantitative Analysis,* June 1969, pp. 201–8. George E. Pinches and Kent A. Mingo, "A Multivariate Analysis of Industrial Bond Ratings," *Journal of Finance,* March 1973, pp. 1–18.

Table 10—5 Description of bond ratings

Quality	Moody's	Standard & Poor's	Description
High-grade	Aaa	AAA	Bonds that are judged to be of the best quality. They carry the smallest degree of investment risk and are generally referred to as "gilt edge." Interest payments are protected by a large or exceptionally stable margin, and principal is secure.
	Aa	AA	Bonds that are judged to be of high quality by all standards. Together with the first group, they comprise what are generally known as high-grade bonds. They are rated lower than the best bonds because margins of protection may not be as large.
Medium-grade	A	A	Bonds that possess many favorable investment attributes and are to be considered as upper medium-grade obligations. Factors giving security to principal and interest are considered adequate.
	Baa	BBB	Bonds that are considered as medium-grade obligations, i.e., they are neither highly protected nor poorly secured.
Speculative	Ba	BB	Bonds that are judged to have speculative elements; their future cannot be considered as well assured. Often the protection of interest and principal payments may be very moderate.
	B	B	Bonds that generally lack characteristics of the desirable investment. Assurance of interest and principal payments or of maintenance of other terms of the contract over any long period of time may be small.
Default	Caa	CCC	Bonds that are of poor standing. Such issues may be in default, or there may be elements of danger present with respect to principal or interest.
	Ca	CC	Bonds that represent obligations which are speculative to a high degree. Such issues are often in default or have other marked shortcomings.
	C		The lowest rated class in Moody's designation. These bonds can be regarded as having extremely poor prospects of attaining any real investment standing.
		C	Rating given to income bonds on which interest is not currently being paid.
		D	Issues in default with arrears in interest and/or principal payments.

SOURCES: *Moody's Bond Record* (Moody's Investors Service) and *Bond Guide* (Standard & Poor's).

distinctions. It is also possible for a corporation to have issues outstanding in more than one category. For example, highly secured mortgage bonds of a corporation may be rated AA, while unsecured issues carry an A rating.

The level of interest payment on a bond is inverse to the quality rating. If a bond rated AAA by Standard & Poor's pays 12 percent, an A-quality bond might pay 13 percent; a BB, 13.75 percent; and so on. The spread between these yields changes from time to time and is watched closely by the financial community as a barometer of future movements in the financial markets. A relatively small spread between two rating categories would indicate investors generally

have confidence in the economy. As the yield spread widens between higher and lower rating categories, this may indicate some loss of confidence. Investors are demanding increasingly higher yields for lower-rated bonds. Their loss of confidence indicates they will demand progressively higher returns for taking risks.

The relative positioning of different types of corporate bonds within the various rating categories is presented in Table 10–6. We see the predominance of bonds ranked in the top four categories, with one exception being the transportation industry (rails, airlines).

BOND QUOTES

The Wall Street Journal and a number of other sources publish bond values on a daily basis. In Table 10–7, we see an excerpt from the daily quote sheet for corporate bonds.

In the first column, note the company name followed by the annual coupon rate and the maturity date. For example, the sixth entry in the table shows Alabama Power with a coupon rate of 7⅞ percent maturing in 02 (the year 2,002). The current yield (cur. yld.) represents the annual interest or coupon payment divided by the price and is 12 percent (rounded). The volume (vol.) is indicated to be three bonds traded, and the closing price is 66½ percent. The bond quote does not represent actual dollars but percent of par value. Since corporate bonds trade in units of $1,000 par values, 66½ represents $665. Other issues of Alabama Power also trade at different prices.

A student interested in further information on a bond could proceed to *Moody's Bond Record,* published by Moody's Investors Service, or the *Bond Guide,* published by Standard & Poor's. For example, using the aforementioned *Moody's Bond Record,* the reader could determine, in Table 10–8, that the Avco 7½s of 1993 are subordinated debentures with a Moody's bond rating of Ba and a current call price of 100 percent of par, or $1,000 (no premium in this case). The *Moody's Bond Record* further indicates that the bonds were initially issued

Table 10–6   **Percentage distribution of corporate bonds by rating categories (based on par value outstanding)**

	Total corporate	Utilities	Industrial	Finance	Transportation
AAA	23%	26%	21%	19%	7%
AA	26	25	26	33	10
A	33	32	34	34	27
BBB	13	16	10	5	18
BB	2	1	3	1	8
B	1	—	2	1	8
CCC and lower	2	—	4	7	22
	100%	100%	100%	100%	100%

SOURCE: Salomon Brothers.

Table 10—7 **Daily quotes on corporate bonds**

Bonds	Cur Yld	Vol	High	Low	Close	Net Chg
APL 10¾97	14.	15	76⅜	76⅜	76⅜	+ ⅜
ARA 4⅜s96	cv	7	55	55	55	+3½
ATO 4⅜s87	cv	11	63	63	63	....
AbbtL 6¼93	9.0	5	69⅝	69⅝	69⅝	+1
AlaBn 13½99	13.	94	101½	101¼	101¼	- ¾
—AlaP 7⅞s02	12.	3	68	66½	66½	+1
AlaP 8⅞s03	12.	10	74½	74	74½	....
AlaP 9⅞s04	12.	20	81¾	81¾	81¾	- ⅜
AlaP 10½s05	12.	2	87⅛	87⅛	87⅛	-1⅞
AlaP 8⅞06	12.	20	72⅛	72⅛	72⅛	+ ⅛
AlaP 8¾07	12.	10	72⅝	72⅝	72⅝	+ ⅛
AlaP 9¼07	12.	1	76⅜	76⅜	76⅜	+1⅜
AlaP 9⅝08	12.	8	79½	79	79½	+1
AlskIn 12¾99	13.	10	98⅞	98½	98½	- ⅜
AlldC 7⅞s96	10.	10	77¼	77¼	77¼	- ¾
AlldSt 4½92	cv	5	99½	99½	99½	+13½
Alcoa 5¼s91	cv	10	110½	110¾	110⅜	+2⅝
Alcoa 9s95	10.	15	90	88	90	+3
AMAX 8s86	9.1	1	87¾	87¾	87¾	+ ¼
AFoP 4.8s87	7.0	17	68⅛	68	68⅛	+ ⅛
AAirl 4¼92	8.4	10	51	50¾	50¾	....
AAirl 11s88	11.	1	96⅛	96⅛	96⅛	+ ⅛
AAirl 10⅞88	11.	4	95	95	95	+1⅜
AAirl 10s89	11.	1	87½	87½	87½	+ ⅜
ACeM 6¾91	cv	5	59½	59½	59½	....
AExC 9½s82	9.5	4	100½	100½	100½	- ¼
AHoist 5½93	cv	11	89	88	88	-2
AHosp 5⅜99	cv	7	121	120½	120½	- ½
AmMot 6s88	cv	22	70½	70	70	- ½
ATT 3¼s84	4.0	76	80½	80½	80½	+ ¼
ATT 4⅜s85	5.3	35	82½	82	82½	+ ⅝
ATT 2⅜s86	3.8	20	69⅛	69⅛	69⅛	+ ⅛
ATT 2⅞s87	4.2	11	68½	68	68	....
ATT 3⅞s90	6.0	13	65½	65⅛	65⅛	- ⅜
ATT 8¾00	9.8	308	89½	87¾	89	+1
ATT 7s01	9.3	220	75½	73½	75¼	+ ¾
ATT 7⅛s03	9.4	149	76	74⅞	76	+1¼
ATT 8.80s05	9.9	590	89	86½	89	+2
ATT 7¾s82	8.0	28	97⅜	96½	97¼	- ⅛
ATT 8⅜s07	10.	170	86½	85	86½	+1½
Amfac 5¼94	cv	5	77	77	77	....
Ampx 5½94	cv	7	64½	64	64	+ ½
Arco 8s82	8.2	41	98	97⅝	97⅝	+ ⅛
Arco 8⅞s88	8.7	4	96	96	96	+ ¼
Arco 8s84	8.5	10	94½	94½	94½	- ½
Arco 7¾86	8.6	10	90½	90½	90½	+1½
ArizP 7.45s82	11.	25	69	69	69	+ ⅛
ArizP 9½s82	9.5	30	100¼	100	100¼	+ ¼
ArizP 10½00	11.	5	92⅞	92⅞	92⅞	+2
ArizP 12⅛09	12.	10	104	103¼	103¼	- ¾
ArCk 8.45s84	8.8	1	95¾	95¾	95¾	+5⅝
AshO 11.1s04	12.	11	93⅞	93¾	93⅞	+ ⅛
AsInv 7⅜88	9.8	10	75	75	75	+1½
Atchn 4s95st	8.0	4	50	50	50	+2
Atchn 4s95r	7.7	15	52	52	52	...
ARich 5⅝97	9.2	5	61	61	61	-
ARich 7¾03	10.	2	75	75		
ARich 11?		5				

on January 1, 1969, and interest is payable on March 31 and November 30 of each year.

In Table 10—9, we turn our attention to quotes on U.S. government securities (as opposed to corporate issues).

Note that while Treasury notes and bonds are quoted on the basis of price (i.e., the first issue is trading for $913 bid and $926 asked), Treasury bills are quoted on the basis of yield.

Table 10–8 Background data on bond issues

Issue	Interest Dates	Current Call Price	Moody's Rating	Current Price	Yield to Mat.	Price —1981— High	Low	Range —1946–80— High	Low	Amt. Outst. Mil.$	Sink. Fund Prov.	Legal Status	Fed. Tax	(Mil. Dol.) Current Assets	Liab.	Times Charges Earned —Annual— 1978	1979	1980	Interim
• AVCO CORP. sr.nts.12.00 1990 · · · · · · · ·	J&D15	¹² 100.00	Baa r	77 bid	17.32	90	72¾	93½	81½	75.0	No	———	N	Issued 6-19-80	@ 100.00	-yield 12.00			
— • do sub.deb. 7.50 1993 ¹³· · · · · · · ·	M31&N30	100.00	Ba r	52¼ sale	17.02	59	49	94½	30½	77.1	No	———	N	Issued Jan.1969	@	-yield			
Avco Fin. Ser.Can.Ltd. gtd.nts.9.50 1982 · ·	AUG 1	N.C.	A	———	———	94	89½	99¾	86¼	20.0	No	———	F	Issued 7-12-77	@	-yield			
do gtd.nts. 9.75 1984· · · · · · · · ·	A&O 4	N.C.	—	———	———	84	81½	99¾	86¾	33.4	No	———	F	Issued 9-6-78	@ 99.50	-yield 9.865			
• Avco Finan. Ser.Inc. sr.nts.10.50 1982· ·	J&D 1	100.00	A r	98½ sale	18.45	98¾	94	109¾	89¾	50.0	No		3 N	4,436	1,033	1.74	1.65	1.54	———

SOURCE: *Moody's Bond Record*, March, 1982, published by Moody's Investors Service, Inc., New York, New York.

BOND MARKETS, CAPITAL MARKET THEORY, AND EFFICIENCY

In many respects, the bond market appears to demonstrate a high degree of rationality in recognition of risk and return. Corporate issues promise a higher yield than government issues to compensate for risk, and furthermore, federally sponsored credit agencies pay a higher return than Treasury issues for the same reason. Also, lower-rated bonds consistently trade at higher yields than quality bonds to provide a risk premium.

Taking this logic one step further, bonds should generally pay a lower return than equity investments. Why? The reason is because the equity holder is in a riskier position because of the absence of a contractual obligation to receive payment. As was pointed out in Chapter 5, over the long term, Fisher and Lorie,[8] and Ibbotson and Sinquefield[9] have attributed superior returns to equity investments relative to debt.

However, in the highly inflationary, high-interest rate periods of the 1970s and 80s, the aforementioned researchers as well as others have indicated a reversal of this pattern; that is, "lower-risk" debt investments have at times provided a higher return (for example, virtually riskless bank CDs have paid as much as 17 percent).

A number of studies have also investigated the efficiency of the bond market. A primary item under investigation was the extent of price change that was associated with a change in a bond rating. If the bond market is efficient, much of the information that led to the rating change was already known to the public and should have been impounded into the value of the bond before the rating change.

---

[8]Lawrence Fisher and James H. Lorie, *A Half Century of Returns on Stocks and Bonds,* (Chicago: University of Chicago Graduate School of Business, 1977). Also, James H. Lorie and Lawrence Fisher, "Rates of Return on Investment in Common Stock," *Journal of Business,* January 1964, pp. 1–17. Lawrence Fisher and James H. Lorie, "Rates of Return on Investment in Common Stock: The Year-by-Year Record 1926–1965," *Journal of Business,* July 1968, pp. 219–316.

[9]Roger G. Ibbotson and Rex A. Sinquefield, "Stocks, Bonds, Bills, and Inflation: Year-by-Year Historical Returns (1926–1974)," *Journal of Business,* January 1976, 11–47.

Table 10–9 Daily quotes on government issues

Treasury notes and bonds

Rate	Mat.	Date	Bid	Asked	Bid Chg.	Yld.
10⅜s,	1985	May n........	91.30	92.6	− .2	13.47
14⅜s,	1985	May n........	102.4	102.12	− .10	13.43
14s,	1985	Jun n........	100.20	100.28	− .6	13.66
8¼s,	1985	Aug n........	85.30	86.6	− .2	13.40
9⅝s,	1985	Aug n........	89.16	89.24	− .2	13.45
15⅞s,	1985	Sep n........	105.13	105.21	....	13.81
11¾s,	1985	Nov........	94.24	95	− .8	13.52
14⅛s,	1985	Dec n........	100.30	101.6	− .10	13.72
13½s,	1986	Feb n........	99.20	99.28	− .4	13.54
7⅞s,	1986	May n........	82.2	82.10	− .10	13.55
13¾s,	1986	May n........	100.4	100.12	− .2	13.63
8s,	1986	Aug n........	82.2	82.10	− .10	13.42
6⅛s,	1986	Nov........	76.14	77.14	− .14	12.32
13⅞s,	1986	Nov n........	100.24	101	− .2	13.58
16⅛s,	1986	Nov n........	107.8	107.16	− .6	13.89
9s,	1987	Feb n........	84.6	84.14	− .8	13.41
12¾s,	1987	Feb n........	96.31	97.7	− .7	13.55
12s,	1987	May n........	95.1	95.9	− .9	13.29
14s,	1987	May n........	101.4	101.8	− .10	13.61
7⅞s,	1987	Nov n........	77.24	78.8	− .14	13.17
12⅜s,	1988	Jan n........	95.3	95.11	− .15	13.55
13¼s,	1988	Apr n........	98.20	98.28	− .11	13.53
8¼s,	1988	May n........	78.26	79.2	− .14	13.32
14s,	1988	Jul n........	101.6	101.14	− .26	13.65
15⅜s,	1988	Oct n........	106.5	106.13	− .25	13.86
8¾s,	1988	Nov n........	79.15	79.31	− .2	13.38
14⅜s,	1989	Jan........	103.21	103.25	− .5	13.76
9¼s,	1989	May n........	80.27	81.3	− .12	13.43
10¾s,	1989	Nov n........	87.6	87.14	− .2	13.42
3½s,	1990	Feb........	85.2	86.2	+1.6	5.71
8¼s,	1990	May........	75.12	76.12	+ .4	13.03
10¾s,	1990	Aug n........	86.14	86.22	+ .10	13.43
13s,	1990	Nov n........	97.10	97.18	+ .6	13.49
14½s,	1991	May n........	104.5	104.13	+ .6	13.65
14⅞s,	1991	Aug n........	106.2	106.10	+ .1	13.67
14¼s,	1991	Nov n........	103.2	103.10	....	13.62
14⅝s,	1992	Feb n........	105	105.8	− .4	13.65
4¼s,	1987-92	Aug........	84.7	85.7	+ .3	6.19
7¼s,	1992	Aug........	65.30	66.30	− .10	13.17
4s,	1988-93	Feb........	84.28	85.28	+ .6	5.76
6¾s,	1993	Feb........	62.19	63.19	− .13	13.11
7⅞s,	1993	Feb........	68.8	69.8	−1.4	13.29
7½s,	1988-93	Aug........	65.22	66.22	− .4	13.23
8⅝s,	1993	Aug........	71.21	71.29	− .19	13.52
8⅝s,	1993	Nov........	71.16	71.24	− .20	13.50
9s,	1994	Feb........	73.6	73.14	− '	13.55
4⅛s,	1989-94	May........	84.22	85 '		
8¾s,	1994	'	71.27		....	

Treasury bills

U.S. Treas. Mat. date	Bills Bid	Asked	Yield Discount	Mat. date	Bid	Asked	Yield Discount
-1982-				7- 1	12.40	12.22	12.88
				7- 8	12.42	12.24	12.93
3-11	13.52	12.96	0.00	7-15	12.45	12.31	13.04
3-18	13.51	12.97	13.18	7-22	12.48	12.36	13.13
3-25	13.56	13.02	13.27	7-29	12.48	12.36	13.16
4- 1	12.79	12.57	12.84	8- 5	12.56	12.40	13.24
4- 8	12.73	12.53	12.83	8-12	12.58	12.40	13.28
4-15	12.66	12.46	12.79	8-19	12.56	12.38	13.29
4-22	12.61	12.37	12.78	8-26	12.54	12.36	13.30
4-29	12.50	12.30	12.68	9- 2	12.49	12.35	13.32
5- 6	12.39	12.23	12.64	9- 9	12.40	12.34	13.34
5-13	12.39	12.23	12.67	10- 7	12.39	12.25	13.26
5-20	12.38	12.22	12.69	11- 4	12.37	12.33	13.29
5-27	12.36	12.20	12.70	12- 2	12.38	12.22	13.33
6- 3	12.38	12.24	12.78	12-30	12.37	12.2?	? 41
6-10	12.36	' ?	?2 85	-1983-			
6-17	1?			1-27			
◄-24							

Thus, the rating change should not have led to major price movements. Major research has generally been supportive of this hypothesis.[10] Nevertheless, there is evidence that the bond market may still be less efficient than the stock market (as viewed in terms of short-term trading profits).[11] The reason behind this belief is that the stock market is heavily weighted toward being a secondary market in which *existing* issues are constantly trading back and forth between investors.

[10]Steven Katz, "The Price Adjustment Process of Bonds to Rating Classifications: A Test of Bond Market Efficiency," *Journal of Finance,* May 1974, pp. 551–59. George W. Hettenhouse and William S. Sartoris, "An Analysis of the Informational Content of Bond Rating Changes," *Quarterly Review of Economics and Business,* Summer 1976, pp. 65–78.

[11]George E. Pinches and Clay Singleton, "The Adjustment of Stock Prices to Bond Rating Changes," *Journal of Finance,* March 1978, pp. 29–44.

The bond market is more of a primary market, with the emphasis on new issues. Thus, bond investors are not constantly changing their portfolio with each new action of the corporation.

OTHER FORMS OF FIXED-INCOME SECURITIES

Our interest so far in this chapter has been on fixed-income securities, primarily in the form of bonds issued by corporations and various sectors of the government. There are other significant forms of debt instruments from which the investor may choose, and they are primarily short-term in nature.

Certificates of deposit (CDs) These instruments are issued by commercial banks and savings and loans (or other thrift institutions) and have traditionally been in amounts of $10,000 or $100,000 (jumbo CDs). The procedure is that the investor provides the funds and receives an interest-bearing certificate in return. The $10,000 CDs generally have a fixed maturity period of six months, and the jumbo CDs, 30 to 90 days. The $10,000 CDs have a fixed rate set at a slightly higher yield than that on Treasury bills of a comparable duration (by 1986, all such interest rate regulations and ceilings will be phased out, and the free market will determine return). Jumbo CDs are said to be topless in that there is no legal limitation on maximum interest paid. It should be pointed out that in May of 1982, the government also approved a new $7,500 CD with a 91 day maturity.

A variation of the basic CD is the "small savers" certificate, which may be purchased from banks and savings and loans in as small a unit as $100. These instruments have maturities up to 2½ years.

At times, banks and savings and loans have been allowed to issue certificates that carry special, tax-exempt privileges. For example, between October 1, 1981, and December 31, 1982, these financial institutions were allowed to issue 12-month "all savers" certificates on which interest to the recipient was tax-exempt.[12] The maximum interest rate paid was set at 70 percent of the effective yield on Treasury bill instruments of a similar duration. Under the 1981 Economy Recovery Tax Act, a person filing a single return could enjoy up to $1,000 of tax-exempt income ($2,000 for those filing a joint return).[13]

In all of the certificates previously described, there are penalties for cashing in the security prior to maturity, and part of the anticipated interest payments may have to be sacrificed with an early withdrawal.

Commercial paper Another form of a short-term credit instrument is commercial paper, which is issued by large business corporations to the public. Com-

---

[12]Seventy-five percent of the proceeds to the financial institutions had to go into the real estate market.

[13]Under the same tax act, beginning January 1, 1985, $450 of interest will be tax-exempt for a single return and $900 for a joint return. To arrive at the interest subject to the exemption, the person must take interest income and subtract from this interest paid on consumer loans.

mercial paper usually comes in minimum denominations of $25,000 and represents an unsecured promissory note. Commercial paper will carry a higher yield than small CDs or government Treasury bills and will be in line with the yield on jumbo CDs. The maturity is usually 30, 60, or 90 days (though up to six months is possible).

Bankers' acceptance   This instrument often arises from foreign trade. The acceptance is a draft which is drawn on a bank for approval for future payment and is subsequently presented to the bank for payment. The investor buys the bankers' acceptance from an exporter (or other third party) at a discount with the intention of presenting it to the bank at face value at a future date. Bankers' acceptances provide yields comparable to commercial paper and jumbo CDs and have an active secondary or resale market.

Money market funds   These funds, previously discussed in Chapter 4, are not a direct form of fixed-income security, but rather represent a vehicle for individuals to buy fixed-income securities through a mutual fund arrangement. An individual with a small amount to invest may pool his or her funds with others to buy high-yielding jumbo CDs and other similar instruments. There is a great deal of flexibility in withdrawing funds through check-writing privileges (usually in minimums of $500).

PREFERRED STOCK AS AN ALTERNATIVE TO DEBT

Finally, we look at preferred stock as an alternative to debt because some investors may elect to purchase preferred stock to satisfy their fixed-income needs. A $50 par value preferred stock issue paying $6.40 in annual dividends would provide an annual yield of 12.80 percent.

Preferred stock as an investment falls somewhere between bonds and common stock as far as protective provisions for the investor. In the case of debt, the bondholders have a contractual claim against the corporation and may force bankruptcy proceedings if interest payments are not forthcoming. Common stockholders have no such claim but are the ultimate owners of the firm and may receive dividends and other distributions after all prior claims have been satisfied. Preferred stockholders, on the other hand, are entitled to receive a stipulated dividend and must receive the dividend prior to any payment to common stockholders. However, the payment of preferred stock dividends is not compelling to the corporation as is true in the case of debt. In bad times, preferred stock dividends may be omitted by the corporation.

While preferred stock dividends are not tax deductible to the corporation, as would be true with interest on bonds, they do offer certain investors some unique tax advantages. The tax law provides that any corporation which receives *preferred* or common stock dividends from another corporation must add only 15 percent of such dividends to its taxable income. Thus, if a $5 dividend is re-

ceived, only 15 percent of the $5, or 75 cents, would be taxable to the corporate recipient.[14]

Because of this tax feature, preferred stock may carry a slightly lower yield than corporate bond issues of similar quality.[15] As indicated in Table 10–10, since the late 1960s, preferred stock has actually carried a yield of ¼ to 1 percent below comparable corporate bond issues.

**Features of
preferred stock**

Preferred stock may carry a number of features that are similar to a debt issue. For example, a preferred stock issue may be *convertible* into common stock. Also, preferred stock may be *callable* by the corporation at a stipulated price, generally slightly above par. The call feature of a preferred stock issue may be of particular interest in that preferred stock has no maturity date as such. If the corporation wishes to take preferred stock off the books, it must call in the issue or purchase the shares in the open market at the going market price.

An important feature of preferred stock is that the dividend payments are usually *cumulative* in nature. That is, if preferred stock dividends are not paid in any one year, they accumulate and must be paid before common stockholders can receive any cash dividends. If preferred stock carries a $6.40 dividend and divi-

Table 10–10   **Yields on corporate bonds and high-grade preferred stock**

Year	Aa bonds (percent)	High-grade preferred stock (percent)
1947	2.70%	3.79%
1952	3.04	4.13
1957	4.03	4.63
1962	4.47	4.50
1967	5.66	5.46
1970	8.32	7.29
1972	7.49	6.85
1975	8.77	8.01
1976	8.75	7.97
1977	8.24	7.60
1978	8.92	8.25
1979	10.46	9.50
1980	12.85	12.35

SOURCES: Moody's Investor Service and Standard & Poor's.

---

[14]An individual investor does not enjoy the same tax benefit. The purpose of the corporate exemption is to avoid triple corporate taxation (that is, the issuing corporation is taxed once, and the receiving corporation's stockholders are taxed on subsequent dividend distributions, but the receiving corporation itself is only lightly taxed).

[15]Beginning January 1982, investors in selected utility stocks may also exclude $750 ($1,500 for a joint return) of dividends for tax purposes if the dividends are used to purchase more shares (a provision of the 1981 Economic Recovery Tax Act).

dends are not paid for three years, the full $19.20 must be paid before any dividends go to common stockholders. This provides a strong incentive to the corporation to meet preferred stock dividend obligations on an annual basis even though preferred stock does not have a fixed, contractual obligation as is true of bonds. If the corporation gets behind in preferred stock dividends, it may create a situation that is quite difficult to get out of in the future. Being behind or in arrears on preferred stock dividends can make it almost impossible to sell new *common stock* because of the preclusion of common stock dividends until the preferred stockholders are satisfied.

An example of existing preferred stock issues is presented in Table 10–11. The issues are listed in *Moody's Bond Record*, and the daily price quotes may be found in the NYSE Composite Stock Transactions section of the *The Wall Street Journal* or other newspapers.

SUMMARY

Debt continues to play an important role in our economy from both the issuer's and investor's viewpoints. The primary fund raisers in the bond market are the U.S. Treasury, federally sponsored credit agencies, state and local governments, and corporations. The corporate sector is made up of industrials, public utilities, and rails and transportation, as well as financial issues. The amount of new, long-term debt financing in the United States greatly exceeds the volume of equity financing.

Bond instruments are evaluated on the basis of a number of factors including yield, maturity, method of repayment, security provisions, and tax treatment. The greater the protection and privileges accorded the bondholder, the lower the yield. Thus, U.S. Treasury securities generally provide a lower yield than federally sponsored credit agency issues, and corporate securities provide a higher yield than governmental offerings. Because interest received on municipal bonds is

Table 10–11   **Examples of outstanding preferred stock issues, February 2, 1981**

Issuer	Moody's rating	Par value	Call price	Market price	Yield (percent)
American Telephone & Telegraph $4.00 cumulative *convertible* preferred	aaa*	$ 50	$ 50.00	54½	7.3%
Gulf States Utilities Co. $8.80 cumulative preferred	a*	100	107.00	66½	13.0
Tenneco $7.94 cumulative preferred	a*	100	106.62	62	12.8

*Lowercase letters are used by Moody's to rate preferred stock.

SOURCES: *Moody's Bond Record* (Moody's Investor Service) and *The Wall Street Journal.*

tax-exempt to the recipient, they provide the lowest promised yield. However, when one converts this figure to an equivalent before-tax return on a taxable investment, the return may be quite attractive. Preferred stock also offers some unique tax advantages in the form of an 85 percent tax exemption on dividends paid to corporate purchasers.

A significant feature for a bond issue is the rating received by Moody's Investors Service, or Standard & Poor's. The ratings generally range from AAA to D and determine the required yield to sell a security in the marketplace. Although there are no firm and fast rules to determine a rating, strong attention is given to such factors as cash flow and earnings generation in relation to interest and other obligations (coverage ratios) as well as to operating margins and return on invested capital and total assets. Financial ratio analysis makes up perhaps 50 percent of the evaluation, with other factors of importance including the nature of the industry, the relative position of the firm within the industry, the pricing ability of the firm, and the overall quality of management (similar criteria have also been developed for municipal bonds).

The bond market appears to be reasonably efficient in terms of absorbing new information into the price of existing issues. Some researchers have suggested that the bond market may be slightly less efficient than the stock market in pricing outstanding issues because of the lack of a highly active secondary or resale market for certain issues. Insurance companies, pension funds, and bank trust departments are not normally active traders in their bond portfolios.

Short-term investors with a need for fixed income may look to certificates of deposit, commercial paper, bankers' acceptances, money market funds (and, of course, previously discussed government securities) as sources of investment. Such factors as maturity, yield, and minimum amount must be considered.

Finally, preferred stock may also be thought of as an alternative form of a fixed-income security. Although dividends on preferred stock do not represent a contractual obligation to the firm as would be true of interest on debt, they must be paid before common stockholders can receive any payment. The preferred stock alternative may be important to the issuing firm because it provides some balance to the corporate capital structure.

IMPORTANT WORDS AND CONCEPTS	Indenture	Government securities
	Par value	Treasury bill, note, bond
	Coupon rate	Agency issues
	Maturity date	Municipal securities
	Perpetual bonds	General obligation bonds
	Serial bonds	Revenue bonds
	Sinking fund	Private placements
	Call provision	CDs
	Secured bond	Commercial paper

After-acquired clause
Debenture
Equipment trust certificate
Subordinated debenture
Income bonds

Bankers' acceptance
Money market funds
Preferred stock (callable,
   convertible, cumulative)

QUESTIONS AND PROBLEMS

1. What are some of the major provisions found in the bond indenture?

2. What are four common means of repaying the principal on a bond issue?

3. Explain how a sinking fund works.

4. Why do you think the right to call a bond is often deferred for a period of time?

5. What is the nature of a mortgage agreement?

6. What is a senior security?

7. Explain an after-acquired clause.

8. How does an equipment trust certificate differ from a secured bond?

9. Discuss the statement, "A debenture may not be more risky than a secured bond."

10. What is an agency issue?

11. Explain the concept of a pass-through certificate.

12. What tax advantages are associated with municipal bonds?

13. Distinguish between general obligation and revenue bonds.

14. How might an investor reduce the risk in buying a municipal bond issue?

15. What is an industrial bond?

16. What is meant by the private placement of a bond issue?

17. What is a split bond rating?

18. What does a bond quote of 72¼ represent in dollar terms?

19. What is a jumbo CD? What is a small savers certificate?

20. Why would an investor consider preferred stock over a bond? What is meant by the cumulative feature in preferred stock issues?

21. If an investor is in the 42 percent marginal tax bracket and can purchase a municipal bond paying 8 percent, what would the equivalent before-tax return from a nonmunicipal have to be to equate the two?

22. Assume a $10,000 Treasury bill is quoted to pay 12 percent interest over a six-month time period.
    a. How much interest would the investor receive?

    b. What will be the price of the Treasury bill?

    c. What will be the true rate of return?

23. In problem 22, if the Treasury bill had only three months to maturity:

    a. How much interest would the investor receive?

    b. What will be the price of the Treasury bill?

    c. What will be the true rate of return?

SELECTED REFERENCES

Ang, James S., and K. A. Patel. "Bond Rating Methods: Comparison and Validation." *Journal of Finance,* May 1975, pp. 631–40.

Bond Guide. Standard & Poor's Corporation, selected issues.

Fisher, Lawrence, and James H. Lorie. *A Half Century of Returns on Stocks and Bonds.* Chicago: University of Chicago Graduate School of Business, 1977.

Grier, Paul, and Steven Katz. "The Differential Effects of Bond Rating Changes among Industrial and Public Utility Bonds by Maturity." *Journal of Business,* April 1976, pp. 226–39.

Hettenhouse, George W., and William S. Sartoris. "An Analysis of the Informational Content of Bond Rating Changes." *Quarterly Review of Economics and Business,* Summer 1976, pp. 65–78.

Homer, Sidney. "Historical Evolution of Today's Bond Market." *Journal of Portfolio Management,* Spring 1975, pp. 6–11.

Horrigan, James O. "The Determination of Long Term Credit Standing with Financial Ratios." *Empirical Research in Accounting.* Supplement to *Journal of Accounting Research,* 1966, pp. 44–62.

Ibbotson, Roger G., and Rex A. Sinquefield. "Stocks, Bonds, Bills, and Inflation: Year-by-Year Historical Returns (1926–1974)." *Journal of Business,* January 1976, pp. 11–47.

Katz, Steven. "The Price Adjustment Process of Bonds to Rating Classifications: A Test of Bond Market Efficiency." *Journal of Finance,* May 1974, pp. 551–59.

Moody's Bond Record. Moody's Investors Service, selected issues.

Pinches, George E., and Kent A. Mingo. "A Multivariate Analysis of Industrial Bond Ratings." *Journal of Finance,* March 1973, pp. 1–18.

Pinches, George E.; Kent A. Mingo; and Clay Singleton. "The Adjustment of Stock Prices to Bond Rating Charges." *Journal of Finance,* March 1978, pp. 29–44.

Pogue, Thomas F., and Robert M. Soldofsky. "What's in a Bond Rating?" *Journal of Financial and Quantitative Analysis,* June 1969, pp. 201–8.

Reilly, Frank K., and Michael D. Joehnk. "The Association between Market-Determined Risk Measures for Bonds and Bond Ratings." *Journal of Finance,* December 1976, pp. 1387–1403.

Ross, Irwin. "Higher Stakes in the Bond Rating Game." *Fortune,* April 1976, pp. 133–42.

Yawitz, Jess B. "Risk Premia on Municipal Bonds." *Journal of Financial and Quantitative Analysis,* September 1978, pp. 475–85.

Yawitz, Jess B., and William J. Marshall. "Risk and Return in the Government Bond Market." *Journal of Portfolio Management,* Summer 1977, pp. 48–52.

Yawitz, Jess B.; George H. Hempel; and William J. Marshall. "A Risk-Return Approach to the Selection of Optimal Government Bond Portfolios." *Financial Management,* Autumn 1976, pp. 36–45.

11

Principles of bond valuation and investment

The old notion that a bond represents an inherently conservative investment can be quickly dispelled. A $1,000, 10 percent coupon rate bond with 25 years to maturity could rise $214.80 or fall $157.60 in response to a 2 percent change in interest rates in the marketplace. According to a study by Ibbotson and Sinquefield, investors enjoyed a total return of 14.64 percent on long-term corporate bonds in 1975 and a return of over 18 percent in 1970 and 1976. By contrast, the same investor would have lost 8.09 percent on his bond portfolio in 1969.[1] While bond prices may not be as volatile as those of stocks, there are still many opportunities for wide fluctuations in value.

In this chapter, we will examine the valuation process for bonds, the relationship of interest rate changes to the business cycle, and various investment and speculative strategies related to bond maturity, quality, and pricing.

FUNDAMENTALS OF THE BOND VALUATION PROCESS

The price of a bond at any point in time represents the present value of future interest payments plus the present value of the par value of the bond at maturity. We say that:

$$V = \sum_{t=1}^{n} \frac{C_t}{(1 + i)^t} + \frac{P_n}{(1 + i)^n} \qquad (11-1)$$

where:

V = Market value or price of the bond.
n = Number of periods.
t = Each period.
C_t = Coupon or interest payment for each period, t.
P_n = Par or maturity value.
i = Interest rate in the market.

---

[1]Roger G. Ibbotson and Rex A. Sinquefield, "Stocks, Bonds, Bills, and Inflation: The Past (1926–1976) and the Future (1977–2000)," Financial Analysts Research Foundation.

Table 11—1

Present value of an annuity of $1 (coupon payments ($C_t$)

Number of perionds (n)	Interest rate (i)					
	4 percent	5 percent	6 percent	8 percent	10 percent	12 percent
1	.962	.952	.943	.926	.909	.893
2	1.886	1.859	1.833	1.783	1.736	1.690
3	2.775	2.723	2.673	2.577	2.487	2.402
4	3.630	3.546	3.465	3.312	3.170	3.037
5	4.452	4.329	4.212	3.993	3.791	3.605
10	8.111	7.722	7.360	6.710	6.145	5.650
20	13.590	12.462	11.470	9.818	8.514	7.469
30	17.272	15.373	13.765	11.258	9.427	8.055
40	19.798	17.160	15.046	11.922	9.777	8.244

We can use logarithms and various mathematical calculations to find the value of a bond or simply use Table 11–1 and Table 11–2 to determine the present value of C_t and P_n and add the two together. (Expanded versions of these two tables are presented in appendixes at the end of the text.)

Assume a bond pays 10% interest or $100 ($C_t$) for 20 years (n) and has a par (P_n) or maturity value of $1,000. The interest rate (i) in the marketplace is assumed to be 12 percent. The present value of the bond is shown to be:

Present value of coupon payments (C_t)
(from Table 11–1)

$n = 20, i = 12\%$

$100 × 7.469 = $746.90

Present value of maturity value (P_n)
(from Table 11–2)

$n = 20, i = 12\%$

$1,000 × .104 = $104.00

Present value of coupon payments	$746.90
Present value of maturity value	104.00
Value of bond	$850.90

Table 11—2

Present value of a single amount of $1 (par or maturity value P_n)

Number ot periods (n)	Interest rate (i)					
	4 percent	5 percent	6 percent	8 percent	10 percent	12 percent
1	.962	.952	.943	.926	.909	.893
2	.925	.907	.890	.857	.826	.797
3	.889	.864	.840	.794	.751	.712
4	.855	.823	.792	.735	.683	.636
5	.822	.784	.747	.681	.621	.567
10	.676	.614	.558	.463	.386	.322
20	.456	.377	.312	.215	.149	.104
30	.308	.231	.174	.099	.057	.033
40	.208	.142	.097	.046	.022	.011

Because the bond pays 10 percent interest and the market rate is 12 percent, investors are unwilling to pay the par value for the bond and thus discount it to $850.90. Actually, coupon payments on most bonds are paid semiannually. To adjust for this, we *divide* the annual coupon payment and required interest rate in the market by two and *multiply* the number of periods by two. Using the same example as before but with appropriate adjustments, we show:

Present value of coupon payments (C_t) (from Table 11–1)	Present value of maturity value (P_n) (from Table 11–2)
$n = 40, i = 6\%$	$n = 40, i = 6\%$
$50 × 15.046 = $752.30	$1,000 × .097 = $97.00

Present value of coupon payments $752.30
Present value of maturity value   97.00
Value of bond $849.30

We see a minor adjustment in price as a result of using the more exacting process. To check our answer, in Table 11–3 we present an excerpt from a bond table indicating prices for 10 percent and 12 percent annual coupon rate bonds at various market rates of interest (yields to maturity) and time periods. Though the values are quoted on an annual basis, the assumption is that semiannual discounting, such as that shown in our second example, was utilized. Note that for a bond with a 10 percent coupon rate, a 12 percent market rate (yield to maturity), and 20 years to run, the value in the table is 84.93. This is assumed to represent 84.93 percent of par value. Since the par value of the bond in our example was $1,000, the answer would be $849.30 ($1,000 × 84.93%). This is precisely the answer we got in our second example. A typical modern bond table may be 1,000 pages long and cover time periods up to 30 years and interest rates from ¼ to 30 percent.

Table 11–3 Excerpts from bond value table

Yield to maturity (percent)	Coupon rate (10 percent)					Coupon rate (12 percent)				
	1 year	5 years	10 years	20 years	30 years	1 year	5 years	10 years	20 years	30 years
8%	101.89%	108.11%	113.50%	119.79%	122.62%	103.77%	116.22%	127.18%	139.59%	145.25%
9	100.94	103.96	106.50	109.20	110.32	102.81	111.87	119.51	127.60	130.96
10	100.00	100.00	100.00	100.00	100.00	101.86	107.72	112.46	117.16	118.93
11	99.08	96.23	94.02	91.98	91.28	100.92	103.77	105.98	108.02	108.72
12	98.17	92.64	88.53	84.93	83.84	100.00	100.00	100.00	100.00	100.00
13	97.27	89.22	83.47	78.78	77.45	99.09	96.41	94.49	92.93	92.48
14	96.38	85.95	78.81	73.34	71.92	98.19	92.98	89.41	86.67	85.96

RATES OF RETURN

Bonds are evaluated on a number of different types of returns including current yield, yield to maturity, yield to call, and anticipated realized yield.

Current Yield

The current yield, which is shown in *The Wall Street Journal* and many daily newspapers, is the annual interest payment divided by the price of the bond. An example might be a 12 percent coupon rate $1,000 par value bond selling for $900. The current yield would be:

$$\frac{\$120}{\$900} = 13.3\%$$

The problem with current yield is that is does not take into consideration the maturity date of a debt instrument. A bond with 1 year to run and another with 20 years to run would have the same current yield quote if interest payments were $120 and the price were $900. Clearly, the one-year bond would be preferable under this circumstance because the investor would not only get $120 in interest, but also a gain in value of $100 ($1000 − $900) within a one-year time period, and this amount could be reinvested.

Yield to maturity

Yield to maturity takes into consideration annual interest received, the difference between the current price of the bond and the maturity value, and the number of years to maturity. Returning to our earlier example, if a bond pays $100 in annual interest and sells for $849.30 with 20 years to maturity, the investor would be receiving $100 annually plus the $150.70 differential spread over 20 years, or $7.54 per year. This would indicate a total annual return of $107.54. We would also think of the investor's average investment as being approximately the midpoint between the initial investment of $849.30 and the ending value of $1,000. Thus, the average investment would be $924.65. The yield to maturity is the total return an investor would receive from income plus capital appreciation assuming the bond is held to maturity. The *approximate* yield to maturity would be:

$$\frac{\$107.54}{\$924.65} = 11.63\%$$

The preceding calculations can be summarized into a formula in which we show:

$$Y' = \frac{\text{coupon payment } (C_t) + \dfrac{\text{Par value } (P_n) - \text{Market value } (V)}{\text{Number of periods } (n)}}{\dfrac{\text{Market value } (V) + \text{Par value } (P_n)}{2}} \qquad (11-2)$$

On an annual basis, we indicate:

Y' = Approximate yield to maturity.
Coupon payment = $100.
Par or maturity value = $1,000.

Market value = $849.30.
Number of periods = 20.

$$Y' = \frac{\$100 + \dfrac{\$1,000 - \$849.30}{20}}{\dfrac{\$849.30 + \$1,000}{2}}$$

$$= \frac{\$100 + \dfrac{\$150.70}{20}}{\$924.65}$$

$$= \frac{\$107.54}{\$924.65}$$

$$= 11.63\%$$

This answer is merely an approximation of exact yield to maturity. The precise answer can only be found mathematically by returning to Formula 11–1 and determining the precise interest rate (i) that allows us to discount back all future coupon payments (C_t) and the par or maturity value (P_n) at the end of n periods to arrive at the current price. The yield to maturity may be thought of as the internal rate of return or yield on the bond. Since computing the exact yield to maturity is a very involved, trial-and-error process, bond tables are readily available to allow us to determine this value. As a matter of fact, all we have to do is return to Table 11–3, the bond value table, and use it in a slightly different fashion. We pick our coupon rate, read across the table for number of years, into the table for price, and then read to the left-hand column to determine yield. A 10 percent coupon rate bond with 20 years to run, selling at $849.30, provides the investor with a yield to maturity of 12 percent.[2]

Note the exact answer in this case is .37 percent above the approximation (12 percent versus 11.63 percent). In the jargon of bond trading, each 1/100th of 1 percent is referred to as a basis point, so we say the difference is 37 basis points. The approximate yield to maturity method tends to understate exact yield to maturity for issues trading at a discount (in this case, the bond is priced at $849.30). The opposite effect takes place for bonds trading above par. The extent of the discrepancy is directly related to the magnitude of the discount or premium and the life span on the bond. For a $950 bond with five years to maturity, the difference between approximate yield and exact yield is a mere .03 percent, or three basis points.[3]

The concept of *yield to maturity* is used interchangeably with the term *market rate of interest*. When we say the market rate of interest is 12 percent, it is the equivalent of saying the required yield to maturity is 12 percent.

_____

[2] Interpolation may also be used to find intermediate values in the table.

[3] It should be pointed out that in all our bond problems, we are assuming that we are buying the bond at the beginning of an interest payment period. To the extent there is accrued interest, we would have to modify our calculations slightly.

Yield to call　　　　As discussed in the preceding chapter on bond fundamentals, not all fixed-income securities are held to maturity. To the extent a debt instrument may be called in prior to maturity, a separate calculation is necessary to determine yield to the call date. Assume a 20-year bond was initially issued at a 13.5 percent interest rate, and after two years, rates have dropped. Let us assume the bond is currently selling for $1,180 and the yield to maturity on the bond is 11.15 percent. However, the investor who purchases the bonds for $1,180 may not be able to hold the bonds for the remaining 18 years because the issue can be called. Under these circumstances, yield to maturity may not be the appropriate measure.

In the present case, we shall assume the bonds can be called in five years after issue at $1,090. Thus, the investor who buys the bonds two years after issue can have his bonds called back after three more years at $1,090. To compute yield to call, we determine the approximate interest rate that will equate an $1,180 investment today with $135 (13.5 percent) per year for the next three years plus a payoff or call price value of $1,090 at the end of three years. We can adjust Formula 11–2 (approximate yield to maturity) to Formula 11–3 (approximate yield to call).

$$Y_c' = \frac{\text{Coupon payment } (C_t) + \dfrac{\text{Call price } (P_c) - \text{Market price } (V)}{\text{Number of periods to call } (n_c)}}{\dfrac{\text{Market value } (V) + \text{Call price } (P_c)}{2}} \qquad (11\text{–}3)$$

On an annual basis, we show:

Y_c' = Approximate yield to call.
Coupon payment = $135.
Call price = $1,090.
Market value = $1,180.
Number of periods to call = 3.

$$Y_c' = \frac{\$135 + \dfrac{\$1,090 - \$1,180}{3}}{\dfrac{\$1,180 + \$1,090}{2}}$$

$$= \frac{\$135 + \dfrac{-\$90}{3}}{\$1,135}$$

$$= \frac{\$135 - \$30}{\$1,135}$$

$$= \frac{\$105}{\$1,135}$$

$$= 9.25\%$$

The yield to call figure of 9.25 percent is 190 basis points less than the yield to maturity figure of 11.15 percent. Clearly, the investor needs to be aware of the

differential. Generally speaking, any time the market price of a bond is equal to or greater than the call price, the investor should do a separate calculation for yield to call.[4]

Anticipated realized yield

Finally, we have the case where the investor purchases the bond with the intention of holding the bond for a period that is different from either the call date or the maturity date. Under this circumstance, we examine the anticipated realized yield for the holding period. Assume an investor buys a bond for $900 providing 12.5 percent interest. Based on his forecasts of lower interest rates, he anticipates the bond will go to $1,050 in three years. The formula for the approximate realized yield is:

$$Y_r' = \frac{\text{Coupon payment } (C_t) + \dfrac{\text{Realized price } (P_r) - \text{Market price } (V)}{\text{Number of periods to realization } (n_r)}}{\dfrac{\text{Market value } (V) + \text{Realized price } (P_r)}{2}} \quad (11-4)$$

The terms are:

Coupon payment = $125.
Realized price = $1,050.
Market price = $900.
Number of periods to realization = 3.

$$Y_r' = \frac{\$125 + \dfrac{\$1,050 - \$900}{3}}{\dfrac{\$900 + \$1,050}{2}}$$

$$= \frac{\$125 + \dfrac{\$150}{3}}{\$975}$$

$$= \frac{\$125 + \$50}{\$975}$$

$$= \frac{\$175}{\$975}$$

$$= 17.95\%$$

The anticipated return of 17.95 percent would not be unusual in a period of falling interest rates.

Reinvestment assumption

Throughout our analysis, when we have talked about yield to maturity, call, or realization, we have assumed that the determined rate also represents an appro-

---

[4]Bond tables may also be used to find the exact value for yield to call. A source is *Thorndike Encyclopedia of Banking and Financial Tables* (Boston: Warren, Gorham & Lamont, 1981).

priate rate for reinvestment of funds. If yield to maturity is 11 percent or 12 percent, then it is assumed that coupon payments, as they come in, can also be reinvested at that rate. To the extent that this is an unrealistic assumption, the investor will wish to temper his thinking. For example, if it is anticipated that returns can be reinvested at a higher rate in the future, this increases true yield, and the opposite effect would be present for a decline in interest rates. Though it is beyond the intention of this book and most introductory texts to go through an explicit analysis of the reinvestment assumption, the interested student can consult *Inside the Yield Book: New Tools for Bond Market Strategy* for desired information.[5]

THE MOVEMENT OF INTEREST RATES

In developing our discussion of bond valuation and investments, we have observed that lower interest rates bring higher bond prices and profits. A glance at previously presented Table 11–3 indicates that a 12 percent coupon rate bond with 20 years to run will sell for $1,171.60 if interest rates decline to a 10 percent yield to maturity and at $1,276.00 at a 9 percent level of interest. The maturity of the bond is also important, with the impact on price being much greater for longer-term obligations.

The investor who wishes to make a substantial profit in the bond market must make an attempt to anticipate the turns and directions of interest rates. While much of the literature on efficient markets would indicate this is an extremely difficult task,[6] nevertheless, some historical perspective is useful.

Interest rates have long been viewed as a coincident indicator in our economy; that is to say, they are thought to move in concert with industrial production, gross national product, and similar measures of general economic health. This is generally true, although in the recessions of 1969–70 and 1973–75 interest rates actually lagged behind the decline in industrial production.

This pattern of lag between interest rate changes and the business cycle, witnessed since the mid-1960s, can be explained in terms of inflationary expectations. In earlier time periods, the occurrence of a recession tended to immediately break off inflationary expectations. Since the mid-60s, a decline in inflationary rates has only taken place well into the recession, deferring the drop-off of interest rates.

While inflationary expectations have their greatest influence on long-term rates, a number of other factors also influence overall interest rates. The demand for

---

[5]S. Homer and M. L. Leibowitz, *Inside the Yield Book: New Tools for Bond Market Strategy* (Englewood Cliffs, N.J.: Prentice-Hall, 1972).

[6]Michael J. Prell, "How well do the Experts Forecast Interest Rates?" Federal Reserve Bank of Kanses City, *Monthly Review,* September–October, 1973, pp. 3–13. Oswald D. Bowlin and John D. Martin, "Extrapolations of Yields over the Short Run: Forecast or Folly?" *Journal of Monetary Economics* (1975), pp. 275–88. Richard Roll, *The Behavior of Interest Rates* (New York: Basic Books, 1970).

funds by individuals, business, and the government represent one side of the equation, with the desire for savings and Federal Reserve policy influencing the supply side. A classic study by Feldstein and Eckstein found that bond yields were inversely related to the money supply (the slower the growth, the higher the interest rates) and directly related to economic activity, the demand for loanable funds by the government, the level of inflation, and changes in short-term interest rate *expectations.*[7]

Term structure of interest rates

Of general importance to understanding the level of interest rates is the development of an appreciation for the relationship between the level of interest rates and the maturity of the debt obligation. In truth, there is no one single interest rate, but rather a whole series of interest rates associated with the given maturity of an obligation.

The term *structure of interest rates* depicts the relationship between maturity and interest rates for a 20- to 25-year time horizon (though sensitivity diminishes after 15 years). In order to eliminate any business risk consideration, the securities analyzed are usually U.S. Treasury issues. However, the same general principles would apply for corporate securities. Examples of four different types of term structures are presented in Figure 11–1.

In panel (a), we see an ascending term structure pattern in which interest rates increase with the lengthening of the maturity dates. When the term structure is in this posture, it is a general signal that interest rates will rise in the future. In panel (b), we see a descending pattern of interest rates, with this pattern generally predictive of lower interest rates. Panel (c) is a variation of panel (b) but with a hump indicated for intermediate-term interest rates—and this particular configuration is an even stronger indicator that interest rates may be declining in the future. Finally, in panel (d), we see a flat-term structure indicating investor indifference between debt instrument maturity. This generally indicates there is no discernable pattern for the future of interest rates.

The rationale for the shape of the term structure of interest rates rests in a phenomenon called the expectations hypothesis. The hypothesis is that any long-term rate is an average of the expectations of future short-term rates over the applicable time horizon. Thus, if lenders expect short-term rates to be continually increasing in the future, they will demand higher long-term rates. Conversely, if they anticipate short-term rates to be declining, they will accept lower long-term rates.

The expectations hypothesis tends to be reinforced by lender/borrower strategy. If investors (lenders) expect interest rates to increase in the future, they will attempt to lend short term and avoid long-term obligations so as to diminish losses on long maturity obligations when interest rates go up. Borrowers have exactly

[7]Martin Feldstein and Otto Eckstein, "The Fundamental Determinants of the Interest Rate," *The Review of Economics and Statistics,* November 1970, pp. 363–75.

Figure 11—1   **Term structure of interest rates**

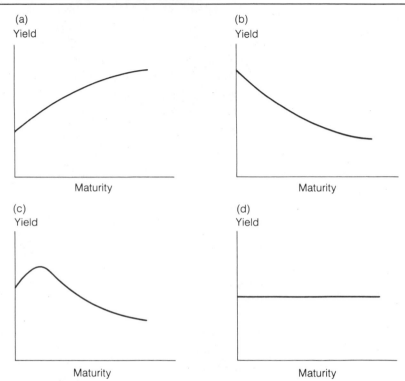

the opposite incentive. When interest rates are expected to go up, they will attempt to borrow long term to lock in the lower rates. Thus the desire of lenders to lend short term (and avoid the long term) and the desire of borrowers to borrow long term (and avoid short term) accentuates the expected pattern of rising interest rates. The exact opposite motivations take place when interest rates are expected to decline.

The shape of the term structure curve tends to be upward sloping more than any other pattern. This reflects a general bias toward expected higher interest rates and a recognition of the fact that long maturity obligations are subject to greater price change movements when interest rates change (causing the risk-averse investor to ask for higher returns on long-term obligations). Nevertheless, the curve takes on many different shapes over time.

For example, in August of 1974, the curve was downsloping in anticipation of lower interest rates as viewed in Figure 11—2. Lower rates came, and by May of 1975, the curve was upward sloping in expectation of higher rates (also in Figure 11—2). The latter shape of the curve held for a good while and successfully indicated the return to higher interest rates in the late 1970s.

Figure 11–2   **Yield curves and their patterns**

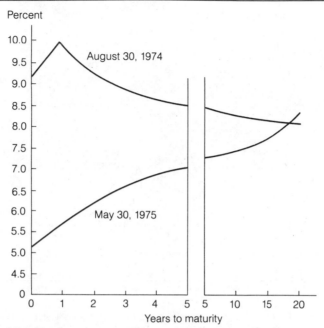

SOURCE: Federal Reserve Bank of St. Louis, December 1976.

Before concluding our discussion of the term structure of interest rates and proceeding to the development of investment strategies, one final observation is significant. Short-term rates, which are most influenced by Federal Reserve policy in attempting to regulate the money supply and economy, are much more volatile in nature than long-term rates. An examination of Figure 11–3 indicates that *short-term* prime commercial paper rates move much more widely than *long-term,* high-grade corporate bond rates.

INVESTMENT STRATEGY— INTEREST RATE CONSIDERA- TIONS

Thus far in this chapter, we have examined different valuation procedures for determining the price or yield on a bond as well as methods for evaluating the future course of interest rates. We now bring this knowledge together in the form of various investment strategies.

When the bond investor believes that interest rates are going to fall, he will take a buy position in the market and try to maximize the price movement pattern associated with a change in interest rates. He can do this by considering the *maturity, coupon rate,* and *quality* of the issue.

Figure 11—3   **Relative volatility of short-term and long-term interest rates**

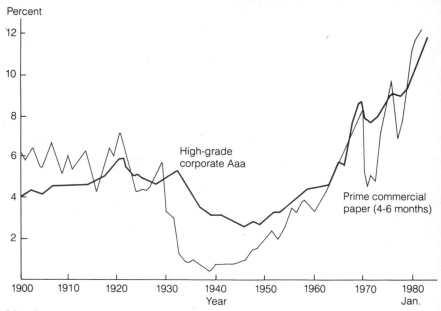

SOURCE: *Federal Reserve Historical Chart Book* (Washington, D.C.: Federal Reserve Board of Governors).

Because the impact of an interest rate change is much greater on long-term securities, the investor will generally look for extended maturities. The impact of various changes in yields on bond prices for a 12 percent coupon rate bond can be examined in Table 11—4. For example, looking at the second line from the bottom, we see a 2 percent drop in interest rates would cause a 1.86 percent increase in value for a bond with one year to maturity, but a 18.93 percent increase for a bond with 30 years to maturity.

Table 11—4   **Change in market prices of bonds for shifts in yields to maturity 12 percent coupon rate**

Yield change (percent)	Maturity (years)				
	1	5	10	20	30
+3%	−2.69%	−10.30%	−15.29%	−18.89%	−19.74%
+2	−1.81	− 7.02	−10.59	−13.33	−14.04
+1	− .91	− 3.57	− 5.01	− 7.08	− 7.52
−1	+ .92	+ 3.77	+ 5.98	+ 8.02	+ 8.72
−2	+1.86	+ 7.72	+12.46	+17.16	+18.93
−3	+2.81	+11.87	+19.51	+27.60	+30.96

We can also observe that the effect of interest rate changes is not symmetrical. Drops in interest rates will cause proportionally greater gains than increases in interest rates will cause losses, particularly as we expand the maturity. An evaluation of the 30-year column running from −19.74 percent to +30.96% will confirm this point.[8]

Though we have emphasized the need for long maturities in maximizing price movement, the alert student will recall that short-term interest rates generally move up and down more than long-term interest rates as previously indicated in Figure 11–3. What if short-term rates are more volatile—even though long-term rates have a greater price impact—which then do we choose? The answer is fairly direct. The mathematical impact of long maturities on price changes far outweighs the more volatile feature of short-term interest rates. A one-year debt instrument would need to have an interest rate *change* of over *10 percent* to have the equivalent impact of a 1 percent change in a 30-year debt obligation.

Another consideration in maximizing price movement is the coupon rate level of the bond. Assume two bonds have "roughly" the same yield to maturity and that one possesses a 13.5 percent coupon rate and is trading well above par, while the other has a 5 percent coupon rate and is trading substantially below par. The price of the lower coupon rate bond is more sensitive to interest rate changes. For example, a 5 percent coupon rate, 30-year bond will advance 30.42 percent as a result of a 2 percent decline in interest rates, whereas the 13.5 percent coupon rate bond will move only 16.71 percent.[9] This is an important point if the investor expects to trade bonds actively over the interest rate cycle.

A final consideration is the quality of the offering. High-quality securities are more sensitive to *pure* interest rate changes than are lower-quality issues. Most of the movement in Treasury securities or Aaa utilities is a function of interest rates, whereas lower-grade corporates may also be influenced by GNP, industry projections, and corporate profits. To take advantage of a perceived interest rate move, quality should be stressed. (For other investment strategies related to a perceived improvement in business conditions, lower-quality corporates may be an ideal investment outlet.)

Actual example

Let's look at an actual example of an interest rate change. Assume we buy 20-year, Aaa utility bonds at par providing a 12 percent coupon rate. Further assume that interest rates on these bonds in the market fall to 10 percent.[10]

---

[8]A sophisticated investor would also consider the concept of duration. Duration is defined as the weighted average time to recover interest and principal. For a bond that pays interest (which includes most cases), duration will be shorter than maturity in that interest payments start almost immediately. Portfolio strategy may call for maximizing duration rather than maturity in order to achieve maximum movement.

[9]Tax benefits and protection from call provisions are other advantages of low coupon rate bonds and are discussed in a subsequent section.

Based on Table 11–5, the new price on the bonds would be $1,171.60 ($1,000 × 117.16).

Though we have assumed the gain in price from $1,000 to $1,171.60 took place very quickly, even if the time horizon were one year, the gain is still 17.16 percent annually. This is only part of the picture. An integral part of many bond interest plays is the use of margin or borrowed funds. For government securities, it is possible to margin as low as 5 percent, and on high-quality utility or corporate bonds, the requirement is generally 30 percent. In the above case, if we had put down 30 percent and borrowed the balance, the rate of return on invested capital could have been 57.2 percent. The 17.16 percent war leveraged 3.33 times by borrowing 70 percent of the purchase price.

$$\frac{\text{Return}}{\text{Investment}} = \frac{\$171.60}{\$300.00} = 57.2\%$$

Though we would have had to pay interest on the $700 we borrowed, the interest on the bonds (which belongs to the borrower/investor) would have partially or fully covered this expense. If interest rates drop down further to 8 percent, our leveraged return could be over 100 percent on our original investment.

Lest the overanxious student sell all his or her worldly possessions to participate in this impressive gain, there are many admonitions. Even though we think interest rates are going down, they may do quite the opposite. A 2 percent *increase* in interest rates would cause a $134.50 loss or a negative return on a leveraged investment of $300 of 44.8 percent. At the very time it appears that interest rates should be falling due to an anticipated or actual recession, the Federal Reserve may generate the opposite effect by tightening the money supply as an antiinflation weapon as it did in 1970, 1974, 1979, and 1981. Having

Table 11–5 **Bond value table (coupon rate 12 percent)**

Yield to maturity (percent)	Number of years		
	10	20	30
8%	127.18%	139.59%	145.25%
10	112.46	117.16	118.93
12	100.00	100.00	100.00
14	89.41	86.55	85.96

SOURCE: Reprinted by permission from the *Thorndike Encyclopedia of Banking and Financial Tables*, 1981, copyright © 1981, Warren, Gorham and Lamont Inc., 210 South Street, Boston, Mass. All rights reserved.

---

[10]Buying bonds at a lower coupon rate when they are trading at a discount from par would provide greater price volatility as previously indicated, but it would complicate our analysis unnecessarily. We will also not worry about calls for now; this matter will be given attention in the next section.

now given adequate warning, the authors would summarize the discussion of interest rate plays by saying there are opportunities for unusually large profits with the anticipated and associated risks.

INVESTMENT STRATEGY— DEEP DISCOUNT VERSUS PAR BONDS

Another feature in analyzing a bond is the current pricing of the bond in regard to its par value. Bonds that were previously issued at interest rates significantly lower than current market levels may trade at deep discounts from par. The long-term secular upward trend in interest rates since World War II has made the deep discount bond very common. As an example, consider the pricing pattern for a number of American Telephone and Telegraph bonds in mid-1981.

Coupon rate (percent)	Maturity year	Price
4.375%	1985	$765.00
3.875	1990	540.00
4.75	1992	520.00
7.00	2000	533.75
8.80	2005	640.00

Deep discount bonds generally trade at a lower yield to maturity than bonds selling at close to par. There are two reasons for this. One is that a deep discount bond has almost no chance to be called away even if prices go up because the value is already far removed from par. The investor is willing to accept a lower yield for this protection. Secondly, the deep discount bond offers the investor certain tax advantages; namely, that part of his return will represent capital gains as opposed to the ordinary income tax provision associated with pure interest income. For this reason also, the investor is willing to accept a lower yield to maturity.

Let us examine how the tax feature might influence an investment decision. Assume we are evaluating three bonds that each have 20 years to run. Their coupon rates, price, and yield to maturity are presented in Table 11–6.

Our first inclination may be to invest in bond C because it provides the highest yield to maturity. But in bond A and B, we get both interest income and capital

Table 11–6   **Characteristics of potential bond investments**

Bond	Coupon rate (percent)	Price	Yield to maturity (percent)
A	6%	$612.60	10.75%
B	10	866.20	11.75
C	12	1,000.00	12

appreciation by holding the bond to maturity. As an approximate measure, in bond A we are getting 6 percent per year in interest and the balance in capital gains. Let us assume that interest on ordinary income is taxed at 50 percent and capital gains at 20 percent. In Table 11–7, we evaluate each bond on an aftertax basis to see which provides the highest yield.

As indicated in the table, we have divided the yield to maturity (1) between the coupon portion (2) and the capital gains portion (3) and then examined aftertax return in columns 4 and 5. The coupon payment in column 2 is assumed to be taxed at 50 percent providing the value in column 4, while the capital gains portion in column 3 is assumed to be taxed at 20 percent providing the figures in column 5. Total aftertax return is presented in column 6. In the measures utilized, the lowest yield to maturity bonds actually provides the highest aftertax yields.

Investment strategy—yield spread considerations

As discussed in the previous chapter, different types or grades of bonds provide different yields. For example, the yield on Baa corporate bonds is always above that of corporate Aaa obligations to compensate for risk. Similarly, Aaa corporates pay a higher yield than long-term government obligations. In Figure 11–4, we observe the actual yield spread between Moody's corporate Baa's, Moody's Corporate Aaa's, and long-term government securities.

Let's direct our attention to total spread between corporate Baa bonds and government securities (corporate Aaa's fall somewhere in between). Over the long term, the spread appears to be between 75 and 100 basis points. For example, in 1973, corporate Baa's were yielding 8 percent, while government securities provided a return of 7.25 percent. Nevertheless, at certain phases of the business cycle, the yield spread changes. For example, in the early phases of a recession, confidence tends to be at a low ebb, and as a consequence, investors will attempt to shift out of low-grade securities into stronger instruments. The impact on the yield spreads can be observed in the recessions of 1969–70 and 1974–75. In both cases, the yield spread between corporate Baa's and government securities went over 200 basis points only to narrow again during the recovery.

The individual investor must determine how the yield spread affects his strat-

Table 11–7 Total aftertax yield (percent)

Bond	(1) Yield to maturity	(2) Coupon portion of yield	(3) (1) − (2) Capital gains portion of yield	(4) Aftertax yield on coupon (50% tax)	(5) Aftertax yield on capital gains (20% tax)	(6) (4) + (5) Total aftertax yield
A	10.75%	6.00%	4.75%	3.00%	3.80%	6.80%
B	11.75	10.00	1.75	5.00	1.40	6.40
C	12.00	12.00	–0–	6.00	–0–	6.00

Figure 11—4   **Yield spread differentials on long-term bonds**

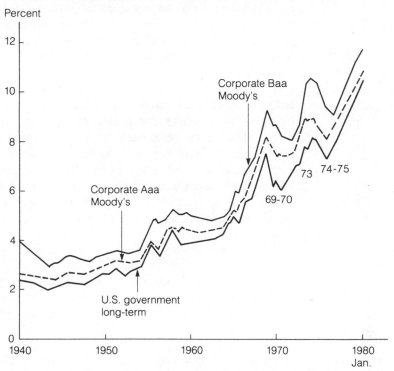

SOURCE: *Federal Reserve Historical Chart Book* (Washington, D.C.: Federal Reserve Board of Governors).

egy. If he does not need to increase the quality of his portfolio during the low-confidence periods of a recession, he can enjoy unusually high returns on lower-grade instruments relative to higher grades.

Investment strategy—swaps

The term *swap* refers to the procedure of selling out of a given bond position and immediately buying into another one with similar attributes in an attempt to improve overall portfolio return or performance.

Often there are bonds that appear to be comparable in every respect with the exception of one characteristic. For example, newly issued bonds that are the equivalent in every sense to outstanding issues generally trade at a slightly higher yield. The rationale behind this phenomenon is discussed further in Chapter 16 under a general discussion of special situations.

Swaps may also be utilized for tax adjustment purposes or for arbitrages associated with interest payment dates, call transactions, conversion privileges, or any quickly changing factor in the market.

SUMMARY

The price of a bond is based on the concept of the present value of future interest payments plus a single-sum payment at maturity. The true return on a bond investment may be measured by yield to maturity, yield to call, or anticipated realized yield. A study of interest rates in the business cycle indicates that while interest rates were at one time a coincident indicator, their movement has tended to lag behind the drop in business activity during recent recessions.

The term structure of interest rates depicts the relationship between maturity and interest rates over a long time horizon. The slope of the curve gives some indication as to future movements, with an ascending pattern generally followed by higher interest rates and a descending pattern associated with a possible decline in the future. While these movements generally hold true in the long run, it is somewhat difficult to project interest movements in the short run.

An investor who wishes to capture maximum gains from an anticipated interest rate decline should maximize the length of his portfolio while investing in low coupon, interest-sensitive securities. Deep discount bonds also offer some protection from call provisions and a lower tax obligation associated with capital gains.

A complete analysis of a bond portfolio will also include a consideration of the yield spreads between low- and high-quality issues. The spread between long-term U.S. government bonds and corporate Baa's has been as high as 200 basis points during periods in the 1970s. Investors with different quality requirements should consider new portfolio strategies during such changes in the market.

IMPORTANT WORDS AND CONCEPTS

Current yield	Yield curve
Yield to maturity	Expectations hypothesis
Coupon rate	Duration
Basis point	Deep discount bond
Market rate	Par bonds
Yield to call	Yield spread
Anticipated realized yield	Swaps
Term structure of interest rates	

QUESTIONS AND PROBLEMS

1. Why are bonds not necessarily a conservative investment?

2. How can the market price of a bond be described in terms of present value?

3. Given a 20-year bond that originally sold for $1,000 with an 11 percent coupon rate, what would be the market price of the bond if present interest rates on similar bonds are now 12 percent? Interest is paid semiannually. (Do the two-step calculation.)

4. Given the facts in problem 3, what would be the price if interest rates go

down to 8 percent? (Once again, do a semiannual analysis and use two steps).

5. Why does a bond price change when interest rates change?

6. What is the current yield of a 10 percent coupon rate bond priced at $885?

7. Why is current yield not a good indicator of bond returns?

8. What is the approximate yield to maturity of a 10 percent coupon rate, $1,000 par value bond priced at $865 if it has nine years to maturity? Use Formula 11–2.

9. What is the significance of the yield to call calculation?

10. Using the facts given in problem 8, what would be the yield to call if the call can be made in four years at a price of $1,050? Does this calculation have significance in this case? Use Formula 11–3.

11. Using the facts given in problem 8, what would be the anticipated realized yield if the forecast is that the bond can be sold in three years for $985? Use Formula 11–4.

12. What is the bond interest reinvestment assumption and its effect on yield calculations?

13. What is the meaning of term structure of interest rates?

14. What does an ascending-term structure pattern tend to indicate?

15. Under what circumstance would the yield spread on different classes of debt obligations tend to be largest?

16. In preparing a strategy to invest in bonds, what variables should be considered to maximize return? Assume a decline in interest rates is anticipated.

17. How do margin requirements affect investor strategy for bonds?

18. Assume an investor purchases a 20-year bond with a coupon rate of 10 percent. The market rate falls to 8 percent. What would be the return on investment if the buyer borrowed part of the funds with a 20 percent margin requirement? Assume the interest payments on the bond cover the interest expense on the borrowed funds.

    Note: you can use Table 11–3 in this problem to determine the new value of the bond.

19. Explain the benefits derived from investing in deep discount bonds.

20. Assume that a 5 percent coupon rate deep discount bond provides an 11.5 percent yield to maturity to the investor. Further assume the investor pays a 50 percent tax on ordinary income (such as interest) and a 20 percent tax on capital gains. Use the methodology in Table 11–7 to determine the total after tax yield to the investor.

SELECTED REFERENCES

Cohen, Kalman J.; Robert L. Kramer; and W. Howard Waugh. "Regression Yield Curves for U.S. Government Securities." *Management Science,* December 1966, pp. 68–175.

Feldstein, Martin, and Otto Eckstein. "The Fundamental Determinants of the Interest Rate." *The Review of Economics and Statistics,* November 1970, pp. 363–75.

Ferri, Michael G. "How Do Call Provisions Influence Bond Yields?" *Journal of Portfolio Management,* Winter 1979, pp. 55–57.

Hastie, K. Larry. "Determinants of Municipal Bond Yields." *Journal of Financial and Quantitative Analysis,* June 1972, pp. 1729–48.

Homer, S., and M. L. Leibowitz. *Inside the Yield Book: New Tools for Book Market Strategy* (Englewood Cliffs, N.J.: Prentice-Hall. 1972).

Jen, Frank C., and James E. Wert. "The Effect of Call Risk on Corporate Bond Yields." *Journal of Finance,* December 1967, pp. 637–52.

Joehnk, Michael D., and James F. Nielsen. "Return and Risk Characteristics of Speculative Grade Bonds." *Quarterly Review of Economics and Business,* Spring 1975, pp. 27–46.

Leibowitz, Martin L. "Goal Oriented Bond Portfolio Management." *Journal of Portfolio Management,* Summer 1979, pp. 13–18.

McCulloch, J. Huston. "Measuring the Term Structure of Interest Rates." *Journal of Business,* January 1971, pp. 19–31.

Malkiel, Burton. "Expectations, Bond Prices, and the Term Structure of Interest Rates." *Quarterly Journal of Economics,* May 1962, pp. 197–218.

Prell, Michael J. "How Well Do The Experts Forecast Interest Rates?" Federal Reserve Bank of Kansas City, *Monthly Review,* September–October, 1973, pp. 3–13.

Roll, Richard. *The Behavior of Interest Rates.* New York: Basic Books, 1970.

Schaefer, Stephen M. "The Problem With Redemption Yields." *Financial Analysts Journal,* July–August 1977, pp. 29–35.

Thorndike Encyclopedia of Banking and Financial Tables. Boston: Warren, Gorham & Lamont, 1981.

Zaentz, Neil. "Relative Price Performance among Coupon Areas in Corporate Bonds." *Financial Analysts Journal,* July–August 1969, pp. 146–55.

12

Convertible securities and warrants

An investment in convertible securities or warrants offers the market participant special opportunities to meet investment objectives. For conservative investors, convertible securities can offer regular income and potential downside protection against falling stock prices. Convertibles also offer capital gains opportunities for an investor desiring the appreciation potential of an equity investment. Warrants are more speculative securities and offer the chance for leveraged returns.

These securities have been used as financing alternatives for corporations in periods of high interest rates or tight money and specifically for mergers, using convertibles as an exchange for the common stock of the acquired company. Convertibles and warrants have advantages to the corporation and to the owner of the security. It is important to realize as we go through this chapter that what is an advantage to the corporation is often a disadvantage to the investor, and visa versa. These securities involve trade-offs between the buyer and the corporation that are taken into consideration in the pricing of each security.

CONVERTIBLE SECURITIES

A convertible security is a bond or share of preferred stock than can be converted into common stock at the option of the holder. Thus, the owner has a fixed-income security that can be transferred to a common stock interest if and when the affairs of the firm indicate that such a conversion is desirable. For purposes of our discussion, we will use a Tandy Corp. 6½ percent convertible bond (debenture) rated Aa by Moody's. The same principles of analysis would apply to convertible preferred stock.

CONVERSION PRICE AND CONVERSION RATIO

The following quote from the footnotes to Tandy's 1979 Annual Report indicates the kind of information available to the bond- or stockholder. Although the initial convertible bondholder also will receive a detailed prospectus, someone purchasing the convertible six months or more after issue would not have the benefit of a prospectus and might rely on the Annual Report.

> On October 31, 1978, the Company issued $100,000,000 of 6½ percent convertible subordinated debentures due 2003. These debentures are convertible at the option of the holder into common stock of the Company at $29 per share, unless previously redeemed. The debentures may be redeemed, at the Company's option, at any time in whole or in part on not less than 30 nor more than 60 days notice at 106.50 percent of their principal amount on or before December 31, 1979. The redemption price declines annually to 100.00 in 1998. Mandatory sinking fund payments are required, beginning in 1989, sufficient to redeem on December 31 of each year $5,000,000 principal amount of debentures at par. Proceeds from the sale of these debentures and other cash funds were used to repay the $110,000,000 outstanding under the revolving credit agreement described below.

Most of the terms contained in the quote are simply a review of your knowledge on bonds. However, one question is not answered directly. How many shares of common stock are you entitled to receive upon conversion? Notice that the debentures are convertible at $29 per share. This is called the *conversion price.* The face value ($1,000) or par value never changes (the market price does), so by dividing the face value by the conversion price, we get the number of shares received upon conversion of one $1,000 bond. This is called the *conversion ratio.*

$$\frac{\text{Face value}}{\text{Conversion price}} = \text{Conversion ratio} \qquad (12-1)$$

For the Tandy convertible bond, an investor would receive 34.4827 shares for each bond.

$$\frac{\$1000 \text{ (face value)}}{\$29/\text{share (conversion price)}} = \frac{34.4827 \text{ shares}}{\text{(conversion ratio)}}$$

Value of the convertible bond

Let us follow the October 31, 1978, issue of Tandy's 6½ percent convertible bond through conversion on September 10, 1980. The bond was originally sold at $1,000, and the common stock price on the day of this offering closed at 23⅛ on the New York Stock Exchange. If the bondholder converted the bond into 34.48 shares of common stock, what would be the market value of the common stock received? We can find this by multiplying the conversion ratio by the market price per share of the common stock, and we get a value of $797.35.

$$\text{Conversion ratio} \times \text{Common stock price} = \text{Conversion value} \qquad (12-2)$$
$$34.48 \text{ shares} \quad \times \quad \$23.125 \quad = \$797.35 \text{ (round to \$797)}$$

This value is called the *conversion value* and represents the value of the underlying shares of common stock each bond represents.

The convertible bond also has what is called a *pure bond value.* This represents its value as a straight bond (nonconvertible). In the case of Tandy Corp., there was also a straight debenture outstanding carrying a coupon of 10 percent and a market price of $960. Based on this information, the yield to maturity on a nonconvertible Tandy bond would be 10.45 percent at the time the convertible bond was issued. If the 6½ percent Tandy bond were valued as a straight debenture at this 10.45 percent yield to maturity, it would have a pure bond value of $654.[1] This is considered the floor price or minimum value of the bond. The conversion value and the pure bond value can be seen in Figure 12–1, which depicts the Tandy convertible bond.

Bond price and premiums

You may wonder how a company can originally sell a bond for $1,000 when the conversion value is $797 and the pure bond value is $654. Let's examine these values. The difference between the bond's market price ($1,000) and the conversion value ($797) is a premium of $203; it is usually expressed as a percentage of the conversion value and thus is called the *conversion premium.* In this case, the conversion premium at issue was 25.47 percent.

Figure 12–1   **Tandy convertible bond on day of issue, October 31, 1978**

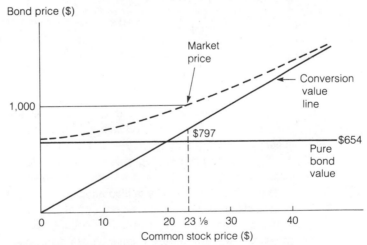

SOURCE: Tandy Annual Report, 1979.

---

[1]Using present value procedures from Chapter 11, the interest payment of $65 per year for 25 years would have a present value at 10.45 percent of $570.17, and the principal of $1,000 would have a present value of 83.34 for a total value of $653.51. We round to $654.

$$\text{Conversion premium} = \frac{\text{Market price of bond} - \text{Conversion value}}{\text{Conversion value}}$$

$$= \frac{\$1000 - \$797}{\$797} \tag{12-3}$$

$$= 25.47 \text{ percent}$$

The $203 premium indicates the extra amount paid for the 34.48 shares of stock. Remember, in essence you paid $29 per share for 34.48 shares by purchasing the bond, but you could have had the same number of shares purchased on the NYSE for 23⅛.

There are several reasons why people pay the conversion premium. In the case of Tandy's bond, the premium is somewhat larger than the usual 15 to 20 percent. First, Tandy common stock pays no dividend, while the bond pays $65 per year in interest. If the bondholder owns the bond for a little over three years, he recovers almost all the premium through the $65 yearly differential between dividend and interest income. Many companies do pay dividends on their common stock, and an analysis of interest income versus dividend income is always important in comparing a stock purchase to a convertible bond purchase.

Additionally, the bond price will rise as the stock price rises because of the convertible feature, but there is a downside limit if the stock should decline in price. This downside limit is established by the pure bond value, which in this case is $654. This downside protection is further justification for the conversion premium. One way to compute this downside protection is to calculate the difference between the market price of the bond and the pure bond value as a percentage of the market price.

$$\text{Downside risk} = \frac{\text{Market price of bond} - \text{Pure bond value}}{\text{Market Price of bond}}$$

$$= \frac{\$1000 - \$654}{\$1000} \tag{12-4}$$

$$= 34.6 \text{ percent}$$

In the case of Tandy, there is a downside limit of 34.6 percent. This is the maximum percentage the bond will decline in value if the stock price falls. One important warning is necessary—the pure bond value is sensitive to market interest rates. As competitively rated Aa bond interest rates rise, the pure bond value will decline. Therefore, downside risk can vary with changing interest rates.

The conversion premium is also affected by several other variables. The more volatile the stock price as measured by beta or standard deviation of returns, the higher the conversion premium. This occurs because of the potential for larger capital gains than on less volatile stocks. The longer the term to maturity, the higher the premium because there is a greater chance that the stock price could rise making the bond more valuable.

Figure 12–2 presents a graph of the Tandy convertible bond and depicts the conversion premium in the left panel and the downside risk in the right panel. Point *P* represents the parity point where the conversion value equals the pure

**Figure 12–2   Tandy convertible bond—6½ percent, 2003
Maturity (convertible into 34.4827 shares of
common stock as of October 31, 1978)**

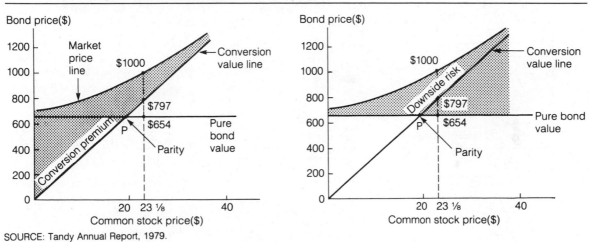

SOURCE: Tandy Annual Report, 1979.

bond value. Notice that the market price follows the conversion value to the right of point *P* and is more influenced by the pure bond value to the left of point *P*. As the common stock price rises, the conversion value rises accordingly, and the market price also rises. Furthermore, the conversion premium shrinks and the downside risk increases, which gives the bondholder less downside protection should the stock decline. As the stock declines, the conversion value falls and the conversion premium increases, but the downside risk declines as the pure bond value acts as a "floor value."

Let us track the Tandy bond from issue to conversion. The straight 10 percent Tandy bond that we used to calculate the pure bond value stayed relatively stable in price and yield during the 22 months this bond was outstanding, so we will assume a constant pure bond value in all three panels of Figure 12–3. In panel (a) we see the original information on the convertible issue. Approximately seven months later, as shown in panel (b), Tandy common stock had declined to 18⅝ and the bond to $880, creating a conversion value of $642 and a conversion premium of 37 percent. The downside risk had declined from 34.6 percent on October 31, 1978, to 25.7 percent by May 16, 1979. In retrospect, this would have been a good price at which to buy the bond. By September 10, 1980, we see in panel (c) that the stock skyrocketed to 71¾ and the bond had a conversion value of $2474. This was exactly equal to the market price as there was no conversion premium. On this date, the Tandy Corporation also called the bond at $1,061.60. Thus, the investor could allow the bond to be redeemed at a mere $1061.60 or convert it into common shares worth $2,474.[2]

---

[2] As the third alternative, the investor might immediately sell the bonds and allow another investor to convert.

Figure 12–3 Tandy 6½ convertible bond closing prices

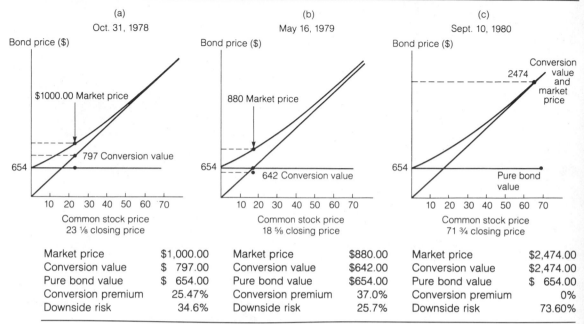

Market price	$1,000.00	Market price	$880.00	Market price	$2,474.00
Conversion value	$ 797.00	Conversion value	$642.00	Conversion value	$2,474.00
Pure bond value	$ 654.00	Pure bond value	$654.00	Pure bond value	$ 654.00
Conversion premium	25.47%	Conversion premium	37.0%	Conversion premium	0%
Downside risk	34.6%	Downside risk	25.7%	Downside risk	73.60%

SOURCE: Tandy Annual Report, 1979.

Comparison to common stock

Would you have been better off putting $1,000 in Tandy stock on October 31, 1978, or $1,000 into the convertible bond? One thousand dollars in Tandy stock at 23⅛ would have purchased 43.24 shares, while $1,000 invested in the bond got the investor 34.48 shares plus interest. On the day of redemption (September 10, 1980), a stock investment would have been worth $3,103 and the convertible bond, $2,474 plus $128 in interest over the life of the issue, or $2,602. The common stock investor would have been better off, but if the stock had gone down sharply, then the convertible with its floor value would have been the better investment. Table 12–1 shows the comparison between a stock investment and a convertible bond investment.

Actually, we have picked one of the more successful convertible bond offerings in recent years. If the convertible bondholder had taken common shares on

Table 12–1 Comparative Tandy Corp. investments

	October 31, 1978— amount invested	Shares	September 10, 1980— stock prices	Ending value	Total dividends	Total interest	Total value
Stock	$1,000	43.24	71¾	$3,103	$0	$—	$3,103
Convertible bond	1,000	34.48	71¾	2,472	—	128	2,602

SOURCE: Tandy Annual Report, 1979.

the call date, these 34.48 shares would have increased to 137.93 shares by June 6, 1981, through several 2-for-1 stock splits, and they would have a value of $4,965. The danger in using such a good example is that you may think convertible bonds are always a good investment. Table 12–2 is a page from Shearson, Loeb Rhoades May 1981 issue of *Convertible Survey.* A glance down the column for bond prices will point out there were many bonds above $1,000 where the stock price has risen like Cooper Laboratories, Inc. However, many companies' convertible bonds have suffered substantial losses, such as Cordis Corp., DPF Incorporated, Fedders Corporation, and First Pennsylvania Corporation. These "losers" all have substantial conversion premiums with bond prices well below the $1,000 initial offering price. In a period of rising interest rates, these "losers'" pure bond values also have declined, offering little floor support until substantial losses have been incurred.

Disadvantages to convertibles

It has been said that everything has a price, and purchasing convertible securities at the wrong price can eliminate one of its main advantages. For example, once convertible debentures begin going up in value, the downside protection becomes pretty meaningless. In the case of Tandy Corp. in our earlier example, the floor price is at $654. If an investor were to pay $1,400 for the convertible bond, he or she would be exposed to $746 in potential losses (hardly adequate protection for a true risk averter). Also, don't forget if interest rates in the market rise, the floor price, or pure bond value, could fall, thus creating greater downside risk.

Another drawback with convertible bonds is that the purchaser is invariably asked to accept below-market rates of interest on the debt instrument. The interest rate on convertibles is generally one third below that for instruments in a similar risk class (e.g., 10 percent instead of 15 percent). In the sophisticated environment of the bond and stock markets, one seldom gets an additional benefit without having to suffer a corresponding disadvantage.

The student will also recall that the purchaser of a convertible bond pays a premium over the conversion value. For example, if a $1,000 bond were convertible into 20 shares of common at $45 per share, a $100 conversion premium would be involved initially. If the same $1,000 were invested directly in common stock at $45 per share, 22.2 shares could be purchased. If the shares go up in value, we have 2.2 more shares on which to garner a profit.

When to convert into common stock

Convertible securities generally have a call provision, such as the Tandy bond (see earlier description) which gives the corporation the option of redeeming the bond at a specified price before maturity. The call price is usually at a premium over par value ($1,000) in the early years of callability, and it generally declines over time to par value. We know that as the price of the common stock goes up, the convertible security will rise along with the stock so that the investor has no

Table 12—2

Convertible Securities Analysis/ Bonds
Pricing Date: May 1 1981

ISSUE	COUPON	MT YR	CALL PRC	RAT ING	OUTS TNDG	SHS./ BOND	COM PRICE	CONVR VALUE$	BOND PRC$	%B PRM	%YLD BOND	Y-T-M	COM. DIVD	%YLD COM	BREK EVEN	BOND-R-LTM HIGH	BOND-R-LTM LOW	STK-R-LTM HIGH	STK-R-LTM LOW	PREM-R-LTM HIGH	PREM-R-LTM LOW
CINCINNATI FINL CORP	9.375	05	S1094	BBB	20.0	24.39	44.62	1088.4	1070	-	8.8	8.68	1.6	3.7	-	1100	0	45.7	25.2	-1.7	-1.7
CITICORP	5.750	000	1038	NR	350.0	24.39	25.37	618.9	682	10	8.4	9.34	1.6	6.1	49	698	580	26.9	18.9	26.0	6.4
CITY INVESTING CO	7.500	90	S1034	B	39.9	60.61	28.13	1704.5	1695	=	4.4	.18	1.6	5.7	5	1755	1090	30.2	18.2	-.6	-4.3
COLUMBIA PICTURES IN	5.750	94	S1033	BB	9.9	32.65	41.62	1359.0	1440	5	4.0	2.01	.6	1.4	26	1600	940	47.2	27.0	6.6	3.7
COLUMBIA PICTURES IN	9.500	05	S1100	BB	50.0	25.00	41.62	1040.6	1122	7	8.5	8.32	.6	1.4	12	1240	0	47.2	27.0	7.9	7.9
COMPUTER SCIENCES CO	6.000	94	S1030	R	49.5	37.04	21.75	805.6	917	13	6.5	6.96	.0	.0	22	1135	640	29.7	15.5	13.9	3.0
CONN GEN MTG & RLTY	6.000	96	S1033	NR	72.8	30.77	27.00	830.8	815	-	7.4	8.16	2.2	8.1	29	960	630	30.5	21.0	-1.9	-1.9
CONTINENTAL AIR LINE	3.500	92	S1010	B	27.4	31.41	10.87	341.6	448	31	7.8	13.09	.0	.0	36	494	400	13.0	7.0	81.9	21.1
CONTINENTAL TEL CORP	5.250	86	S1005	BB	19.9	41.77	16.75	699.7	775	10	6.8	11.00	1.4	8.6	-	960	720	18.1	13.7	25.4	10.8
CONTROL DATA CORP DE	3.750	89	S1018	BB	26.0	12.85	79.25	1018.4	990	-	3.8	3.90	.9	1.1	-	1020	770	80.0	47.1	27.2	-2.8
COOPER LABS INC	7.500	91	S1030	B	10.3	52.27	39.75	2077.9	2290	10	3.3	.00	.8	2.0	88	2320	960	44.7	16.4	12.2	-.8
CORDIS CORP	8.500	00	S1085	B	25.0	22.22	20.00	444.4	700	57	12.1	12.69	.0	.0	36	943	0	37.7	18.2	57.5	12.4
CROCKER NATL CORP	5.750	96	S1032	NR	14.4	22.73	37.00	840.9	830	-	6.9	7.67	2.4	6.5	-	960	630	40.2	27.1	2.2	-1.3
CRYSTAL OIL CO	11.375	00	S1080	B	50.0	49.50	32.75	1621.3	1635	0	7.0	5.81	.4	1.1	1	1840	163	38.2	11.5	.8	-2.8
DPF INC	5.500	87	S1030	R	18.7	27.93	10.50	293.3	567	93	9.7	16.84	.0	.0	59	650	510	11.1	5.4	239.7	93.5
DAYCO CORP	5.750	94	1027	BB=	9.9	43.98	13.00	571.7	606	6	9.5	11.82	.6	4.3	13	670	546	14.4	10.1	22.7	6.0
DAYCO CORP	6.000	94	1000	BB=	47.5	47.80	13.00	621.4	657	5	9.1	11.10	.6	4.3	13	699	570	14.4	10.1	17.8	1.7
DAYCO CORP	6.250	96	S1036	BB=	16.6	65.62	13.00	853.0	862	1	7.2	7.83	.6	4.3	4	930	700	14.4	10.1	5.4	-1.4
DEERE & CO	5.500	01	S1044	A-	100.0	30.53	43.87	1339.7	1380	3	4.0	2.94	2.0	4.6	-	1480	870	49.7	28.6	3.0	-2.6
DORCHESTER GAS CORP	8.500	05	S1085	BB	50.0	28.37	17.87	507.1	795	56	10.7	10.91	.2	.9	44	1013	0	29.4	13.0	56.8	21.5
DURO TEST CORP	5.750	92	S1025	NR	3.1	66.40	13.50	896.4	950	5	6.1	6.37	.4	3.3	24	1150	820	16.7	10.6	16.9	3.6
EG & G INC	3.500	87	S1010	BBB	5.4	43.23	39.37	1702.3	1750	2	2.0	.00	.5	1.3	44	2135	1200	48.6	27.4	2.8	1.6
EASTERN AIR LINES IN	11.500	99	S1107	B	150.0	62.50	10.75	671.9	835	24	13.8	14.03	.0	.0	17	945	105	11.5	6.9	24.3	24.3
EASTERN AIR LINES IN	11.750	05	S1118	R	35.0	76.92	10.75	826.9	950	14	12.4	12.40	.0	.0	12	990	0	11.5	6.9	14.9	11.9
ECONOMICS LAB INC	5.125	91	S1025	BBB	19.9	31.25	22.06	689.5	800	16	6.4	8.05	1.0	4.7	97	860	690	24.6	18.2	21.4	12.0
EDWARDS A G & SONS	110.500	06	S1100	BBB	25.0	40.00	26.00	1040.0	1100	5	9.5	9.44	.9	3.7	11	1160	0	28.2	9.6	5.8	2.7
EL PASO NAT GAS CO	6.000	93	S1020	BB	16.0	59.03	23.12	1365.1	1350	-	4.4	2.54	1.5	6.4	16	1685	960	29.5	16.1	.9	-3.2
EMPIRE INC	9.000	05	S1090	B	25.0	20.51	26.75	548.7	810	47	11.1	11.30	.4	1.5	40	925	0	49.5	14.0	47.6	-8.9
EQUITABLE GAS CO	9.500	06	S1095	A	50.0	26.79	28.25	756.8	950	25	10.0	10.05	1.3	4.7	45	1280	0	34.3	17.1	25.5	25.5
FMC CORP	4.250	92	S1015	BBB	83.6	24.10	33.62	810.2	810	-	5.2	6.68	1.6	4.8	-	960	630	35.7	22.1	18.2	-.0
FARAH MFG INC	5.000	94	S1023	CCC	9.9	26.58	12.75	338.9	520	53	9.6	12.69	.0	.0	43	525	370	14.9	3.6	364.0	32.8
FEDDERS CORP	5.000	96	S1028	R	30.0	20.00	7.75	155.0	395	154	12.7	15.49	.0	.0	57	430	351	9.2	3.0	485.4	132.4
FEDERAL NATL MTG ASS	4.375	94	S1025	NR	45.0	50.94	10.25	522.2	612	17	7.1	9.10	.6	6.2	196	960	590	17.4	9.9	17.3	8.5
FIRST BK SYS INC	6.250	00	1053	AA	50.0	20.62	46.12	951.0	970	1	6.4	6.52	2.4	5.3	20	970	790	46.7	34.2	11.9	.6
FIRST INTL BANCSHARE	7.750	05	1070	AA	100.0	19.42	55.00	1068.0	1115	4	7.0	6.78	1.1	2.0	10	1280	0	56.9	37.0	4.4	4.4
FIRST PA CORP	5.000	93	1050	NR	60.0	23.26	4.75	110.5	395	257	12.7	16.89	.0	.0	68	485	370	6.3	4.9	297.7	233.7
FIRST SEC CORP DEL	9.500	06	S1090	AA	40.0	35.40	25.56	904.9	1000	10	9.5	9.50	1.0	3.9	20	1003	0	26.8	17.4	10.5	5.6
1ST UN RL EST EV MTG	10.000	06	S1095	BBB	40.0	38.46	23.75	913.5	1022	11	9.8	9.89	1.5	6.3	36	1280	0	25.0	14.5	11.9	11.9
FISCHBACH CORP	4.750	97	S1028	BB	25.0	17.86	39.62	707.6	740	4	6.4	7.59	1.6	4.0	22	940	530	42.0	0	*******	4.6
FISCHBACH CORP	8.500	05	S1085	BH	30.0	27.78	39.62	1100.7	1170	6	7.3	7.19	1.6	4.0	22	1190	0	42.0		6.3	2.0
FISHER FOODS INC	6.500	94	S1030	R	15.3	31.30	11.75	438.3	611	39	10.6	12.65	.5	4.3	53	642	525	13.5	6.7	108.5	27.5
FISHER SCIENTIFIC CO	8.500	05	S1085	BB+	25.0	27.40	39.37	1078.8	1060	-	6.0	7.94	.5	1.3	-	1080	0	44.2	16.7	-1.7	-10.9
FLEXI VAN CORP	4.750	97	S1034	BB	25.0	40.82	28.37	1158.2	1150	-	4.1	3.54	.8	2.8	-	1303	640	32.1	16.4	-.7	-.7
FLORIDA PWR & LT CO	4.375	86	1012	BBB	19.5	45.45	27.87	1267.0	639	-	6.8	13.90	3.0	10.9	289	661	231	28.5	23.2	-49.5	-49.5

Explanation Key

ISSUE	ISSUE NAME
COUPON	COUPON RATE
MT.YR	MATURITY YEAR
	AN O INDICATES A CONVERTIBLE WITH LISTED OPTIONS ON THE UNDERLYING STOCK
	AN S INDICATES SINKING FUND
CALL/PRC	CALL PRICE IN DOLLARS
RAT.ING	S & P RATING
OUTS.TNDG	OUTSTANDING PRINCIPAL AMOUNT IN $MILLIONS
SHS/.BOND	# OF SHARES OF COMMON RECEIVED PER BOND
COM.PRICE	COMMON PRICE
CONVR.VALUE$	CONVERSION VALUE IN DOLLARS
BOND.PRC$	BOND PRICE IN DOLLARS
%B.PRM	PERCENT BOND PREMIUM OVER CONVERSION VALUE
%YLD.BOND	BOND CURRENT YIELD (%)
Y-T-M	BOND YIELD TO MATURITY (%)
COM.DIVD	COMMON DIVIDEND ($)
%YLD.COM	COMMON CURRENT YIELD (%)
BREK.EVEN	BREAKEVEN IN MONTHS (MONTHS NEEDED TO OVERCOME BOND PREMIUM FROM YIELD SPREADS
BOND-R-LTM.HIGH	BOND HIGH PRICE, LAST 12 MONTH ($)
BOND-R-LTM.LOW	BOND LOW PRICE, LAST 12 MONTH ($)
STK-R-LTM.HIGH	STOCK HIGH PRICE, LAST 12 MONTH ($)
STK-R-LTM.LOW	STOCK LOW PRICE, LAST 12 MONTH ($)
PREM-R-LTM.HIGH	HIGH BOND PREMIUM LAST 12 MONTH (%)
PREM-R-LTM.LOW	LOW BOND PREMIUM LAST 12 MONTH (%)

SOURCE: Shearson, Loeb Rhoades, *Convertible Survey*, May 1981, Lloyd Haas, CFA.

incentive to convert his bonds into stock. However, the corporation may use the call privilege to force conversion before maturity. Companies usually force conversion when the conversion value is well above the call price, like the Tandy offer which forced conversion on September 10, 1980 when the conversion value was $2,474 and the call price was slightly over $1,000. Investors will take the shares rather than the call price since the shares are worth more. This enables the company to turn debt into equity on its balance sheet and makes a new debt issue a better risk for future lenders because of higher interest coverage and a lower debt-to-equity ratio.

Corporations may also encourage voluntary conversion by using a step-up in the conversion price over time. When the bond is issued, the contract may specify the following conversion provisions.

	Conversion price	Conversion ratio
First five years	$40	25.0 shares
Next three years	45	22.2 shares
Next two years	50	20.0 shares
Next five years	55	18.2 shares

At the end of each time period, there is a strong inducement to convert rather than accept an adjustment to a higher conversion price and a lower conversion ratio. This is especially true if the bond's conversion value is the dominating influence on the market price of the bond. In the case where the conversion value is below the pure bond value and where the interest income is greater than the dividend income, an investor will most likely not be induced to convert through the step-up feature.

About the only other reason for voluntarily converting is if the dividend income received on the common stock is greater than the interest income on the bond. Even in this case, investors who are risk averse may want to hold the bond because interest is guaranteed whereas dividends are not and may be reduced. As with most investment decisions, investors must consider their expectations of future corporate and market conditions. Hard and fast rules are difficult to find, and different investors may react according to their own risk aversion and objectives.

ADVANTAGES AND DISADVANTAGES TO THE ISSUING CORPORATION

Having established the fundamental characteristics of the convertible security from the investor viewpoint, let us now turn the coin over and examine the factors a corporate financial officer must consider in weighing the advisability of a convertible offer for the firm.

Not only has it been established that the interest rate paid on convertible

issues is lower than that paid on a straight debt instrument, but also the convertible feature may be the only device for allowing smaller corporations access to the bond market. In this day of debt-ridden corporate balance sheets, investor acceptance of new debt may be contingent upon a special sweetener, such as the ability to convert to common stock.

Convertible debentures are also attractive to a corporation that feels its stock is currently undervalued. For example, assume a corporation's $1,000 bonds are convertible into 20 shares of common stock at a conversion price of $50. Also assume the company's common stock has a current price of $45, and new shares of stock might be sold at only $44.[3] Thus, the corporation will effectively receive $6 over current market price, assuming future conversion. Of course, one can also argue that if the firm had delayed the issuance of common stock or convertibles for a year or two, the stock might have gone up from $45 to $60 or $65, and new common stock might have been sold at this lofty price.

To translate this to overall numbers for the firm, if a corporation needs $10 million in funds and offers straight stock now at a new price of $44, it must issue 227,272 shares ($10 million shares/$44). With convertibles, the number of shares potentially issued is only 200,000 shares ($10 million/$50). Finally, if no stock or convertible bonds are issued now and the stock goes up to a level at which new shares can be offered at a new price of $60, only 166,667 will be required ($10 million/$60).

Another matter of concern to the corporation is the accounting treatment accorded to convertibles. In the funny-money days of the 1960's conglomerate merger movement, corporate management often chose convertible securities over common stock because the convertibles had a nondilutive effect on earnings per share. As is indicated in the following section on reporting earnings for convertibles, the rules were changed in 1969, and this is no longer the case.

ACCOUNTING CONSIDERATIONS WITH CONVERTIBLES

Prior to 1969, the full impact of the conversion privilege as it applied to convertible securities, warrants (long-term options to buy stock), and other dilutive securities was not adequately reflected in reported earnings per share. Since all of these securities may generate additional common stock in the future, the potential effect of dilution should be considered. Let us examine the unadjusted (for conversion) financial statements of the XYZ Corporation in Table 12–3.

An analyst would hardly be satisfied in accepting the unadjusted earnings per share figure of $1 for the XYZ Corporation. In computing earnings per share, we have not accounted for the 400,000 additional shares of common stock that could be created by converting the bonds. How then do we make this full disclosure? According to Accounting Principles Board *Opinion No. 15,* issued by the American Institute of Certified Public Accountants in 1969, we need to compute earn-

---

[3]There is always a bit of underpricing to ensure the success of a new offering.

Table 12–3	**XYZ Corporation**

1. Capital section of balance sheet

Common stock (1 million shares at $10 par)	$10,000,000
4.5% convertible debentures (10,000 debentures of $1,000; convertible into 40 shares per bond, or a total of 400,000 shares)	10,000,000
Retained earnings	20,000,000
Net worth	$40,000,000

2. Condensed income statement

Earnings before interest and taxes	$ 2,450,000
Interest (4.5% of $10 million)	450,000
Earnings before taxes	2,000,000
Taxes (50%)	1,000,000
Earnings after taxes	$ 1,000,000

3. Earnings per share

$$\frac{\text{Earnings after taxes}}{\text{Shares of common}} = \frac{\$1,000,000}{1,000,000} = \$1$$

ings per share using two different methods when there is potential dilution of a material nature.

1. Primary earnings per share

$$= \frac{\text{Adjusted earnings after taxes}}{\text{Shares outstanding + Common stock equivalents}} \quad (12\text{–}5)$$

Common stock equivalents include warrants, other options, and any convertible securities that paid less than two thirds of the going interest rate at time of issue.[4]

2. Fully diluted earnings per share

$$= \frac{\text{Adjusted earnings after taxes}}{\substack{\text{Shares outstanding + Common stock} \\ \text{equivalents + All convertibles} \\ \text{regardless of the interest rate}}} \quad (12\text{–}6)$$

The intent in computing both primary and fully diluted earnings per share is to consider the effect of potential dilution. Common stock equivalents represent those securities that are capable of generating new shares of common stock in the future. Note that convertible securities may or may not be required in computing

---

[4]The going interest rate was initially defined as the prime interest in Accounting Principles Board *Opinion No. 15* (1969). In 1982, the Financial Accounting Standards Board was considering changing the going interest rate to a designated long-term rate at time of issue.

primary earnings per share depending on rates, but they must be included in computing fully diluted earnings per share.

In the case of the XYZ Corporation in Table 12–3, the convertibles pay 4.5 percent interest. We assume that the going interest rate was 9 percent at the time they were issued, so they are considered as common stock equivalents and are included in both primary and fully diluted earnings per share.

We get new earnings per share for the XYZ Corporation by assuming that 400,000 new shares will be created from potential conversion, while at the same time allowing for the reduction in interest payments that would take place as a result of the conversion of the debt to common stock. Since before-tax interest payments on the convertibles are $450,000, the aftertax interest cost will be saved and can be added back to income. Making the appropriate adjustments to the numerator and denominator, we show adjusted earnings per share.

$$\text{Primary earnings per share}^5 = \frac{\text{Adjusted earnings after taxes}}{\text{Shares outstanding} + \text{Common stock equivalents}}$$

$$= \frac{\overset{\text{Reported earnings}}{\$1,000,000} + \overset{\text{Interest savings}}{\$225,000}}{1,000,000 + 400,000} = \frac{\$1,225,000}{1,400,000} = \$.875$$

We see a 12½-cent reduction from the earnings per share figure of $1 in Table 12–3. The new figure is the value that a sophisticated security analyst would utilize.

SPECULATING THROUGH WARRANTS

A warrant is an option to buy a stated number of shares of stock at a specified price over a given time period. For example, the warrants of Chrysler Corporation enable the holder to buy one share of stock at a price of $13 any time between now and 1990. If Chrysler becomes a profitable automobile company once again, the stock could rise to over $20 per share, and these warrants could become quite valuable. However, if Chrysler stock does not reach a price of $13 by 1990, the warrants would be worthless. Warrants are usually issued as a sweetener to a bond offering, and they may enable the firm to issue debt when this would not be feasible otherwise. The warrants allow the bond issue to carry a lower coupon rate and are usually detachable from the bond after the issue date. After being separated from the bond, warrants have their own market price and are primarily traded on the American Stock Exchange, with a few issues traded on the New York Stock Exchange. After the warrants are exercised, the initial debt with which they were sold remains in existence.

---

[5]Same as fully diluted in this instance.

The financial company Bache Group (Bache Halsey Stuart Shields), which is known for its retail brokerage business, had a bond offering October 30, 1980. They offered 35,000 units of $1,000 debentures due in the year 2000 with a coupon interest rate of 14 percent. To each bond, 30 warrants were attached. Each warrant allowed the holder to buy one share of stock at $18.50 until November 1, 1985. At the time of issue, the warrant had no true value since the common stock was selling below $18.50. During 1981, however, the stock went up as several merger offers were made for retail brokerage companies.[6] On May 29, 1981, Bache common stock was selling at 31½, and each warrant traded at 13⅝. The 30 warrants received with each bond were now worth $408.75 and provided the sweetener every bondholder had hoped for.

Because a warrant is dependent on the market movement of the underlying common stock and has no "security value" as such, it is highly speculative in nature. If the common stock of the firm is volatile, the value of the warrants may change dramatically.

Tri-Continental Corporation warrants went from ⅟₃₂ to 75¾ between 1942 and 1969, while United Airlines warrants moved from 4½ to 126 in the 1962-to-1966 time span. Of course, this is not a one-way street, as holders of LTV warrants will attest when they saw their holdings dip from 83 to 2¼ in the 1968–70 bear market.

Valuation of warrants

Because the value of a warrant is closely tied to the underlying stock price, we can develop a formula for the minimum or intrinsic value of a warrant.

$$\begin{array}{l}\text{Minimum or intrinsic} \\ \text{value of a warrant}\end{array} = \left(\begin{array}{l}\text{Market value of} \\ \text{common stock}\end{array} - \begin{array}{l}\text{Option price} \\ \text{of warrant}\end{array}\right) \quad (12\text{--}7)$$
$$\times \begin{array}{l}\text{Number of shares each warrant} \\ \text{entitles holder to purchase}\end{array}$$

Assume that the common stock of the Graham Corporation is $25 per share, and each warrant carries an option to purchase one share at $20 over the next 10 years. Using Formula 12–7, the minimum value is $5. [($25 − $20) × 1]. Since the warrant has 10 more years to run and is an effective vehicle for speculative trading, it may well trade for over $5. If the warrant were selling for $9, we would say that it had an intrinsic or formula value of $5 and a premium of $4.

Even if the stock were trading at less than $20 (the option price on the warrant), the warrant might still have some value in the market. Speculators might purchase the warrant in the hope that the common stock value would increase sufficiently in the future to make the option provision valuable. If the common stock were selling for $15 per share, thus giving the warrant a negative intrinsic value of $5, the warrant might still command a value of $1 or $2 in anticipation

---

[6]Bache was subsequently acquired by Prudential Insurance Company.

of increased common stock value. In Table 12–4, we see warrant prices (column 2) and a comparison with their intrinsic value (column 5). In column 6, we see the premium (warrant price minus intrinsic value).

As an example of an extreme case in the table, Resorts International stock price was 26.625 points below the option price on the warrant, and yet the warrant still traded for 6. The typical relationship between the warrant price and the intrinsic value of a warrant is depicted in Figure 12–4. We assume the warrant entitles the holder to purchase one new share of common stock at $20.

Note that although the intrinsic value of the warrant is negative at a common stock price between 0 and $20, the warrant still carries some value in the market. Also, observe that the difference between the market price of the warrant and its intrinsic value is diminished at the upper ranges of value. Two reasons may be offered for the declining premium.

First, the speculator loses the ability to use leverage to generate high returns as the price of the stock goes up. When the price of the stock is relatively low, say $25, and the warrant is in the $5-to-$10 range, a 10-point movement in the stock could mean a 200 percent gain in the value of the warrant, as indicated in part A of Table 12–5. At the upper levels of stock value, much of this leverage is lost, as indicated in part B of the same table. At a stock value of $50 and a warrant value of approximately $30, a 10-point movement in the stock would produce only a 33 percent gain in the warrant.

Another reason why speculators pay a very low premium at higher stock prices is that there is less downside protection. A warrant selling at $30 when the stock price is $50 is more vulnerable to downside movement than is a $5 to $10 warrant when the stock is in the 20s.

Table 12–4 Selected warrants as of May 1981

(1) Firm, warrant listing, and stock listing*	(2) Warrant price	(3) Stock price	(4) Option price	(5) Intrinsic value	(6) Premium	(7) Due date
Allegheny Corp: Am, NY	$35½	$38½	$ 3.75	34.750	$ .750	Perpetual
American Airlines: NY, NY	8¼	20⅜	14.00	6.375	1.875	4-1-84
Braniff: Am, NY	2⅞	4	22.94	−21.056	23.930	12-1-86
Bache: NY, NY	13⅝	31½	18.50	13.000	.625	11-1-84
Chrysler: NY, NY	3	6⅜	13.00	−6.625	.625	1990
Frontier Airlines: Am, Am	17⅝	26⅛	9.99	16.135	1.490	3-1-87
Mattel: NY, NY	6⅛	9⅛	4.00	5.125	1.000	1987
Pier One: Am, NY	⅛	3⅛	19.14	−16.015	16.140	2-28-82
Resorts International: Am, Am	6	26⅜	53.00	−26.625	32.625	8-1-84
Textron: Am, NY	26	37¾	11.25	26.500	.500	5-1-84
U.S. Air: Am, NY†	14⅞	25	17.31	8.690	6.185	4-1-87
Warner Communications: Am, NY	23⅞	57¼	55.00	2.250	21.625	4-30-86

*Am = American Stock Exchange; NY = New York Stock Exchange. The first abbreviation indicates where the warrant trades, and the second abbreviation indicates where the common stock trades.

†Holder may purchase 1.04 shares at the option price; this gives stock price a value of $26.

Figure 12—4   **Market price relationships for a warrant**

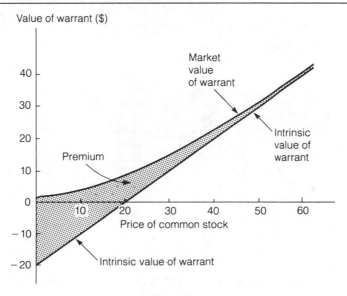

Premiums are also influenced by the same factors that affect convertible bond premiums. More volatile common stocks will have greater potential to create short-run profits for warrant speculators, so the higher the price volatility (use beta as an estimate), the greater the premium. Also, the longer the option has before expiration, the higher the premium will be. This "time premium" is worth more the longer the common stock has to reach and surpass the option price of the warrant.

Table 12—6 covers the same warrants as Table 12—4 and shows prices between November 1980 and May 1981. The results indicate the potential profits and a few surprises.

It can be seen that even in some cases like Chrysler or Resorts International,

Table 12—5   **Leverage in valuing warrants**

(A)	(B)
Stock price, $25; warrant price, $5* + 10-point movement in stock price. New warrant price, $15 (10-point gain)	Stock price, $50; warrant price, $30 + 10-point movement in stock price. New warrant price, $40 (10-point gain)
Percentage gain in warrant $= \dfrac{\$10}{\$5} \times 100 = 200\%$	Percentage gain in warrant $= \dfrac{\$10}{\$30} \times 100 = 33\%$

*The warrant price would, of course, be greater than $5 because of the speculative premium. Nevertheless, we use $5 for ease of computation.

Table 12–6 Stock versus warrant performance

	Stock price			Warrant price		
	November 21, 1980	May 29, 1981	Percent gain/ loss	November 21, 1980	May 29, 1981	Percent gain/ loss
Allegheny Corp.	36¾	38½	4.76%	32	35½	10.93%
American Airlines	9¾	20⅜	108.97	3⅜	8¼	144.44
Braniff	5⅜	4	−25.58	4¼	2⅞	−32.35
Bache	19⅜	31½	62.58	9¾	13⅝	39.74
Chrysler	6¾	6⅜	− 5.55	2⅞	3	4.34
Frontier Airlines	17⅞	26⅛	46.15	11⅞	17⅝	48.42
Mattel	15¾	9⅛	−42.06	11⅝	6⅛	−47.31
Pier One	3⅝	3⅛	−13.79	5/16	⅛	−60.00
Resorts International	26½	26⅜	− .47	5	6	20.00
Textron	28¾	37¾	31.30	17¼	26	50.72
U.S. Air	18⅜	25	36.05	8	14⅞	85.93

a decline in stock prices is not always followed by a decline in warrant price. Speculative stocks such as these are highly influenced by investor expectation. In the case of Bache, a tender offer was made for a merger, and a fixed buy-out price eliminated much of the premium that might have existed if expectations for a higher stock price were still possible. Firms like American Airlines, Textron, and U.S. Air demonstrate the potential for positive leverage.

Usage of warrants by corporations

As previously indicated, warrants may allow for the issuance of debt under difficult circumstances. While a straight debt issue may not be acceptable or may be accepted only at extremely high rates, the same security may be well received because detachable warrants are included. Warrants may also be included as an add-on in a merger or acquisition agreement. A firm might offer $20 million in cash plus 10,000 warrants in exchange for all the oustanding shares of the acquisition candidate.

The use of warrants has traditionally been associated with such aggressive, "high-flying" firms as real estate investment trusts, airlines, and conglomerates. However, in 1970, American Telephone and Telegraph came out with a $1.57 billion debt offering sweetened by the use of warrants.

As a financing device for creating new common stock, warrants may not be as desirable as convertible securities. A corporation with convertible debentures outstanding may force the conversion of debt to common stock through a call, while no similar device is available to the firm with warrants. The only possible inducement might be a step-up in option price—whereby the warrant holder may pay a progressively higher option price if he does not exercise by a given date.

The capital structure of the firm after the exercise of a warrant is somewhat different from that created after the conversion of a debenture. In the case of a warrant, the original debt outstanding remains in existence after the detachable warrant is exercised, whereas the conversion of a debenture extinguishes the former debt obligation.[7]

ACCOUNTING CONSIDERATIONS WITH WARRANTS

As with convertible securities, the potential dilutive effect of warrants must be considered. All warrants are included in computing both primary and fully diluted earnings per share.[8] The accountant must compute the number of new shares that could be created by the exercise of all warrants, with the provision that the total can be reduced by the assumed use of the cash proceeds to purchase a partially offsetting amount of shares at the market price. Assume that warrants to purchase 10,000 shares at $20 are outstanding and that the current price of the stock is $50. We show the following:

1. New shares created   10,000
2. Reduction of shares from cash proceeds (computed below)   4,000

    Cash proceeds—10,000 shares at $20 = $200,000
    Current price of stock—$50
    Assumed reduction in shares outstanding from cash
    proceeds = $200,000/$50 = 4,000

3. Assumed net increase in shares from exercise of warrants
    (10,000 − 4,000)   6,000

In computing earnings per share, we will add 6,000 shares to the denominator with no adjustment to the numerator, which will lower earnings per share. If earnings per share had previously been $1 based on $100,000 in earnings and 100,000 shares outstanding, EPS would now be reduced to $.943

$$\frac{\text{Earnings } \$100,000}{\text{Shares } 106,000} = \$.943$$

With warrants included in computing both primary and fully diluted earnings per share, their impact on reported earnings is important from both the investor and corporate viewpoints.

---

[7]It should be pointed out that a number of later financing devices can blur this distinction. See Jerry Miller, "Accounting for Warrants and Convertible Bonds," *Management Accounting,* January 1973, pp. 36–38.

[8]Under most circumstances, if the market price is below the option price, dilution need not be considered (APB *Opinion No. 15*).

SUMMARY

Convertible securities and warrants offer the investor an opportunity for participating in increased common stock values without owning common stock directly. Convertible securities may be in the form of debt or preferred stock, though most of our examples refer to debt.

Convertible securities provide a guaranteed income stream and a floor value based on required yield on the investment. At the same time, they have an established conversion ratio to common stock (par value/conversion price). The conversion value of an issue is equal to the conversion ratio times the current value of a share of common stock. The conversion value is generally less than the current market price of the convertible issue. Actually, the difference between the market price of the convertible issue and the conversion value is referred to as the conversion premium. The conversion premium is influenced by the volatility of the underlying common stock, the time of maturity, the dividend payment on common stock relative to the interest rate on the convertibles, and other lesser factors. Generally, when the common stock price has risen well above the conversion price (and the convertible is trading well above par), the conversion premium will be quite small as indicated in the left-hand portion of Figure 12–2. The small premium is attributed to the fact that the investor no longer enjoys significant downside protection.

A convertible issue is considered to be potentially dilutive to the reported earnings of the corporation, and since 1969, primary and/or fully diluted earnings per share must consider the impact of potential conversion. Actually, the corporation may ultimately have the opportunity to force conversion through calling the issue at slightly over par when in fact it is selling at a substantially higher price. In the absence of a call, there is generally little incentive to convert since the convertible security will move up and down with the common stock issue.

A warrant is an option to buy a stated number of shares of stock (usually one) at a specified price over a given time period. Warrants are often issued as a sweetener to a bond issue and may allow the firm to issue debt where it would not normally be feasible. The warrants are generally detachable from the bond issue. Thus, if the warrants are exercised, the bond issue still remains in existence (this is clearly different from a convertible security). The difference between the market price of a warrant and its minimum or intrinsic value represents a premium that the investor is willing to pay. This premium represents the speculative potential in the warrant. Warrants are dilutive to earnings and must generally be considered in computing primary and fully diluted earnings per share.

IMPORTANT WORDS AND CONCEPTS

Convertible securities	Downside risk
Warrants	Floor value
Conversion price	Dilution
Conversion ratio	Primary earnings per share
Conversion value	Fully diluted earnings per share
Pure bond value	Intrinsic value (of warrant)

Conversion premium   **Speculative premium**
Downside protection   **Option price (of warrant)**

QUESTIONS AND PROBLEMS

1. Why would an investor have an interest in convertible securities?

2. What are the disadvantages of investing in convertible securities?

3. A convertible bond has a face value of $1,000, and the conversion price is $40 per share. The stock is selling at $35 per share. The bond pays $80 per year interest and is selling in the market for $980. It matures in 10 years. Market rates are 12 percent per year.
   a. What is the conversion ratio?
   b. What is the conversion value?
   c. What is the floor value or pure bond value? (You may wish to review material in Chapter 11 for computing bond values.)
   d. What is the conversion premium (in dollars and percent)?

4. Compute the downside risk as a percentage in problem 3. What does this mean?

5. Under what circumstance might the downside risk increase? Relate your answer to interest rates in the market.

6. Assume that the stock in problem 3 rises in price to $43 per share and that the firm forces investors to convert to common stock by calling the bond. This occurs two years after purchasing the bond. Would you have been better off if you (a) had bought the stock directly or (b) bought the convertible bond and eventually converted it to common stock? The stock paid a 50-cent dividend per share each year. Assume you invested $980. Disregard taxes, commissions, etc. Hint: consider appreciation in value plus annual income received.

7. How does the volatility of a stock influence the conversion premium?

8. How might a step-up in the conversion price force conversion?

9. Why do corporations use convertible bonds?

10. What is meant by the dilutive effect of convertible securities?

11. Given the following data, compute fully diluted earnings per share. There are no other potentially dilutive securities outstanding, and the 8 percent interest is greater than two thirds of the going interest rate at time of issue.

Common stock (500,000 shares at $5 par)	= $2,500,000
Eight percent convertible debentures (5,000 at $1,000 each; convertible into 50 shares per bond)	5,000,000
Retained earnings	5,000,000
Earnings before interest and taxes	3,000,000
Interest	400,000
Earnings before taxes	2,600,000
Earnings after taxes (50 percent)	$1,300,000

12. What is a warrant?

13. For what reasons do firms issue warrants?

14. Assume a firm has warrants oustanding that permit the holder to buy one new share of stock at $30 per share. The market price of the stock is now $35.
    a. What is the intrinsic value of the warrant?
    b. Why might the warrant sell for $2 on the market even if the stock price is $28.

15. Once again, assume a firm has warrants outstanding that allow the holder to buy one share of stock at $30 per share. Also assume the stock is selling for $35 per share, and the warrants are now selling for $7 per warrant (this, of course, is above intrinsic value). You can invest $1,000 in the stock or the warrants (for purposes of the computation, round to two places to the right of the decimal point). Assume the stock goes to $40, and the warrants trade at their intrinsic value when the stock goes to $40. Would you have a larger total dollar profit by initially investing in the stocks or the warrants?

16. Why do investors tend to pay less premium for a warrant as the price of the stock goes up?

17. If warrants were initially a detachable part of a bond issue, will the amount of debt be reduced if the warrants are eventually exercised? Contrast this with a convertible security.

18. Assume a corporation has $300,000 in earnings and 150,000 shares outstanding ($2 in earnings per share). Also assume there are warrants outstanding to purchase 20,000 shares at $30 per share. The stock is currently selling at $40 per share. In considering the effect of the warrants oustanding, what would revised earnings per share be?

SELECTED REFERENCES

Alexander, Gordon J., and Roger D. Stover. "Pricing in the New Issue Convertible Debt Market." *Financial Management,* Fall 1977, pp. 35–39.

Bierman, Harold J., Jr., "The Cost of Warrants." *Journal of Financial and Quantitative Analysis,* June 1973, pp. 499–504.

Brennan, M. J., and E. S. Schwartz. "Convertible Bonds; Valuation and Optimal Strategies for Call and Conversion." *Journal of Finance,* December 1977, pp. 1699–1715.

Brigham, Eugene F. "An Analysis of Convertible Debentures." *Journal of Finance,* March 1966, pp. 35–54.

Jennings, Edward H. "An Estimate of Convertible Bond Premiums." *Journal of Financial and Quantitative Analysis,* January 1974, pp. 33–56.

Hayes, Samuel L. III, and Henry B. Reiling. "Sophisticated Financing Tool: The Warrant." *Harvard Business Review,* January–February 1969, pp. 137–50.

Ingersoll, Jonathan. "An Examination of Corporate Call Policies on Convertible Securities." *Journal of Finance,* May 1977, pp. 463–78.

Kassouf, Sheen T. "Warrant Price Behavior 1945–1964." *Finance Analysts Journal,* January–February 1968, pp. 123–26.

Miller, Jerry D., "Effects of Longevity on Values of Stock Purchase Warrants." *Financial Analysts Journal,* November–December 1971, pp. 78–85.

———. "Accounting for Warrants and Convertible Bonds." *Management Accounting,* January 1973, pp. 36–38.

Parkinson, Michael. "Empirical Warrant-Stock Relationships." *Journal of Business,* October 1972, pp. 563–69.

Noodings, Thomas C. *The Dow Jones-Irwin Guide to Convertible Securities.* Homewood, Ill.: Dow Jones-Irwin, 1973.

Rush, David F., and Ronald W. Melicher. "An Empirical Examination of Factors Which Influence Warrant Prices." *Journal of Finance,* December 1974, pp. 1449–66.

Stone, Bernell K. "Warrant Financing." *Journal of Financial and Quantitative Analysis,* March 1976, pp. 143–53.

Water, James E., and Agustin V. Que. "The Valuation of Convertible Bonds." *Journal of Finance,* June 1973, pp. 713–32.

13 Put and call options

The word *option* has many different meanings, but most of them include the ability or right to choose a certain alternative. One definition provided by *Webster's* is "the right, acquired for a consideration, to buy or sell something at a fixed price within a specified period of time." This definition is very general and applies to puts, calls, warrants, real estate options, or any other contracts entered into between two parties where a choice of action or decision can be put off for a limited time at a cost. The person acquiring the option pays an agreed-upon sum to the person providing the option. For example, someone may want to buy your house for its sale price of $75,000. The buyer does not have the money but will give you $2,000 in cash if you give him the right to buy the house for the next 60 days at $75,000. If you accept, you have given the buyer an option and have agreed not to sell the house to anyone else for the next 60 days. If the buyer raises $75,000 within the 60-day limit, he may buy the house giving you the $75,000. Perhaps he finds the $75,000 but also finds another house he likes better for $72,000. He will not buy your house, but you have $2,000 and must now find someone else to buy your house. By selling the option, you tied up the sale of your house for 60 days, and if the option is unexercised, you have foregone an opportunity to sell the house to someone else.

Puts and calls are options on common stock. A put is an option to sell 100 shares of common stock at a specified price for a given period of time for which the option buyer pays the seller (writer) a premium or option price. Calls are the opposite of puts and allow the owner the right to buy 100 shares of common stock from the option writer. Contracts on listed puts and calls have been standardized at date of issue for periods of three, six, and nine months, although as these contracts approach expiration, they may be purchased with a much shorter life.

Before the days of options trading on exchanges, puts and calls were traded over-the-counter by the Put and Call Dealers Association. These dealers would

buy and sell puts and calls for their own accounts for stocks traded on the New York Stock Exchange and then try to find an investor, hedger, or speculator to take the other side of the option. For example, if you owned 1,000 shares of General Motors and you wanted to write a call option giving the buyer the right to buy 1,000 shares of General Motors at $50 per share for six months, the dealer might buy the calls and look for someone who would be willing to buy them.

There were several disadvantages to this system. Dealers had to have contact with the buyers and sellers, and the financial stability of the option writer had to be endorsed (guaranteed) by a brokerage house. The option writer either had to keep the shares on deposit with the brokerage firm or put up a cash margin. Options in the same stock could exist in the market at various strike prices (price at which the option could be exercised) and scattered expiration dates. This meant that when an option buyer wanted to exercise or terminate the contract before expiration, he or she would have to deal directly with the option writer. This does not make for an efficient, liquid market. Unlisted options also reduced the striking price of a call by any dividends paid during the option period, which did not benefit the writer of the call.

Listed option exchanges

The Chicago Board Options Exchange (CBOE) was established in 1973 as the first exchange for call options. The market response was overwhelming, and within three years, the American, Pacific, and Philadelphia exchanges were also trading call options. By 1982, the list of stocks with available option contracts increased dramatically over the original list of 20 companies to 370 companies, and puts as well as calls were traded for many companies. Table 13–1 presents a comprehensive list of available options as well as the principal trading exchange for the option. On many days, the number of underlying shares of stock represented by options traded on the option exchanges is greater than the number of actual shares traded on the NYSE in those same issues.[1]

Several reasons exist that make the listed options markets so successful compared to the previous method of over-the-counter trading. The contract period was standardized with three-, six-, and nine-month expiration dates on three calendar cycles. Table 13–1 also lists the cycles of each contract as follows:

Cycle 1:   January/April/July/October.

Cycle 2:   February/May/August/November.

Cycle 3:   March/June/September/December.

As one month's expiration date comes up, another month in the cycle is added. For example, as the January option expires, the October nine-month option is added, and the cycle is continued. The use of three cycles spreads out the expiration dates for the options so that not all contracts come due on the same day.

---

[1]"How to Play the Option Game," *Business Week*, December 22, 1980, p. 88.

Table 13–1 Listing of stocks with options

Underlying stock/symbol	Exchange1	Expiration cycle2	Underlying stock/symbol	Exchange1	Expiration cycle2
Abbott Labs/**ABT**	PH	2	Capital Cities Comm./**CCB**	C	*
Advanced Micro Devices/**AMD**	P	1	Caterpillar/**CAT**	A	2
Aetna Life/**AET**	A	1	CBS/**CBS**	C	2
Air Products & Chemicals/**APD**	PH	3	Celanese/**CZ**	C	*
Allied/**ALD**	PH	1	Cessna Aircraft/**CEA**	C	2
Allis Chalmers/**AH**	PH	1	Champion Intern'l./**CHA**	C	3
Aluminum Co. of America/**AA**	C	1	Charter/**CHR**	PH	3
Amax/**AMX**	A	3	Chase Manhattan/**CMB**	A	3
Amdahl/**AMH**	C	2	Church's Fried Chicken/**CHU**	PH	*
Amerada Hess/**AHC**	PH	2	CIGNA/**CI**	C	1
American Brands/**AMB**	A	*	Cincinnati Milacron/**CMZ**	PH	2
American Broadcasting/**ABC**	P	2	Citicorp/**FNC**	C	1
American Can/**AC**	A	*	Cities Service/**CS**	PH	3
American Cyanamid/**ACY**	A	1	City Investing/**CNV**	PH	1
American Electric Power/**AEP**	C	2	Clorox/**CLX**	PH	1
American Express/**AXP**	C,A	1	Coastal/**CGP**	C,A	3
American Home Products/**AHP**	A	1	Coca-Cola/**KO**	C	2
American Hospital Supply/**AHS**	C	2	Colgate Palmolive/**CL**	C	2
American Medical Intern'l./**AMI**	P	3	Colt Industries/**COT**	PH	2
American Telephone & Telegraph/**T**	C	1	Combustion Eng./**CSP**	P	3
AMF/**AMF**	A	2	Commodore Intern'l./**CBU**	PH	2
AMP/**AMP**	C	2	Commonwealth Edison/**CWE**	C	2
Anacomp/**AAC**	PH	*	Communications Satellite/**CQ**	PH	1
Anheuser-Busch/**BUD**	PH	3	Community Psychiatric Ctrs./**CMY**	PH	*
Apache/**APA**	C	3	Computer Sciences/**CSC**	C	3
Archer-Daniels-Midland/**ADM**	PH	3	Computervision/**CVN**	PH	2
ARMCO/**AS**	PH	2	Consolidated Edison/**ED**	A	2
ASA, Ltd./**ASA**	A	2	Continental Telephone/**CTC**	A	1
Asarco/**AR**	A	3	Control Data/**CDA**	C	2
Ashland Oil/**ASH**	PH	1	Corning Glass/**GLW**	C	2
Atlantic Richfield/**ARC**	C	1	Cooper Industries/**CBE**	A	*
Automatic Data Processing/**AUD**	PH	2	Cray Research/**CYR**	P	3
Avco/**AV**	PH	3	Crown Zellerbach/**ZB**	A	*
Avnet/**AVT**	A	2	CSX Corp./**CSX**	P	2
Avon/**AVP**	C	1	Dart & Kraft/**DKI**	A	*
Baker Intern'l./**BKO**	P	3	Data General/**DGN**	P	3
Baldwin-United/**BDW**	P	1	Datapoint/**DPT**	C	2
Bally Mfg./**BLY**	C,A	2	Dataproducts/**DPC**	P	1
BankAmerica/**BAC**	C	1	Dayton-Hudson/**DH**	P	*
Bard (C.R.)/**BCR**	PH	*	Deere/**DE**	A	3
Bausch & Lomb/**BOL**	A	1	Delta Air Lines/**DAL**	C	1
Baxter Travenol Labs/**BAX**	C	2	Denny's/**DEN**	P	*
Beatrice Foods/**BRY**	A	3	Diamond Shamrock/**DIA**	P	1
Becton, Dickinson/**BDX**	PH	3	Diebold/**DBD**	C	2
Bethlehem Steel/**BS**	C	1	Digital Equipment/**DEC**	C,A	1
Black & Decker/**BDK**	C	2	Disney/**DIS**	C,A	1
Blue Bell/**BBL**	PH	1	Dr. Pepper/**DOC**	A	2
Boeing/**BA**	C	2	Dome Mines/**DM**	PH	2
Boise Cascade/**BCC**	C	2	Dorchester Gas/**DGS**	P	2
Bristol-Myers/**BMY**	C	3	Dow Chemical/**DOW**	C	3
Browning-Ferris Industries/**BFI**	A	3	Dresser/**DI**	PH	1
Brunswick/**BC**	C	3	Duke Power/**DUK**	PH	1
Bucyrus-Erie/**BY**	A	3	duPont/**DD**	C,A	1
Burlington Northern/**BNI**	C	1	Eastern Gas & Fuel Assoc./**EFU**	PH	1
Burroughs/**BGH**	C,A	1	Eastman Kodak/**EK**	C	1

Table 13–1 *(continued)*

Underlying stock/**symbol**	Exchange¹	Expiration cycle²	Underlying stock/**symbol**	Exchange¹	Expiration cycle²
Jack Eckerd/**ECK**	C	*	Hughes Tool/**HT**	C	3
EG & G/**EGG**	PH	3	Humana/**HUM**	C	2
Electronic Data Systems/**EDS**	PH	*	Hutton (E.F.)Group/**EFH**	A	1
El Paso/**ELG**	A	2	Inexco Oil/**INX**	PH	2
Emerson Electric/**EMR**	A	3	Intern'l. Business Machines/**IBM**	C	1
Engelhard/**EC**	C	*	Intern'l. Flavors & Fragrances/**IFF**	C	2
Enserch/**ENS**	P	2	Intern'l. Harvester/**HR**	C	1
Esmark/**ESM**	C	3	Intern'l. Minerals & Chemical/**IGL**	C	1
E-Systems/**ESY**	P	*	Intern'l. Paper/**IP**	C	1
Exxon/**XON**	C	1	Intern'l. Telephone & Telegraph/**ITT**	C	3
Federal Express/**FDX**	C	1	Johnson & Johnson/**JNJ**	C	1
First Charter Financial/**FCF**	A	1	Joy Mfg./**JOY**	PH	2
Fleetwood Enterprises/**FLE**	A	*	Kaneb Services/**KAB**	A	3
Flow General/**FGN**	A	2	Kerr McGee/**KMG**	C	1
Fluor/**FLR**	C	1	Key Pharmaceuticals/**KPH**	P	*
Ford Motor/**F**	C	3	K Mart/**KM**	C	3
Foster Wheeler/**FWC**	P	1	Lear Siegler/**LSI**	PH	3
Freeport-McMoRan/**FTX**	C	2	Lehman/**LEM**	PH	*
Fuqua Industries/**FQA**	PH	3	Levi Strauss/**LVI**	P	1
GAF/**GAF**	PH	1	Lifemark/**LMK**	C	3
GCA/**GCA**	A	2	Lilly (Eli)/**LLY**	A	1
General American Oil/**GAO**	C	*	Litton Industries/**LIT**	C	3
General Dynamics/**GD**	C	2	Lockheed/**LK**	P	3
General Electric/**GE**	C	3	Loral/**LOR**	C	*
General Foods/**GF**	C	2	Louisiana Land & Explor./**LLX**	PH	2
General Instruments/**GRL**	PH	3	Louisiana Pacific/**LPX**	A	2
General Motors/**GM**	C	3	LTV/**LTV**	A	3
General Telephone & Electronics/**GTE**	A	3	M/A Com/**MAI**	A	2
Genuine Parts/**GPC**	P	3	Manville/**MAN**	C	2
Geo International/**GX**	A	*	MAPCO/**MDA**	P	1
Georgia Pacific/**GP**	PH	1	Marriott/**MHS**	PH	1
Getty Oil/**GET**	PH	3	Martin Marietta/**ML**	PH	3
Gillette/**GS**	A	3	Mary Kay Cosmetics/**MKY**	C	3
Global Marine/**GLM**	A	3	Mattel/**MAT**	A	2
Goodyear Tire/**GT**	A	1	MCA/**MCA**	PH	2
Gould/**GLD**	A	1	McDermott/**MDE**	PH	2
Grace (W.R.)/**GRA**	A	2	McDonald's/**MCD**	C	3
Great Western Financial/**GWF**	C	1	McDonnell Douglas/**MD**	P	2
Greyhound/**G**	A	1	Medtronic/**MDT**	C	2
Gulf + Western/**GW**	C	3	Merck/**MRK**	C	1
Gulf Canada Ltd./**GOC**	PH	2	Merrill Lynch/**MER**	C,A	1
Gulf Oil/**GO**	A	1	Mesa Petroleum/**MSA**	A	1
Halliburton/**HAL**	C	1	Middle South Utilities/**MSU**	C	3
Harris/**HRS**	C	2	Minnesota Mining & Mfg./**MMM**	C	1
Hercules/**HPC**	A	3	Mitchell Energy & Devel./**MND**	P	*
Heublein/**HBL**	P	2	Mitel/**MLT**	A	3
Hewlett-Packard/**HWP**	C	2	Mobil/**MOB**	C	2
Hilton Hotels/**HLT**	P	2	Mohawk Data Sciences/**MDS**	P	3
Hitachi/**HIT**	C	1	Monsanto/**MTC**	C	1
Holiday Inns/**HIA**	C	2	Morgan (J.P.)/**JPM**	PH	*
Homestake Mining/**HM**	C	1	Motorola/**MOT**	A	1
Honeywell/**HON**	C	2	Murphy Oil/**MUR**	P	*
Hospital Corp. of Amer./**HCA**	P	1	NCR/**NCR**	C	3
Household Finance/**HI**	A	1	Nat'l. Distillers/**DR**	A	2
Houston Natural Gas/**HNG**	P	1	Nat'l. Medical Ent./**NME**	A	2

Table 13–1 *(continued)*

Underlying stock/**symbol**	Exchange1	Expiration cycle2	Underlying stock/**symbol**	Exchange1	Expiration cycle2
Nat'l. Semiconductor/**NSM**	C,A	2	Schlumberger Ltd./**SLB**	C	2
Natomas/**NOM**	A	3	Scientific Atlanta/**SFA**	P	3
Newmont Mining/**NEM**	PH	3	Scott Paper/**SPP**	PH	1
NL Industries/**NL**	PH	2	Seagram/**VO**	P	*
NLT/**NLT**	A	3	Searle (G.D.)/**SRL**	A	2
Noble Affiliates/**NBL**	A	*	Sears, Roebuck/**S**	C	3
Norfolk Southern/**NSC**	C	3	Sedco/**SED**	A	3
Northern Telecom/**NT**	C	3	Shell Oil/**SUO**	P	2
Northrop/**NOC**	C	2	Signal Cos./**SGN**	P	2
Northwest Airlines/**NWA**	C	1	Singer/**SMF**	A	*
Northwest Industries/**NWT**	C	3	Skyline/**SKY**	C	2
Norton Simon/**NSI**	A	2	Smith International/**SII**	P	*
Novo Industries/**NVO**	A	2	Smith Kline/**SKB**	P	3
Oak Industries/**OAK**	PH	1	Sony/**SNE**	P	2
Occidental Petroleum/**OXY**	C	2	Southern/**SO**	C	2
Ocean Drilling & Explor./**ODR**	A	2	Southern Pacific/**SX**	C	*
Owens-Corning Fiber/**OCF**	PH	3	Southland Royalty/**SRO**	P	1
Owens-Illinois/**OI**	C	2	Southwest Airlines/**LUV**	C	3
Paradyne/**PDN**	C	3	Sperry/**SY**	C	1
Parker Drilling/**PKD**	P	*	Squibb/**SQB**	C	1
Penn Central/**PC**	PH	3	Standard Oil of Calif./**SD**	A	3
Penney (J.C.)/**JCP**	A	2	Standard Oil of Ind./**SN**	C	2
Pennzoil/**PZL**	C	1	Standard Oil of Ohio/**SOH**	A	3
PepsiCo/**PEP**	C	1	Sterling Drug/**STY**	A	2
Perkin-Elmer/**PKN**	P	3	Storage Technology/**STK**	C	1
Petrolane/**PTO**	PH	*	Storer Broadcasting/**SBK**	A	2
Pfizer/**PFE**	A	3	Sun/**SUN**	PH	2
Phelps Dodge/**PD**	A	1	Superior Oil/**SOC**	C	3
Phibro-Salomon/**PSB**	PH	1	Sybron/**SYB**	A	*
Philip Morris/**MO**	A	3	Syntex/**SYN**	C	3
Phillips Petroleum/**P**	A	2	Tandy/**TAN**	C,A	1
Pitney Bowes/**PBI**	A	1	Tei/**TEI**	A	2
Pittston/**PCO**	PH	2	Tektronix/**TEK**	C	3
Pogo Producing/**PPP**	P	1	Teledyne/**TDY**	C,P	1
Polaroid/**PRD**	C,P	1	Tennaco/**TGT**	A	2
PPG Industries/**PPG**	PH	2	Tesoro Petroleum/**TSO**	PH	2
Prime Computer/**PRM**	A	3	Texaco/**TX**	A	1
Procter & Gamble/**PG**	A	1	Texas Instruments/**TXN**	C	1
Ralston Purina/**RAL**	C	3	Texas Oil & Gas/**TXO**	PH	3
Raytheon/**RTN**	C	2	Tidewater/**TDW**	C	*
RCA/**RCA**	C	3	TIE Communications/**TIE**	P	1
Reading & Bates/**RB**	P	2	Tiger Intern'l./**TGR**	A	2
Resorts Intern'l./**RTA**	P	1	Time/**TL**	PH	3
Revlon/**REV**	C	3	Tosco/**TOS**	A	2
Reynolds Metals/**RLM**	P	2	Toys "R" Us/**TOY**	C	3
Reynolds (R.J.)/**RJR**	C	2	Transamerica/**TA**	PH	2
Rockwell Intern'l./**ROK**	C	2	Trans World/**TW**	P	3
ROLM/**RM**	C	3	Travelers/**TIC**	P	2
Rowan/**RDC**	PH	2	Tri-Continental/**TY**	PH	*
Royal Dutch Petroleum/**RD**	A	2	TRW/**TRW**	A	1
Ryder Systems/**RDR**	P	2	Tymshare/**TYM**	PH	2
Sabine/**SAB**	C	*	UAL/**UAL**	C	2
Safeway Stores/**SA**	C	2	UNC Resources/**UNC**	C	2
Sante Fe Industries/**SFF**	A	3	Union Carbide/**UK**	A	1
Schering-Plough/**SGP**	P	2	Union Oil (Calif.)/**UCL**	P	1

Table 13—1 *(concluded)*

Underlying stock/**symbol**	Exchange[1]	Expiration cycle[2]	Underlying stock/**symbol**	Exchange[1]	Expiration cycle[2]
Union Pacific/**UNP**	PH	2	Waste Management/**WMX**	PH	2
United States Steel/**X**	A	1	Wendy's Intern'l./**WEN**	P	3
United Technologies/**UTX**	C	2	Western Co. of North Amer./**WSN**	A	1
Upjohn/**UPJ**	C	1	Western Union/**WU**	PH	1
U.S. Air/**U**	P	3	Westinghouse/**WX**	A	1
U.S.Home/**UH**	A	3	Weyerhaeuser/**WY**	C	1
Valero Energy/**VLO**	A	3	Whittaker/**WKR**	A	3
Viacom Intern'l./**VIA**	C	3	Williams/**WMB**	C	2
Virginia Electric & Power/**VEL**	PH	1	Williams Electronics/**WMS**	PH	*
Wal-Mart/**WMT**	C	*	Woolworth (F.W.)/**Z**	PH	2
Walter, Jim/**JWC**	C	2	Xerox/**XRX**	C,P	1
Wang Labs B/**WAN.B**	P	1	Zapata/**ZOS**	P	3
Warner Communications/**WCI**	C	2	Zenith Radio/**ZE**	A	2
Warner-Lambert/**WLA**	A	1			

1. Exchange
   A Amex
   P Pacific
   C CBOE
   PH Philadelphia
2. Expiration Cycle
   1 January/April/July/October
   2 February/May/August/November
   3 March/June/September/December
*Not yet trading
SOURCE: Chicago Board Options Exchange, Chicago, June 11, 1982.

Each contract expires at 11:59 P.M. eastern time on the Saturday immediately following the third Friday of the expiration month. For all practical purposes, any closing out of positions must be done on that last Friday while the markets are open.

The exercise price (striking price) is also standardized. For all stocks under $50 per share, the striking price changes by $5 intervals; for stock between $50 and $100 per share, the strike price changes by $10 a share; and stocks selling over $200 have 20-point differences in striking price.[2] As the underlying stocks change prices in the market, options with new striking prices are added. For example, a stock selling at $30 per share when the January option is added will have a striking price of $30, but if the stock gets to 32½ (half way to the next striking price), the exchange may add another option (to the class of options) with a $35 strike price.

An example of an actual call option is presented on the next page for Exxon. Note the different strike prices (30, 35, 40) and expiration months (January, April, July). Exxon common stock is selling for 34¾. The values within the table, such

---

[2]The SEC has approved 5-point intervals for stocks under $100 per share and 10-point intervals for stocks over $100. As of this writing, the exchanges have not implemented this change.

as 5⅜ or 1½, reflect the price of the various option contracts. Much of this type of information will take on greater meaning as we go through the chapter.

Option and NY close	Strike price	Calls—last		
		January	April	July
Exxon	30	5⅜	6	6⅝
34¾	35	1½	2⅝	3½
34¾	40	¼	⅞	1⁹⁄₁₆

This standardization of expiration dates and strike prices creates more certainty when buying and selling options in a changing market and allows more efficient trading strategies because of better coordination between stock prices, strike prices, and expiration dates. Dividends no longer affect the option contract as they did in the unlisted market. Transactions occur at arms length between buyer, seller, and writer without any matchmaking needed on the part of the broker. The ultimate result of these changes in the option market is a highly liquid, efficient market where speculators, hedgers, and arbitrageurs all operate together.

THE OPTIONS CLEARING CORPORATION

Much of the liquidity and ease of operation of the option exchanges is due to the role of the Options Clearing Corporation, which functions as the issuer of all options listed on the four exchanges—the CBOE, the AMEX, the Pacific Coast Exchange, and the Philadelphia Exchange. Investors who want to trade puts and calls need to have an approved account with a member brokerage firm; upon opening an account, they receive a prospectus from the Options Clearing Corporation detailing all aspects of option trading.

Options are bought and sold or written through a member broker the same as other securities. The exchanges allow special orders, such as limit, market, and stop orders, as well as orders used specifically in options trading, like spread orders and straddle orders. The order process originates with the broker and is transacted on the floor of the exchange. Remember that for every order there must be a buyer and seller or buyer and writer so that the orders can be "matched." Once the orders are matched, they are filed with the Options Clearing Corporation, which then issues the necessary options or closes the position. There are four basic transactions listed in the prospectus of the Options Clearing Corporation.[3]

Opening purchase transaction—A transaction in which an investor intends to become the holder of an option.

---

[3]Prospectus, The Options Clearing Corporation, October 30, 1980, p. 3.

Opening sale transaction—A transaction in which an investor intends to become the writer of an option.

Closing purchase transaction—A transaction in which an investor who is obligated as a writer of an option intends to terminate his obligation as a writer. This is accomplished by "purchasing" an option in the same series as the option previously written. Such a transaction has the effect, upon acceptance by the Options Clearing Corporation, of canceling the investor's preexisting position as a writer.

Closing sale transaction—A transaction in which an investor who is the holder of an outstanding option intends to liquidate his position as a holder. This is accomplished by "selling" an option in the same series as the option previously purchased. Such a transaction has the effect, upon acceptance by the Options Clearing Corporation, of liquidating the investor's preexisting position as a holder of the option.

What occurs in a transaction is that holders and writers of options are not contractually linked together but are committed to the Options Clearing Corporation. Since there are no certificates issued for options, a customer must maintain a brokerage account as long as he or she holds an option position and must liquidate the option through the broker originating the transaction unless a brokerage transfer is completed before an ensuing transaction. If an option is traded on more than one exchange, it may be bought, sold, or closed out on either exchange and cleared through the Options Clearing Corporation. Basically, the aggregate obligation of the option holders is backed up by the aggregate obligation of the option writers. If holders choose to exercise their options, they must do so through the Clearing Corporation, which randomly selects a writer from all Clearing member accounts in the same option series. This would be true whether the holder chooses to exercise early or at expiration. Upon notice from the Options Clearing Corporation, a call writer must sell 100 shares of the underlying common stock at the exercise price, while the put writer must buy 100 shares from the holder exercising the put.

All option contracts are adjusted for stock splits, stock dividends, or other stock distributions. For example, a 2-for-1 stock split for a stock selling at 60, with options available at 70, 60, and 50 strike prices, would cause the stock to trade at 30 and the strike prices to be 35, 30, and 25. Now the option holder would have two puts or calls at the adjusted price.

OPTION PREMIUMS

Before one can understand various option strategies, an investor or speculator must be able to comprehend what creates option premiums (prices). Look at Table 13–2. Using Eastman Kodak (EK) as an example, we can see that the common stock closed at $72 per share on the NYSE and that puts and calls are available at strike prices—60, 70, 80 and 90. The October 70 call closed at 6⅛

Table 13–2 Listed option quotes

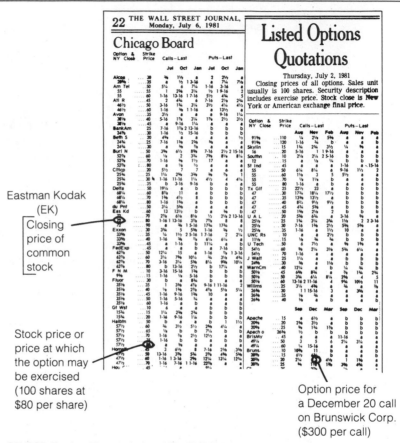

Eastman Kodak
(EK)
Closing
price of
common
stock

Stock price or
price at which
the option may
be exercised
(100 shares at
$80 per share)

Option price for
a December 20 call
on Brunswick Corp.
($300 per call)

SOURCE: Reprinted by permission of *The Wall Street Journal,* © Dow Jones & Company, Inc. (July 6, 1981). All rights reserved.

($612.50 for one call on 100 shares), while the October 80 call closed at 1¹³⁄₁₆. The 70 call is said to be "in-the-money" because the market price (72) is above the strike price (70), but the 80 call is "out-of-the-money" since the strike price is above the market price.

In-the-money options have an intrinsic value equal to the market price minus the strike price. In the case of the EK October 70 call, the intrinsic value is $2 as indicated by Formula 13–1. Options that are out of the money have no tangible intrinsic value.

$$\text{Intrinsic value}_{call} = \text{Market price} - \text{Strike price}$$
$$\text{Intrinsic value}_{EK\ 70\ October\ call} = \$72 - 70 \tag{13-1}$$
$$= \$2$$

The EK October 80 call would have a negative $8 intrinsic value derived by Formula 13–1. When the market price minus the strike price is negative, the negative value represents the amount the stock price must increase to have the option "at-the-money" where the strike price and market price are equal.

Returning to the Eastman Kodak 70 October call, we see that the total premium is 6⅛, while the intrinsic value is $2. This call option has an additional premium of 4⅛ due to other factors. The total premium (option price) is a combination of the intrinsic value plus a speculative premium which is a function of common stock volatility and risk, time to expiration, dividend yield on the underlying common stock, potential leverage, and market expectations.

$$\text{Total premium} = \text{Intrinsic value} + \text{Speculative premium}$$
$$\$6\tfrac{1}{8} = \$2 + \$4\tfrac{1}{8}$$
(13–2)

Generally, the higher the beta on the common stock and the lower the dividend yield, the greater the speculative premium. The longer the exercise period, the higher the speculative premium, especially if market expectations over the duration of the option are positive. Finally, the deeper the option is in the money, the smaller the leverage potential and therefore the smaller the speculative premium. Most often, we examine the speculative premium separately to see if it is a reasonable premium to pay for the possible benefits.

The speculative premium can be expressed in dollars or as a percentage of the common stock price. A speculative premium expressed in percent indicates the increase in the stock price needed for the purchaser of a call option to break even on the expiration date. Table 13–3 shows this point.

Notice that the 60 option, which is deep in-the-money, has the lowest speculative premium, while the 80 option has the highest. Realize that the 80 option only has a cash value of 1¹³⁄₁₆ (the total premium) and that the other $8 represents the required increase in the stock price for the strike price and market price to be equal. The 13.62 percent premium, however, does represent the percentage movement in stock price by the expiration date for a break-even position. Remember that at expiration there will be no speculative premium. The option will only reflect the intrinsic value and possibly even a discount because of commission expenses incurred upon exercise. Table 13–4 provides a better look at premiums for in-the-money and out-of-the-money options from 15 days to six months of expiration.

Table 13–3   **Speculative premiums**

Market price ($)	Eastman Kodak strike price ($)	Total premium ($) −	Intrinsic value ($) =	Speculative premium ($) =	Speculative premium as percent of CSP*
72	60 October call	13½	12	1½	2.08%
72	70 October call	6⅛	2	4⅛	5.73
72	80 October call	1¹³⁄₁₆	(8)	9¹³⁄₁₆	13.62

*Common stock price.

Table 13–4 Speculative premiums over time (Eastman Kodak calls, July 2, 1981, beta 1.05)

Market price	Strike price	July total premium*	Speculative premium Dollars	Speculative premium Percent	October total premium†	Speculative premium Dollars	Speculative premium Percent	January total premium‡	Speculative premium Dollars	Speculative premium Percent
72	60	13	1	1.38	13½	1½	2.08	Not offered		
72	70	2⅞	⅞	1.21	6⅛	4⅛	5.73	8⅛	6⅛	8.50
72	80	¹⁄₁₆	8¹⁄₁₆	11.19	1¹³⁄₁₆	9¹³⁄₁₆	13.62	3⅞	11⅞	16.49

*July—15 days to expiration.

†October—91 days to expiration.

‡January—182 days to expiration.

Eastman Kodak's speculative premiums are not very high due to a low-risk beta, an expected dividend yield of 5 percent, and an uninspired stock market in July 1981. Several relationships are evident, however. The speculative premiums increase with time for all strike prices but are very low for the 60 calls because of low leverage potential and a high chance of being exercised on the expiration date. The 80 calls have high speculative premiums, but an option writer would *not reap much cash inflow.* The July 80 is almost worthless because there is very little chance that EK would rise more than 11.19 percent in 15 days. The October 80 is in similar shape, but the January 80 would generate $387.50 to a call writer and require more than a 16.5 percent increase in stock price over six months for a call buyer to break even.

Table 13–5 demonstrates the relationship between betas and dividend yields to the speculative premium. The three options listed are all October calls from Table 13–2, and they are either at-the-money or slightly in-the-money.

Notice the rising premiums as the betas increase and dividend yields fall. This, of course, is not always true since other factors, such as market attitudes toward the industry, can have a strong bearing on the speculative premium in addition to other influences mentioned previously.

Premiums can be deceiving. The novice may attempt to write the options with the highest total premium or speculative premium, while the buyer may think the smallest investment provides the greatest leverage. These are not usually true if

Table 13–5   Speculative premiums related to betas and dividend yields

Stock	October strike	Market	Total premium	Speculative premium Dollars	Speculative premium Percent	Beta	Expected dividend yield
AT&T	55	55	2⅜	2⅜	4.31	.65	10.5%
Citicorp	25	25¾	2⅝	1⅞	7.28	1.15	6.8%
Fluor	35	35⅛	3⅜	3¼	9.25	1.40	2.6%

we look at speculative premiums on a per-day basis. For example, the EK 70 calls have the following speculative premiums per day.

			Speculative premiums per day
July 70	1.21% / 15 days	=	.0866% per day
October 70	5.75% / 91 days		.0629% per day
January 70	8.50% / 182 days		.0467% per day

An examination of daily premiums would suggest that call writers should write short-lived calls and then roll them over if they don't get exercised. On the other hand, call buyers get more time for less premium by purchasing long-lived calls.

Although this section has examined call premiums, puts have most of the same relationship except for the definitions of in-the-money and out-of-the money. Since puts allow the owner to sell stock at the strike price, in-the-money put options exist where the strike price is above the market price of the stock. Out-of-the-money puts have market values for common stock above the strike price. Since the owner of the stock can sell the stock for more in the market than by exercising a put, the put has no intrinsic value. The speculative premium of a put as a percentage of the stock price then represents the percentage decline in the stock price necessary to break even.

Understanding option premiums is important in order to make sense out of options strategies. Various strategies involving puts and calls are covered in the next section. Do not go on unless you are comfortable with this section on option premiums.

BASIC OPTION STRATEGIES

Option strategies can be very aggressive and risky, or they can be quite con-servative and used as a means of reducing risk. Option buyers and writers both attempt to take advantage of the option premiums discussed in the preceding section. In this section, we discuss the possible uses of puts and calls to achieve different investment goals. Table 13–6 provides option quotes at three separate time periods for our examples. We have ignored commissions in most examples, but we do advise that commissions can be a significant hidden cost in some types of option strategies.

Buying call options

The leverage strategy Leverage is a very common reason for buying call options when the market is expected to rise during the exercise period. The use of calls in this way is similar to warrants discussed in Chapter 12, but calls have shorter lives and lower premiums. The call option is priced much lower than the common stock, and the leverage is derived from a small change in the price of

Table 13—6

Chicago Board

Listed Options Quotations

Wednesday, March 11, 1981

Closing prices of all options. Sales unit usually is 100 shares. Security description includes exercise price. Stock close is New York or American exchange final price. p-Put option. o-Old shares.

		– Apr –		– Jul –		– Oct –		
Alcoa	30	15	4¾	6	5¾	a	a	34⅝
Alcoa	35	172	15-16	15	2⅞	a	a	34⅝
Alcoa	40	53	⅛	32	½	a	a	34⅝
Am Exp	40	8	4¾	a	a	a	a	44⅝
Am Exp	45	2	1⅜	a	a	a	a	44⅝
Am Tel	50	220	2⅜	20	3⅜	a	a	51⅜
Am Tel	55	129	3-16	83	15-16	419	1¾	51⅜
Att R p	40	5	1-16	b	b	b	b	54⅛
Att R	45	5	9½	b	b	b	b	54⅛
Att R p	45	1	3-16	b	b	b	b	54⅛
Att R	50	410	5½	7	7⅞	4	9¾	54⅛
Att R p	50	413	¾	99	2⅝	5	3⅝	54⅛
Att R	60	435	¾	46	2 11-16	27	4½	54⅛
Att R p	60	169	6½	13	7¾	17	8¾	54⅛
Att R	70	181	1-16	44	15-16	33	1⅞	54⅛
Att R p	70	5	15½	21	15¾	19	16½	54⅛
Avon	30	2	7¼	a	a	a	a	37
Avon	35	254	2¾	52	3⅞	56	4¾	37
Avon p	35	123	7-16	13	1¼	2	2	37
Avon	40	170	⅜	53	1½	25	2 7-16	37
Avon p	40	15	3	a	a	1	4½	37
BankAm	25	6	2¼	20	3¼	a	a	26⅝
BankAm	30	19	¼	52	15-16	5	8½	26⅝
Beth S	20	a	a	a	a	a	a	28
Beth S	25	338	3⅞	32	4¾	a	a	28
Beth S	30	50	11-16	55	1½	40	2½	28
Burl N	40	2	21¾	b	b	b	b	60⅝
Burl N	45	59	16⅜	b	b	b	b	60⅝
Burl N	50	39	11¾	40	14	b	b	60⅝
Burl N p	50	224	5-16	69	1	b	b	60⅝
Burl N	60	578	4⅛	23	7½	1	10	60⅝
Burl N p	60	998	2 7-16	47	3¾	1	6	60⅝
Burl N	70	597	⅜	32	3¼	71	4⅞	60⅝
Burl N p	70	459	9	35	9¾	1	11	60⅝
Burl N	80	518	1-16	117	15-16	133	2⅜	60⅝
Citicp	20	146	2¼	283	2⅞	5	3½	21⅞
Citicp	25	234	¼	70	11-16	28	1 5-16	21⅞
Delta	45	a	a	10	24½	b	b	69½
Delta	50	105	19¼	1	20½	a	a	69½
Delta	60	220	10	43	12	1	13	69½
Delta	70	282	2½	103	5⅜	335	6¾	69½
Delta p	70	a	a	2	1½	a	a	69½
du Pnt	35	484	14⅜	a	a	b	b	49⅛
du Pnt p	35	475	1-16	a	a	b	b	49⅛
du Pnt	40	475	9½	a	a	a	a	49⅛
du Pnt p	40	495	1-16	a	a	a	a	49⅛
du Pnt	45	5	5	a	a	2	3¼	49⅛
du Pnt p	45	a	a	a	a	a	a	49⅛
du Pnt	50	15	1⅞	a	a	a	a	49⅛
du Pnt p	50	31	2¾	a	a	a	a	49⅛
Eas Kd	50	1	29¼	b	b	b	b	79¾
Eas Kd	60	76	19⅞	6	20¾	a	a	79¾
Eas Kd p	60	191	1-16	118	⅝	39	1 1-16	79¾
Eas Kd	70	948	10½	178	12¾	26	15	79¾
Eas Kd p	70	1380	⅜	433	2 7-16	105	3¾	79¾
Eas Kd	80	4321	3¼	322	6⅝	34	8¾	79¾
Eas Kd p	80	2887	3⅜	92	4¾	72	7½	79¾
Eas Kd	90	b	b	270	2¾	92	4⅜	79¾
Exxon	40	291	10⅝	a	a	1	13	69¾
Exxon	60	114	½	25	9-16	9	⅞	69¾
Exxon p	70	654	2 1-16	92	4¾	36	5⅜	69¾
Exxon	70	314	2	37	3¼	16	4¼	69¾
Exxon	80	139	¼	110	1 1-16	48	2¼	69¾
Exxon	80	21	10¼	16	16½	a	a	69¾
Exxon	90	15	1-16	82	¼	5	⅞	69¾
Exxon p	90	4	20	a	a	a	a	69¾
FedExp	35	10	1-16	6	½	b	b	48⅞
FedExp p	40	22	8⅜	a	a	5	11¼	48⅞
FedExp	40	154	¼	73	1	15	2¼	48⅞
FedExp	45	161	5⅛	74	7¾	83	8¾	48⅞
FedExp	45	246	1 3-16	30	2½	2	3⅝	48⅞
FedExp	50	119	2½	47	4	87	5⅝	48⅞
FedExp	50	136	3¼	18	4½	51	5½	48⅞
F N M	10	61	¾	13	1¼	46	1¾	10½
F N M	15	3	1-16	16	¼	35	½	10½
Fluor	40	23	8	b	b	b	b	48
Fluor	40	76	¾	b	b	b	b	48
Fluor	45	341	4¾	19	7¾	63	10	48
Fluor p	45	166	1½	47	2⅜	5	3½	48
Fluor	50	570	2¼	134	5¼	24	7	48
Fluor p	50	277	3½	21	5⅜	7	6	48
Fluor	60	361	⅜	210	2	158	3¾	48
Fluor	60	18	12¼	a	a	1	12⅞	48
Fluor	70	41	1-16	42	¾	b	b	48
Gt Wst	10	b	b	a	a	6	6	15⅝
Gt Wst	15	201	1¾	117	2 9-16	81	3	15⅝
Gt Wst	20	171	⅛	105	⅜	16	1¾	15⅝
Gt Wst	25	a	a	10	¼	b	b	15⅝

Listed Options Quotations

Thursday, May 7, 1981

Closing prices of all options. Sales unit usually is 100 shares. Security description includes exercise price. Stock close is New York or American exchange final price. p-Put option. o-Old shares.

		– Jul –		– Oct –		– Jan –		
Alcoa	30	15	3¼	a	a	a	a	31⅞
Alcoa	35	53	11-16	3	1 9-16	a	a	31⅞
Alcoa	40	2	3-16	10	¾	5	1¼	31⅞
Am Exp	40	15	2¾	a	a	a	a	42⅛
Am Exp p	40	22	⅞	5	2	a	a	42⅛
Am Exp	45	20	3⅞	10	4⅜	a	a	42⅛
Am Tel	45	23	9¾	500	10½	b	b	54⅞
Am Tel	50	104	5¼	96	5½	a	a	54⅞
Am Tel p	50	1	¼	a	a	a	a	54⅞
Am Tel	55	349	1 5-16	90	2 5-16	27	3	54⅞
Am Tel p	55	178	1 7-16	a	a	52	2¾	54⅞
Am Tel	60	86	¼	126	13-16	42	1¼	54⅞
Att R	40	5	⅛	a	a	10	¾	51¼
Att R	45	60	7½	17	9	a	a	51¼
Att R	45	109	9-16	21	1	2	1½	51¼
Att R	50	1141	3¾	279	5½	44	7	51¼
Att R	50	506	1 13-16	78	2½	10	3⅞	51¼
Att R	60	531	⅜	376	1⅞	88	3	51¼
Att R	60	11	8¼	10	9¼	a	a	51¼
Att R	70	99	3-16	111	½	b	b	51¼
Avon	35	24	4	a	a	a	a	38⅛
Avon	35	58	½	5	1	5	1½	38⅛
Avon	40	39	1⅜	12	2¼	10	2¾	38⅛
Avon	40	42	2¾	19	3½	10	4½	38⅛
Avon	45	15	¼	a	a	12	1⅜	38⅛
BankAm	25	9	1	8	2⅛	a	a	24⅝
BankAm	30	63	3-16	17	½	10	13-16	24⅝
Beth S	25	a	a	8	a	2	4¾	27¼
Beth S	30	32	⅞	18	1¾	a	a	27¼
Beth S p	30	5	3	a	a	a	a	27¼
Burl N	50	27	11½	7	14¼	1	13½	59¾
Burl N p	50	527	13-16	a	a	a	a	59¾
Burl N	60	388	4⅜	6	7½	8	8¾	59¾
Burl N	60	786	3⅞	67	5¼	13	6	59¾
Burl N	70	403	1⅛	147	3⅜	60	4½	59¾
Burl N	70	118	10½	36	11¼	a	a	59¾
Burl N	80	138	¼	81	1¼	61	2¼	59¾
Burl N	80	35	20	a	a	a	a	59¾
Citicp	20	149	5	4	a	a	a	24¾
Citicp	25	563	1 1-16	116	2⅛	12	2½	24¾
Citicp	30	32	3-16	13	½	11	13-16	24¾
Delta	50	6	19	a	a	b	b	68
Delta	60	38	9½	111	11¾	a	a	68
Delta	70	123	3⅞	32	6¼	a	a	68
Delta	80	130	¾	5	2½	a	a	68
Eas Kd p	50	30	3½	a	a	a	a	74¾
Eas Kd	60	5	15½	a	a	b	b	74¾
Eas Kd p	60	302	⅛	72	½	b	b	74¾
Eas Kd	70	311	7¼	10	9½	19	11¼	74¾
Eas Kd p	70	632	1¼	116	2⅜	98	3¼	74¾
Eas Kd	80	1192	1⅞	224	4½	41	6¼	74¾
Eas Kd p	80	668	6	17	6¾	47	7¾	74¾
Eas Kd	90	436	5-16	144	1⅜	157	2⅜	74¾
Eas Kd p	90	28	15¾	4	15½	a	a	74¾
Exxon	60	27	8¾	5	10¼	3	11½	68⅛
Exxon	60	4	16	13-16	2	1	68⅛
Exxon	70	340	2	39	2¼	21	5¾	68⅛
Exxon	70	33	3½	18	4¾	5	5¼	68⅛
Exxon	80	265	5-16	66	15-16	b	b	68⅛
Exxon	80	2	13	2	13	b	b	68⅛
FedExp	40	23	21½	a	a	b	b	60⅛
FedExp	40	2	⅛	100	9½	b	b	60⅛
FedExp	45	a	a	1	18½	a	a	60⅛
FedExp	45	25	⅜	9	1	a	a	60⅛
FedExp	50	70	11-16	19	2⅛	a	a	60⅛
FedExp	60	46	5¼	17	8¼	51	10¼	60⅛
FedExp	60	50	4	48	5⅞	35	7	60⅛
FedExp	70	215	1½	41	4	14	5¾	60⅛
FedExp	70	a	a	12	11¾	7	12	60⅛
F N M	10	848	½	477	1 1-16	70	1½	9¾
F N M	15	30	1-16	73	3-16	57	7-16	9¾
Fluor	35	19	7½	a	a	a	a	41¼
Fluor	40	262	4	8	a	a	a	41¼
Fluor p	40	87	1¼	a	a	23	2¾	41¼
Fluor	45	134	1 13-16	33	3¾	6	5¼	41¼
Fluor	45	60	4¼	24	5¼	30	5½	41¼
Fluor	50	206	11-16	33	2⅛	4	3½	41¼
Fluor p	50	4	8½	11	8½	a	a	41¼
Fluor	60	50	3-16	10	⅝	b	b	41¼
Fluor	60	a	a	3	18⅝	b	b	41¼
Fluor	70	11	1-16	b	b	b	b	41¼
Gt Wst	10	3	5¼	a	a	a	a	15⅜
Gt Wst	15	201	1½	109	2⅛	40	2¾	15⅜
Gt Wst	20	248	7-16	37	⅞	a	a	15⅜

Listed Options Quotations

Wednesday, July 8, 1981

Closing prices of all options. Sales unit usually is 100 shares. Security description includes exercise price. Stock close is New York or American exchange final price.

Option & NY Close	Strike Price	Calls—Last			Puts—Last		
		Jul	Oct	Jan	Jul	Oct	Jan
Alcoa	25	b	5⅜	b	a	b	½
28⅞	30	¼	a 2 11-16	1⅜	1¾	2¾	
28⅞	35	a	7-16 15-16	a	a	a	
Am Exp	45	9¾	a	b	a	a	a
Am Tel	45	9¾	a	b	a	a	a
55	50	5	6	7¾	a	⅜	½
55	55	½	2¾	3⅜	7-16 1 15-16	1⅞	
55	60	1-16	⅜	1¼	5	4⅜	a
Att R	40	9½	a	a	a	⅜	b
48⅞	45	4	6¾	7	1-16 1 11-16	2⅛	
48⅞	50	9-16	3⅜	4¾	1¾	2½	a
48⅞	60	1-16	⅜	1⅜	11½	10¾	a
48⅞	70	1-16	⅛	b	a	a	b
Avon	30	a	a	b	a	3-16	b
38	35	3	4⅛	5⅛	a	13-16	1¼
38	40	3-16	1½	2¾	2	2¾	3
38	45	1-16	½	1⅛	a	a	a
BankAm	25	1¼	1¾	2⅜	b	b	b
Beth S	20	a	4⅛	a	a	a	⅜
23¼	25	1	⅞	1¾	1¾	2	a
23¼	30	1-16	¼	½	a	a	a
23¼	35	a	1-16	a	a	a	a
Burl N	50	2⅞	6	7⅞	¼	2 3-16	3
52⅜	60	a	1⅞	3¾	7½	8	8¾
52⅜	70	a	7-16	a	17¾	a	a
52⅜	80	a	⅛	a	a	a	a
Citicp	20	5¼	a	6½	a	a	a
25¼	25	⅞	2½	3	⅜	1	1¼
25¼	30	1-16	13-16	1¼	4½	4¼	4⅝
25¼	35	b	3-16	a	b	a	a
Delta	60	5	8¾	10¼	b	b	b
65½	70	⅜	3½	a	b	b	b
65½	80	1-16	1¼	3¾	b	b	b
65½	90	b	½	a	b	b	b
Dig Eq	110	1-16	a	a	b	b	b
Disney	60	⅜	a	a	b	b	b
46¼	45	a	a	a	½	a	a
Eas Kd	50	11¾	13¼	b	a	5-16	b
72⅜	70	2	4¾	6¾	1¼	2⅛	3¼
72⅜	80	1-16 1 13-16	3¼	7¾	7¾	8⅛	
72⅜	90	a	¼	1⅜	18	a	16¾
Exxon	30	4⅜	5	6	a	¼	7-16
34½	35	a 1 13-16	2¾	¾	1½	1 13-16	
34½	40	1-16	½	1 1-16	a	a	a
34½	45	a	⅛	a	a	a	a
FedExp	40	16½	a	a	a	3-16	b
58¼	45	12	a	a	a	⅜	b
58¼	50	8	11	12¾	1-16 1 13-16	b	
58¼	60	½	4⅜	7	2½	5¼	6½
58¼	70	1-16	2	3½	13½	12½	12¼
58¼	80	b	½	1½	a	a	a
F N M	10	1⅜	a 1 3-16	b	b	b	b
9¼	15	1-16	⅜	b	b	b	b
9¼	20	1-16	b	b	b	b	b
Fluor	30	b	6¾	b	b	5⅜	a
34¾	35	7-16	2⅞	4⅛	1	2	2⅞
34¾	40	1-16	1	2⅜	5¾	a	6¼
34¾	45	1-16	½	1¼	10½	10½	a
34¾	50	1-16	¼	15½	a	a	a
34¾	60	1-16	b	b	a	a	b
Gt Wst	10	6	a	a	b	b	b
15¼	15	1	2¼	2⅝	b	b	b
15¼	20	a	⅜	1	b	b	b

the common stock that can cause a large change in the price of the call option. For example, on March 11, 1981, Federal Express common closed at 48⅞, and the 50 October call closed at 5⅝. Two months later, the stock closed at 60⅛ for an 11¼ gain of 23 percent. The 50 October call closed at 14¾ for a 9⅛ gain of 162 percent. The option increased by more than seven times the percentage move in the common stock.

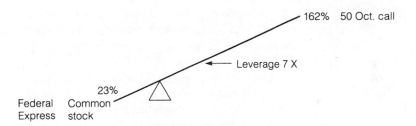

Part of the gain is due to a speculative premium of 4⅝ which still exists because five months remain until expiration.

Figure 13–1 depicts the relationship between profit and loss opportunities for

Figure 13–1   **Federal Express 50 October call buy 1 option (excludes commissions)**

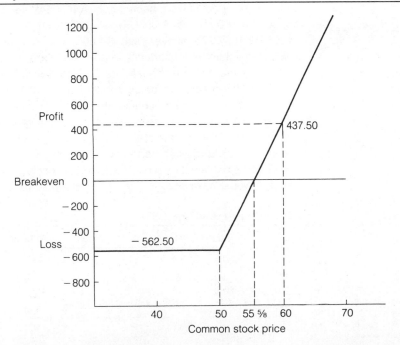

the Federal Express 50 October call option given the market price at expiration (no speculative premium exists at expiration).

As long as the common stock closes under 50, the call buyer loses the whole premium. At a price of 55⅝, the call buyer breaks even as the option is worth an intrinsic value of 5⅝. As the stock increases past 55⅝, the profit starts accumulating. If the option is sold before expiration, a speculative premium may alter the profit potential.

As of March 11, 1981, Federal Express calls had three October strike prices of 40, 45, and 50. Each strike price did not provide the same amount of leverage. The deeper in the money, the less leverage available. This is demonstrated in Table 13–7.

Playing the leverage game doesn't always work out. If a speculator had assumed that Federal Express would continue its rapid price rise, he may have purchased an in-the-money July 60 call on May 7, 1981. Although the stock declined almost $2 from 60⅛ to 58¼ by July 8, 1981, the call option declined from 5¼ to ½ (−90 percent) as the expiration date approached. On May 7, 1981, 5⅛ of the 5¼ total premium was speculative, and two months later it was almost all gone. It is not hard to lose all your money under these circumstances—leverage works in reverse too.

Call options instead of stock   Many people do not like to risk losing large amounts of money and view call options as a way of controlling 100 shares of stock without a large dollar commitment. For example, on March 11, 1981, Fluor common stock could have been purchased at $48 per share or $4,800 plus commission for 100 shares. A July 50 call could also be bought for 5¼ ($525) which would leave $4,275 leftover cash ($4,800 − $525) for an investment elsewhere and still maintain the opportunity to buy 100 shares at 50.

Assume the call is purchased for $525 and $4,275 is left to be invested in a money market fund at 15 percent until July 8, 1981. The interest income would be almost $212. In the meantime, the stock declined to 34⅜, and the option is trading at 1/16 (for our purposes, we will assume a value of 0). The strategy saved a large loss of 13⅝ on the stock. Instead, the potential investor lost $525 on the option plus a $20 dividend she could have received on the stock, but she also earned $212 in interest for a net loss of $333. That is a lot better than the $1,342.50 loss that would have occurred on the common stock.

Table 13–7   **Leverage relationship**

October strike price	March 11, 1981		May 7, 1981		Percent change stock	Percent change call	Leverage
	Call	Stock	Call	Stock			
40	11¾	48⅞	22	60⅛	23%	87%	3.8×
45	8⅝	48⅞	18½	60⅛	23	114	5.0×
50	5⅝	48⅞	14¾	60⅛	23	162	7.0×

Buy call; invest rest		Buy stock	
March 11, 1981			
$ 525	Call	$4,800	Fluor common stock
4,275	Money market fund		
$4,800	Total invested	$4,800	Total invested
July 8, 1981			
$ 0	Call	$3,437.50	Fluor common stock
4,275	Money market fund	20.00	Dividend
	Interest (15 percent for		
212	119 days)		
(20)	Dividend foregone		
$4,467	Ending value	$3,457.50	Ending value
(333)	Loss	(1,342.50)	Loss

Of course, there is always the possibility that the common stock would have risen to $60 per share, and the owner of the call would have exercised her right to purchase the stock at 50. Under these circumstances, a sizable gain could be enjoyed with a relatively small investment.

Protecting a short position Calls are often used to cover a short sale against the risk of rising stock prices. This is called hedging your position; by purchasing a call, the short seller guarantees a loss of no more than a fixed amount while at the same time reducing any potential profit by the total premium paid for the call. Assume you had sold Citicorp short at 21⅞ on March 11 and had bought an October 20 call for 3½ as protection against a rise in the price of the stock. By July 8, the stock has risen to 25¾ for a 3⅞ loss on the short position. This loss has been partially offset by an increase in the option price to 6 or a 2½ gain. Instead of losing $387.50, the short position is only out 1⅜ so far (3⅞ − 2½). This strategy has locked in a maximum loss potential of 1⅝ plus commissions. The 1⅝ is the speculative premium paid for the October 20 call; as the stock rises, the speculative premium evaporates at expiration, but otherwise the call goes up dollar for dollar with the stock. If Citicorp was a good short at 21⅞, the speculator may sell the call for 6 on July 8 and be left with an unprotected short position with the stock at 25¾, hoping for an eventual decline in the stock price.

Consider the 3½ call premium insurance. If the stock goes up, it limited your loss, but if the stock goes down, your profit on the short position is reduced by the call premium. In the case of Citicorp, the stock would have to reach 18⅜ (21⅞ − 3½) before the short seller with call protection would break even. A decline of 16 percent in the stock price would have to take place before the short seller would begin to profit, and this ignores commissions.

Guaranteed price   Often an investor thinks a stock will rise over the short term and long term but does not currently have the cash available to purchase the stock. The important point for this strategy is that the investor wants to own this stock eventually but does not want to miss out on a good buying opportunity (based on his or her expectations). Perhaps the oil stocks are depressed or semiconductors have hit bottom. The investor could be anticipating a cash inflow at a specific time in the future when he plans to exercise the call option with a tax refund, a book royalty, or even the annual Christmas bonus.

For example, on March 11, 1981, Mrs. Harris buys a July 35 call option in Avon Products for $3\frac{7}{8}$, which is a $1\frac{7}{8}$ speculative premium since Avon is selling at 37 per share. By July, she has received her $3,500 anticipated check and exercises the option when the stock is selling at $38. For tax purposes, the cost or basis of this 100 shares of Avon is the strike price plus the option premium, or $38\frac{7}{8}$ per share. Since most investors will not pursue this strategy if they expect prices to fall, they will usually seek out the deepest in-the-money option that they can afford because it is likely to have the lowest speculative premium.

Writing call options

Writers of call options take the opposite side of the market from the buyers. The writer is similar to a short seller in that he or she expects the stock to decline or stay the same. In order for short sellers to profit, prices must decline, but since writers of call options receive a premium, they can make a profit if prices stay the same or even rise less than the speculative premium. Option writers can write covered options, meaning they own the underlying common stock, or they can write naked call options, meaning they do not own the underlying stock.

Writing covered call options is often considered a hedged position because, if the stock price declines, the writer's loss on the stock is partially offset by the option premium. A writer of a covered call must decide if he is willing to sell the underlying stock if it closes above the strike price and the option is exercised. He also must consider any adverse tax consequences, such as short-term capital gains.

Returning to Table 13–6 for another set of option quotes, find Atlantic Richfield (Atl R) options. The market price of common is $54\frac{1}{8}$ on March 11, 1981, and the writer for a July option can choose from the following strike prices reprinted in Table 13–8.

Remember, the writer agrees to sell 100 shares at the strike price for the consideration of the premium. The 50 strike price has the highest premium and would be a good write if the stock closed at less than 50 because the call would not get exercised and the writer would profit the amount of the premium ($7\frac{7}{8}$). If

Table 13–8   **Atlantic Richfield July strike prices**

March 11, 1981	Strike	July premiums	Market
Atl R	50	$7\frac{7}{8}$	$54\frac{1}{8}$
Atl R	60	$2\frac{11}{16}$	$54\frac{1}{8}$
Atl R	70	$\frac{15}{16}$	$54\frac{1}{8}$

the stock closed above 50, then the call could get exercised, and the writer would have to deliver 100 shares at 50. If the stock closed at more than 57⅞, the call writer would be at a loss. Figure 13–2 shows this relationship between profit and loss and the common stock price.

By July 24, the date of expiration, Atlantic Richfield stock closed at 48½, and the option was worthless. Both a covered writer and a naked writer would have pocketed $787.50 (less commissions) in profit. The covered writer would have collected a dividend and still have possession of 100 shares of stock now valued at $4,850 instead of $5,412.50. The following is an analysis of how the two types of call writers fared.

Covered writer		Naked writer	
Initial investment 100 at 54⅛	$(5,412.50)	Margin 30 percent stock price	$(1,623.75)
Option premium	787.50	Option premium	787.50
Dividend	55.00	Ending value	1,623.75
Ending value	4,850.00		
Profit	$ 280.00	Profit	$ 787.50
Percent return	5.17%	Percent return	48.49%

Figure 13–2   **Atlantic Richfield July calls write 1 call (excludes commissions)**

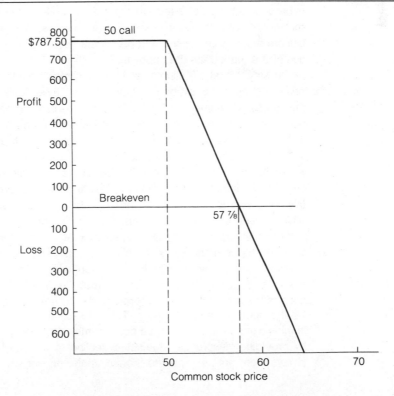

The covered writer hedged the losses on his stock by collecting an option premium. In spite of a declining stock price, he still managed a positive return. Our naked writer was required to put up margin on 30 percent of the value of the stock to ensure her ability to close out the option write if the stock should rise significantly. The capital was returned to her when it was no longer needed as collateral, and she profited with almost a 50 percent return. If the stock price had risen, the naked writer was exposed to unlimited risk as she either had to close out her position at a loss or purchase the stock above the strike price and deliver it at a loss. The covered writer had limited risk because he locked in the cost of his stock and can deliver it or close out his position before it is called.

Another critical decision for a call writer is the choice of months. In the section on option premiums, we examined percentage premiums per day and found that the shortest expiration dates provided the highest daily speculative premium. In most cases, the call writer will choose the shorter options and, as they expire, write another short-term option. Annualized returns of 20 percent are not uncommon for continuously covered writing strategies.

Buying put options

The owner of a put may sell 100 shares of stock to the put writer at the strike price. The strategy behind a put is similar to selling short or writing a call except losses are limited to the total investment (premium), and no more risk exposure is possible if the stock rises. Buying a put in anticipation of a price decline is one method of speculating on market price changes. The same factors influencing call premiums also apply to put premiums except that expectations for the direction of the market are the opposite.

On May 7, 1981, Burlington Northern Railroad's common stock price was 59¾, and a 60 July put could be purchased for 3⅞ (see Table 13–6 with "p" following the company's name on May 7). The put was in the money by ¼, and the speculative premium was 3⅝. Two and one half months remained until expiration. The buyer of the put would expect a price decline with the idea that the intrinsic value of the put would increase. By July 8, Burlington Northern had declined to 52⅝ with the July 60 put at 7½. (See "Puts" section in last three columns for July 8.) The intrinsic value was now 7⅜, and the speculative premium was ⅛. At this point in time, the owner of the put had a 3⅝ gain on a 3⅞ investment or a 93.5 percent return while the market was declining.

Puts can make money in a down market without risking a large loss in the value of the common stock. In this case, an owner of 100 shares of Burlington Northern could have bought a put to hedge against a loss in the value of the stock. Burlington's stock dropped 7⅛ (59¾ − 52⅝), and the gain of 3⅝ on the put offset some of the loss suffered on the common stock.

The comparison of returns in Table 13–9 demonstrates the benefits of a put in minimizing losses. A hedged position may do better than a pure stock position by providing "insurance" against a decline in the stock price. Hedges do not always work out as expected. For example, on May 7, 1981, the owner of 100

Table 13—9   **Profit potential on Burlington Northern July 60 put, stock, hedge**

	100 shares	July 60 put	Hedge = 100 shares + put
May 7, 1981	$5,975.00	$387.50	$6,362.50
July 8, 1981	5,262.50	750.00	6,012.50
Gain (Loss)	$ (712.50)	$362.50	$ (350.00)
Percent return	(11.9%)	93.5%	(5.5%)

shares of American Telephone and Telegraph (AT&T) anticipated a price decline because of expectations of rising interest rates, but he did not want to sell the stock. Instead he bought a July 55 put for 1⁷⁄₁₆ when the stock was at 54⁷⁄₈. By July 8, AT&T stock was up ⅛ (the decline never materialized), and the July 55 put was worth ⁷⁄₁₆, a loss of $100 on the put. This $100 loss is insurance against a price decline that never happened—much like auto insurance, we pay a premium for something we hope never happens.

USING OPTIONS IN COMBINATIONS

Spreads

Now that you have a basic understanding of puts and calls from both the buyer's and writer's perspective, we proceed with a discussion of spreads. Most combinations of options are called spreads and consist of buying one option (going long) and writing an option (going short) on the same underlying stock. Spreads are for the sophisticated investor and involve many variations on a theme. Vertical spreads involve buying and writing two contracts at different striking prices with the same month of expiration. Horizontal spreads consist of buying and writing two options with the same strike price but different months, and a diagonal spread is a combination of the vertical and horizontal spread. These spreads are all constructed using call options. Table 13–10 presents an example of Fluor Corporation demonstrating the options, months, and strike prices involved in each type of spread. There are more complicated spreads than these, such as the butterfly spread, variable spread, and domino spread. We cannot attempt to explain all of these spreads in the space available and so will concentrate on vertical bull spreads and bear spreads.

Since spreads require the purchase of one call and the sale of another call, a speculator's account will have either a debit or credit balance. If the cost of the long call is greater than the revenue from the short position, the speculator has a net cash outflow and a debit in his account. When your spread is put on with a debit, it is said that you have "bought the spread." You have "sold the spread" if the receipt from writing the call is greater than the cost of the long call and you have a credit balance. In either case, the profit or loss from a spread position results in the change between the two option prices over time as the price of the underlying common stock goes up or down. For example, the difference between

the option prices for a vertical spread on Fluor Corporation in Table 13–10 with October strike prices of 35 and 40 is $2 ($4 − $2). The $2 difference between these two option prices is sometimes called the price spread and could be either a debit or credit depending on whether a bull or bear spread is used.

Vertical bull spread Being a bull spread, the expectation is that the common stock price will rise. The speculator can buy the common stock outright, or if he wants to profit from an expected price increase but reduce his risk of loss, he can enter into a bull spread. Vertical bull spreads limit both the maximum gain and maximum loss available. They are usually debit positions because the spreader buys the higher-priced, in-the-money option and shorts (writes) an inexpensive, out-of-the-money option. Using Table 13–10 for a Fluor October bull spread, we would buy the October 35 at 4 and short the October 40 at 2 for a debit of 2 (price spread). This represents a $200 investment. Assume that three weeks later, Fluor stock rises from 36⅜ to 42 with the October 35 selling at 7½ (previously purchased at 4) and the October 40 at 4½ (previously sold at 2). Table 13–11 shows the result of closing out the spread.

Table 13–10 Spreads (call options)

Vertical Spreads

Option & Mkt. Price	Strike Price	Oct.	Jan.	April
FLUOR 36⅜	35	4	6	6½
36⅜	40	2	3⅜	4
36⅜	45	11⁄16	1½	6

Horizontal Spread (Time Spread)

Option & Mkt. Price	Strike Price	Oct.	Jan.	April
FLUOR 36⅜	35	4	6	6½
36⅜	40	2	3⅜	4
36⅜	45	11⁄16	1½	6

Diagonal Spread

Option & Mkt. Price	Strike Price	Oct.	Jan.	April
FLUOR 36⅜	35	4	6	6½
36⅜	40	2	3⅜	4
36⅜	45	11⁄16	1½	6

Table 13–11   **Profit on vertical bull spread**

	Fluor October 35 (stock price 36⅜)		Fluor October 40 (stock price 42)		Price spread
Bought at	4	Sold at	2		2
Sold at	7½	Bought at	4½		3
Gain	3½	(Loss)	(2½)		1
Net gain	$100				
Investment	$200				
Return	50%				

Because the investment was only $200, the total return of $100 provided a 50 percent return. However, returns on spreads can be greatly altered by commissions. If the following spread incurred commissions of $50 in and out, the percentage return could be cut in half to 25 percent.

The maximum profit at expiration is equal to the difference in strike prices ($5 in this case) minus the initial price spread ($2 in this case). For the Fluor bull spread, the maximum profit is $300, and the maximum loss is the original debit of $200. At expiration, all speculative premiums are gone, and each option sells at its intrinsic value. Table 13–12 shows maximum profit and loss at various closing market prices at expiration. Remember, our initial investment is $200.

As Table 13–12 shows, profit does not increase after the stock moves through the $40 call price. The stock price must increase from 36⅜ to 40 (10 percent) to generate a 150 percent spread profit. Every dollar of increased profit on the long position is offset by $1 of loss on the short position after the stock passes a price of 40. One of the important but difficult aspects of spreading is forecasting a range of prices rather than just the direction prices will move. If a speculator is bullish, he or she may buy a call instead of spreading. The potential loss is higher but still limited, but the possible gain is not. The relationship between long calls and bull spreads appears in the bottom of Figure 13–3. Note the maximum loss with the bull spread is $200 and $400 with a long call. The break-even point is also $2 less for the bull spread ($37 versus $39). However, the long call has

Table 13–12 Fluor vertical bull spread

Fluor stock price at expiration 35				Fluor stock price at expiration 40				Fluor stock price at expiration 45			
October 35		October 40		October 35		October 40		October 35		October 40	
Bought at	4	Sold at	2	Bought at	4	Sold at	2	Bought at	4	Sold at	2
Expired at*	0	Expired at*	0	Sold at*	5	Expired at*	0	Sold at*	10	Bought at*	5
(Loss)	(4)	Gain	2	Gain	1	Gain	2	Gain	6	Loss	(3)
(Net loss) (2)				Net gain 3				Net gain 3			
$(200) 100 percent loss				$300 150 percent gain				$300 150 percent gain			

*All call options on date of expiration equal their intrinsic value.

unlimited profit potential, and the bull spread is locked in at $300 at a stock price of $40 or higher. The spread positions lower the break-even point by $2 per share but also limit potential returns—a classic case of risk-return trade-off.

Vertical bear spreads   The speculator enters a bear spread anticipating a decline in stock prices. Instead of selling short or writing a call with both having unlimited risk, he spreads by selling short the call with the lower strike price (highest premium) and covers the upside risk with the purchase of a call having a higher strike price. This creates a credit balance. In a sense, the bear spread does the opposite of the vertical bull spread as seen in Table 13–13 in which we show profits and losses from the strategy if Fluor ends up at $35 or at $40.

With a bear spread, the price spread of 2 is the maximum gain if the stock closes at $35 or less at expiration, while the maximum loss equals 3, the difference between the exercise prices minus the price spread. The relationships between bear spreads and writing a call option is also demonstrated in Figure 13–3.

Straddles

A straddle is a combination of a put and call on the same stock with the same strike price and expiration date. It is used to play wide fluctuations in stock prices and is usually applied to individual stocks with high betas and a history of large, short-term fluctuations in price. The speculator using a straddle may be unsure of the direction of the price movement but may be able to make a large enough profit on one side of the straddle to cover the cost of both options even if one option expires worthless.

For example, assume a put and a call can be bought for $5 apiece on an XYZ October 50 when XYZ Corporation is selling at 50 with six months to expiration. The total investment is 10 ($1,000). If the stock should rise from 50 to 65 at expiration, the call would provide a profit of 10 (15 value − 5 cost), and the put would be left to expire worthless for a loss of 5. This would provide a net gain of 5, or $500. The same type of example can be drawn if the price goes way down. Some who engage in spreads or straddles might attempt to close out one position before the other. This expands the profit potential but also increases the risk.

Table 13–13   **Fluor vertical bear spread**

Fluor stock price at expiration 35				Fluor stock price at expiration 40			
October 35		October 40		October 35		October 40	
Sold at	4	Bought at	2	Sold at	4	Bought at	2
Expired at	0	Expired at	0	Bought at	5	Expired at	0
Gain	4	(Loss)	(2)	(Loss)	1	(Loss)	2
	Net gain 2				(Net loss) (3)		
	$200				$(300)		

Figure 13–3 Profit and loss relationships on spreads and calls

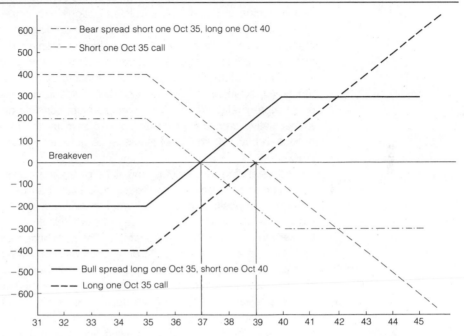

Many factors have not been covered in detail because of their changing nature over time. Tax laws relating to options are constantly changing, and some items, such as capital gains holding periods for determination of long-term and short-term tax treatment, have been revised several times in the last several years. We do know that tax laws have a significant impact on spread positions and also on the long-term tax treatment where put options are involved. The best advice we can give is to check the tax consequences of any option strategy with your accountant or stockbroker.

Commissions vary between different brokerage houses and are not easy to pinpoint for option transactions since quantity discounts exist. We can assure you that because many option positions involve small dollar outlays, commissions of $25 to $50 buying and selling can significantly alter your returns and even create losses. Commissions on exercising common stock through options are higher than the transaction costs of options, and these are a motivating force in causing closing option transactions before expiration. Overall, commissions on options tend to be more significant than commissions on commodities or other highly leveraged investments.

SUMMARY

Put and call options are an exciting area of investment and speculation. We have discussed the past history of over-the-counter options trading and more recent trading of options on the listed options exchanges, such as the CBOE. The markets are more efficient, and the standardized practices of the listed exchanges have made options more usable for many investors and widened the number of options strategies that can be efficiently employed.

Option premiums (option prices) are affected by many variables, such as time, market expectations, stock price volatility, dividend yields, and in-the-money, out-of-the-money relationships. The total premium consists of an intrinsic value plus a speculative premium which declines to zero by the expiration date. Calls are options to buy 100 shares of stock, while puts are options to sell 100 shares of stock.

Understanding the benefits and risks of trading options is complicated. Options can be risky or used to reduce risk. Calls can be bought for leverage, to cover a short position, or as an alternative to investing in the underlying common stock while buying time to purchase the stock (waiting for the financial resources to exercise the call). Calls are written either as a hedge on a long position in the underlying stock or to speculate on a price decline. Puts are bought to hedge a long position against a price decline or as an alternative to selling short. A writer of a put may speculate on a price increase or use the write as a hedge against a short position (if the price goes up, he will come out ahead on the writing of the put to partially offset the loss on the short sale).

Spreads are combinations of buying and writing the same options for an underlying common stock. In general, spreads reduce the risk of loss while at the same time limiting the gain. Spreads can be created to profit from rising prices, falling prices, or no price change at all. The important part is having the correct expectations. Straddles are a combination of a put and a call in a stock at the same exercise date and strike price. They are used to profit from stocks showing large, short-term price fluctuations.

Other factors affect option profitability, such as taxes and commissions, and in general, each investor or speculator should check out his or her own situation and factor in the appropriate information with regard to taxes and commissions.

IMPORTANT WORDS AND CONCEPTS

Bull spread	Intrinsic value
Buying-the spread	Opening purchase transaction
Call	Opening sale transaction
CBOE	Option
Closing purchase transaction	Option premium
Closing sale transaction	Option Clearing Corporation
Covered writer	Put
Diagonal spreads	Spreads
Exercise price	Straddle
In-the-money	Vertical spread

1. What exchanges trade in options?

2. Explain how the Options Clearing Corporation operates.

3. Look at the option quotes in Table 13–2. *(a)* What is the closing price of the common stock of Warner Communications? *(b)* What is the highest strike price listed? *(c)* What is the price of a February 60 call option? *(d)* What is the price of a February 60 put option? *(e)* Why is there a difference between the prices of the put and the call?

4. What are factors that influence a speculative premium on an option?

5. Why might an option reflect a discount at expiration?

6. Why does an option that is deep in-the-money often have a low speculative premium?

7. Why would a high-beta stock often have a greater speculative premium than a low-beta stock?

8. Assume that a stock is selling for $52 with options available at 40, 50, and 60 strike prices. The 50 call option is at 5¼.
   a. What is the intrinsic value of the 50 call?
   b. Is the 50 call in-the-money?
   c. What is the speculative premium on the 50 call option?
   d. What percent does the speculative premium represent of common stock price?
   e. Are the 40 and 60 call options in-the-money?

9. In the case of Warner Communications in Table 13–2, what is the intrinsic value of the 45 August call? What is the total premium? How much is the speculative premium?

10. What does the speculative premium as a precent of stock price indicate for a call option?

11. Briefly describe what leverage is in purchasing a call option.

12. In Table 13–6, calculate the leverage from holding a Citicorp option (July 20 call option) from March 11 until May 7. (The best approach for doing this is to compute the percentage gain from holding the option, then compute the percentage gain from holding the stock, and finally divide the first value by the second value.)

13. Assume that a party writes a call for 100 shares at a strike price of 40 for a premium of 5¼. This is a naked option. What would her gain or loss be if the stock closed at 35? What would the break-even point be in terms of the closing price of the stock?

14. Assume you purchase 100 shares of stock at $64 per share and wish to hedge your position by writing a 100-share call option on your holdings. The option has a $60 strike price and a premium of $8. If the stock is selling at $58 at the time of expiration, what will be the overall gain or loss on this

covered option play? (Consider the change in stock value as well as the gain or loss on the option.) Note that the stock does not pay a cash dividend.

15. In question 14, what would be the overall gain or loss if the stock ended up at *(a)* $60, *(b)* $40, *(c)* $70. (Disregard the stock being called away in *a* and *c*.)

16. Though commissions would not explicitly be considered in problems 13 through 15, might they be significant?

17. Assume a 35 July put option is purchased for $7 on a stock selling at $30 per share. If the stock ends up on expiration at $26½, what will be the value of the put option?

18. At what ending stock price would the investor break even?

19. Vertical bull spread: a stock is selling for $47. You buy a July 45 call option for 3½ and short (write) a July 50 call option for 1. If the stock is $53 at expiration, what will your profit or loss be on the spread? (Note: you do not own any stock directly.)

20. What is a straddle? Why is it used?

**SELECTED
REFERENCES**

Black, Fisher. "Fact and Fantasy in the Use of Options." *Financial Analysts Journal,* July–August 1975, pp. 36–41.

Black, Fisher, and Myron Scholes. "The Valuation of Option Contracts and a Test of Market Efficiency." *Journal of Finance,* May 1972, pp. 399–417.

Chicago Board of Options Exchange. Selected material.

Clasing, Henry. *The Dow Jones-Irwin Guide to Put and Call Options.* Homewood, Ill.: Dow Jones-Irwin, 1975.

Dawson, Frederic S. "Risk and Returns in Continuous Option Writing." *Journal of Portfolio Management,* Winter 1979, pp. 58–63.

Finnerty, Joseph E. "The Chicago Board Options Exchange and Market Efficiency." *Journal of Financial and Quantitative Analysis,* March 1978, pp. 29–38.

Galai, Dan. "Tests of Market Efficiency of the Chicago Board Options Exchange." *Journal of Business,* April 1977, pp. 167–97.

Gastineau, Gary L. "An Index of Listed Option Premiums." *Financial Analysts Journal,* May–June 1977, pp. 70–75.

Gambola, Michael J.; Rodney L. Roenfeldt; and Philip L. Cooley. "Spreading Strategies in CBOE Options: Evidence on Market Performance." *Journal of Financial Research,* Winter 1978, pp. 35–44.

Hettenhouse, George W., and Donald J. Puglisi. "Investor Experience with Put and Call Options." *Financial Analysts Journal,* July–August 1975, pp. 53–58.

"How to Play the Option Game." *Business Week,* December 22, 1980, p. 88.

Malkiel, Burton, and Richard Quandt. *Strategies and Rational Decisions in the Securities Option Market.* Cambridge, Mass.: MIT Press, 1969.

Merton, Robert C.; Myron S. Scholes; and Mathew L. Gladstein. "The Returns and Risk of Alternative Call Option Investment Strategies." *Journal of Business,* April 1978, pp. 183–242.

"Options—A Pension Management Tool for Controlling Risk and Return." *Financial Executive,* March 1979, pp. 37–43.

Reback, Robert. "Risk and Return in Option Trading." *Financial Analysts Journal,* July–August 1975, pp. 42–52.

Rendleman, Richard J., Jr. "Optimal Long-Run Option Investment Strategies." *Financial Management,* Spring 1981, pp. 61–76.

Scholes, Myron. "Taxes and the Pricing of Options." *Journal of Finance,* May 1976, pp. 319–32.

Smith, Clifford W., Jr. "Option Pricing: A Review." *Journal of Financial Economics,* January–March 1976, pp. 3–51.

Stoll, Hans R. "The Relationship between Put and Call Option Prices." *The Journal of Finance,* December 1969, pp. 801–24.

PART 4 INTRODUCTION TO PORTFOLIO MANAGEMENT

The contemporary portfolio manager is continually called upon to assess the nature of his or her performance over a period of time. A couple of decades ago, an analysis that merely indicated the extent of gains and losses would have been sufficient. This is no longer the case. There are at least two dimensions to every modern portfolio evaluation: the rate of return that was earned as well as the amount of *risk* that was taken. Many of the earlier concepts related to risk (introduced in Chapter 1) will now be more formally developed.

In Chapter 14, we evaluate the risk measurement tools for an individual asset as well as a portfolio of assets. We also review the concept that most investors are risk averse (dislike risk) and will therefore require proportionally higher returns as risks increase.

If we accept the concept of a premium return for risk, we must then consider what type of risk should be rewarded. Portfolio theory suggests that much of the risk in individual assets can be diversified away in a cross section or portfolio of investments and that only risk which cannot be diversified is likely to receive a higher return in a competitive marketplace. These topics are developed (and briefly debated) in the first of the two chapters on portfolio management.

In Chapter 15, we examine empirical studies of portfolio managers and the nature of their performance. A typical question for consideration is, "Have mutual fund or pension fund managers actually provided superior investment returns on a risk-adjusted basis? We also evaluate how effective they have been in pursuing investment policies that are consistent with their stated objectives. Finally, we consider the various types of investors that are part of the category of institutional investor (as opposed to individual investor) and some of the investment management characteristics of each.

14

A basic look at portfolio management and capital market theory

In this chapter, we develop a more complete understanding of how the investor perceives risk and demands compensation for it. We eventually build toward a theory of portfolio management that incorporates many of these concepts. While the use of mathematical terms is an essential ingredient to a basic understanding of portfolio theory, more involved or complicated concepts are treated in appendixes at the end of the chapter.

As indicated in Chapter 1, risk is generally associated with uncertainty about future outcomes. The greater the range of possible outcomes, the greater the risk. We also observed in Chapter 1 that most investors tend to be risk averse; that is, all things being equal, investors prefer less risk to more risk and will only increase their risk-taking position if a premium for risk is involved. Each investor has a different attitude toward risk. The inducement necessary to cause a given investor to withdraw his funds from a savings account to drill an oil well may be quite different from yours. For some, only a very small premium for risk is necessary, while others may not wish to participate unless there are exceptionally high rewards. We begin the chapter with a more formal approach toward the measurement of risk.

FORMAL MEASUREMENT OF RISK

Having defined risk as uncertainty about future outcomes, how do we actually measure risk? The first task is to design a probability distribution of anticipated future outcomes. This is no small task. The possible outcomes and associated probabilities are likely to be based on economic projections, past experience, subjective judgments, and many other variables. For the most part, we are forcing ourselves to write down what already exists in our head. Having established the probability distribution, we then determine the *expected value* and the dispersion around that expected value. The greater the dispersion, the greater the risk.

Expected value

To determine the expected value, we multiply each possible outcome by its probability of occurrence. Assume we are considering two investment proposals where K represents a possible outcome and P represents the probability of that outcome based on the state of the economy. If we were dealing with stocks, K would represent the price appreciation potential plus the dividend yield (total return). Assume that for our first investment (investment i) the following data are indicated.

Investment i

K	P	Based on state of the economy
5%	.20	Recession
7	.30	Slow growth
13	.30	Semi-strong economy
15	.20	Strong economy

We will say that $\overline{K}_i$ (the expected value of investment i) equals ΣKP. In this case, our answer would be 10.0 percent.

$$\overline{K}_i = \Sigma KP \qquad (14-1)$$

K	P	KP
5%	.20	1.0%
7	.30	2.1
13	.30	3.9
15	.20	3.0
		10.0% $= \Sigma KP$

$\overline{K}_i$, or the expected value for investment i, equals 10.0 percent.

Standard deviation

The commonly used measure of dispersion is the standard deviation, which is a measure of the spread of the outcomes around the expected value.[1] The formula for the standard deviation is:

$$\sigma_i = \sqrt{\Sigma(K - \overline{K}_i)^2 P} \qquad (14-2)$$

Let's determine the standard deviation for investment i around the expected value $(\overline{K}_i)$ of 10 percent.

---

[1]Rather than being the average difference of each K value from $\overline{K}_i$, it is the quadratic mean of the difference; that is, we square the differences, average these squared differences, and then reverse the process by taking the square root.

K	$\bar{K}_i$	P	$(K - \bar{K}_i)$	$(K - \bar{K}_i)^2$	$(K - \bar{K}_i)^2 P$
5%	10%	.20	−5%	25%	5.0%
7	10	.30	−3	9	2.7
13	10	.30	+3	9	2.7
15	10	.20	+5	25	5.0

$$15.4\% = \Sigma(K - \bar{K}_i)^2 P$$

$$\sigma_i = \sqrt{\Sigma(K - \bar{K}_i)^2 P} = \sqrt{15.4\%} = 3.9\%$$

The standard deviation of investment i is 3.9 percent (rounded). In order to have some feel for the relative risk characteristics of this investment, we compare it to a second proposal, investment j.

We assume that investment j is a countercyclical investment. It does well during a recession and poorly in a strong economy. Perhaps it represents a firm in the housing industry that is most profitable when the economy is sluggish and interest rates are low. Under these circumstances, people will avail themselves of low-cost financing to purchase a new home, and the stock of the firm will do well. In a booming economy, interest rates will advance rapidly, and there will be little money for housing. Thus, we have a countercyclical investment. The outcomes and probabilities of outcomes for investment j are as follows:

Investment j

K	P	Based on state of the economy
20%	.20	Recession
8	.30	Slow growth
8	.30	Semi-strong economy
6	.20	Strong economy

The expected value and standard deviation for investment j are as follows.

Expected value

$$\bar{K}_j = \Sigma KP$$

K	P	KP
20%	.20	4.0%
8	.30	2.4
8	.30	2.4
6	.20	1.2
	$\bar{K}_j =$	10.0%

Standard deviation

$$\sigma_j = \sqrt{\Sigma(K - \bar{K}_j)^2 P}$$

K	$\overline{K}_j$	P	$(K - \overline{K}_j)$	$(K - \overline{K}_j)^2$	$(K - \overline{K}_j)^2 P$
20%	10%	.20	+10%	100%	20.0%
8	10	.30	−2	4	1.2
8	10	.30	−2	4	1.2
6	10	.20	−4	16	3.2
					25.6% $= \Sigma(K - \overline{K}_j)^2 P_j$

$$\sigma_j = \sqrt{\Sigma(K - \overline{K}_j)^2 P} = \sqrt{25.6\%} = 5.1\% \text{ (rounded)}$$

We now see we have two investments, each with an expected value of 10 percent but with varying performances in different types of economies and different standard deviations (3.9 percent versus 5.1 percent).

PORTFOLIO EFFECT

An investor who is holding only investment i may wish to consider bringing investment j into the portfolio. If the stocks are weighted evenly, the new portfolio expected value will be 10 percent. We define K_p as the expected value of the portfolio.

$$K_p = X_i \overline{K}_i + X_j \overline{K}_j \qquad (14\text{–}3)$$

The X values represent the weights assigned by the investor to each component in the portfolio and are 50 percent for both investments. The K_i and K_j values were previously determined to be 10 percent. Thus we have:

$$K_p = .5\ (10\%) + .5\ (10\%) = 5\% + 5\% = 10\%$$

What about the standard deviation for the combined portfolio (σ_p)? If a weighted average were taken of the two investments, the new standard deviation would be 4.5 percent.

$$X_i \sigma_i + X_j \sigma_j$$
$$.5\ (3.9\%) + .5\ (5.1\%) = 1.95\% + 2.55\% = 4.5\%$$

The interesting element is that the investor in investment i would appear to be losing from the combined investment. His expected value remains at 10 percent, but his standard deviation has increased from 3.9 percent to 4.5 percent. Given that he is risk averse, he appears to be getting more risk rather than less risk by expanding his portfolio.

There is one fallacy in the analysis. The standard deviation of a portfolio is not based on the simple weighted average of the individual standard deviations (as the expected value is). Rather, it takes into consideration significant interaction between the investments. If one investment does well during a given economic condition while the other does poorly and vice versa, there may be significant risk reduction from combining the two, and the standard deviation for the

portfolio may be less than the standard deviation for either investment (this is the reason we do not simply take the weighted average of the two).

Note in Figure 14–1, the risk reduction potential from combining the two investments under study. Investment *i* alone may produce outcomes anywhere from 5 to 15 percent and investment *j* from 6 to 20 percent. By combining the two, we narrow the range for investment *(i, j)* from 7.5 percent to 12.5 percent. Thus, we have reduced the risk while keeping the expected value constant at 10 percent. We now examine the appropriate standard deviation formula for the two investments.

Standard deviation for a two-asset portfolio

The standard deviation for a two-asset portfolio (Formula 14–4) appears complicated but is actually quite easy to calculate.[2]

$$\sigma_p = \sqrt{X_i^2\sigma_i^2 + X_j^2\sigma_j^2 + 2X_iX_jr_{ij}\sigma_i\sigma_j} \tag{14-4}$$

The only new term in the entire expression is r_{ij}, which represents the correlation coefficient or measurement of joint movement between the two variables. If two variables move in completely opposite directions, the coefficient correlation has a maximum negative value of -1. If two variables move in precisely the same direction, the maximum positive correlation coefficient is $+1$. For most variables, the coefficient correlation falls somewhere in between. The actual

Figure 14–1 **Investment outcomes under different conditions**

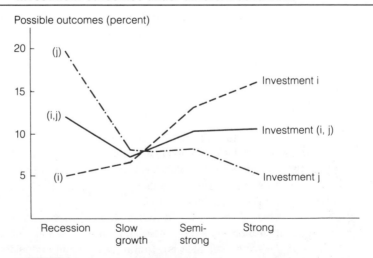

Possible outcomes (percent)

----

[2]For a multiple asset portfolio, the expression is written as:

$$\sigma_p = \sqrt{\sum_{i=1}^{N} X_i^2\sigma_i^2 + 2\sum_{i=1}^{N-1}\sum_{j=1+1}^{N} X_iX_jr_{ij}\sigma_i\sigma_j}$$

N is the number of securities in the portfolio.

computation of the correlation coefficient for investments i and j is covered in Appendix 14–A. It is not necessary to go through Appendix 14–A before proceeding with our discussion, though some readers may wish to do so. As indicated there, the correlation coefficient (r_{ij}) between investment i and investment j is −.70. This indicates that the investments show a high degree of negative correlation. Plugging this value into Formula 14–4, along with other previously determined values, the standard deviation (σ_p) for the two-asset portfolio can be computed.[3]

$$\sigma_p = \sqrt{X_i^2 \sigma_i^2 + X_j^2 \sigma_j^2 + 2X_i X_j r_{ij} \sigma_i \sigma_j}$$

where:

$X_i = .5, \ \sigma_i = 3.9$
$X_j = .5, \ \sigma_j = 5.1$
$r_{ij} = -.70$

$$
\begin{aligned}
\sigma_p &= \sqrt{(.5)^2(3.9)^2 + (.5)^2(5.1)^2 + 2(.5)(.5)(-.7)(3.9)(5.1)} \\
&= \sqrt{(.25)(15.4) + .25(25.6) + 2(.25)(-.7)(19.9)} \\
&= \sqrt{3.85 + 6.4 + (.5)(-13.93)} \\
&= \sqrt{3.85 + 6.4 - 6.97} \\
&= \sqrt{3.28} = 1.8\%
\end{aligned}
$$

The interesting factor is that the newly computed standard deviation of the portfolio of 1.8 percent is less than the standard deviation of either investment i or j (3.9 percent or 5.1 percent) or the weighted average of the individual investments (4.5 percent). Any time two investments have a correlation coefficient (r_{ij}) less than +1 (perfect positive correlation), the standard deviation of the portfolio (σ_p) will be less than the weighted average of the standard deviation for the individual investments and some risk reduction will be possible. In the real world most items are positively correlated; to the extent that we can still get risk reduction from positively correlated items gives extra meaning to portfolio management. Note the impact of various assumed correlation coefficients for the two investments previously described in terms of individual standard deviations.[4]

r_{ij}	σ_p
+1.0	4.5
+.5	3.9
0	3.2
−.5	2.3
−.7	1.8
−1.0	0

[3]Note that the squared values, such as $(3.9)^2 = 15.4$, are the reverse of earlier computations. Previously we found the square root of 15.4 to be 3.9 (see computation under Formula 14–2). The use of rounding introduces slight discrepancies where we square numbers for which we previously found the square root.

[4]Each is assumed to represent 50 percent of the portfolio.

The conclusion to be drawn from our portfolio analysis discussion is that the most significant risk factor associated with an individual investment may not be its own standard deviation but how it affects the standard deviation of a portfolio through correlation. As we shall later see in this chapter, there is not considered to be a risk premium for the total risk or standard deviation of an individual security, but only for that risk component which can not be eliminated by various portfolio diversification techniques.

DEVELOPING AN EFFICIENT PORTFOLIO

We have seen how the combination of two investments has allowed us to maintain our return of 10 percent, but it reduces the portfolio standard deviation to 1.8 percent. We also saw in the preceding table that different coefficient correlations produce many different possibilities for portfolio standard deviations. A shrewd portfolio manager may wish to consider a large number of portfolios, each with a different expected value and standard deviation, based on the expected values and standard deviations of the individual securities and, more importantly, on the correlations between the individual securities. Though we have been discussing a two-asset portfolio case, our example may be expanded to cover 5-, 10- or even 100-asset portfolios.[5] The major tenets of portfolio theory that we are currently examining were developed by Professor Harry Markowitz in the 1950s, and we shall later refer to it as Markowitz portfolio theory.

Assume we have identified the following risk-return possibilities for eight different portfolios (there may also be many more, but we will restrict ourselves to this set for now).

Portfolio number	K_p	σ_p
1.	10%	1.8%
2.	10	2.1
3.	12	3.0
4.	13	4.2
5.	13	5.0
6.	14	5.0
7.	14	5.8
8.	15	7.2

In diagramming our various risk-return points, we show the values in Figure 14–2.

[5]The incremental benefit from reduction of the portfolio standard deviation through adding securities appears to diminish fairly sharply with a portfolio of 10 securities and is quite small with a portfolio as large as 20. A portfolio of 12 to 14 securities is generally thought to be of sufficient size to enjoy the majority of desirable portfolio effects. W. H. Wagner and S. C. Lau, "The Effect of Diversification on Risk," *Financial Analysts Journal*, November–December 1971, pp. 48–53.

Figure 14—2   **Diagram of risk-return trade-offs**

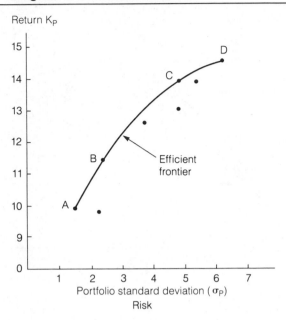

Though we have only diagrammed eight possibilities, we see an efficient set of portfolios would lie along the *ABCD* line. That is, along this *efficient frontier,* we can receive a maximum return for a given level of risk or a minimum risk for a given level of return. Points above this line are asumed not to exist (they are not part of the feasible set of investment alternatives). Points below this line do not offer acceptable alternatives to points along the line. As an example of maximum return for a given level of risk, consider point C. Along the efficient frontier, we are receiving a 14 percent return for a 5 percent risk level, whereas directly below point C, we are only receiving a return of 13 percent for a 5 percent risk level.

To demonstrate that we also are getting minimum risk for a given return level, we can examine point A in which we receive a 10 percent return for a 1.8 percent risk level, whereas to the right of point A, we get the same 10 percent return but a less desirable 2.1 percent risk level. Though we have shown but eight points, a fully developed efficient frontier may be based on a virtually unlimited number of observations as is presented in Figure 14–3.

In Figure 14–3, we once again view the efficient frontier in relationship to the feasible set and note certain risk-return possibilities are not attainable (and should be disregarded). At this point in the analysis, we can stipulate that the various points along the efficient frontier are all considered potentially optimal and that a given investor must choose the most appropriate single point based on his or her individualized risk-return trade-off desires. (In a later section of this chapter on

Figure 14—3   **Expanded view of efficient frontier**

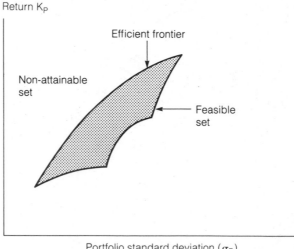

Return K_P

Efficient frontier

Non-attainable
set

Feasible
set

Portfolio standard deviation (σ_P)
Risk

the capital asset pricing model, this analysis changes somewhat.) For now, we would say that a low risk oriented investor might prefer point A or B in Figure 14–2, whereas a more risk oriented investor would prefer point C or D. At each of these points, the investor is getting the best risk-return trade-off for his or her own particular risk-taking propensity.

Risk-return indifference curves

To actually pair up an investor with an appropriate point along the efficient frontier, we look at his or her indifference curve as illustrated in Figure 14–4.

The indifference curves show the investor's trade-off between risk and return. The steeper the slope of the curve, the more risk averse the investor is. For example, in the case of investor B (I_B in Figure 14–4), the indifference curve has a steeper slope than that for investor A (I_A). This means that investor B will require more incremental return (more of a risk premium) for each additional unit of risk. Note that to take risks, investor B requires approximately twice as much incremental return as investor A between points C and D. Investor A is still somewhat risk averse and perhaps represents a typical investor in the capital markets.

Once the shape of an investor's indifference curve is determined, a second objective can be established—to attain the highest curve possible. For example, investor A, initially shown in Figure 14-4, would have a whole set of similarly shaped indifference curves as presented in Figure 14–5.

While he is indifferent to any point along a given curve (such as I_{A4}), he is not indifferent to achieving the highest curve possible (I_{A4} is clearly superior to I_{A1}). It

Figure 14—4   **Risk-return indifference curves**

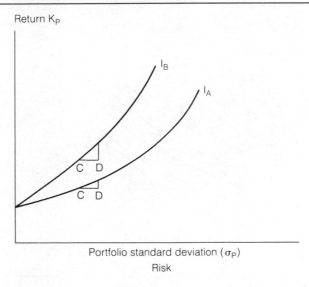

provides more return at all given risk levels. The only limitation to achieving the highest possible indifference curve is the feasible set of investments that are available.

Optimum portfolio   The investor must theoretically match his own risk-return indifference curve with the best investments that are available in the market as represented by

Figure 14—5   **Indifference curves for investor A**

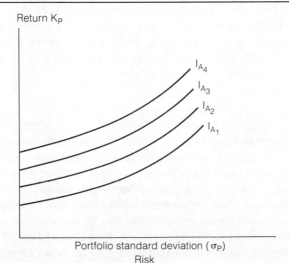

Figure 14—6   **Combining the efficient frontier and indifferent curves**

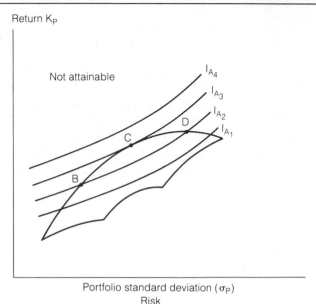

Return K_P

Not attainable

I_{A_4}

I_{A_3}

I_{A_2}

I_{A_1}

D

C

B

Portfolio standard deviation (σ_P)
Risk

points on the efficient frontier. We see in Figure 14—6 that investor A will achieve the highest possible indifference curve at point C along the efficient frontier.

This is the point of tangency between his own indifference curve (I_{A_3}) and the efficient frontier. Both curves have the same slope or risk-return characteristics at this point. While a point along indifference curve (I_{A_4}) might provide a higher level of utility, it is not attainable in relationship to the efficient frontier. Also, any other point along the efficient frontier would cross a lower level indifference curve and be inferior to point C. For example, points B and D cross I_{A_2}, providing less return for a given level of risk. Investors must relate the shape of their *own* risk-return indifference curves to the efficient frontier to determine that point of tangency providing maximum benefits.

CAPITAL ASSET PRICING MODEL

The development of the efficient frontier in the previous section gives insight into optimum portfolio mixes in an appropriate risk-return context. Nevertheless, the development of multiple portfolios is a rather difficult and tedious task. Professors Sharpe, Lintner, and others have allowed us to take the philosophy of efficient portfolios into a more generalized and meaningful context through the capital asset pricing model. Under this model, we examine the theoretical underpinnings through which assets are valued based on their risk characteristics.

The capital asset pricing model (CAPM) takes off where the efficient frontier

concluded through the introduction of a new investment outlet, the risk-free asset *(R_F)*. A risk-free asset has a standard deviation of 0 ($\sigma_{RF} = 0$) and is the lowest assumed safe return that can be earned. A U.S. Treasury bill or Treasury bond is often considered representative of a risk-free asset. Under the capital asset pricing model, we introduce the notion of combining the risk-free asset and the efficient frontier with the development of the *R_FMZ* line as indicated in Figure 14–7.

The R_FMZ line opens up the possibility of a whole new set of superior investment opportunities. That is, by combining some portion of the risk-free asset (R_F) with M (a point along the efficient frontier), we create new investment opportunities that will allow us to reach higher indifference curves than would be possible simply along the efficient frontier. We see in Figure 14–8 that points O and P provide higher utility than points on the efficient frontier. The only point along the efficient frontier that now has significance is point M, where the straight line from R_F is tangent to the old efficient frontier.

We can reach points along the R_FMZ line in a number of different ways. To be at point R_F, we would simply buy a risk-free asset. To be at a point between R_F and M, we would buy a combination of R_F and the M portfolio along the efficient frontier. To be at a point between M and Z, we buy M with our available funds and then borrow additional funds to further increase our purchase of the M portfolio (an example of this would be to be at point P in Figure 14–8). To the extent that M is higher than R_F and we can borrow at a rate equal to R_F or slightly higher, we can get larger returns with a combination of buying M and borrowing additional funds to buy M. (Of course, this calls for greater risk as well.)

Figure 14–7   **Basic diagram of the capital asset pricing model**

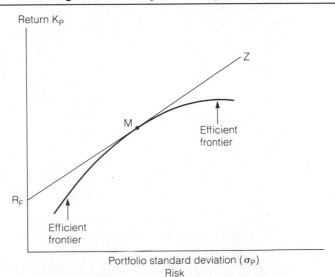

Return K_P

Z

M

Efficient frontier

R_F

Efficient frontier

Portfolio standard deviation (σ_P)
Risk

Figure 14–8   **The CAPM and indifference curves**

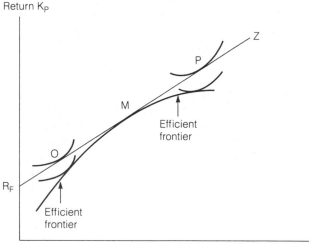

We also note that point M is considered the optimum "market basket" of investments that is available (though you may wish to combine this market basket with risk-free assets or borrowing). If you took all the possible investments that investors could acquire and determined the optimum basket of investments, you would come up with point M (because it is along the efficient frontier and tangent to the R_F line). Point M can be measured by the total return on the Standard & Poor's 500 Stock Average, the Dow Jones Industrial Average, the New York Stock Exchange Index, or similar measures. If point M or the market were not represented by the optimum risk-return portfolio for all investments at a point in time, then it is assumed there would be an instantaneous change and the market measure (point M) would once again be in equilibrium.

Capital market line   The previously discussed $R_F MZ$ line is called the capital market line (CML) and is once again presented in Figure 14–9.

The formula for the capital market line in Figure 14–9 may be written as:

$$K_P = R_F + \left(\frac{K_M - R_F}{\sigma_M - 0} \right) \sigma_P \qquad (14-5)$$

We indicate that the expected return on any portfolio (K_P) is equal to the risk-free rate of return (R_F) plus the slope of the line times a value along the horizontal axis (σ_P) indicating the amount of risk undertaken. We can relate the formula for the capital market line to the basic equation for a straight line as follows:

Figure 14—9   **Illustration of the capital market line**

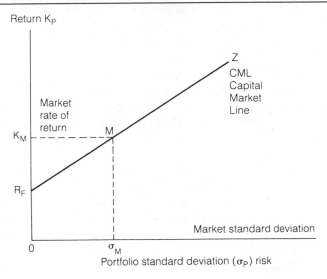

Straight line $Y = a + b \cdot X$

Capital market line $K_P = R_f + \left(\dfrac{M_K - R_F}{\sigma_M - 0} \right) \cdot \sigma_P$

In using the capital market line, we start with a minimum rate of return of R_F and then say any additional return is a reward for risk. The reward for risk or risk premium is equal to the market rate of return (M_K) minus the risk-free rate (R_F) divided by the market standard deviation (σ_M). If the market rate of return (K_M) is 9 percent and the risk-free rate of return (R_F) is 6 percent, with a market standard deviation (σ_M) of 10 percent, there is a risk premium of 3 percent. Then if the standard deviation of our portfolio (σ_P) is 14 percent, we can expect a return of 10.2 percent along the CML.

$$K_P = R_F + \left(\frac{M_K - R_F}{\sigma_M - 0} \right) \sigma_P$$

$$K_P = 6\% + \left(\frac{9\% - 6\%}{10\% - 0} \right) 14\%$$

$$= 6\% + \left(\frac{3\%}{10\%} \right) 14\%$$

$$= 6\% + (.3)\, 14\%$$

$$= 6\% + 4.2\% = 10.2\%$$

The essence of the capital market line is that the way to get larger returns is to take increasingly higher risks. Thus, the only way to climb up the K_P *return* line in Figure 14–9 is to extend yourself out of the σ_P *risk* line. Portfolio managers who claim highly superior returns may have taken larger than normal risks and thus may not really be superior performers on a risk-adjusted basis. We shall see in the following chapter that the best way to measure a portfolio manager is to evaluate his returns relative to the risks taken. Average to slightly above average returns on low risk may be superior to high returns on high risk. One does not easily exceed market-dictated constraints for risk and return.

RETURN ON AN INDIVIDUAL SECURITY

We have been examining return expectations for a portfolio; we now turn our attention to an individual security. Once again, the return potential is closely tied to risk. However, when dealing with an individual security, the premium return for risk is not related to *all* the risk in the investment as measured by the standard deviation (σ).[6] The reason for this is that the standard deviation is made up of two types of risks, but only one is accorded a premium return under the capital asset pricing model.

We now begin an analytical process that allows us to get at the two forms of risk in an individual security. The first form of risk is measured by the beta coefficient.

Beta coefficient In analyzing the performance of an individual security, it is first important to measure its relationship to the market through the beta coefficient. Let us lay the ground-work for understanding beta. In the case of a potential investment, stock i, we can observe its relationship to the market by tracing its total return performance relative to market total return over the last five years.[7]

	Stock i return *(K)*	Market return *(K_M)*
1978	4.8%	6.5%
1979	14.5	11.8
1980	19.1	14.9
1981	3.7	1.1
1982	15.6	12.0

---

[6]Actually, rather than use the standard deviation, we often use its squared value, termed the *variance,* to describe risk. That is we may use σ^2 (the standard deviation squared) to describe risk in an individual security.

[7]Though monthly or quarterly calculations would be desirable, we can satisfy our same basic objectives with annual data.

We see that stock i moves somewhat with the market. Plotting the values in Figure 14–10, we observe a line that is upward sloping at slightly above a 45-degree angle.

A straight line of best fit has been drawn through the various points representing the following formula:

$$K_i = a_i + b_i K_M + e_i \qquad (14{-}6)$$

K_i represents the anticipated stock return based on the formula; a_i (alpha) is the point at which the line crosses the vertical axis; b_i (beta) is the slope of the line; K_M is the independent variable of market return; and e_i is the random error term. The $a_i + b_i K_M$ portion of the formula describes a straight line, and e_i represents deviations or random, nonrecurring movements away from the straight line. In the present example, the formula for the straight line is $K_i = .42 + 1.20 \ K_M$ (indicating a beta or line slope of 1.2). These values can be approximated by drawing a line of best fit as indicated in Figure 14–10 or through the use of least squares regression analysis presented in Appendix 14–B. Basically, the equation tells us how volatile our stock is relative to the market through the beta coefficient. In the present case, if the market moves up or down by a given percent, our stock is assumed to move by 1.2 times that amount. With a beta of 1.2, our

Figure 14–10　　　**Relationship of individual stock to the market**

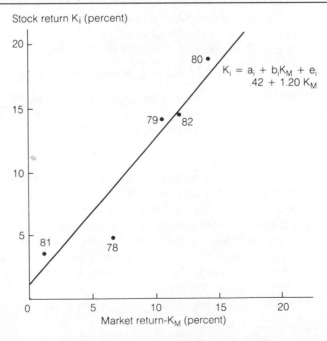

stock is considered to be 20 percent more volatile than the market. A stock with average volatility would have a beta of 1, while one with less than normal volatility would have a beta of under 1.

Systematic and unsystematic risk

Previously, we mentioned that there are two major types of risk associated with a stock. One is the market movement or beta (b_i) risk. If the market moves up or down, a stock is assumed to change in value. This type of risk is referred to as *systematic* risk. The second type of risk is represented by the error term (e_i) and indicates changes in value not associated with market movement. It may represent the temporary influence of a competitor's new product, changes in raw material prices, or unusual economic and government influences on a given firm. These changes are peculiar to an individual security or industry at a given point in time and are not directly correlated with the market. This second type of risk is referred to as *unsystematic* risk.

Recall that one type of risk is assumed to be compensated for under the capital asset pricing model, while another is not. The investor is presumed to receive a risk premium for the beta or systematic risk but not for unsystematic risk. Since the latter is associated with an individual company or industry, it may be diversified away in a large portfolio and is not a risk inherent in investing in common stocks. Thus, by picking stocks that are less than perfectly correlated, unsystematic risk may be eliminated. For example, the inherent risks of investing in semiconductor stocks may be diversified away by investing in the countercyclical housing stocks. Researchers have indicated that all but 15 percent of unsystematic risk may be eliminated with a carefully selected portfolio of 10 stocks and all but 11 percent with a portfolio of 20 stocks.[8]

$$\text{Total risk} = \text{Systematic risk} + \text{Unsystematic risk}$$

But unsystematic risk can be diversified away, so that systematic risk (b_i) is the only relevant risk under the capital asset pricing model for which the investor can expect to receive compensation.

Security market line

We actually express the trade-off between risk and return for an *individual stock* through the security market line (SML) in Figure 14–11. Whereas in Figure 14–10 we graphed the relationship that allowed us to compute the *beta* (b_i) for a security, in Figure 14–11, we now take that *beta* and show what the anticipated or required return in the marketplace is for a stock with that characteristic. The security market line (SML) is a generalized concept to show the risk-return trade-off for an individual stock just as the capital market line (CML) accomplished that same objective for a portfolio.

Once again, we stress that the return is not plotted against the total risk (σ)

---

[8] Wagner and Lau, "The Effect of Diversification on Risk."

Figure 14—11   **Illustration of the security market line**

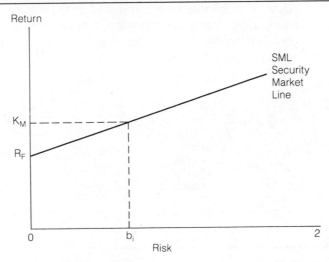

for the stock but only that part of the risk that can not be diversified away, commonly referred to as the systematic or beta risk. The actual formula for the security market line (SML) is:

$$K_i = R_F + b_i (K_M - R_F) \qquad (14-7)$$

The mathematical derivation of the formula is presented in Appendix 14—C. As was true of the capital market line for portfolio returns, with the security market line, we start out with a basic rate of return for a risk-free asset (R_F) and add a risk premium. In this case, the premium is equal to the beta on the stock times the difference between the market rate of return (K_M) and the risk-free rate of return (R_F). If $R_F = 6\%$, $K_M = 9\%$, and the stock has a beta (b_i) of 1, the anticipated rate of return, using Formula 14–7, would be the same as that in the market, or 9 percent.

$$K_i = 6\% + 1 (9\% - 6\%) = 6\% + 3\% = 9\%$$

Since the stock has the same degree of risk as the market in general, this would appear to be logical. If the stock has a beta of 1.5, the added systematic risk would call for a return of 10.5 percent, whereas a beta of .5 would indicate the return should be 7.5 percent.

$$\text{Beta} = 1.5$$

$$K_i = 6\% + 1.5 (9\% - 6\%) = 6\% + 1.5 (3\%) = 6\% + 4.5\% = 10.5\%$$

$$\text{Beta} = .5$$

$$K_i = 6\% + .5 (9\% - 6\%) = 6\% + .5 (3\%) = 6\% + 1.5\% = 7.5\%$$

Since the beta factor is deemed to be important in analyzing potential risk and return, there is much emphasis placed on knowing the beta for a given security. Merrill Lynch, Value Line, and other brokerage houses and investment services publish information on beta for various securities. A representative list is presented in the table below.

Corporation	Beta (December 1980)
Tandy Corp.	1.40
Digital Equipment	1.30
Eastman Kodak	1.15
Eli Lilly	1.05
Ford Motor	.90
Cincinnati Gas and Electric	.65

ASSUMPTIONS OF THE CAPITAL ASSET PRICING MODEL

Having evaluated some of the implications of the CAPM, it is important that the student be aware of some of the assumptions that go into the model.

1. All investors can borrow or lend an unlimited amount of funds at a given risk-free rate.
2. All investors have the same one-period time horizon.
3. All investors wish to maximize their expected utility over this time horizon and evaluate investments on the basis of means and standard deviations of portfolio returns.
4. All investors have the same expectations—that is to say, all investors estimate identical probability distributions for rates of return.
5. All assets are perfectly divisible—it is possible to buy fractional shares of any asset or portfolio.
6. There are no taxes or transactions costs.
7. The market is efficient and in equilibrium or quickly adjusting to equilibrium.

The purpose of listing these assumptions is to indicate some of the necessary conditions to create the CAPM. While at first they may appear to be severely limiting, they are similar to those often used in the standard economic theory of the firm and in other basic financial models.

The primary usefulness in examining this model or similar risk-return trade-off models is to provide some reasonable basis for relating return opportunity with risk on the investment. Portfolio managers find risk-return models helpful in explaining their performance or the performance of their competitors to clients. A competitor's portfolio that has unusually high returns may have been developed primarily on the basis of high-risk assets. To the extent that this can be explained on the basis of capital market theory, the competitor's performance may look less like superior money management and more like a product of high risk taking. As

we shall see in Chapter 15, "Measuring Risk and Returns of Portfolio Managers," many of the techniques for assessing portfolio performance on Wall Street are explicitly or implicitly related to the risk-return concepts discussed in this chapter.

Though empirical tests have somewhat supported the capital asset pricing model, a number of testing problems remain. In order to develop the SML in, which stock returns (vertical axis) can be measured against beta (horizontal axis), an appropriate line must be drawn. Researchers have some disagreement about R_F. (Is it represented by short-term or long-term Treasury rates?) There is also debate about what is the appropriate K_M, or market rate of return. Some suggest the market proxy variable will greatly influence beta and that difficulties in dealing with this problem can bring the whole process under attack.[9]

When empirical data is compared to theoretical return expectations, there is some discrepancy in that the theoretical SML may have a slightly greater slope than the actual line fitted on the basis on real-world data as shown in Figure 14–12.[10]

There may also be a possible problem in that betas for individual securities are not necessarily stable over time (rather than remaining relatively constant at 1.3 or perhaps .7, they tend to approach 1 over time). Thus, a beta based on past risk may not always reflect current risk.[11] Because the beta for a portfolio may be more stable than an individual stock's beta, portfolio betas are also used

Figure 14–12 | **Test of the security market line**

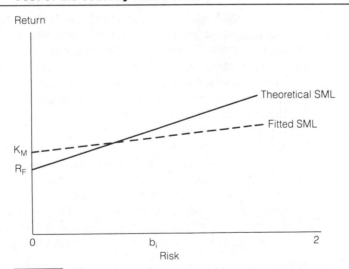

[9]Richard Roll, "A Critique of the Asset Pricing Theory's Test," *Journal of Financial Economics,* March 1977, pp. 129–76. Also, "Ambiguity When Performance is Measured by the Securities Market Line," *Journal of Finance,* September 1978, pp. 1051–69.

[10]Franco Modigliani and Gerald A. Pogue, "An Introduction to Risk and Returns," *Financial Analysts Journal,* March–April 1974, pp. 68–86, and May–June 1974, pp. 69–86.

as a systematic risk variable. A portfolio beta is simply the weighted average of the betas of the individual stocks. We can say:

$$b_P \text{ (portfolio beta)} = \Sigma X_i b_i \qquad (14-8)$$

and

$$K_P = R_F + b_P (K_M - R_F) \qquad (14-9)$$

By examining portfolio betas rather than individual stock betas, we overcome part of the criticism leveled at the instability of betas in the capital asset pricing model. Many of the other criticisms have also evoked new research that may provide different approaches or possible solutions to past deficiencies in the model.[12]

REVIEW OF CONCEPTS IN THE CHAPTER

The investor is basically risk averse and therefore will demand a premium for incremental risk. In an efficient market context, the ability to achieve high returns may be more directly related to absorption of additional risk than superior ability in selecting stocks (this remains a debatable point which proponents of fundamental and technical analysis would argue).

Risk for an individual stock is measured in terms of the standard deviation (σ_i) around a given expected value $(\overline{K}_i)$. The larger the standard deviation, the greater the risk. For a portfolio of stocks, the expected value (K_P) is the weighted average of the individual returns; but this is not true for the portfolio standard deviation (σ_P). The portfolio standard deviation is also influenced by the interaction between the stocks. To the extent the correlation coefficient (r_{ij}) is less than $+1$, there will be some reduction from the weighted average of the standard deviation of the individual stocks that we are combining. A negative correlation coefficient will provide substantial reduction in the portfolio standard deviation.

Under classic Markowitz portfolio theory, we look at a large array of possible portfolios in an attempt to construct an efficient frontier that represents the best possible risk-return trade-off at different levels of risk. Individuals then match their own risk-return indifference curves with the efficient frontier to determine where they should be along this optimal scale.

This was the prevailing theory until the capital asset pricing model (CAPM) was developed in the 1960s and 70s. The CAPM supersedes some of the findings of classic portfolio theory with the introduction of the risk-free asset (R_F) into the analysis. The assumption is that an individual can choose an investment

---

[11]Robert A. Levy, "On the Short-term Stationary of Beta Coefficients," *Financial Analysts Journal,* November–December 1971, pp. 55–62. Also Marshall E. Blume, "Beta and Their Regression Tendencies," *Journal of Finance,* June 1975, pp. 785–95.

[12]J. Fred Weston, "Developments in Financial Theory," *Financial Management,* 10th anniversary issue, 1981, pp. 5–22.

combining the return on the risk-free asset with the market rate of return, and this will provide superior returns to the efficient frontier at all points except M, where they are equal. The investor may invest in any combination of R_F and M to achieve the risk-return positions described by the capital market line in Figure 14–9.

The capital market line describes the general trade-off between risk and return for portfolio managers in the economy. Any attempt to get higher portfolio returns must be matched by higher portfolio risks. Although the portfolio manager is investing in stocks and bonds, the general pattern set out for the risk-free asset and market combination is perceived to establish the limits for investment performance of any nature. Any increase in portfolio returns (K_P) must be associated with an increase in the portfolio standard deviation (σ_P).

The capital asset pricing model also calls for an evaluation of individual assets (rather than portfolios). The security market line in Figure 14–11 shows the same type of risk-return trade-off for individual securities as the capital market line did for portfolios. Investors in individual assets are only assumed to be rewarded for systematic, market-related risk, known as the beta (b_i) risk. All other risk is assumed to be susceptible to diversification.

There are a number of assumptions associated with the capital asset pricing model that are subject to close review and challenge. Furthermore, there is some question about the appropriate measure for R_F and K_M as well as the stability of beta and the appropriate slope of the SML line. Nevertheless, the capital asset pricing model represents a generally useful device for portraying the relationship of risk and return in the capital markets over the long term.

IMPORTANT WORDS AND CONCEPTS	Risk Expected value Dispersion Standard deviation Portfolio effect Correlation coefficient Efficient portfolio Efficient frontier	Capital asset pricing model (CAPM) Capital market line (CML) Beta coefficient Systematic risk Unsystematic risk Security market line (SML)

QUESTIONS AND PROBLEMS

1. Define risk.

2. How is risk measured?

3. What is an expected value?

4. What is the most commonly used measure of dispersion?

5. An investment has the following range of outcomes and probabilities.

Outcomes (percent)	Probability of outcome
6%	.20
9	.60
12	.20

    Calculate the expected value and the standard deviation (round to two places after the decimal point where necessary).

6. Given another investment with an expected value of 12 percent and a standard deviation of 2.2 percent that is countercyclical to the investment in problem 5, what is the expected value of the portfolio and its standard deviation if both are combined into a portfolio with 40 percent invested in the first investment and 60 percent in the second? Assume the correlation coefficient (r_{ij}) is $-.40$.

7. What would be the portfolio standard deviation if the two investments in the previous problem had a correlation coefficient (r_{ij}) of $+.40$?

8. Over what range can the correlation coefficient (r_{ij}) fall?

9. What is the efficient frontier?

10. What does the steepness of the slope at the risk-return indifference curve indicate?

11. Describe the optimum portfolio for an investor in terms of indifference curves and the efficient frontier.

12. In examining the capital market line as part of the capital asset pricing model, in order to increase portfolio return (K_p), what other variable must you increase?

13. Using the formula for the capital market line (Formula 14–5), if the risk free rate (R_F) is 8 percent, the market rate of return (M_K) is 12 percent, the market standard deviation (σ_M) is 10 percent, and the standard deviation of the portfolio (σ_P) is 12 percent, compute the anticipated return (K_P).

14. For an individual security, if a stock has a beta of 1.2, what does this indicate?

15. In terms of the capital asset pricing model:
    a. Indicate the two types of risks associated with an individual security.
    b. Which of these two is the beta risk?
    c. What risk is assumed not to be compensated for in the marketplace under the capital asset pricing model and why?

16. What does the security market line indicate? In general terms, how is it different from the capital market line?

17. Using the formula for the security market line (Formula 14–7), if the risk-free rate (R_F) is 8 percent, the beta (b_i) is 1.4, and the market rate of return (K_M) is 12 percent, compute the anticipated rate of return (K_i).

18. If another security had a lower beta than indicated in question 17, would K_I be lower or higher? What is the logic behind your answer in terms of risk?

19. In regard to the capital asset pricing model, comment on disagreements or debates related to R_F (the risk-free rate) and K_M (market rate of return).

20. Are betas of individual stocks necessarily stable (constant) over time? What about portfolio betas?

SELECTED REFERENCES

Baker, H. Kent; Michael B. Hargrove; and John A. Haslem. "An Empirical Analysis of the Risk-Return Preferences of Individual Investors." *Journal of Financial and Quantitative Analysis*, September 1977, pp. 377–89.

Black, Fischer. "Capital Market Equilibrium with Restricted Borrowing." *Journal of Business*, July 1972, pp. 444–54.

Blume, Marshall E. "Betas and Their Regression Tendencies." *Journal of Finance*, June 1975, pp. 785–95.

————. "Betas and Their Regression Tendencies: Some Further Evidence." *Journal of Finance*, March 1979, pp. 265–67.

Blume, Marshall E., and Irwin Friend. "The Asset Structure of Individual Portfolios and Some Implications for Utility Functions." *Journal of Finance*, May 1975, pp. 585–603.

Elgers, Pieter T.; James R. Haltiner; and William H. Hawthorne. "Beta Regression Tendencies: Statistical and Real Causes." *Journal of Finance*, March 1979, pp. 261–63.

Elton, Edwin J.; Martin J. Gruber; and Thomas J. Ulrich. "Are Betas Best?" *Journal of Finance*, December 1978, pp. 1375–84.

Fabozzi, Frank J., and Jack Clark Francis. "Stability Tests for Alphas and Betas over Bull and Bear Market Conditions." *Journal of Finance*, September 1977, pp. 1093–99.

Friend, Irwin; Randloph Westerfield; and Michael Granito. "New Evidence on the Capital Asset Pricing Model." *Journal of Finance*, June 1978, pp. 903–17.

Hill, Joanne M. "Reducing Forecast Error in Portfolio Management: Sample Clustering and Alternative Risk Specifications." *Financial Management*, Winter 1980, pp. 42–50.

Jensen, Michael C., ed. *Studies in the Theory of Capital Markets*. New York: Praeger Publishers, 1972.

Levy, Robert A. "On the Short-Term Stationarity of Beta Coefficients." *Financial Analysts Journal*, November–December 1971, pp. 55–62.

Linter, John. "The Evaluation of Risk Assets and the Selection of Risky Investments in Stock Portfolios and Capital Budgets." *Review of Economics and Statistics*, February 1965, pp. 13–37.

Martin, John D., and Arthur Keown. "A Misleading Feature of Beta for Risk Measurement." *Journal of Portfolio Management*, Summer 1977, pp. 31–34.

Markowitz, Harry H. "Portfolio Selection." *Journal of Finance,* March 1952, pp. 77–91.

————. *Portfolio Selection: Efficient Diversification of Investments.* New York: John Wiley & Sons, 1959.

Modigliani, Franco, and Gerald A. Pogue "An Introduction to Risk and Returns." *Financial Analysts Journal,* March–April 1974, pp. 68–80, and May–June 1974, pp. 69–86.

Roll, Richard. "Ambiguity When Performance is Measured by the Securities Market Line." *Journal of Finance,* September 1978, pp. 1051–70.

————. "A Critique of the Asset Pricing Theory's Test." *Journal of Financial Economics,* March 1977, pp. 129–76.

Ross, Stephen A. "The Current Status of the Capital Asset Pricing Model." *Journal of Finance,* June 1978, pp. 885–901.

Sharpe, William F. "A Simplified Model for Portfolio Analysis." *Management Science,* January 1963, pp. 277–93.

————. "Capital Asset Prices: A Theory of Market Equilibrium under Conditions of Risk." *Journal of Finance,* September 1964, pp. 425–42.

————. "Bonds versus Stocks: Some Lessons from Capital Market Theory." *Financial Analysis Journal,* November–December 1973, pp. 74–80.

Wagner, W. H., and S. C. Lau. "The Effect of Diversification on Risk." *Financial Analysts Journal,* November–December 1971, pp. 48–53.

Weston, J. Fred. "Investment Decisions Using the Capital Asset Pricing Model." *Financial Management,* Spring 1973, pp. 25–33.

————. "Developments in Financial Theory." *Financial Management,* 10th anniversary issue, 1981, pp. 5–22.

Yawitz, Jess B.; George H. Hempel; and William J. Marshall. "A Risk-Return Approach to the Selection of Optimal Government Bond Portfolios." *Financial Management,* Autumn 1976, pp. 36–47.

APPENDIX 14–A—THE CORRELATION COEFFICIENT

There are a number of formulas for the correlation coefficient. We shall use the statement:

$$r_{ij} = \frac{\text{cov}_{ij}}{\sigma_i \sigma_j} \qquad (14A-1)$$

Cov$_{ij}$ (covariance) is an *absolute* measure of the extent to which two sets of variables move together over time. Once we have determined this value, we simply divide by $\sigma_i \sigma_j$ to get a relative measure of correlation (r_{ij}).

The formula for the covariance is:

$$\text{cov}_{ij} = \Sigma (K - \overline{K}_i)\,(K - \overline{K}_j)\,P \qquad (14A-2)$$

We take our K and P values from investment i and investment j in Chapter 14 to compute the following:

K	$\overline{K}_i$	$(K - \overline{K}_i)$	K	$\overline{K}_j$	$(K - \overline{K}_j)$	$(K - \overline{K}_i)(K - \overline{K}_j)$	P	$(K - \overline{K}_i)(K - \overline{K}_j)P$
5%	10%	−5%	20%	10%	+10%	−50%	.20	−10.0%
7	10	−3	8	10	−2	+6	.30	+1.8
13	10	+3	8	10	−2	−6	.30	−1.8
15	10	+5	6	10	−4	−20	.20	−4.0
								−14.0%

$$\text{cov}_{ij} = \Sigma(K - \overline{K}_i)(K - \overline{K}_j)P = -14.0\%$$

Using the values in the chapter for σ_i and σ_j, we determine:

$$r_{ij} = \frac{\text{cov}_{ij}}{\sigma_i\sigma_j} = \frac{-14.0}{(3.9)(3.1)} = \frac{-14.0}{19.9} = -.70$$

APPENDIX 14–B—LEAST SQUARES REGRESSION ANALYSIS

We shall show how least squares regression analysis can be used to develop a linear equation to explain the relationship between the return on a stock and return in the market.

We will develop the terms in the expression:

$$K_i = a_i + b_iK_M + e_i$$

(e_i is the random error term and will not be quantified in our analysis).

Using the data from the chapter,

	K	K_M
1978	4.8%	6.5%
1979	14.5	11.8
1980	19.1	14.9
1981	3.7	1.1
1982	15.6	12.0

The normal or mathematical equation to solve for b_i is:

$$b_i = \frac{N\Sigma KK_M - \Sigma K\Sigma K_M}{N\Sigma K_M^2 - (\Sigma K_M)^2} \qquad (14B-1)$$

For a_i, we use the following formula (which is dependent on prior determination of b_i).

$$a_i = \frac{\Sigma K - b_i\Sigma K_M}{N} \qquad (14B-2)$$

We compute four columns of data and plug the value into our formulas.

K	K_M	KK_M	$K_M{}^2$
4.8	6.5	31.20	42.25
14.5	11.8	171.10	139.24
19.1	14.9	284.59	222.01
3.7	1.1	4.07	1.21
15.6	12.0	187.20	144.00
$\Sigma K = 57.7$	$\Sigma K_M = 46.3$	$\Sigma K K_M = 678.16$	$\Sigma K_M{}^2 = 548.71$

Also N (number of observations) $= 5$.

$$b_i = \frac{N\Sigma K K_M - \Sigma K \Sigma K_M}{N\Sigma K_M{}^2 - (\Sigma K_M)^2}$$

$$b_i = \frac{5(678.16) - 57.7(46.3)}{5(548.71) - (46.3)^2}$$

$$= \frac{3390.80 - 2671.51}{2743.55 - 2143.69} = \frac{719.29}{599.86} = 1.20$$

Using our beta value, we now compute alpha:

$$a_i = \frac{\Sigma K - b_i \Sigma K_M}{N}$$

$$a_i = \frac{57.7 - 1.2(46.3)}{5}$$

$$= \frac{57.7 - 55.6}{5} = \frac{2.1}{5} = .42$$

In summary:

$$K_i = a_i + b_i K_M$$

$$K_i = .42 + 1.20\, K_M$$

APPENDIX 14–C —DERIVATION OF THE SECURITY MARKET LINE (SML)

First of all, we graph the SML based on covariance (Figure 14C–1).[13]

Along the vertical axis, we show return and along the horizontal axis, covariance of return with the market.[14] We can describe our equation for the SML in terms of the slope of the line.

---

[13]The concept of covariance is described in Appendix 14–A.

[14]Actually, $\sigma_M{}^2$ represents the covariance of the market with the market (a bit redundant). The cov_{MM} equals $\sigma_M{}^2$. The covariance of a variable with itself is equal to the variance.

Figure 14C–1   **Derivation of the SML**

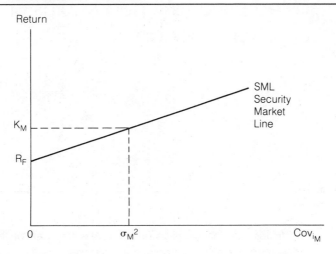

$$K_i = R_F + \frac{(K_M - R_F)}{(\sigma_M^2 - 0)}\, cov_{iM} \qquad\qquad (14C–1)$$

We then rearrange our terms:

$$K_i = R_F + \left[\frac{cov_{iM}}{\sigma_M^2}\right](K_M - R_F) \qquad\qquad (14C–2)$$

The systematic risk of an individual asset is measured by its covariance with the market (cov_{iM}). We can convert this to a relative measure by dividing through by the market variance (σ_M^2). The *relative* systematic movement of an individual asset with the market is referred to as the beta regression coefficient. Thus, we show in Formula 14C–3.

$$b_i = \frac{cov_{iM}}{\sigma_M^2} \qquad\qquad (14C–3)$$

Plugging this in to equal Formula 14C–2, we show:

$$K_i = R_F + b_i\,(K_M - R_F) \qquad\qquad (14C–4)$$

15 Measuring risks and returns of portfolio managers

In the bull market days of the 1950s and part of the 1960s, many portfolio managers turned in performances that were vastly superior to the market averages. These high returns were often achieved by taking larger than normal risks through investing in small, growth companies or concentrating in a limited number of high-return industries. These portfolio managers or their representatives proclaimed their superior ability in managing money and often extrapolated past returns into the future to indicate the potential returns to the investor. A typical statement might be: "The Rapid Growth Fund has earned 20 percent per year over the past 10 years. The investor who places his or her funds with us has the possible opportunity to see the funds grow from a $100 investment today to $672.70 in 10 years at this historical growth rate of 20 percent." There was very little attempt to relate rate of return directly to risk exposure or to provide caveats about the likelihood of replicating past performance. In terms of generating returns, people were simply superior money managers or they were not.

Nevertheless, with the end of the bull market era of the 1960s, a new mentality developed. Many of the gunslinging super performers of the past were the worst performers in a bear market. It could be reasonably inferred that their high returns of the past were not so much a function of clairvoyance or unusual insight, but rather the utilization of unusually high risk. Actually, some portfolio managers began to welcome the notion of risk-adjusted returns. A mutual fund manager or bank trust department head could rationally explain to a client, "although a competitor had a 2 percent higher return, it was actually inferior to our performance on a risk-adjusted basis."

In this chapter, we will examine actual studies of risk-return performance for professional money managers. We will evaluate the setting of objectives, the achievement of efficient diversification, and the measurement of return related to risk. In some of this discussion, we will relate back to the capital asset pricing model developed in Chapter 14.

Though the majority of comments in this chapter relate to mutual funds, there

are many other important participants among professional money managers. These include pension funds, life insurance companies, property and casualty insurance companies, and endowments and foundations. These institutional investors are examined in a later section of this chapter, particularly in light of earlier comments on risk-return characteristics.

STATED OBJECTIVES AND RISK

A first question to be posed to a mutual fund manager is, Have you followed the basic objectives that were established? These objectives might call for maximum capital gains, a combination of growth plus income, or simply income (with many variations in between). The objectives should be set with an eye toward the capabilities of the money managers and the financial needs of the investors. The best way to measure adherence to these objectives is to evaluate the risk exposure that the fund manager has accepted. Anyone who aspires to maximize capital gains must, by nature, absorb more risk. An income-oriented fund should have a minimum risk exposure.

A study by John McDonald published in the *Journal of Financial and Quantitative Analysis* indicates that mutual fund managers generally follow the objectives they initially set out. As indicated in Figure 15–1, he measured the betas and standard deviations for 123 mutual funds and compared these to the funds' stated objectives. In panel a, we see the fund's beta dimension along the horizontal axis and the fund's stated objective along the vertical axis. Inside the panel, we see the association between the two. For example, funds with an objective of maximum capital gains had an average beta of 1.22, those with a growth objective had an average beta of 1.01, and so on all the way down to an average beta of .55 for income-oriented funds. In panel b of Figure 15–1, a similar approach was used to compare the fund's objective to the portfolio standard deviation.

In both cases of using betas and portfolio standard deviations, we see that the risk absorption was carefully tailored to the fund's stated objectives. Funds with aggressive capital gains and growth objectives had high betas and portfolio standard deviations, while the opposite was true of balanced and income-oriented funds.

Adherence to objectives as measured by risk exposure is important in evaluating a fund manager because risk is one of the variables a money manager can directly control. While short-run return performance can be greatly influenced by unpredictable changes in the economy, the fund manager has almost total control in setting the risk level. He can be held accountable for doing what was specified or promised in regard to risk. Most lawsuits brought against money managers are not for inferior profit performance but for failure to adhere to stated risk objectives. Though it may be appropriate to shift the risk level in anticipation of changing market conditions (lower the beta at a perceived peak in the market), long-run adherence to risk objectives is advisable.

Figure 15–1 **Risk and fund objectives for 123 mutual funds, 1960–1969**

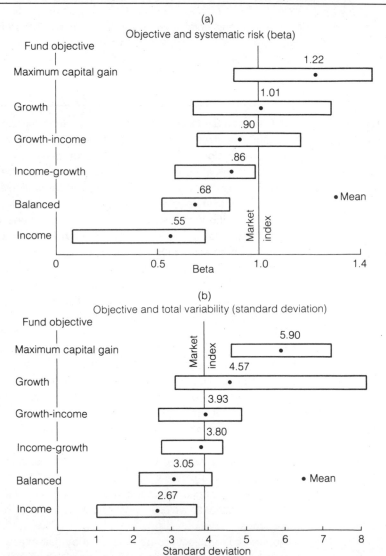

(a)
Objective and systematic risk (beta)

Fund objective

Maximum capital gain — 1.22

Growth — 1.01

Growth-income — .90

Income-growth — .86

Balanced — .68

Income — .55

Market index

• Mean

0   0.5   1.0   1.4
Beta

(b)
Objective and total variability (standard deviation)

Fund objective

Maximum capital gain — 5.90

Growth — 4.57

Growth-income — 3.93

Income-growth — 3.80

Balanced — 3.05

Income — 2.67

Market index

• Mean

1   2   3   4   5   6   7   8
Standard deviation

SOURCE: John G. McDonald, "Objectives and Performance of Mutual Funds, 1960–1969," *Journal of Financial and Quantitative Analysis*, June 1974, p. 316.

MEASUREMENT OF RETURN IN RELATION TO RISK

In examining the performance of fund managers, the return measure commonly used is "excess returns." Though excess returns has many definitions, one often used is total return (capital appreciation plus dividends) minus the return on Treasury bills. Thus, a fund that earns 12 percent when the Treasury bill

rate is 6 percent has excess returns of 6 percent. Excess returns are then compared to risk. Early studies compared excess returns to units of risk by developing a ratio of excess returns to the portfolio beta or standard deviation.[1]

Market line

    With the development of the capital asset pricing model, the use of the "market line" became a more popular approach. In terms of evaluating portfolios, excess returns are shown on the vertical axis, the portfolio beta is shown on the horizontal axis, and the market line describes the relationship between the two as indicated in Figure 15–2. This presentation is very similar to the security market line shown for individual stocks and betas in Chapter 14, only now the interest is in a portfolio of stocks rather than an individual security.[2] Also, we are dealing with excess returns rather than actual returns, though the basic principles are the same.

    In Figure 15–2, the market line connects risk-free excess returns of 0 with market excess returns of 3 percent. In the present case, we will assume the Treasury bill rate is 6 percent and the return on the Standard & Poor's 500 Stock

Figure 15–2   **Risk-adjusted portfolio returns**

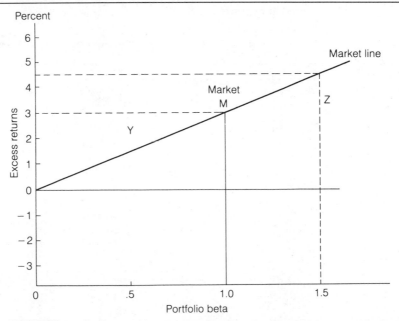

[1]William F. Sharpe, "Mutual Fund Performance," *Journal of Business,* January 1966, pp. 119–38, and Jack L. Treynor, "How to Rate Management of Investment Funds," *Harvard Business Review,* January–February 1965, pp. 63–74.

[2]If risk were measured in terms of the portfolio standard deviation instead of the portfolio beta, we could use the CML in Chapter 15.

Average is 9 percent, thus proving market excess returns of 3 percent. Based on Figure 15–2, we say that a portfolio manager with a 0 beta portfolio (riskless) should expect no excess returns; while a beta of 1 should provide excess returns of 3 percent, and a beta of 1.5, excess returns of 4.5 percent.

Adequacy of performance

Using this approach, the adequacy of a portfolio manager's performance can be judged against the market line. While it would appear that portfolio manager y in Figure 15–2 had inferior excess returns in comparison to portfolio manager z (2.1 percent versus 3.9 percent), this notion is quickly dispelled when one considers risk. Actually, portfolio manager y performed above risk-return expectations as indicated by the market line, while portfolio manager z was below his risk-adjusted expected level. The vertical difference from a fund's performance point to the market line can be viewed as a measure of performance. This value, termed *alpha* or *average differential return,* indicates the difference between the return on the fund and a point on the market line that corresponds to a beta equal to the fund. In the case of fund z, the beta of 1.5 indicated an excess return of 4.5 percent along the market line, and the actual excess return was only 3.9 percent. We thus have a negative alpha of .6 percent (3.9% − 4.5%). Clearly, a positive alpha indicates a superior performance, while a negative alpha leads to the opposite conclusion.

Figure 15–3   **Empirical study of risk-adjusted portfolio returns—systematic risk and return**

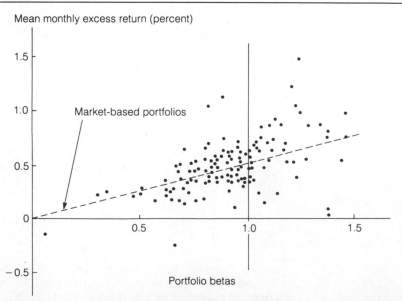

SOURCE: John G. McDonald, "Objectives and Performance of Mutual Funds, 1960–1969," *Journal of Financial and Quantitative Analysis,* June 1974, p. 321.

A key question for portfolio managers in general is, Can they consistently perform at positive alpha levels? Can they generate returns better than those that are available along the market line and which are theoretically available to anyone? The results of a study conducted by John McDonald on 123 mutual funds are presented in Figure 15–3.

The upward-sloping dotted line is the market line or anticipated level of performance based on risk. The small dots represent performance of the funds. About as many funds underperformed (negative alpha below the line) as overperformed (positive alpha above the line). Although a few high-beta funds had an unusually strong performance on a risk-adjusted basis, there is no consistent pattern of superior performance. Note in this case that the excess returns are presented on a monthly basis and must be multiplied by 12 to get annualized excess returns.

Other studies

There are many other studies of a similar nature. In Figure 15–4, we see the results of a landmark study by Michael Jensen in which he computed the alpha

Figure 15–4   **Frequency distribution of estimated alphas**

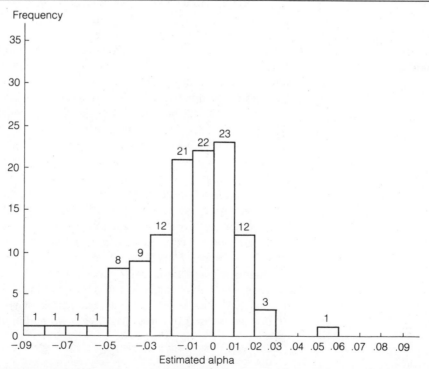

SOURCE: Michael C. Jensen, "The Performance of Mutual Funds in the Period 1945–1964," *Journal of Finance*, May 1968, p. 404.

values of 115 mutual funds between 1945 and 1964. The average alpha value was −1.1 percent per year, and only 39 out of 115 funds had a positive alpha.

A number of other important studies have been conducted by the Securities and Exchange Commission, Merrill Lynch, and various professors throughout the country (Friend, Blume, Marshall, Crockett, Gentry, Schlarbaum, Williamson, etc.).[3] Although they worked with different data bases over varying time periods, their general results were similar. Professional money managers have generally not outperformed the market over the long term on a risk-adjusted basis.

Transaction costs

One frequently cited reason for no better than average performance over the long term is the potentially high transaction costs associated with fund management. A study by the Securities and Exchange Commission indicated that fund performance could not be positively correlated with the size of the fund, the method of selling the fund (load or no-load), or size of assets managed. However, performance was negatively correlated with rate of portfolio turnover. On average, a 10 percent increase in portfolio turnover was associated with a .3 percent to .6 percent reduction in net performance per year.[4] Although some portfolio managers thought they were improving their returns by active trading, in most instances, this was simply not the case.

Performance reviews

Each year *Forbes* magazine publishes a list of mutual funds and their average returns over a 10 to 15-year period as well as in the last 12 months. An excerpt from this survey is presented in Table 15–1.

In examining the *Forbes* data, the reader may also compare the fund's performance to the Standard & Poor's 500 Stock Average and the *Forbes* Stock Fund Composite Average as well as other averages. On the left-hand margin are listed performance ratings for the funds in up and down markets. For example, American General Pace Fund is shown as having an A+ rating in an up market and a C rating in a down market. In terms of grading, the top 12.5 percent get an A+; the next 12.5 percent, an A; the next 25 percent, a B; and so on. The *Forbes* survey comes out in August of each year.

Wiesenberger Investment Companies Service also provides excellent information on mutual funds as indicated by the excerpt in Table 15–2 for the T. Rowe Price Growth Stock Fund. In the section on statistical history, we see the total assets managed and other important data. In the box inside the table we see what would have happened to a $10,000 investment in the T. Rowe Price Growth Stock Fund over a 10-year time period. While the original investment of $10,000 would have grown to $13,062, if we add in shares accepted as capital

---

[3]Complete citations for these sources are presented under selected references at the end of this chapter.

[4]*Institutional Investor Study Report of the Securities and Exchange Commission* (Washington, D.C.: U.S. Government Printing Office, 1971).

Table 15–1 Forbes mutual fund performance review

1981 Fund Ratings

Performance in UP markets	Performance in DOWN markets		Average annual total return 1968-81	Latest 12 months return from capital growth	Latest 12 months return from income dividends	Total assets 6/30/81 (millions)	Total assets % change '81 vs. '80	Maximum sales charge	Annual expenses per $100
		Standard & Poor's 500 stock average	5.7%	14.9%	4.9%				
		FORBES stock fund composite	5.8%	25.2%	3.4%				
		FORBES balanced fund composite	4.7%	3.0%	8.3%				
		FORBES bond and preferred stock fund composite	3.6%	–13.4%	12.5%				
		Stock funds (load) *Group averages*	5.6%	24.6%	3.7%				
D	D	Affiliated Fund	7.5%	14.8%	6.2%	$1,736.5	10.5	7.25%	$0.38
A	B	AMCAP Fund	10.0	26.3	3.8	254.1	91.2	8.50	0.80
•C	•A	American Birthright Trust	—*	14.8	none	129.7	77.2	8.50	1.32
B	B	American General Comstock Fund[1]	10.0	33.0	4.3	179.5	39.7	8.50	0.90
B	F	American General Enterprise Fund	4.2	44.2	1.0	605.0	20.9	8.50	0.75
— A+	•C	American General Pace Fund[2]	—*	51.7	2.7	59.6	210.4	8.50	1.05
•B	•C	American General Venture Fund	—*	34.5	2.9	60.4	205.1	8.50	1.12
C	A	American Growth Fund	8.4	14.8	5.1	28.2	26.5	7.25	1.49
C	B	American Insurance & Industrial Fund	9.6	13.1	6.3	15.1	5.6	8.50	1.00
D	•D	American Leaders Fund	—*	9.1	7.9	48.1	0.4	6.50	1.37
D	B	American Mutual Fund	9.1	22.7	4.7	508.0	30.5	8.50	0.54
C	C	American National Growth Fund	8.0	23.0	4.3	57.7	41.4	8.50	0.79
D	F	Anchor Growth Fund	0.1	23.9	4.4	139.0	7.3	8.50	0.65
D	C	Axe-Houghton Stock Fund	4.4	25.2	1.4	122.4	64.7	8.50	0.88
B	•D	BLC Growth Fund	—*	37.0	2.3	14.6	40.4	8.50	1.04
D	•B	BLC Income Fund	—*	25.3	5.2	16.4	32.3	8.50	0.94
C	C	Broad Street Investing Corp	7.9	20.3	4.8	377.0	17.1	7.25	0.45
C	D	Bullock Fund	6.4	17.5	4.0	140.4	5.5	8.50	0.78
C	D	The Cardinal Fund	4.5	16.2	4.0	13.5	4.7	8.50	0.93
C	D	Century Shares Trust	6.5	16.9	4.6	71.9	10.8	7.25	0.99
B	F	CG Fund	5.7	23.4	3.9	152.2	28.8	7.50	0.68
A+	A	Charter Fund	13.5	26.2	3.1	40.6	60.5	8.50	1.35
B	C	Chemical Fund	6.2	21.2	3.0	1,032.6	20.0	8.50	0.62
B	F	Colonial Growth Shares	2.8	24.5	2.1	67.0	11.1	8.50	1.18
C	F	Common Stock Fund State Bond & Mortgage Co	3.1	17.3	3.2	33.8	5.3	8.50	1.15
D	D	Commonwealth Fund Indenture Trust Plans A & B	2.8	5.5	7.8	10.2	–5.6	7.50	0.40
D	C	Commonwealth Fund Indenture of Trust Plan C	4.2	6.5	6.5	35.4	0.6	7.50	0.75
D	D	Composite Fund	4.8	24.6	3.8	26.0	21.5	7.00	0.91
C	C	Corporate Leaders Tr Fund Certificates, Series "B"	6.7	14.8	6.3	49.6	7.1	†	0.10
C	D	Country Capital Growth Fund	3.7	26.0	2.7	47.0	16.3	7.50	0.85
D	C	Decatur Income Fund	8.4	13.6	6.3	376.3	29.5	8.50	0.69
D	D	Delaware Fund	6.0	25.5	4.1	255.9	7.8	8.50	0.77
D	D	Delta Trend Fund	2.2	46.9	2.7	10.3	27.2	8.50	1.60
D	C	Diversified Fund of State Bond and Mtge Co	6.1	12.7	4.9	7.4	17.5	8.50	1.00
D	C	Dividend Shares	5.1	11.0	5.4	251.8	1.7	8.50	0.80
C	C	The Dreyfus Fund	6.4	26.8	3.9	1,752.2	15.9	8.50	0.74
B	•C	The Dreyfus Leverage Fund	—*	9.4	4.4	322.4	1.9	8.50	1.00
		Eaton & Howard Funds							
A	F	Growth	4.2	41.3	1.0	36.5	21.7	7.25	0.95
D	F	Stock	1.1	7.2	4.7	73.2	–5.6	7.25	0.67
A+	F	Fairfield Fund	3.2	48.3	0.6	32.8	36.7	8.50	1.13
•B	•B	Fidelity Destiny Fund	—*	33.4	2.9	233.1	48.0	‡	0.75
A+	D	Fidelity Magellan Fund[3]	13.0	67.9	2.7	104.4	161.7	2.00	1.23
C	•F	First Investors Discovery Fund	—*	48.2	0.3	6.0	42.9	8.50	1.50
A	F	First Investors Fund for Growth	3.7	31.3	2.2	69.9	16.3	8.50	1.01
D	C	First Investors Natural Resources Fund[4]	2.5	–4.8	10.0	11.1	–9.0	8.50	1.30
D	B	First Investors Option Fund	3.4	14.3	4.7	81.8	97.1	7.25	1.10
C	C	Founders Mutual Fund	4.5	16.3	4.5	132.8	5.1	4.00	0.52

• Fund rated for two periods only; maximum allowable rating A. *Fund not in operation for full period. †Fund not currently selling new shares; existing shares traded over-the-counter. ‡ Available only through contractual plan. [1]Formerly Comstock Fund. [2]Formerly Pace Fund. [3]Formerly Magellan Fund. [4]Formerly First Investors Fund.

SOURCE: "1981 Fund Ratings," *Forbes*, August 31, 1981, p. 64.

Table 15–2   T. Rowe Price Growth Stock Fund

Statistical History

	Total Net Assets ($)	Number of Share- holders	Net Asset Value Per Share ($)	Yield (%)	Cash & Equiv- alent	Bonds & Pre- ferreds	Com- mon Stocks	Income Div- idends ($)	Capital Gains Distribu- tion ($)	Expense Ratio (%)	Offering Price ($) High	Low
Year						— % of Assets in —						
1980	1,133,745,871	105,748	15.08	2.8	11	—	89	0.419	—	0.49	15.58	10.39
1979	942,946,894	116,794	12.02	2.8	5	—	95	0.331	—	0.51	12.33	10.43
1978	974,832,394	138,034	11.12	2.5	4	—	96	0.277	—	0.52	12.64	9.24
1977	986,066,265	159,140	10.25	2.2	2	—	98	0.226	—	0.51	11.23	9.46
1976	1,174,928,903	179,108	11.26	2.1	3	—	97	0.231	—	0.51	11.68	10.26
1975	1,112,897,758	196,103	10.19	1.3	6	1*	93	0.129	—	0.53	11.21	7.73
1974	797,177,531	197,742	7.65	2.7	12	—	88	0.215	0.23	0.55	12.05	6.87
1973	1,121,029,445	198,438	11.91	1.1	9	1	90	0.14	0.54	0.51	16.81	11.19
1972	1,370,912,433	181,236	16.66	0.7	6	1*	93	0.12	0.32	0.49	17.22	14.55
1971	1,000,368,709	147,660	14.81	1.0	5	3*	92	0.15	0.20	0.53	14.94	11.41

* Includes a substantial proportion of convertible issues.   Note: Figures adjusted for 2-for-1 split effective May 1, 1973.

Directors: E. Kirkbride Miller, Chmn.; Robert E. Hall, Pres.; Cornelius C. Bond, Jr.; Richard W. Case; Donald W. Dick; James E. Halbkat, Jr.; Albert Keidel, Jr.; John K. Major; D. Reid Weedon, Jr.

Investment Adviser: T. Rowe Price Associates, Inc. Compensation to the Adviser is ½ of 1% annually of first $50 million of average net assets; 4/10 of 1% of next $100 million; 35/100 of 1% of the next $850 million, and 3/10 of 1% on asets in excess of $1 billion, payable quarterly.

Custodian and Transfer Agent: State Street Bank and Trust Co., Boston, MA 02107.

Distributor: None. Shares are sold directly by the fund.

Sales Charge: None. Shares are issued at net asset value. Minimum initial investment is $500. Minimum subsequent investment is $50.

Dividends: Income dividends are paid annually in January. Capital gains, if any, are paid in January.

Shareholder Reports: Issued quarterly. Fiscal year ends December 31. The 1980 prospectus was effective in May.

Qualified for Sale: In all states, DC and PR.

Address: 100 East Pratt St., Baltimore, MD 21202.

Telephone: (301) 547-2308. Toll Free: (800) 638-5660.

An assumed investment of $10,000 in this fund, with capital gains accepted in shares and income dividends reinvested, is illustrated below. The explanation on Page 155 must be read in conjunction with this illustration.

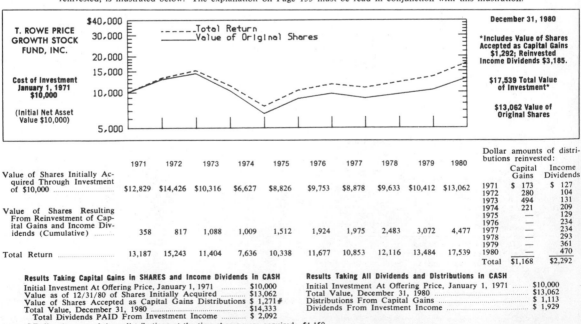

	1971	1972	1973	1974	1975	1976	1977	1978	1979	1980
Value of Shares Initially Acquired Through Investment of $10,000	$12,829	$14,426	$10,316	$6,627	$8,826	$9,753	$8,878	$9,633	$10,412	$13,062
Value of Shares Resulting From Reinvestment of Capital Gains and Income Dividends (Cumulative)	358	817	1,088	1,009	1,512	1,924	1,975	2,483	3,072	4,477
Total Return	13,187	15,243	11,404	7,636	10,338	11,677	10,853	12,116	13,484	17,539

Dollar amounts of distributions reinvested:

	Capital Gains	Income Dividends
1971	$ 173	$ 127
1972	280	104
1973	494	131
1974	221	209
1975	—	129
1976	—	234
1977	—	234
1978	—	293
1979	—	361
1980	—	470
Total	$1,168	$2,292

Results Taking Capital Gains in SHARES and Income Dividends in CASH

Initial Investment At Offering Price, January 1, 1971 .... $10,000
Value as of 12/31/80 of Shares Initially Acquired $13,062
Value of Shares Accepted as Capital Gains Distributions $ 1,271#
Total Value, December 31, 1980 .... $14,333
    Total Dividends PAID From Investment Income .... $ 2,092

Dollar Amount of these distributions at the time shares were acquired: $1,150

Results Taking All Dividends and Distributions in CASH

Initial Investment At Offering Price, January 1, 1971 .... $10,000
Total Value, December 31, 1980 .... $13,062
Distributions From Capital Gains .... $ 1,113
Dividends From Investment Income .... $ 1,929

gains and reinvested dividend income, the total is $17,539. The Wiesenberger survey book comes out annually and covers virtually every mutual fund.

Past performance and future performance

Even with this wealth of data available to investors, a key question that must be considered is How well does past performance indicate future performance? Will a fund that has provided high positive alphas or A's on the *Forbes* scale necessarily do the same in the future? Will a fund that has the most impressive record in the Wiesenberger survey necessarily do the best in the future?

Substantial research by the SEC and Professor Jensen found that this is not necessarily the case. In Table 15–3, we see results from the Jensen study of 115 mutual funds from 1955 through 1964.

In the left-hand column of Table 15–3, we see the number of years that selected funds beat a passive (unmanaged) portfolio with equal market risk, and in the right-hand column, we see the percent of those funds that beat the same measure in the next year. Even for funds with good prior year's performance, the odds on beating the control group in the next year was not particularly high.

Though past performance does not offer significant promise for the future, historical perspective does take on some importance. Clearly, you would not wish to buy a fund that has had consistently negative alphas or performance below the norm measured on some other basis. They may be overtrading the portfolio or inefficiently diversifying. By the same token, you should be most hesitant about paying any kind of premium sales commission or high management fee purely on the basis of a fund's strong past performance, which may or may not be replicated in the future. A good rule to follow is to go for the best past performance but pay no extra premium for it. This is often possible because money managers with prior success may have large asset bases and low percentage management fees.

Diversification

An important service that a money manager can provide is effective diversification of asset holdings. Once we at least partially accept the fact that superior

Table 15–3

Relating past and future performance

Number of consecutive years funds' performance exceeded that of a passive portfolio with similar risk	Percentage of group with performance exceeding that of a passive portfolio with similar market risk in the next year
1	50.4%
2	52.0
3	53.4
4	55.8
5	46.4
6	35.3
7	25.0

SOURCE: Michael C. Jensen, "Risk, Capital Assets, and Evaluation of Portfolios," *The Journal of Business*, April 1969, p. 239.

performance on a risk-adjusted basis is a difficult achievement, we begin to look hard at other attributes that money managers may possess. We can ask, Are mutual fund managers effective diversifiers of their holdings?

As previously discussed in Chapter 14, there are two measures of risk: systematic and unsystematic. Systematic risk is measured by the portfolio (or individual stock's) beta. Under the capital asset pricing model, higher betas are rewarded with relatively high returns, and vice versa. As the market goes up 10 percent, our portfolio might go up 12 percent (beta of 1.2), and a similar phenomenon may occur on the downside. Unsystematic risk is random or nonmarket related and may be generally diversified away by the astute portfolio manager. Under the capital asset pricing model, there is no market reward for unsystematic risk since it can be eliminated through diversification.

The question for a portfolio manager then becomes, How effective have you been at diversifying away the nonrewarded, unsystematic risk? Put another way, to what extent can a fund's movements be described as market related rather than random in nature? If we plot a fund's excess returns over an extended period of time against market excess returns, we can determine the joint movement between the two as indicated in Figure 15–5. In Figure 15–5(a), we plot our basic points. In Figure 15–5(b), we draw a regression line through these points. Of importance to the present discussion is the extent to which our line fits the data. If the points of observation fall very close to the line, the independent variable, excess market returns, is largely responsible for describing the dependent variable, excess returns for fund x.

The degree of association between the independent and dependent variable is measured by R^2 [5] (coefficient of determination). R^2 may take on a value anywhere between 0 and 1. A high degree of correlation between the independent and dependent variable will produce an R^2 of .7 or better. In Figure 15–5(b), it is assumed to be .90.

In Figure 15–6, the points do not fall consistently close to the regression line, and the R^2 value is assumed to be only .55. In this instance, we say that the independent variable (excess market returns) was not the only major variable in explaining changes in the dependent variable (excess returns for fund y).

The points in Figure 15–6 imply that the portfolio manager for fund y may have not been particularly effective in his diversification efforts. Many other factors besides market returns appear to be affecting the portfolio returns of fund y, and these could have been diversified away rather than allowed to influence returns. In this instance, we say there is a high degree of unsystematic or non-

---

[5] R^2 also represents the correlation coefficient squared. Thus, we can square Formula 14A–1 in Chapter 14. Another statement is

$$R^2 = 1 - \frac{\Sigma(y - y_c)^2/n}{\Sigma(y - \overline{y})^2/n}$$

where y_c represents points along the regression line and y is the average value of the independent variable.

Figure 15—5   **Relationship of fund's excess returns to market excess returns**

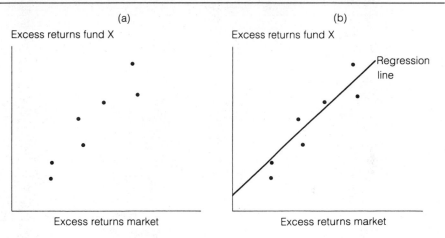

market-related risk. Since unsystematic risk is presumed to go unrewarded in the marketplace under the capital asset pricing model, there is evidence of inefficient portfolio management.

What does empirical data tell us about the effectiveness of portfolio managers in achieving diversification. How have they stacked up in terms of R^2 values for their portfolios? As indicated in Figure 15–7, their record is generally quite good.

The Merrill Lynch study of 100 mutual funds between 1970 and 1974 shows an average R^2 value of approximately .90 with very few funds falling below .70.

Figure 15—6   **Example of lower correlation**

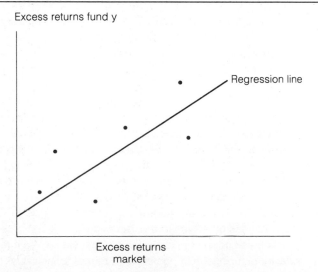

Figure 15—7   **Quarterly returns attributable to market fluctuations: 100 mutual funds, 1970—1974**

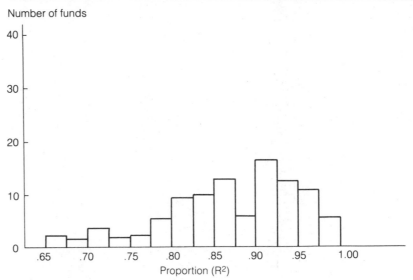

SOURCE: Merrill Lynch, Pierce, Fenner & Smith, *Investment Performance Analysis, Comparative Survey, 1970–1974.*

The actual range is between .66 and .98. Studies by McDonald, Jensen, Gentry, and Williamson have led to similar conclusions (see selected references for complete citation).

Although many mutual funds invest in 80 to 100 securities to achieve effective diversification, this is often more than is necessary. A high degree of diversification can be achieved with between 10 and 20 efficiently selected stocks as is indicated in Table 15—4. The Wagner and Lau study shows the number of securities in the portfolio, the portfolio standard deviation, and correlation with return on the market index *(R²).*

STABILITY OF BETAS

In Chapter 14, the lack of stability of the beta coefficient of an individual security was mentioned as a possible drawback to the use of the capital asset pricing model. Instability means prior beta values may not be reflective of future beta values. If this is the case, then use of a beta based on prior performance may not be entirely accurate in reflecting future return potential. Since the beta coefficient is such an integral part of our analysis in Chapters 14 and 15, we must address ourselves to this issue.

We break down our discussion on beta stability as it relates to individual stocks, industry groupings, and portfolios. In regard to individual stocks, a study by Blume

Table 15—4 **Reduction in portfolio risk through diversification**

Number of securities in portfolio	Standard deviation of portfolio returns, σ_p (percent per month)	Correlation with return on market index*
1	7.0	0.54
2	5.0	0.63
3	4.8	0.75
4	4.6	0.77
5	4.6	0.79
10	4.2	0.85
15	4.0	0.88
20	3.9	0.89

*The market here refers to an unweighted index of all NYSE stocks.

SOURCE: W. H. Wagner and S. C. Lau, "The Effect of Diversification on Risk," *Financial Analysts Journal,* November–December 1971, p. 53.

provided evidence that the betas of individual stocks tend to regress or approach 1 over time.[6] That is, a stock with a beta of 1.5 may tend to have a beta of 1.4 in the next period, 1.3 in a subsequent period, and so on. Stocks with betas below 1 also tend to approach 1 over time. While this is not an automatic occurrence, there is a tendency to follow this pattern.

The same pattern of instability would apply to betas for various industry groupings as indicated in Table 15–5. The Valentine study shows the changing betas for different industry groupings over time. The pattern of typical change can be found in such industries as canned goods and department stores.

While betas of individual stocks and industries may not be particularly stable over time, there is some evidence that portfolio betas are stable. This stability can be achieved with reasonably sized diversified portfolios of 10 to 20 stocks. We once again look to the research of Marshall Blume.

As indicated in Table 15–6, he measured the correlation between portfolio betas during different time periods. In each case, he compared one period to the next and determined the extent of correlation for different size portfolios. A high degree of correlation would indicate a stable beta as the past would be correlated with the future. For example, the last column shows the correlation of betas between the seven-year time periods from July 1954 to June 1961 and from July 1961 to June 1968. With only one security, there was a correlation coefficient of .60; with 10 securities, .92; with 20, securities, .97; and finally with 50 securities, .98. The presumption is that reasonably large portfolios have stable betas over time, and this may be useful in assessing future risk considerations.

---

[6]Marshall E. Blume, "Betas and Their Regression Tendencies," *Journal of Finance,* June 1975, pp. 785–95.

Table 15—5   **Industry beta values 1951—1970**

	1951–55	1956–60	1961–65	1966–70
Aerospace	.96247	.66585	.72409	1.31815
Agricultural machinery	.78687	.90875	.81422	1.14613
Aluminum	1.18617	1.60756	1.13980	1.21376
Apparel manufacturing	.50733	.47428	1.23344	1.52437
Auto parts and accessories	.87577	1.03116	.84302	1.17786
Autos	1.21383	1.00899	.87593	1.00869
Auto tires and rubber goods	1.18350	1.20016	1.16497	.97226
Auto trucks and parts	.96299	1.24551	1.21358	1.24255
Biscuit bakers	.34377	.18935	.76037	.68711
Bituminous coal	1.02612	1.14341	1.11203	.80200
Bread and cake bakers	.35396	.35301	.93734	1.91074
Brewers	.18364	.56817	.74847	1.03782
Business and office equipment	1.12362	1.12134	1.44912	1.09700
Canned foods	.65238	.55939	1.04155	1.01861
Cement	1.01518	.87642	.82306	1.53511
Chemicals	1.06482	1.04785	.94006	.85256
Cigarettes	.29077	.23970	1.29410	.55432
Confectionery	.35793	.35514	1.04756	.59934
Construction and material handling machinery	1.14771	1.18300	.91518	1.19976
Copper	1.17911	.97515	.94643	1.08206
Corn refiners	.32177	.44286	1.02606	.93099
Crude oil producers	.69844	1.03158	1.12971	.95093
Dairy products	.40212	.35200	.98700	1.04501
Department stores	.60589	.53718	.66176	1.21765
Distillers	.74801	.79331	.86246	.90287
Drugs	.54110	1.05861	1.29238	.95521
Electrical equipment	.96542	1.25540	1.04542	1.19990
Electrical household appliances	.76593	1.01648	.91009	1.15041
Electronics	.90328	1.31251	1.55722	1.56784
Food chain stores	.38349	.51301	1.00418	.73317
Gold mining	.54291	.63910	.06125	.07090
Heating and plumbing	.64976	.86583	.95464	1.27624
Home furnishings	.45473	.76023	1.18308	1.60301
Industrial machinery	.81678	1.18670	1.03285	1.33398
Integrated domestic oil companies	.79546	1.09107	.82772	.96288
Integrated international oil companies	1.05360	.98599	.70443	.73875
Lead and zinc	.91563	.99167	1.07584	.72259

SOURCE: Jerome L. Valentine, "Investment Analysis and Capital Market Theory," *Occasional Paper No. 1* (Charlottesville, Va.: The Financial Research Foundation, 1975), p. 34.

THE MAKEUP OF INSTITUTIONAL INVESTORS

Having discussed measurement and portfolio management techniques for institutional investors, we will now take a more specific look at the participants. Institutional investors (as opposed to individual investors) represent organizations that are responsible for bringing together large pools of capital for purposes of

Table 15-6   **Correlation coefficients of betas for portfolios of N securities**

Number of securities per portfolio	7/26-6/33 and 7/33-6/40	7/33-6/40 and 7/40-6/47	7/40-6/47 and 7/47-6/54	7/47-6/54 and 7/54-6/61	7/54-6/61 and 7/61-6/68
1	0.63	0.62	0.59	0.65	0.60
2	0.71	0.76	0.72	0.76	0.73
4	0.80	0.85	0.81	0.84	0.84
7	0.86	0.91	0.88	0.87	0.88
10	0.89	0.94	0.90	0.92	0.92
20	0.93	0.97	0.95	0.95	0.97
35	0.96	0.98	0.95	0.97	0.97
50	0.98	0.99	0.98	0.98	0.98

SOURCE: Abstracted from Marshall Blume, "On the Assessment of Risk," *Journal of Finance*, March 1971, p. 7.

reinvestment. Our coverage will center on investment companies (including mutual funds), pension funds, life insurance companies, bank trust departments, and endowments and foundations.

Investment companies (including mutual funds)

Investment companies take the proceeds of individual investors and reinvest them in other securities according to their specific objectives. Income and capital gains are generally distributed to stockholders and are subject to single taxation under Subchapter M of the Internal Revenue Code. Investment companies were discussed at some length in Chapter 4.

Other institutional investors

Other institutional investors and their extent of market participation are presented in Table 15-7. We will briefly comment on pension funds, insurance companies, bank trust departments, and foundations and endowments.

Pension funds   Pension funds represent an important and growing sector of the institutional market. Pension funds may be private or public in nature. Private funds represent over 50 percent of the total. The benefits that accrue under private pension funds may be insured or uninsured, with the latter arrangement occurring most frequently. Public pension funds are run for the benefit of federal, state, or local employees.

Insurance companies   Insurance companies may be categorized as either "life" or "property and casualty." Life insurance companies must earn a minimum rate of return assumed in calculating premiums, and public policy places great emphasis on safety of assets. Approximately 70 percent of life insurance company assets are in privately placed debt or mortgages, with the balance in bonds

**Table 15–7 Market value of stockholdings of institutional
investors and others ($ billions, end of year)**

		1971	1972	1973	1974	1975	1976	1977	1978
1.	Private noninsured pension funds	88.7	115.2	90.5	63.3[1]	88.6	109.7	101.9	107.9
2.	Open-end investment companies	52.6	58.0	43.3	30.3	38.7	43.0	36.2	34.1
3.	Other investment companies	6.9	7.4	6.6	4.7	5.3	5.9	3.1	2.7
4.	Life insurance companies	20.6	26.8	25.9	21.9	28.1	34.2	32.9[1]	35.5
5.	Property-liability insurance companies[2]	16.6	21.8	19.7	12.8	14.2	16.9	17.3[1]	19.7
6.	Personal trust funds[3]	94.1	110.2	94.7	67.7	81.0	93.0	90.5[1]	93.1
7.	Common trust funds[3]	5.8	7.4	6.6	4.3	5.9	7.8	n.a.[1]	n.a.
8.	Mutual savings banks	3.5	4.5	4.2	3.7	4.4	4.4	4.8	4.8
9.	State and local retirement funds	15.4	22.2	20.2	20.3	24.3	30.1	30.0	33.3
10.	Foundations	25.0	28.5	24.5	18.4	22.7	27.1	26.1	27.0
11.	Educational endowments	9.0	10.7	9.6	6.7	8.8	10.4	9.8	10.2
12.	Subtotal	338.2	412.7	345.8	254.1[1]	322.0	382.5	352.7[1]	368.3
13.	Less: Institutional holdings of investment company shares	5.8	6.5	6.7	6.5	8.6	10.0	10.5	10.3
14.	Total institutional investors	332.4	406.2	339.1	247.6[1]	313.4	372.5	342.2[1]	358.0
15.	Foreign investors[4]	32.9	41.3	37.0	28.4	52.6	63.9	60.1	64.7
16.	Other domestic investors[5]	638.4	690.6	525.3	365.7[1]	483.5	623.3	593.0	618.6
17.	Total stock oustanding[6]	1003.7	1138.1	901.4	641.7	849.5	1059.7	995.3[1]	1041.3

[1]Revised.

[2]Excludes holdings of insurance company stock.

[3]Data for years through 1976 exclude common trust fund holdings which were separately available. Common trust data were not separately available after 1976 and personal trust fund data therefore include assets held in these commingled funds.

[4]Includes estimate of stock held as direct investment.

[5]Computed as residual (line 16 = 17 − 14 − 15). Includes both individuals and institutional groups not listed above.

[6]Includes both common and preferred stock. Excludes investment company shares but includes foreign issues outstanding in the United States.

SOURCE: Annual Report of the Securities and Exchange Commission, 1979.

and stocks. Property and casualty insurance companies enjoy more lenient regulation of their activities and generally have a larger percentage of their assets in bonds and stocks.

Bank trust departments The emphasis in bank trust departments is on managing other people's funds for a fee. Banks may administer individual trusts or commingled (combined) funds in a common trust fund. Often a bank will establish more than one common trust fund to serve varying needs and objectives. The overall performance of bank trust departments has been mixed, with the usual number of leaders and laggards. Bank trust management is highly concentrated with a relatively small number of trust departments holding the majority of funds. Out of approximately 4,000 bank trust departments, the top 10 hold one third of all assets, and the largest 60 hold two thirds.

Foundations and endowments Foundations represent nonprofit organizations set up to accomplish social, educational, or charitable purposes. They are often established through the donation of a large block of stock in which the donor was one of the corporate founders. Examples include the Ford, Carnegie, and Rockefeller Foundations. Endowments, on the other hand, represent permanent capital funds that are donated to universities, churches, or civic organizations. The management of endowment funds is often quite difficult because of the pressure for current income to maintain operations (perhaps the university library), while at the same time there is a demand for capital appreciation. Measurement of performance for foundations and endowments has gone much more to a total-return basis (dividends plus capital appreciation) rather than the traditional interest-earned or dividend-received basis.

COMMENTS ON INSTITUTIONAL PERFORMANCE

Performance studies similar to those presented earlier in the chapter on mutual funds have been conducted on other institutional portfolios by Gentry, Schlarbaum, Williamson, and others.[7] The conclusion of this research is very similar to that on mutual funds; that is, on a risk-adjusted basis, they have not provided superior performance to a generally accepted market average or a randomly selected portfolio.

Another question that frequently arises in regard to institutional investors is whether they effectively control the movements in the market due to their large size. Although they represent approximately 35 percent of equity wealth and conduct 75 to 85 percent of the daily trading volume, empirical research indicates they do not control the market for their own purpose. Researchers Kraus and Stoll found little evidence to support a market dominance theory.[8] While there is a tendency for *similar* institutions to follow a given pattern, there is a compensating tendency for *different* institutions to take offsetting positions. This, of course, does not guarantee the absence of problems in the future as increased concentration continues.

SUMMARY

The ability of portfolio managers to meet various goals and objectives is considered in this chapter. Many portfolio managers appeared to demonstrate superior performances during the market boom years of the 1950s and part of the 1960s. However, when this performance is adjusted for risk, any perceived superiority quickly vanishes.

---

[7]Complete citations are provided under selected references at the end of the chapter.
[8]Alan Kraus and Hans K. Stoll, "Parallel Trading by Institutional Investors," *Journal of Financial and Quantitative Analysis,* December 1972, pp. 2107–38. Also, Frank K. Reilly, "Institutions on Trial: Not Guilty!" *Journal of Portfolio Management,* Winter 1977, pp. 5–10.

Some concepts related to the capital asset pricing model may be used to evaluate the performance of money managers. Portfolio beta values are shown along the horizontal axis, while the market line indicates expected returns. Portfolio managers that are able to operate above the line (positive alphas) are thought to be superior managers, while the opposite would be true of those falling below the line. Research by McDonald, Jensen, and others indicates that, on average, portfolio managers do not beat the popular averages or random portfolios on a risk-adjusted basis. One possible reason is the high transaction costs involved in active portfolio management. Some portfolio managers have even set up index funds in which they directly replicate the performance of the Standard & Poor's 500 Stock Average to minimize transaction costs or to insure that they will not underperform the averages.

Empirical research has also indicated that those funds that have done well in the past do not necessarily promise superior returns in the future. Although it may be helpful to examine past records to eliminate clearly unsatisfactory performers, the stars of the past may not necessarily be the stars of the future. Nevertheless, mutual funds (or other managed portfolios) do have some desirable attributes. As indicated by a Merrill Lynch study (and others as well), mutual funds tend to be very efficient diversifiers. Their average correlation with the market (R^2) tends to be approximately 90 percent, indicating only 10 percent unsystematic or nonrewarded risk. In general, mutual fund managers also do a good job of constructing portfolios that are consistent with their initially stated objectives (i.e., maximum capital gains, growth, income, etc).

The beta for a diversified portfolio also tends to be more stable than that for a given stock or group of stocks within an industry. Thus, the historical portfolio beta may be more reflective of current and future risk than would be the case with individual securities.

The market of institutional investors is made up of investment companies (closed-end and mutual funds), pension funds, insurance companies, foundations, endowments, and other participants. Although the great weight of empirical research has dealt with mutual funds, the same basic conclusions about risk-adjusted returns can be applied to other institutional investors. Research also indicates that large institutional investors do not control the market. While there is a tendency for similar institutions to follow a given pattern, there is also a compensating tendency for other institutions to follow an offsetting pattern.

IMPORTANT WORDS AND CONCEPTS

Risk-adjusted return
Excess returns
Alpha
Market line
Beta stability
Institutional investors

Investment companies
Efficient diversification
Average differential return
Wiesenberger Financial Services
R^2
Institutional investor

QUESTIONS AND PROBLEMS

1. What is a risk-adjusted return?

2. In evaluating a mutual fund manager, what would be the first point to analyze?

3. How can adherence to portfolio objectives be measured?

4. How can risk exposure be measured?

5. How are excess returns defined?

6. How is the market line related to excess returns?

7. Explain alpha as a measure of performance.

8. What conclusions can be drawn from the empirical studies of portfolio (fund) managers' performances?

9. Is the past performance of portfolio managers of any significance?

10. What is the meaning of beta instability versus stability? Relate this to individual firms, industries, and portfolios.

11. If investment companies do not offer returns which are, on average, any better than the market in general, why would someone invest in them?

12. "The vast holdings of institutions and their large trading volume could mean they effectively control the market." Do you agree based on the discussion in the latter part of the chapter?

13. Examining the information in Table 15–1 for the Fairfield Fund, would you think it has a high or low beta?

14. What is meant by an institutional investor? Give some examples.

SELECTED REFERENCES

Altman, Edward I., and Robert A. Schwartz. "Common Stock Price Volatility Measures." *Journal of Financial and Quantitative Analysis,* January 1970, pp. 603–25.

Blume, Marshall E. "Betas and Their Regression Tendencies." *Journal of Finance,* June 1975, pp. 785–95.

————. "On the Assessment of Risk." *Journal of Finance,* March 1971, pp. 1–10.

Fielitz, Bruce D. "Indirect vs. Direct Diversification." *Financial Management,* Winter 1974, pp. 54–62.

"Forbes 1981 Mutual Fund Survey." *Forbes,* August 31, 1981, pp. 58–87.

Friend, Irwin, Marshall Blume and Jean Crockett. *Mutual Funds and Other Institutional Investors* New York: McGraw-Hill, 1970.

Gentry, James A. "Capital Market Line Theory, Insurance Company Portfolio Performance, and Empirical Anomalies." *Quarterly Review of Economics and Business,* Spring 1975, pp. 8–16.

Institutional Investor Study Report of the Securities and Exchange Commission. Washington D.C.: U.S. Government Printing Office, 1971.

Jensen, Michael C. "The Performance of Mutual Funds in the Period 1945–1964." *Journal of Finance,* May 1968, pp. 389–416.

—————. "Risk, Capital Assets, and Evaluation of Portfolios." *Journal of Business,* April 1969, pp. 167–247.

Kraus, Alan, and Hans K. Stoll. "Parallel Trading by Institutional Investors." *Journal of Financial and Quantitative Analysis,* December 1972, pp. 2107–38.

McDonald, John G. "Objectives and Performance of Mutual Funds, 1960–1969." *Journal of Financial and Quantitative Analysis,* June 1974, pp. 311–33.

Pinches, George E., and William R. Kinney, Jr. "The Measurement of the Volatility of Common Stock Prices." *Journal of Finance,* March 1971, pp. 119–25.

Reilly, Frank K. "Institutions on Trial: Not Guilty." *Journal of Portfolio Management,* Winter 1977, pp. 5–10.

Schlarbaum, Gary G. "The Investment Performance of the Common Stock Portfolios of Property-Liability Insurance Companies." *Journal of Financial and Quantitative Analysis,* January, 1974, pp. 89–106.

Sharpe, William F. "Mutual Fund Performance." *Journal of Business,* January 1966, pp. 119–38.

Treynor, Jack L. "How to Rate Management of Investment Funds." *Harvard Business Review,* January–February 1965, pp. 63–74.

Valentine, Jerome L. "Investment Analysis and Capital Market Theory." Occasional Paper No. 1., Charlottesville, Va.: The Financial Research Foundation, 1975.

Wagner, W. H., and S. C. Lau. "The Effect of Diversification on Risk." *Financial Analysts Journal,* November–December 1971, pp. 48–53.

Wiesenberger Investment Companies Service. Boston: Warren, Gorham & Lamont, 1981.

Williamson, J. Peter. "Measuring Mutual Fund Performance." *Financial Analysts Journal,* November–December 1972, pp. 78–84.

PART 5 BROADENING THE INVESTMENT PERSPECTIVE

In the final section, we expand the investment horizon to consider many different types of investment strategies.

We begin in chapter 16 with a consideration of "special situations" that at times exist in the stock and bond markets. Empirical research has indicated that some of these investment alternatives may provide superior returns on a risk-adjusted basis. Topics for consideration include investing in mergers and acquisitions, in new stock or bond issues, in securities that are initially listed on major exchanges, and in firms that are repurchasing their own shares in the market.

Another consideration for the investor expanding the investment horizon is that of commodity and financial futures (discussed in Chapter 17). Commodities include such items as wheat, copper, and pork bellies, whereas financial futures include such categories as currencies and Treasury securities. In the chapter, we consider the mechanics of various trading strategies and the risks that are involved.

The emphasis in Chapter 18 is on real assets, which include real estate, gold and silver, precious gems, collectibles, and many other forms of tangible assets. Real assets are thought to represent a strong inflation hedge; however, they also have drawbacks in terms of illiquidity and high transaction costs. In the chapter, we also go through a detailed analysis of a real estate investment project.

In the final chapter, the investment perspective is broadened not only by type of investment, but also by time horizon. The emphasis is on lifelong planning with special attention devoted to retirement and estate considerations. Not only is the material potentially important to an individual's planning, but also to a financial advisor who may be expected to address many of these issues in dealing with his or her clientele. Particular attention is directed to the effect of the 1981 Economic Recovery Tax Act on retirement plans and estate taxes.

16

Investments in special situations

In a previous discussion of market efficiency in Chapter 9, we suggested that while the security markets were generally efficient in the valuing of securities, there were still opportunities for special returns in a limited number of circumstances. Just what these circumstances are is subject to debate as not all researchers agree.

In most instances, special or abnormal returns refer to gains beyond what the market would normally provide after adjustment for risk. In this chapter, we will explore such topics as market movements associated with mergers and acquisitions, the underpricing of new stock issues, the impact of an exchange listing on a stock's valuation, the stock market impact of a firm repurchasing its own shares, and market movements associated with stock splits and stock dividends. Additionally, in the bond market, we will look at a special situation associated with interest rate premiums on new bond issues.

We will attempt to separate some of the market folklore from significant analysis. Furthermore, when a valid investment opportunity is perceived to exist, we attempt to suggest under what circumstances it is most likely to prove profitable. Let's begin our analysis with a discussion of investment opportunities in mergers and acquisitions.

MERGERS AND ACQUISITIONS

Many stocks that were leaders in daily volume and price movement in the late 1970s and early 1980s represented firms that were merger candidates; that is, companies that were being acquired or anticipated being acquired by other firms. The stocks of these acquisition candidates often increased by 60 percent or more over a relatively short period of time. The list of participants included such well-known names as Conoco, Seven-Up, Avis, Pizza Hut, Marathon Oil, and Anaconda Copper.

Premiums for acquired companies

The primary reason for the upward market movement in the value of the acquisition candidate is the high premium that is offered over current market value in a merger or acquisition. The premium represents the difference between the candidate's offering price per share and the market price per share (before the impact of the offer). For example, a firm that is selling for $25 per share may attract a purchase price of $40 per share. Quite naturally, the stock will go up in response to the offer and the anticipated consummation of the merger.

As expected, researchers have consistently found that there are abnormal returns for acquisition candidates.[1] A recent study has indicated that the average premium paid in the 1975–78 time period was approximately 60 percent, and there was an associated upward price movement of a similar magnitude.[2] This is a much larger average premium than in prior time periods and may be attributed to the recognition of high replacement value in relationship to current market value. The premium was based on the difference between the price paid and the value of the acquisition candidate's stock *three months* before announcement of the merger. Some examples of recent premiums are presented in Table 16–1.

The only problem from an investment viewpoint is that approximately two thirds of the price gain related to large premiums takes place before public announcement. It is clear that people close to the situation are trading on information leaks. The highly prestigious investment banking house of Morgan Stanley was recently embarrassed by charges brought by the U.S. Attorney's Office that two of its

Table 16–1 Premiums paid in mergers and acquisitions, 1975–1978

Acquiring firm	Acquired firm	Price paid in cash or acquiring company's stock	Value of acquired firm three months before announcement	Premium paid (percent)
Beatrice Food Co	Harmon International Industries	$35.25	$20.00	81.25%
Parker Pen Co.	Manpower, Inc.	15.20	11.50	32.18
Colt Industries	Menaso Man.	26.60	15.00	77.33
Pepsico, Inc.	Pizza Hut, Inc.	38.00	22.375	69.83
Walter Kidde & Co.	Victor Comptometer	11.75	7.375	59.32
Dana Corporation	Weatherford Co.	14.00	9.375	49.33
Allis Chalmers Corporation	American Air Filter	19.50	34.00	74.36
Time, Inc.	Inland Containers	35.00	20.75	68.67

[1]Gershon Mandelker, "Risk and Return: The Case of Merging Firms," *Journal of Financial Economics,* December 1974, pp. 303–35; Donald R. Kummer and J. Ronald Hoffmeister, "Valuation Consequences of Cash Tender Offers," *Journal of Finance,* May 1978, pp. 505–16; and Peter Dodd, "Merger Proposals, Management Discretion and Stockholder Wealth," *Journal of Financial Economics,* December 1980, pp. 105–38.

[2]Henry Oppenheimer and Stanley Block, "An Examination of Premiums and Exchange Ratios Associated with Merger Activity During the 1975–78 Period" (Financial Management Association Meeting, 1980).

former merger and acquisition specialists were conspiring to use privileged information on takeovers to make profits on secret trading accounts.[3]

Those who attempt to legitimately profit by investing in mergers and acquisitions can follow a number of routes. First of all, there are investors who try to identify merger candidates before public announcement to capture maximum profits. This is a difficult process. While researchers have attempted to identify financial and operating characteristics of acquisition candidates, the information is often contradictory and may even change over time.[4] In prior time periods (such as the 1960s), acquisition candidates were often firms with sluggish records of performance, whereas many of the current acquirees are high-quality companies that have unusually good records of performance (Alcon Labs, Coca Cola Bottling of Los Angeles, Steak and Ale).

Some alert analysts do keep a close eye on such sources as the *Financial Weekly's* "Stocks in the Spotlight," which pinpoints securities that are undergoing unusual volume or pricing patterns (of course, this could be for any number of reasons). Other investors identify industries where companies are being quickly absorbed and attempt to guess which firm will be the next to be acquired. Prime examples of such industries in recent times were natural resource firms being acquired by multinational oils companies and brokerage houses being absorbed by insurance companies or other firms in the financial services industry.

While trying to guess an acquisition candidate prior to public announcement can be potentially profitable, it requires that an investor tie up large blocks of capital in betting on an event that may never come to pass. Others prefer to invest at the time of announcement of a merger or acquisition. A gain of the magnitude of 20 percent or more may still be available (over a few months' time period). Perhaps a stock that was $25 before any consideration of merger is up to $34 on announcement. If the actual purchase price is $40, there may still be a nice profit to be made. The only danger is that the announced merger may be called off, in which case the stock may sharply retreat in value, perhaps all the way back down to $25 (that is, assuming another potential acquiring company does not immediately come into the picture). Examples of price drops associated with merger cancellations are shown in Table 16–2.

The wise investor must carefully assess the likelihood of cancellation. Special attention must be given to such factors as the possibility of antitrust action, the attitude of the target company's management toward the merger, the possibility of unhappy stockholder suits, and the likelihood of poor earnings reports or other negative events. In a reasonably efficient market environment, the potential price gain that exists at announcement may be well correlated with the likelihood of the merger being successfully consummated. That is to say, if it appears that the

---

[3]"Two Former Morgan Stanley Executives Accused of Plot Involving Takeover Data," *The Wall Street Journal*, February 4, 1981, p. 2.

[4]Robert J. Monroe and Michael A. Simkowitz, "Investment Characteristics of Conglomerate Targets: A Discriminant Analysis," *Southern Journal of Business*, November 1971, pp. 1–15. Donald J. Stevens, "Financial Characteristics of Merger Firms: A Multivariate Analysis," *Journal of Financial and Quantitative Analysis*, March 1973, pp. 149–58.

Table 16–2   **Stock movement of potential acquirees in cancelled mergers**

Acquirer-potential acquiree	Preannouncement	One day after announcement	One day after cancellation
Mead Corporation—Occidental Petroleum	$20^3/_8$	$33^1/_4$	$23^1/_4$
Olin Corp.—Celanese	16	$23^3/_4$	$16^3/_4$
Chicago Rivet—MITE	$20^3/_4$	$28^1/_8$	$20^3/_4$

merger is almost certain to go through, the stock may be up to $37.50 at announcement based on an anticipated purchase price of $40. If a serious question remains, the stock may only be at $31. When a merger becomes reasonably certain, arbitrageurs come in and attempt to lock in profits by buying the acquisition candidate at a small spread from the purchase price.

One of the most interesting features of the current merger movement has been the heavy incidence of unfriendly takeovers; that is, the bidding of one company for another against its will. This strategy has occurred in 20 to 25 percent of announced mergers in various time periods.[5] Such events often lead to the appearance of a third company on the scene, referred to as a white knight, whose function is to save the target company by buying them out instead of the undesired suitor. The new suitor is generally deemed to be friendly to the interests of the target company and may be specifically invited by it to partake in the process. Examples of white knights occurred when Sea World thwarted an offer from MCA and went with Harcourt Brace Jovanovich in 1976. Along these same lines, Babcock and Wilcox rejected an offer from United Technologies to go with J. Ray McDermott in 1978 and Marathon Oil rejected an offer from Mobil Oil to merge with U.S. Steel in 1982.

As one might guess, these multiple-suitor bidding wars often lead to unusually attractive offers. A 40 to 60 percent premium may ultimately parlay into an 80 to 100 percent gain. For example, the bidding for Babcock and Wilcox sent the stock from 34¾ to 65.

Acquiring company performance

What about the acquiring company's stock in the merger and acquisition process? Is this a special situation; that is, does this stock also show abnormal market gains associated with the event? A study by Mandelker has indicated that it does not.[6] Long-term economic studies have indicated that many of the anticipated results from mergers may be difficult to achieve.[7] There is often an initial

---

[5]Anna Merjos, "Costly Propositions—Some Big Mergers Have Lately Fallen Through," *Barron's*, May 14, 1979, p. 9.

[6]Gershon Mandelker, "Risk and Return: The Case of Merging Firms," *Journal of Financial Economics*, December 1974, pp. 303–35.

[7]T. Hogarty, "The Profitability of Corporate Mergers," *Journal of Business*, July 1970, pp. 317–27.

feeling of optimism that is not borne out in reality. The synergy or "2 + 2 = 5" effect associated with broadening product lines or eliminating overlapping functions may be offset by the inability of management to mesh divergent philosophies together. However, companies do appear to be more adapt at the process than in prior time periods; now conservatively managed firms, such as General Electric, R. J. Reynolds, and Atlantic Richfield, are replacing the funny-money conglomerate gunslingers of the 1960s. Nevertheless, most investors would prefer to position themselves with the acquired firm, which is certain to receive a high premium, rather than with the acquiring firm, which has to pay it.

Form of payment

A final consideration in a merger is the form of payment. Cash offers usually carry a slightly higher premium than stock offers because of the immediate tax consequences to the acquired firm's shareholders. When stock is offered, the tax obligation usually may be deferred until the stock of the acquiring firm is sold. This may occur relatively soon or many years in the future.

The merger movement of the late 1970s and early 1980s has seen a much heavier utilization of cash as a medium of payment than in prior time periods (in the 50 percent range as opposed to 25 percent in the 1960s).[8] Many of the old accounting advantages associated with stock or residual stock items (convertibles, warrants) in mergers have been diminished by accounting rule changes. Many financial management texts have whole chapters covering mergers and acquisitions, which could further expand your knowledge of the subject.

NEW STOCK ISSUES

Another form of a special situation is the initial issuance of stock by a corporation. There is a belief in the investment community that securities may be underpriced when they are issued to the public for the first time. That is to say, when a company goes public by selling formerly privately held shares to new investors in the over-the-counter market, the price may not fully reflect the value of the security.

Why does this so-called underpricing take place, and what is the significance to the investor? The underpricing may be the result of the firm commitment to buy the shares that an investment banker makes in distributing the issue. That is, the investment banker agrees to buy the stock from company A at a set price and then resells it to the public (along with other investment bankers, dealers, and brokers). The investment banker must be certain that the issue will be fully subscribed to at the initial market price to the public or he (and others) will absorb losses or build up unwanted inventory. In order to protect his position, the investment banker may underprice the issue by 5 to 10 percent to insure adequate demand.

---

[8] 1978 Merger Survey (Chicago: W. T. Grimm and Co., 1978).

Studies by Reilly,[9] McDonald and Fisher,[10] and Ibbotson[11] have indicated there are positive abnormal returns in the new issues market for one week and one month after issue. Reilly, for example, observed positive excess returns of 10.9 percent one week after issue and 11.6 percent one month after issue. However, the efficiency of the market comes into play after the stock is actively trading on a regular basis, and any excess returns begin to quickly disappear. The lesson to be learned here is that, on average, the best time to buy a new, unseasoned issue is on initial distribution from the underwriting syndicate (investment bankers, dealers, brokers), and the best time to sell is in the first few weeks of trading.

Participating in the distribution of a new issue is not always as easy as it sounds. A really hot new issue may be initially oversubscribed, and only good customers of a brokerage house may be allocated shares. Such was the case in the feverish atmosphere that surrounded the initial public trading of Apple Computer and Genentech. Genentech actually went from $35 to $89 in the first 20 minutes of trading (only to quickly come back down). For the most part, customers with a regular brokerage account and a desire to participate in the new-issues market can find adequate opportunities for investment, though perhaps in less spectacular opportunities than those described above.

Performance of investment bankers

Investors closely watch the performance of investment bankers. As indicated in Table16–3, some analysts actually keep a scorecard on the after-market performance of investment bankers. The 10 best performers in the two categories, associated with frequency of offerings, have been selected from hundreds of investment banking candidates. The "batting average" refers to the percentage of new issues underwritten in which the price six months after distribution exceeded the offering price (this was for a bullish time period in 1971–72). Though there is only nominal predictive value in such an analysis, it illustrates Wall Street's interest in after-market performance.

Actual research studies indicate that large, prestigious investment banking houses do not generally provide the highest initial returns to investors in the new issues they underwrite.[12] The reason for this is that the upper tier investment bankers tend to underwrite the issues of the strongest firms coming into the market. These firms generally shop around among the many investment bankers that are interested in their business and eventually negotiate terms that would allow

[9]Frank K. Reilly, "New Issues Revisited," *Financial Management,* Winter 1977, pp. 28–42.

[10]J. G. McDonald and A. K. Fisher, "New Issue Stock Price Behavior," *Journal of Finance,* March 1974, pp. 97–102.

[11]Roger G. Ibbotson, "Price Performance of Common Stock New Issues," *Journal of Financial Economics,* September 1975, pp. 235–72.

[12]Brian M. Neuberger and Carl T. Hammond, "A Study of Underwriters' Experience with Unseasoned New Issues," *Journal of Financial and Quantitative Analysis,* March 1974, pp. 165–74. Also, see Dennis E. Logue, "On the Pricing of Unseasoned New Issues, 1965–1969," *Journal of Financial and Quantitative Analysis,* January 1973, pp. 91–103.

Table 16—3   **The scorecard on new issues, 1971–1972**

Rank	Ten offerings or more	Number of offerings	Batting average	Average gain after six months
1.	E. F. Hutton	12	86%	48%
2.	Wheat, First Securities	10	73	47
3.	D. H. Blair	10	71	25
4.	Goldman Sachs	50	79	36
5.	Hornblower & Weeks	13	74	29
6.	Shearson, Hammill	21	63	45
7.	Smith, Barney	16	83	19
8.	Kidder, Peabody	25	72	15
9.	Loeb, Rhoades	14	59	38
10.	Du Pont Glore Forgan	16	61	9
	Four to nine offerings			
1.	Flaks, Zaslow	4	100%	343%
2.	Amherst Securities	4	92	81
3.	Smith, Jackson	5	69	122
4.	McDonald & Co.	4	89	103
5.	Edwards & Hanly	9	85	61
6.	Butcher & Sherrerd	8	71	88
7.	Dillon, Read	5	83	60
8.	New York Securities	6	79	43
9.	Alex, Brown & Sons	5	90	38
10.	Mitchum, Jones & Templeton	5	56	80

SOURCE: Underwriters Performance Record (Wayne, N.J.), 1973.

for very little underpricing when they reach the market. (They want most of the benefits to go to the corporation not to the initial stockholders.)

Factors to consider in a new issue

First of all, the investor should consider the management of the firm and their prior record of performance. In most cases, a firm that is going public will have past sales and profit figures that can be compared to others in the industry. In the 1974–78 time period, the average sales volume for a firm approaching the new issues market was $22.9 million with $1.8 million in aftertax profits and $14.6 million in assets.[13]

The investor also should take a close look at the intended use of funds from the public distribution. There are many legitimate purposes, such as the construction of new plant and equipment, the expansion of product lines, or the reduction of debt. The investor should be less enthusiastic about circumstances in which funds are being used to buy out old stockholders or to acquire property from existing shareholders.

---

[13]Stanley Block and Marjorie Stanley, "The Financial Characteristics and Price Movement Patterns of Companies Approaching the Unseasoned Securities Market in the Late 1970's," *Financial Management,* Winter 1980, pp. 30–36.

The investor should also be sensitive to the industry and nature of the product involved. Examples of changing industry patterns for new issues are presented in Table 16–4.

Wall Street West

A discussion of the market for new issues would not be complete without a few comments on the "Denver Stock Exchange." This is a special market for low-priced, untested securities that are somewhat different in character from the issues previously discussed. They are often referred to as "penny" stocks. Investors may be looking for a gamble here, and there is plenty of opportunity. Of the 270 new issues taking place between January 1, 1979, and January 30, 1980, 199 were initially offered for $1 or less.[14] Many of these infant, wildcatter companies provided astronomical returns for investors shortly after trading, while others were hardly ever heard of again.

EXCHANGE LISTINGS

A special situation of some interest to investors is an exchange listing, in which a firm trading over-the-counter now lists its shares on an exchange (such as the American or New York Stock Exchange). Another version of a listing is for

Table 16—4   **Industry groupings for new public issues (based on samples)**

Lines of business	1969–1972	1974–1978
Computers	8	18
Electronics	5	9
Retailing	7	3
Wholesaling	2	0
Financial services	11	11
Energy	3	9
Health care	6	8
Light manufacturing	21	6
Heavy manufacturing	7	12
Entertainment	4	1
Restaurants	1	1
Construction	7	1
Transportation	0	2
Food processing	4	4
Other	16	17
	102	102

SOURCE: Stanley Block and Marjorie Stanley, "The Financial Characteristics and Price Movement Patterns of Companies Approaching the Unseasoned Securities Market in the Late 1970's," *Financial Management,* Winter 1980, p. 36.

---

[14]"Penny Stocks, New Issues are Still the Rage; Risks, Fraud Charges Don't Deter Investors," *The Wall Street Journal,* March 30, 1981, p. 42.

a firm to step up from an American Stock Exchange listing to a New York Stock Exchange listing.

An exchange listing may well generate interest in a security (particularly in reference to moving up from the over-the-counter market to an organized exchange). The issue will now be assigned a specialist who has responsibility for maintaining a continuous and orderly market.[15] Furthermore, there may be greater marketability for the issue as well as more readily available price quotes (particularly in small-town newspapers). An exchange listing may also make the issue more acceptable for margin trading and short selling. Large institutional investors and foreign investors may also consider a listed security more appropriate for inclusion in their portfolio.

Listed firms must meet certain size and performance criteria provided in Table 16–5 (and previously mentioned in Chapter 2 for the NYSE). Although the criteria are not highly restrictive, meeting these standards may still signal a favorable message to investors.

A number of research studies have specifically examined the stock market impact of exchange listings. As might be expected, there is a strong upward movement associated with securities that are to be listed, but there is also a strong sell-off after the event has taken place. Research by Van Horne,[16] Fabozzi,[17] and others[18] indicate that the total effect may be neutral. Research by

Table 16–5   **Minimum requirements for exchange listing**

	American Stock Exchange	New York Stock Exchange
Number of shares publicly held	400,000	1,000,000
Market value of publicly held shares	$3 million	$16 million
Number of stockholders owning 100 shares	1,200	2,000
Pretax income, last fiscal year	$750,000	$2.5 million
Pretax income, each of last two years	—	$2.0 million
Net income last fiscal year after all charges	$400,000	—
Net tangible assets	$4 million	$16 million

[15]This is not always a superior arrangement to having multiple market makers in the over-the-counter market. It depends on how dedicated the specialist is to maintaining the market. Some banks and smaller industrial firms may prefer the competitive dealer system in the over-the-counter market to the assigned specialist.

[16]James C. Van Vorne, "New Listings and their Price Behavior," *Journal of Finance,* September 1970, pp. 783–94.

[17]Frank J. Fabozzi, "Does Listing on the AMEX Increase the Value of Equity?" *Financial Management,* Spring 1981, pp. 43–50.

[18]Richard W. Furst, "Does Listing Increase the Market Value of Common Stock?" *Jour-*

Ying, Lewellen, Schlarbaum, and Lease (YLSL) would tend to indicate an overall gain.[19]

The really significant factor is that regardless of whether a stock has a higher net value a few months after listing as opposed to a few months before listing, there still may be profits to be made. This would be true if the investor simply bought the stock four to six weeks before listing and sold it upon listing. Because an application approval for listing is published in the weekly bulletin of the American Stock Exchange or New York Stock Exchange well before the actual date of listing, this is often possible. The study by YLSL, sighted above, indicates there may be an opportunity for abnormal returns on a risk-adjusted basis in the many weeks between announcement of listing and actual listing (between 4.40 percent and 16.26 percent over normal market returns depending on the time period involved). In this case, YLSL actually reject the semi-strong form of the efficient market hypothesis by suggesting there are still substantial profits to be made even after announcement of a new listing. The wise investor may wish to sell on the eventual date of listing because sometimes a loss in value may take place at that point.

The reader should also be aware of the potential impact of delisting on a security; that is, the formal removal from New York Stock Exchange or American Stock Exchange listing and a resumption of trading over-the-counter. This may take place because the firm has fallen substantially below the requirements of the exchange.[20] As you would expect, this has a large negative effect on the security. Merjos found that 48 of the 50 firms in her study declined between the last day of trading on an exchange and the resumption of trading over-the-counter.[21] The average decline was 17 percent. While the value was not risk adjusted, it is large enough to indicate the clear significance of the event.

STOCK REPURCHASE

The repurchase by a firm of its own shares provides for an interesting special situation. The purchase price is generally over current market value and tends to increase the demand for the shares while decreasing the effective supply. Before we examine the stock market effects of a repurchase, we will briefly examine the reasons behind the corporate decisions.

---

nal of Business, April 1970, pp. 174–80. Waldemar M. Goulet, "Price Changes, Managerial Accounting and Insider Trading at the Time of Listing," Financial Management, Spring 1974, pp. 303–306.

[19]Louis K. W. Ying, Wilbur G. Lewellen, Gary G. Schlarbaum, and Ronald C. Lease, "Stock Exchange Listing and Securities Returns," Journal of Financial and Quantitative Analysis, September 1977, pp. 415–32.

[20]Firms may also be delisted because they have been acquired in a merger or acquisition, in which case the shares are no longer traded.

[21]Anna Merjos, "Stricken Securities," Barron's, March 4, 1963, p. 9.

Reasons for repurchase

In some cases, management believes their stock is undervalued in the market. Prior research studies have indicated that repurchased securities have generally underperformed the popular market averages before announcement of repurchase.[22] Thus, management or the board of directors may perceive this to be an excellent opportunity because of depressed prices. Others, however, might see the repurchase as a sign that management is not creative or that it lacks investment opportunities for the normal redeployment of capital.[23] Empirical study indicates that firms that engage in repurchase transactions often have lower sales and earnings growth and lower return on net worth than other, comparable firms.[24] There also tends to be a concentration of these firms in the lower-growth areas, such as apparels, steel, food products, tobacco, and aerospace.

Tax factors may also play a role in the repurchase decision. In the literature of finance, it is suggested that a stock repurchase will put a stockholder in a better aftertax position than the direct payment of cash dividends.[25] Assume a corporation has $2 million in excess cash with 1 million shares of stock outstanding. One strategy would be to pay the stockholders a $2 cash dividend. An alternate strategy, however, would be to repurchase a portion of the outstanding shares in the market. Through reducing the shares outstanding, earnings per share would increase, and with an assumed constant P/E ratio, the market price would increase. Thus, corporate management may determine that stockholders could receive additional value either in the form of dividends, which are taxable as ordinary income, or appreciation in value, which is taxable at a lower capital gains tax rate. The lower capital gains rate may therefore provide support for a repurchase strategy. This line of reasoning is largely theoretical; the market may or may not provide the appreciation in value associated with an increase in earnings per share in each individual case.

Another reason for the repurchase of shares is the acquisition of treasury stock to be used in future mergers and acquisitions or to fulfill obligations under an employee stock option plan. Shares may also be acquired to reduce the number of voting shares outstanding and thus diminish the vulnerability of the corporation to an unwanted or unsolicited takeover attempt by another corporation. Finally, the repurchase decision may be closely associated with a desire to reduce stockholder servicing cost; that is, to eliminate small stockholder accounts that are particularly unprofitable for the corporation to maintain.

---

[22]Richard Norgaard and Connie Norgaard, "A Critical Evaluation of Share Repurchase," *Financial Management,* Spring 1974, pp. 44–50. Larry Y. Dann, "Common Stock Repurchases: An Analysis of Returns to Bondholders and Stockholders," *Journal of Financial Economics,* June 1981, pp. 113–38.

[23]Charles D. Ellis and Allen E. Young, *The Repurchase of Common Stock* (New York: The Ronald Press, 1971), p. 61.

[24]Norgaard and Norgaard, "A Critical Evaluation."

[25]Harold Bierman, Jr. and Richard West, "The Acquisition of Common Stock by the Corporate Issuer," *Journal of Finance,* December 1966, pp. 687–96.

Actual market effect

From the viewpoint of a special situation, the key question is, What is the stock market impact of the repurchase? Is there money to be made here or not? Much of the earlier research said no.[26] However, recent research would tend to indicate there might well be positive returns to investors in a repurchase situation.[27] Most of the higher returns are confined to formal tender offers to repurchase shares (perhaps 10 to 20 percent of the shares outstanding) rather than the use of informal, unannounced, open-market purchases. Under a formal tender offer, the corporation will specify the purchase price, the date of purchase, and the number of shares it wishes to acquire.

Table 16—6

Summary statistics for the tender offer sample, 1962—1976 (143 observations)

Characteristic of offers	Mean	Median
Tender offer premium relative to closing market price one *day* prior to announcement	22.46%	19.40%
Tender offer premium relative to closing market price one *month* prior to announcement	20.85%	18.83%
Percentage of outstanding shares sought	15.29%	12.57%
Percentage of outstanding shares acquired	14.64%	11.93%
Percentage of outstanding shares tendered	18.04%	14.27%
Number of shares tendered ÷ number of shares sought	142.30%	115.63%
Number of shares acquired ÷ number of shares sought	111.35%	100.00%
Value of proposed repurchase relative to preoffer market value of equity	19.29%	15.28%
Value of actual repurchase relative to preoffer market value of equity	18.63%	13.90%
Duration of offer	22 days	20 days

SOURCE: Larry Y. Dann, "Common Stock Repurchases: An Analysis of Returns to Bondholders and Stockholders," *Journal of Financial Economics,* June 1981, p. 122.

---

[26]A good example is Charles D. Ellis and Allen E. Young, *The Repurchase of Common Stock* (New York: Ronald Press, 1971), p. 156.

[27]Terry E. Dielman, Timothy J. Nantell, and Roger L. Wright, "Price Effects of Stock Repurchasing: A Random Coefficient Regression Approach," *Journal of Financial and Quantitative Analysis,* March 1980, p. 175–89. Larry Y. Dann, "Common Stock Repurchases: An Analysis of Returns to Bondholders and Stockholders," *Journal of Financial Economics,* June 1981, pp. 113–38. Theo Vermaelen, "Common Stock Repurchases and Market Signaling: An Empirical Study," *Journal of Financial Economics,* June 1981, pp. 139–83. R. W. Masulis, "Stock Repurchase by Tender Offer: An Analysis of the Causes of Common Stock Price Changes," *Journal of Finance,* May 1980, pp. 305–19.

Of particular interest is the fact that most of the positive market movement comes *on* and *after* the announcement rather than before it. The implications are that there may be trading profits to be made here.

Dann determined that the average premium paid over the stock price (the day prior to announcement) was 22.46 percent as indicated on the top line of Table 16–6.

This high premium helps to generate a return of 8.946 percent on the day of announcement and 6.832 percent one day after announcement. This represents a two-day return of approximately 15.8 percent.[28] Dann further indicated that the price movements shortly *before* announcement were negligible as indicated in Table 16–7.

Table 16–7   **Common stock rates of return over a 121-day period around announcement of common stock repurchase tender offer**

Trading day	Mean rate of return (percent)	Trading day	Mean rate of return (percent)
−60	.217%	0	8.946%
−50	−.034	1	6.832
−40	.058	2	.908
−30	−.562	3	−.041
−25	−.125	4	.133
−20	−.071	5	.158
−19	.026	6	.230
−18	−.346	7	.129
−17	−.317	8	.051
−16	−.413	9	−.211
−15	.377	10	.213
−14	−.228	11	.172
−13	−.738	12	−.024
−12	.051	13	.181
−11	−.424	14	−.143
−10	−.578	15	.497
− 9	.188	16	−.105
− 8	−.391	17	−.236
− 7	.107	18	.148
− 6	.417	19	.141
− 5	−.169	20	−.057
− 4	.943	25	−.003
− 3	.239	30	−.025
− 2	.490	40	.133
− 1	.959	50	−.069
		60	.161

SOURCE, Larry Y. Dann, "Common Stock Repurchases: An Analysis of Returns to Bondholders and Stockholders," *Journal of Financial Economics*, June 1981, p. 124.

[28]Professor Dann's observations are based on raw data rather than normalized returns. However, they are of sufficient magnitude to be important.

The predominant argument for the beneficial effects of the repurchase is that management knows what they are doing when they purchase their *own* shares. In effect, they are acting as insiders for the benefit of the corporation, and we previously observed in Chapter 9 that insiders tend to be correct in their investment decisions. This factor, combined with the high premium, may provide positive investment results. Of course, these are merely average results over many transactions, and not all tender offers will prove to be beneficial events. The investor must carefully examine the premium offered, the number of shares to be repurchased, the reasons for repurchase, and the future impact on earnings and dividends per share.

STOCK SPLITS AND STOCK DIVIDENDS

Stock splits and stock dividends tend to receive much attention in the financial press. Most investors, at one time or another, have received a call from their broker indicating a company is announcing a stock split or stock dividend. It is important that investors be able to assess the probable market impact of such events.

First, we shall briefly distinguish between a stock split and a stock dividend. A stock split represents an increase in the number of shares outstanding with a proportionate decrease in par value (if it is stated). A firm with 1 million shares outstanding and a $10 par value that announced a 2-for-1 stock split would increase shares outstanding to 2 million and decrease par value to $5 per share. Earnings per share would also go down by a proportionate amount. In a stock split, there is no transfer of funds between the retained earnings and capital stock accounts.

A stock dividend usually represents a smaller adjustment to shares outstanding (frequently 5 to 10 percent). Furthermore, there is no restatement of par value, but there is a transfer of funds from retained earnings to the capital stock accounts.

Neither a stock split nor stock dividend affects the asset side or operating capability of the firm. There are simply more shares of stock outstanding. In fact, even the term stock *dividend* could be misleading. A dividend implies that something of value is being distributed, yet the question can be asked whether more shares that represent the same proportionate ownership interest are something of value.

Then why all the excitement in the financial press? Stock splits and stock dividends do serve the purpose of placing a stock in a more desirable trading range. For example, a $60 stock may be at the upper limit of what an average investor would be willing to buy in a 100-share, round-lot transaction. A 2-for-1 stock split may bring the stock into a more popular $30 trading range. By attracting smaller stockholders, the firm may also attract potential customers for its products (transistor radios, toothpaste, etc.). Now that larger investors dominate the marketplace, these factors are perhaps less important than in the past, but they certainly merit some consideration.

The key question that we are interested in is, What is the stock market effect of stock splits and stock dividends? Though we will confine most of our attention to splits, the same basic principles would apply to stock dividends (only to a lesser extent). First of all, we can say that stocks tend to show a very positive market performance many months prior to the announcement of a stock split.[29] This, however, becomes a chicken-and-egg-type proposition. Did the stock go up as a result of the anticipated stock split, or was the stock split necessary because of the previous run-up in the stock price? The answer is that probably both of these circumstances were at play. In other words, a stock has a strong operating performance that leads to an increase in market value; at some point, the management of the firm determines that the price of the stock is moving out of the popular trading range and decides a stock split would be useful, and the stock goes up further in value.

Note, however, in Figure 16–1, that almost all this positive movement comes before the announcement of the stock split (assumed to be the vertical line).

Thus, the investor who makes an investment at point of announcement has very little to gain in terms of excess returns. This would appear to represent a situation where the market is highly efficient in absorbing the information into the value of the security before public announcement. There are other lessons to be learned as well on the relationship between the dividend-paying policies of the

Figure 16–1 Abnormal price changes before and after stock splits

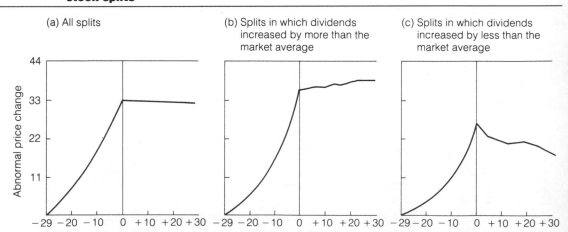

SOURCE: Eugene F. Fama, Lawrence Fisher, Michael G. Jensen, and Richard Roll, "The Adjustment of Stock Prices to New Information," *International Economic Review*, February 1969, pp. 1–21.

[29]Eugene F. Fama, Lawrence Fisher, Michael G. Jensen, and Richard Roll, "The Adjustment of Stock Prices to New Information," *International Economic Review*, February 1969, pp. 1–21. Also, W. H. Hausman, R. R. West, and J. A. Largay, "Stock Splits, Price Changes and Trading Profits: A Synthesis," *Journal of Business*, January 1971, pp. 69–77.

firm and the impact of the stock split on stock values. We see in panel a that the market performance by all firms after the announcement of the stock split is flat; however, in panels b and c, we see the impact on valuation of differing dividend policies associated with the stock split. Firms that had a relative increase in dividends show a neutral to slightly positive pattern (panel b), while those that do not have a relative increase in cash dividends show a negative price movement pattern (panel c).

The investor may attempt to segregate more desirable stock split situations from others. If a company has a strong performance and reflects this through increased dividend payouts to stockholders, this may represent a buy-and-hold situation. Assume the stock presently pays a cash dividend of $1 per share. After an announced 2-for-1 split, perhaps the cash dividend per share will only be reduced to 60 cents, so that total dividends will be $1.20. This could be a slightly positive sign and might indicate that the stock should be held.

Of course, many stocks that utilize stock splits and stock dividends do not pay cash dividends. In this case, the investor must evaluate the pure fundamentals of the situation.[30] As a general overview of most stock split situations, we would say that an investment in a stock split or stock dividend before public announcement is likely to bring profits (perhaps you have access to nonpublic information). However, if your broker calls you on the announcement, in most cases there is little justification for excitement.

A special situation in the bond market—new bond issues

The student should be aware of the situation that exists in the new issues market for bonds. As indicated in Figure 16–2, new bond issues are consistently priced to provide higher yields than existing (seasoned) issues of the same quality, maturity, and other similar features. The lines descending from the dots on each graph represent the difference between the yield on old and new issues. This yield differential provides a special-situation opportunity for higher returns to the investor.

What is the reason for the gap in yields between new and seasoned issues? It could be that investment bankers choose to overprice the yield (underprice the bond) in order to insure the successful distribution of the issue and reduce the risk. Investment bankers are particularly vulnerable to taking losses on new bond issues when interest rates are rising rapidly. A new issue they thought was attractively priced when interest rates were 12 percent may prove to be almost unmarketable if interest rates shoot up. For this reason, it is hypothesized that investment bankers may garner an extra margin of protection by overpricing yields on new issues in relation to seasoned issues, particularly when interest rates are moving upward, such as in 1979 and 1980. The danger of getting trapped into too low a rate is illustrated by what happened to the securities firm of Salomon

---

[30]A similar case would also be that the total amount of dividends paid is not changed by the stock split or stock dividend.

Figure 16–2 Yields on corporate bonds—new issues versus seasoned issues

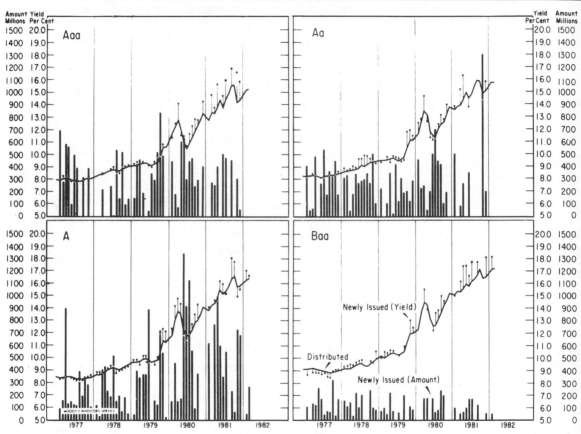

SOURCE: *Moody's Bond Record,* February, 1982, Moody's Investor's Service, Inc., New York, New York.

Brothers in its distribution of a high-quality IBM offering in October of 1979. Federal Reserve Board Chairman Paul Volker announced an unexpected, extreme credit tightening policy during the distribution process, and bond prices fell dramatically leaving Salomon Brothers and other investment bankers with approximately $10 million in losses.

One important piece of research has taken a slightly different approach to explain the gap between yields on new and existing issues of the same quality. Lindvall has suggested that dealers or market makers in the existing bond market are slow to change the value of their inventory to reflect current market conditions.[31] Because trading in existing bond issues is not as intense as similar trad-

---

[31]John R. Lindvall, "New Issue Corporate Bonds, Seasoned Market Efficiency and Yield Spreads," *Journal of Finance,* September 1977, pp. 1057–67.

ing in the stock market, dealers are more arbitrary in setting prices. This may be particularly true when interest rates are going up and dealers do not wish to mark down the value of their inventory. The essence of the Lindvall argument is that, in the bond market, new offerings may come closer to reflecting current market conditions than seasoned issues.

Regardless of the reasoning, it is clear that new issues tend to carry a higher yield than existing issues of the same quality most of the time. The consequences are twofold. First, investors should prefer new issues to seasoned issues with other things being equal. Second, there may be short-term arbitrage or swap possibilities between old and new issues.

SUMMARY

In this chapter, we examined various forms of special situations for the investor. Perhaps none has gotten more attention than the great wave of mergers and acquisitions in the late 1970s and early 1980s. Because of the premiums paid by the acquiring companies, there is substantial upward potential in the stocks of the acquired firms. However, two thirds of the gain comes before public announcement, and for that reason, some analysts attempt to identify potential target companies before announcements are made. One of the problems of investing in mergers and acquisitions is that announced plans may be called off, and there may be substantial retractions in value for the stock of the target company. A final point of observation is that stocks of acquiring firms generally do no better than the market in general.

Next we observe the price patterns of firms going public (selling their stock to the general public for the first time). There appears to be abnormal returns for the first week and month after issue, and then the efficiency of the market comes strongly into play. The reason for the initial excess returns is the underpricing by investment bankers to insure a good reception for the new issue. Stocks of firms underwritten by prestigious underwriters may show smaller returns because of the bargaining power of the issuing firm.

Exchange listings may or may not provide higher values for the securities involved; the research is somewhat contradictory in this regard. However, the interesting feature suggested by the Ying, Lewellen, Schlarbaum, and Lease research is that there may be excess returns between point of announcement and listing (regardless of whether or not there is a sell-off after listing). This is somewhat at variance with the semi-strong form of the efficient market hypothesis.

There is also conflicting evidence on the impact of a firm's repurchase of its own shares in the marketplace. Recent research, however, does indicate that the high premiums paid (22.46 percent) on cash tender often may provide upward market movement at and immediately after the point of announcement.

Stock splits and stock dividends tend to generate much interest in the financial press. Research by Fama, Fisher, Jensen, and Roll indicates that there may be upward price movement but that almost all the gain comes before the point of

announcement. The gain may be either the cause of the stock split or the result of the stock split (or a combination of both). What happens subsequent to the announcement of the stock split is closely related to the cash dividend policy of the firm. The market movement may be neutral to slightly positive if there is an increase in cash dividends and negative if there is a decrease.

Finally, new bond issues may be considered for purchase on the premise that they provide higher yields than equivalent existing securities. The gap in yield may be explained by either the underpricing (over-yielding) activities of investment bankers to ensure the success of a distribution or by the hesitancy of dealers in the bond market to mark down seasoned issues to reflect current interest rate conditions.

IMPORTANT WORDS AND CONCEPTS		
Abnormal return	Merger price premium
Stock split	Going public
Stock dividend	Unseasoned issue
Unfriendly takeover	Exchange listing
White knight	Ying, Lewellen, Schlarbaum, and
Synergy	Lease study
Batting average	Stock repurchase
Trading range	Underpricing
After-market performance	

QUESTIONS AND PROBLEMS

1. Define special or abnormal returns.

2. What is the basis for upward movement in the stock of an acquisition candidate?

3. What is an unfriendly takeover?

4. What is the primary danger in investing in merger and acquisition candidates?

5. What factor(s) will determine the extent of upward price potential for an acquisition candidate at the time of merger announcement?

6. Do the stocks of acquiring companies tend to show strong upward market movement as a result of the merger process? Comment on the reasoning behind your answer.

7. Why do cash tender offers frequently carry a higher premium than stock offers?

8. Why does abnormal return potential sometimes exist in the new-issues market?

9. What are some factors to consider before buying a new issue?

10. Why might firms that are underwritten by large, prestigious, investment banking houses not necessarily provide the highest initial returns to investors in the new-issues market?

11. What are some reasons why a firm may wish to have its security listed on an exchange?

12. What was the major finding of the Ying, Lewellen, Schlarbaum, and Lease study? How does this relate to the semi-strong form of the efficient market hypothesis?

13. What are some reasons a firm may repurchase its own stock?

14. What are some negative connotations associated with a firm repurchasing its own shares?

15. Indicate how the repurchase of shares may increase the stock price if the P/E ratio remains constant.

16. Relate the existence of positive returns on stock repurchases to the type of offer (formal versus informal).

17. Explain the difference between a stock split and a stock dividend.

18. Why do firms split their stock?

19. Relate the price movements associated with stock splits to the time periods before and after announcement.

20. What is the Lindvall reasoning as to why the interest rate on new bond issues may be higher than the interest rate on comparable, outstanding, old bond issues.

21. Project: Identify a recently announced merger or acquisition. Determine the price of the acquisition candidate's stock three months before announcement. Compare this to the actual offer by the acquiring company in terms of cash or stock. Also compare this to the acquisition candidate's stock price at point of announcement. Determine the percentage premium over the acquisition candidate's stock value in each case. Do these premiums seem reasonable in light of the quality of the companies involved and the likelihood of the merger going through? Note: You can use old issues of *The Wall Street Journal* to determine the first date of announcement and the stock prices.

SELECTED REFERENCES

Bierman, Harold J., and Richard West. "The Acquisition of Common Stock by the Corporate Issuer." *Journal of Finance,* December 1966, pp. 687–96.

Block, Stanley, and Marjorie Stanley. "The Financial Characteristics and Price

Movement Patterns of Companies Approaching the Unseasoned Securities Market in the Late 1970's." *Financial Management,* Winter 1980, pp. 30–36.

Dann, Larry Y. "Common Stock Repurchases: An Analysis of Returns to Bondholders and Stockholders." *Journal of Financial Economics,* June 1981, pp. 113–38.

Dielman, Terry E.; Timothy J. Nantell; and Roger L. Wright. "Price Effects of Stock Repurchasing: A Random Coefficient Regression Approach." *Journal of Financial and Quantitative Analysis,* March 1980, pp. 175–89.

Dodd, Peter. "Merger Proposals, Management Discretion and Stockholder Wealth." *Journal of Financial Economics,* December 1980, pp. 105–38.

Ellis, Charles D., and Allen E. Young. *The Repurchase of Common Stock.* New York: The Ronald Press, 1971.

Fabozzi, Frank J. "Does Listing Increase the Market Value of Common Stock?" *Journal of Business,* April 1970, pp. 174–80.

Fama, Eugene F.; Lawrence Fisher; Michael G. Jensen; and Richard Roll. "The Adjustment of Stock Prices to New Information." *International Economic Review,* February 1969, pp. 1–21.

Furst, Richard W. "Does Listing Increase the Market Value of Common Stock?" *Journal of Business,* April 1970, pp. 174–80.

Goulet, Waldemar. "Price Changes, Managerial Accounting and Insider Trading at the Time of Listing." *Financial Management,* Spring 1974, pp. 303–306.

Hausman, W. H., R. R. West; and J. A. Largay. "Stock Splits, Price Changes and Trading Profits: A Synthesis." *Journal of Business,* January 1971, pp. 69–77.

Hogarty, T. "The Profitability of Corporate Mergers." *Journal of Business,* July 1970, pp. 317–27.

Ibbotson, Roger G. "Price Performance of Common Stock New Issues." *Journal of Financial Economics,* September 1975, pp. 235–72.

Kummer, Donald R., and J. Ronald Hoffmeister. "Valuation Consequences of Cash Tender Offers." *Journal of Finance,* May 1978, pp. 505–16.

Lindvall, John R. "New Issue Corporate Bonds, Seasoned Market Efficiency and Yield Spreads." *Journal of Finance,* September 1977, pp. 1057–67.

Logue, Dennis E. "On the Pricing of Seasoned New Issues, 1965–1969." *Journal of Financial and Quantitative Analysis,* January 1973, pp. 91–103.

Mandelker, Gershon. "Risk and Return: The Case of Merging Firms." *Journal of Financial Economics,* December 1974, pp. 303–35.

Masulis, R. W. "Stock Repurchase by Tender Offer: An Analysis of the Causes of Common Stock Price Changes." *Journal of Finance,* May 1980, pp. 305–19.

McDonald, J. G., and A. K. Fisher. "New Issue Stock Price Behavior." *Journal of Finance,* March 1974, pp. 97–102.

Merjos, Anna. "Stricken Securities." *Barron's,* March 4, 1963, p. 9.

_____. "Costly Propositions—Some Big Mergers have Lately Fallen Through." *Barron's,* May 14, 1979, pp. 9–16.

Monroe, Robert J., and Michael A. Simkowitz. "Investment Characteristics of Conglomerate Targets: A Discriminant Analysis." *Southern Journal of Business,* November 1971, pp. 1–15.

Neuberger, Brian M., and Carl T. Hammond. "A Study of Underwriters' Experience with Unseasoned New Issues, 1965–1969." *Journal of Financial and Quantitative Analysis,* January 1973, pp. 91–103.

Norgaard, Richard, and Connie Norgaard. "A Critical Evaluation of Share Repurchase." *Financial Management,* Spring 1974, pp. 44–50.

Oppenheimer, Henry, and Stanley Block. "An Examination of Premiums and Exchange Ratios Associated with Merger Activity During the 1975–78 Period." Financial Management Association Meeting, 1980.

"Penny Stocks, New Issues are Still the Rage; Risks, Fraud Charges Don't Deter Investors." *The Wall Street Journal,* March 30, 1981, p. 42.

Reilly, Frank K. "New Issues Revisited." *Financial Management,* Winter 1977, p. 28–42.

Stevens, Donald J. "Financial Characteristics of Merger Firms: A Multivariate Analysis." *Journal of Financial and Quantitative Analysis,* March 1973, pp. 149–58.

"Two Former Morgan Stanley Executives Accused of Plot Involving Takeover Data." *The Wall Street Journal,* February 4, 1981, p. 2.

Van Horne, James C. "New Listings and Their Price Behavior." *Journal of Finance,* September 1970, pp. 783–94.

Vermaelen, Theo. "Common Stock Repurchases and Market Signaling: An Empirical Study." *Journal of Financial Economics,* June 1981, pp. 139–83.

Ying, Louis K. W.; Wilbur G. Lewellen; Gary G. Schlarbaum; and Ronald C. Lease. "Stock Exchange Listing and Securities Returns." *Journal of Financial and Quantitative Analysis,* September 1977, pp. 415–32.

17 Commodities and financial futures

What do pork bellies, soybeans, Japenese yen, and Treasury bills have in common? They are all items on which contracts may be traded in the commodities and financial futures markets.

A futures contract is an agreement that provides for the delivery of a specific amount of a commodity at a designated time in the future at a given price. An example might be a contract to deliver 5,000 bushels of corn in September of 1982 at $3.50 per bushel. The person who sells the contract does not need to have actual possession of the corn, nor does the purchaser of the contract need to plan on taking possession of the corn. Almost all commodity futures contracts are closed out or reversed before the actual transaction is to take place. Thus, the seller of a futures contract for the delivery of 5,000 bushels of corn may simply buy back a similar contract for the purchase of 5,000 bushels and close out his position. The initial buyer also reverses his position. Over 97 percent of all contracts are closed out in this fashion rather than through actual delivery.[1] The commodities futures market is similar to the options market in that there is a tremendous volume of activity but very few actual items ever change hands.

The futures markets were originally set up to allow grain and livestock producers and processors to hedge their positions in a given commodity. For example, a wheat producer might have a five-month lead time between the planting of his crop and the actual harvesting and delivery to the market. While the current price of wheat is $4.50 a bushel, there is a tremendous risk that the price might change before delivery to the market. The wheat producer can hedge his position by offering to sell futures contracts for the delivery of wheat. Even though he will probably close out or reverse these futures contracts prior to the call for actual delivery, he will still have effectively hedged his position. Let's see how this works. If the price of wheat goes down, he will have to sell his crop for less than he anticipated when he planted the wheat, but he will make up the difference on the

---

[1]"Speculating on Inflation: Futures Trading in Interest Rates, Foreign Currencies and Precious Metals," Merrill Lynch, Pierce, Fenner & Smith, July 1979.

wheat futures contracts. That is, he will be able to buy back the contracts for less than he sold them. Of course, if the price of the wheat goes up, the extra profit he makes on the crop will be lost on the futures contracts as he now has to buy back the contracts at a higher price.[2]

A miller who uses wheat as part of his processing faces the opposite dilemma in terms of pricing. The miller is afraid the price of wheat might go up and ultimately cut into his profit margin when he takes actual delivery of his product. He can hedge his position by buying futures contracts in wheat. If the actual price of wheat does go up, the extra cost of producing his product will be offset by the profits he makes on his futures contracts.

The commodities market allows the many parties in need of hedging opportunities to acquire contracts. While some of this could be accomplished on a private basis (one party in Kansas City calls another party in Chicago on the advice of his banker), this would be virtually impossible to handle on a large-scale basis. Liquid, fluid markets, such as those provided by the commodity exchanges, are necessary to accomplish this function.

While the hedgers are the backbone and basic reason for existence of the commodity exchanges, they are not the only significant participants. We also have the speculators who take purely long or short positions without any intent to hedge actual ownership. Thus, there is the speculator in wheat or silver who believes that the next major price move can be predicted to such an extent that a substantial profit can be made. Because commodities are purchased on the basis of a small investment in the form of margin (usually running 5 to 10 percent of the value of the contract), there is substantial leverage on the investment, and percentage returns and losses are greatly magnified. The typical commodities trader often suffers many losses with the anticipation of a few very substantial gains. Commodities speculation, as opposed to hedging, represents somewhat of a gamble, and stories have been told of reformed commodities speculators who gave up the chase to spend the rest of their days merely playing the slot machines.

The volatility of commodity prices can be seen in Figure 17–1. While the price trend for the 27 commodities in the index has been strongly upward, note the up and down patterns particularly in the mid–1970s and early 1980s.

TYPES OF COMMODITIES AND EXCHANGES

Commodities and financial futures can be broken down into a number of categories based on their essential characteristics. As indicated in Table 17–1, there are six primary categories. In each case, we show representative items that fall under each category.

---

[2]The hedger not only reduces risk of loss but also eliminates additional profit opportunities. This may be appropriate for farmers since they are not in the risk-taking business but rather in agriculture.

Figure 17—1

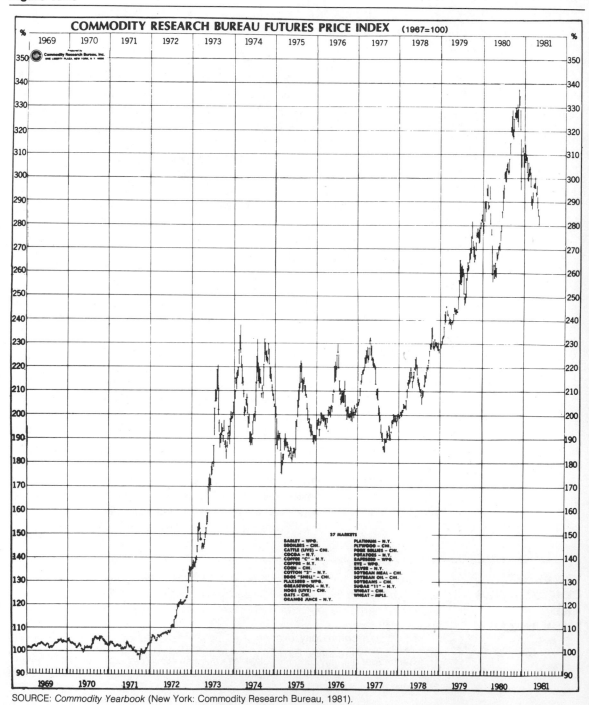

SOURCE: *Commodity Yearbook* (New York: Commodity Research Bureau, 1981).

Table 17–1 **Categories of commodities and financial futures**

(1)	(2)	(3)
Grains and oilseeds:	Livestock and meat:	Food and fiber:
Corn	Cattle—feeder	Cocoa
Oats	Cattle—live	Coffee
Soybeans	Hogs—live	Cotton
Wheat	Pork bellies	Orange juice
Barley	Turkeys	Potatoes
Rye	Broilers	Sugar
		Rice
		Butter

(4)	(5)	(6)
Metals and petroleum:	Wood:	Financial futures:
Copper	Lumber	a. Foreign exchange
Gold	Plywood	(pound, yen, franc, etc.)
Platinum		b. Interest rate futures
Silver		GNMA certificates
Mercury		Treasury bonds
Heating oil no. 2		Treasury bills
		Certificates of deposit
		Commercial paper

The first five categories represent traditional commodities, but category 6 came into prominence in the 1970s with foreign exchange futures originating in 1972 and interest rate futures beginning in 1975. Because financial futures have tremendous implications for financial managers, we will give them special attention in a later section of this chapter. Just as a farmer may wish to hedge his wheat crop, a bond portfolio manager or bank officer may wish to hedge his position with interest rate futures.

The possibilities for additional commodity futures contracts are endless. On the drawing boards are contracts to buy and sell almost any financial commodity. Furthermore, in the European capital markets, there are actually options to buy commodity contracts. This is thought to be the ultimate bang for your bucks.

The commodities previously listed in Table 17–1 trade on various commodity exchanges in the United States and Canada (see Table 17–2). While the exchanges are well-organized and efficient in their operation, they are still run by an open auction complete with outcries of bids and various hand-signal displays.

The largest commodity exchange is the Chicago Board of Trade (CBT) with the Chicago Mercantile Exchange (CME) in second place. While some exchanges are highly specialized, such as the New York Cotton Exchange, most exchanges trade in a wide number of securities. For example, the Chicago Board

Table 17—2   **Major United States and Canadian commodity exchanges**

American Commodities Exchange (ACE)
Chicago Board of Trade (CBT)
Chicago Mercantile Exchange (CME)
　Also controls International Monetary
　Market (IMM)
Commodity Exchange (CMX)
Kansas City Board of Trade (KC)
Minneapolis Grain Exchange (MPLS)
New Orleans Commodity Exchange
New York Coffee, Sugar, and Cocoa Exchange (CSCE)
New York Cotton Exchange (CTN)
New York Futures Exchange (NYFE)
　Subsidiary of the New York Stock Exchange
New York Mercantile Exchange (NYM)
Pacific Commodities Exchange (PCE)
Winnipeg Grain Exchange (WPG)

of Trade deals in such diverse products as corn, oats, soybeans, wheat, plywood, GNMA certificates, and Treasury bonds.

The American Commodities Exchange (ACE), part of the American Stock Exchange, and the New York Futures Exchange (NYFE), part of the New York Stock Exchange, are rather new in the game and specialize in financial futures. As the Chicago Board of Trade and Chicago Mercantile Exchange moved into this territory with financially oriented securities (such as GNMA futures and Treasury bill futures), members of Wall Street felt compelled to get into the financial futures game as well.

The activities of the commodity exchanges are primarily regulated by the Commodity Futures Trading Commission (CFTC), a federal regulatory agency established by Congress in 1975. The CFTC has had a number of jurisdictional disputes with the SEC over the regulation of financial futures.

Types of commodities contracts

The commodity contract lists the type of commodity and the denomination in which it is traded (bushels, pounds, troy ounces, metric tons, percentage points, etc.). The contract will also specify the standardized unit for trade (5,000 bushels, 30,000, pounds, etc.). A further designation will indicate the month in which the contract ends, with most commodities having a whole range of months from which to choose. Typically contracts run as far as a year into the future, but some interest rate futures contracts extend as far as three years.

Examples of the sizes of futures contracts are presented in Table 17–3. Be aware that there may be many different forms of the same commodity (such as spring wheat or amber/durum wheat).

Table 17—3   **Size of commodity contracts**

Contract	Trading units	Size of contract based on mid-1981 prices
Corn	5,000 bushels	$ 17,500
Oats	5,000 bushels	10,000
Wheat	5,000 bushels	22,500
Pork bellies	38,000 pounds	22,800
Coffee	37,500 pounds	38,000
Cotton	50,000 pounds	40,500
Sugar	112,000 pounds	17,920
Copper	25,000 pounds	20,000
Gold	100 troy ounces	41,000
Silver	5,000 troy ounces	45,000
Treasury bonds	$100,000	66,000
Treasury bills	$1,000,000	858,000

ACTUAL COMMODITIES CONTRACT

To examine the potential gain or loss in a commodities contract, let's go through a hypothetical investment. Assume we are considering the purchase of a December wheat contract (it is now August 1). The price on the futures contract is $4.50 per bushel. Since wheat trades in units of 5,000 bushels, the total price is $22,500. As we go through our example, we will examine many important features associated with commodity trading—beginning with margin requirements.

Margin requirements

Commodity trading is based on the use of margin rather than actual cash dollars. Margin requirements are typically 5 to 10 percent of the value of the contract and may vary over time or even from exchange to exchange for a given commodity. For our example, we will assume a $1,500 margin requirement. This would represent 6.7 percent of the value of the contract ($22,500).

Margin requirements on commodities contracts are much lower than those on stock transactions, where 50 percent of the purchase price has been the requirement since 1974. Furthermore, in the commodities market, the margin payment is merely considered to be a good-faith payment against losses. There is no actual borrowing or interest to be paid.[3] This, of course, contrasts with the traditional use of margin in the stock or bond markets.

In addition to the initial margin requirements, there are also margin maintenance requirements that run 70 to 80 percent of the value of the initial margin. In the case of the previously described wheat contract, the margin maintenance requirement might be $1,200 (80% × $1,500). If our initial margin of $1,500 is

---

[3]It should also be pointed out that we may need a minimum account balance of $5,000 or greater to open a commodity account.

reduced by $300 due to losses on our contract, we will be required to replace the $300 to cover our margin position. If we do not do so, our position will be closed out and we will take our losses.

The margin requirement, relative to size, is even less for financial futures. For example, on a $1 million Treasury bill contract, the investor generally must only post an initial margin of $1,500. Similar requirements exist for other types of financial futures.

Note that the high risk inherent in a commodities contract is not so much a function of volatile price movements as it is the impact of high leverage made possible by the low initial margin requirements. A 10 percent price move may equal or exceed the size of our initial investment in the form of the margin deposit. This is similar to the type of leverage utilized in the options market as described in Chapter 13. However, the action in the commodities market is much quicker. You can be asked to put up additional margin within hours after you establish your initial position.

Market conditions

Because the price of every commodity moves in response to market conditions, each investor must determine the key market variables that influence the value of his or her contract. In the case of wheat, the investor may be particularly concerned about such factors as weather and crop conditions in the Midwest, the price of corn as a substitute product, the carryover of wheat supply from the previous year, and the potential wheat sales to Russia and other foreign countries. A rumor about an impending transaction with Russia has often caused market prices to change radically.

Gains and losses

In the present example, assume we guessed right in our analysis of the wheat market; we purchased a December futures contract for $4.50 per bushel, and the price goes to $4.85 per bushel (recall that the contract was for 5,000 bushels). With a 35-cent increase per bushel, we have established a dollar gain of $1,750 (5,000 bushels × $.35 per bushel profit). With an initial margin requirement of $1,500, we have made a percentage profit of 116.7 percent.[4]

$$\frac{\text{Dollar gain}}{\text{Amount of margin deposit}} = \frac{\$1,750}{\$1,500} \times 100 = 116.7\%$$

If this transaction took place over a one-month time period, the annualized gain would be 1,400 percent (116.7% × 12 = 1,400.4%). Note that this was all accomplished by a 35-cent movement in the price of a December wheat contract from $4.50 to $4.85, a percentage change of 7.8 percent ($.35/$4.50). Actually, the investor may choose to close out his contract or attempt to let his profits run. He also may use his profits to establish the basis for margin on

---

[4]This does not include commissions, which are generally less than $60 to $70 for a complete transaction (buy and sell).

additional futures contracts. A paper gain of $1,750 is more than enough to provide the $1,500 margin on another wheat contract. Actually, a gain of only 30 cents per bushel would have accomplished this by providing $1,500 in profits (5,000 bushels × $.30).

The investor is now in a position to use an inverse pyramid to expand his position. With two contracts outstanding, a mere 15-cent price change will provide $1,500 in profits.

$$
\begin{array}{rl}
\$ \ .15 & \text{Price change} \\
\times \ \underline{10,000} & \text{Bushels (Two contracts)} \\
\$1,500 & \text{Profits (can be applied} \\
& \text{to third contract)}
\end{array}
$$

The $1,500 in profits can be used to purchase a third contract, and now with 15,000 bushels under control, a 10-cent price change will generate enough profits for a fourth contract.

$$
\begin{array}{rl}
\$ \ .10 & \text{Price change} \\
\times \ \underline{15,000} & \text{Bushels (Three contracts)} \\
\$1,500 & \text{Profits (can be applied to} \\
& \text{fourth contract)}
\end{array}
$$

The process of inverse pyramiding begins to sound astounding since eventually a 1-cent or ½-cent change in the price of wheat will trigger off enough profits for a new contract. Of course, there are great risks associated with such a process. It is like building a house with playing cards. If one card tumbles, the whole house comes down. The investor can become so highly leveraged that any slight reversal in price can trigger off tremendous margin calls. While it is often wise to let profits run and perhaps do some amount of pyramiding, great prudence must be exercised.

Our primary attention up to this point has been on contracts that are making money. What are the implications if there is an immediate price reversal after we have purchased our December wheat contract? You will recall there was a margin maintenance requirement of $1,200 based on our initial margin of $1,500. In this case, a $300 loss would call for an additional deposit to bring our margin position up to $1,500. How much would the price of wheat have to decline for us to get this margin call to increase our deposit? With a 5,000-bushel contract, we are talking about a mere decline of 6 cents per bushel.

$$
\frac{\$300 \text{ loss}}{5,000 \text{ bushels}} = \$.06 \text{ per bushel}
$$

This could happen in a matter of hours or days after our initial purchase. When we get the margin call, we can either elect to put up the additional $300 and continue with the contract or tell our commodities broker to close out our contract and take our losses. If we put up the $300, our broker could still be on the phone two hours later asking for more margin because the price has shown

further deterioration. Because investors often buy multiple contracts, such as 10 December wheat contracts, the process can be all the more intense. In the commodities market, the old adage of "cut your losses short and let your profits run" probably has its greatest significance. Even a seasoned commodities trader might determine that he is willing to lose 80 percent of the time and only win 20 percent of the time, but those victories will represent home runs and the losses mere singles.

Price movement limitations

Because of the enormous opportunities for gains and losses in the commodities markets, the commodity exchanges do place some broad limitations on maximum daily price movements in a commodity. Some examples are shown in Table 17–4.

These daily trading limits obviously must affect the efficiency of the market somewhat. If market conditions indicate the price of wheat should decline by 30 cents and the daily limit is 20 cents, then obviously the price of wheat is not in equilibrium as it opens the following morning. However, the desire to stop market panics tends to override the desire for total market efficiency in the commodity markets. Nevertheless, the potential intraday trading range is still large. Recall, for example, that a 20-cent change in the price of wheat, which is the daily limit, is more than enough to place tremendous pressure on the investor to repeatedly increase his margin position. On the typical 5,000-bushel contract, this would represent a daily loss of $1,000.

READING MARKET QUOTES

We now turn our attention to interpreting market quotes in the daily newspaper. In Figure 17–2, we show an excerpt from the July 22, 1981, edition of *The Wall Street Journal* covering 22 different types of contracts (this represents about half of the contracts reported for that day).

In each case, we see there is a wide choice of months for which a contract

Table 17–4   **Maximum daily price changes**

Commodity	Exchange	Normal price range	Maximum daily price change (from previous close)*
Corn	CBT	$3.00–$4.00	$.10 per bushel
Oats	CBT	$1.80–$2.40	$.06 per bushel
Wheat	CBT	$3.50–$5.50	$.20 per bushel
Pork bellies	CBT	$.40–$.80	$.02 per pound
Copper	CME	$.70–$1.50	$.03 per pound
Silver	CMX	$8.00–$50.00	$.50 per ounce
Treasury bills	IMM of CME	85% of par and up	50 basis points

*These values may change slightly from exchange to exchange and are often temporarily altered in response to rampent speculation.

Figure 17–2 **Examples of price quotes on commodity futures**

Futures Prices

Tuesday, July 21, 1981

Open Interest Reflects Previous Trading Day

–GRAINS AND OILSEEDS–

CORN (CBT)–5,000 bu.; cents per bu.

	Open	High	Low	Settle	Change	Lifetime High	Lifetime Low	Open Interest
July	331½	333	326	331¾	– ½	419¼	312	324
Sept	337½	339¾	334	338¾	....	407	331½	34,178
Dec	344	349½	342¼	349¼	+ 2½	396¼	332½	5,623
Mar82	358	363	355¾	362¾	+ 2¾	406½	353	15,436
May	367	371¼	364¼	370¾	+ 4	410¾	360¾	4,137
July	372	375½	369½	375½	+ 3½	399	365	2,390

Est vol 55,359; vol Mon 50,409; open int 112,695, –142.

OATS (CBT)–5,000 bu.; cents per bu.

	Open	High	Low	Settle	Change	Lifetime High	Lifetime Low	Open Interest
July	200½	203¾	200	203¾	+ 6	241	192½	384
Sept	188	190¾	187¼	190½	+ 3½	237	186¼	2,866
Dec	197½	200½	197	200½	+ 3¼	235	196½	2,083
Mar82	207½	209¾	206	209¾	+ 3¾	239	206	211
May	211½	213½	210	213½	+ 2½	231½	210	63

Est vol 2,081; vol Mon 1,496; open int 5,557, –360.

SOYBEANS (CBT)–5,000 bu.; cents per bu.

	Open	High	Low	Settle	Change	Lifetime High	Lifetime Low	Open Interest
July	719	720	710	719½	+ 1½	1024	673	566
Aug	720	722	711	720¾	+ 1¼	1083	685	18,562
Sept	726½	730	719½	729½	+ 3	933	697	12,089
Nov	747	751	738	750¼	+ 4¼	900	714	33,980
Jan82	763½	769	756	768½	+ 4¼	916½	732½	11,763
Mar	784	790	777	790	+ 7	908	755	11,902
May	799½	807	794	805	+ 5½	922	772	7,398
July	812	818	805	818	+ 5½	866	786	2,577

Est vol 34,225; vol Mon 45,744; open int 98,837, –3,599.

SOYBEAN MEAL (CBT)–100 tons; $ per ton.

	Open	High	Low	Settle	Change	Lifetime High	Lifetime Low	Open Interest
July	199.00	200.50	197.80	200.00	+ .50	301.00	191.20	649
Aug	201.00	201.70	198.70	201.30	+ .60	295.00	194.90	10,875
Sept	203.00	204.50	201.70	204.20	+ 1.20	278.50	198.60	5,617
Oct	205.50	206.50	204.10	206.30	+ .30	262.00	200.40	5,882
Dec	211.50	212.50	209.60	212.30	+ 1.00	259.00	206.00	12,463
Jan82	214.50	216.00	213.00	216.00	+ 2.00	259.00	209.50	4,832
Mar	220.80	223.00	219.00	222.30	+ .80	259.00	217.00	2,059
May	225.00	225.00	223.00	225.00	+ .50	260.50	221.00	898
July	228.00	229.00	226.50	227.50	– .30	242.20	224.00	343
Aug	229.50	229.50	228.00	228.30	– .70	244.00	228.00	10

Est vol 9,108; vol Mon 13,405; open int 43,628, –327.

SOYBEAN OIL (CBT)–60,000 lbs.; cents per lb.

	Open	High	Low	Settle	Change	Lifetime High	Lifetime Low	Open Interest
July	23.45	23.65	23.15	23.65	+ .15	32.00	21.15	202
Aug	23.65	23.80	23.27	23.78	– .06	31.60	21.63	17,020
Sept	24.10	24.25	23.70	24.23	– .15	31.20	22.05	10,571
Oct	24.55	24.65	24.10	24.58	+ .13	30.05	22.45	7,363
Dec	25.20	25.45	24.80	25.37	+ .20	29.73	23.10	12,347
Jan82	25.53	25.80	25.25	25.70	+ .28	29.65	23.45	4,272
Mar	26.20	26.44	25.95	26.39	+ .26	28.77	24.15	2,867
May	26.55	26.89	26.50	26.87	+ .24	28.50	24.70	1,326
July	27.05	27.40	26.95	27.37	+ .22	29.50	25.34	619
Aug	....	....	....	27.35	+ .20	27.70	25.53	22

Est vol 12,946; vol Mon 11,236; open int 56,409, –1,664.

WHEAT (CBT)–5,000 bu.; cents per bu.

	Open	High	Low	Settle	Change	Lifetime High	Lifetime Low	Open Interest
July	386	389½	383	389½	+ 6¾	552	365	739
Sept	398	404	396½	403	+ 5	558½	384	22,412
Dec	428½	433½	426½	432½	+ 4¾	569	412½	25,626
Mar82	452½	458	451	456¾	+ 5¾	538	436	8,288
May	467	472	465	471	+ 6	526	447	2,484
July	473½	478½	472	478½	+ 7	497½	457	2,110

Est vol 14,087; vol Mon 23,252; open int 61,659, +1,457.

WHEAT (KC)–5,000 bu.; cents per bu.

	Open	High	Low	Settle	Change	Lifetime High	Lifetime Low	Open Interest
July	414	414	414	414	– 1	544	402½	16
Sept	426½	449½	425½	429¾	+ 3	550	419	11,895
Dec	449	452½	447½	451	+ 2½	525	421¼	5,806
Mar82	465	469	464¼	469	+ 3½	505	455	1,181
May	474	474	473	473	– 4	495	475	42

Est vol 4,300; vol Mon 3,599; open int 18,940, +299.

WHEAT (MPLS)–5,000 bu.; cents per bu.

	Open	High	Low	Settle	Change	Lifetime High	Lifetime Low	Open Interest
July	419	419	419	419	+ 4	544½	402½	16
Sept	421	423	418½	421¾	+ 1	545	400	3,785
Dec	439½	442	438	441½	+ 2¼	500	427½	1,701
Mar82	457	459	56	458	....	478¾	447	251
May	483	483	483	483	....	485	483	2

Est vol 900; vol Mon 1,006; open int 5,754, +88.

BARLEY (WPG)–20 metric tons; Can$ per ton

	Open	High	Low	Settle	Change	Lifetime High	Lifetime Low	Open Interest
July	144.00	147.30	144.00	147.00	+ .70	165.50	129.50	754
Oct	132.20	134.50	132.20	134.50	+ 2.00	166.40	129.50	4,514
Dec	133.00	134.60	132.60	134.50	+ 2.00	165.20	129.60	6,559
Mr82	137.50	138.00	137.50	137.90	+ 1.50	152.50	131.60	2,007
May	139.00	140.00	138.50	139.90	+ 1.50	144.20	133.60	515

Est vol 2,740; vol Mon 3,915; open int 14,349, +115.

FLAXSEED (WPG)–20 metric tons; Can$ per ton

	Open	High	Low	Settle	Change	Lifetime High	Lifetime Low	Open Interest
July	360.00	360.50	360.00	360.50	+ 1.20	463.00	341.70	465
Oct	373.00	375.10	370.00	375.10	+ 2.10	455.00	361.70	5,132
Nov	....	....	....	371.50	– .50	411.00	393.50	103
Dec	372.00	373.00	369.00	373.00	+ .70	415.00	364.70	2,918
My82	....	....	....	391.00	– .10	413.00	385.10	250

Est vol 1,300; vol Mon 2,044; open int 8,868, –27.

RAPESEED (WPG)–20 metric tons; Can$ per ton

	Open	High	Low	Settle	Change	Lifetime High	Lifetime Low	Open Interest
Sept	334.00	338.00	333.00	337.90	+ 4.50	393.50	330.40	8,546
Nov	348.00	351.00	346.70	351.00	+ 3.50	392.00	343.50	5,610
Jan82	360.00	363.70	359.80	363.70	+ 3.60	387.80	353.70	849
Mar	371.50	374.50	371.50	374.50	+ 3.30	384.30	371.20	35
June	....	....	....	384.00	– 2.00	....	....	2

Est vol 1,130; vol Mon 3,007; open int 15,042, –536.

RYE (WPG)–20 metric tons; Can. $ per ton

	Open	High	Low	Settle	Change	Lifetime High	Lifetime Low	Open Interest
July	....	....	....	212.20	– 2.50	237.80	166.50	706
Oct	170.10	170.30	170.10	170.10	....	213.00	145.50	3,279
Dec	168.50	168.60	168.50	168.60	....	205.50	141.50	364
May82	....	....	....	174.00	– .50	164.00	160.00	35

Est vol 123; vol Mon 296; open int 4,384, +12.

–LIVESTOCK & MEAT–

CATTLE–FEEDER (CME)–42,000 lbs.; cents per lb.

	Open	High	Low	Settle	Change	Lifetime High	Lifetime Low	Open Interest
Aug	63.50	64.37	62.60	62.90	– .95	83.00	62.35	4,029
Sept	62.70	63.35	61.80	62.27	– .42	82.40	61.65	976
Oct	62.25	63.15	61.65	61.82	– .67	80.10	61.55	4,360
Nov	63.40	63.90	62.60	62.82	– .80	77.05	62.60	1,120
Jan82	65.25	65.25	64.00	64.00	– 1.00	75.57	64.00	274
Mar	65.25	65.50	64.25	64.60	– .40	74.25	64.25	266
Apr	65.00	65.90	65.00	65.00	– .70	70.80	65.00	22
May	....	....	....	65.10	– .60	72.00	65.60	99

Est vol 3,866; vol Mon 2,783; open int 11,146, +198.

CATTLE–LIVE (CME)–40,000 lbs.; cents per lb.

	Open	High	Low	Settle	Change	Lifetime High	Lifetime Low	Open Interest
Aug	65.50	65.70	64.30	64.75	– 1.00	76.25	63.50	21,812
Oct	62.45	63.27	62.10	62.30	+ .50	75.20	61.67	13,909
Dec	63.90	64.30	62.90	63.30	– .35	75.85	62.60	6,401
Feb82	64.50	64.85	63.35	63.90	– .37	72.55	63.35	3,441
Apr	65.55	65.75	64.15	64.85	– .32	72.40	64.15	2,358
June	66.00	66.60	65.10	65.82	– .35	72.30	65.10	417

Est vol 17,474; vol Mon 11,610; open int 48,338, –335.

HOGS–LIVE (CME)–30,000 lbs.; cents per lb.

	Open	High	Low	Settle	Change	Lifetime High	Lifetime Low	Open Interest
Aug	50.80	50.90	50.17	50.17	– 1.50	62.70	43.67	9,558
Oct	49.00	49.05	48.17	48.17	– 1.50	61.35	43.00	6,091
Dec	51.00	51.70	50.72	50.72	– 1.50	61.75	47.40	4,045
Feb82	53.00	53.40	52.37	52.50	– 1.37	61.85	50.00	1,187
Apr	52.62	52.90	51.50	51.50	– 1.50	61.50	49.50	350
June	55.45	55.60	54.40	54.40	– 1.50	59.90	54.40	150
July	55.65	55.70	54.60	54.60	– 1.50	59.97	54.60	65
Aug	....	....	....	52.80	– 1.50	59.50	53.75	41

Est vol 7,249; vol Mon 6,308; open int 21,487, –658.

PORK BELLIES (CME)–38,000 lbs.; cents per lb.

	Open	High	Low	Settle	Change	Lifetime High	Lifetime Low	Open Interest
July	51.50	51.50	50.70	50.70	– 2.00	79.05	42.50	262
Aug	50.20	50.60	49.90	49.90	– 2.00	78.40	42.00	8,814
Feb82	63.90	64.35	63.05	63.05	– 2.00	74.45	54.80	4,786
Mar	63.90	64.30	63.15	63.15	– 2.00	74.80	56.00	945
May	64.60	65.15	64.10	64.10	– 2.00	75.90	63.60	293
July	65.60	66.00	65.20	65.20	– 2.00	77.40	64.85	63
Aug	64.80	64.80	64.80	64.80	– 2.00	75.00	64.80	40

Est vol 5,416; vol Mon 9,263; open int 15,203, –842.

–FOOD & FIBER–

COCOA (CSCE)–10 metric tons; $ per ton.

	Open	High	Low	Settle	Change	Lifetime High	Lifetime Low	Open Interest
July	1,925	1,925	1,925	1,924	+ 70	2,750	1,330	8
Sept	1,935	1,962	1,928	1,939	+ 65	2,745	1,422	4,227
Dec	2,040	2,065	2,030	2,033	+ 56	2,595	1,538	4,738
Mar82	2,105	2,140	2,095	2,101	+ 49	2,280	1,625	2,446
May	2,165	2,170	2,135	2,140	+ 53	2,318	1,690	786
July	2,180	2,180	2,180	2,175	+ 53	2,365	1,740	470
Sept	....	....	....	2,210	+ 53	2,370	1,790	448
Dec	....	....	....	2,250	+ 53	2,250	2,040	393

Est vol 2,525; vol Mon 1,023; open int 13,516, –71.

COFFEE (CSCE)–37,500 lbs.; cents per lb.

	Open	High	Low	Settle	Change	Lifetime High	Lifetime Low	Open Interest
July	116.00	124.40	116.00	127.63	+ 17.08	196.75	85.50	205
Sept	110.63	110.63	110.63	110.63	+ 4.00	198.00	83.75	3,863
Dec	104.59	104.59	104.59	104.59	+ 4.00	165.50	82.00	2,887
Mr82	100.60	100.60	100.60	100.60	+ 4.00	137.00	81.00	1,312
May	100.40	100.40	100.40	100.40	+ 4.00	131.00	80.50	351
July	100.13	100.13	100.13	100.13	+ 4.00	131.00	81.00	187
Sept	100.00	100.00	100.00	100.00	+ 4.00	124.00	81.00	186
Dec	....	....	....	100.00	+ 4.00	81.25	81.25	12

Est vol 948; vol Mon 3,040; open int 9,003, –120.

COTTON (CTN)–50,000 lbs.; cents per lb.

	Open	High	Low	Settle	Change	Lifetime High	Lifetime Low	Open Interest
July	....	....	....	....	....	....	....	46
Aug	78.15	80.00	78.15	80.00	– .15	89.25	78.10	188
Oct	76.70	77.20	76.55	77.14	+ .59	89.95	75.50	4,860
Dec	77.20	77.60	76.96	77.35	+ .25	86.10	75.50	15,268
Mr82	78.80	79.50	78.71	79.30	+ .35	86.80	77.15	3,541
May	80.70	80.70	80.70	80.80	+ .30	87.00	78.70	667
July	82.48	82.48	82.48	82.48	+ .48	86.10	80.00	919
Oct	80.80	80.80	80.80	81.00	+ .40	85.00	79.50	185
Dec	80.20	80.75	80.50	80.70	+ .20	80.75	78.65	232

Est vol 3,450; vol Mon 4,960; open int 25,906, –126.

ORANGE JUICE (CTN)–15,000 lbs.; cents per lb.

	Open	High	Low	Settle	Change	Lifetime High	Lifetime Low	Open Interest
July	....	....	....	....	....	....	....	499
Sept	126.70	128.00	125.05	126.55	– .15	156.80	89.95	5,944
Nov	130.40	131.60	128.80	130.50	+ .10	156.00	92.70	1,447
Jan82	133.85	135.00	132.30	133.60	– .05	154.50	91.50	2,538
Mar	134.90	134.90	134.00	135.30	+ .05	155.00	92.75	716
May	....	....	....	137.00	+ .15	155.75	99.25	349
July	138.90	138.90	137.50	138.70	+ .25	152.50	137.25	183
Sept	....	....	....	140.40	+ .35	152.00	140.00	27
Nov	....	....	....	142.10	+ .45	151.25	141.00	18

Est vol 1,300; vol Mon 2,306; open int 11,715, +273.

POTATOES (NYM)–50,000 lbs.; cents per lb.

	Open	High	Low	Settle	Change	Lifetime High	Lifetime Low	Open Interest
Nov	7.37	7.40	7.31	7.34	– .05	9.07	6.81	1,262
Feb82	....	....	....	8.39	– .08	10.00	7.35	46
Mar	8.75	8.75	8.70	8.72	– .07	11.50	7.80	726
Apr	9.99	10.02	9.92	9.95	– .12	12.44	8.85	2,447

Est vol 477; vol Mon 512; open int 4,481, –39.

SUGAR–WORLD (CSCE)–112,000 lbs.; cents per lb.

	Open	High	Low	Settle	Change	Lifetime High	Lifetime Low	Open Interest
Sept	16.00	16.34	15.95	16.27	+ .24	41.50	14.45	10,797
Oct	16.10	16.49	16.05	16.43	+ .33	40.90	14.70	22,310
Jan82	16.25	16.25	16.25	16.62	+ .34	37.80	14.85	630
Mar	16.45	16.88	16.45	16.85	+ .36	36.60	15.40	19,437
May	16.73	17.10	16.71	17.10	+ .38	26.50	15.70	5,574
July	16.95	17.36	16.95	17.36	+ .50	23.75	15.90	3,905
Sept	17.25	17.60	17.25	17.60	+ .47	19.15	16.22	883
Oct	17.60	17.60	17.60	17.73	+ .38	19.17	16.35	1,991

Est vol 7,655; vol Mon 9,601; open int 65,527, –606.

Table 17–5   Price quotes for wheat contracts

1.	Open	High	Low	Settle	Change	Lifetime High	Low	Open Interest
2. **Wheat (CBT)—5,000 bu.; cents per bu.**								
July	386	389½	383	389½	+6¾	552	365	739
Sept	398	404	396½	403	+5	358½	384	22,412
Dec	428½	433½	426½	432½	+4¾	569	412½	25,626
Mar 82	452½	458	451	456¾	+5¾	538	436	8,288
May	467	472	465	471	+6	526	447	2,484
June	473½	478½	472	478½	+7	497½	457	2,110

SOURCE: *The Wall Street Journal,* July 22, 1981, p. 38.

may be purchased. For example, corn, which trades on the Chicago Board of Trade (CBT), has futures contracts for July, September, December, March, and May. Some commodities offer a contract for virtually every month. In order to directly examine some of the terms in Figure 17–2, we reproduce the portion related to the first wheat contract (CBT) in Table 17–5.

We initially read the second line in the table that indicates we are dealing in wheat traded on the Chicago Board of Trade (CBT). We then note that wheat is traded in 5,000-bushel units and quoted in cents per bushel. Quotations in cents per bushel require some mental adjustment. For example, 400 cents per bushel would actually represent four dollars ($4) per bushel. We generally move the decimal point two places to the left and quote in terms of dollars. For example, the May 1982 opening price was 467, or $4.67 per bushel.

Across the top of the table we observe that we are given information on the open, high, low, settle (close), and change for the day as well as the lifetime high and low for that particular contract. The last column represents the open interest or the number of actual contracts presently outstanding for that delivery month. Note that there are not many July 1981 contracts outstanding as most investors have reversed their initial position by closing out contracts for that month (the table was dated in July of 1981). In September and December, the same thing will happen as investors shift their contracts to March and May of 1982.

The progressively higher prices with the passage of time represent both a carrying cost for holding the commodities for longer periods of time and inflationary expectations. Because of the wide options available in delivery dates, the producer, processor, or speculator can carefully tailor the contract month to his or her needs.

THE CASH MARKET AND THE FUTURES MARKET

Many commodity futures exchanges provide areas where buyers and sellers can negotiate cash (or spot) prices. The cash price is the actual dollar value paid for the immediate transfer of a commodity. Unlike a futures contract, there must be a transfer of the physical possession of the goods. Prices in the cash market

are somewhat dependent on prices in the futures market. Thus, it is said that the futures markets (12 in the United States and 1 in Canada) provide an important service as a price discovery mechanism. By cataloging price trends in everything from corn to cattle, producers, processors, and handlers of over 40 commodities are able to observe the present worth and price trends in categories of interest.

In Figure 17–3 we observe price quotes in the cash market for various commodities. These cash prices are very close to the prices in the near-term futures market that we presented in Figure 17–2.

Let's take the category of grains and feeds to show our example. In Table 17–6, we compare the most recent cash prices for corn, oats, and soybeans in Figure 17–3 to the near-term July future prices in Figure 17–2. You can observe the similarity.

Figure 17–3 **Price quotes in the cash market**

Cash Prices

Tuesday, July 21, 1981
(Quotations as of 4 p.m. Eastern time)

	Tues.	Mon.	Yr. Ago
FOODS			
Flour, hard winter KC cwt	$10.05-10.15	$9.90-10.00	$9.90
Coffee, Brazilian, NY lb	n1.25	1.15	1.70
Cocoa, Accra NY lb	z	z	z
Potatoes, rnd wht. 50 lb. NY del	y5.00	5.00	5.00
Sugar, cane, raw NY lb del	.1891	.1868	.2866
Sugar, cane, ref NY lb fob	.3010	.3110	.4010
Sugar, beet, ref Chgo-W lb fob	.2790	.2790	.3690
Orange Juice, frz con, NY lb	b1.22	1.18	.8400
Butter, AA, Chgo., lb.	1.47¼	1.47¼	1.38¼
Eggs, Lge white, Chgo doz.	.70½-.71	.70½	.69¾
Broilers, Dressed "A" NY lb	x.5299	.5307	.5914
Beef, 700-900 lbs, Midw lb fob	1.06-1.07	1.06-1.07	1.12
Pork Loins, 14 down Mdw lb fob	1.02	1.04	.84½
Hams, 14-17 lbs, Midw lb fob	.84	.80	.70
Pork Bellies, 12-14lbMdw lb fob	.62	.62	.46
Hogs, Sioux City avg cwt	e50.60	51.30	42.90
Hogs, Omaha avg cwt	e49.75	50.50	42.90
Steers, Omaha choice avg cwt	67.19	67.50	71.10
Steers, Sioux City ch avg cwt	67.38	68.06	71.90
Feeder Cattle, Okl Cty, av cwt	e61.00	62.00	73.60
Pepper, black NY lb	a.63	.63	.84
GRAINS AND FEEDS			
Alfalfa Pellets, dehy, Neb., ton	89.-90.	89 -90.	88.00
Barley, top-quality Mpls., bu	2.80-3.05	2.80-3.05	3.05-3.65
Bran, (wheat middlings) KC ton	84.00	86.00	97.50
Brewer's Grains, Mlwke, ton	82.00	82.00	85.00
Corn, No. 2 yellow Chgo., bu bi	3.21¾	3.21¾	3.10¾
Corn Gluten Feed, Chgo., ton	97.50	97.50	120.00
Cottonseed Meal, Memphis, ton	175.00	175.00	160.00
Flaxseed, Mpls., bu	8.00	8.00	7.35
Hominy Feed, Ill., ton	93.00	93.00	92.00
Linseed Meal, Mpls., ton	145.00	145.00	162.50
Meat-Bonemeal 50%-pro, Ill.,ton	240.-245.	245.00	270.00
Oats, No. 2 milling, Mpls., bu	1.94-1.97	1.95-2.02	1.80
Rice, No. 2 milled fob Ark. cwt	27.-28.	27.-28.	20.-21.
Rye, No. 2 Mpls., bu	3.50	3.50 -3.55	2.90-2.95
Sorghum, (Milo), No. 2 Gulf cwt	5.51	5.51	6.08
Soybean Meal, Decatur, Ill. ton	195.00	195.50	190.75
Soybeans No1 yellow Chgo bu bi	7.20¾	7.19½	7.14¼
Sunflower Seed, No. 1 Mpls. cwt	12.30	12.30	11.10
Wheat, Spring 14%-pro Mpls. bu	4.46¾	4.43¾	4.63¼
Wheat, amber durum, Mpls., bu	4.40-5.25	4.40-5.25	7.10-7.35
Wheat No2 soft red Chgo bu bi	3.73	3.68	4.12½
Wheat, No. 2 hard KC, bu	4.21½	4.18½	4.16¾
FATS AND OILS			
Coconut Oil, crd, N. Orleans lb	n.28½	.28½	.30½
Corn Oil, crd wet mill, Chgo. lb	.24	.24½	.26½
Corn Oil, crd dry mill, Chgo. lb	n.26	.26	.30
Cottonseed Oil, crd Miss Vly lb	.27½	.27	.28
Grease, choice white, Chgo lb	.19½	.19	.17¼
Lard, Chgo lb	.23	23	23
Linseed Oil, raw Mpls lb	.33	.33	.30
Palm Oil, Neutral, N.Y. lb	n.29	.29	.28
Peanut Oil, crd, Southeast lb	n.38	.38	.28
Soybean Oil, crd Decatur, lb	.2340	.2325	.2663
Tallow, bleachable, Chgo lb	.20	.19¼	.20
Tallow, edible, Chgo lb	.24	.24	.25
FIBERS AND TEXTILES			
Burlap, 10 oz. 40-in. NY yd	n.2455	.2445	.3285
Cotton 1 1-16 in str lw-md Mphs lb	.7464	.7405	.8175
Print Cloth, cotton, 48-in NY yd	s.82	.83	.67
Print Cloth, pol/cot 48-in NY yd	t.58¼	.58½	.49½
Satin Acetate, NY yd	.64	.64	.58
Sheetings, 60x60 48-in. NY yd	.88½	.88½	.69
Wool, fine staple terr. Boston lb	2.87	2.87	2.48
METALS			
Aluminum ingot lb	p.76	.76	.72
Copper cathodes lb	p.82½-.83	.83-.84	1.04-1.05¾
Copper Scp, No. 2 wire NY lb.	k.62½	.63½	.79
Lead, lb.	p.42	.42	.36
Mercury 76 lb. flask NY	430.00	430.00	405.00
Nickel plating grade lb	p3.50	3.50	3.50
Steel Scrap 1 hvy mlt Chgo ton	93.00	100.00	75.00
Tin Metals Week composite lb.	7.0328	7.0319	8.5119
Zinc High Grade lb	p.46¼	.46¼	.35½
MISCELLANEOUS			
Hides, lt native cows Chgo lb	.48½	.48½	.51-.52
Newspapers, old No.1 Chgo ton	35.00	35.00	45.00-50.00
Rubber, smoked sheets, lb	n.54½	.54½	.67¼
PETROLEUM			
Crude, Saudi Arabia light, brl	32.00	32.00	28.00
Fuel Oil, No. 2 NY, gal	g.9375	.9300	.7700
Gasoline, Reg NY, gal	g1.0125	1.0125	.8750
Gasoline, Unld NY, gal	g1.06	1.06	.8900
PRECIOUS METALS			
Gold, troy oz			
Engelhard indust bullion	406.00	412.50	613.00
Engelhard fabric prods	422.24	429.00	634.46
Handy & Harman base price	406.00	412.50	613.00
London fixing AM 408.00 PM	406.00	412.50	613.00
Krugerrand, whol	a419.50	423.00	656.00
Platinum, troy ounce	p475.00	475.00	420.00
Silver, troy ounce			
Engelhard indust bullion	8.570	8.660	15.460
Engelhard fabric prods	9.137	9.233	16.286
Handy & Harman base price	8.620	8.710	15.510
London (in pounds)			
Spot (U.S. equiv. $8.500)	4.600	4.640	6.630
3 months	4.756	4.799	6.895
6 months	4.927	4.977	7.125
1 year	5.241	5.297	7.560
Coins, whol $1,000 face val	a8,745	8,705	12,885

a-Asked. b-Bid c-Corrected. d-Dealer market. e-Estimated g-f.o.b. harbor barge. Source: Oil Buyers' Guide. i-To arrive by rail within 30 days. k-Dealer selling price in lots of 40,000 pounds or more, f.o.b. buyer's works. n-Nominal. p-Producer price. r-Day's trading range. s-Thread count 78x76. t-Thread count 78x54. x-Less than truckloads. y-Delaware origin; varies seasonally. z-Not quoted.

SOURCE: *The Wall Street Journal*, July 22, 1981, p. 38.

Table 17—6   **Comparison of cash and near-term futures prices**

Grains and feeds	Cash price (Figure 17–3)	Futures price July 1981 (Figure 17–2)*
Corn	$3.21¾	$3.31½
Oats	$1.94–$1.97	$2.00½
Soybeans	$7.20¾	$7.19

*Note that we have shifted the decimal point two places to the left to convert from cents per bushel to dollars per bushel.

THE FUTURES MARKET FOR FINANCIAL INSTRUMENTS

The major event in the commodities markets for the last decade has been the development of financial futures contracts. With the great volatility in the foreign exchange markets and in interest rates, corporate treasurers, investors, and others have felt a great need to hedge their positions. Financial futures also have an appeal to speculators because of their low margin requirements and wide swings in value.

Financial futures may be broken down into two major categories, currency futures and interest rate futures.[5] Trading in currency futures began in May of 1972 on the International Monetary Market (part of the Chicago Mercantile Exchange). Interest rate futures started trading on the Chicago Board of Trade in October of 1975 with the GNMA certificate.[6] Trading in financial futures, regardless of whether they are currency or interest rate futures, is very similar to trading in traditional commodities, such as corn, wheat, copper, or pork bellies. There is a stipulated contract size, month of delivery, margin requirement, and so on. We will first look at currency futures and then shift our attention to interest rate futures.

CURRENCY FUTURES

These futures are generally available in eight different currencies. They include the following:

British pound.	West German mark.
Canadian dollar.	French franc.
Japanese yen.	Mexican peso.
Swiss franc.	Dutch guilder.

---

[5] A new type of financial future on common stock trading was also initiated in 1982. It relates to a futures contract on the Value Line 1700 Stock Index and trades on the Kansas City Board of Trade. Other stock-related futures contracts based on the Standard and Poor's 500 Stock Index and NYSE Index have followed.

[6] A GNMA (Ginnie Mae) certificate represents an interest in a pool of federally insured

The futures market in currencies provides many of the same functions as the older and less formalized market in "foreign exchange" operated by banks and specialized brokers, who maintain communication networks throughout the world. In either case, one can speculate or hedge. The currency futures market, however, is different in that it provides standardized contracts and a strong secondary market.

Let's examine how the currency futures market works. Assume you wish to purchase a currency futures contract in Japanese yen. The standardized contract is 12.5 million yen. The value of the contract is quoted in cents per yen. Assume that you purchase a December futures contract in July, and the price on the contract is .4342 cents per yen. The total value of the contract is $54,275 (12.5 million yen × $.004342). The typical margin on a yen contract is $3,000.

We will assume that the yen strengthens relative to the dollar. This might happen because of decreasing U.S. interest rates, declining inflation in Japan, or any number of other reasons. Under these circumstances, the currency might rise to .4530 cents per yen (the yen is now equivalent to more cents than it was previously). The value of the contract has now risen to $56,625 (12.5 million × $.004530). This represents an increase in value of $2,350.

$$\begin{array}{r} \$56,625 \\ -54,275 \\ \hline \$\ 2,350 \end{array}$$

With an original margin requirement of $3,000, this represents a return of 78.3 percent.

$$\frac{\$2,350}{\$3,000} \times 100 = 78.3\%$$

On an annualized basis, it would even be higher. Of course, the contract could produce a loss if the yen weakens against the dollar as a result of higher interest rates in the United States or increasing inflation in Japan. With a normal margin maintenance requirement of $2,400, a $600 loss on the contract will call for additional margin beyond the original $3,000.

Corporate treasurers often try to hedge an exposed position in their foreign exchange dealings through the currency futures market. Assume a treasurer closes a deal today to receive payment in two months in Japanese yen. If the yen goes down relative to the dollar, he will have less value than he anticipated. One solution would be to sell a yen futures contract (go short). If the value of the yen

---

mortgages. Actually, GNMA (the Government National Mortgage Association) buys a pool of mortgages from various lenders at a discount and then issues securities to the public against the mortgages. They are pass-through in nature in that the holder of a GNMA certificate receives the interest and principal payment on the mortgages on a monthly basis.

Table 17—7   **Contracts in currency futures**

Currency	Trading units	Size of contract based on mid–1981 prices
British pound	25,000	$46,250
Canadian dollar	100,000	$83,000
Swiss franc	125,000	$60,000
West German mark	125,000	$51,250

goes down, he will make money on his futures contract that will offset the loss on the receipt of the Japanese yen in two months.

In Table 17—7, we see the typical size of contracts for four other foreign currencies that trade on the International Monetary Market (part of the Chicago Mercantile Exchange).

INTEREST RATE FUTURES

Since the inception of the interest rate futures contract with GNMA certificates in October of 1975, the market has been greatly expanded to include Treasury bonds, Treasury bills, Treasury notes, commercial paper, and certificates of deposits. There is almost unlimited potential for futures contracts on interest-related items (though the Commodity Futures Trading Commission has been cautious in its approval of new items).

Interest rate futures trade on a number of major exchanges including the Chicago Board of Trade, the International Monetary Market of the Chicago Mercantile Exchange, the New York Futures Exchange, and the American Commodities Exchange. As we mentioned earlier, there is competition between Chicago and New York on interest rate futures. The most popularly traded contracts in the early 1980s were Treasury bonds and GNMA certificates traded on the Chicago Board of Trade and Treasury bills traded on the International Monetary Market of the Chicago Mercantile Exchange. However, the New York Futures Exchange was coming on strong with their Treasury bond and certificates of deposit futures, and the American Commodities Exchange was also moving into various Treasury futures, such as Treasury bonds and Treasury bills.

A comparison of the monthly volume on an interest rate future (Treasury bonds) and a traditional commodity (cattle) is presented in Figure 17—4. As would be expected, the growth in interest rate futures has been explosive.

Figure 17—5 shows an example of quotes on interest rate futures. Direct your attention to the second category, Treasury bonds (CBT), trading on the Chicago Board of Trade.

They trade in units of $100,000, and the quotes are in percent of par taken to 32ds of a percentage point. Although it is not shown in this data, the bonds on which the futures are based are assumed to be new, 15-year instruments paying

Figure 17–4 **Increasing emphasis on interest rate futures**

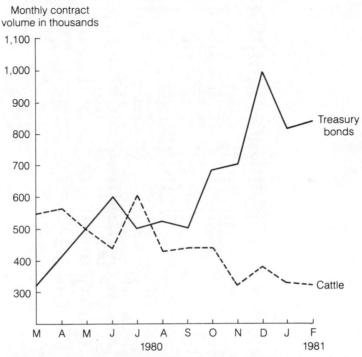

Data from Chicago Board of Trade and Chicago Mercantile Exchange.

8 percent interest. Since long-term rates tend to be above 8 percent, the quoted price is usually at a discount from $100,000. In the first column for the September contract for Treasury bonds, we see a price of 61–21. This indicates a value of $61^{21}/_{32}$ percent of par. We thus show a contract value of $61,656.25 ($61^{21}/_{32}$ × $100,000). This represents the opening value. The entire line would read as follows.

	Open	High	Low	Settle	Change	Yield Settle	Change	Open Interest
Sept	61–21	62–00	62–11	61–28	+3	13.581	−.020	52,877

We see the settle or closing price is 61–28, which represents a change (chg.) of $^9/_{32}$ from the close from the previous day. The reader should be aware that the close for the previous day is not necessarily the same as the open for the current

Figure 17—5   **Examples of price quotes on interest rate futures**

```
        GNMA 8% (CBT) — $100,000 prncpl; pts., 32nds of 100%
                                          Yield        Open
        Open  High  Low  Settle  Chg  Settle  Chg  Interest
Sept   59-27 60-13 59-26 60-10  + 11  15.563 − .096  13,008
Dec    60-14 60-26 60-07 60-24  + 11  15.441 − .096  13,368
Mar82  60-26 61-09 60-25 61-08  + 12  15.304 − .103  11,599
June   61-11 61-21 61-10 61-21  + 15  15.194 − .127  12,401
Sept   61-14 61-31 61-14 61-31  + 17  15.110 − .143  12,277
Dec    61-26 62-07 61-24 62-07  + 18  15.043 − .151  12,478
Mar83  61-28 62-14 61-28 62-14  + 19  14.985 − .158  12,653
June   62-04 62-20 62-04 62-20  + 21  14.935 − .175   9,628
Sept   62-08 62-25 62-08 62-25  + 23  14.894 − .191  11,486
Dec    62-10 62-30 62-10 62-30  + 26  14.853 − .215   8,553
Mar84  ..... ..... ..... 63-02  + 28  14.821 − .230  10,378
June   62-14 63-06 62-14 63-06  + 30  14.788 − .247   4,688
Sept   62-16 63-10 62-16 63-10  + 32  14.756 − .262   1,503
Dec    ..... ..... ..... 63-14  + 34  14.723 − .279     481
Mar85  ..... ..... ..... 63-18  + 36  14.691 − .294       1
     Est vol 7,700; vol Mon 10,636; open int 134.532, − 26.
         TREASURY BONDS (CBT) — $100,000; pts. 32nds of 100%
Sept   61-21 62-00 61-11 61-28  +  3  13.581 − .020  52,877
Dec    62-11 62-28 62-07 62-24  +  6  13.392 − .040  33,709
Mar82  63-07 63-18 63-00 63-15  +  7  13.240 − .046  28,986
June   63-23 64-02 63-19 64-01  +  8  13.124 − .051  27,386
Sept   64-05 64-17 64-01 64-16  +  9  13.028 − .057  27,655
Dec    64-17 64-30 64-17 64-30  + 11  12.939 − .070  29,035
Mar83  65-01 65-10 64-30 65-10  + 12  12.864 − .075  22,642
June   65-03 65-21 65-03 65-21  + 13  12.796 − .081  17,197
Sept   65-14 65-31 65-13 65-31  + 14  12.735 − .086  23,571
Dec    65-27 66-08 65-26 66-08  + 15  12.680 − .091  21,574
Mar84  65-29 66-16 65-29 66-16  + 15  12.631 − .091  20,646
June   66-10 66-23 66-10 66-23  + 15  12.589 − .091   9,867
Sept   66-20 66-30 66-20 66-30  + 15  12.547 − .090   2,640
Dec    ..... ..... ..... 67-05  + 15  12.506 − .089     562
     Est vol 52,000; vol Mon 50,747; open int 318,329, +3,230.
         TREASURY BONDS (NYFE) — $100,000; pts. 32nds of 100
Aug    67-10 67-27 67-07 67-22  +  4  13.788 − .026     495
Nov    68-07 68-15 68-07 68-15  +  4  13.629 − .025     799
Feb82  ..... ..... ..... 69-01  +  4  13.516 − .025   1,559
May    69-07 69-07 69-07 69-13  +  4  13.442 − .024   1,216
Aug    ..... ..... ..... 69-21  +  4  13.392 − .025     607
Nov    ..... ..... ..... 69-28  +  4  13.350 − .024     473
Feb83  70-03 70-03 70-03 70-10  +  5  13.265 − .030     173
May    70-18 70-18 70-18 70-25  +  7  13.175 − .042     100
     Est vol 656; vol Mon 547; open int 5,422, − 53.
         TREASURY BILLS (IMM) — $1 mil.; pts. of 100%
                                         Discount    Open
        Open  High  Low  Settle  Chg  Settle  Chg  Interest
Sept   85.40 85.53 85.20 85.29  − .49  14.71 + .49  19,199
Dec    86.15 86.28 86.00 86.10  − .29  13.90 + .29  10,128
Mar82  86.75 86.83 86.57 86.71  − .14  13.29 + .14   7,533
June   87.02 87.12 86.91 87.04  − .01  12.96 + .01   2,848
Sept   87.10 87.25 87.08 87.19  + .03  12.81 − .03   1,715
Dec    87.25 87.30 87.17 87.28  + .03  12.72 − .03     901
Mar83  87.25 87.37 87.23 87.29  + .01  12.71 − .01     768
June   ..... ..... .... 87.30  ....  12.70               7
     Est vol 22,265; vol Mon 17,200; open int 43,099, +1,783.
```

day.[7] We also see what yield the settle (closing) price represents on a 15-year bond paying an 8 percent coupon rate. In this case, it is 13.581 percent, which is a decline in yield from the previous day of .020 percent. The decline in yield is consistent with the increase in settle price (and vice versa). Finally, we see there is an open interest of 52,877 indicating the number of contracts that are presently outstanding for September.

Assume we buy a September futures contract for 61-28 or $61,875 ($61^{28}/_{32}$ × $100,000). The margin requirement for this contract on the Chicago Board of

---

[7]A number of overnight events can cause the difference. In this case, we can assume the close for the previous day was 61–25 based on the change of +3.

Trade is $2,000 with a $1,600 margin maintenance requirement. In this case, it may be that we have bought the futures contract because we anticipate easier monetary policy by the Federal Reserve, which will trigger a decline in interest rates and an increase in bond prices. If interest rates decline by .3 percent (30 basis points), Treasury bond prices will increase by approximately $1^{30}/_{32}$.[8] On a $100,000 par value futures contract, this would represent a gain of $1,937.50 as indicated below.

$$\times \quad \frac{\$100,000}{\$1,937.50} \quad 1^{30}/_{32}\% \ (1.9375\%)$$

With a $2,000 initial margin, the $1,937.50 profit represents an attractive return. Note, however, that if interest rates go up by even a small amount, our Treasury bond futures contract value will fall, and there will be a margin call.

As is true of other commodities, when we trade in interest rate futures, we do not take actual title or possession of the commodity unless we fail to reverse our initial position. The contract merely represents a bet or hedge on the direction of future interest rates and bond prices.

Quotes on Treasury bill futures

One type of interest rate future that requires special attention is the Treasury bill future. Particular reference in this case is made to the 90-day, $1 million, T bill futures contract that trades on the International Monetary Market of the Chicago Mercantile Exchange and is shown on the bottom portion of Figure 17–5. We reproduce the first line below.

	Open	High	Low	Settle	Change	Yield Settle	Change	Open Interest
Sept	85.40	83.53	85.20	85.29	−.49	14.71	+.49	19,199

The items of particular interest are the settle price of 85.29 and the settle yield of 14.71 percent. Unlike other interest rate futures, such as Treasury bonds or GNMA certificates, we cannot simply multiply the settle price of 85.29 (percent) times par value of $1 million to get the value of the contract. Why? Because this Treasury bill represents a 90-day instrument, and the annual yield of 14.71 percent must be converted to a 90-day rate in order to determine value. We thus take the annual rate of 14.71 percent and multiply it by $^{90}/_{360}$ to get an equivalent 90-day yield of 3.68 percent.

$$14.71\% \times \frac{90}{360} = 3.68\%$$

---

[8]This is derived from a standard bond table and not explicitly calculated in their example.

We then subtract this value from 100 percent to get the appropriate percentage to multiply times par value to get the value of the contract. For the $1 million Treasury bill, the actual converted price is:

$$(100\% - 3.68\%) \times \$1,000,000$$
$$96.32\% \times \$1,000,000 = \$963,200$$

Each time the yield on a Treasury bill changes by .01 percent ($\frac{1}{100}$ of 1 percent or 1 basis point), the price of the T bill future will change by $25 as indicated in the two steps below.

$$.01\% \text{ of } \$1,000,000 = \$100$$

we convert this from an annual rate to a 90-day rate by multiplying by $\frac{90}{360}$.

$$\$100 \times \frac{90}{360} = \$25$$

Thus, if you buy a Treasury bill futures contract and interest rates on Treasury bills change by .50 percent (50 basis points), you will gain or lose $1,250.

$$
\begin{array}{ll}
\$25 & \text{For each .01\% or basis points} \\
\underline{\times\ 50} & \text{Basis points} \\
\$1,250 &
\end{array}
$$

The initial margin requirement for a $1 million Treasury bill on the International Monetary Market of the Chicago Mercantile Exchange is only $1,500, with a $1,200 margin maintenance requirement. The daily trading limit is 50 basis points, so a $1,250 change in value is possible in one day.[9]

Hedging with interest rate futures

Interest rate futures have opened up opportunities for hedging that can only be compared to the development of the traditional commodities market over a century ago. Consider the following potential hedges against interest rate risks.

a. A corporate treasurer is awaiting a new debt issue that will take place in 60 days. The underwriters are still putting the final details together. The great fear is that interest rates will rise between now and then. The treasurer could hedge his or her position in the futures market by selling a Treasury bond, Treasury bill, GNMA certificate, or other similar security short. If interest rates go up, the price to buy back the interest rate futures will go down, and a profit will be made on the short position. This will partially or fully offset the higher interest costs on the new debt issue.

b. A corporate treasurer is continually reissuing commercial paper at new interest rates or borrowing under a floating prime agreement at the bank. He or she fears that interest rates will go up and make a big dent in projected

---

[9]The American Commodity Exchange and other markets have even smaller margin requirements and larger daily limits for price movements, so there is plenty of opportunity for action.

profits. By selling (going short) on commercial paper, certificates of deposit, or other interest rate futures, the corporate treasurer can make enough profit on interest rate futures if interest rates go up to compensate for the higher costs of money.

c. A mortgage banker has made a forward commitment to provide a loan at a set interest rate one month in the future. If interest rates go up, the resale value of the mortgage in the secondary market will go down. He or she can hedge the position by selling or going short on a GNMA certificate futures contract or other interest rate futures contract.

d. A pension fund manager has been receiving a steady return of 15 percent on his short-term portfolio in 90-day Treasury bills. He is afraid that interest rates will go down and he will have to adjust to receiving lower returns on the managed funds. His strategy might be to buy (go long) on a Treasury bill futures contract. If interest rates go down, he will make a profit on his futures contract that will partially or fully offset his decline in interest income. Of course, if he is heavily invested in long-term securities and fearful of an interest rate rise, a sell or short position that would provide profits on an interest rate rise would be advisable. This, of course, would offset part of the loss in the portfolio value due to increasing interest rates.

e. A commercial banker has most of his loans on a floating prime basis, meaning that the rate that he charges will change with the cost of funds. However, some of the loans have a fixed rate associated with them. If the cost of funds go up, the fixed-rate loans will become unprofitable. By selling or going short in interest rate futures, the danger of higher interest rates can be hedged away by the profits he will make on the interest rate futures. Similarly, a banker may make a commitment to pay a set amount of interest on certificates of deposit for the next six months. If interest rates go down, the banker may have to loan the funds at a lower rate than he is currently paying. If he buys a futures contract in certificates of deposit, then lower interest rates will increase the value of the contract and provide a profit. This will offset the possible negative profitability spread described above.

An actual example   Assume an industrial corporation has a $10 million, 15-year bond to be issued in 60 days. Long-term rates for such an issue are currently 13.75 percent, and there is concern that interest rates will go up by ¼ percent by the time of the issue. The corporate treasurer has figured out that the extra ¼ percent would have a present value cost of $153,550 over the life of the issue (on a before-tax basis).

$$\begin{array}{ll} \underline{\begin{array}{r} \$10,000,000 \\ \tfrac{1}{4}\% \end{array}} & \\ \underline{\begin{array}{r} \$25,000 \\ 6.142 \end{array}} & \text{Present value factor for 15 years at 14 percent} \\ \$153,550 & \text{Present value of futures costs} \end{array}$$

To establish a hedge position, he sells 161 Treasury bond futures short. We assume they are currently selling at 62 (62 percent of $100,000), equaling $62,000 each. The total value of the hedge would be $9,982,000. This is roughly the equivalent to the $10 million size of the corporate bond issue. If interest rates go up by ¼ percent, the profit on the Treasury bond futures contract (due to falling prices with a short position) will probably offset the present value of the increased cost of the corporate bond issue.

Of course, we do not suggest that both rates (on Treasury bonds and corporate bonds) would move exactly together. However, the general thrust of the example should be apparent. We are actually establishing a *cross-hedging* pattern by using one form of security (Treasury bonds) to hedge another form of security (corporate bonds). This is often necessary. Even when the same security is used, there may be differences in maturity dates or quality characteristics so that a perfect hedge is difficult to establish.

Many financial managers prefer partial hedges to complete hedges. They are willing to take away part of the risk but not all of it. Others prefer no hedge at all because it locks in their position. While a hedge insures them against loss, it precludes the possibility of an abnormal gain.

Nevertheless, in a risk-averse financial market environment, most financial managers can gain by hedging their position as described in the many examples in this section. Companies such as Burlington Northern, Esmark, and Stauffer Chemical have established reputations for just such actions.[10] Others have not yet joined the movement because of a lack of appreciation or understanding of the highly innovative financial futures market. Much of this will change with the passage of time.

FINAL COMMENT ON COMMODITIES AND FINANCIAL FUTURES

Those who want to invest in commodities may do so through individual accounts (usually requiring a minimum $5,000 balance), through managed accounts (in which a professional advisor calls most of the shots), or through a commodity fund. The latter distributes the risk among many investors and provides additional management skill.

As previously mentioned in this chapter, the commodities futures contract is somewhat similar to the options contract covered in Chapter 13 in that both provide a high degree of leverage on a minimal investment. The Chicago Board Options Exchange (CBOE) has actually received permission to trade options on GNMA certificates. However, there is an essential difference between options and commodities. In the options market, the investor who buys an option can lose no more than his or her purchase price and will never be called upon to put up more funds. In the commodities futures market, an initial margin for a contract that has six months to termination can be wiped out in the first hours of trading.

[10]"Hedging with Interest Rate Futures," *Business Week,* December 8, 1980, p. 96.

SUMMARY

In this chapter, we break down the commodities futures markets into traditional commodities, such as grains and wheat, livestock, and meat, and financial futures primarily in currencies and interest rates.

A commodities futures contract is an agreement that provides for the delivery of a specific amount of a commodity at a designated time in the future. It is not intended that the purchaser of a contract take actual possession of the goods, but rather that he or she reverse or close out the contract before delivery is due. The same is true for the seller.

Primary participants in the commodities market include both speculators and hedgers. We first examine speculators. A speculator buys a commodities contract (goes long) or sells a commodities contract (goes short) because he believes he can effectively anticipate the direction in which the market is going to move. Because of low margin (initial deposit) requirements of 5 to 10 percent, large profits or losses are possible with small price movements. If the market moves against someone who has a commodity contract, they may be asked to put up additional margin.

A hedger buys or sells a commodities futures contract to protect an underlying position he might have in the actual commodity. For example, a wheat farmer may sell (go short) on a futures contract in wheat to protect against a price decline. If prices go down, he can buy back his contract at a lower price than he sold it and record a profit on the transaction. This may offset any losses he incurs as a result of selling wheat at a lower price to its intended user. Of course, if the price goes up, he will lose on his futures contract but make up the difference on the actual sale of wheat. Millers or bakers who know they will have to purchase wheat in the future may buy (go long) on a futures contract. If the price goes up, they will make money on the contract, and this will offset the added production costs.

Many commodity futures exchanges provide areas where buyers and sellers can negotiate cash (or spot) prices. The cash price is the actual dollar paid for the immediate delivery of the goods. Near-term futures prices and cash prices tend to approximate each other.

Financial futures are composed primarily of currency and interest rate futures. Although these markets only came into existence in the 1970s, they have seen explosive growth. The contract on financial futures is very similar to that on basic, traditional commodities; only the items traded and units of measurement are different.

Currency futures relate to eight different currencies and enable the financial manager to hedge this position in foreign markets. There is also active participation by the speculators.

Interest rate futures cover Treasury bonds, Treasury bills, GNMA certificates, Treasury notes, commercial paper, and certificates of deposit. Many other items are on the drawing board. Interest rate futures generally trade in units of $100,000 or $1 million with extremely low margin requirements. There is a battle between the traditional commodity exchanges in Chicago and the New York Futures Exchange (part of the New York Stock Exchange) and the Amex Commodity Ex-

change (part of the American Stock Exchange) to see who will ultimately have a dominant position in the financial futures markets.

In the current environment of volatile interest rates, interest rate futures offer an excellent opportunity to hedge dangerous interest rate risks. Possible hedgers include corporate financial officers, pension fund managers, mortgage bankers, and commercial bankers. As sophistication and understanding in the use of these hedging techniques increase, the market in financial futures will continue to expand.

IMPORTANT WORDS AND CONCEPTS	Futures contract	Currency futures
	Commodity markets	Interest rates futures
	Hedging	Settle price
	Margin requirement	Bases point
	Margin maintenance requirement	Cross hedge
	Inverse pyramiding	Partial hedge
	Spot market	

QUESTIONS AND PROBLEMS

1. What is a futures contract?

2. Do you have to take delivery or deliver the commodity if you are a party to a futures contract?

3. Explain what hedging is.

4. Why is there substantial leverage in commodity investments?

5. What are the basic categories of items traded on the commodities exchanges?

6. What group has primary regulatory responsibility for the activities of the commodity exchanges?

7. What is a maintenance margin requirement?

8. You purchase a 5,000-bushel contract for wheat at $5 per bushel with an initial margin requirement of 5 percent. The price goes up to $5.15 in one month. What is your percentage profit and the annualized gain?

9. Problem 8 generally assumed you were a speculator. Now assume you are a hedger. If you were a potential purchaser of wheat (perhaps a miller), explain how the commodities contract in problem 8 would allow you to hedge against future price changes before you actually buy the wheat for cash.

10. With a 5,000-bushel contract for $30,000, assume the margin requirement is $2,500 and maintenance margin is 80 percent. How much would the price per bushel have to fall before additional margin is required?

11. If contracts are written on a 5,000-bushel basis requiring $2,000 of margin and you control 10 contracts, how much would the price per bushel have to change to generate enough profit to purchase an additional contract?

12. Referring to number 11, how many contracts would need to be controlled to generate enough profit for a new margin contract if the price changed by only 1 cent per bushel?

13. What is meant by a daily trading limit on a commodities contract?

14. Refer to Figure 17–2, and explain the quotation for December wheat on the Chicago Board of Trade (CBT).

15. How does the cash market differ from the futures market for commodities?

16. What are the two main categories of financial futures?

17. How does the currency futures market differ from the foreign exchange market?

18. What is the value of the June 1982 Treasury bill contract in Figure 17–5? Remember to convert settle yield (12.96 percent) from an annual basis to a 90-day basis as the first step in the calculation.

19. If you purchase a Treasury bill futures contract and interest rates change by 25 bases points, how much does this represent in dollars?

20. How can using the financial futures market help financial managers through hedging? Briefly explain and give one example.

SELECTED REFERENCES

Angell, George. *Winning in the Commodities Market.* New York: Doubleday & Co., 1979.

Bacon, Peter W., and Richard Williams. "Interest Rate Futures Trading: New Tool for the Financial Manager." *Financial Management,* Spring 1976, pp. 32–38.

Bear, Robert M. "Margin Levels and the Behavior of Futures Prices." *Journal of Financial and Quantitative Analysis,* September 1972, pp. 1907–30.

Dusak, Katherine. "Futures Trading and Investor Returns: An Investigation of Commodity Market Risk Premiums." *Journal of Political Economy,* November–December 1973, pp. 1387–1406.

Harlow, Charles V., and Richard J. Teweles. "Commodities and Securities Compared." *Financial Analysts Journal,* September–October 1972, pp. 64–70.

"Hedging with Interest Rate Futures." *Business Week,* December 8, 1980, p. 96.

Peterson, Richard L. "Investor Preferences for Futures Straddler." *Journal of Financial and Quantitative Analysis,* March 1977, pp. 105–20.

Powers, Mark J. "Does Futures Trading Reduce Price Fluctuations in the Cash Markets?" *American Economic Review,* June 1970, pp. 460–64.

Robichek, Alexander; Richard Cohn; and John Pringle. "Returns on Alternative Investment Media and Implications for Portfolio Construction." *Journal of Business,* July 1972, pp. 427–43.

Senchach, Andrew J., Jr., and Donald M. Heep. "Auction Profits in the Treasury Bill Market." *Financial Management,* Summer 1975, pp. 45–52.

Shellenbarger, Susan. "Boom in Financial Futures Trading Transforms Commodities Markets." *The Wall Street Journal,* March, 23, 1981, p. 25.

"Speculating on Inflation: Futures Trading in Interest Rates, Foreign Currencies and Precious Metals." Merrill Lynch, Pierce, Fenner & Smith, July 1979.

Stevenson, Richard A., and Robert M. Bear. "Commodity Futures: Trends or Random Walks." *Journal of Finance,* March 1970, pp. 65–82.

Telser, Lester G., and Harlow N. Higinbotham. "Organized Futures Markets: Costs and Benefits." *Journal of Political Economy,* October 1977, pp. 969–1000.

"The Zooming Futures Market." *Business Week,* June 11, 1979, pp. 62–73.

18

Investments in real assets

In this chapter, we turn our attention to real assets; that is, tangible assets that may be seen, felt, held, or collected. Examples of such assets are real estate, gold, silver, diamonds, coins, stamps, and antiques. This is no small area from which to consider investments. For example, the total market value of all real estate holdings in the United States in 1980 was $3 trillion as compared to $1 trillion in stocks and bonds.

As further evidence of value, in 1980 Rubens's painting, *Samson and Delilah,* sold for $5.4 million, and a 132-carat diamond earring set sold for $6.6 million. Coins and stamps also sold for values well into the hundreds of thousands.

A number of the traditional stock brokerage houses have moved into the area of real assets with such firms as Merrill Lynch participating in real estate and Thomson McKinnon Securities managing a diamond fund. Likewise, Citicorp of New York has an art investment program. No less than 25 million people in the United States are stamp collectors, and 8 million collect and invest in coins.

As was pointed out in Chapter 5, in inflationary environments, real assets have at times outperformed financial assets (such as stocks and bonds), at least in the short run. With this in mind, the reader is well advised to become familiar with these investment outlets—not only to take advantage of the investment opportunities, but to be well aware of the pitfalls. A money manager who is challenged by clients to include real assets in a portfolio (such as real estate or precious metals) must be conversant not only with the opportunities, but also with the drawbacks.

ADVANTAGES AND DISADVANTAGES OF REAL ASSETS

As previously mentioned, real assets may offer an opportunity as an inflation hedge. This is because inflation means higher replacement costs for real estate, precious metals, and other physical items. Real assets also serve as an investment hedge against the unknown and feared. When people become concerned about world events, gold and other precious metals may be perceived as the last, safe haven for investments.

435

Real assets also may serve as an effective vehicle for portfolio diversification. Since financial and real assets at times move in opposite directions, some efficient diversification may take place. A study by Robichek, Cohn, and Pringle in the *Journal of Business* actually indicates that movements between various types of real and monetary assets are less positively correlated than are those for monetary assets alone.[1] The general findings indicate that enlarging the universe of investment alternatives would benefit the overall portfolio construction in terms of risk-return alternatives. The reader who wishes to follow the performance of a wide range of investments can consult the monthly investment scorecard of *Money* magazine as a source. An example is presented in Table 18–1.

A final advantage of an investment in real assets is the psychic pleasure that may be provided. One can easily relate to a beautiful painting in the living room, a mint gold coin in a bank lockbox, or an attractive real estate development.

There are many disadvantages to consider as well. Perhaps the largest drawback is the absence of large, liquid, and relatively efficient markets. Whereas stocks or bonds can generally be sold in a few minutes at a value close to the latest quoted trade, such is not likely to be the case for real estate, diamonds, art, and other forms of real assets. It may take many months to get the desired price for a real asset, and even then, there is an air of uncertainty about the impending transaction until it is consummated.

Furthermore, there is the problem of dealer spread or middleman commission. Whereas in the trading of stocks and bonds, spreads or commissions are very small (usually 1 or 2 percent), dealer spreads for real assets can be as large as 20 to 25 percent or more. This is particularly true for small items that do not have great value. On more valuable items, such as rare paintings, valuable jewels, or mint gold coins, the dealer spread tends to be smaller (perhaps 5 to 10 percent) but still more than that on securities.

The investor in real assets generally receives no current income (with the possible exception of real estate) and may in fact incur storage and insurance costs. Furthermore, there may be the problem of high unit cost for investments. You cannot easily acquire multiple art masterpieces.

A final drawback or caveat in real assets is the hysteria or overreaction that tends to come into the marketplace from time to time. Gold, silver, diamonds, and coins may be temporarily bid all out of proportion to previously anticipated value. The last buyer, who arrives too late, may end up owning a very unprofitable investment. The trick is to get into the recurring cycle early enough to take advantage of the large capital gains opportunities that regularly occur for real assets. Also, you should buy items of high enough quality so that you can ride out the setbacks if your timing is incorrect.

In the remainder of this chapter, we will examine real estate, gold, silver, dia-

[1]Alexander A. Robichek, Richard A. Cohn, and John J. Pringle, "Return on Alternative Media and Implications for Portfolio Construction," *Journal of Business,* July 1972, pp. 427–43.

Table 18–1 Investment scorecard

	End of July	A month earlier	A year earlier	One-month change	12-month change
Stocks:					
Standard & Poor's 500 Index	121.67	114.24	103.81	+6.5%	+17.2%
American Stock Exchange Index	314.49	293.61	198.69	+7.1%	+58.3%
Growth stock average	116.64	104.40	102.68	+11.7%	+13.6%
Fixed-income securities (yields):					
Long-term Treasury bonds	10.60%	9.94%	8.95%	+6.6%	+18.4%
Intermediate-term utility bonds	11.63%	10.75%	9.20%	+8.2%	+26.4%
Six-month Treasury bills	8.68%	7.92%	9.40%	+9.6%	−7.7%
Currencies:					
British pound	$2.33	$2.36	$2.24	−1.3%	+4.0%
Japanese yen (100)	$4.42	$4.59	$4.61	−3.7%	−4.1%
Commodities:					
Gold (ounce)	$614.25	$653.50	$296.45	−6.0%	+107.2%
Silver (ounce)	$15.80	$16.48	$9.05	−4.1%	+ 74.6%
Sugar (pound)	30.1¢	32.3¢	8.5¢	−6.8%	+254.1%
Copper (pound)	95.8¢	91.3¢	81.3¢	+4.9%	+17.8%
Real estate:					
Real Estate Investment Trust Index	38.57	35.61	35.30	+8.3%	+9.3%
Iowa farmland (per acre)	$1,581	—	$1,550	—	+2.0%
Collectibles:					
Art Nouveau posters portfolio	$68,200	—	$45,750	—	+49.1%
Ceylon sapphire (one carat)	$2,300	—	$1,600	—	+43.8%
Oriental rugs (Caucasion Shirvan)	$9,500	—	$6,500	—	+46.2%
Mickey Mantle 1960 baseball card	$22.75	$22.50	$6.00	+1.1%	+279.2%

Notes: Percentages are based on month-end figures, except in the case of most collectibles, for which the only reliable data are semiannual. In the fixed-income market, new investors earn the yields shown; since prices fall as yields rise and vice versa, securities already owned gain or lose investment value as yields change. Data gathered from Smith Barney Harris Upham; Salomon Bros.; Commodity Research Bureau; National Association of Real Estate Investment Trusts; U.S. Department of Agriculture and Federal Reserve Bank of Chicago; Reinhold-Brown Gallery, New York; PreciouStones Newsletter; the Ghiordian Knot, New York; Baseball Hobby News.
SOURCE: *Money,* September 1980, p. 12.

monds, and other collectibles as investment outlets. Because real estate lends itself more directly to analytical techniques familiar to students of finance, it will receive a proportionately larger share of our attention.

REAL ESTATE AS AN INVESTMENT

Approximately one half of the households in the United States own real estate as a home or investment. Also, many firms in the brokerage and investment community have also moved into the real estate sector. As examples, Merrill Lynch, Lehman Brothers, Kuhn Loeb, and Shearson/American Express have acquired real estate affiliates to broker property, conduct mortgage banking activi-

ties, or package real estate syndications. While only 1 percent of pension fund assets are currently in real estate, predictions indicate that the number may grow to 10 percent by the end of the current decade.[2]

Some insight into changing real estate values may be gained from viewing Figure 18–1. We see the gain for a dollar invested in 1946 (as compared to fixed-income investments).

In Table 18–2, we see the change in conventional mortgage rates and median home prices in the United States during the decade of the 1970s. The gain in home prices is over threefold.

Real estate investments may include such outlets as your own home, du-

Figure 18–1   **Growth in value, 1946–1980 ($1 of investment)**

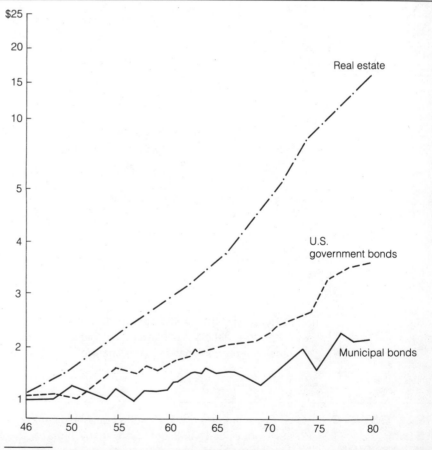

[2]"Soaring Real Estate Values are Enticing Big Securities Concerns into the Field," *The Wall Street Journal,* August 6, 1980, p. 32.

Table 18—2   **Mortgage rates and home prices**

Year	Average conventional mortgage rate	Median price of a new home
1970	8.40	$23,258
1971	7.71	24,998
1972	7.56	27,110
1973	7.98	30,823
1974	8.97	34,055
1975	9.11	37,237
1976	9.05	41,179
1977	9.02	45,867
1978	9.56	52,242
1979	13.00	75,000

SOURCES: Federal Home Loan Bank Board (Washington, D.C.); National Association of REALTORS® (Chicago); Moody's (New York), Jim Kaden, economist; and the U.S. League of Savings Associations (Chicago).

plexes and apartment buildings, office buildings, shopping centers, industrial buildings, hotels and motels, as well as raw land. The investor may participate as an individual, as part of a limited partnership real estate syndicate, or through a real estate investment trust. These forms of ownership will receive further coverage toward the end of this section.

We have already talked generally about the advantages and disadvantages of real assets (on the positive side, an inflation hedge and the associated psychic value, and on the negative side, illiquidity and high transaction costs). Over and above these considerations, real estate also has some unique features of its own. A major advantage of real estate relates to tax considerations. Accelerated depreciation and interest payments can provide substantial tax benefits. Also, real estate provides for a high degree of leverage with a cash down payment of 20 to 25 percent supporting a large asset base. Most other forms of real assets do not serve so readily as collateral. An issue associated with real estate is the high degree of government regulation (particularly at the local level). Thus, the investor must be prepared to deal with zoning regulations, building codes, and the incidence of relatively high property taxes. On the other hand, the government also serves in a positive role by providing guarantees for FHA and VA loans and a secondary market for mortgages (the original lender can dispose of the initial mortgage).

Throughout the rest of this section on real estate, we will evaluate a typical real estate investment and the related tax aspects, consider new methods of real estate financing, and examine limited partner syndicates and real estate investment trusts.

INVESTMENT EXAMPLE

Assume we are considering investing $170,000 in a new fourplex (four-unit apartment housing project). Our land costs will be $30,000, and the actual physical structure will cost $140,000. This latter amount will be the value to be depreciated. Though we are dealing with relatively small numbers for ease of computation, the same types of considerations would apply to a multimillion-dollar shopping center or office building. Before we actually evaluate our cash inflows and outflows, we will consider tax and accounting factors related to depreciation in real estate.

Depreciation effects

In the present case, we can write off depreciation on real estate over 15 years under the provisions of the 1981 Economic Recovery Tax Act. The act further specifies that we can use 175 percent declining balance as the most rapid depreciation write-off method on real estate. Actually, we will start out using 175 percent declining balance and shift to straight-line depreciation in order to optimize our position. Let's see how this works. Under 175 percent declining balance, we take depreciation at 175 percent of straight line. On a 15-year asset, straight line would be 6.67 percent per year—so 175 percent declining balance would be 11.67 percent (6.66% × 175%). The IRS actually rounds this value off at 12% for first year depreciation. In the second year, depreciation would be 11.67% × (100% − 11.67%) or 11.67 × 88.33%. The answer is 10.3%. The IRS rounds this value off to 10%. In Table 18–3, we actually see allowable accelerated depreciation on real estate as specified under the 1981 Economic Recovery Tax Act. The table approximates 175 percent declining balance depreciation with an assumed shift to straight-line during the life of the asset.

Applying the depreciation schedule in table 18–3 to our $140,000 physical structure (fourplex building), we show the depreciation schedule in Table 18–4. The $30,000 land value cannot be written off for depreciation purposes.

Most real estate investors prefer the most rapid depreciation possible in the early years because it provides a tax shelter for other income. However, there are two issues here. One is that a rapid rate of depreciation in the early life of the asset dictates a slower rate in the later years as depreciation runs out.

Table 18–3

Accelerated depreciation allowance on real estate under the 1981 Economic Recovery Tax Act (approximates 175 declining balance depreciation with an eventual shift to straight-line)

Year of depreciation	Percentage depreciation
1	12
2	10
3	9
4	8
5	7
6–9	6
10–15	5

Table 18–4   **Accelerated depreciation schedule for investment**

Year	Percentage depreciation	Initial asset value	Dollar depreciation
1	12%	$140,000	$16,800
2	10%		14,000
3	9%		12,600
4	8%		11,200
5	7%		9,800
6	6%		8,400
7	6%		8,400
8	6%		8,400
9	6%		8,400
10	5%		7,000
11	5%		7,000
12	5%		7,000
13	5%		7,000
14	5%		7,000
15	5%		7,000

A second issue related to accelerated depreciation is that of *recaptured depreciation,* which can take place upon selling the property. When accelerated depreciation is taken and the property is sold at a profit, part of the profit may be taxed as ordinary income rather than capital gains.[3] This part of the profit is considered to be recaptured depreciation.

Cash flow considerations

The only aspect of our investment we have considered so far is depreciation. We have established the fact that on a $170,000 investment with $30,000 in land and $140,000 in the building, we could take 12 percent in first-year depreciation or $16,800 (see Table 18–4). Depreciation is a noncash, tax-deductible item. We now must consider various cash flow items, such as the receipt of rent and the payment of interest, property taxes, insurance, maintenance expenses, and so on. An example of overall cash flow analysis is presented in Table 18–5. This is for the first year of operations.

We see in Table 18–5 that we have a loss of $16,470 for federal income tax purposes and that this provides a tax shelter benefit of $8,235 against other income. We also add depreciation back in to get cash flow because it was previously subtracted out but is really a noncash item. The negative and two positive values provide a positive cash flow figure of $8,565 at the bottom of Table 18–5.

---

[3]On commercial real estate (that is nonresidential), the treatment of recaptured depreciation may be even more penalizing. The investor should check this in each case.

Table 18–5 **Cash flow analysis for an apartment (fourplex) investment**

Gross annual rental (4 units at $425 per month/$5,100 per year)		$20,400
Less 5 percent vacancy		1,020
Net rental income		$19,380
Interest expense on a loan of 75 percent of property value at 12 percent interest:		
(75%) × 170,000 = $127,500		
(12%) × 127,500 = $15,300	$15,300	
Property taxes	2,000	
Insurance	750	
Maintenance	1,000	
Depreciation	16,800	
Total expenses		$35,850
Before-tax income or (loss)		(16,470)
Tax shelter benefit—assumes 50 percent tax rate		8,235
Depreciation		16,800
Cash flow		$ 8,565

We should point out that in considering the cost of the loan in Table 18–5, we have only evaluated interest payments. We might wish to consider repayment of principal as well. In the present case, we are assuming that in the first year we are paying 12 percent interest on a loan balance of $127,500, or $15,300 (as shown on the ninth line in Table 18–5). Assuming a 20-year loan (it is not unusual for the life of the loan to be different from the depreciation period), the total first-year payment for interest and principal is actually $17,070, indicating that $1,770 is applied toward the repayment of principal.

$$\text{Payment} - \text{Interest} = \text{Repayment of principal}$$
$$\$17,070 - \$15,300 = \$1,770$$

On this basis, our cash flow figure will be reduced to $6,795.

$$\text{Cash flow} - \text{Repayment of principal} = \text{Net cash flow}$$
$$\$8,565 - \$1,770 = \$6,795[4]$$

Of course, this value only applies to the first year. Rental income, interest, depreciation, and many other expense items will change each year. (For example, we will eventually run out of depreciation.)

---

[4]One could argue that we are building up equity or ownership interest through the repayment of principal. However, our focus for now is simply on the amount of cash flow going in and out. We will consider buildup in equity in a subsequent discussion.

In terms of investor return in the first year, the initial cash investment is $42,500. This is based on the total value of the property of $170,000 minus the initial loan amount of $127,500, requiring the investor to put up $42,500 in cash. With a net cash inflow of $6,795 in the first year, the cash on cash investor return in the first year is 15.99 percent ($6,795/$42,500). This represents the cash return on the investment divided by the actual "cash" investment. The investor will also build up his or her equity or ownership interest by the amount of repayment toward principal as well as any increase in property value resulting from inflation. If the property increases by 10 percent in the first year, this represents an added benefit of $17,000 (10 percent times the $170,000 value of the property). Actually, return benefits associated with inflation may exceed all other considerations. An investor may be willing to accept little or no cash flow if he or she can enjoy inflation-related gains. Note that in the present case, the $17,000 gain from inflation alone would represent a first-year return on cash investment of 40 percent ($17,000/$42,500).

You can readily see the twin factors that make real estate attractive are depreciation write-off and appreciation in value due to inflationary effects. Apartments, office buildings, warehouses, and shopping centers have served particularly well as good performers in inflationary environments.

FINANCING OF REAL ESTATE

One of the essential considerations in any real estate investment analysis is the cost of financing. In the prior example, we said a loan for $127,500 over 20 years at 12 percent interest would have yearly payments of $17,070. Note, in Table 18–6, the effects of various interest rates on annual payments.

We see the difference in annual payments ranges from $12,986 at 8 percent up to $21,504 at 16 percent. Even more dramatic is the increase in total interest paid over the life of the loan; it goes from $132,220 at 8 percent to $302,580 at 16 percent. (Keep in mind that the total loan was only $127,500.)

An investor who has the unlikely opportunity to shift out of the loan at 16 percent into one at 8 percent might be willing to pay as much as $83,692.72 for the priviledge. (Tax effects are not specifically considered here.)

Table 18–6

Interest rates and annual repayment obligations for a 20-year loan (principal amount equals $127,500)

	8 percent	10 percent	12 percent	14 percent	16 percent
Annual payment	$ 12,986	$ 14,975	$ 17,070	$ 19,251	$ 21,504
Total interest over the life of the loan	132,220	172,000	213,900	257,520	302,580

16 percent interest − 8 percent interest = Dollar difference in annual payments
$21,504 − $12,986 = $8,518

Present value of $8,518 over 20 years assuming an 8 percent discount rate (see Appendix D).

$$\$8,518 \times 9.818 = \$83,629.72$$

Thus, it is easy to appreciate the role of interest rates in a real estate investment decision. No industry is more suspectible to the impact of changing interest rates than real estate. Each time the economy overheats and interest rates skyrocket, the real estate industry comes to a standstill. With the eventual easing of interest rate pressures, the industry once again enjoys a recovery.

Much of the same pattern has continued into the 1980s. It is within this environment that many traditional lenders have hesitated to commit themselves to long-term lending on a fixed interest rate basis. A 20-year loan commitment at a fixed rate of 10 percent can be both embarrassing and expensive to the lender when interest rates advance to 14 or 15 percent.

New types of mortgages

In actuality, a whole new set of mortgage arrangements have appeared as alternatives to the fixed interest rate mortgage (particularly for home mortgages). The borrower must now be prepared to consider such alternative lending arrangements as the *variable rate mortgage,* the *graduated payment mortgage,* and the *shared appreciation mortgage.*

Variable rate mortgage (VRM)   Under a variable rate mortgage, the interest rate is adjusted regularly. Recent pronouncements by federal regulatory authorities have indicated a tendency to allow the rate to *float* more and more with market conditions (originally there were many restrictions). If interest rates go up, borrowers may either increase their normal payments or extend the maturity date of the loan at the same, fixed-payment level to fully compensate the lender. Similar downside adjustments can also be made if interest rates fall. Generally, variable rate mortgages are initially made at rates 1 to 2 percent below fixed interest rate mortgages because the lender enjoys the flexibility of changing interest rates and is willing to share the benefits with the borrower.

Graduated payment mortgage (GPM)   Under this type of financial arrangement, the payments start out on a relatively low basis and increase over the life of the loan. This type of mortgage may be well suited to the young borrower who has an increasing repayment capability over the life of the loan. An example would be a 30-year, $50,000 loan at 12 percent which would normally require monthly payments of $503.20 under a standard fixed-payment mortgage. With a graduated payment mortgage, monthly payments might start out as $350 or $400 and eventually progress to over $600. The GPM plan has been referred

to by a few of its critics as the "gyp em" plan in that early payments may not be large enough to cover interest and therefore later payments must cover not only the amortization of the loan, but also interest on the accumulated, unpaid, early interest. This is not an altogether fair criticism but merely an interpretation of what the graduated payment stream represents.

Shared appreciation mortgage (SAM)   Perhaps the newest and most innovative of the mortgage payment plans is the shared appreciation mortgage. This provides the lender with a direct hedge against inflation because he directly participates in any increase in value associated with the property being mortgaged. The lender may enjoy as much as 30 to 40 percent of the appreciation in value over a specified time period when the property is sold. In return for this privilege, the lender may advance funds at well below current market rates (perhaps at three quarters of current rates). The shared appreciation mortgage is not yet legal in all states.

Somewhat similar to the shared appreciation mortgage is the concept of *equity participation* that is popular in commercial real estate. Under an equity participation arrangement, the lender not only provides the borrowed capital, but part of the equity or ownership funds as well. A major insurance company or savings and loan thus may acquire an equity interest of 10 to 25 percent (or more). This financing arrangement becomes popular each time inflation rears its head. Some lenders are simply unwilling to commit capital for long time periods without a participation feature.

Borrowers may also look toward a *second mortgage* for financing. Here a second lender provides additional financing in return for a secondary claim or lien. The second mortgage is generally for a shorter period of time than the initial mortgage. Primary suppliers of second mortgages in the early 1980s have been sellers of property. Quite often, in order to consummate a sale, it is necessary for the seller to supplement the financing provided by a financial institution. Sellers providing second mortgages generally advance the funds at rates below the first mortgage rate to facilitate the sale, whereas other second mortgage lenders (nonsellers) will ask for a few percentage points above the first mortgage rate to compensate for the extra risk of being in a secondary claim position.

One way to get around a second mortgage is through a *wraparound mortgage*. This may be appropriate when there is an existing low interest rate loan on a piece of property and the buyer needs additional financing because the property has gone up in value. Perhaps it is being sold for an amount that is twice the original loan balance. The participating parties may wrap a new mortgage around the old mortgage. If there is an old $50,000 mortgage at 6 percent, the buyer will write a new wraparound mortgage with the seller (or a second financial institution) for $100,000 at perhaps 10 percent (which is also below market). The seller or second financial institution can afford to make the loan at the 10 percent rate because part of the financing is coming from the low interest rate 6 percent, $50,000 mortgage already in existence. On a $100,000 loan, they

must provide only $50,000 of the financing now; the other $50,000 is from the old mortgage. The lender will receive payments on the $100,000, 10 percent new mortgage while paying off the old $50,000 loan at 6 percent.

Some of the financial arrangements discussed in this section imply the new buyer can *assume* the mortgage of the prior owner (and perhaps add a second mortgage). While this *assumption* privilege was common in the 1960s and 70s, this is not always the case in the 1980s. Many financial institutions will attempt to disallow assumption of an old loan. If they do allow an assumption, they will often ask for an alteration of terms.

FORMS OF REAL ESTATE OWNERSHIP

Ownership of real estate may take many forms. The investor may participate as an individual, in a regular partnership, through a real estate syndicate (generally a limited partnership), or through a real estate investment trust (REIT).

Individual or regular partnership

Investing as an individual or with two or three others in a regular partnership offers the simplest way of getting into real estate from a legal viewpoint. The investors pretty much control their own destinies and can take advantage of personal knowledge of local markets and changing conditions to enhance their returns.

As is true with most smaller and less complicated business arrangements, there is a well-defined center of responsibility that often leads to quick corrective action. However, there may be a related problem of inability to pool adequate capital to engage in large-scale investments as well as the absence of expertise to develop a wide range of investments. Furthermore, there is unlimited liability to the investor(s).

Syndicate or limited partnership

In order to expand the potential for investor participation, a syndicate or limited partnership may be formed.[5] The purpose of the limited partnership is to combine the limited liability protection of a *corporation* with the tax provisions of a *regular partnership*. The limited partnership works as follows: a general partner forms the limited partnership and has unlimited liability for the partnership liabilities. The general partner then sells participation units to the limited partners whose liability is generally limited to the extent of their initial investment (such as $5,000 or $10,000). Limited liability is particularly important in real estate because mortgage debt obligations may exceed the net worth of the participants.

The other significant feature of the limited partnership (or any partnership) is that all profits or losses are directly assigned to the partners rather than ac-

---

[5]A syndicate may take the form of a corporation, but this is not common. The term *real estate syndicate* has become virtually synonymous with the limited partnership form of operation.

counted for in the business unit. Thus, there is avoidance of double taxation as would be true in a corporation. The direct assignment of tax losses in the early years of a project may be particularly attractive as a tax shelter device for a wealthy individual. As we showed in Table 18–5, a typical investment might be an apartment project that has a $16,470 first-year tax loss, in spite of the fact that there was a positive cash flow of $8,565 and perhaps another $17,000 appreciation in value due to inflation. Investors can claim the tax losses directly rather than have them go through business or corporate taxation first. Thus, we see the limited partnership offers the dual benefits of limited liability to limited partners (similar to a corporation) as well as the avoidance of double taxation and therefore the direct assignment of losses as tax shelters (similar to individuals or regular partnerships).

As previously indicated, the limited partnership allows the investor to participate in much larger, more diversified holdings than the individual or normal partnership could hope to achieve. A wealthy investor in Connecticut can acquire an interest in apartments in Dallas, shopping centers in Phoenix, and so on. Furthermore, he or she will have full-time managers to look after the holdings.

As is true in almost any form of investment, there are also drawbacks to the limited partnership. As implied by the title, the *limited* partner has very little to say in the operations of the partnership. It is the general partner who represents the operation and makes the day-to-day decisions. This is fine as long as the general partner is operating in a prudent and effective manner. However, it is quite difficult for limited partners to replace the general partner when other forms of behavior appear.

Furthermore, the limited partners must be particularly sensitive to the front-end fees and commissions that the general partner might charge. These can vary anywhere from 5 to 10 percent to as large as 20 to 25 percent.[6] The investor must also be sensitive to any double-dealing that the general partner might be doing. An example would be selling property back and forth between different syndicates that the general partner has formed and taking a commission each time. The inflated paper profits may prove quite deceptive and costly to the uninformed limited partner.

In assessing a general partner and his associated real estate deal, the investor should look at a number of items. First of all, prior record of performance should be reviewed. Is this the 1st or 10th deal that the general partner has put together? The investor will also wish to be sensitive to any lawsuits against the general partner that might exist. The investor might also wish to ascertain whether he or she is investing in a *blind pool* arrangement where funds are provided to the general partner to ultimately select properties for investment or if specific projects have already been identified and analyzed.

Finally the investor may have to decide whether to invest in a limited partnership/syndication that is either *public* or *private* in nature. A public offering gen-

---

[6]Kenneth R. Harvey, *Beating Inflation with Real Estate* (New York: Random House, 1980), p. 230.

erally involves much larger total amounts and has gone through the complex and rigorous process of SEC registration. Of course, SEC registration only attempts to insure that full disclosure has taken place—it does not judge the prudence of the venture. A private offering of a limited partnership syndication is usually local in scope and restricted to a maximum of 35 investors.

Real estate investment trusts

Another form of real estate investment is the real estate investment trust (REIT). REITs are similar to mutual funds or investment companies and trade on organized exchanges or over-the-counter. They pool investor funds, along with borrowed funds, and invest them directly in real estate or use them to make construction or mortgage loans to investors.

The advantage to the investor of an REIT is that he or she can participate in the real estate market for as little as $5 to $10 per share. Furthermore, this is the most liquid type of real estate investment because of the large secondary market for the shares.

REITs were initiated under the Real Estate Investment Trust Act of 1960. Like other investment companies, they enjoy the privilege of single taxation of income (only the stockholder pays and not the trust). In order to qualify for the tax privilege of an REIT, a firm must pay out at least 90 percent of its income to shareholders, have no less than 75 percent of its assets in real estate, and concurrently obtain at least 75 percent of its incomes from real estate.

REITs may take any of three different forms or combinations thereof. *Equity trusts* buy, operate, and sell real estate as an investment; *construction and development trusts* make short-term loans to developers during their construction period; and *mortgage trusts* make long-term loans to real estate investors. REITs are generally formed and advised by affiliates of commercial banks, insurance companies, mortgage bankers, and other financial institutions. Representative issues include Bank America Realty, Continental Illinois Property, and Connecticut General Mortgage.

Although REITs were enormously popular investments during the 1960s and early 1970s, the bottom fell out of the REIT market in the mid-1970s. Many had made questionable loans that came to the surface in the tight money, recessionary period of 1973–75. Nevertheless, REITs have now regained some of their earlier popularity. Many investors look at the equity trust, which owns real estate directly, as a hedge against inflation. Somewhat less popular are the construction and development trusts and mortgage trusts (many REITs combine these various functions). The investor in REITs hopes to receive a reasonably high yield because 90 percent of income must be paid out in the form of dividends plus a modest capital appreciation in stock value.

There are over 200 REITs from which the investor may choose. Further information on REITs may be acquired from the National Association of Real Estate Investment Trusts, 1101 17th St., N.W., Washington, D.C. 20036. In Figure 18–2, a Value Line data sheet is presented for First Union, an example of a reasonably successful REIT.

Figure 18-2 Data sheet for a REIT

FIRST UNION NYSE- FUR

RECENT PRICE **15**	P/E RATIO **8.7** (Trailing: 8.4 / Median: NMF)	EARN'S YLD **11.5%**	DIV'D YLD **7.7%** **1172**

| High→ | 8.5 | 8.9 | 10.7 | 9.2 | 9.1 | 8.9 | 8.6 | 7.9 | 7.1 | 8.3 | 8.8 | 8.7 | 13.0 | 16.6 | 17.9 | Feb. 19, 1982 Value Line |
| Low→ | 7.2 | 7.3 | 7.2 | 6.1 | 7.3 | 7.4 | 6.5 | 3.9 | 4.4 | 6.6 | 7.3 | 7.0 | 7.2 | 9.0 | 14.0 | 1984 1985 1986 |

Insider Decisions 1981

	O N D J F M A M J J A S O N D
to Buy	0 1 1 1 0 1 1 0 1 3 0 0 0 0 1
to Sell	0 1 0 0 0 0 1 1 0 0 0 0 0 0 0

(Continued from Capital Structure)
Incl. $31.0 mill. 8⅞% debs. ('99), callable 108.75 each conv. into 83.33 shs. at $12; $40.0 mill. 10% debs. ('06), callable 110.00, each conv. into 57.69 shs. at $17.33.

3-for-2 split

1.2 X Dividends p sh divided by Interest Rate

Relative Price Strength

Target Price Range
TIMELINESS **3** Average (Relative Price Performance Next 12 Mos.)
SAFETY **3** Average (Scale: 1 Highest to 5 Lowest)
BETA .75 (1.00 = Market)

1984-86 PROJECTIONS

	Price	Gain	Ann'l Total Return
High	30	(+100%)	24%
Low	20	(+35%)	14%

© Arnold Bernhard & Co., Inc.

Institutional Decisions

	3Q'80	4Q'80	1Q'81	2Q'81	3Q'81
to Buy	3	4	1	5	4
to Sell	4	0	5	4	5
Hldg's(000)	1207	1326	1306	1285	1361

Percent shares traded 3.0 / 2.0 / 1.0

1966	1967	1968	1969	1970	1971	1972	1973	1974	1975	1976	1977	1978	1979	1980	1981	1982	1983		84-86E
6.40	6.09	6.10	6.22	6.14	6.03	6.16	6.10	6.10	5.96	5.91	5.86	5.91	6.35	6.80	**7.80**	**8.75**		(A)Book Value per sh	**8.50**
.71	.74	.58	.75	.69	.86	.96	1.07	1.08	1.20	1.16	1.14	1.42	1.38	1.93	**2.60**	**1.90**		(B)"Cash Flow" per sh	**2.20**
.23	.25	.23	.34	.40	.47	.51	.53	.54	.60	.57	.57	.73	.83	1.28	**1.79**	**1.20**		(C)Earnings per sh	**1.40**
.52	.55	.53	.56	.57	.59	.60	.63	.64	.64	.65	.67	.70	.76	.90	1.02	**1.15**		(D)Div'ds Decl'd per sh ■	**1.60**
14.09	14.57	13.14	14.85	12.71	15.81	23.88	25.04	25.37	26.06	27.50	28.78	30.87	26.56	27.89	**31.10**	**27.90**		Loans & Real Est per sh	**32.25**
2.91	2.91	3.81	3.86	5.34	5.34	5.45	5.56	5.91	5.94	5.99	6.36	6.44	8.36	8.55	**9.00**	**10.75**		Common Shs Outst'g	**12.40**
20%	22%	28%	52%	17%	33%	35%	36%	10%	3%	26%	43%	40%	59%	96%	**110%**			Premium over Book	**180%**
33.7	30.8	33.4	27.5	18.2	17.0	16.1	15.2	11.9	9.9	12.6	14.2	10.9	11.4	15.0	8.5	Bold figures are		Avg Ann'l P/E Ratio	**17.0**
3.0%	3.3%	3.0%	3.6%	5.5%	5.9%	6.2%	6.6%	8.4%	11.0%	7.9%	7.1%	9.6%	8.8%	6.7%	11.7%	Value Line estimates		Avg Ann'l Earn's Yield	**8.0%**
6.6%	7.3%	6.8%	6.0%	7.8%	7.3%	7.4%	7.8%	10.0%	10.8%	9.0%	8.2%	8.8%	8.0%	4.7%	6.7%			Avg Ann'l Div'd Yield	**6.7%**

CAPITAL STRUCTURE as of 9/30/81

ST Debt $28.9 mill. (10% of Cap'l)
LT Debt $188.6 mill. (64% of Cap'l)
Due in 5 Yrs $38.4 mill. LT Interest $16.6 mill.
(Total interest coverage in 1980: 1.8x)
(Continued on Chart)

Pfd Stock $8.0 mill. Pfd Div'd $.7 mill.
80,000 shs. $100 par participating 95% cv. conv. to 11.33 com. shs., $9.00 min. div'd rate (3% of Cap'l)
Common Stock 8,895,000 shs. (23% of Cap'l)
(14.7 mill. fully diluted shares)

14.5	18.4	20.8	23.2	25.5	27.8	34.7	43.7	52.5	**66.0**	**83.0**		(A)Gross Income ($mill)	**90.0**
2.7	2.9	3.0	3.6	3.4	4.1	5.6	7.4	11.9	17.0	12.5		Net Profit ($mill)	**17.6**
18.9%	15.9%	14.5%	15.3%	13.5%	14.8%	16.1%	17.0%	22.6%	**26.0%**	**20.0%**		Net Profit Margin	**19.6%**
130.0	139.3	149.9	154.9	164.8	183.1	198.8	222.0	238.6	**280**	**300**		Loans & Real Est ($mill)	**400**
13.1	16.2	17.1	19.6	22.9	26.0	31.2	40.7	45.9	**53.0**	**58.0**		Rental Income ($ mill)	**85.0**
6.3%	6.9%	7.7%	7.4%	7.3%	6.9%	6.8%	7.9%	8.2%	**9.0%**	**9.0%**		Avg Interest Paid	**9.5%**
15.1	12.0	20.3	26.0	28.9	19.2	22.1	15.9	14.6	**10.0**	**25.0**		Short-Term Debt ($mill)	**35.0**
86.0	89.3	92.1	97.8	105.3	121.0	133.3	158.7	198.0	**200**	**185**		Long-Term Debt ($mill)	**260**
33.6	33.9	36.1	35.4	35.4	47.3	48.0	62.5	67.1	**78.0**	**94.0**		Net Worth ($mill)	**105**
39.3%	36.0%	34.0%	32.9%	30.7%	33.2%	30.6%	41.1%	50.4%	**51.0%**	**49.0%**		% Cap Funds to Tot Cap	**51.0%**
.5%	.6%	.7%	.8%	.9%	1.0%	1.2%	.7%	.5%	**1.0%**	**.7%**		% Expenses to Assets	**.7%**
6.9%	7.3%	8.0%	8.0%	7.9%	7.6%	7.9%	9.3%	11.4%	**14.0%**	**11.0%**		% Earned Total Cap'l	**11.5%**
8.2%	8.6%	8.9%	10.2%	9.0%	9.0%	9.2%	11.8%	13.4%	**20.0%**	**13.5%**		% Earned Net Worth	**16.5%**

FUNDS FLOW

	1978	1979	1980
Net Profit Plus			
Noncash Charges	10.0	12.6	17.2
Investments Repaid	11.7	12.0	8.7
Net New Debt	22.2	37.3	41.5
New Equity	— —	2.6	— —
Investments Funded	30.8	40.8	30.0
Dividends Declared	5.3	7.4	7.6

BUSINESS: First Union Real Estate Equity and Mortgage Investments is a nationwide equity-oriented real estate investment trust. At 12-31-80, properties comprised 95% of real estate investments; loans, 5%. About 47% of office space is in Ohio, primarily in Cleveland. Investments by property type are office bldgs. (40%) & enclosed mall shopping centers (57%), the two property categories that continue to receive most emphasis. Has 9,920 shrhldrs. Insiders own 2.5% of stk.; Unicorp Financial Corp. owns 17% of fully-diluted stock; Merchant Navy Officers Pension Fund, 3.5%. Org.: Ohio. Chrmn.: J.A. Hughes. Pres.: D.S. Schofield. Address: 55 Public Sq., Cleveland, Ohio 44113.

FINANCIAL POSITION

	9/30/80	9/30/81
Senior Debt	$133.6 mill.	$146.4 mill.
Subordinated Debt	$34.7 mill.	$71.0 mill.
Sr Debt/Cap'l Funds	1.3:1	1.0:1
Total Debt/Equity	2.5:1	2.8:1

PORTFOLIO CONDITION

	Year Ago	Latest
Mtges Repaid in Quarter	None	$13.2 mill.
Loss Reserve—% of Invests	Nil	Nil
Non-Earn Assets—% of Invests	None	None

LOANS & REAL ESTATE ($mill.)(A)

Fiscal Year Ends	Mar. 31	June 30	Sept. 30	Dec. 31
1979	201.5	212.9	220.0	222.0
1980	221.9	229.8	232.4	238.6
1981	238.0	239.2	278.4	**280**
1982	**285**	**290**	**290**	**300**
1983				

EARNINGS PER SHARE (A)

Fiscal Year Ends	Mar. 31	June 30	Sept. 30	Dec. 31	Full Fiscal Cl Year
1979	.20	.19	.15	.29	.83
1980	.17	.69	.19	.23	1.28
1981	.35	.27	.94	.23	1.79
1982	**.27**	**.28**	**.30**	**.35**	**1.20**
1983					

QUARTERLY DIVIDENDS PAID (D)

Calendar	Mar. 31	June 30	Sept. 30	Dec. 31	Full Year
1978	.173	.173	.173	.18	.70
1979	.18	.18	.20	.20	.76
1980	.213	.213	.227	.227	.88
1981	.233	.25	.25	.26	.99
1982	.26				

Asset value per share jumped 25% last year. The figure, which includes properties at market value rather than book, was $25.11 per fully diluted share at December 31st, compared with $22.73 six months earlier and $20.17 a year ago. The increase is particularly encouraging when you consider that prices of real estate generally have slipped for several reasons, including the difficulty of arranging suitable financing, the ongoing recession, and the possibility that inflation has been conquered, thus removing the need to buy inflation hedges such as real estate.

But one major shareholder is willing to sell its stock at a big discount. Unicorp Financial Corp. owns First Union securities equal to 17% of the total if all convertible securities were converted into common shares. First Union and Unicorp have been locked in a legal battle, with First Union contending that its bylaws restrict concentrated ownership to 9.8% of the total. The dispute set the stage for Britain's Merchant Navy Officers Pension Fund, already a holder of 3.5% of the fully diluted stock, to make an offer for Unicorp's position at the equivalent of $18 per First Union share. The agreement is conditioned on First Union waiving its bylaw restriction, which it has refused to do. This last move evoked plans for a proxy fight by Unicorp to gain control of First Union. The stock's price action doesn't evidence the existence of a "white knight" willing to buy all the shares at asset value or higher—although that is a possibility.

1982 will be a year of uninspiring share earnings comparisons, unless management comes up with a number of property sales. First Union was rich in short-term investments for the first three quarters of 1981, and the high-yielding instruments added about 7¢ a share to quarterly earnings. But now that the money has been invested in properties that provide a lower initial return, earnings will probably be under pressure. First Union also realized its largest (63¢ a share) capital gain ever in the September quarter. **Watch for the dividend to continue upward.** Recent years' increases have outpaced the inflation rate, and management intends to maintain this happy trend. The stock is of interest for income and for the possibility that some development in the skirmish with Unicorp will spur better year-ahead relative price action than fundamentals alone are likely to produce.
D.L.H./N.R.W.

(A) Calendar year. Fiscal yr. ended Oct. 31 thru '78. (B) Incl. intangible assets. In '80: $5.1 mill., 59¢/sh. At 12/31/81 est'd current value of real estate was $25.11 per fully diluted share. (C) Primary earnings. Next egs. report due late Apr. (D) Next dividend meeting about Mar.10. Goes ex about Mar. 25. Div'd paym't dates: end of Jan., Apr., July, Oct. ■ Div'd reinvest. plan av'ble.

Company's Financial Strength	B++
Stock's Price Stability	85
Price Growth Persistence	70
Earnings Predictability	55

Factual material is obtained from sources believed to be reliable but cannot be guaranteed.

GOLD AND SILVER

We now examine a number of other forms of real asset investments. Precious metals represent the most volatile of the investment alternatives. Gold and silver tend to move up in troubled times and show a decline in value during stable, predictable periods. Observe the movement in the price of gold between January 1976 and March 1981 in Figure 18–3. The movement up and down is even more impressive when one considers the price of gold was a mere $35 an ounce in 1967.

Gold

Major factors that tend to drive up gold prices are fear of war, political instability, and inflation (these were particularly evident in 1979 with the takeover of U.S. embassies and double-digit inflation). Conversely moderation in worldwide tensions and high interest rates caused a decline in gold prices in 1980. High interest rates may make it prohibitively expensive to carry gold as an investment.

Figure 18–3   **Dollar per troy ounce**

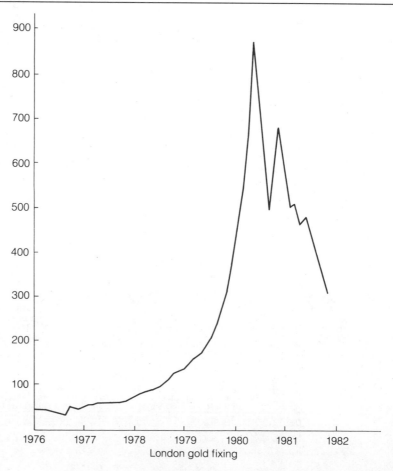

London gold fixing

Gold may be owned in many different forms, and a 1977 survey by *Changing Times* indicated that 30 percent of the United States population with incomes over $30,000 per year owned gold or other forms of precious metals. Let's examine the different forms of gold ownership.

Gold bullion Gold bullion includes gold bars or wafers. The investor may own anywhere from 1 troy ounce to 10,000 troy ounces (valued at approximately $5 million in 1981). Smaller bars generally trade at a 6 to 8 percent premium over pure gold bullion value, with larger bars trading at a 1 to 2 percent premium. Gold bullion may provide storage problems, and unless the gold bars remain in the custody of the bank or dealer who initially sells them, they must be reassayed before being sold.

Gold coins Many of the storing and assaying costs associated with gold bullion can be avoided by investing directly in gold coins. There are three basic outlets for investing in gold coins. First, there are *gold bullion coins,* such as the South African Kruggerand, the Mexican 50 peso, and the Austrian or Hungarian 100 korona. These coins trade at a small premium of 2 to 3 percent over pure bullion value and afford the investor an excellent outlet for taking a position in the market. A second form is represented by *common date gold coins* that are no longer minted, such as the United States double eagle, the British sovereign, or the French Napoleon. These coins may trade at as much as 50 to 100 times their pure gold bullion value. Finally, there are gold coins that are *old* and *rare* and that may trade at a numismatic value into the thousands or hundreds of thousands of dollars.

Gold stocks In addition to gold bullion and gold coins, the investor may choose to take a position in gold by simply buying common stocks that have heavy gold mining positions. Examples of companies listed on U.S. exchanges include Campbell Red Lake (Canadian based), Dome Mines (Canadian based), and Homestake Mining (U.S. based). Because these securities often move in the opposite direction of the stock market as a whole, they may provide excellent portfolio diversification. The investor may also examine closed-end investment companies with heavy gold mining positions (such as ARA Limited).

Gold futures contracts Finally, the gold investor may consider trading in futures contracts. Gold futures are traded on five different U.S. exchanges and on many foreign exchanges.

Silver

Silver has many of the same investment characteristics as gold in terms of being a hedge against inflation and a safe haven for investment during troubled times. Silver has moved from $4 a troy ounce in 1976 to over $50 an ounce in early 1980 and then back to below $9 an ounce in early 1981. An additional

factor causing volatility in the silver market during this time period was the speculative investment activity of the Hunt brothers of Texas (who many thought were trying to corner the market).

More so than gold, silver has heavy industrial and commercial applications. Areas of utilization include photography, electronic and electrical manufacturing, electroplating, dentistry, and silverware and jewelry. It is estimated that industrial uses of silver exceed annual production by 150 million ounces per year. Furthermore, supply of silver does not necessarily increase with price because silver is a byproduct of copper, lead, zinc, and gold. Because of the undersupply factor, many consider silver to be appropriate for long-term holding.

Investment in silver can also take many different forms. Some may choose to buy *silver bullion* in the form of silver bars. Because the price of silver generally is 1/20th to 1/40th the price of gold and larger bulk is involved for an equivalent dollar size investment, the storage and carrying costs can be quite high. Secondly, *silver coins* may be bought in large bags or as rare coins for their numismatic value. Keep in mind that dimes, quarters, and half-dollars minted during and prior to 1965 were 90 percent pure silver. As a third outlet, the investor may wish to consider *silver futures contracts.* Finally, the investor may purchase *stocks* of firms that have interests in silver mining, such as Callahan Mining, Hecla Mining, or Rosario Resources.

PRECIOUS GEMS

Precious gems include diamonds, rubies, sapphires, and emeralds. Investments in diamonds have received major attention in recent years. In 1980, there were 15 different banks that allowed diamonds in their investment portfolios, and Thomson, McKinnon Securities established a diamond trust fund for investors.[7]

Diamonds and other precious gems have appeal to investors because of their small size, easy concealment, and great durability. They are particularly popular in Europe because of a long-standing distrust of paper currencies as a store of value.

The reason diamonds are so valuable can be best understood by considering the production process. It is estimated that 50 to 200 *tons* of rock or sand is required to uncover one carat (1/142 of an ounce) of quality diamonds.

The distribution of diamonds is under virtual monopolistic control by De Beers Consolidated Mines of South Africa, Ltd. They control the distribution of approximately 80 percent of the world's supply and have a stated policy of maintaining price control. Diamonds have generally enjoyed a steady, somewhat spectacular movement in price. For example, the price of a "D" color, one-carat, flawless, polished diamond increased over 10-fold between 1974 and 1980.

Of course, not all diamonds have done so well. Furthermore, there have been

---

[7]"Your Money Matters," *The Wall Street Journal,* July 1980, p. 18.

substantial breaks in the market, such as in 1974 and 1980–81 when diamond prices declined by 20 to 25 percent. Even with large increases in value, the diamond investor does not automatically come out ahead. There may be dealer markups anywhere from 10 percent to 100 percent so that three to five years of steady gain may be necessary to show a substantial profit.

In no area of investment is product and market knowledge more important. Either you must be an expert yourself or know that you are dealing with an "honest" expert. Diamonds are judged on the basis of the four c's (color, clarity, carat weight, and cut), and the assessment of any stone should be certified by the Gemological Institute of America. As is true of most valuable items, the investor is well advised to purchase the highest quality possible. You are considerably better off using the same amount of money to buy a higher-quality, smaller-carat diamond than a lesser-quality, high-carat diamond.

OTHER COLLECTIBLES

A listing of other collectibles for investment might include art, antiques, stamps, Chinese ceramics, rare books, and other items that appeal to various sectors of our society. Each offers psychic pleasure to the investor as well as the opportunity for profit.

Anyone investing in a collectible should have some understanding of current market conditions and of the factors that determine the inherent worth of the item. Otherwise, you may be buying someone else's undesirable holding at a premium price. It is important not to get swept away in a buying euphoria. The best time to buy art, antiques, or stamps is when the bloom is off the market and dealers are overburdened with inventory, not when there is a weekly story in *The Wall Street Journal* or *Business Week* about overnight fortunes being made. There seems to be a pattern or cycle in the collectibles market the same as in other markets (arts, antiques, and stamps actually do move together). The market was very strong in the 1970s with a pause in the mid-1970s caused by the recession. The market gained tremendous momentum from 1975 to 1980, with a sell-off in late 1980 and early 1981.

As is true of other markets, the wise investor in the collectibles market must be sensitive to dealer spreads. A price guide that indicates a doubling in value every two or three years may be meaningless if the person with whom you are dealing sells for $100 and buys back for $50. The wise investor/collector can best maintain profits by dealing with other collectors or investors and eliminating the dealer or middleman from the transaction where possible.

Such periodicals as *Money* magazine and the *Collector/Investor* provide excellent articles on the collectibles market. Specialized periodicals, such as *American Arts and Antiques, Coin World, Linn's Stamp News, The Sports Collectors Digest,* and *Antique Monthly,* also are helpful. For an extended discussion of periodical sources and other data, see a special report by the editors of *Con-*

sumer Guide on *How to Make Money During Inflation/Recession;* it covers collectibles as well as many other items.[8]

SUMMARY

Investments in real assets have gained increasing popularity in the last decade. They offer a measure of inflation protection, an opportunity for efficient portfolio diversification, and psychic pleasure to the investor.

A disadvantage is the absence of a large, liquid market, such as that provided by the securities markets. There also may be a large dealer or middleman spread, and the investor may have to forgo current income.

The hysteria that grips these markets from time to time not only creates substantial opportunities for profit, but also dictates that the investor must be particularly cautious about market timing. It can be quite expensive to be the last buyer in a gold or silver boom.

Investors in real estate must be sensitive to tax aspects related to the investment, particularly the impact of accelerated depreciation in the early years of the investment and the associated effect of recaptured depreciation when the property is sold. Although real estate may show a loss for federal income tax purposes, related tax savings and the adding back of depreciation may well create a positive cash flow. Real estate also may enjoy substantial appreciation benefits in an inflationary economy.

The financing of real estate is becoming increasingly complicated as lenders seek alternatives to fixed-rate mortgages. Thus, we have seen the creation of the variable rate mortgage (VRM) and other floating-rate plans, the graduated payment mortgage (GPM), and the shared appreciation mortgage (SAM).

Gold and silver represent two highly volatile forms of real assets in which price movements often run counter to events in the economy and the world. Bad news is good news (and vice versa) for precious metal investors. Gold and silver may generally be purchased in bullion or bulk form, as coins, in the commodities futures market, or indirectly through securities of firms specializing in gold or silver mining.

Precious gems and other collectibles, such as art, antiques, stamps, Chinese ceramics, and rare books, have caught the attention of investors in recent times. Although there are many warning signs, the wise and patient investor can do well over the long run. The investor should understand the factors that determine value before taking a serious investment position.

IMPORTANT WORDS AND CONCEPTS

Real assets	Shared appreciation mortgage
REIT	Wraparound mortgage
Straight-line depreciation	Limited partnership

[8]The editors of *Consumer Guide,* with Peter A. Dickinson, *How to Make Money During Inflation/Recession* (New York: Harper & Row, 1980).

175 percent declining-balance
   depreciation
Recaptured depreciation
Variable rate mortgage
Graduated payment
   mortgage

Blind pool
Equity trust
Construction and development
   trust
Mortgage trust
Equity participation

QUESTIONS AND PROBLEMS

1. Why might real assets offer an opportunity as an inflation hedge?

2. Explain why real assets might add to effective portfolio diversification.

3. What are some disadvantages of investing in real assets?

4. In what way does real estate provide for a high degree of leverage?

5. There is a motel complex with land valued at $250,000 and a building valued at $1 million. The depreciation method is 175 percent declining-balance over 15 years as shown in Table 18–3.
   a. What is the first year depreciation deduction?
   b. Assume revenue minus all other expenses besides depreciation equals – $10,000. Now considering depreciation, how much will cash flow in the first year be? Use a tax rate of 50 percent.
   c. Assume a 20-year loan equal to 75 percent of the total value of the property at 14 percent interest. Annual payments will be $141,552. How much of the annual payment will go toward interest and how much toward repayment of principal in the first year.
   d. Based on information in b and c, compute net cash flow (cash flow minus repayment of principal).
   e. What is the ratio of net cash flow to initial cash investment? Initial cash investment equals total investment minus the loan.
   f. If there is 8 percent inflation related to the total property value in the first year, what will be the ratio of inflationary gains to initial cash investment?

6. If a $100,000 piece of real estate is depreciated over a 15-year life using Table 18–3, how much is the third year's depreciation?

7. By how much does the answer to question 6 exceed the allowable depreciation under straight-line depreciation for a $100,000 asset with a 15-year life?

8. What is a variable rate mortgage?

9. Explain a shared appreciation mortgage.

10. How is liability handled in a limited partnership?

11. What are REITs? What are the various types of REITs?

12. What are some factors that drive up the price of gold? What are factors that drive it down?

13. Suggest some commercial and industrial uses of silver. What forms can silver investments take?

14. Explain how the dealer spread can affect the rate of return on a collectible item.

SELECTED REFERENCES

Bleck, Erich K. "Real Estate Investments and Rates of Return." *The Appraisal Journal,* October 1973, pp. 535–47.

Cooper, James R., and Stephen A. Pyhrr. "Forecasting the Rates of Return on an Apartment Investment: A Case Study." *The Appraisal Journal,* July 1973, pp. 312–37.

The editors of *Consumer Guide,* with Peter A. Dickinson. *How to Make Money During Inflation/Recession.* New York: Harper & Row, 1980.

Freedman, Michael. *The Diamond Book.* Homewood, Ill.: Dow Jones-Irwin, 1980.

Harvey, Kenneth R. *Beating Inflation with Real Estate.* New York: Random House, 1980.

Lipscomb, Joseph. "Discount Rates for Cash Equivalent Analysis." *The Appraisal Journal,* January 1981, pp. 23–33.

McQuade, Walter. "Invest in the Art Market? Soybeans Might Be Safer." *Fortune,* May 1974, pp. 201–6.

Robichek, Alexander A; Richard A. Cohn; and John J. Pringle. "Return on Alternative Media and Implications for Portfolio Construction." *Journal of Business,* July 1972, pp. 427–43.

Rosen, Lawrence R. *When and How to Profit from Buying and Selling Gold.* Homewood, Ill.: Dow Jones-Irwin, 1975.

Roulac, Stephen E. "Can Real Estate Returns Outperform Common Stocks?" *Journal of Portfolio Management,* Winter 1976, pp. 26–43.

Rush, Richard H. *Antiques as an Investment.* New York: Bonanza Books, 1968.

"Soaring Real Estate Values are Enticing Big Securities Concerns into the Field." *The Wall Street Journal,* August 6, 1980, p. 32.

Shenkel, William M. *Modern Real Estate Principles.* Rev. ed. Plano, Tex.: Business Publications, 1980.

Van Caspel, Venita. *Money Dynamics for the 1980's.* Reston, Va.: Reston Publishing, 1980.

Wendt, Paul F., and Alan R. Cerf: *Real Estate Investment Analysis and Taxation.* New York: McGraw-Hill, 1979.

19

An overview of investment management: Retirement and estate planning

In the 18 preceding chapters, we have examined many different investment outlets ranging from traditional investments in common stocks and fixed-income securities to convertibles, warrants, options, commodities, and real assets. Each investor must assess his or her goals and objectives as well as anticipated economic circumstances to determine the appropriate portfolio mix. Investors must further examine their willingness to take risks, their needs for liquidity, the tax consequences of investment decisions, and many other variables.

Finally, investors must also determine whether they want to take an active or passive posture in investment management. In the context of a reasonably efficient market environment, highly active portfolio management may not necessarily provide superior returns because of the large commission costs involved. The key may be to set realistic objectives and then select a portfolio that moves one toward the accomplishment of those objectives. The investor, of course, must always remain active in terms of adjusting to the implications of new tax legislation or reorienting a portfolio to a change in financial conditions (you just inherited a million dollars or your gold mine is worthless).

THE CONCEPT OF LIFELONG PLANNING

The various investment outlets described in the text may be related to investment for immediate income and capital gains or to retirement and estate planning needs; indeed, the concepts of current and future needs are closely related. However, because most of the text has dealt with current investment strategy, in this chapter we will focus on retirement and estate planning.

Planning is a difficult task, and the unpredictability and uncertainty of politics and economics in recent years has made financial planning and forecasting even more difficult. Of course, these conditions make careful financial planning, especially retirement planning, critical to the accomplishment of lifelong goals.

Even though the future is uncertain and returns from various investments may fluctuate greatly, future time is as much a benefit as it is a detriment to invest-

457

ments. Over time, unusual variations tend to smooth out and follow long-term trends that override short-term aberrations. This will be helpful when analyzing specific strategies for building retirement funds.

Assume that someone wishes to retire at age 65 and anticipates a 10-year retirement period to age 75 based on life expectancy tables. Further assume that the individual will need $18,000 for the first year and that this requirement will go up by 8 percent per year based on inflation. We will assume that the individual can earn 10 percent on investments, and this will be the discount rate to equate the future with the present.[1] The future needs and associated present values are presented in Table 19–1.

The present value factors are found in Appendix B. We see the individual will need to accumulate $150,872 for retirement. We further assume the individual is 48 years old, so that he or she has 17 years to accomplish this goal. If we once again assume a 10 percent discount rate, a current investment of $29,872.66 will allow the investor to achieve this objective.

$$\$150,872 \times .198 = \$29,872.66$$
$$\uparrow$$
Present value factor
for 17 years at 10 percent

This analysis assumes that the proceeds from the investment are being reinvested on a tax-free basis. This is somewhat difficult to accomplish on a lump-sum investment of this nature. On the other hand, the individual may wish to set aside an annual annuity that will grow to $150,872 if invested at 10 percent for 17 years. Employing various tax deferral devices discussed later in this chapter (such as pension plan contributions, Keogh plans, IRAs, and other forms of annuities), this may be possible to accomplish with little or no tax liability as the funds are accumulating. Using Appendix C for the compound sum of an annuity,

Table 19–1 **Financial needs at retirement**

Year	Annual requirement (assumes 8 percent increase)	Present value factor (10 percent)	Present value
1	$18,000	.909	$ 16,362
2	19,440	.826	16,057
3	20,995	.751	15,767
4	22,675	.683	15,487
5	24,489	.621	15,208
6	26,448	.564	14,917
7	28,564	.513	14,653
8	30,849	.467	14,406
9	33,317	.424	14,126
10	35,982	.386	13,889
	Financial needs at retirement		$150,872

[1]Taxes are not explicitly considered at this point.

we see the annual annuity contribution would be $3719.99 in order to accumulate $150,872 in 17 years at 10 percent.

$$\frac{\$150,827}{40.545} = \$3719.99$$

Compound sum factor
for 17 years at 10 percent

Note that a relatively small contribution will accomplish the objective of raising $150,872 because of the time horizon involved and the relatively high reinvestment rate of 10 percent. At 6 percent, we must contribute $7,640.11 annually and at 13 percent, $2,807.49.

$$\frac{\$150,872}{20.213} = \$7464.11 \qquad \frac{\$150,872}{53.739} = \$2807.50$$

Compound sum factor   Compound sum factor
for 17 periods at 6   for 17 periods at 13
percent   percent

Also consider that social security benefits will reduce the need for accumulated funds or, conversely, that a desire to leave a lump sum in a final estate will increase the need for annual payments.

As previously specified, one of the advantages of long-term planning is the ability to smooth out short-term variations in investment returns. For example, if we make an annual purchase of a diversified common stock portfolio to achieve part of our investment objectives, we may have some years in which stock values are up or down, but over the long run, we should receive a normal return of perhaps 9 percent. Even bonds can be bought with 17-year maturities (in this instance) so that we can be assured of the return of the initial principal at retirement (plus the accumulated interest over the life of the bond).

Of course, this smoothing out principle is not true for all investments. Who can say what the price of gold or silver will be 17 years from now? We can retire as millionaires or in poverty if all our holdings are in precious metals. For this reason, it is generally advisable that an individual who is doing retirement planning attempt to achieve a sufficiently diversified portfolio so that long-term returns are reasonably predictable. For example, gold or silver may represent an important inflation hedge in a retirement portfolio but should generally represent a relatively small percentage because of the impact of price volatility.

DOLLAR-COST AVERAGING

In building a portfolio over the long term, we may also wish to utilize dollar-cost averaging in purchasing stocks or other assets. Under dollar-cost averaging, we place a fixed-dollar investment in a given security each year regardless of its

price or the current market outlook. The use of dollar-cost averaging is a concession to the principle that most investors cannot outsmart the market (at least in the short run). All too often, investors buy when a stock is high on a wave of good news only to find themselves with a desire to liquidate when the stock is low due to negative events. A recent example of this was the boom in energy stocks in 1979–80 due to a belief in an energy shortage and the need for domestic oil production. In 1981, the tables turned. An oil glut was present in world markets, and energy issues were under sharp selling pressure.

The intent with dollar-cost averaging is to avoid the common practice of buying high and selling low. In fact, you are forced to do the opposite. Why? You are committing a fixed dollar amount each year (or month) and buying the stock at the current market price regardless of what it is. When the price is high, you will be buying relatively fewer shares. When the price is low, your fixed-dollar investment will allow you to accumulate more shares. An example is presented in Table 19–2, in which we are purchasing $1,000 of stock each year over a five-year time period. The price is assumed to reach a low of $97 and a high of $130 a share. To facilitate the analysis, a purchase of fractional shares is assumed possible (such as 8.3 shares in 1983).

Note that when the stock price is relatively low, such as in 1984 or 1986, we purchase relatively more shares. When it is high, such as 1987, we purchase fewer shares. On balance, we are buying more shares at lower prices. In this case, there is a happy ending in that the stock ends up at $130 in 1987.

What would happen if the price merely ended up at the average price over the five-year time period? The values in column 3 total to 565, so that the average price over five years is $113 (565/5). Actually, we would still make money under this assumption because the average *cost* is less than this amount. Consider that we invested $5,000 and purchased 44.8 shares. This translates to an average cost of only $111.61.

$$\frac{\text{Investment}}{\text{Shares}} = \frac{\$5,000}{44.8} = \$111.61$$

The reason that the average cost ($111.61) is less than the average price ($113) is that we bought relatively more shares at the lower price levels and they weigh more heavily in our calculations. Thus, under dollar-cost averaging, we

Table 19–2   **Dollar cost averaging**

(1) Year	(2) Investment	(3) Stock price	(4) Shares purchased
1983	$1,000	120	8.3
1984	1,000	100	10.0
1985	1,000	118	8.5
1986	1,000	97	10.3
1987	1,000	130	7.7
	$5,000	565	44.8

have shown that you can make money if the stock ends up at a relatively high level ($130) or even at the average price over the time horizon of $113 (565/5).[2]

The only time you would lose money is if the eventual price falls below the average cost ($111.61) and you sell at that point in time. While dollar-cost averaging has its advantages, it is not without criticism. Clearly, if a stock continues to go down over a long period of time, it is hard to convince yourself that you are doing the right thing to continue buying. For example, Polaroid stock fell from 149½ to 25½ between 1972 and 1977. To continue with dollar-cost averaging may have been too painful or foolish to endure. Also, one of the advantages of dollar-cost averaging is a disadvantage as well; namely, that you are removing all human judgment from the decision-making process. You simply buy x dollars worth when it's time to buy. The plan could be carried out by a computer or robot. Many investors are uncomfortable with this approach.

Of course, you could arrange various alterations or modifications to basic dollar-cost averaging by saying, "I will only follow the plan if such and such happens to the stock." This altered version may dilute some of the presumed advantages of dollar-cost averaging. It is like a person on a diet outlining the circumstances when they will or will not eat chocolate.

ELEMENTS OF RETIREMENT PLANS

In examining actual retirement plans, we look at government sponsored social security as well as private sector plans. In both cases, we will look at costs and benefits involved as well as other features of the programs. Let's first look at social security.

Social security

Ninety percent of those employed in the United States participate in the social security system, which provides not only retirement benefits, but also payments for dependents of the deceased, disability income for workers and their dependents, and health care expenses for elderly and low-income families. Those exempt from participation in the social security program are employees of state and local governments, employees of tax-exempt charities or service institutions, civilian employees of the federal government, and other less important categories. Many of these people participate in similar programs outside of the social security system.

When social security was initiated under the Social Security Act in 1935, the social security tax was levied against 1 percent of wages up to $3,000. Thus, the maximum payment into the program was $30 per year. In 1981, the employee's share of the annual contribution (to be added with similar payments by the employer) was 6.65 percent on a maximum base of $29,700. Thus, someone making $29,700 or higher paid $1,975.05 in social security taxes. The tax is currently

---

[2]This, of course, does not consider commissions, which could be important.

scheduled to go up each year through 2011. Since the social security tax is not a tax-deductible item for federal income tax purposes, it is a heavy burden to the payer. Many of the tax reduction benefits from the 1981 Economic Recovery Tax Act will be offset by increased social security taxes to those in the work force.

What are the benefits of social security and how do they influence retirement planning?[3] In Table 19–3, we see a description of social security benefits for retirees. If we were computing benefits for 1981, the values in the table must be adjusted upward for cost of living increases in 1979 and 1980. For example, assume a worker at age 65 retires with a dependent spouse of the same age. Further assume that the average earnings of the worker over a number of years were $7,600. The total unadjusted benefits would be $465.60 plus $232.80, or a total of $698.40 per month. We now adjust the tabular values for cost of living increases of 9.9 percent in 1979 and 14.3 percent in 1980. Thus, the payment

Table 19–3 Monthly retirement benefits for workers who reach 62 in 1979 to 1983

Average yearly earnings	Retirement for workers at age				Dependents—Child, or spouse at age*			
	65	64	63	62	65	64	63	62
$ 923 or less	121.80	113.70	105.60	97.50	60.90	55.90	50.80	45.70
1,200	156.70	146.30	135.90	125.40	78.40	71.90	65.40	58.80
2,600	230.10	214.80	199.50	184.10	115.10	105.50	95.90	86.40
3,000	251.80	235.10	218.30	201.50	125.90	115.40	104.90	94.50
3,400	270.00	252.00	234.00	216.00	135.00	123.80	112.50	101.30
4,000	296.20	276.50	256.80	237.00	148.10	135.70	123.40	111.10
4,400	317.30	296.20	275.00	253.90	158.70	145.40	132.20	119.10
4,800	336.00	313.60	291.20	268.80	168.00	153.90	140.00	126.00
5,200	353.20	329.70	306.20	282.60	176.60	161.80	147.20	132.50
5,600	370.60	345.90	321.20	296.50	185.30	169.80	154.40	139.00
6,000	388.20	362.40	336.50	310.60	194.10	177.80	161.70	145.60
6,400	405.60	378.60	351.60	324.50	202.80	185.80	169.00	152.10
6,800	424.10	395.90	367.60	339.30	212.10	194.30	176.70	159.10
7,200	446.00	416.30	386.60	356.80	223.00	204.30	185.80	167.30
7,600	465.60	434.60	403.60	372.50	232.80	213.30	194.00	174.60
8,000	482.60	450.50	418.30	386.10	241.30	221.10	201.10	181.00
8,400	492.90	460.10	427.20	394.40	246.50	225.80	205.40	184.90
8,800	505.10	471.50	437.80	404.10	252.60	231.40	210.50	189.50
9,200	516.00	481.60	447.20	412.80	258.00	236.40	215.00	193.50
9,400	520.40	485.80	451.10	416.40	260.20	238.40	216.80	195.20
9,600	524.60	489.70	454.70	419.70	262.30	240.30	218.50	196.80
9,800	530.40	495.10	459.70	424.40	265.20	243.00	221.00	198.90
10,000	534.70	499.10	463.50	427.80	267.40	245.00	222.80	200.60

*If a person is eligible for both a worker's benefit and a spouse's benefit, the payable check is limited to the larger of the two.

SOURCE: Social Security Administration (Washington, D.C.), 1981.

---

[3]It should be pointed out that a work history of 7 to 10 years is necessary to qualify for the benefits.

for 1981 would be $877.30 per month. In 1982 and subsequent years, there will be similar adjustments to the basic tabular values.

Also, note that the worker or spouse receives lesser benefits if retirement is at age 62, 63, or 64 as opposed to age 65. Maximum benefits would be computed on an income of $10,000, so that executives retiring from $100,000 or $200,000 salaries would not receive payments proportionate to their total income. An important attribute is that social security payments are not taxable to the recipient.

Those receiving benefits can continue to work without losing benefits if annual earnings do not exceed $6,000 until age 70. At that age, earnings restrictions are removed. The penalty prior to age 70 is 50 cents on the dollar—if you earn $2 above $6,000, a dollar in benefits is subtracted. Only earnings from employment or self-employment are counted. No penalty applies to income from pensions, dividends, interest, or sale of assets.

Most experts and observers agree that the social security system will not be permitted to disintegrate. However, most assume that some relatively major changes will be forthcoming. Such ideas as raising the normal retirement age from 65, raising the qualifications for receiving benefits, changing the "indexing" of benefits, and other new rules are likely.

If we have 8 percent inflation over the next 20 years and social security benefits are adjusted accordingly, total social security benefits could be at least four times higher than they are today. This is a heavy burden for the system to bear. Social security operates on a current-funding basis. That is, taxes that are paid into the system now are used to fund the retirement benefits of workers who have worked in the past. Each current generation pays the benefits of past generations. Although there is a social security trust fund, it merely serves as a short-term cushion in periods when revenues are not sufficient to meet expenses. Those who plan to retire 40 to 50 years from now can only hope that their children and grandchildren are prepared to work hard enough to support their social security payments.

PRIVATE PENSION PLANS

Clearly, there is a need to supplement social security benefits for many in the population. About 60 percent of nongovernmental employees are also covered by private pension plans. Actually, in terms of total retirement benefits paid in 1980, $105 billion was from social security, $20 billion from private pension plans, and $22 billion from other federal, state, and local retirement programs.

In our discussion of private pension plans, we will consider those that apply to employees of business firms as well as individual plans. We first examine employee pension plans.

Legal considerations

No employer is required to have a pension plan. However, if a plan exists, it is regulated by law.

Several major features of the law protect those covered by a pension. The

law having the most impact on pensions is the Employee Retirement Income Security Act of 1974 (ERISA), commonly called the Pension Reform Act of 1974, which requires that vesting must take place after a period of time. Vesting means that pension benefits or rights cannot be taken away. Typically, vesting occurs after 10 years of service or is based on a formula. The law requires full vesting after 10 years if there is no partial vesting prior to that; or if graduated vesting occurs after 4 years of service, full vesting must take effect after 15 years.

ERISA also prescribes minimum standards of eligibility for participation in plans, required disclosure to participants, and employer fiscal responsibility. All newly initiated *private* pension plans by firms engaged in interstate commerce are covered by ERISA (most older plans are covered as well). ERISA does not regulate plans sponsored by governmental bodies, charitable organizations, or those involved in intrastate commerce (other regulatory organizations are generally responsible).

Understanding benefits and contributions

Understanding the features of a plan is critical to good retirement planning. Some plans base the pension on average earnings over a period of years, often the two to five years prior to retirement. Others use formulas based on such things as years of service, age, or job class. Knowledge of the way contributions and benefits are calculated and of the options available can have a significant effect on retirement income.

The law does not attempt to specify the features of a pension plan; it only requires that they be fully disclosed and meet minimum standards. A first question to be considered is whether the plan is *contributory* or *noncontributory*. Many private pension plans are noncontributory, meaning the employer makes the full contribution and the employee does not have to contribute. In a contributory plan, both the employer and employee contribute. Contributory plans are common for federal, state, and local governments and in many colleges and universities. Under a contributory plan, the employer might pay in 50 or 60 percent of the annual contribution with the balance coming from the employee through payroll deductions.

If an employee leaves a job covered by a contributory plan before retirement, he usually receives his contribution plus interest. In some cases, the funds may be left in the plan, and a pension is paid when a particular age is reached. The noncontributory plans usually pay only a pension that is based on the vested rights of the employee if vesting has occurred when the employee leaves.

We've been discussing methods of contribution into a plan, but what about the receipt of benefits? There are two different approaches that may be applied. The first is called a *defined benefit plan*. Under a defined benefit plan, the employee can calculate his pension based on a formula using years of service and average earnings. Thus, the employee might be assured of receiving 1½ percent of the average of his last two year's salary for each year of service. If the average

is $30,000 and the employee has been with the firm 20 years, the annual retirement benefit will be $9,000.

$$\text{Percentage} \times \text{Salary} \times \text{Number of years} = \text{Yearly benefit}$$
$$1\frac{1}{2}\% \quad \times 30{,}000 \times \qquad 20 \qquad = \$9{,}000$$

The second type of benefit plan is *the defined contribution plan.* Under this arrangement, retirement benefits are a function of total contributions over the life of the plan. The responsibility for those contributions are defined between employer and employee. Needless to say, large contributions will lead to substantial retirement benefits, with the opposite outcome for meager contributions. Conditions in the financial markets over the life of the contributions will also influence the total payoff.

The previously described *defined benefit plan* generally allows for greater predictability in planning. Many retirement plans combine elements of both the defined benefit plan and defined contribution plan, in which retirement benefits are based on annual contributions, years of service, average earnings, and a number of other factors.

Impact of changing employers

One of the major errors that occurs in retirement planning is to overlook the effect of changing jobs. The present law requiring vesting of benefits has eliminated some of the problem by permitting employees to retain some pension rights if they leave a firm *after* vesting has taken place. Of course, if no vesting has occurred, then all benefits may be lost. Even if rights have been vested, a financial loss may occur from the perspective that most plans pay benefits based on the salary earned at the time of employment. This means that with inflation and normally greater salaries just prior to retirement, benefits based on a job that was left, say, 20 years ago, will probably be so small in terms of today's needs that they are nearly worthless. This is particularly true if you have not built up similar benefits in a new job because of employment shifts.

The uninitiated might believe that being in three different plans (due to changing jobs) each for 10 years would give the same total pension income as being in one plan for 30 years. However, this is not true. Most plans base benefits on the salary earned in the last few years of employment or on some average of earnings as well as years of service. To receive a reasonable retirement benefit, most plans require at least 20 years of service—more for a really good pension. Thus, it is sad but true that most people cannot really afford to change jobs after age 40 or 45 unless they have other means of financing their retirement.

The ability to take pension rights earned on one job directly to another job is called "portability." Very few jobs and pension plans have portability. Some public employees, university teachers, and members of certain unions have portability to some extent. Even in these cases, some of the credit for a pension may not transfer.

Funding and tax considerations

Two other important considerations for a plan are the nature of its funding and tax provisions. *Funded plans* charge current income with pension liabilities in advance of the actual payment, and funds are set aside. To do this, an estimate of the ultimate liability must be made. Experts called actuaries evaluate data concerning the probable number of employees who will qualify for a pension, when they will take the pension, and how much it will be. The objective is to arrive at amounts that permit the plan to be reasonably funded to meet its obligations.

An *unfunded* plan is similar to our social security system in that payments to retirees are made out of current income. In an unfunded plan, the employees must hope that sufficient resources are available to cover retirement.

Even a funded plan may not assure that all necessary resources will be available. If the actuarial assumptions that have gone into the computations allow too small an actual contribution, inadequate funding may take place. ERISA attempts to regulate and control such practices.

Finally, the employer and employee must determine if the plan is *qualified* for federal tax purposes. A qualified pension plan, under the provisions of the Internal Revenue Service, allows the employer to deduct annual contributions to the pension plan as a tax-deductible item. From the employees' perspective, a qualified plan allows funds in the plan to earn income without taxation, and no tax is paid on the employer's contribution until benefits are received. A qualified pension plan must meet the appropriate requirements established under ERISA.

INDIVIDUAL PENSION PLANS

Our discussion of pension plans up until now has centered on employee-employer related pension plans. We now shift our attention to individual pension or retirement plans.

Many individuals are self-employed or are employed by firms without pension plans. Under the Economic Recovery Tax Act of 1981 and prior legislation, those who are not covered by employer-sponsored pension plans, and even those who are covered, can establish individual personal pension plans which allow some major tax advantages and thus conserve dollars for retirement years. The two types of individual retirement plans receiving the greatest attention are Keogh plans and individual retirement accounts.

Keogh plans

Keogh plans are pension plans for self-employed individuals. These plans originally stem from the Self-Employment Individuals Tax Retirement Act of 1962-HR10 (Keogh Act) and give participants the same tax advantages that qualified pension plans of corporations enjoy. The current rules allow 15 percent of earned income up to a maximum of $15,000 to be deducted from taxable income and to earn returns on a nontaxable basis until paid out at retirement. The money must be put in legally approved investments for retirement. The funds can be managed

by a variety of financial institutions or self-administered. The custodians can be changed once per year without penalty, and movement into different kinds of investments can be made as often as desired. An applicant and the particular plan must be approved by the IRS. Funds may not be withdrawn from the Keogh plan until the participant is at least 59½ years old, and withdrawal must begin by the end of the year in which age 70½ is reached. Most users of Keogh plans are self-employed doctors, dentists, lawyers, accountants, farmers, and business-people. Only those who become totally disabled or the dependents of those who die can withdraw funds early without penalty. The penalty for withdrawing without meeting the proper conditions is to nullify the plan and cause regular taxes and penalty taxes to become due. Also, another Keogh plan cannot be instituted for five years.

It is possible to pay in more than 15 percent of earned income or $15,000, but the additional amount is not to exceed $2,000 or 10 percent of net income. This can be done simply by making the greater contribution; however, the additional amount is not tax deductible, but the earnings in the additional contributions are not taxed until disbursement.[4]

Individual retirement accounts

Individual retirement accounts (IRAs) are similar to Keogh plans except that they were originally intended to be open to employees of firms who were not covered by an employer-sponsored plan. In the 1981 tax revisions, the idea is retained, but now the plans are also open to employees already covered by a sponsored plan. The maximum annual deduction is $2,000 for one person or $2,250 if there is also a nonworking spouse. If there are two working spouses, the maximum deduction is $4,000. Deductions reduce taxable income and allow for the accumulation of funds that are not currently taxed. Taxation only begins when withdrawals are made.

It is now permissible to deduct the appropriate dollar amount without any percentage limitation. In other words, if a person earns only $2,000, the *whole* $2,000 can be deducted and put into an IRA. The same rule would apply to larger permitted deductions up to $4,000. Prior to the Economic Recovery Tax Act of 1981, you could only put 15 percent of income into an IRA, with a maximum of $1,500. Thus, $10,000 of income was necessary to utilize the full $1,500 deduction. As with Keogh plans, the funds can not be withdrawn without penalty before the age of 59½ and withdrawals must begin by the end of the year in which age 70½ is reached.

---

[4]There is also a plan, called a defined benefit Keogh plan, which allows even larger amounts to be tax deductible. Under this plan, the beneficiary of the plan is allowed to pay an amount into the plan depending on the amount of payout to be received upon retirement. The basic idea is to figure how much would have to be set aside each year until retirement year to receive a particular sum each year after retirement. Limitations do apply. The amount of the benefit cannot be larger than the amount earned when the plan was established regardless of the age of the person at that time.

Individual retirement accounts are formally established when contributions are turned over to a trustee. Often the trustee is a bank or savings and loan association. The trustee then invests the funds in such outlets as certificates of deposit, savings accounts, mutual fund shares, or other allowable investments. Similarly, an *individual retirement annuity* can be purchased from a life insurance company to serve the same purpose. The interested investor may wish to consult a banker, insurance agent, or stockbroker to determine what is the most appropriate avenue to follow.

A number of other tax-advantaged retirement plans are also available. These include simplified employee pension IRAs, profit sharing plans, tax-sheltered annuities under Section 403B of the Internal Revenue Code, and the use of professional corporations. These topics go beyond the intended scope of this chapter and may be found in texts specifically dealing with personal financial planning or life insurance.

ESTATE PLANNING

In developing a comprehensive financial plan, one must look beyond the requirements of retirement planning to consider estate planning as well. Many believe that estate planning is only for the wealthy. While the wealthy do have greater needs in terms of disposing of assets, those who are not wealthy may have equal needs in terms of carefully directing the application of their estate to take care of dependents or to effectively use limited resources. As an example, a young married person with several children needs to make sure that funds are available for the childrens' education if the breadwinner dies; whereas a wealthy person in the same situation may know, within reason, that plenty is available for education and other purposes.

Another problem is that people lack awareness of the size of their estates. With the considerable inflation that has taken place over the years, estates are often much larger than assumed. If no estate planning takes place, unnecessary problems, unwarranted taxes, and misdirection of resources may occur. The conclusion is that almost everyone should at least review his or her potential estate and the needs and responsibilities of disposing of it. The subsequent discussion in this section centers around wills, trusts, and estate taxes.

Wills

One of the first steps of estate planning is to draft a will. This requires some preliminary homework to determine such items as a list of assets, approximate net worth, legal residence, and special family situations (divorces, children, remarriages, etc.). All of these items will be needed and helpful for other parts of estate planning as well.

A will is a legal document that directs the disposition of the owner's property upon death. If no will exists, a person who dies is said to have died intestate. In this case, the laws of each state provide how the property is to be dispersed.

Thus, a primary reason for having a will is because a person may not want his estate to be divided in the amounts and order of preference that state laws require.

Trusts

The legal device called a trust is a valuable tool for estate planners. The concept of a trust is that of a legal entity in which transfer of ownership of property takes place from an original owner (the creator of the trust) to another person (the trustee) for the benefit of someone else (the beneficiary). Many variations of this concept are possible. For example, it is possible for one person to be both creator and beneficiary or creator and trustee or trustee and beneficiary. When a trust is created, a trust agreement is drawn, and the trustee must act in good faith as a fiduciary party.

Trusts may be testamentary or living, revocable or irrevocable. A testamentary trust is one created by will. A living trust *(inter vivos)* is one that is established during the lifetime of the creator. If a trust is defined so that the creator may dissolve it and retake ownership of the property, it is a revocable trust. When the trust is irrevocable, the trust cannot be changed and the property it owns cannot be taken back by the creator.

Trusts are created for many reasons. Management of property is one. The property is taken care of by the trustee, and this may provide for expertise, continuity of management, and objectivity in management.

Decreasing or deferring taxes is also a major reason for using trusts. Property that produces income can be transferred to a trust so that the income is paid to the trust or to the beneficiaries of the trust, such as minor children. The transfer of income from the creator's tax return lowers his taxes, and the tax bracket of a minor is often low enough so that little or no tax is required.

A problem relating to trusts is the fact that changes occurring long after the trust was established may make provisions of the trust inadequate. This is especially true with payments to beneficiaries when inflation exists. Income from the earnings of the trust may be inadequate to pay for a college education 20 years from now. This can be relieved by allowing use of part of the principal assets of the trust to supplement the funds earned. Use of the principal is termed "invasion" of the trust and can be written into the trust agreement. Other problems that develop over time can be partially or completely avoided by giving the trustee adequate flexibility to manage the trust's assets.

Estate and gift taxes

Estate taxes are imposed on the estate of a deceased person, and gift taxes are imposed on lifetime gifts that exceed the $10,000 per year gift allowance. For the purpose of computation of taxes payable, the two types of tax obligations are combined (estate and gift), and a unified tax rate is applied to both. Thus, the lifetime gifts subject to taxation and the value of an estate at time of death are added together to determine the total tax base against which the unified rate schedule is applied.

As implied above, anyone can give away $10,000 per year to any number of people without incurring a subsequent tax obligation. Actually, each spouse can give a child $10,000 per year ($20,000 total per year). This is known as gift-splitting. Thus, a husband and wife with three children could give away $60,000 per year without further tax obligation. Over 20 years, $1.2 million could be transferred in such a fashion.

Computation of unified federal gift and estate tax

In Table 19–4, we see a unified tax rate schedule for federal gift and estate taxes. The tax obligation can be found by using column 3 (and column 4 where necessary). For example, on $40,000, the basic tax amount is $8,200 (column 3). On $50,000, we take the basic tax amount on $40,000 ($8,200) and multiply the additional $10,000 by 24 percent (the additional or marginal tax rate in column 4). This $2,400 is added to $8,200 to arrive at $10,600.

Table 19–4 **Unified rate schedules for federal gift and estate taxes***

(1) Taxable estate more than	(2) Taxable estate less than or equal to	(3) Tax on amount in column 1	(4) Rate of tax on excess over amount in column 1 (percent)
$ 0	$ 10,000	0	18%
10,000	20,000	1,800	20
20,000	40,000	3,800	22
40,000	60,000	8,200	24
60,000	80,000	13,000	26
80,000	100,000	18,200	28
100,000	150,000	23,800	30
150,000	250,000	38,800	32
250,000	500,000	70,800	34
500,000	750,000	155,800	37
750,000	1,000,000	248,300	39
1,000,000	1,250,000	345,800	41
1,250,000	1,500,000	448,300	43
1,500,000	2,000,000	555,800	45
2,000,000	2,500,000	780,800	49
2,500,000	3,000,000	1,025,800	53
3,000,000	3,500,000	1,290,800	57
3,500,000	4,000,000	1,575,800	61
4,000,000	4,500,000	1,880,800	65
4,500,000	5,000,000	2,205,800	69
5,000,000	—	2,550,800	70

*Changes in upper-bracket rates of 50 percent or higher will take place between 1982 and 1985. The maximum rate will eventually be 50 percent, starting at $2.5 million (as specified in the 1981 Economic Recovery Tax Act).

Prior to passage of the 1981 Economic Recovery Tax Act, a $47,000 unified tax credit was allowed. This $47,000 tax credit effectively freed the first $175,625 in an estate from taxation. Let's see how this works.

Tax on $150,000	$38,800
Tax on additional $25,625 (at 32 percent)	8,200
Total tax obligation	$47,000
Unified tax credit	− 47,000
Tax obligation	$ 0

Only on amounts greater than $175,625 would a tax obligation occur. With the passage of the 1981 Economic Recovery Tax Act, the unified tax credit was changed each year from 1982 through 1987, allowing progressively larger estates to be exempt from taxation as indicated in Table 19–5.

For example, in 1985, the unified tax credit is $121,800. This will exempt a $400,000 estate from taxation. Referring back to Table 19–4 for tax rates, we see:

Tax on $250,000	$70,800
Tax on additional $150,000 (at 34 percent)	51,000
Total tax obligation	$121,800
Unified tax credit	− 121,800
Tax obligation	$ 0

In 1987 and thereafter, $600,000 of a taxable estate will be exempt from taxation. Thus on a $1 million estate, we would compute taxes as follows.

Taxes on $1,000,000 (Table 19–4)	$345,800
United tax credit (Table 19–5 for 1987)	192,800
Actual taxes owed	$153,000

Table 19–5   **Unified credits under the 1981 Economic Recovery Tax Act (ERTA)**

Year	Unified credit	Equivalent exemption
1981	$ 47,000	$175,625
1982	62,800	225,000
1983	79,300	275,000
1984	96,300	325,000
1985	121,800	400,000
1986	155,800	500,000
1987 and forward	192,800	600,000

On the $1 million estate, this only represents an average tax of 15.3 percent. Another way to look at this is to say that $153,000 represents the tax on estate values between $600,000 and $1 million. As indicated in Table 19–4, the marginal tax rate between $600,000 and $750,000 would be 37 percent, and between $750,000 and a $1 million, it would be 39%. The computed tax is:

$600,000-$750,000 (representing $150,000) × 37% = $ 55,500
$750,000-$1,000,000 (representing $250,000) × 39% = 97,500
Total tax = $153,000

Other consequences of the 1981 Economic Recovery Tax Act related to estate planning

The act also allowed all qualifying transfers between spouses to be free of gift or estate taxes (unlimited marital deduction). Thus, one spouse may completely transfer or leave an estate to his or her spouse without any immediate tax consequences. This is different from prior legislation in which the greater of $250,000 or one half of the adjusted estate could be passed on to a spouse. Previously, on a $1 million estate, one spouse could leave up to $250,000 to another spouse without tax consequences. Now the full amount is exempt from estate taxes. Of course, descendants of the surviving spouse may ultimately have to pay the estate taxes. The surviving spouse and the future heirs must be particularly aware of the ultimate tax consequences because the estate, which is free of taxes on the first pass due to the unlimited marital deduction, is likely to be larger than it would have been in the past.

The bill also provided an estate tax break for farmers, whose land is passed on to heirs categorized as "special use" land—that is, property valued as farmland rather than its "highest and best use." Previously, special use land could be transferred in an estate up to $500,000 below the highest and best use value. Under the 1981 Economic Recovery Tax Act, this was raised to $750,000

Additional comments on estate planning

A few additional comments about estate planning need to be made. We have made no specific points about state inheritance taxes, which naturally vary from state to state. Traditionally, they are smaller and of less consequence than federal estate taxes. Furthermore, state inheritance taxes may be used as credits against federal taxes. Nevertheless, it is possible that in the future with substantially reduced federal estate taxes (a $600,000 exemption in 1987), the only taxes that many families will pay will be relatively low state inheritance taxes.

In taking an overview of estate planning, some have suggested that the $600,000 exemption and other liberal provisions of the 1981 Economic Recovery Tax Act will make estate planning for tax purposes less important. However, with the presence of even modest inflation, estate values are likely to be substantially increased by the end of the century. While estate planning for tax purposes may have reduced importance for many, others must continue to contend with these

issues. Financial advisors must remain aware of the various vehicles for passing along property and deferring taxes.[5]

Life insurance must also be considered as a necessary *protective* device. Also, many favorable tax arrangements can be established through insurance contracts that use present contributions to provide future benefits.

SUMMARY

Retirement and estate planning considerations are important to comprehensive financial planning. First, objectives must be set based on a thorough evaluation of personal circumstances.

Even though the future is uncertain and returns from various investments may fluctuate greatly, future time is as much a benefit as it is a detriment to financial planning. Over time, unusual variations tend to smooth out and follow long-term trends that override short-term changes. Although common stock portfolios may go up or down 10 or 20 percent in a given year, over the long term, a normal anticipated return can be considered.

Many sources of retirement income are available to those who plan ahead. Common examples include social security, private pension plans, and individual retirement plans which include Keogh plans, individual retirement accounts (IRAs), and annuities. These can be combined with current investments in common stocks and real assets to provide a comprehensive investment package. Essentials of estate planning concern wills, trusts, and taxes. Wills permit transfer of property at death according to the wishes of the owner within legal limits. Trusts are legal entities that allow for control of property before and/or after death by transferring assets from an owner to a trustee. Numerous reasons for establishing trusts can be described, but tax advantages and management of assets are the most common.

Major taxes involved with estate planning are gift and estate taxes. The 1981 Economic Recovery Tax Act has increased the size of an exempt estate from $175,625 to $600,000 by 1987, increased the annual allowable gift from $3,000 to $10,000, provided for an unlimited marital deduction, and lowered maximum gift-estate tax rates. All of these factors are essential to estate planning and determining future tax exposure.

IMPORTANT WORDS AND CONCEPTS

Dollar-cost averaging	Individual retirement accounts
Private pension plans	(IRAs)
Vesting	Individual retirement annuity

---

[5]For example, the $600,000 exemption actually can become a $1.2 million exemption for a married couple. One spouse leaves $600,000 tax exempt to the heirs or descendants and the remaining $600,000 tax free to the other spouse, who ultimately utilizes the $600,000 tax exemption to pass on the estate tax free to the heirs.

ERISA
Contributory pension plan
Noncontributory pension plan
Defined benefit plan
Defined contribution plan
Funded pension plan
Unfunded pension plan
Qualified pension plan
Keogh plan

Trust
Testamentory trust
Living trust *(inter vivos)*
Revocable trust
Irrevocable trust
Estate and gift taxes
Uniform tax rate schedule
Unified tax credit
Marital deduction

QUESTIONS AND PROBLEMS

1. Why does dollar-cost averaging force the investor to buy relatively more shares at lower stock prices?

2. What is meant by the fact that social security operates on a current-funding basis?

3. What is meant by the term *vesting* in a pension plan?

4. What is the difference between a contributory and noncontributory pension plan?

5. Explain why frequent job shifts may reduce retirement benefits.

6. What are the maximum contributions (deductions) that can be made to an individual retirement account (IRA) under the 1981 tax revisions?

7. What is the earliest age one can begin withdrawing funds from an IRA without penalty? By what age must withdrawals begin?

8. Explain how a trust set up for the benefit of minors may lower taxes.

9. What is the difference between a revocable and irrevocable trust?

10. Explain how gift taxes and estate taxes are combined.

11. Explain the general effect of the 1981 Economic Recovery Tax Act on the unified credit.

12. An individual will need $21,000 per year during retirement over a 14-year period. With an 8 percent discount rate, what is the present value of the annual needs?

13. Assume, funds will be set aside each year for 12 years at 10 percent to meet the retirement need computed in problem 12. How much will the annual contribution be?

14. Under dollar-cost averaging, an investor will purchase $4,000 worth of stock each year for three years. The stock price is $25 in year 1, $16 in year 2, and $32 in year 3.
    a. Compute the average price.
    b. Compute the average cost.
    c. Explain why the average cost is less than the average price.

15. An estate has a value of $475,000. Compute the estate tax obligation before tax credits.

16. In 1984, how much would the tax obligation be after tax credits for problem 15?

SELECTED REFERENCES

"A Long Life Can Strain Your Finances." *Changing Times,* August 1980, pp. 61–62.

Ashley, Paul Prichard. *You and Your Will: The Planning and Management of Your Estate.* New York: McGraw-Hill, 1975.

Ball, Robert M. *Social Security Today and Tomorrow.* New York: Columbia University Press, 1978.

"Economic Recovery Tax Act of 1981." (An analysis). Chicago: Arthur Andersen & Co., 1981.

Hemphill, Charles F., Jr. *Wills and Trusts.* Englewood Cliffs, N.J.: Prentice-Hall, 1980.

Jacoby, Susan. "All about Pensions and Other Retirement Plans." *Working Woman,* April 1977, pp. 14–18.

Kahn, Arnold D. *Family Security through Estate Planning.* New York: McGraw-Hill, 1979.

Lippett, Peter E. *Estate Planning: What Anyone Who Owns Anything Must Know.* Reston, Va.: Reston Publishing, 1979.

Platt, Charles M. "Social Security, Will It Be There When You Need It?" *U.S. News & World Report,* April 1979, pp. 24–27.

Scharff, Edward E. "Planning Now for Retirement Later." *Money,* July 1979, pp. 33–37.

Unthank L. L., and Harry M. Behrendt. *What You Should Know about Individual Retirement Accounts.* Homewood, Ill.: Dow Jones-Irwin, 1978.

Glossary

Abnormal return Gains beyond what the market would normally provide after adjustment for risk.

Advances Increases in the prices of various stocks as measured between two points in time. Significant advances in a large number of stocks indicate a particular degree of market strength. See also **Declines.**

After-acquired property clause The stipulation in a mortgage bond (secured by real estate) indenture requiring all real property subsequently obtained by the issuing firm to serve as additional bond security.

After-market performance The price experience of new issues in the market.

Alpha The value representing the difference between the return on a portfolio and a point on the market line that corresponds to a beta equal to the portfolio. If a portfolio manager performs at positive alpha levels, he would generate returns better than those available along the market line, which is available to everyone.

Anticipated realized yield The return received on a bond held for a period other than that ending on the call date or the maturity date. In computing the anticipated realized yield, the investor considers both coupon payments and expected capital gains.

Asset utilization ratios Ratios that indicate the number of times per year that assets are turned over. They show the activity in the various asset accounts.

Average differential return The alpha value which indicates the difference between the return on a portfolio or fund and a point on the market line that corresponds to a beta equal to the portfolio or fund.

Balance sheet A financial statement that indicates, at a given point in time, what the firm owns and how these assets are financed in the form of liabilities and ownership interest.

Balanced fund A type of mutual fund that invests in common stock, bonds, and often preferred stock to try to provide income plus some capital gains.

Bankers' acceptance A short-term debt instrument issued in conjunction with a foreign trade transaction. The acceptance is a draft that is drawn on a bank for approval for future payment and is subsequently presented to the payer.

Barron's Confidence Index An indicator utilized by technical analysts who follow smart money rules. Movements in the index measure the expectations of bond investors, whom some technical analysts see as astute enough to foresee economic trends before the stock market has time to react.

Basis point The unit of measure of change on interest-bearing instruments. One basis point is equal to .01 percent.

Batting average Percentage of new issues underwritten in which the price six months after distribution exceeded the offering price.

Beta A measurement of movement of a security with the market in general. It measures relative volatility. A high beta coefficient indicates high amounts of systematic risk.

Beta stability The amount of consistency in beta values over time. Instability means prior beta values may not be reflective of future beta values.

Blind pool A form of limited partnership for real estate investment in which funds are provided to the general partner to select properties for investment.

Breadth of market indicators Overall market rules used by technical analysts in comparing broad market activity with trading activity in a few stocks. By comparing all advances and declines in NYSE-listed stocks, for example, with the Dow Jones Industrial Average, analysts attempt to judge when the market has changed directions.

Bull spread An option strategy utilized when the expectation is that the stock price will rise. The opposite is a bear spread.

Business cycle Short-term swings in economic activity

encompassing expansionary and recessionary periods and generally occurring over two- to four-year periods.

Buying the spread A term indicating the cost from writing the call is more than the revenue of the short position. The opposite results in "selling the spread."

Call An option to buy 100 shares of common stock at a specified price for a given period of time.

Call provision A mechanism for repaying funds advanced through a bond issue. A provision of the indenture allows the issuer to retire bonds prior to maturity by paying holders a premium above principal and accrued interest.

CBOE Chicago Board Options Exchange, the first exchange for call options.

Capital appreciation A growth in the value of a stock or other investment as opposed to earnings, such as dividends or interest.

Capital asset pricing model A model by which assets are valued based on their risk characteristics. It allows for viewing the possibility of a set of superior investment opportunities by combining some portion of a risk-free asset with the efficient frontier.

Capital market line The graphic representation of the range of risks and returns with various portfolios of assets.

Certificate of deposit A fixed-income security issued by a depository institution. Examples include the $10,000 money market CD, the $100,000 jumbo CD, and the tax-free all savers certificate. Holders of smaller certificates receive government insurance on their deposits but must sacrifice liquidity during the fixed holding periods.

Chartered Financial Analyst (CFA) A security analyst or portfolio manager who has been appropriately certified through experience requirements and testing (via the University of Virginia).

Charting The use by technical analysts (chartists) of numerical charts and graphs to plot past stock price movements, which are used to predict future prices.

Closed-end fund An investment fund with a limited number of shares. Shares are available in the market only if present owners wish to sell their holdings. See **Open-end fund.**

Closing purchase transaction A transaction in which an investor who is a writer of an option intends to terminate his obligation.

Closing sale transaction A transaction in which an investor who is the holder of an outstanding security intends to liquidate his position as a holder.

Combined earnings and dividend model A model combining earnings per share and an earnings multiplier with a finite dividend model. Value is derived from both the present value of dividends and the present value of the future price of the stock based on the earnings multiplier (P/E).

Commercial paper A short-term, unsecured debt instrument of large dollar denomination issued to the public by a major corporation.

Commission broker An individual who represents a stock brokerage firm at an exchange and who executes sales and purchases stocks for the firm's clients across the nation.

Commodities Such tangible items as livestock, farm produce, and precious metals. Users and producers of commodities hedge against future price fluctuations by transferring risks to speculators through futures contracts.

Constant dollar method Adjusting for inflation in the financial statements by using the consumer price index.

Constant growth model A dividend valuation model that assumes a constant growth rate for dividends.

Construction and development trust A type of REIT that makes short-term loans to developers during their construction period.

Consumer price index An index used to measure the changes in the general price level.

Contrary opinion rules Guidelines, such as the odd-lot or the short sales position, used by technical analysts who predict stock market activity based on the assumption that such groups as small traders or short sellers are often wrong. Such groups can then be observed so that actions opposite to theirs can be taken. Also see **Smart money rules.**

Contributory pension plan An arrangement in which both the employer and employee contribute to the pension plan.

Conversion premium The amount, expressed as a dollar value or as a percentage, by which the price of the convertible security exceeds the current market value of the common stock into which it may be converted.

Conversion price The face value of a convertible security divided by the conversion ratio, giving the price of the underlying common stock at which the security is convertible. An investor would usually not convert the security into common stock unless the market price was greater than the conversion price.

Conversion ratio The number of shares of common stock an investor receives in exchanging convertible bonds or shares of convertible preferred stock for shares of common stock.

Conversion value The value of the underlying common stock represented by convertible bonds or convertible preferred stock. This dollar value is obtained by multiplying the conversion ratio by the per-share market price of the common stock.

Convertible security A corporate bond or a share of preferred stock which, at the option of the holder, can be converted into shares of common stock of the issuing corporation.

Correlation coefficient The measurement of joint movement between two variables.

Coupon rate The stated, fixed rate of interest paid on a bond.

Covered writer A writer of an option who owns the stock upon which the option is written. If the stock is not owned, the writer is deemed naked.

Cross hedge A hedging position in which one form of security is used to hedge another form of security (often because differences in maturity dates or quality characteristics make a perfect hedge difficult to establish).

Currency futures Futures contracts for speculation or hedging in different nations' currencies.

Current cost method Adjusting for inflation in the financial statements by revaluing assets at their current cost.

Current ratio Current assets divided by current liabilities.

Current yield The annual dollar amount of interest paid on a bond divided by the price at which the bond is currently trading in the market.

Cyclical indicators Factors that economists can observe to measure the progress of economic cycles. Leading indicators move in a particular direction in advance of the movement of general business conditions, while lagging indicators change direction after general conditions, and coincident indicators move in unison with the economy.

Cyclical industry An industry, such as automobiles, whose financial health is closely tied to the condition of the general economy. Such industries tend to make the type of products whose purchase can be postponed until the economy improves.

Debenture An unsecured corporate bond.

Debt utilization ratios Ratios that indicate how the firm is financed between debt (lenders) and equity (owners), and the firm's ability for meeting cash payments due on fixed obligations, such as interest, lease payments, licensing fees, or sinking fund charges.

Declines Decreases in the prices of various stocks as measured between two points in time. Significant declines in a large number of stocks indicate a particular degree of market weakness. See also **Advances**.

Deep discount bond A bond that has a coupon rate far below rates currently available on investments and which consequently can be traded only at a significant discount from par value. It may offer an opportunity for capital appreciation.

Defined benefit plan Under a defined benefit plan, the employee can calculate his or her pension based on a formula using years of service and average earnings.

Defined contribution plan Under a defined contribution plan, retirement benefits are a function of total contributions over the life of the plan and are not based on such factors as years of service or average earnings.

Diagonal spreads A combination of vertical and horizontal spreads.

Dilution The reduction in earnings per share that occurs when earnings remain unchanged yet the number of shares outstanding increases, as in the conversion of convertible bonds or preferred stock into common stock.

Direct equity claim Representation of ownership interests, such as common stock or other instruments, to purchase common stock, such as warrants and options.

Discount rate The interest rate at which future cash flows are discounted to a present value.

Dispersion The spread of values or outcomes around an expected value.

Diversification Lack of concentration in any one item. A portfolio composed of many different securities is diversified.

Dividend valuation model Any one of a number of stock valuation models based on the premise that the value of stock lies in the present value of its future dividend stream.

Dividend yield Annual dividends per share divided by market price.

Dollar-cost averaging Under this system, a fixed-dollar investment is placed in a given security (or portfolio) each year regardless of its price or the current market outlook. This reflects an attempt to buy more shares at a lower average price.

Double-declining-balance depreciation A method of depreciation in which the rate under straight-line depreciation is doubled on the declining-balance.

Dow Jones Industrial Average An index of stock market activity based on price movements of the stocks of 29 large industrial corporations and American Telephone & Telegraph (30 stocks in total).

Dow theory The theory, developed by Charles Dow in the late 1890s and still in use today, states that the analysis of long-term (primary) stock market trends can yield accurate predictions of future price movements.

Downside protection The protection that a convertible bond investor enjoys during a period of falling stock prices. While the underlying common stock and the convertible bond may both fall in value, the bond will fall only to a particular level because it has a fundamental or pure bond value based on its assured income stream.

Downside risk The possibility that an asset, such as a security, may fall in value as a result of fundamental factors or external market forces. The limit of the downside risk for a convertible bond can be computed as the difference between the bond's market price and its pure bond value divided by the market price.

Du Pont analysis A system of analyzing return on assets through examining the profit margin and asset turnover. Also, the value of return on equity is analyzed through evaluating return on assets and the debt/total assets ratio. Figure 8–2 summarizes the major components of the Du Pont system of analysis.

Duration The weighted average time that must pass before the investor recovers the interest and principal on

a bond. If the cash flows are higher in the earlier years of the investment, then the duration is shorter; this is more favorable for the investor than a longer duration.

Earnings per share The earnings available to common stockholders divided by the number of common stock shares outstanding.

Earnings valuation model Any one of a number of stock valuation models based on the premise that a stock's value is some appropriate multiple of earnings per share.

Effective diversification The amount of diversification of a portfolio to remove unsystematic risk. The amount of a fund's excess return related to market excess return can define whether a portfolio manager has been effective in diversifying away unsystematic risk.

Efficient frontier A set of portfolios of investments in which the investor receives maximum return for a given level of risk or a minimum risk for a given level of return.

Efficient market The capacity of the market to react to new information, to avoid rapid price fluctuations, and to engage in an increased or reduced trading volume without realizing significant price changes. In an efficient market environment securities are assumed to be correctly priced at any point in time.

Efficient market hypothesis The thought that there are many participants in the securities markets who are profit maximizing and alert to information so that there is almost instant adjustment to new information. The weak form of this hypothesis considers that there is no relationship between past and future prices. The semi-strong form considers that all forms of public information are already reflected in the price of a security so fundamental analysis cannot determine under- or overvaluation. The strong form suggests that all information, insider as well as public, is impounded in the value of a security.

Efficient portfolio A portfolio that combines assets so as to minimize the standard deviation for a given level of return.

Equipment trust certificate A secured debt instrument used by firms in the transportation industry that provides for bond proceeds to purchase new equipment, which in turn is collateral for the bond issue.

Equity participation The lender also participates in an ownership interest in the property.

Equity trust A type of REIT that buys, operates, and sells real estate as an investment as opposed to construction and development trusts and mortgage trusts.

ERISA Employee Retirement Income Security Act of 1974 (commonly called the Pension Reform Act of 1974). The act requires that vesting after a certain period of time must take place. ERISA also prescribes minimum standards of eligibility for participation, disclosure to participant rules, and employer fiscal responsibility.

Estate and gift taxes Estate taxes are imposed on the estate of a deceased person, and gift taxes are imposed on lifetime gifts that exceed the $10,000-per-year gift al-

lowance. For purposes of computation of taxes payable, the two types of tax obligations are combined (estate and gift), and a unified tax is applied to both.

Excess returns A measure used in evaluating fund manager performance. It is total return (capital appreciation plus dividends) minus the return on Treasury bills or other market measures.

Exchange listing A firm formerly trading over-the-counter lists its shares on an exchange (such as the American or New York Stock Exchange).

Exercise price (also called the striking price). The price at which each share of stock can be bought or sold; standardized in trading at $5 intervals for stock between $50 and $100, $10 intervals for those between $100 and $200, and $20 for those over $200.

Expected value The sum of possible outcomes times their probability of occurrence to obtain a measure of value.

Expectations hypothesis The hypothesis which explains the term structure of interest rates, stating that a long-term interest rate is the average of expected short-term interest rates over the applicable time period. If, for example, long-term rates are lower than short-term rates, then according to the expectations hypothesis, investors must expect that short-term rates will be falling in coming periods.

Extraordinary gains and losses Gains or losses from the sale of corporate fixed assets, lawsuits, or similar events that would not be expected to occur often, if ever again.

Fed The Federal Reserve serves as the central banking authority for the United States. The Fed enacts monetary policy, and it plays a major role in regulating commercial banking operations and controlling the money supply.

Federal deficit A situation in which the federal government spends more money than it receives through taxes and other revenue sources. Deficits are financed through borrowing by the U.S. Treasury.

Federal surplus A situation in which taxes and other government revenues provide more money than is needed to cover government expenditures.

FIFO A method of inventory valuation in which it is assumed that inventory purchased first is sold first (first-in, first-out).

Financial asset A financial claim on an asset (rather than physical possession of a tangible asset) usually documented by a legal instrument, such as a stock certificate.

Fiscal policy Government spending and taxing practices designed to promote or inhibit various economic activities.

Floor broker An independent stock broker who is a member of a stock exchange and who executes trades, for a fee, for commission brokers experiencing excessive volumes of trading.

Floor value A value which an income-producing security will not fall below because of the fundamental value attributable to its assured income stream.

Flow of funds analysis Analysis of the pattern of financial payments between business, government, and households.

Fourth market The direct trading between large institutional investors in blocks of listed stocks. The participants avoid paying brokerage commissions

Fully diluted earnings per share The value of earnings per share that would be realized if all outstanding securities convertible into common stock were in fact converted.

Fundamental analysis The valuation of stocks based on fundamental factors, such as company earnings or dividend receipts.

Funded pension plan Current income is charged with pension liabilities in advance of the actual payment, and funds are set aside.

Futures contract An agreement that provides for the delivery of a specific amount of a commodity at a designated time in the future at a given price.

General obligation bond A municipal bond backed by the full financial strength, including the taxing power, of the issuing governmental unit.

Gift splitting Each spouse giving a child $10,000 per year for a total of $20,000, rather than the usual $10,000 available under the 1981 Economic Recovery Tax Act.

Going public Selling formerly privately held shares to new investors on the over-the-counter market for the first time.

Government securities Bonds issued by federal, state, or local governmental units or government agencies. Whereas corporate securities' returns are paid through company earnings, government securities are repaid through taxes or the revenues from projects financed by the bonds.

Graduated payment mortgage A type of mortgage in which payments start out on a relatively low basis and increase over the life of the loan.

Gross national product implicit price deflator A calculation made by the Department of Commerce which adjusts the prices of all goods and services in the GNP estimate for the effects of price change.

Growth company A company that exhibits rising returns on assets each year and sales that are growing at an increasing rate (growth phase of the life-cycle curve). Growth companies may not be as well known as growth stocks.

Growth stock The stock of a firm generally growing faster than the economy or market norm.

Hedging A process for lessening or eliminating risk by taking a position in the market opposite to your original position. For example, someone who owns wheat can sell a futures contract to protect against future price declines.

Horizontal spread Buying and writing two options with the same strike price but maturity in different months.

Ibbotson and Singuefield study A University of Chicago study examining comparative returns on stocks and fixed-income securities from the mid-1920s into the 1970s. It is similar to the Lorie and Fisher study in many respects.

Income bond A corporate debt instrument on which interest is paid only if funds are available from current income.

Income statement A financial statement that shows the profitability of a firm over a given period of time.

Income statement method A method of forecasting earnings per share based on a projected income statement.

Indenture A lengthy, complicated legal document which spells out the borrowing firm's responsibilities to the individual lenders in a bond issue.

Index fund A mutual fund investing in a portfolio of corporate stocks, the composition of which is determined by the Standard & Poor's 500 or some other index.

Indirect equity claim A claim on investments in common stock or other assets such as that achieved by placing funds in investment companies.

Individual retirement accounts (IRAs) Individual retirement plans open to all persons under the 1981 tax revisions. The maximum annual contribution is $2,000 for one person and $2,250 if there is a nonworking spouse. If there are two working spouses, the maximum contribution in $4,000. Contributions reduce taxable income and allow for the accumulation of funds that are not currently taxed. Taxation only begins when withdrawals are made.

Individual retirement annuity A tax-deferred retirement annuity purchased from an insurance company. Benefits may be guaranteed in advance.

Industry factors The unique attributes that must be considered in analyzing a given industry or group of industries. Examples include industry structure, supply/demand of labor and materials, and government regulation.

Industry life cycle The movement of a firm or industry through stages of development, growth, expansion, and maturity.

Inflation A general increase in the prices of goods and services.

Inflation-adjusted accounting Restating financial statements to show the effect of inflation on the balance sheet and income statement. This is supplemental to the normal presentation based on historical data.

Inflationary expectations Expectations about inflation that tend to influence investing and purchasing decisions. A change in expectations can modify the required rate of return for the investor.

Institutional investor A type of investor (as opposed to individual investors) representing organizations re-

sponsible for bringing together large pools of capital for investment. Institutional investors include investment companies, pension funds, life insurance companies, bank trust departments, and endowments and foundations.

Interest rate futures Futures contracts involving Treasury bills, Treasury bonds, Treasury notes, commercial paper, certificates of deposit, and GNMA certificates.

In-the-money A term that indicates when the market price of a stock is above the striking price of the option. When the strike price is above the market price, the option is out-of-the-money.

Intrinsic value Value of an option equal to market price minus the strike price.

Inverse pyramiding A process of leveraging to control commodities contracts in which the profits from one contract are used to purchase another contract on margin, and profits on this contract are applied to a third, and so on.

Investment The commitment of current funds in anticipation of the receipt of an increased return of funds at some point in the future.

Investment banker One who is primarily involved in the distribution of securities from the issuing corporation to the public. An investment banker also advises corporate clients on their financial strategy and may help to arrange mergers and acquisitions.

Investment banking The underwriting and distribution of a new securities issue in the primary market. The investment banker advises the issuing concern on price and other terms and normally guarantees sale, while overseeing distribution of the securities through the selling brokerage houses.

Investment companies A type of financial institution that takes proceeds of individual investors and reinvests them in securities according to their specific objectives. A popular type of investment company is the mutual fund.

Irrevocable trust The creator may not dissolve the trust and take back the property.

K_e The term representing anticipated rate of return equal to dividend yield plus expected growth in earnings and dividends. It is the discount rate applied to future dividends.

Keogh plan A retirement plan for self-employed individuals. The current rules allow 15 percent of earned income up to a maximum of $15,000 to be deducted from taxable income and to earn returns on a nontaxable basis until paid out at retirement.

Key indicators Various market observations used by technical analysts to predict the directions of future market trends. Examples include the contrary opinion and smart money rules.

Least squares trendline A statistically developed linear trendline that minimizes the distance of the individual observations from the line.

LIFO A method of inventory valuation in which it is as-

sumed that inventory purchased last is sold first (last-in, first-out).

Limit order A condition placed on a transaction executed through a stock broker to assure that securities will be sold only if a specified minimum is received or purchased only if the price to be paid is no more than a given maximum.

Limited partnership A business arrangement in which there is the limited liability protection of a corporation with the tax provisions of a regular partnership. All profits or losses are directly assigned to the partners for tax purposes. The general partner has unlimited liability.

Liquidity The capacity of an investment to be retired for cash in a short period of time with a minimum capital loss.

Liquidity ratios Ratios that demonstrate the firm's ability to pay off short-term obligations as they come due.

Living trust (inter vivos) A trust that is established during the lifetime of the creator.

Long position A market transaction in which an investor purchases securities with the expectation of holding the securities for cash income or for resale at a higher price in the future. See also **Short position.**

Lorie and Fisher study A University of Chicago study indicating comparative returns on financial assets over half a decade. It is similar to the Ibbotson and Sinquefield study in many respects.

Margin account A trading account maintained with a brokerage firm on which the investor may borrow a percentage of the funds for the purchase of securities. The broker loans the fund at interest slightly above the prime rate.

Margin maintenance requirement The amount of money that must be "deposited" to hold a margin position if losses reduce the initial margin that was put up.

Margin requirements The amount of money that must be "deposited" to purchase a commodity contract or shares of stock on margin.

Marital deduction The avoidance of any immediate tax consequence in passing an estate from one spouse to another.

Market A mechanism for facilitating the exchange of assets through buyer-seller communication. The communication, and not a central negotiating location, is the requisite condition for a market to exist, though some transactions (e.g., trades at the various stock exchanges) do involve a direct meeting of buyers and sellers or their agents.

Market line On a graph excess returns are shown on the vertical axis and the portfolio beta is shown on the horizontal axis and the market line describes the relationship between the two.

Market rate The coupon rate of interest paid on bonds currently issued. Of course, a previously issued bond which is currently traded may be sold at a discount or a premium so that the buyer in effect receives the market

rate even if the coupon rate on this older bond is substantially higher or lower than market. The market rate is also known as the yield to maturity.

Maturity date The date at which outstanding principal must be repaid to bondholders.

Merger price premium The difference between the offering price per share and the market price per share of the merger candidate (before the impact of the offer).

Monetarist An economic analyst who feels that monetary policy tools, and not fiscal policy, can best provide a stable environment of sustained economic growth.

Monetary policy Direct control of interest rates or the money supply undertaken by the Federal Reserve to achieve economic objectives. Used in some cases to augment or offset the use of fiscal policy.

Money market fund A type of mutual fund which invests in short-term government securities, commercial paper, and repurchase agreements. Most offer check-writing privileges in minimums of $500.

Money supply The level of funds available at a given time for conducting transactions in our economy. The Federal Reserve can influence the money supply through its monetary policy tools. There are many different definitions of the money supply. For example, M1 is currency in circulation plus private checking deposits, including those in interest-bearing NOW accounts. M2 adds in savings accounts and money market mutual funds.

Mortgage trust A form of REIT in which long-term loans are made to real estate investors.

Mutual fund A type of investment company in which the investor owns a share of the portfolio assets equal to his number of shares in the fund.

Mutual fund cash position An overall market rule which asserts that by examining the level of uncommitted funds held by large institutional investors, analysts can measure the potential demand for stocks and thereby anticipate market movements.

National Association of Securities Dealers Automated Quotations System (NASDAQ) A computerized system that provides up-to-the-minute price quotations on over 3,000 of the more actively traded OTC stocks.

Net asset value A term often used in reference to the price of a share of a mutual fund. It is equal to the market value of the portfolio minus liabilities divided by the total number of shares outstanding in the fund.

Net debtor-creditor hypothesis Since inflation makes each dollar worth less, it is often argued that a person or firm that is a net debtor gains from inflation because payments of interest and return of principal are made with continually less valuable dollars. Conversely, a net creditor loses real capital because the loans are repaid in less valuable dollars.

Net working capital Current assets minus current liabilities.

New York Stock Exchange Index A market value weighted measure of stock market changes for all stocks listed on the NYSE.

No-load mutual fund A mutual fund on which no sales commission must be paid. The funds' shares are sold not through brokers, but rather through the mail or other direct channels.

Nominal return A return that has not been adjusted for inflation.

Nonconstant growth model A dividend valuation model that does not assume a constant growth rate for dividends.

Noncontributory pension plan An arrangement in which only the employer contributes to the pension plan. It is noncontributory for the employee.

Odd-lot dealer A member of a stock exchange who maintains an inventory of a particular firm's stock in order to sell odd lots (trades of less than 100 shares) to customers of the exchange.

Odd-lot theory The contrary opinion rule stating that small traders (who generally buy or sell odd lots) often misjudge market trends, selling just before upturns and buying before downturns. The theory has not been useful in predicting trends observed in recent years.

One hundred seventy-five percent declining-balance depreciation An accelerated depreciation method which represents the most rapid write-off of depreciation allowable on real estate (over 15 years) under the 1981 Economic Recovery Tax Act. In the IRS tables, there is also an assumed shift to straight-line in the mid-life of the asset.

Open-end fund A mutual fund without a specified number of shares for trading; new shares can be created for new investors. See **Closed-end fund.**

Open-market operations The Federal Reserve's action of buying or selling government securities in order to expand or contract the amount of money in the economy.

Opening purchase transaction A transaction in which an investor intends to become the holder of an option.

Opening sale transaction A transaction in which an investor intends to be a writer of an option.

Operating margin Operating income divided by sales.

Option The right acquired for a consideration to buy or sell something at a fixed price within a specified period of time.

Option premium The intrinsic value plus a speculative premium.

Option price The specified price at which the holder of a warrant may buy the shares to which the warrant entitles purchase.

Options Clearing Corporation Issues all options listed on the four exchanges which trade in options.

Organized exchanges Institutions, such as the New York Stock Exchange, the American Stock Exchange, or any

of the smaller regional exchanges, that provide a central location for the buying and selling of securities.

Overall market rules Guidelines, such as breadth of market indicators or mutual fund cash positions, used by technical analysts who predict stock market activity based on past activity.

Over-the-counter market Not a specific location but rather a communications network through which trades of bonds, nonlisted stocks, and other securities take place. Trading activity is overseen by the National Association of Securities Dealers (NASD).

Par bonds Bonds that are selling at their par or maturity values rather than at premium or discounted prices. Par value on a corporate bond is generally $1,000.

Par value (bond) The face value of a bond, generally $1,000 for corporate issues, higher denominations for government issues.

Partial hedge A hedge position in which only part of the risk is eliminated or lessened.

Payout ratio Annual dividends per share divided by annual earnings per share.

Peak The point in an economic cycle at which expansion ends and a recession begins.

Perpetual bond A bond with no maturity date.

Personal savings/personal disposable income The rate at which people are saving their disposable income. This has implications for the generation of funds to modernize plant and equipment and increase productivity.

Portfolio effect The effect obtained when assets are combined into a portfolio. The interaction of the assets can provide risk reduction such that the portfolio standard deviation may be less than the standard deviation of any one asset in it.

Preferred stock A hybrid security that generally provides fixed returns. Preferred stockholders are paid returns after bondholder claims are satisfied but before any returns are paid to common stockholders. Though preferred stock returns are fixed in amount, they are classified as dividends (not interest) and are not tax-deductible to the issuing firm.

Portfolio The term applied to a collection of securities or investments.

Portfolio manager One who has responsibility for managing large pools of funds. Portfolio managers may be employed by insurance companies, mutual funds, bank trust departments, pension funds, and other institutional investors.

Price/earnings ratio The multiplier applied to earnings per share to determine current value. The P/E ratio is influenced by the earnings and sales growth of the firm, the risk or volatility of its performance, the debt-equity structure, and other factors.

Price ratios Ratios that relate the internal performance of the firm to the external judgment of the marketplace in terms of value.

Primary earnings per share A firm's adjusted earnings after taxes divided by the number of shares of common stock outstanding plus common stock equivalents. Common stock equivalents include warrants and other options along with convertible securities that are paying low returns and are therefore likely to be converted to common stock.

Primary market A market in which an investor purchases an asset directly from the issuer of that asset. The purchase of newly issued shares of corporate stock is an example of primary market activity. Subsequent transfers of the particular asset take place in the secondary market. Also see **Secondary market.**

Private pension plans Nongovernment-sponsored pension plans. About 60 percent of nongovernmental employees are covered by a private pension plan.

Private placement The sale of securities by the issuing concern directly to an investor (generally a large institutional investor) rather than through the public markets.

Profitability ratios Ratios that allow the analyst to measure the ability of the firm to earn an adequate return on sales, total assets, and invested capital.

Prospectus A document that must accompany a new issue of securities. It contains the same information appearing in the registration statement, such as a list of directors and officers, financial reports certified by a CPA, the underwriters, the purpose and use for the funds, and other reasonable information that investors need to know.

Pure bond value The fundamental value of a bond that represents a floor price below which the bond's value should not fall. The pure bond value is computed as the present values of all future interest payments added to the present value of the bond principal.

Put An option to sell 100 shares of common stock at a specified price for a given period of time.

Qualified pension plan Under the provisions of the internal Revenue Service, a qualified pension plan allows the employer to deduct annual contributions to the pension plan as a tax-deductible item. From the employees' perspective, a qualified plan allows funds in the plan to earn income without immediate taxation, and no tax is paid on the employer's contribution until benefits are received. A qualified pension plan must meet the appropriate requirements established under ERISA.

Quick ratio Current assets minus inventory (i.e. cash, marketable securities, and accounts receivables) divided by current liabilities.

R^2 A statistical measure that indicates the degree of association between the independent and dependent variable(s).

Real asset A tangible piece of property that may be seen, felt, held, or collected, such as real estate, gold, diamonds, etc.

Real estate investment trust (REIT) An organization similar to a mutual fund where investors pool funds that

are invested in real estate or used to make construction or mortgage loans.

Real return A return that has been adjusted for inflation. Real returns are equal to nominal returns minus the rate of inflation during the time period under study.

Recaptured depreciation When accelerated depreciation is taken and then the property is sold, part of the profit may be considered recaptured depreciation for tax purposes.

Registered trader A member of a stock exchange who trades for his or her own account rather than for the client of a brokerage firm.

Reported income versus adjusted earnings Reported income is generally based on historical cost accounting whereas adjusted earnings have been modified for the effect of inflation (on inventory and plant and equipment).

Reserve requirements Percentages of bank deposit balances stipulated by the Federal Reserve as unavailable for lending. By increasing or reducing reserve requirements, the Fed can contract or expand the money supply.

Resistance level The technical analyst's view that as long as a given long-term trend continues, prices of a particular stock or of the market as a whole will not rise above the upper end of the normal trading range (the resistance level) because at that point investors sell in an attempt to get even or take a profit.

Return on equity Net income divided by stockholders' equity.

Revenue bond A municipal bond issued to procure funding for a specific project of a governmental unit or agency. Such a bond issue can be repaid only with funds generated by the project financed.

Revocable trust The creator may eventually dissolve the trust and take back the property.

Risk Uncertainty concerning the outcome of an investment or other situation. It is often defined as variability of returns of an investment. The greater the range of possible outcomes, the greater the risk.

Risk-adjusted return The amount of return after adjustment for the level of risk incurred to achieve the return.

Secondary market A market in which an investor purchases an asset from another investor rather than the issuing corporation. The activity of secondary markets sets prices and provides liquidity. Also see **Primary market.**

Secured bond A bond which is collateralized by the pledging of assets.

Securities Act of 1933 Enacted by Congress to curtail abuses by securities issuers, the law requires full disclosure of pertinent investment information and provides for penalties to officers of firms that do not comply.

Securities Acts Amendments of 1975 Enacted to increase competition in the securities markets, this legis-

lation prohibits fixed commissions on public offerings of securities and directs the Securities and Exchange Commission to develop a single, nationwide securities market.

Securities and Exchange Commission (SEC) The federal government agency created in 1934 to enforce securities laws. Issuers of securities must register detailed reports with the SEC, and the SEC policies such activities as insider trading, investor conspiracies, and the functionings of the securities exchanges.

Securities Exchange Act of 1934 Created the Securities and Exchange Commission to regulate the securities markets. The act further empowers the Board of Governors of the Federal Reserve System to control margin requirements.

Securities Investor Protection Corporation Created under the Securities Investor Protection Act of 1970, this agency oversees the liquidation of insolvent brokerage firms and provides insurance on investors' trading accounts in amounts up to $50,000.

Security analyst One who studies various industries and companies and provides research reports and valuation studies.

Security market line The graphic representation of risk and return for an individual security.

Semi-strong form of efficient market hypothesis The hypothesis states that all public information is already impounded into the value of a security.

Selling short against the box A short sale of securities with the objective of deferring the payment of taxes. This requires a short sale against shares already owned so that shares owned are delivered to cover the short position as the transaction is completed.

Serial bond A mechanism for repaying funds advanced through a bond issue. Regular payments systematically retire individual bonds with increasing maturities until, after many years, the entire series has been repaid.

Settle price The term for the closing price of quotes on prices of futures contracts.

Shared appreciation mortgage A type of mortgage in which the lender participates in any increase in value associated with the property being mortgaged.

Short position (short sale) A market transaction in which an investor sells borrowed securities in anticipation of a price decline. The investor's expectation is that the securities can be repurchased (to replace the borrowed shares) at a lower price in the future. See also **Long position.**

Short sales position theory The contrary opinion rule stating that large volumes of short sales (meaning short sellers expect a downturn) can signal an impending market upturn because short sales must be covered and thereby create their own demand.

Sinking fund A mechanism for repaying funds advanced through a bond issue. The issuer makes periodic

payments to the trustee, who retires part of the issue by purchasing the bonds in the open market.

Smart money rules Guidelines, such as *Barron's* Confidence Index, used by technical analysts who predict stock market activity based on the assumption that sophisticated investors will correctly predict market trends and that their lead should be followed. See also **Contrary opinion rules.**

Sources and uses of funds statement A presentation of how changes in the balance sheet were financed over a period of time. Sources of funds include increases in stockholders' equity, decreases in assets, and increases in liabilities. Uses are represented by decreases in stockholders' equity, increases in assets, and decreases in liabilities.

Specialist A member of a stock exchange who performs specialized functions in connection with one or a few stocks. Such activities include executing special orders for brokers' clients and maintaining inventories in order to make markets when trading is inactive.

Speculative premium The difference between a warrant's price and its intrinsic value. That an investor would pay something in excess of the intrinsic value indicates a speculative desire to hold the warrant in anticipation of future increases in the price of the underlying stock.

Spot market The term applied to the cash price for immediate transfer of a commodity as opposed to the futures market where no physical transfer takes place immediately.

Spreads A combination of options which consists of buying one option (going long) and writing an option (going short) on the same stock.

Standard & Poor's 500 Composite Index An index which measures price movements in the stocks of 500 large industrial, utility, and transportation corporations listed on the New York Stock Exchange.

Standard & Poor's 400 Industrial Index An index which measures price movements in the stocks of 400 large industrial corporations listed on the New York Stock Exchange.

Standard deviation A measure of dispersion that measures the spread of outcomes around the expected value.

Stock dividend A dividend paid by issuing more stock which results in retained earnings being capitalized.

Stock repurchase A purchase by a firm of its own shares in the marketplace.

Stock split The result of a firm dividing its shares into more shares with a corresponding decrease in par value.

Stop order A mechanism for locking in gains or limiting losses on securities transactions. The investor is not assured of paying or receiving a particular price but rather agrees to accept the price prevailing when the broker is able to execute after prices have reached some predetermined figure.

Strong form of the efficient market hypothesis A hypothesis that says that all information, insider as well as public, is reflected in the value of a security.

Straddle A combination of a put and call on the same stock with the same strike price and expiration date.

Straight-line depreciation A method of depreciation in which the project cost is divided by the project life to calculate each year's depreciation amount.

Support level The technical analyst's view that as long as a given long-term trend continues, prices of a particular stock or of the market as a whole will not fall below the lower end of normal trading range (the support level) because at that point low prices stimulate demand.

Swaps The procedure of selling out of a given bond position and immediately buying into another one with similar attributes in an attempt to improve overall portfolio return or performance.

Syndicate A group of investment bankers which jointly shares the underwriting and distribution responsibilities in a large offering of new securities. Each participant is responsible for a predetermined sales volume. One or a few firms serve as the managing underwriters.

Synergy A more than proportionate increase in performance from the combination of two or more parts.

Systematic risk Risk inherent in an investment related to movements in the market that cannot be diversified away.

Technical analysis An analysis of price and volume data as well as other related market indicators to determine past trends that are believed to be predictable into the future.

Term structure of interest rates This depicts the relationship between maturity and interest rates for a 20- to 25-year time horizon.

Testamentary trust A trust created by a will.

Third market The trading between dealers and institutional investors, through the over-the-counter market, of NYSE- or AMEX-listed stocks. The third market accounts for an extremely small share of total trading activity.

Trading range The spread of prices that a stock normally sells within.

Treasury bill A short-term U.S. government obligation. A T bill is purchased at a discount and is negotiable.

Treasury bond A long-term (7 to 25 years) U.S. government bond.

Treasury note An intermediate-term (one to seven years) U.S. government bond.

Treasury stock Stock issued but not outstanding by virtue of being held (after it is repurchased) by the firm.

Trend analysis Comparative analysis of performance over time.

Trough The point in an economic cycle at which recession ends and expansion begins.

Trust A legal entity in which transfer of ownership of property from an original owner (the creator of the trust)

to another person (the trustee) takes place for the benefit of someone else (the beneficiary).

Underpricing In selling formerly privately held shares to new investors in the over-the-counter market, the price might not fully reflect the value of the issue. Underpricing is used to attempt to insure the success of the initial distribution.

Underwriting The acceptance of risk in return for payment. In a new securities issue, the investment banker may perform an underwriting function by purchasing the securities at a fixed price from the issuer. Subsequent profits or losses then accrue to the underwriter.

Unfriendly takeover A merger or acquisition in which the firm acquired does not wish to be acquired.

Unfunded pension plan Payments to retirees are made out of current income and not out of prior funding.

Unified tax credit A credit against the estate and gift tax. Under the 1981 Economic Recovery Tax Act, the credit will go from $47,000 in 1981 to $192,800 in 1987. In 1987, this will provide an equivalent exemption of $600,000 for estate taxes.

Unified tax rate schedule The schedule applied to estate and gift taxes on a unified basis.

Unseasoned issue An issue that has not been formerly traded in the public markets.

Unsystematic risk Risk of an investment that is random in nature. It is not related to general market movements. It may represent the temporary influence of a competitor's new product, changes in raw material prices, or unusual economic or government influences on a firm. It may generally be diversified away.

Valuation The process of attributing a value to a security based on expectations of the future performance of the issuing concern, the relevant industry, and the economy as a whole.

Valuation model A representation of the components that provide the value of an investment, such as a dividend valuation model used to show the value of a common stock.

Variable rate mortgage A mortgage in which the interest rate is adjusted regularly.

Variability The possible different outcomes of an event. As an example, an investment with many possible different levels of return would have great variability.

Vertical spread Buying and writing two contracts at different striking prices with the same month of expiration.

Vesting A legal term meaning that pension benefits or rights cannot be taken away.

Warrant A right or option to buy a stated number of shares of stock at a specified price over a given time period. It is usually of longer duration than a call option.

Weak form of efficient market hypothesis A hypothesis suggesting there is no relationship between past and future prices of securities.

White knight A firm that "rescues" another firm from an unfriendly takeover by a third firm.

Wiesenberger Financial Services An advisory service that provides important information on mutual funds.

Wraparound mortgage A means of financing in which the participating parties wrap a new mortgage around the old, existing mortgage. The seller-lender thus receives payments on the new, larger mortgage and pays off the older, smaller mortgage.

Yield curve A curve that shows interest rates at a specific point in time for all securities having equal risk but differing maturity dates. Usually, government securities are used to construct such curves. The yield curve is also referred to as the term structure of interest rates.

Yield spread The difference between the yields received on two different types of bonds with different ratings. It is important to investment strategy because during periods of economic uncertainty, spreads increase because investors demand larger premiums on risky issues to compensate for the greater chance of default.

Yield to call The interest yield that will be realized on a callable bond if it is held from a given purchase date until the date when it can be called by the issuer. The yield to call reflects the fact that lower overall returns may be realized if the issuer avoids some later payments by retiring the bonds early.

Yield to maturity The annualized rate of return that an investor will receive if a bond is held until its maturity date. It is the market rate of return. The yield to maturity formula includes any capital gains or losses that arise because the par value is greater or less than the market price.

Ying, Lewellen, Schlarbaum, and Lease study A research study that indicates there may be an opportunity for abnormal returns on a risk-adjusted basis in the many weeks between announcement of listing and actual listing of a security.

Appendixes

Appendix A
Compound sum of $1

Percent

Period	1%	2%	3%	4%	5%	6%	7%	8%	9%	10%	11%
1	1.010	1.020	1.030	1.040	1.050	1.060	1.070	1.080	1.090	1.100	1.110
2	1.020	1.040	1.061	1.082	1.103	1.124	1.145	1.166	1.188	1.210	1.232
3	1.030	1.061	1.093	1.125	1.158	1.191	1.225	1.260	1.295	1.331	1.368
4	1.041	1.082	1.126	1.170	1.216	1.262	1.311	1.360	1.412	1.464	1.518
5	1.051	1.104	1.159	1.217	1.276	1.338	1.403	1.469	1.539	1.611	1.685
6	1.062	1.126	1.194	1.265	1.340	1.419	1.501	1.587	1.677	1.772	1.870
7	1.072	1.149	1.230	1.316	1.407	1.504	1.606	1.714	1.828	1.949	2.076
8	1.083	1.172	1.267	1.369	1.477	1.594	1.718	1.851	1.993	2.144	2.305
9	1.094	1.195	1.305	1.423	1.551	1.689	1.838	1.999	2.172	2.358	2.558
10	1.105	1.219	1.344	1.480	1.629	1.791	1.967	2.159	2.367	2.594	2.839
11	1.116	1.243	1.384	1.539	1.710	1.898	2.105	2.332	2.580	2.853	3.152
12	1.127	1.268	1.426	1.601	1.796	2.012	2.252	2.518	2.813	3.138	3.498
13	1.138	1.294	1.469	1.665	1.886	2.133	2.410	2.720	3.066	3.452	3.883
14	1.149	1.319	1.513	1.732	1.980	2.261	2.579	2.937	3.342	3.797	4.310
15	1.161	1.346	1.558	1.801	2.079	2.397	2.759	3.172	3.642	4.177	4.785
16	1.173	1.373	1.605	1.873	2.183	2.540	2.952	3.426	3.970	4.595	5.311
17	1.184	1.400	1.653	1.948	2.292	2.693	3.159	3.700	4.328	5.054	5.895
18	1.196	1.428	1.702	2.206	2.407	2.854	3.380	3.996	4.717	5.560	6.544
19	1.208	1.457	1.754	2.107	2.527	3.026	3.617	4.316	5.142	6.116	7.263
20	1.220	1.486	1.806	2.191	2.653	3.207	3.870	4.661	5.604	6.727	8.062
25	1.282	1.641	2.094	2.666	3.386	4.292	5.427	6.848	8.623	10.835	13.585
30	1.348	1.811	2.427	3.243	4.322	5.743	7.612	10.063	13.268	17.449	22.892
40	1.489	2.208	3.262	4.801	7.040	10.286	14.974	21.725	31.409	45.259	65.001
50	1.645	2.692	4.384	7.107	11.467	18.420	29.457	46.902	74.358	117.39	184.57

Appendix A *(continued)*
Compound sum of $1

Percent

Period	12%	13%	14%	15%	16%	17%	18%	19%	20%	25%	30%
1	1.120	1.130	1.140	1.150	1.160	1.170	1.180	1.190	1.200	1.250	1.300
2	1.254	1.277	1.300	1.323	1.346	1.369	1.392	1.416	1.440	1.563	1.690
3	1.405	1.443	1.482	1.521	1.561	1.602	1.643	1.685	1.728	1.953	2.197
4	1.574	1.630	1.689	1.749	1.811	1.874	1.939	2.005	2.074	2.441	2.856
5	1.762	1.842	1.925	2.011	2.100	2.192	2.288	2.386	2.488	3.052	3.713
6	1.974	2.082	2.195	2.313	2.436	2.565	2.700	2.840	2.986	3.815	4.827
7	2.211	2.353	2.502	2.660	2.826	3.001	3.185	3.379	3.583	4.768	6.276
8	2.476	2.658	2.853	3.059	3.278	3.511	3.759	4.021	4.300	5.960	8.157
9	2.773	3.004	3.252	3.518	3.803	4.108	4.435	4.785	5.160	7.451	10.604
10	3.106	3.395	3.707	4.046	4.411	4.807	5.234	5.696	6.192	9.313	13.786
11	3.479	3.836	4.226	4.652	5.117	5.624	6.176	6.777	7.430	11.642	17.922
12	3.896	4.335	4.818	5.350	5.936	6.580	7.288	8.064	8.916	14.552	23.298
13	4.363	4.898	5.492	6.153	6.886	7.699	8.599	9.596	10.699	18.190	30.288
14	4.887	5.535	6.261	7.076	7.988	9.007	10.147	11.420	12.839	22.737	39.374
15	5.474	6.254	7.138	8.137	9.266	10.539	11.974	13.590	15.407	28.422	51.186
16	6.130	7.067	8.137	9.358	10.748	12.330	14.129	16.172	18.488	35.527	66.542
17	6.866	7.986	9.276	10.761	12.468	14.426	16.672	19.244	22.186	44.409	86.504
18	7.690	9.024	10.575	12.375	14.463	16.879	19.673	22.091	26.623	55.511	112.46
19	8.613	10.197	12.056	14.232	16.777	19.748	23.214	27.252	31.948	69.389	146.19
20	9.646	11.523	13.743	16.367	19.461	23.106	27.393	32.429	38.338	86.736	190.05
25	17.000	21.231	26.462	32.919	40.874	50.658	62.669	77.388	95.396	264.70	705.64
30	29.960	39.116	50.950	66.212	85.850	111.07	143.37	184.68	237.38	807.79	2,620.0
40	93.051	132.78	188.88	267.86	378.72	533.87	750.38	1,051.7	1,469.8	7,523.2	36,119.
50	289.00	450.74	700.23	1,083.7	1,670.7	2,566.2	3,927.4	5,988.9	9,100.4	70,065.	497,929.

Source: Maurice Joy, *Introduction to Financial Management* (Homewood, Ill.: Richard D. Irwin, Inc. 1977).

Appendix B
Present value of $1

Percent

Period	1%	2%	3%	4%	5%	6%	7%	8%	9%	10%	11%	12%
1	0.990	0.980	0.971	0.962	0.952	0.943	0.935	0.926	0.917	0.909	0.901	0.893
2	0.980	0.961	0.943	0.925	0.907	0.890	0.873	0.857	0.842	0.826	0.812	0.797
3	0.971	0.942	0.915	0.889	0.864	0.840	0.816	0.794	0.772	0.751	0.731	0.712
4	0.961	0.924	0.885	0.855	0.823	0.792	0.763	0.735	0.708	0.683	0.659	0.636
5	0.951	0.906	0.863	0.822	0.784	0.747	0.713	0.681	0.650	0.621	0.593	0.567
6	0.942	0.888	0.837	0.790	0.746	0.705	0.666	0.630	0.596	0.564	0.535	0.507
7	0.933	0.871	0.813	0.760	0.711	0.665	0.623	0.583	0.547	0.513	0.482	0.452
8	0.923	0.853	0.789	0.731	0.677	0.627	0.582	0.540	0.502	0.467	0.434	0.404
9	0.914	0.837	0.766	0.703	0.645	0.592	0.544	0.500	0.460	0.424	0.391	0.361
10	0.905	0.820	0.744	0.676	0.614	0.558	0.508	0.463	0.422	0.386	0.352	0.322
11	0.896	0.804	0.722	0.650	0.585	0.527	0.475	0.429	0.388	0.350	0.317	0.287
12	0.887	0.788	0.701	0.625	0.557	0.497	0.444	0.397	0.356	0.319	0.286	0.257
13	0.879	0.773	0.681	0.601	0.530	0.469	0.415	0.368	0.326	0.290	0.258	0.229
14	0.870	0.758	0.661	0.577	0.505	0.442	0.388	0.340	0.299	0.263	0.232	0.205
15	0.861	0.743	0.642	0.555	0.481	0.417	0.362	0.315	0.275	0.239	0.209	0.183
16	0.853	0.728	0.623	0.534	0.458	0.394	0.339	0.292	0.252	0.218	0.188	0.163
17	0.844	0.714	0.605	0.513	0.436	0.371	0.317	0.270	0.231	0.198	0.170	0.146
18	0.836	0.700	0.587	0.494	0.416	0.350	0.296	0.250	0.212	0.180	0.153	0.130
19	0.828	0.686	0.570	0.475	0.396	0.331	0.277	0.232	0.194	0.164	0.138	0.116
20	0.820	0.673	0.554	0.456	0.377	0.312	0.258	0.215	0.178	0.149	0.124	0.104
25	0.780	0.610	0.478	0.375	0.295	0.233	0.184	0.146	0.116	0.092	0.074	0.059
30	0.742	0.552	0.412	0.308	0.231	0.174	0.131	0.099	0.075	0.057	0.044	0.033
40	0.672	0.453	0.307	0.208	0.142	0.097	0.067	0.046	0.032	0.022	0.015	0.011
50	0.608	0.372	0.228	0.141	0.087	0.054	0.034	0.021	0.013	0.009	0.005	0.003

Appendix B (continued)
Present value of $1

Percent

Period	13%	14%	15%	16%	17%	18%	19%	20%	25%	30%	35%	40%	50%
1	0.885	0.877	0.870	0.862	0.855	0.847	0.840	0.833	0.800	0.769	0.741	0.714	0.667
2	0.783	0.769	0.756	0.743	0.731	0.718	0.706	0.694	0.640	0.592	0.549	0.510	0.444
3	0.693	0.675	0.658	0.641	0.624	0.609	0.593	0.579	0.512	0.455	0.406	0.364	0.296
4	0.613	0.592	0.572	0.552	0.534	0.515	0.499	0.482	0.410	0.350	0.301	0.260	0.198
5	0.543	0.519	0.497	0.476	0.456	0.437	0.419	0.402	0.320	0.269	0.223	0.186	0.132
6	0.480	0.456	0.432	0.410	0.390	0.370	0.352	0.335	0.262	0.207	0.165	0.133	0.088
7	0.425	0.400	0.376	0.354	0.333	0.314	0.296	0.279	0.210	0.159	0.122	0.095	0.059
8	0.376	0.351	0.327	0.305	0.285	0.266	0.249	0.233	0.168	0.123	0.091	0.068	0.039
9	0.333	0.300	0.284	0.263	0.243	0.225	0.209	0.194	0.134	0.094	0.067	0.048	0.026
10	0.295	0.270	0.247	0.227	0.208	0.191	0.176	0.162	0.107	0.073	0.050	0.035	0.017
11	0.261	0.237	0.215	0.195	0.178	0.162	0.148	0.135	0.086	0.056	0.037	0.025	0.012
12	0.231	0.208	0.187	0.168	0.152	0.137	0.124	0.112	0.069	0.043	0.027	0.018	0.008
13	0.204	0.182	0.163	0.145	0.130	0.116	0.104	0.093	0.055	0.033	0.020	0.013	0.005
14	0.181	0.160	0.141	0.125	0.111	0.099	0.088	0.078	0.044	0.025	0.015	0.009	0.003
15	0.160	0.140	0.123	0.108	0.095	0.084	0.074	0.065	0.035	0.020	0.011	0.006	0.002
16	0.141	0.123	0.107	0.093	0.081	0.071	0.062	0.054	0.028	0.015	0.008	0.005	0.002
17	0.125	0.108	0.093	0.080	0.069	0.060	0.052	0.045	0.023	0.012	0.006	0.003	0.001
18	0.111	0.095	0.081	0.069	0.059	0.051	0.044	0.038	0.018	0.009	0.005	0.002	0.001
19	0.098	0.083	0.070	0.060	0.051	0.043	0.037	0.031	0.014	0.007	0.003	0.002	0
20	0.087	0.073	0.061	0.051	0.043	0.037	0.031	0.026	0.012	0.005	0.002	0.001	0
25	0.047	0.038	0.030	0.024	0.020	0.016	0.013	0.010	0.004	0.001	0.001	0	0
30	0.026	0.020	0.015	0.012	0.009	0.007	0.005	0.004	0.001	0	0	0	0
40	0.008	0.005	0.004	0.003	0.002	0.001	0.001	0.001	0	0	0	0	0
50	0.002	0.001	0.001	0.001	0	0	0	0	0	0	0	0	0

Source: Maurice Joy, *Introduction to Financial Management* (Homewood, Ill.: Richard D. Irwin, Inc. 1977).

Appendix C
Compound sum of an annuity of $1

Percent

Period	1%	2%	3%	4%	5%	6%	7%	8%	9%	10%	11%
1	1.000	1.000	1.000	1.000	1.000	1.000	1.000	1.000	1.000	1.000	1.000
2	2.010	2.020	2.030	2.040	2.050	2.060	2.070	2.080	2.090	2.100	2.110
3	3.030	3.060	3.091	3.122	3.153	3.184	3.215	3.246	3.278	3.310	3.342
4	4.060	4.122	4.184	4.246	4.310	4.375	4.440	4.506	4.573	4.641	4.710
5	5.101	5.204	5.309	5.416	5.526	5.637	5.751	5.867	5.985	6.105	6.228
6	6.152	6.308	6.468	6.633	6.802	6.975	7.153	7.336	7.523	7.716	7.913
7	7.214	7.434	7.662	7.898	8.142	8.394	8.654	8.923	9.200	9.487	9.783
8	8.286	8.583	8.892	9.214	9.549	9.897	10.260	10.637	11.028	11.436	11.859
9	9.369	9.755	10.159	10.583	11.027	11.491	11.978	12.488	13.021	13.579	14.164
10	10.462	10.950	11.464	12.006	12.578	13.181	13.816	14.487	15.193	15.937	16.722
11	11.567	12.169	12.808	13.486	14.207	14.972	15.784	16.645	17.560	18.531	19.561
12	12.683	13.412	14.192	15.026	15.917	16.870	17.888	18.977	20.141	21.384	22.713
13	13.809	14.680	15.618	16.627	17.713	18.882	20.141	21.495	22.953	24.523	26.212
14	14.947	15.974	17.086	18.292	19.599	21.015	22.550	24.215	26.019	27.975	30.095
15	16.097	17.293	18.599	20.024	21.579	23.276	25.129	27.152	29.361	31.772	34.405
16	17.258	18.639	20.157	21.825	23.657	25.673	27.888	30.324	33.003	35.950	39.190
17	18.430	20.012	21.762	23.698	25.840	20.213	30.840	33.750	36.974	40.545	44.501
18	19.615	21.412	23.414	25.645	28.132	30.906	33.999	37.450	41.301	45.599	50.396
19	20.811	22.841	25.117	27.671	30.539	33.760	37.379	41.446	46.018	51.159	56.939
20	22.019	24.297	26.870	29.778	33.066	36.786	40.995	45.762	51.160	57.275	64.203
25	28.243	32.030	36.459	41.646	47.727	54.865	63.249	73.106	84.701	98.347	114.41
30	34.785	40.588	47.575	56.085	66.439	79.058	94.461	113.28	136.31	164.49	199.02
40	48.886	60.402	75.401	95.026	120.80	154.76	199.64	259.06	337.89	442.59	581.83
50	64.463	84.579	112.80	152.67	209.35	290.34	406.53	573.77	815.08	1,163.9	1,668.8

Appendix C *(continued)*
Compound sum of an annuity of $1

Percent

Period	12%	13%	14%	15%	16%	17%	18%	19%	20%	25%	30%
1	1.000	1.000	1.000	1.000	1.000	1.000	1.000	1.000	1.000	1.000	1.000
2	2.120	2.130	2.140	2.150	2.160	2.170	2.180	2.190	2.200	2.250	2.300
3	3.374	3.407	3.440	3.473	3.506	3.539	3.572	3.606	3.640	3.813	3.990
4	4.779	4.850	4.921	4.993	5.066	5.141	5.215	5.291	5.368	5.766	6.187
5	6.353	6.480	6.610	6.742	6.877	7.014	7.154	7.297	7.442	8.207	9.043
6	8.115	8.323	8.536	9.754	8.977	9.207	9.442	0.683	9.930	11.259	12.756
7	10.089	10.405	10.730	11.067	11.414	11.772	12.142	12.523	12.916	15.073	17.583
8	12.300	12.757	13.233	13.727	14.240	14.773	15.327	15.902	16.499	19.842	23.858
9	14.776	15.416	16.085	16.786	17.519	18.285	19.086	19.923	20.799	25.802	32.015
10	17.549	18.420	19.337	20.304	21.321	22.393	23.521	24.701	25.959	33.253	42.619
11	20.655	21.814	23.045	24.349	25.733	27.200	28.755	30.404	32.150	42.566	56.405
12	24.133	25.650	27.271	29.002	30.850	32.824	34.931	37.180	39.581	54.208	74.327
13	28.029	29.985	32.089	34.352	36.786	39.404	42.219	45.244	48.497	68.760	97.625
14	32.393	34.883	37.581	40.505	43.672	47.103	50.818	54.841	59.196	86.949	127.91
15	37.280	40.417	43.842	47.580	51.660	56.110	60.965	66.261	72.035	109.69	167.29
16	42.753	46.672	50.980	55.717	60.925	66.649	72.939	79.850	87.442	138.11	218.47
17	48.884	53.739	59.118	65.075	71.673	78.979	87.068	96.022	105.93	173.64	285.01
18	55.750	61.725	68.394	75.836	84.141	93.406	103.74	115.27	128.12	218.05	371.52
19	63.440	70.749	78.969	88.212	98.603	110.29	123.41	138.17	154.74	273.56	483.97
20	72.052	80.947	91.025	102.44	115.38	130.03	146.63	165.42	186.69	342.95	630.17
25	133.33	155.62	181.87	212.79	249.21	292.11	342.60	402.04	471.98	1,054.8	2,348.80
30	241.33	293.20	356.79	434.75	530.31	647.44	790.95	966.7	1,181.9	3,227.2	8,730.0
40	767.09	1,013.7	1,342.0	1,779.1	2,360.8	3,134.5	4,163.21	5,529.8	7,343.9	30,089.	120,393.
50	2,400.0	3,459.5	4,994.5	7,217.7	10,436.	15,090.	21,813.	31,515.	45,497.	280,256.	165,976.

Source: Maurice Joy, *Introduction to Financial Management* (Homewood, Ill.: Richard D. Irwin, Inc. 1977).

Appendix D
Present value of an annuity of $1

Percent

Period	1%	2%	3%	4%	5%	6%	7%	8%	9%	10%	11%	12%
1	0.990	0.980	0.971	0.962	0.952	0.943	0.935	0.926	0.917	0.909	0.901	0.893
2	1.970	1.942	1.913	1.886	1.859	1.833	1.808	1.783	1.759	1.736	1.713	1.690
3	2.941	2.884	2.829	2.775	2.723	2.673	2.624	2.577	2.531	2.487	2.444	2.402
4	3.902	3.808	3.717	3.630	3.546	3.465	3.387	3.312	3.240	3.170	3.102	3.037
5	4.853	4.713	4.580	4.452	4.329	4.212	4.100	3.993	3.890	3.791	3.696	3.605
6	5.795	5.601	5.417	5.242	5.076	4.917	4.767	4.623	4.486	4.355	4.231	4.111
7	6.728	6.472	6.230	6.002	5.786	5.582	5.389	5.206	5.033	4.868	4.712	4.564
8	7.652	7.325	7.020	6.733	6.463	6.210	5.971	5.747	5.535	5.335	5.146	4.968
9	8.566	8.162	7.786	7.435	7.108	6.802	6.515	6.247	5.995	5.759	5.537	5.328
10	9.471	8.983	8.530	8.111	7.722	7.360	7.024	6.710	6.418	6.145	5.889	5.650
11	10.368	9.787	9.253	8.760	8.306	7.887	7.499	7.139	6.805	6.495	6.207	5.938
12	11.255	10.575	9.954	9.385	8.863	8.384	7.943	7.536	7.161	6.814	6.492	6.194
13	12.134	11.348	10.635	9.986	9.394	8.853	8.358	7.904	7.487	7.103	6.750	6.424
14	13.004	12.106	11.296	10.563	9.899	9.295	8.745	8.244	7.786	7.367	6.982	6.628
15	13.865	12.849	11.939	11.118	10.380	9.712	9.108	8.559	8.061	7.606	7.191	6.811
16	14.718	13.578	12.561	11.652	10.838	10.106	9.447	8.851	8.313	7.824	7.379	6.974
17	15.562	14.292	13.166	12.166	11.274	10.477	9.763	9.122	8.544	8.022	7.549	7.102
18	16.398	14.992	13.754	12.659	11.690	10.828	10.059	9.372	8.756	8.201	7.702	7.250
19	17.226	15.678	14.324	13.134	12.085	11.158	10.336	9.604	8.950	8.365	7.839	7.366
20	18.046	16.351	14.877	13.590	12.462	11.470	10.594	9.818	9.129	8.514	7.963	7.469
25	22.023	19.523	17.413	15.622	14.094	12.783	11.654	10.675	9.823	9.077	8.422	7.843
30	25.808	22.396	19.600	17.292	15.372	13.765	12.409	11.258	10.274	9.427	8.694	8.055
40	32.835	27.355	23.115	19.793	17.159	15.046	13.332	11.925	10.757	9.779	8.951	8.244
50	39.196	31.424	25.730	21.482	18.256	15.762	13.801	12.233	10.962	9.915	9.042	8.304

Appendix D *(continued)*
Present value of an annuity of $1

Percent

Period	13%	14%	15%	16%	17%	18%	19%	20%	25%	30%	35%	40%	50%
1	0.885	0.877	0.870	0.862	0.855	0.847	0.840	0.833	0.800	0.769	0.741	0.714	0.667
2	1.668	1.647	1.626	1.605	1.585	1.566	1.547	1.528	1.440	1.361	1.289	1.224	1.111
3	2.361	2.322	2.283	2.246	2.210	2.174	2.140	2.106	1.952	1.816	1.696	1.589	1.407
4	2.974	2.914	2.855	2.798	2.743	2.690	2.639	2.589	2.362	2.166	1.997	1.849	1.605
5	3.517	3.433	3.352	3.274	3.199	3.127	3.058	2.991	2.689	2.436	2.220	2.035	1.737
6	3.998	3.889	3.784	3.685	3.589	3.498	3.410	3.326	2.951	2.643	2.385	2.168	1.824
7	4.423	4.288	4.160	4.039	3.922	3.812	3.706	3.605	3.161	2.802	2.508	2.263	1.883
8	4.799	4.639	4.487	4.344	4.207	4.078	3.954	3.837	3.329	2.925	2.598	2.331	1.922
9	5.132	4.946	4.772	4.607	4.451	4.303	4.163	4.031	3.463	3.019	2.665	2.379	1.948
10	5.426	5.216	5.019	4.833	4.659	4.494	4.339	4.192	3.571	3.092	2.715	2.414	1.965
11	5.687	5.453	5.234	5.029	4.836	4.656	4.486	4.327	3.656	3.147	2.752	2.438	1.977
12	5.918	5.660	5.421	5.197	4.988	4.793	4.611	4.439	3.725	3.190	2.779	2.456	1.985
13	6.122	5.842	5.583	5.342	5.118	4.910	4.715	4.533	3.780	3.223	2.799	2.469	1.990
14	6.302	6.002	5.724	5.468	5.229	5.008	4.802	4.611	3.824	3.249	2.814	2.478	1.993
15	6.462	6.142	5.847	5.575	5.324	5.092	4.876	4.675	3.859	3.268	2.825	2.484	1.995
16	6.604	6.265	5.954	5.668	5.405	5.162	4.938	4.730	3.887	3.283	2.834	2.489	1.997
17	6.729	6.373	6.047	5.749	5.475	5.222	4.988	4.775	3.910	3.295	2.840	2.492	1.998
18	6.840	6.467	6.128	5.818	5.534	5.273	5.033	4.812	3.928	3.304	2.844	2.494	1.999
19	6.938	6.550	6.198	5.877	5.584	5.316	5.070	4.843	3.942	3.311	2.848	2.496	1.999
20	7.025	6.623	6.259	5.929	5.628	5.353	5.101	4.870	3.954	3.316	2.850	2.497	1.999
25	7.330	6.873	6.464	6.097	5.766	5.467	5.195	4.948	3.985	3.329	2.856	2.499	2.000
30	7.496	7.003	6.566	6.177	5.829	5.517	5.235	4.979	3.995	3.332	2.857	2.500	2.000
40	7.634	7.105	6.642	6.233	5.871	5.548	5.258	4.997	3.999	3.333	2.857	2.500	2.000
50	7.675	7.133	6.661	6.246	5.880	5.554	5.262	4.999	4.000	3.333	2.857	2.500	2.000

Source: Maurice Joy, *Introduction to Financial Management* (Homewood, Ill.: Richard D. Irwin, Inc. 1977).

Appendix E
Tables of squares and square roots

N	N^2	$\sqrt{N}$	$\sqrt{10N}$	N	N^2	$\sqrt{N}$	$\sqrt{10N}$
				50	2 500	7.071 068	22.36068
1	1	1.000 000	3.162 278	51	2 601	7.141 428	22.58318
2	4	1.414 214	4.472 136	52	2 704	7.211 103	22.80351
3	9	1.732 051	5.477 226	53	2 809	7.280 110	23.02173
4	16	2.000 000	6.324 555	54	2 916	7.348 469	23.23790
5	25	2.236 068	7.071 068	55	3 025	7.416 198	23.45208
6	36	2.449 490	7.745 967	56	3 136	7.483 315	23.66432
7	49	2.645 751	8.366 600	57	3 249	7.549 834	23.87467
8	64	2.828 427	8.944 272	58	3 364	7.615 773	24.08319
9	81	3.000 000	9.486 833	59	3 481	7.681 146	24.28992
10	100	3.162 278	10.00000	60	3 600	7.745 967	24.49490
11	121	3.316 625	10.48809	61	3 721	7.810 250	24.69818
12	144	3.464 102	10.95445	62	3 844	7.874 008	24.89980
13	169	3.605 551	11.40175	63	3 969	7.937 254	25.09980
14	196	3.741 657	11.83216	64	4 096	8.000 000	25.29822
15	225	3.872 983	12.24745	65	4 225	8.062 258	25.49510
16	256	4.000 000	12.64911	66	4 356	8.124 038	25.69047
17	289	4.123 106	13.03840	67	4 489	8.185 353	25.88436
18	324	4.242 641	13.41641	68	4 624	8.246 211	26.07681
19	361	4.358 899	13.78405	69	4 761	8.306 824	26.26785
20	400	4.472 136	14.14214	70	4 900	8.366 600	26.45751
21	441	4.582 576	14.49138	71	5 041	8.426 150	26.64583
22	484	4.690 416	14.83240	72	5 184	8.485 281	26.83282
23	529	4.795 832	15.16575	73	5 329	8.544 004	27.01851
24	576	4.898 979	15.49193	74	5 476	8.602 325	27.20294
25	625	5.000 000	15.81139	75	5 625	8.660 254	27.38613
26	676	5.099 020	16.12452	76	5 776	8.717 798	27.56810
27	729	5.196 152	16.43168	77	5 929	8.774 964	27.74887
28	784	5.291 503	16.73320	78	6 084	8.831 761	27.92848
29	841	5.385 165	17.02939	79	6 241	8.888 194	28.10694
30	900	5.477 226	17.32051	80	6 400	8.944 272	28.28427
31	961	5.567 764	17.60682	81	6 561	9.000 000	28.46050
32	1 024	5.656 854	17.88854	82	6 724	9.055 385	28.63564
33	1 089	5.744 563	18.16590	83	6 889	9.110 434	28.80972
34	1 156	5.830 952	18.43909	84	7 056	9.165 151	28.98275
35	1 225	5.916 080	18.70829	85	7 225	9.219 544	29.15476
36	1 296	6.000 000	18.97367	86	7 396	9.273 618	29.32576
37	1 369	6.082 763	19.23538	87	7 569	9.327 379	29.49576
38	1 444	6.164 414	19.49359	88	7 744	9.380 832	29.66479
39	1 521	6.244 998	19.74842	89	7 921	9.433 981	29.83287
40	1 600	6.324 555	20.00000	90	8 100	9.486 833	30.00000
41	1 681	6.403 124	20.24846	91	8 281	9.539 392	30.16621
42	1 764	6.480 741	20.49390	92	8 464	9.591 663	30.33150
43	1 849	6.557 439	20.73644	93	8 649	9.643 651	30.49590
44	1 936	6.633 250	20.97618	94	8 836	9.695 360	30.65942
45	2 025	6.708 204	21.21320	95	9 025	9.746 794	30.82207
46	2 116	6.782 330	21.44761	96	9 216	9.797 959	30.98387
47	2 209	6.855 655	21.67948	97	9 409	9.848 858	31.14482
48	2 304	6.928 203	21.90890	98	9 604	9.899 495	31.30495
49	2 401	7.000 000	22.13594	99	9 801	9.949 874	31.46427
50	2 500	7.071 068	22.36068	100	10 000	10.00000	31.62278

Source: Donald H. Sanders, A. Franklin Murphy, Robert J. Eng, *Statistics, A Fresh Approach* (New York: McGraw-Hill, Inc. 1976). Reprinted by permission..

N	N^2	$\sqrt{N}$	$\sqrt{10N}$	N	N^2	$\sqrt{N}$	$\sqrt{10N}$
100	10 000	10.00000	31.62278	150	22 500	12.24745	38.72983
101	10 201	10.04988	31.78050	151	22 801	12.28821	38.85872
102	10 404	10.09950	31.93744	152	23 104	12.32883	39.98718
103	10 609	10.14889	32.09361	153	23 409	12.36932	39.11521
104	10 816	10.19804	32.24903	154	23 716	12.40967	39.24283
105	11 025	10.24695	32.40370	155	24 025	12.44990	39.37004
106	11 236	10.29563	32.55764	156	24 336	12.45000	39.49684
107	11 449	10.34408	32.71085	157	24 649	12.52996	39.62323
108	11 664	10.39230	32.86335	158	24 964	12.56981	39.74921
109	11 881	10.44031	33.01515	159	25 281	12.60952	39.87480
110	12 100	10.48809	33.16625	160	25 600	12.64911	40.00000
111	12 321	10.53565	33.31666	161	25 921	12.68858	40.12481
112	12 544	10.58301	33.46640	162	26 244	12.72792	40.24922
113	12 769	10.63015	33.61547	163	26 569	12.76715	40.37326
114	12 996	10.67708	33.76389	164	26 896	12.80625	40.49691
115	13 225	10.72381	33.91165	165	27 225	12.84523	40.62019
116	13 456	10.77033	34.05877	166	27 556	12.88410	40.74310
117	13 689	10.81665	34.20526	167	27 889	12.92285	40.86563
118	13 924	10.86278	34.35113	168	28 224	12.96148	40.98780
119	14 161	10.90871	34.49638	169	28 561	13.00000	41.10961
120	14 400	10.95445	34.64102	170	28 900	13.03840	41.23106
121	14 641	11.00000	34.78505	171	29 241	13.07670	41.35215
122	14 884	11.04536	34.92850	172	29 584	13.11488	41.47288
123	15 129	11.09054	35.07136	173	29 929	13.15295	41.59327
124	15 376	11.13553	35.21363	174	30 276	13.19091	41.71331
125	15 625	11.18034	35.35534	175	30 625	13.22876	41.83300
126	15 876	11.22497	35.49648	176	30 976	13.26650	41.95235
127	16 129	11.26943	35.63706	177	31 329	13.30413	42.07137
128	16 384	11.31371	35.77709	178	31 684	13.34166	42.19005
129	16 641	11.35782	35.91657	179	32 041	13.37909	42.30839
130	16 900	11.40175	36.05551	180	32 400	13.41641	42.42641
131	17 161	11.44552	36.19392	181	32 761	13.45362	42.54409
132	17 424	11.48913	36.33180	182	33 124	13.49074	42.66146
133	17 689	11.53256	36.46917	183	33 489	13.52775	42.77850
134	17 956	11.57584	36.60601	184	33 856	13.56466	42.89522
135	18 225	11.61895	36.74235	185	34 225	13.60147	43.01163
136	18 496	11.66190	36.87818	186	34 596	13.63818	43.12772
137	18 769	11.70470	37.01351	187	34 969	13.67479	43.24350
138	19 044	11.74734	37.14835	188	35 344	13.71131	43.35897
139	19 321	11.78983	37.28270	189	35 721	13.74773	43.47413
140	19 600	11.83216	37.41657	190	36 100	13.78405	43.58899
141	19 881	11.87434	37.54997	191	36 481	13.82027	43.70355
142	20 164	11.91638	37.68289	192	36 864	13.85641	43.81780
143	20 449	11.95826	37.81534	193	37 249	13.89244	43.93177
144	20 736	12.00000	37.94733	194	37 636	13.92839	44.04543
145	21 025	12.04159	38.07887	195	38 025	13.96424	44.15880
146	21 316	12.08305	38.20995	196	38 416	14.00000	44.27189
147	21 609	12.12436	38.34058	197	38 809	14.03567	44.38468
148	21 904	12.16553	38.47077	198	39 204	14.07125	44.49719
149	22 201	12.20656	38.60052	199	39 601	14.10674	44.60942
150	22 500	12.24745	38.72983	200	40 000	14.14214	44.72136

N	N²	√N	√10N	N	N²	√N	√10N
200	40 000	14.14214	44.72136	250	62 500	15.81139	50.00000
201	40 401	14.17745	44.83302	251	63 001	15.84298	50.09990
202	40 804	14.21267	44.94441	252	63 504	15.87451	50.19960
203	41 209	14.24781	45.05552	253	64 009	15.90597	50.29911
204	41 616	14.28296	45.16636	254	64 516	15.93738	50.39841
205	42 025	14.31782	45.27693	255	65 025	15.96872	50.49752
206	42 436	14.35270	45.38722	256	65 536	16.00000	50.59644
207	42 849	14.38749	45.49725	257	66 049	16.03122	50.69517
208	43 264	14.42221	45.60702	258	66 564	16.06238	50.79370
209	43 681	14.45683	45.71652	259	67 081	16.09348	50.89204
210	44 100	14.49138	45.82576	260	67 600	16.12452	50.99020
211	44 521	14.52584	45.93474	261	68 121	16.15549	51.08816
212	44 944	14.56022	46.04346	262	68 644	16.18641	51.18594
213	45 369	14.59452	46.15192	263	69 169	16.21727	51.28353
214	45 796	14.62874	46.26013	264	69 696	16.24808	51.38093
215	46 225	14.66288	46.36809	265	70 225	16.27882	51.47815
216	46 656	14.69694	46.47580	266	70 756	16.30951	51.57519
217	47 089	14.73092	46.58326	267	71 289	16.34013	51.67204
218	47 524	14.76482	46.69047	268	71 824	16.37071	51.76872
219	47 961	14.79865	46.79744	269	72 361	16.40122	51.86521
220	48 400	14.83240	46.90415	270	72 900	16.43168	51.96152
221	48 841	14.86607	47.01064	271	73 441	16.46208	52.05766
222	49 284	14.89966	47.11688	272	73 984	16.49242	52.15362
223	49 729	14.93318	47.22288	273	74 529	16.52271	52.24940
224	50 176	14.96663	47.32864	274	75 076	16.55295	52.34501
225	50 625	15.00000	47.43416	275	75 625	16.58312	52.44044
226	51 076	15.03330	47.53946	276	76 176	16.61325	52.53570
227	51 529	15.06652	47.64452	277	76 729	16.64332	52.63079
228	51 984	15.09967	47.74935	278	77 284	16.67333	52.72571
229	52 441	15.13275	47.85394	279	77 841	16.70329	52.82045
230	52 900	15.16575	47.95832	280	78 400	16.73320	52.91503
231	53 361	15.19868	48.06246	281	78 961	16.76305	53.00943
232	53 824	15.23155	48.16638	282	79 524	16.79286	53.10367
233	54 289	15.26434	48.27007	283	80 089	16.82260	53.19774
234	54 756	15.29706	48.37355	284	80 656	16.85230	53.29165
235	55 225	15.32971	48.47680	285	81 225	16.88194	53.38539
236	55 696	15.36229	48.57983	286	81 796	16.91153	53.47897
237	56 169	15.39480	48.68265	287	82 369	16.94107	53.57238
238	56 644	15.42725	48.78524	288	82 944	16.97056	53.66563
239	57 121	15.45962	48.88763	289	83 521	17.00000	53.75872
240	57 600	15.49193	48.98979	290	84 100	17.02939	53.85165
241	58 081	15.52417	49.09175	291	84 681	17.05872	53.94442
242	58 564	15.55635	49.19350	292	85 264	17.08801	54.03702
243	59 049	15.58846	49.29503	293	85 849	17.11724	54.12947
244	59 536	15.62050	49.39636	294	86 436	17.14643	54.22177
245	60 025	15.65248	49.49747	295	87 025	17.17556	54.31390
246	60 516	15.68439	49.59839	296	87 616	17.20465	54.40588
247	61 009	15.71623	49.69909	297	88 209	17.23369	54.49771
248	61 504	15.74802	49.79960	298	88 804	17.26268	54.58938
249	62 001	15.77973	49.89990	299	89 401	17.29162	54.68089
250	62 500	15.81139	50.00000	300	90 000	17.32051	54.77226

N	N²	√N	√10N	N	N²	√N	√10N
300	90 000	17.32051	54.77226	350	122 500	18.70829	59.16080
301	90 601	17.34935	54.86347	351	123 201	18.73499	59.24525
302	91 204	17.37815	54.95453	352	123 904	18.76166	59.32959
303	91 809	17.40690	55.04544	353	124 609	18.78829	59.41380
304	92 416	17.43560	55.13620	354	125 316	18.81489	59.49790
305	93 025	17.46425	55.22681	355	126 025	18.84144	59.58188
306	93 636	17.49288	55.31727	356	126 736	18.86796	59.66574
307	94 249	17.52142	55.40758	357	127 449	18.89444	59.74948
308	94 864	17.54993	55.49775	358	128 164	18.92089	59.83310
309	95 481	17.57840	55.58777	359	128 881	18.94730	59.91661
310	96 100	17.60682	55.67764	360	129 600	18.97367	60.00000
311	96 721	17.63519	55.76737	361	130 321	19.00000	60.08328
312	97 344	17.66352	55.85696	362	131 044	19.02630	60.16644
313	97 969	17.69181	55.94640	363	131 769	19.05256	60.24948
314	98 596	17.72005	56.03670	364	132 496	19.07878	60.33241
315	99 225	17.74824	56.12486	365	133 225	19.10497	60.41523
316	99 856	17.77639	56.21388	366	133 956	19.13113	60.49793
317	100 489	17.80449	56.30275	367	134 689	19.15724	60.58052
318	101 124	17.83255	56.39149	368	135 424	19.18333	60.66300
319	101 761	17.86057	56.48008	369	136 161	19.20937	60.74537
320	102 400	17.88854	56.56854	370	136 900	19.23538	60.82763
321	103 041	17.91647	56.65686	371	137 641	19.26136	60.90977
322	103 684	17.94436	56.74504	372	138 384	19.28730	60.99180
323	104 329	17.97220	56.83309	373	139 129	19.31321	61.07373
324	104 976	18.00000	56.92100	374	139 876	19.33908	61.15554
325	105 625	18.02776	57.00877	375	140 625	19.36492	61.23724
326	106 276	18.05547	57.09641	376	141 376	19.39072	61.31884
327	106 929	18.08314	57.18391	377	142 129	19.41649	61.40033
328	107 584	18.11077	57.27128	378	142 884	19.44222	61.48170
329	108 241	18.13836	57.35852	379	143 641	19.46792	61.56298
330	108 900	18.16590	57.44563	380	144 000	19.49359	61.64414
331	109 561	18.19341	57.53260	381	145 161	19.51922	61.72520
332	110 224	18.22087	57.61944	382	145 924	19.54483	61.80615
333	110 889	18.24829	57.70615	383	146 689	19.57039	61.88699
334	111 556	18.27567	57.79273	384	147 456	19.59592	61.96773
335	112 225	18.30301	57.87918	385	148 225	19.62142	62.04837
336	112 896	18.33030	57.96551	386	148 996	19.64688	62.12890
337	113 569	18.35756	58.05170	387	149 769	19.67232	62.20932
338	114 224	18.38478	57.13777	388	150 544	19.69772	62.28965
339	114 921	18.41195	58.22371	389	151 321	19.72308	62.36986
340	115 600	18.43909	58.30952	390	152 100	19.74842	62.44998
341	116 281	18.46619	58.39521	391	152 881	19.77372	62.52999
342	116 694	18.49324	58.48077	392	153 664	19.79899	62.60990
343	117 649	18.52026	58.56620	393	154 449	19.82423	62.68971
344	118 336	18.54724	58.65151	394	155 236	19.84943	62.76942
345	119 025	18.57418	58.73670	395	156 025	19.87461	62.84903
346	119 716	18.60108	58.82176	396	156 816	19.89975	62.92853
347	120 409	18.62794	58.90671	397	157 609	19.92486	63.00794
348	121 104	18.65476	58.99152	398	158 404	19.94994	63.08724
349	121 801	18.68154	59.07622	399	159 201	19.97498	63.16645
350	122 500	18.70829	59.16080	400	160 000	20.00000	63.24555

N	N²	√N	√10N	N	N²	√N	√10N
400	160 000	20.00000	63.24555	450	202 500	21.21320	67.08204
401	160 801	20.02498	63.32456	451	203 401	21.23676	67.15653
402	161 604	20.04994	63.40347	452	204 304	21.26029	67.23095
403	162 409	20.07486	63.48228	453	205 209	21.28380	67.30527
404	163 216	20.09975	63.56099	454	206 116	21.30728	67.37952
405	164 025	20.12461	63.63961	455	207 025	21.33073	67.45369
406	164 836	20.14944	63.71813	456	207 936	21.35416	67.52777
407	165 649	20.17424	63.79655	457	208 849	21.37756	67.60178
408	166 464	20.19901	63.87488	458	209 764	21.40093	67.67570
409	167 281	20.22375	63.95311	459	210 681	21.42429	67.74954
410	168 100	20.24846	64.03124	460	211 600	21.44761	67.82330
411	168 921	20.27313	64.10928	461	212 521	21.47091	67.89698
412	169 744	20.29778	64.18723	462	213 444	21.49419	67.97058
413	170 569	20.32240	64.26508	463	214 369	21.51743	68.04410
414	171 396	20.34699	64.34283	464	215 296	21.54066	68.11755
415	172 225	20.37155	64.42049	465	216 225	21.56386	68.19091
416	173 056	20.39608	64.49806	466	217 156	21.58703	68.26419
417	173 889	20.42058	64.57554	467	218 089	21.61018	68.33740
418	174 724	20.44505	64.65292	468	219 024	21.63331	68.41053
419	175 561	20.46949	64.73021	469	219 961	21.65641	68.48357
420	176 400	20.49390	64.80741	470	220 900	21.67948	68.55655
421	177 241	20.51828	64.88451	471	221 841	21.70253	68.62944
422	178 084	20.54264	64.96153	472	222 784	21.72556	68.70226
423	178 929	20.56696	65.03845	473	223 729	21.74856	68.77500
424	179 776	20.59126	65.11528	474	224 676	21.77154	68.84706
425	180 625	20.61553	65.19202	475	225 625	21.79449	68.92024
426	181 476	20.63977	65.26808	476	226 576	21.81742	68.99275
427	182 329	20.66398	65.34524	477	227 529	21.84033	69.06519
428	183 184	20.68816	65.42171	478	228 484	21.86321	69.13754
429	184 041	20.71232	65.49809	479	229 441	21.88607	69.20983
430	184 900	20.73644	65.57439	480	230 400	21.90800	69.28203
431	185 761	20.76054	65.65059	481	231 361	21.93171	69.35416
432	186 624	20.78461	65.72671	482	232 324	21.95450	69.42622
433	187 489	20.80865	65.80274	483	233 280	21.97726	69.50820
434	188 356	20.83267	65.87868	484	234 256	22.00000	69.57011
435	189 225	20.85665	65.95453	485	235 225	22.02272	69.64194
436	190 096	20.88061	66.03030	486	236 196	22.04541	69.71370
437	190 969	20.90454	66.10598	487	237 169	22.06808	69.78530
438	191 844	20.92845	66.18157	488	238 144	22.09072	69.85700
439	192 721	20.95233	66.25708	489	239 121	22.11334	69.92853
440	193 600	20.97618	66.33250	490	240 100	22.13594	70.00000
441	194 481	21.00000	66.40783	491	241 081	22.15852	70.07139
442	195 364	21.02380	66.48308	492	242 064	22.18107	70.14271
443	196 249	21.04757	66.55825	493	243 049	22.20360	70.21396
444	197 136	21.07131	66.63332	494	244 036	22.22611	70.28513
445	198 025	21.09502	66.70832	495	245 025	22.24860	70.35624
446	198 916	21.11871	66.78323	496	246 016	22.27106	70.42727
447	199 809	21.14237	66.85806	497	247 009	22.29350	70.49823
448	200 704	21.16601	66.93280	498	248 004	22.31519	70.56912
449	201 601	21.18962	67.00746	499	249 001	22.33831	70.63993
450	202 500	21.21320	67.08204	500	250 000	22.36068	70.71068

N	N²	√N	√10N	N	N²	√N	√10N
500	250 000	22.36068	70.71068	550	302 500	23.45208	74.16198
501	251 001	22.38303	70.78135	551	303 601	23.47339	74.22937
502	252 004	22.40536	70.85196	552	304 704	23.49468	74.29670
503	253 009	22.42766	70.92249	553	305 809	23.51595	74.36397
504	254 016	22.44994	70.99296	554	306 916	23.53720	74.43118
505	255 025	22.47221	71.06335	555	308 025	23.55844	74.49832
506	256 036	22.49444	71.13368	556	309 136	23.57965	74.56541
507	257 049	22.51666	71.20393	557	310 249	23.60085	74.63243
508	258 064	22.53886	71.27412	558	311 364	23.62202	74.69940
509	259 081	22.56103	71.34424	559	312 481	23.64318	74.76630
510	260 100	22.58318	71.41428	560	313 600	23.66432	74.83315
511	261 121	22.60531	71.48426	561	314 721	23.68544	74.89993
512	262 144	22.62742	71.55418	562	315 844	23.70654	74.96666
513	263 169	22.64950	71.62402	563	316 969	23.72762	75.03333
514	264 196	22.67157	71.69379	564	318 096	23.74686	75.09993
515	265 225	22.69361	71.76350	565	319 225	23.76973	75.16648
516	266 256	22.71563	71.83314	566	320 356	23.79075	75.23297
517	267 289	22.73763	71.90271	567	321 489	23.81176	75.29940
518	268 324	22.75961	71.97222	568	322 624	23.83275	75.36577
519	269 361	22.78157	72.04165	569	323 761	23.85372	75.43209
520	270 400	22.80351	72.11103	570	324 900	23.87467	75.49834
521	271 441	22.82542	72.18033	571	326 041	23.89561	75.56454
522	272 484	22.84732	72.24957	572	327 184	23.91652	75.63068
523	273 529	22.86919	72.31874	573	328 329	23.93742	75.69676
524	274 576	22.89105	72.38784	574	329 476	23.95830	75.76279
525	275 625	22.91288	72.45688	575	330 625	23.97916	75.82875
526	276 676	22.93469	72.52586	576	331 776	24.00000	75.89466
527	277 729	22.95648	72.59477	577	332 929	24.02082	75.96052
528	278 784	22.97825	72.66361	578	334 084	24.04163	76.02631
529	279 841	23.00000	72.73239	579	335 241	24.06242	76.09205
530	280 900	23.02173	72.80110	580	336 400	24.08319	76.15773
531	281 961	23.04344	72.86975	581	337 561	24.10394	76.22336
532	283 024	23.06513	72.93833	582	338 724	24.12468	76.28892
533	284 089	23.08679	73.00685	583	339 889	24.14539	76.35444
534	285 156	23.10844	73.07530	584	341 056	24.16609	76.41989
535	286 225	23.13007	73.14369	585	342 225	24.18677	76.48529
536	287 296	23.15167	73.21202	586	343 396	24.20744	76.55064
537	288 369	23.17326	73.28028	587	344 569	24.22808	76.61593
538	289 444	23.19483	73.34848	588	345 744	24.24871	76.68116
539	290 521	23.21637	73.41662	589	346 921	24.26932	76.74634
540	291 600	23.23790	73.48469	590	348 100	24.28992	76.81146
541	292 681	23.25941	73.55270	591	349 281	24.31049	76.87652
542	293 764	23.28089	73.62056	592	350 464	24.33105	76.94154
543	294 849	23.30236	73.68853	593	351 649	24.35159	77.00649
544	295 936	23.32381	73.75636	594	352 836	24.37212	77.07140
545	297 025	23.34524	73.82412	595	354 025	24.39262	77.13624
546	298 116	23.36664	73.89181	596	355 216	24.41311	77.20104
547	299 209	23.38803	73.95945	597	356 409	24.43358	77.26578
548	300 304	23.40940	74.02702	598	357 604	24.45404	77.33046
549	301 401	23.43075	74.09453	599	358 801	24.47448	77.39509
550	302 500	23.45208	74.16198	600	360 000	24.49490	77.45967

N	N²	√N	√10N	N	N²	√N	√10N
600	360 000	24.49490	77.45967	650	422 500	25.49510	80.62258
601	361 201	24.51530	77.52419	651	423 801	25.51470	80.68457
602	362 404	24.53569	77.58868	652	425 409	25.53240	80.80130
603	363 609	24.55606	77.65307	653	426 409	25.55386	80.80842
604	364 816	24.57641	77.71744	654	427 716	25.57342	80.87027
605	366 025	24.59675	77.78175	655	429 025	25.59297	80.93207
606	367 736	24.61707	77.84600	656	430 336	25.61250	80.99383
607	368 449	24.63737	77.91020	657	431 649	25.63201	81.05554
608	369 664	24.65766	77.97435	658	432 964	25.65151	81.11720
609	370 881	24.67793	78.03845	659	434 281	25.67100	81.17881
610	372 100	24.69818	78.10250	660	435 600	25.69047	81.24038
611	373 321	24.71841	78.16649	661	436 921	25.70992	81.30191
612	374 544	24.73863	78.23043	662	438 244	25.72936	81.36338
613	375 769	24.75884	78.29432	663	439 569	25.74879	81.42481
614	376 996	24.77902	78.35815	664	440 896	25.76820	81.48620
615	378 225	24.79919	78.42194	665	442 225	25.78759	81.54753
616	379 456	24.81935	78.48567	666	443 556	25.80698	81.60882
617	380 689	24.83948	78.54935	667	444 889	25.82634	81.67007
618	381 924	24.85961	78.61298	668	446 224	25.84570	81.73127
619	383 161	24.87971	78.67655	669	447 561	25.86503	81.79242
620	384 400	24.89980	78.74008	670	448 900	25.88436	81.85353
621	385 641	24.91987	78.80355	671	450 241	25.90367	81.91459
622	386 884	24.93993	78.86698	672	451 584	25.92296	81.97561
623	388 129	24.95997	78.93035	673	452 929	25.94224	82.03658
624	389 376	24.97999	78.99367	674	454 276	25.96151	82.09750
625	390 625	25.00000	79.05694	675	455 625	25.98076	82.15838
626	391 876	25.01999	79.12016	676	456 976	26.00000	82.21922
627	393 129	25.03997	79.18333	677	458 329	26.01922	82.28001
628	394 384	25.05993	79.24645	678	459 684	26.03843	82.34076
629	395 641	25.07987	79.30952	679	461 041	26.05763	82.40146
630	396 900	25.09980	79.37254	680	462 400	26.07681	82.46211
631	398 161	25.11971	79.43551	681	463 761	26.09598	82.52272
632	399 424	25.13961	79.49843	682	465 124	26.11513	82.58329
633	400 689	25.15949	79.56130	683	466 489	26.13427	82.64381
634	401 956	25.17936	79.62412	684	467 856	26.15339	82.70429
635	403 225	25.19921	79.68689	685	469 225	26.17250	82.76473
636	404 496	25.21904	79.74961	686	470 596	26.19160	82.82512
637	405 769	25.23886	79.81228	687	471 969	26.21068	82.88546
638	407 044	25.25866	79.87490	688	473 344	26.22975	82.94577
639	408 321	25.27845	79.93748	689	474 721	26.24881	83.00602
640	409 600	25.29822	80.00000	690	476 100	26.26785	83.06624
641	410 881	25.31798	80.06248	691	477 481	26.28688	83.12641
642	412 164	25.33772	80.12490	692	478 864	26.30589	83.18654
643	413 449	25.35744	80.18728	693	480 249	26.32489	83.24662
644	414 736	25.37716	80.24961	694	481 636	26.34388	83.30666
645	416 025	25.39685	80.31189	695	483 025	26.36285	83.36666
646	417 316	25.41653	80.37413	696	484 416	26.38181	83.42661
647	418 609	25.43619	80.43631	697	485 809	26.40076	83.48653
648	419 904	25.45584	80.49845	698	487 204	26.41969	83.54639
649	421 201	25.47548	80.56054	699	488 601	26.43861	83.60622
650	422 500	25.49510	80.62258	700	490 000	26.45751	83.66600

Tables of squares and square roots

N	N²	√N	√10N	N	N²	√N	√10N
700	490 000	26.45751	83.66600	750	562 500	27.38613	86.60254
701	491 401	26.47640	83.72574	751	564 001	27.40438	86.66026
702	492 804	26.49528	83.78544	752	565 504	27.42262	86.71793
703	494 209	26.51415	83.84510	753	567 009	27.44085	86.77557
704	495 616	26.53300	83.90471	754	568 516	27.45906	86.83317
705	497 025	26.55184	83.96428	755	570 025	27.47726	86.89074
706	498 436	26.57066	84.02381	756	571 536	27.49545	86.94826
707	499 849	26.58947	84.08329	757	573 049	27.51363	87.00575
708	501 264	26.60827	84.14274	758	574 564	27.53180	87.06320
709	502 681	26.62705	84.20214	759	576 081	27.54995	87.12061
710	504 100	26.64583	84.26150	760	577 600	27.56810	87.17798
711	505 521	26.66458	84.32082	761	579 121	27.58623	87.23531
712	506 944	26.68333	84.38009	762	580 644	27.60435	87.29261
713	508 369	26.70206	84.43933	763	582 169	27.62245	87.34987
714	509 796	26.72078	84.49852	764	583 696	27.64055	87.40709
715	511 225	26.73948	84.55767	765	585 225	27.65863	87.46428
716	512 656	26.75818	84.61578	766	586 756	27.67671	87.52143
717	514 089	26.77686	84.67585	767	588 289	27.69476	87.57854
718	515 524	26.79552	84.73488	768	589 824	27.71281	87.63561
719	516 961	26.81418	84.79387	769	591 361	27.73085	87.69265
720	518 400	26.83282	84.85281	770	592 900	27.74887	87.74964
721	519 841	26.85144	84.91172	771	594 441	27.76689	87.80661
722	521 284	26.87006	84.97058	772	595 984	27.78489	87.86353
723	522 729	26.88866	85.02941	773	597 529	27.80288	87.92042
724	524 176	26.90725	85.08819	774	599 076	27.82086	87.97727
725	525 625	26.92582	85.14693	775	600 625	27.83882	88.03408
726	527 076	26.94439	85.20563	776	602 176	27.85678	88.09086
727	528 529	26.96294	85.26429	777	603 729	27.87472	88.14760
728	529 984	26.98148	85.32294	778	605 284	27.89265	88.20431
729	531 411	27.00000	85.38150	779	606 841	27.91057	88.26098
730	532 900	27.01851	85.44004	780	608 400	27.92848	88.31761
731	534 361	27.03701	85.49854	781	609 961	27.94638	88.37420
732	535 824	27.05550	85.55700	782	611 524	27.96426	88.43076
733	537 289	27.07397	85.61542	783	613 089	27.98214	88.48729
734	538 756	27.09243	85.67380	784	614 656	28.00000	88.54377
735	540 225	27.11088	85.73214	785	616 225	28.01785	88.60023
736	541 696	27.12932	85.79044	786	617 796	28.03569	88.65664
737	543 169	27.14774	85.84870	787	619 369	28.05352	88.71302
738	544 644	27.16616	85.90693	788	620 944	28.07134	88.76936
739	546 121	27.18455	85.96511	789	622 521	28.08914	88.82567
740	547 600	27.20294	86.02325	790	624 100	28.10694	88.88194
741	549 081	27.22132	86.08136	791	625 681	28.12472	88.93818
742	550 564	27.23968	86.13942	792	627 264	28.14249	88.99438
743	552 049	27.25803	86.20745	793	628 849	28.16026	89.05055
744	553 536	27.27636	86.25543	794	630 436	28.17801	89.10668
745	555 025	27.29469	86.31338	795	632 025	28.19574	89.16277
746	556 516	27.31300	86.37129	796	633 616	28.21347	89.21883
747	558 009	27.33130	86.42916	797	635 209	28.23119	89.27486
748	559 504	27.34959	86.48609	798	636 804	28.24889	89.33085
749	561 001	27.36786	86.54479	799	638 401	28.26659	89.38680
750	562 500	27.38613	86.60254	800	640 000	28.28427	89.44272

N	N²	√N	√10N	N	N²	√N	√10N
800	640 000	28.28427	89.44272	850	722 500	29.15476	92.19544
801	641 601	28.30194	89.49860	851	724 201	29.17190	92.24966
802	643 204	28.31960	89.55445	852	725 904	29.18904	92.30385
803	644 809	28.33725	89.61027	853	727 609	29.20616	92.35800
804	646 416	28.35489	89.66605	854	729 316	29.22328	92.41212
805	648 025	28.37252	89.72179	855	731 025	29.24038	92.46621
806	649 636	28.39014	89.77750	856	732 736	29.25748	92.52027
807	651 249	28.40775	89.83318	857	734 449	29.27456	92.57429
808	652 864	28.42534	89.88882	858	736 164	29.29164	92.62829
809	654 481	28.44293	89.94443	859	737 881	29.30870	92.68225
810	656 100	28.46050	90.00000	860	739 600	29.32576	92.73618
811	657 721	28.47806	90.05554	861	741 321	29.34280	92.79009
812	659 344	28.49561	90.11104	862	743 044	29.35984	92.84396
813	660 969	28.51315	90.16651	863	744 769	29.37686	92.89779
814	662 596	28.53069	90.22195	864	746 496	29.39388	92.95160
815	664 225	28.54820	90.27735	865	748 225	29.41088	93.00538
816	665 856	28.56571	90.33272	866	749 956	29.42788	93.05912
817	667 489	28.58321	90.38805	867	751 689	29.44486	93.11283
818	669 124	28.60070	90.44335	868	753 424	29.46184	93.16652
819	670 761	28.61818	90.49862	869	755 161	29.47881	93.22017
820	672 400	28.63564	90.55385	870	756 900	29.49576	93.27379
821	674 041	28.65310	90.60905	871	758 641	29.51271	93.32738
822	675 684	28.67054	90.66422	872	760 384	29.52965	93.38094
823	677 329	28.68798	90.71935	873	762 129	29.54657	93.43447
824	678 976	28.70540	90.77445	874	763 876	29.56349	93.48797
825	680 625	28.72281	90.82951	875	765 625	29.58040	93.54143
826	682 276	28.74022	90.88454	876	767 376	29.59730	93.59487
827	683 929	28.75761	90.93954	877	769 129	29.61419	93.64828
828	685 584	28.77499	90.99451	878	770 884	29.63106	93.70165
829	687 241	28.79236	91.04944	879	772 641	29.64793	93.75500
830	688 900	28.80972	91.10434	880	774 400	29.66479	93.80832
831	690 561	28.82707	91.15920	881	776 161	29.68164	93.86160
832	692 224	28.84441	91.21403	882	777 924	29.69848	93.91486
833	693 889	28.86174	91.26883	883	779 689	29.71532	93.96808
834	695 556	28.87906	91.32360	884	781 456	29.73214	94.02027
835	697 225	28.89637	91.37833	885	783 225	29.74895	94.07444
836	698 896	28.91366	91.43304	886	784 996	29.76575	94.12757
837	700 569	28.93095	91.48770	887	786 769	29.78255	94.10868
838	702 244	28.94823	91.54234	888	788 544	29.79933	94.23375
839	703 921	28.96550	91.59694	889	790 321	29.81610	94.28680
840	705 600	28.98275	91.65151	890	792 100	29.83287	94.33981
841	707 281	29.00000	91.70605	891	793 881	29.84962	94.39280
842	708 964	29.01724	91.76056	892	795 664	29.86637	94.44575
843	710 649	29.03446	91.81503	893	797 449	29.88311	94.49868
844	712 336	29.05168	91.86947	894	799 236	29.89983	94.55157
845	714 025	29.06888	91.92388	895	801 025	29.91655	94.60444
846	715 716	29.08608	91.97826	896	802 816	29.93326	94.65728
847	717 409	29.10326	92.03260	897	804 609	29.94996	94.71008
848	719 104	29.12044	92.08692	898	806 404	29.96665	94.76286
849	720 801	29.13760	92.14120	899	808 201	29.98333	94.81561
850	722 500	29.15476	92.19544	900	810 000	30.00000	94.86833

N	N²	√N	√10N	N	N²	√N	√10N
900	810 000	30.00000	94.86833	950	902 500	30.82207	97.46794
901	811 801	30.01666	94.92102	951	904 401	30.83829	97.51923
902	813 604	30.03331	94.97368	952	906 304	30.85450	97.57049
903	815 409	30.04996	·95.02631	953	908 209	30.87070	97.62172
904	817 216	30.06659	95.07891	954	910.116	30.88689	97.67292
905	819 025	30.08322	95.13149	955	912 025	30.90307	97.72410
906	820 836	30.09938	95.18403	956	913 936	30.91925	97.77525
907	822 649	30.11644	95.23655	957	915 849	30.93542	97.82638
908	824 464	30.13304	95.28903	958	917 764	30.95158	97.87747
909	826 281	30.14963	95.34149	959	919 681	30.96773	97.92855
910	828 100	30.16621	95.39392	960	921 600	30.98387	97.97959
911	829 921	30.18278	95.44632	961	923 521	31.00000	98.03061
912	831 744	30.19934	95.49869	962	925 444	31.01612	98.08160
913	833 569	30.21589	95.55103	963	927 369	31.03224	98.13256
914	835 396	30.23243	95.60335	964	929 296	31.04835	98.18350
915	837 225	30.24897	95.65563	965	931 225	31.06445	98.23441
916	839 056	30.26549	95.70789	966	933 156	31.08054	98.28530
917	840 889	30.28201	95.76012	967	935 089	31.09662	98.33616
918	842 724	30.29851	95.81232	968	937 024	31.11270	98.38699
919	844 561	30.31501	95.86449	969	938 961	31.12876	98.43780
920	846 400	30.33150	95.91663	970	940 900	31.14482	98.48858
921	848 241	30.34798	95.96874	971	942 841	31.16087	98.53933
922	850 084	30.36445	96.02083	972	944 784	31.17691	98.59006
923	851 929	30.38092	96.07289	973	946 729	31.19295	98.64076
924	853 776	30.39735	96.12492	974	948 676	31.20897	98.69144
925	855 625	30.41381	96.17692	975	950 625	31.22499	98.74209
926	857 476	30.43025	96.22889	976	952 576	31.24100	98.79271
927	859 329	30.44667	96.28084	977	954 529	31.25700	98.84331
928	861 184	30.46309	96.33276	978	956 484	31.27299	98.89388
929	863 041	30.47950	96.38465	979	958 441	31.28898	98.94443
930	864 900	30.49590	96.43651	980	960 400	31.30495	98.99495
931	866 761	30.51229	96.48834	981	962 361	31.32092	99.04544
932	868 624	30.52868	96.54015	982	964 324	31.33688	99.09591
933	870 489	30.54505	96.59193	983	966 144	31.34021	99.10321
934	872 356	30.56141	96.64368	984	968 256	31.36877	99.19677
935	874 225	30.57777	96.69540	985	970 225	31.38471	99.24717
936	876 096	30.59412	96.74709	986	972 196	31.40064	99.29753
937	877 969	30.61046	96.79876	987	974 169	31.41656	99.34787
938	879 844	30.62679	96.85040	988	976 144	31.43247	99.39819
939	881 721	30.64311	96.90201	989	978 121	31.44837	99.44848
940	883 600	30.65942	96.95360	990	980 100	31.46427	99.49874
941	885 481	30.67572	97.00515	991	982 081	31.48015	99.54898
942	887 364	30.69202	97.05668	992	984 064	31.49603	99.54920
943	889 249	30.70831	97.10819	993	986 049	31.51190	99.64939
944	891 136	30.72458	97.15966	994	988 036	31.52777	99.69955
945	893 025	30.74085	97.21111	995	990 025	31.54362	99.74969
946	894 916	30.75711	97.26253	996	992 016	31.55947	99.79980
947	896 809	30.77337	97.31393	997	994 009	31.57531	99.84989
948	898 704	30.78961	97.36529	998	996 004	31.59114	99.89995
949	900 601	30.80584	97.41663	999	998 001	31.60696	99.94999
950	902 500	30.82207	97.46794	1000	1 000 000	31.62278	100.00000

INDEX

This book has been set VIP in 9 point Helvetica and Helvetica Light leaded 3 points. Part and chapter titles are set in 18 and 16 point Avant Garde Book respectively. The size of the type page is 36 picas by 48 picas overall.